INTRODUCTION TO
SPECIAL
EDUCATION

Deborah Deutsch Smith
Ruth Luckasson

The University of New Mexico

Allyn & Bacon

Boston   London   Toronto   Sydney   Tokyo   Singapore

INTRODUCTION TO
SPECIAL
EDUCATION

Teaching in an Age of Challenge

Series Editor: *Ray Short*
Production Administrator: *Lisa Feder*
Senior Editorial Assistant: *Jo Ellen Caffrey*
Editorial-Production Service: *Barbara Pendergast*
Cover Administrator: *Linda Dickinson*
Composition Buyer: *Linda Cox*
Manufacturing Buyer: *Megan Cochran*
Text Designer: *Lee Goldstein*
Photo Researcher: *Laurel Anderson*

Copyright ©1992 by Allyn and Bacon
A Division of Simon & Schuster, Inc.
160 Gould Street
Needham Heights, MA 02194

Library of Congress Cataloging-in-Publication Data

Smith, Deborah Deutsch.
    Introduction to special education : teaching in an age of
challenge / Deborah Deutsch Smith, Ruth Luckasson.
        p.   cm.
    Includes bibliographical references and index.
    ISBN 0-205-13315-0
    1. Special education—United States.   I. Luckasson, Ruth.
II. Title.
    LC3981.S56   1991
371.9′0973—dc20   91-26970
                                                        CIP

Printed in the United States of America
10 9 8 7 6 5 4 3 2   96 95 94 93

Dedication

To: Steven Smith and Jim Smith
Charles Donald Luckasson Ellis,
Virginia Brudos Luckasson,
and Lindahl Luckasson

CONTENTS

*C*hapter Four

MENTAL RETARDATION 119

*A*nother Perspective: AN OLDER BROTHER WITH MENTAL RETARDATION 120

Chapter Five

COMMUNICATIVE DISORDERS   161

Another Perspective: JOHN CASEY'S SHIP COMES IN 162

Chapter Six

Chapter Seven

*C*hapter Eight

BEHAVIORAL DISORDERS AND EMOTIONAL DISTURBANCE   301

*A*nother Perspective: *"THE ONES WHO ALWAYS GET THE BLAME"; THE WRITINGS OF CHILDREN WITH EMOTIONAL AND BEHAVIORAL HANDICAPS 302*

*C*hapter Nine

VISUAL IMPAIRMENTS 339

*A*nother Perspective: *A WHITE CANE? 340*

One vision sustained us through the three year's work writing this book—a vision of schools in which all children, children with disabilities and children without, are engaged in learning. Schools in which they learn with each other and from each other, with the help of their teachers and other professionals. Schools in which families are integral to the educational process, and in which family traditions, culture, and language are reflected. It is our hope that this book can contribute in some small way to helping make this vision a reality.

We want to transmit a part of the excitement we have felt watching a child who has exceptional learning needs achieve an important goal. We invite you to join us in exploring the teaching and learning of students with disabilities. In this book you will find the basic knowledge of special education and many examples of educational procedures that you can apply immediately. We have attempted to provide you with the most current information based on research findings. We also present some of the dilemmas that currently confront society and people with disabilities.

Special education and opportunities for people with disabilities have changed greatly over the last decade. Today, issues and challenges facing individuals with disabilities are frequently brought to public attention through the media. Access to the benefits of society, such as education, is characterized in terms of rights. Children, youth, and adults with disabilities are asserting a proper place in American society where they have equal access to education, employment, and leisure-time activities. The recent passage of the Americans with Disabilities Act further defines the civil rights of people with disabilities. The nation—the public, policymakers, and the courts—is now discussing issues such as full inclusion, community-based living arrangements, and national prevention programs designed to reduce disabling conditions. In addition, advances in technology are enabling people with disabilities to achieve more independence, autonomy, and greater integration.

ORGANIZATION OF THE BOOK

We begin the book by describing the context of special education. This foundation chapter defines what special education is, provides a brief history of the entire field, and presents the landmark legislation and court cases that define the special educational rights of children with disabilities and their families. Chapter 2 provides a comprehensive look at multicultural and bilingual special education. Because of the growing sensitivity to the unique learning needs of these children, each chapter contains a special box, *Focus: Issues of Diversity*. Individualized educational plans and programs are the keystones to an appropriate special education, and chapter 3 is entirely devoted to these plans: IFSPs, IEPs, and ITPs.

We then present individual chapters on the higher prevalence categories. We placed mental retardation first, not because it is the largest category but because work in this area has formed the foundation for much of special education. The chapter about communicative disorders precedes the one about learning disabilities because so many preschoolers identified as having a language disorder are later identified as having learning disabilities. The next two chapters are about giftedness and creativity, and behavioral disorders and emotional disturbance. The last three chapters present information on disabilities with the lowest prevalence: visual impairments, hearing impairments, and physical disabilities and health impairments.

TOOLS FOR STUDENTS

We included many features to make the book easy to use. For example, we use a *standard organizational outline* for each chapter. This way, as you study, you will know where to find specific types of information in each chapter:

- Definition, measurement, and significance
- History of the field
- Prevalence
- Causes and prevention
- Profile of students with this disability
- Educational considerations
- Families
- Adults with this disability
- Technology
- Concepts and controversies

At the beginning of each chapter, the most important *learning objectives* are listed. Read these first, for they provide advance organizers for your study.

Key terms and brief definitions are found at the tops of the pages where an important concept is first introduced and discussed. The comprehensive end-of-book *glossary* provides expanded definitions for the key terms.

In each chapter you will find a box labeled *Tips for Teachers* containing practical information on simple ways to make any classroom more suitable for students with that disability. The *Teaching Tactics* boxes describe a teaching procedure that has been successful with students.

The *Concepts and Controversies* section at the end of each chapter raises an unresolved issue in that disability area. We summarize the arguments on each side of the controversy, and raise questions for thought.

At the end of every chapter, you will find numbered statements in a *summary* of important points. The summaries provide a way to quickly review the chapter's content to be sure you remember the important points. You will also find *discussion questions* to synthesize or extend what you have learned.

A portrayal of an individual with a particular disability in a book or videotape often suggests a societal or historical context. At the end of each chapter you will find a short list of *popular books* in which people with the disability in that chapter are major characters. A short list of *videotapes* is also included. (Much fuller lists of books, videos, as well as *professional and consumer organizations* in that disability area are included in the *Student Study Guide* and the teacher's materials.)

At the end of the book, you will find the full *references* cited in each chapter and recommendations for some additional reading. They are organized in a special way—by chapter, and in subheadings that correspond to the standard outline. As you want to learn more about a topic or write a paper for class, the arrangement of these references should be helpful.

But facts, research, and techniques, while an important beginning, are insufficient to describe the essence of special education. To approach what is really important about this field, we must listen to individuals with disabilities and their families. To this end, we have included many first-person *accounts* and *vignettes* by people with disabilities and their families. We also included, at the beginning of each chapter, works of art created by artists who have disabilities and whose biographical sketches are included.

ACKNOWLEDGMENTS

We owe a great debt of thanks to many people who helped over the three years it took to prepare this book, for the journey this text took in its development was somewhat unusual. First, we would like to thank Susan Willig at Prentice-Hall who had confidence and believed in our abilities. Because of her encouragement and persistence, we began on what became an incredible adventure. Soon after we began writing, Carol Wada assumed responsibility for this project. It was Carol who listened to the long phone calls, who handled the details, and helped ensure that all was of the highest quality possible during the first two years of the book's development. For all those little and big details, we thank Carol, but most importantly we thank her for arranging for the assignment of our Development Editor, Virginia Feury-Gagnon. Virginia, we share this book with you and hope you are as pleased as we are. As the manuscript was entering the production stage, our book, along with the whole Prentice-Hall Education list, was transferred to Allyn & Bacon. Our thanks also go to Ray Short at Allyn & Bacon, our third editor, for all his support during the difficult transition period, for taking part ownership in the project and referring to "our book" so quickly, and for working with us so closely as we completed this project. We also wish to thank the following people for their special care and attention to our book: Barbara Pendergast, our Production Packager; Mary Beth Finch and Lisa Feder, our Production Supervisor and Coordinator; Laurel Anderson, Art Coordinator, and Jo Ellen Caffrey, Chief Finder and Details Fixer. So, to all of the wonderful and competent people at Prentice-Hall and Allyn & Bacon, thank you.

We wish to thank the many people in our home environment who devoted themselves to us and this project. Dr. Tom Pierce, now of the University of Nevada-Las Vegas, was our "Chief Coordinator" during the beginning of this project, helped us all the way along, and kept us laughing when things did not seem so funny. His attention to details, his loyalty, and his caring made even the difficult times tolerable. We also thank Dr. Diane Bassett who worked so closely with this project as it came to conclusion. Her help with the many details, her rallying resources when we thought there were none left was such a help to us. We offer thanks to so many of our students and friends who offered their assistance as well. In particular we want to mention: Jane Clarke, Dr. Marie Fritz, Patti Huskin, Denis Keyes, Marge McCament, Lori Navarrete, Roger Poppe, Kim Strahan, and Kim Triplett. In addition, we wish to thank others who helped in valuable ways throughout the preparation of the book: Delilah Yao, Paula Lucero, Victor Torres, and Richard Lightfoot. Finally, thanks to Shelle Carter, who chased the last missing reference citations and handled all of the permissions for us.

Many others were helpful to us also. Dr. Diane Rivera wrote the Annotated Teacher's Edition, and also field-tested the text with her students at Florida Atlantic University. We are grateful to Diane and her students for their comments. They helped immeasurably as we refined the text. Our gratitude is extended to the focus group participants who gave us feedback on the entire text and whose input makes this a better product: Dr. Ann C. Chandler of Texas Tech University, Dr. Jo Crain of Valdosta State University, Dr. Deborah Gartland of Towson State University, Dr. Michael Rosenberg of Johns Hopkins University, and Dr. Donald Weber of Miami University of Ohio.

We also wish to acknowledge the following professionals for providing content input on various chapters of this text: Barbara Baskin, SUNY at Stony Brook; John Beattie, University of North Carolina at Charlotte; Gary Best, California State University-Los Angeles; Ann Beckwith, Albuquerque Public Schools; Virginia Cavalluzzo, Children's Psychiatric Hospital of the University of New Mexico; Jozi De Leon, University of New Mexico; Amy Dietrich, Memphis State University; Mary Kay Dykes, SpEdCon, Inc.; Linda Clark, Dept. of Human Services Spokane WA; June H. Elliot, Lydon State College; Jim Ellis, University of New Mexico Law School; Marie Fritz, Indiana State University; Eloy Gonzales, University of New Mexico; Suki Harada, Albuquerque Public Schools; Kathryn Haring, University of Oklahoma; Randall Harley, Peabody College/Vanderbilt University; Bill Healey, University of Arizona; Kyle Higgins, University of Washington; Dick Hood, University of New Mexico; Marcia Horne, University of Oklahoma; Selma Hughes, East Texas State University; Elliot Lessen, Northern Illinois University; David Lovett, University of Oklahoma; Tom Lovitt, University of Washington; Jean Lowe, University of New Mexico Hospital; Sheila Lowenbraun, University of Washington; Barbara MacDonald and the staff of the New Mexico School for the Visually Handicapped; Donald MacMillan, University of California at Riverside; Donald F. Maietta, Boston University; June Maker, University of Arizona; Horace Mann, State University College at Buffalo; Ed Martin, National Center on Employment and Disability; Christine Marvin, University of Nebraska-Lincoln; Cecil Mercer, University of Florida; C. Julius Meisel, University of Delaware; Isaura Barrara Metz, University of New Mexico; Donald Moores, Gallaudet University; Elizabeth Neilsen, University of New Mexico; Bengt Nirje, Swedish Organization of Sports for the Handicapped; A. Harry Passow, Columbia University; Fran Reed, Olivet Nazarene University; Suzanne Robinson, Kansas University; Raymond Rodriquez, Colorado State University; Robert B. Rutherford, Jr.,

Arizona State University; Jerome J. Schultz, Lesley College; Cathe Snyder, Albuquerque Public Schools; Mårten Söder, University of Uppsala; Janet Spector, University of Maine-Orono; Keith Stearns; Nonda Stone, University of Oregon; Qaisar Sultana, Eastern Kentucky University; Janis Tabeck-Keene, Albuquerque Public Schools; Jo Tomason, Council for Administrators of Special Education; James Van Tassel, Ball State University; Phyllis Wilcox, University of New Mexico; and Mary Kay Zabel, Kansas State University.

Finally, we thank our families.

D.D.S.
R.L.

Left: Deborah Smith; right: Ruth Luckasson

ABOUT THE AUTHORS

DEBORAH DEUTSCH SMITH, Ph.D., has taught special education at the college level since 1974. She is currently Professor of Special Education and Regents' Professor at the University of New Mexico. She earned her B.A. in Psychology at Pitzer College, her M.Ed. in Special Education at the University of Missouri-Columbia, and her Ed.D. in Special Education at the University of Washington-Seattle. She was recently elected President of the Higher Education Consortium for Special Education, and has authored *Teaching Students with Learning Disabilities, Effective Discipline,* and *Teaching Students with Learning and Behavior Problems.* Dr. Smith has also written numerous child-use materials in the areas of speech and language development, mathematics, and computer programs to develop thinking skills.

RUTH LUCKASSON, J.D., is currently a Professor in the Special Education Department at the University of New Mexico. She received her M.A. in Special Education and her J.D. from the University of New Mexico School of Law. Professor Luckasson is the former managing attorney for the New Mexico Protection and Advocacy System, is active in national and international disability social policy reforms, and is presently Chair of the American Association on Mental Retardation Terminology and Classification Committee and Chair of the American Bar Association Commission on Mental and Physical Disability Law. She was an editor of *Transition to Adult Life for People with Mental Retardation* and *Mental Retardation and the Criminal Justice System.*

INTRODUCTION TO

SPECIAL

EDUCATION

LIU JINGSHENG, 37, is a resident of Beijing in The People's Republic of China. He is the Director of the Beijing Calligraphy Association, a member of the Association of Foot and Mouth Painting Artists Worldwide, and is currently studying Traditional Chinese Painting at the Special Education Department of Changchun University.

Chapter One

THE CONTEXT OF SPECIAL EDUCATION

*L*earning

Objectives

After studying this chapter, you should be able to:

- Define special education and the categories of special needs

- Discuss the seven major provisions Congress addressed when it passed the Individuals with Disabilities Education Act (IDEA) (formerly called the Education for All Handicapped Children Act (EHA))

- Analyze the principle of least restrictive environment

- Summarize the major roles that legislation and litigation play in special education

A MYTH FOR SPECIAL EDUCATION: WU SONG AND THE TIGER

*E*dwin Martin, the first director of the Bureau of the Education of the Handicapped and one of the creators of the Education for All Handicapped Children Act (now the Individuals with Disabilities Education Act—IDEA), recently described his image of special education. Speaking in China to professionals in the field of special education, he compared the Chinese myth of Wu Song to the universal battles to overcome discrimination against individuals with handicaps.

Outside the Ming tombs, I noticed some cardboard cutouts. One was of a figure fighting and triumphing over a tiger. There was a place for a tourist to put his or her head on the warrior's body, to be photographed as a hero. I recognized this as an ancient myth, one that is represented in many cultures, although I had not yet learned the Chinese story. After some questioning, I learned the story of Wu Song, hero of the epic "Water Margin."

Wu Song had many strengths, but was most famous for his ability to kill tigers. One day during his travels he passed a small inn at the foot of Jin Yang Mountain. A sign in the window read "3 bowls and you will never make it across." His curiosity was piqued and he asked the meaning of the sign. He was told that the mountain was notorious for its ferocious tigers. The sign was a warning not to drink too much. A drunken traveler who lay down to nap would surely be eaten alive!

Wu Song was undaunted. He called for nine bowls of wine, gulped them down and set off to cross Jin Yang Mountain. He began to feel drowsy. He lay down with his club at his side and fell asleep. Soon a tiger came upon the sleeping hero and attacked him with teeth and claws. They battled long and hard, the club split apart; but in the end, Wu Song overcame the tiger with a blow from a stone.

Once again he had proved that individuals can accomplish what common wisdom warns is impossible. You are Wu Song. I am Wu Song. That is the truth the myth seeks to share. We must face the tigers in our own lives. It is interesting to note that Wu Song's club split apart. A detail like that always has meaning. In myths, when the usual tool or weapon fails, the hero has the opportunity to improvise a new solution. In our work, too, we need to go beyond the usual methods, and to use improvisation and imagination to overcome our tiger. Together, as specialists interested in persons with disabilities, we seek to accomplish, as Wu Song did, "what common wisdom warned was impossible." We seek to end centuries of fear and exclusion. Our work has shown each of us that it is possible. We have seen in the lives of children and adults with disabilities the triumph of the human spirit over the tiger. (1988)

1. How is the myth of Wu Song like the battle against discrimination?

2. What role can the professional play in this battle?

The right to education for all young people is one of the most widely held values in the United States. Our leaders have recognized that the success of our democracy depends on citizens who are educated and who actively participate in the political process. In the early days of our nation, education was a right of the privileged—generally, white males. It was not until the midnineteenth century that universal education became a reality. Today, all children in the United States have the right to attend school. In most states, in fact, it is their legal obligation to attend school until they reach age sixteen. Side-by-side, girls and boys, rich and poor, every race and ethnic group, and children of all skill levels and abilities arrive at schools each morning. Such student diversity demands teachers and other professionals who are skilled to meet challenges, who eagerly meet students and pledge to help and guide the process of education.

Special education teachers and other professionals have committed themselves to special challenges. All children with handicaps are now part of our public schools and have a right to education. These students have a wide variety of special needs. Special education children include those with mental retardation, communicative disorders, learning disabilities, gifted and creative abilities, behavioral disorders, visual impairments, hearing impairments, physical disabilities and health impairments, and children who are multicultural and bilingual who also have special education needs. Children who are gifted and creative have historically been included in discussions of special education. Although programs for gifted children exist in many schools, they are not universal as programs for children with handicaps now are in the United States. Special education professionals are needed to ensure the success of all these special students.

Of course, all children are unique individuals, and stereotypes or suggestions that certain children are a "type" must be avoided. While each child is unique, however, children frequently share certain characteristics. This is especially true for children with exceptionalities. This book describes some of those shared characteristics and shows you how you can address the special needs of these students.

> **special education.** Individualized education for children and youth with special needs.

*"Forget it, pal. I thought I recognized you, but, as it turns out,
it was just your type that I recognized."*

Drawing by Zeigler; © 1988. The New Yorker Magazine, Inc.

regular class. A typical classroom designed to serve students without disabilities.

You will learn what causes these special needs and how some disabilities can be prevented or their impact reduced. Special education can make the difference between a child's success or failure in school. You will study the learning characteristics of these children and some practical ways of teaching them.

Special education is controversial. Frequently, professionals in the field of education disagree about issues such as integration of students with disabilities into **regular classes.** Within the field of special education, professionals also disagree about a variety of issues. For example, professionals who work with individuals with hearing impairments disagree over whether to use sign language or oral language (see chapter 10, Hearing Impairments). To help you grapple with some of these thorny issues we introduce you to concepts and controversies in each chapter, raising issues with no one correct answer. You will find your study of people with special needs exciting and we hope that you will accept the challenge of working with these individuals to assist them in achieving their highest potential.

SPECIAL EDUCATION DEFINED

First and foremost, special education is individualized education for children with special needs. According to federal regulations, special education means "specially designed instruction, at no cost to the parent, to meet the unique needs of a handicapped child, including classroom instruction, instruction in physical education,

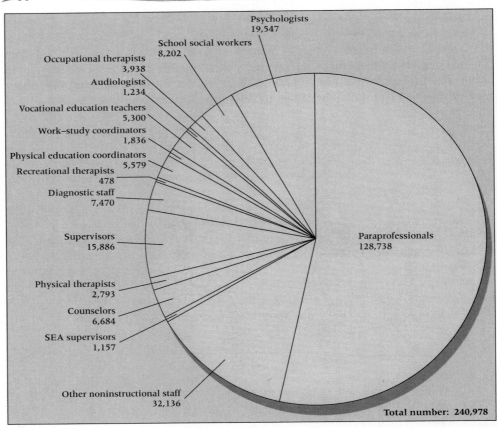

FIGURE 1.1 **Types of Special Education Personnel in Related Services**

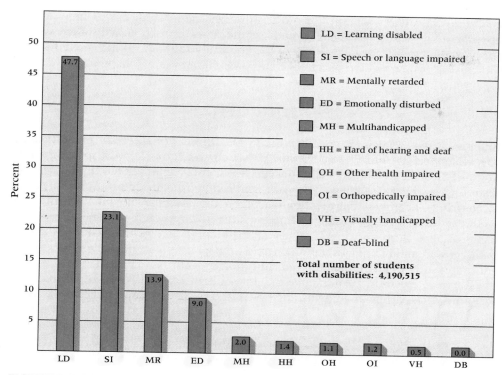

prevention. Avoiding development of a disability.

The chart shows:

LD = Learning disabled
SI = Speech or language impaired
MR = Mentally retarded
ED = Emotionally disturbed
MH = Multihandicapped
HH = Hard of hearing and deaf
OH = Other health impaired
OI = Orthopedically impaired
VH = Visually handicapped
DB = Deaf–blind

Total number of students with disabilities: 4,190,515

Values: LD 47.7, SI 23.1, MR 13.9, ED 9.0, MH 2.0, HH 1.4, OH 1.1, OI 1.2, VH 0.5, DB 0.0

FIGURE 1.2 **Types of Special Education Teachers**

home instruction, and instruction in hospitals and institutions" (34 Code of Federal Regulations (C.F.R.) 300.14 (a)(1)). It also includes all related services (for example, speech pathology, physical therapy) required to meet the unique learning needs of the youngster. (See Figure 1.1, which illustrates the variety of professionals providing related services to students with disabilities.) Special education considers the individual's unique learning needs and arranges the learning opportunities necessary for each youngster. Special education not only provides the materials and services required by the student's handicap but also monitors progress so that no student with special needs is overlooked or neglected.

Special education is a viable, dynamic, changing field. Although great strides have been made in the past 50 years, much work remains to be done. There is a critical shortage of special education personnel. The field needs more trained teachers and support personnel, additional research and development of special education techniques, increased use of advanced technology, improvements in the **prevention** of handicaps, and more sensitive communities and school environments. Figure 1.2 shows the proportion of special education teachers working in each disability area.

Children and youth with intense needs are still excluded from school in some communities. In the future, schools and service agencies will have to find cooperative ways to meet the medical and educational needs of all students with disabilities, particularly those with severe physical disabilities, in classroom settings. Our future must be one in which no youngster faces a verdict of "noneducable." *All children can learn.* The focus of special education must include all students with disabilities.

To enable students with special needs to achieve their maximum potential, special education provides them the opportunity to learn to read, write, and compute so that throughout their lives they can continue to learn and grow. While learning academic skills is appropriate for most youngsters with handicaps, it may not be appropriate for some who need more basic life skills instruction. All students with special needs should develop social and community skills. And they should begin the kind of job preparation necessary to become economically independent.

CLASSIFICATION AND LABELING

Students with special needs are individuals who require special education and related special services in order to achieve their fullest potential. In this book special education needs are grouped into eight categories: mental retardation, communicative disorders, learning disabilities, giftedness and creativity, behavioral disorders, visual impairments, hearing impairments, and physical disabilities and health impairments. Figure 1.3 shows the percentage of students identified in each disability area compared to all children in special education. The book also includes chapters about multicultural and bilingual special education (chapter 2) and the delivery of special education services and individualized education programs and plans (chapter 3).

However, we must keep in mind that individuals themselves cannot be precisely categorized. A particular student might have the special education needs of one or

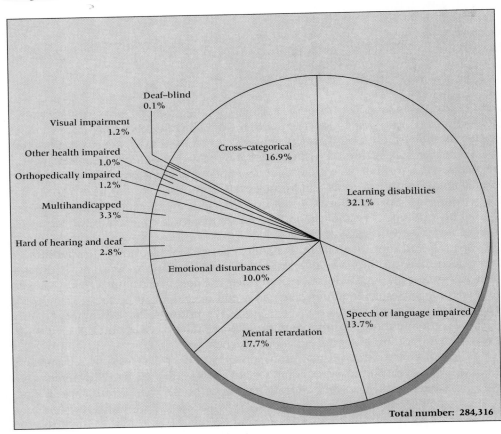

FIGURE 1.3 Percentage of Special Education by Disability*

*National data are not available for students who are gifted/creative or for those who are culturally and linguistically diverse.

more of the categories; some may have multiple handicaps. That is, a child might have a visual impairment, a hearing impairment, a behavioral disorder, *and* a learning disability. Another child might have a different combination of disabilities. The needs of students are as individual as the children themselves. Mere recognition of a handicap cannot dictate either a particular **educational placement** or a label into which the student's individuality is forced.

As we try to refine our definition of special education and students with handicaps we must also contend with issues of classification and labeling. These issues have received widespread attention in the field of special education (Hobbs, 1975a–c; Mercer, 1973). As we all know, the names we use to describe persons with special needs can influence the way people think about these individuals and their abilities. These names or labels can also affect how individuals with special needs regard themselves. Early in the history of mental retardation, for example, people with this disability were labeled "morons," "imbeciles," and "idiots." When first used, these labels may not have had strong negative connotations, but today we all recognize the devaluation in those labels. We realize that to continue using such terms to describe students with mental retardation would negatively influence the way they perceive themselves, the way others regard them, and probably our own attitudes toward them.

Many special educators differentiate classification from labeling. Classification typically refers to a structured system that identifies and organizes characteristics to establish order. Many disciplines, such as biology, chemistry, and geology, have classification systems. For a classification system to be useful, it must meet four criteria: it must be reliable, cover all relevant aspects, be logically consistent, and have clinical utility (Cromwell, Blashfield, and Strauss, 1975). The classification system we use in this text is **categorical,** organizing special education into the categories mental retardation, communicative disorders, learning disabilities, giftedness and creativity, behavioral disorders, visual impairments, hearing impairments, and physical disabilities and health impairments. Each of these categories has its own internal classification system, or subcategorization. For example, the category mental retardation is subcategorized into four levels: mild, moderate, severe, and profound mental retardation.

What are the advantages of a system of classification for special education? First, a classification system enables us to name disabilities, to differentiate them from one another, and to communicate in a meaningful and efficient way about a specific disability. Second, a classification system is essential for research. It would be very difficult to conduct research about physical disabilities, for example, without a system of categorizing the disability and the needs of those who have physical disabilities. Third, the system helps in forming special interest groups to lobby for improved services and promote enlightened attitudes. Finally, categories are helpful in developing particular treatments and therapies. They make it easier to relate a certain treatment to a certain diagnosis or category.

What are the disadvantages of using a system of classification? Many professionals support a **noncategorical** approach to educating children with disabilities. They argue that when categories are used, children with special needs are not treated as individuals, that classification places too much emphasis on the group and not enough emphasis on matching the services to individual needs. However, even when a noncategorical approach is used, it is sometimes necessary to classify according to level of disability, for example, mild, moderate, and severe.

Labeling identifies individuals or groups according to a category assigned to

educational placement. The location or type of classroom program (for example, resource room) arranged for a child's education; the setting in which a student receives educational services.

classification. A structured system that identifies and organizes characteristics to establish order.

categorical approach. A system of classification using specific categories such as learning disabilities or mental retardation.

noncategorical. In special education, not classifying or differentiating among handicaps or exceptionalities in providing services.

labeling. Assigning a special education category to an individual.

diagnostician. A professional trained to test and analyze a student's areas of strength and weakness to determine whether an individual is eligible for special services and to help in setting educational goals and planning for instruction.

All children are individuals, and some have special education needs. It is important to remember them as people first.

them. For example, a child who has been diagnosed as having a behavior disorder might subsequently be labeled "behaviorally disordered." Labeling can be formal, for example, imposed by an authority such as a psychologist or **diagnostician,** or informal, for example, imposed by other children on the playground. Many have criticized labeling as limiting and stigmatizing. Some argue that when you impose a label, the person so labeled is seen as a stereotype of the label rather than as an individual. Certainly labels are harmful when, as a result of that label, individuals are degraded, discriminated against, excluded from society, or placed in classrooms without regard for their individuality. But labels can be helpful, in the ways that classification can be helpful, providing a common language to describe a disability. Labeling may also be inevitable (Soder, 1989).

You will notice that in this book students are referred to as individuals first, with the disability second. We do not refer to "*the* disabled" or "*the* deaf" or "*the* retarded." Children, youth, and adults are described as individuals *who have* a certain disability—for example, "a child *with* a visual impairment," "a girl *with* mental retardation," or "a student *with* a physical disability." A disability is not the student, any more than any other single characteristic becomes the person. Each person is a complicated bundle of many characteristics, of which a certain disability may be one. Professionals must always use care in the language they use to describe their students and their students' special needs. The language a teacher uses affects the students with special needs, other students in the school, other teachers, the families of the students, and the community.

HISTORY OF SPECIAL EDUCATION

How did the field of special education develop? Special education grew from an initial awareness that some children require a type or intensity of education different from typical education in order to achieve their potential. This awareness evolved

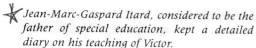 *Jean-Marc-Gaspard Itard, considered to be the father of special education, kept a detailed diary on his teaching of Victor.*

Victor, the wild boy of Aveyron, contributed to the development of special education theory and techniques as a student of Itard's.

over many years, and we can trace its roots to Europe in the 1700s, when certain innovators began to make isolated attempts to provide education to children with handicaps.

One of these people was Jean-Marc-Gaspard <u>Itard,</u> a French physician who is considered to be the father of special education. Itard had been working with children with hearing impairments, but his most important work came out of his efforts to help the so-called wild boy of Aveyron. In 1799 a young boy, later named Victor, was discovered in the woods of France. The boy was thought to be a "wild child," untouched by civilization. It is likely that he had mental retardation as well as environmental deprivation. Most people thought the case was hopeless. But Itard, believing in the power of education, took on the task of teaching Victor all the things that typical children learn from their families and in school. He used carefully designed techniques to teach Victor to speak a few words, to walk upright, to eat with dishes and utensils, and to interact with other people.

Fortunately, Itard wrote detailed reports of his techniques, and his philosophy, as well as Victor's progress. Many of these techniques are still used in modern special education. Below are listed Itard's five aims for Victor's "mental and moral education":

First Aim: To interest him in social life . . .
Second Aim: To awaken his nervous sensibility . . .
Third Aim: To extend the range of his ideas . . .
Fourth Aim: To lead him to the use of speech . . .
Fifth Aim: To make him exercise the simplest mental operations . . .
     (Itard, 1962, pp. 10–11)

Another major early figure in the field of special education is Edouard <u>Seguin,</u> a student of Itard. In 1846 he published *The Moral Treatment, Hygiene, and Education of Idiots and Other Backward Children,* the first special education treatise addressing the needs of children with handicaps. After he moved to the United States, he helped found the Association of Medical Officers of American Institutions for Idiots and Feebleminded Persons in 1876. This organization later became the American Association on Mental Deficiency (AAMD), and later yet the American Association on Mental Retardation (AAMR). The oldest and largest interdisciplinary professional association in the field of mental retardation, AAMR remains a significant influence. Seguin believed that sensorimotor exercises could help stimulate learning for children with handicaps. His ideas were integrated into many schools in the United States in the 1800s. The legacy of Seguin's work can be found today in many aspects of special education. For example, the use of motor exercises as an aid to learning was reintroduced in the 1960s in the United States and is often part of the curriculum in special education (Kephart, 1960; Frostig and Horne, 1964; Barsh, 1965).

Seguin in turn influenced Maria Montessori. Montessori, the first female physician in Italy, worked first with children with mental disabilities before she began the study of young children. She showed that children could learn at young ages and that concrete experiences and an environment rich in manipulative materials facilitated their learning. Her educational methods were published in 1912, helping to spread special education strategies. Today, Montessori is probably most familiar as a leader in early childhood education. It is after her that the Montessori preschool movement is named.

By the early 1800s, residential institutions had been developed in the United States for teaching children with most disabilities. For example, the American Asylum for the Education of the Deaf and Dumb (now the American School for the Deaf) was started in 1817 by Thomas Hopkins Gallaudet. Samuel Gridley Howe, the famous American reformer and abolitionist, founded the New England Asylum for the Blind (later the Perkins Institute) in 1832. He was the first to successfully teach

Maria Montessori, a pioneer in creating concrete experiences and environments that enhanced learning. She first studied children with mental disabilities and then extended her work to the study of young children.

Scattered attempts to provide education to children with disabilities began in the nineteenth century. Regrettably, these opportunities were neither systematic nor available to all children.

a person with both blindness and deafness. Later, in 1848, Howe created the Massachusetts School for Idiotic and Feeble-minded Children. Howe successfully persuaded the Massachusetts legislature to appropriate $2500 to educate children with mental handicaps for an experimental three-year program (Barr, 1913). In 1825 the House of Refuge, the first U.S. institution for juvenile delinquents, was founded in New York (Kauffman, 1989). The first hospital devoted to children with physical disabilities was the Home of the Merciful Saviour founded in 1884 in Philadelphia (Eberle, 1922). By 1917 most states had at least one residential institution where children and adults with disabilities lived, often spending their entire lives (Scheerenberger, 1983).

Special education classes based in regular schools appeared in the late nineteenth century. In 1878 two special education classes opened in Cleveland (Kanner, 1964), apparently for children with behavior problems. Sarason and Doris (1979) describe the early efforts of Elizabeth Farrell, beginning in 1898, to create "ungraded" classes in New York. Farrell's work teaching "backward" students was tied to the settlement house movement, a social service movement to assist the poor and to help immigrants become Americanized. Farrell later founded the Council for Exceptional Children (CEC). Although by the early twentieth century most states had residential institutions, special school classes in neighborhood schools existed in only a few cities. Classes were reported in Providence, Rhode Island; Springfield, Massachusetts; Chicago, Illinois; Boston, Massachusetts; New York, New York; Philadelphia, Pennsylvania; Los Angeles, California; Detroit, Michigan; Elgin, Illinois; Trenton, New Jersey; Bridgeport, Connecticut; Newton, Massachusetts; Rochester, New York; and Washington, D.C.

As today, professionals in the late nineteenth century believed in the individual worth of each student, regardless of that student's special learning needs, and were prepared to work hard to make achievement a reality for all students. In 1891 one institution superintendent described the perfect special education teacher. He urged the teachers to be "sweet-tempered":

> The ideal teacher is well educated, refined, intensely interested in her pupils, and has a professional zeal to grow in her work: she is original, striving to introduce new and bright methods, but not passing hastily from subject to subject before the child has grasped the first. She is patient but energetic, sweet-tempered but persistent, and to the influences of her education and character she adds the charms of personal neatness and attractive manners. She possesses naturally a well grounded religious sense, which finds its best expression in self-sacrifice, conscientious duty, and instinctive kindness. (Isaac N. Kerlin, Manual of Elwyn, 1891, quoted in Nazzaro, 1977 p. 11)

The first training opportunity for teachers of special classes was offered in 1905 at the New Jersey Training School for Feebleminded Boys and Girls (Kanner, 1964). In 1907 the tuition for a six-week summer course in special education was $25.

While the idea of special education was taking root in the early 1900s, special education classes remained rare. Only a small number of all students with special needs were able to attend these classes. As late as 1948, for example, only 12 percent of all children and youth *with handicaps* were receiving a special education (Ballard, Ramirez, and Weintraub, 1982). What happened to the others? Many were probably able to function to some degree in their home communities. Others were forced to enter isolated, segregated institutions. Certainly, some died from lack of care, and others were hidden by families fearing discrimination and prejudice.

The recognition that special education required a particular expertise was important in the development of this new profession. The National Education Association (NEA), a professional educators' organization, approved a Department of Special Education in 1897, although it was disbanded by 1918. In 1922 the International Council for the Education of Exceptional Children (CEC) was founded (Aiello, 1976) when members of a 1922 summer special education class conducted at Teachers' College, Columbia University decided to meet annually in order to continue to share exciting ideas about special education. Their professor, Elizabeth Farrell, became the group's first president. Membership grew and in later years the "International" was dropped from the title and the organization became known as the Council for Exceptional Children, or CEC. CEC affiliated with the National Education Association in 1924 and the World Federation of Education Associations in 1929. To this day, CEC remains the main special education professional organization in the United States. The largest professional organization of special educators across all disabilities, today CEC has approximately 50,000 members.

Other professional organizations important to the development of special education, for example the American Occupational Therapy Association (AOTA), the National Association of Social Workers (NASW), and the American Physical Therapy Association (APTA), were also active during the 1920s. Many volunteer and parent organizations developed in the midtwentieth century. The Association for Retarded Citizens of the United States (ARC-US), founded in 1950 as the National Association of Parents and Friends of Mentally Retarded Children, worked to shape special education services. Also influential were United Cerebral Palsy Associations, Inc. (UCP) (1949), the National Society for Autistic Children (1961), the Learning Disability Association of America (LDAA) founded in 1963 as the Association for

What about ASHA?

The Training School

Entered March 14, 1904, at Vineland, N. J., as second-class matter,
under act of Congress of July 16, 1894.

No. 36.   **FEBRUARY 1907.**   **25c. per Annum.**

"*I gave a beggar from my little store
Of well-earned gold.   He spent the
   shining ore
And came again, and yet again, still
   cold
   And hungry as before.*

*I gave a thought and through that
   thought of mine
He found himself a man, supreme,
   divine,
Bold, clothed, and crowned with bless-
   ings manifold,
   And now he begs no more.*"

THE SUMMER SCHOOL FOR TEACHERS.

The announcements of our Summer School for 1907 are now ready for distribution. The purpose of the School is to give professional training to those who desire to teach in the special classes in the public schools and to fit teachers and others to better understand peculiar, backward and "special" children. We have unusual facilities for this work, a splendid general equipment and quite a complete laboratory. The plan of work includes observation and teaching, laboratory work, lectures and reading. The tuition fee is $25 and those students who first apply may be boarded at the School at an additional cost of $25. The course extends from July 15th to August 24th.

Information concerning the Summer School may be obtained by addressing E. R. Johnstone, Vineland, N. J.

AS IT APPEARS TO THE PSYCHOLOGIST.

You remember the fable of the lion looking at the picture of a man conquering a lion and saying: "If a lion had painted the picture the man would have gotten the worst of it." It makes a difference who paints the picture.

Men strong of intellect have for long had a monopoly of painting the picture of the feeble-minded. While at times the feeble-minded child has been regarded as a supernatural being possessed of a spirit either good or bad, he has been among the more intellectual races more often treated much as the Spartans treated him—regarded as an outcast and either exposed to die or, where some reverence for human life as such has developed, been preserved from death indeed, but preserved for a life that is possibly worse than death. He has been not only useless, but a drag on society, an incurable disease, a horrible nightmare, one of God's blunders.

But how would the picture look if the lion and not the man painted it?

The feeble-minded child is a human being. He differs from those who call themselves normal, in degree, not in kind. No one of us but might have been of his grade had any one of a score of very possible contingencies taken place. Not one of us but might to-morrow become as "defective" as any of these by the slightest change in our organism. (It is true we should call it insanity, but that is only a matter of terminology.)

What then are we and who is this child? He is somewhere near the

normalization. Making available ordinary patterns of life and conditions of everyday living.

legislation. Laws passed by a legislation or congress and signed by a governor or president.

litigation. A lawsuit or legal proceeding.

prevalence. The total number of cases at a given time.

incidence. The number of new cases that occur within a certain time period.

Education for All Handicapped Children Act (EHA). A federal law, PL 94–142, passed in 1975 with many provisions for assuring free appropriate public education for all students with handicaps—later renamed the Individuals with Disabilities Act (IDEA).

Individuals with Disabilities Education Act (IDEA). New name given in 1990 to the Education for All Handicapped Children Act (EHA).

Children with Learning Disabilities, and the Epilepsy Foundation of America (1968), growing out of several earlier epilepsy groups. These organizations have had a profound impact on the development of special education and services to individuals with special needs and their families.

Normalization is an essential dimension of special education. Although the concept was suggested in 1959 by Bank-Mikkelsen of Denmark (Biklen, 1985), the word itself was first coined by Bengt Nirje of Sweden (1969), who encouraged Americans to incorporate this principle in services to people with disabilities. According to Nirje (1985), normalization means "making available to all persons with disabilities or other handicaps, patterns of life and conditions of everyday living which are as close as possible to or indeed *the same as* the regular circumstances and ways of life of society" (p. 67; emphasis in original). The principle of normalization applies to every aspect of a student's life. Nirje referred to a set of normal life patterns: the normal rhythm of the day, the normal rhythm of the week, the normal rhythm of the year, and the normal development of the life cycle. (See also Wolfensberger, 1972).

This brief history describes the birth of special education. Later in this chapter you will read about **legislation** and **litigation** that have brought the field to its present status. In each chapter you will find a more detailed history of the development of educational services in specific categories.

PREVALENCE OF CHILDREN WITH SPECIAL NEEDS

How many students in this country need special education services? There are two ways to describe the number of children with handicaps. Prevalence refers to the *total* number of cases at a given time. A slightly different calculation is made by incidence, which is the number of *new* cases that occur within a certain time period. As you work through this text, you will note that we usually refer to the prevalence of each exceptionality.

What is the prevalence of students requiring special education in the United States? The *Twelfth Annual Report to Congress on the Implementation of the Education of the Handicapped Act* indicates that in the 1988–1989 school year, a total of 4,587,370 children were served in special education programs under the **Education for All Handicapped Children Act (EHA)** (see Figure 1.4). Congress changed the name of this act to **Individuals with Disabilities Education Act (IDEA)** in 1990. This total represents approximately 6.7 percent of children and youth ages three to twenty-one. Because many students are not identified as having a handicap until they are school age, the percentage of children and youth between ages six and seventeen receiving special education services is higher at 9.4 percent. Most of these students have mild disabilities; thus their special education needs are often mild. Other children have disabilities that are more severe, and their special education needs are likely to be more intense and last over a longer period of time.

 Prevalence, however, is influenced by factors other than the number of youngsters with disabilities. The percentage of students receiving special education programs varies from state to state. This is so despite the fact that the federal government creates rules and guidelines, monitors general compliance with those rules, and shapes the overall picture of special education in this country. While the federal government oversees the process, however, individual state education agencies, individual school districts, individual schools, and individual teachers and families

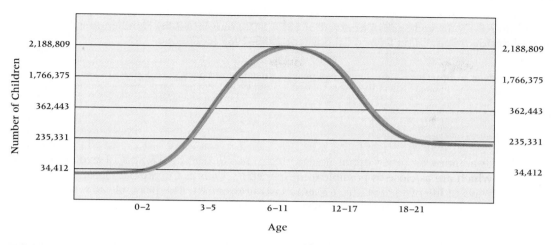

FIGURE 1.4 Number and Age of Children Served by IDEA During the 1988–1989 School Year

carry out the critical details. Table 1.1 shows the percentage of students with each disability served by each state. Find your state on this chart. What percentage of students are provided special education services in your state?

TABLE 1.1. Percentage of Children 6–17 Served under Chapter 1 of ESEA(SOP) and EHA-B by Handicapping Condition Based on Estimated Resident Population During School Year 1988–1989

State	All Conditions	Learning Disabled	Speech Impaired	Mentally Retarded	Emotionally Disturbed	Hard of Hearing and Deaf	Multi-Handicapped	Ortho-pedically Impaired	Other Health Impaired	Visually Handicapped
Alabama	11.12	3.75	2.94	3.26	0.74	0.11	0.12	0.06	0.08	0.05
Alaska	12.57	6.69	2.79	1.93	0.53	0.13	0.26	0.08	0.12	0.04
Arizona	8.14	4.63	1.88	0.62	0.53	0.15	0.17	0.07	0.06	0.04
Arkansas	9.28	4.98	1.54	2.31	0.07	0.12	0.12	0.03	0.05	0.05
California	8.13	4.91	1.94	0.41	0.23	0.13	0.09	0.13	0.24	0.05
Colorado	8.41	4.14	1.41	0.49	1.53	0.13	0.52	0.13	0.00	0.04
Connecticut	10.97	5.93	1.81	0.63	2.15	0.12	0.15	0.05	0.06	0.07
Delaware	10.54	6.05	1.46	0.97	1.45	0.14	0.11	0.18	0.10	0.05
District of Columbia	7.21	3.57	1.24	0.99	1.01	0.05	0.16	0.08	0.05	0.05
Florida	10.45	4.43	3.25	1.23	1.19	0.08	0.00	0.11	0.13	0.04
Georgia	7.01	2.06	1.56	1.74	1.44	0.09	0.00	0.05	0.03	0.04
Hawaii	6.17	3.54	1.16	0.58	0.42	0.12	0.10	0.14	0.07	0.04
Idaho	8.25	4.93	1.53	1.19	0.21	0.13	0.03	0.10	0.11	0.03
Illinois	10.68	5.00	2.81	1.15	1.30	0.14	0.01	0.14	0.08	0.05
Indiana	9.71	3.68	3.54	1.77	0.43	0.11	0.07	0.05	0.01	0.05
Iowa	10.03	4.47	1.92	1.90	1.30	0.14	0.09	0.18	0.00	0.03
Kansas	8.90	3.73	2.55	1.19	0.99	0.13	0.11	0.09	0.05	0.05
Kentucky	9.48	3.04	3.15	2.48	0.41	0.12	0.14	0.06	0.04	0.07
Louisiana	6.87	2.77	2.14	1.03	0.42	0.13	0.08	0.10	0.15	0.04
Maine	11.80	5.17	2.69	1.21	1.91	0.13	0.41	0.11	0.13	0.04
Maryland	10.59	5.43	3.27	0.61	0.50	0.16	0.33	0.08	0.12	0.08

(continued)

TABLE 1.1. Percentage of Children 6–17 Served under Chapter 1 of ESEA(SOP) and EHA-B by Handicapping Condition Based on Estimated Resident Population During School Year 1988–1989 (continued)

State	All Conditions	Learning Disabled	Speech Impaired	Mentally Retarded	Emotionally Disturbed	Hard of Hearing and Deaf	Multi-Handi capped	Ortho-pedically Impaired	Other Health Impaired	Visually Handi-capped
Massachusetts	14.75	5.20	3.38	3.12	2.03	0.21	0.33	0.16	0.21	0.09
Michigan	8.36	3.76	1.99	0.98	1.14	0.13	0.09	0.20	0.03	0.04
Minnesota	9.56	4.60	1.89	1.24	1.40	0.17	0.02	0.15	0.05	0.05
Mississippi	9.64	4.62	3.28	1.42	0.04	0.08	0.05	0.12	0.00	0.03
Missouri	10.56	4.96	2.87	1.54	0.89	0.10	0.05	0.08	0.05	0.03
Montana	9.07	5.02	2.36	0.66	0.41	0.13	0.19	0.07	0.12	0.10
Nebraska	9.80	4.25	2.69	1.34	0.84	0.16	0.12	0.22	0.12	0.06
Nevada	8.26	5.02	1.78	0.53	0.50	0.08	0.13	0.12	0.06	0.04
New Hampshire	8.72	5.35	1.50	0.46	0.86	0.11	0.12	0.08	0.17	0.05
New Jersey	12.51	6.32	4.08	0.38	1.06	0.10	0.45	0.04	0.04	0.03
New Mexico	9.95	4.78	2.96	0.61	1.05	0.13	0.19	0.16	0.03	0.04
New York	8.79	5.29	0.84	0.64	1.44	0.11	0.27	0.06	0.10	0.04
North Carolina	9.16	3.98	2.13	1.69	0.80	0.15	0.10	0.07	0.17	0.05
North Dakota	8.88	4.23	2.92	1.06	0.34	0.13	0.00	0.08	0.05	0.05
Ohio	9.44	3.70	2.61	2.06	0.38	0.10	0.38	0.17	0.00	0.04
Oklahoma	9.75	4.62	2.67	1.81	0.24	0.10	0.19	0.05	0.02	0.04
Oregon	9.48	5.16	2.49	0.62	0.58	0.21	0.00	0.16	0.19	0.07
Pennsylvania	9.46	4.02	2.70	1.60	0.89	0.14	0.00	0.06	0.00	0.06
Puerto Rico	.	.	.	.	.	.	.	.	.	.
Rhode Island	11.43	7.66	1.92	0.54	0.88	0.09	0.05	0.09	0.15	0.04
South Carolina	10.27	4.11	2.79	2.07	0.93	0.14	0.05	0.10	0.02	0.06
South Dakota	9.28	4.16	2.91	1.07	0.39	0.21	0.29	0.13	0.06	0.04
Tennessee	10.52	5.47	2.66	1.37	0.28	0.16	0.19	0.10	0.20	0.10
Texas	8.75	4.95	1.83	0.64	0.71	0.12	0.10	0.10	0.25	0.05
Utah	9.42	4.20	1.80	0.70	2.16	0.14	0.24	0.06	0.08	0.05
Vermont	11.99	5.22	3.60	1.60	0.91	0.19	0.14	0.13	0.15	0.05
Virginia	9.51	4.88	2.35	1.16	0.76	0.11	0.09	0.06	0.05	0.05
Washington	8.26	4.31	1.58	0.84	0.53	0.18	0.22	0.12	0.43	0.03
West Virginia	11.42	5.20	3.12	2.19	0.64	0.10	0.00	0.08	0.02	0.06
Wisconsin	7.63	2.56	1.52	0.47	1.13	0.02	1.84	0.04	0.02	0.02
Wyoming	9.54	5.17	2.64	0.60	0.55	0.15	0.00	0.15	0.22	0.05
American Samoa	.	.	.	.	.	.	.	.	.	.
Guam	.	.	.	.	.	.	.	.	.	.
Northern Marianas	.	.	.	.	.	.	.	.	.	.
Trust Territories	.	.	.	.	.	.	.	.	.	.
Virgin Islands	.	.	.	.	.	.	.	.	.	.
Bureau of Indian Affairs	.	.	.	.	.	.	.	.	.	.
United States and Insular Areas	9.48	4.55	2.31	1.20	0.85	0.13	0.18	0.10	0.11	0.05
50 States, District of Columbia, and Puerto Rico	9.47	4.54	2.31	1.20	0.85	0.13	0.18	0.10	0.11	0.05

NOTES:
The sum of the percents of individual handicapping conditions may not equal the total percent of all conditions because of rounding.
Percentage of children served is based on estimated resident population counts for July 1988.
Resident populations are estimated by the U.S. Bureau of the Census.
Data as of October 1, 1989.
Annual.cntl (CBRPPX1A)

FAMILIES OF CHILDREN WITH SPECIAL NEEDS

Children with special needs cannot be viewed in isolation, but rather as members of their society, community, and also as members of their families. Special education must give strong consideration to the parents of students with exceptionalities. According to Hobbs (1975c), a parent is the "primary helper, monitor, coordinator, observer, record keeper, and decision maker" for the child (p. 286). Others—teachers, therapists, physicians, nurses, and psychologists—are consultants to the parents. Turnbull and Turnbull (1986) propose that professionals use a family systems approach in order to incorporate the family into the work they do with students with exceptionalities. They propose an analysis of four components of an individual's family: family resources, family interaction, family functions, and family life cycle. These components form the framework of a family systems analysis. Attention to these components helps individualize professionals' interactions with families so that the uniqueness in each family is recognized in services to the child. Most important is for families and service providers to develop a partnership so the educational needs of the youngster can be met.

THE EFFECTS OF A CHILD'S DISABILITY ON THE FAMILY

Parents of children with disabilities were asked the following question: "How has your child's disability affected you and your family socially, emotionally, and professionally?" Their answers, in part, reveal the stress and changes in family life caused by a child with a disability. More important, their responses can help educators understand how to work with families more effectively.

Naturally, we went through a similar kind of grieving process that other parents of handicapped children do. I am glad educators in the field are finally beginning to recognize that grieving is recurrent and occurs especially during developmental milestones in a child's life. This is something we parents have known for a long time despite the occasionally aggravating urging of "social work types" to "just deal with it and get on with life."

Emotionally, the effect is ongoing. It seems that one of us is always going in or out of the grief cycle. The family is very much affected emotionally. Financially, I don't feel our child has affected us much. Professionally, as a father, I don't feel it has affected us adversely as a family. I did leave a job for a better school or learning possibilities for our disabled child. Our child could limit my advancements, literally, because of the school system he is now enrolled in.

Socially, we have a few close friends. More friendships are flexible. Some of our very close friends and family too, for a time, almost dropped out of our lives. I think we have grown away from people too . . . our attitudes have changed. It makes us hard to be around. Emotionally, Susan has been a drain on all of us. It was especially hard on her younger sister. Professionally, I guess it hasn't changed our lives from what they would have been except for the statewide connections

(continued)

I've developed because of it. . . . Our attitude toward family, community, and community responsibility has changed.

We didn't change our activities. Emotionally, Stephanie made us aware of others. We are more aware of our responsibilities as the parents of a disabled child. Our picture of parenting has been altered. Our commitment is more long term. Financially, insurance is always an issue and a constant drain for us. We have worked hard to put ourselves in a position not to feel bitter. This affects our entire family.

Professionally, whether you have a Ph.D. or a pilot's license, when you are the mother of a handicapped child, this appears to be the major way in which others view you. Fathers do not have the same problem.

Socially, we have been limited in how and where we go and who we choose for friends (love me, love my child), how long we can be gone, the number of times we can go, how many can go, and what the weather will be like. Many things my husband and I have to do together instead of just with me or just with Roger because, at present, it's lots easier with two to help.

Socially, all of our friends changed initially; that is, we lost some friends and acquired others. Our new friends tended to be people who had more than average concern and caring about social/human needs and rights. We sought out new friends who had common experiences and avoided, in particular, judgmental and biased people. Emotionally, we both matured faster than we would have otherwise. My acceptance of other people's differences rose astronomically. We are also compelled, for reasons of sheer survival, to seek out more effective and structured mechanisms for coping with stress.

Source: The Rubberband Syndrome: Family Life with a Child with a Disability (pp. 11–13) by D. Bower and V. K. Wright, 1986, Nebraska Department of Education and the Iowa Department of Public Instruction. In cooperation with the Mt. Plains Regional Resource Center, Drake University, Des Moines, Ia. Reprinted by permission.

LEGISLATION

Pattern of School Exclusion

Modern special education reflects the thinking of many practicing educators, as well as the contributions of people with disabilities and their families. But special education also reflects the legal and political realities in the United States. Federal and state laws govern many aspects of special education. Let us consider some of these legal issues.

In 1948 it was reported that only 12 percent of all children with handicaps were receiving special education (Ballard, Ramirez, and Weintraub, 1982). Even as late as 1962, only sixteen states in the United States included "educable" mentally retarded

TABLE 1.2. Landmark Court Cases Setting the Stage for Special Education

Case	Date	Ruling	Importance
Brown v. Board of Education	1954	End to white "separate but equal" schools	Basis for future rulings that children with handicaps cannot be excluded from school
Pennsylvania Association for Retarded Children (PARC) v. Commonwealth of Pennsylvania	1972	Guaranteed special education to children with mental retardation	Court case that signaled a new period for special education
Mills v. Board of Education of the District of columbia	1972	Extended the right for special education to children with all disabilities	Reinforced the right to a free, public education to all children with handicaps

PL 94–142. Education for All Handicapped Children Act.

children (the modern terminology would be "children with mild mental retardation") under mandatory school attendance laws (Roos, 1970). In most states, even those children with the mildest levels of disabilities were not allowed to attend school. Children with more severe disabilities were routinely excluded even until the 1970s. While children without handicaps were required to attend school under compulsory school attendance laws, children *with* handicaps were *prevented* from attending school. The excuses presented for excluding children with handicaps from school are shocking by today's standards. One state supreme court justified excluding a young boy with cerebral palsy because he "produces a depressing and nauseating effect upon the teachers and school children" (*State ex rel. Beattie v. Board of Education,* 1919).

But the rights of children with special needs gradually gained momentum. In the 1970s the courts and the U.S. Congress addressed the issue of education for children with disabilities. Table 1.2 summarizes landmark court cases.

New laws finally helped put a stop to slamming school doors in the faces of these children and their families. These laws were the results of extraordinary efforts of people dedicated to helping those with handicaps. The landmark law protecting children with special needs—the Education for All Handicapped Children Act (EHA), **PL 94–142**—was passed in 1975. This law is now called Individuals with Disabilities Education Act (IDEA).

Individuals with Disabilities Education Act (IDEA)

The face of special education has changed steadily in the United States over the past 100 years. The progress achieved in the nineteenth and early twentieth centuries can be attributed to the efforts of individuals. The progress of recent years can be attributed in large part to court cases and the passage of a revolutionary new national law. With this law, the U.S. Congress designed federal legislation that guarantees education to every child with disabilities in the country.

REASONS FOR NATIONAL LEGISLATION. Why did Congress pass this revolutionary law? Let us look at Congress's own words.

The Congress finds that—

1. there are more than 8 million handicapped children in the United States today;

Free Appropriate Public Education (FAPE). One of the provisions of IDEA that assures children with handicaps receive necessary education and services without cost to the child and family.

2. the special educational needs of such children are not being fully met;

3. more than half of the handicapped children in the United States do not receive appropriate educational services which would enable them to have full equality of opportunity;

4. 1 million of the handicapped children in the United States are excluded entirely from the public school system and will not go through the educational process with their peers;

5. there are many handicapped children throughout the United States participating in regular school programs whose handicaps prevent them from having a successful educational experience because their handicaps are undetected;

6. because of the lack of adequate services within the public school system, families are often forced to find services outside the public school system, often at great distance from their residence and at their own expense;

7. developments in the training of teachers and in diagnostic and instructional procedures and methods have advanced to the point that, given appropriate funding, State and local educational agencies can and will provide effective special education and related services to meet the needs of handicapped children;

8. State and local educational agencies have a responsibility to provide education for all handicapped children, present financial resources are inadequate to meet the special educational needs of handicapped children; and

9. it is in the national interest that the Federal Government assist State and local efforts to provide programs to meet the educational needs of handicapped children in order to assure equal protection of the law. (20 U.S.C. section 1400 (b))

Clearly, Congress recognized the importance of special education for children with disabilities, and it was concerned about the widespread discrimination. Congress pointed out that many students with disabilities were excluded from education; and those who had entered the schoolhouse frequently failed to benefit from school experience because their disabilities went undetected or ignored. Congress realized that special education could make a positive difference in the lives of these children and their families with proper financial assistance and educational support. Congress found these facts so compelling that it declared that it was "in the national interest" to stop discrimination against children with disabilities.

What did Congress intend to accomplish with this law? Again, Congress was specific:

> It is the purpose of this chapter to assure that all handicapped children have available to them . . . a free appropriate public education which emphasizes special education and related services designed to meet their unique needs, to assure that the rights of handicapped children and their parents or guardians are protected, to assist States and localities to provide for the education of all handicapped children, and to assess and assure the effectiveness of efforts to educate handicapped children. (20 U.S.C. section 1400(c))

Fundamental Provisions

The seven major provisions of this law are explained below.

 1. Free and appropriate public education (FAPE). Any special education received by a student with handicaps is to be provided at no cost to the student and family. Even though most students with handicaps are served in regular classrooms, extra funds are needed to provide special education services. This extra cost, referred to as **excess cost,** is to be shared by the individual states and the federal government. The share is approximately 12 percent paid by the federal government, and 88 percent paid by the states (Singer and Butler, 1987). Although many people believe that special education is becoming increasingly expensive, Singer and Butler report that "average per child expenditure for special students in relation to average per child expenditure for regular students is about where it was in 1977. Spending the money during the school years is a good investment and saves money ultimately because the individuals are more likely to become independent adults.

Special education must also be appropriate. That is, the education must be suitable to the individual needs of the child. During the course of your study in special education, you will learn about techniques, methods, materials, and approaches designed to provide students with appropriate special education programs.

2. Notification and procedural rights for parents. Parents have the right to examine the records of their child and to obtain an independent educational evaluation of their child. They have the right to receive a clearly written notice that states the school's **evaluation** of the child. If the school believes the student has special needs, it will recommend further evaluation, placement, and other special services. If the school does not believe the child has a disability, the notice will state that as the reason for denying further special services. The parents have the right to consent or object to this notice, to make formal complaints, and to pursue a **due process hearing** and a **judicial hearing** if they disagree with the services provided by the school to the child. These rights are important and include the right to legal counsel and other rights concerning witnesses, written evidence, verbatim documentation of the hearing, and an appeal.

3. Identification and services to all children. The law requires that states specifically seek out and identify *all* the children who require services. A school must actively seek the children through public information campaigns and other types of outreach.

4. Necessary related services. For some children with handicaps, special education alone will not be enough. The law therefore includes a right to related services such as developmental, corrective, and other support services that may be needed to enable a child to benefit from special education (20 U.S.C., section 1401(17)). Typical related services might include transportation, speech pathology and audiology, psychological services, physical and occupational therapy, recreation, and certain medical and counseling services.

★ *so this is where SP & A come in*

5. Individualized assessments. Special education that is truly individualized cannot occur unless a child receives individualized and nondiscriminatory assessments (20 U.S.C., section 1412(5)(C)). Assessments include evaluations and tests by trained professionals to determine what handicaps a child might have and the most appropriate ways for dealing with the handicaps.

6. Individualized education program (IEP) plans. The roadmap for a student's special education is the individualized educational program plan, called IEP. The law requires that each child or youth with a handicap have a written statement developed in a meeting attended by the following people: a qualified representative of the local education agency, generally, the child's proposed special education teacher; the child's current teacher; the parents of the child; and the child (20 U.S.C., section 1401(20)). Because of the importance of this component of IDEA, we devote most of chapter 3 to the development and implementation of these plans.

---

excess cost. Expenses for the education of a child with handicaps that exceeds the average expenses of education for a child without handicaps.

evaluation. Assessment or judgment of special characteristics such as intelligence, physical abilities, sensory abilities, learning preferences, and achievement.

due process hearing. A noncourt proceeding before an impartial hearing officer that can be used if parents and school personnel disagree on a special education issue.

judicial hearing. A hearing before a judge in court.

identification. To seek out and identify children with disabilities.

individualized education program (IEP). A requirement of IDEA that guarantees a specifically tailored program to meet the individualized needs of each student with disabilities.

7. Least restrictive environment (LRE). When the field of special education began, the few services that were available were offered primarily in segregated settings: sometimes special schools in a school district, but more often in residential institutions. These institutions usually were geographically isolated in the rural parts of a state. Students often continued living in these facilities even after school age, frequently living their entire lives in the facility. The students spent their time with

---

*L*east Restrictive Means:

MAXIMUM FREEDOM: Restrictions of the students' ability to physically and intellectually explore their world should be minimized.

SIMILAR TO OTHER STUDENTS OF THE SAME CHRONOLOGICAL AGE: The student should be doing what other students of the same age are doing. Any necessary restrictions imposed on the child are the type that all children of that age experience. For example, five-year-olds are not allowed to play in the street, whether or not they are in special education.

SIMILAR TO OTHER STUDENTS OF THE SAME "MENTAL" AGE: Sometimes students are not ready for all the freedom their age peers experience. It may take longer, for example, for a student with physical disabilities to learn to drive a specially adapted car. Or a person with profound mental retardation may have freedom limited in ways that are similar to mental age peers rather than chronological age peers.

NOT HARMFUL: The special vulnerabilities sometimes resulting from disabilities may require, at least temporarily, restrictions to protect the person from harm. Caution is necessary, however, because this justification is sometimes inadvertently used to unnecessarily limit the freedom of a student with disabilities.

NOT CONTROLLING: All individuals seek to develop the skills and means to bring their world within their own control. Students with disabilities may require special assistance to control their world. Teachers should help students develop control of their worlds.

NOT DANGEROUS: Least restriction should never be used as an excuse to place students in unnecessarily dangerous situations. There will often be a balance, however, between enabling the student to assume the dignity of risk (Perske, 1972) and acknowledging an acceptable level of danger.

NOT INTRUSIVE: It is a difficult task to provide education and services to a student while avoiding intrusion. Respect for the privacy and dignity of each student will help teachers avoid intrusiveness.

MOST RESPECTFUL: Implementation of the principle of least restriction, like all other activities of a good teacher, always involves respect for the student.

MOST APPROPRIATE: The essence of individualization is that the education that results is genuinely suitable, given the student's strengths, weaknesses, personality, family circumstances, age, and all other relevant factors.

MOST INTEGRATED: Nirje (1985) defines integration as "based on recognition of a person's integrity, meaning to be yourself among others—to be able and to be allowed to be yourself among others" (p. 67).

MOST NORMALIZED: Normalization means making available to students with disabilities opportunities for lives similar to others in their society.

other students of similar disabilities, rarely interacting with noninstitutionalized peers or participating in the normal patterns of life. Even students with mild disabilities frequently found themselves in these facilities. Until the 1970s, it was common for much of the day-to-day work in institutions—such as caring for individuals with more severe disabilities or performing farm or laundry work—to be provided by the inmates with mild disabilities. The widely held belief that individuals with disabilities would contaminate the regular population caused many people to spend their entire lives locked away from the mainstream of society.

Many people with disabilities are still isolated and segregated today. Tolerance for such treatment is disappearing, however. New principles focusing on integration and the community guide the design of services for individuals with disabilities. IDEA provides the right to education for all children, but also requires **mainstreaming** or placement in the **least restrictive environment.** But what does this mean for children? According to the law, this means that

> to the extent appropriate, handicapped children, including children in public or private institutions or other care facilities, are educated with children who are not handicapped, and that special classes, separate schooling, or other removal of handicapped children from the regular education environment occurs only when the nature or severity of the handicap is such that education in regular classes with the use of supplementary aids and services cannot be achieved satisfactorily. . . . (20 U.S.C., section 1412(5)(B))

Almost everyone agrees with the principle that segregation harms students, *all* students—those students without handicaps as well as students with handicaps. But not everyone agrees on what the principle of LRE means in the case of a particular child. It is not simply the choice of one type of classroom over another, although that is a tremendously important choice. The simple physical location of students is not the only way of measuring least restrictive environment (LRE). At one level, it must mean that students' environments permit them maximum freedom. But, maximum freedom has to be appropriate to the student's age, doesn't it? What else does least restrictive mean? The box on this topic lists some aspects that have been suggested by commentators on a definition of least restrictive.

The principle of normalization is an essential dimension of LRE. It demands that professionals and parents make choices that provide services as close to normal as possible. For one child, this might mean riding the same bus to school as other children, using ordinary books and materials that have been adapted to his or her disability, receiving all special education services in the regular classroom, and having an after-school job delivering newspapers. For a student with severe disabilities it might mean that designer jeans have Velcro closings to fit over leg braces, that wheelchair wheels are wide enough to enable the student to play on the sandy playground during recess, and that a specially equipped bus does not have reference to special education painted on the side.

Normalization also requires allowing the individual the **"dignity of risk"** (Perske, 1972). Frequently, students with handicaps are overprotected, deprived of the ordinary risks and challenges necessary for human development and essential to growing up. Students with disabilities should be allowed the dignity of risk to succeed or fail like others.

What does *environment* mean? There is no simple answer. A student's educational environment is multifaceted. It includes the physical environment in which the student works, the human environment or the individuals with whom the stu-

---

mainstreaming. Including students with special needs in regular education classrooms for some or all of their school day.

least restrictive environment (LRE). One of the principles outlined in IDEA that must be balanced when considering the "best" educational placement for an individual student with disabilities.

dignity of risk. The principle that taking ordinary risks and chances is part of growing up and is essentially human.

TABLE 1.3. Environmental Features

Physical	Human	Affective	Geographic
Student work area	Family members	Feelings and attitudes of students	Community's culture
Books and materials	Friends	Feelings and attitudes of others	Rural or urban setting
Communication devices	Other students without handicaps	Quality of personal interactions	Proximity to family and friends
Braces, glasses, and clothing	Other students with handicaps		Proximity to services
Sights, sounds, and smells	Teachers		Availability of transportation
The classroom	Related services personnel		Availability of work opportunities
The school			
Transportation			

dent has the opportunity to interact, the affective environment or the feelings and emotional tone surrounding the student, and the geographic environment or the location of the school. Table 1.3 provides some examples of these four aspects of educational environments.

With all these possible interpretations and combinations, it is easy to see why there might be disagreement over what *the* least restrictive environment is for a particular student. (Issues and further discussions about LRE are found throughout this book. In particular, see the diagram titled Considerations for Individualized Determination of LRE in chapter 3.) Professionals and parents must weigh all of the considerations, constantly balancing students' needs for freedom with their needs to learn certain skills, and their needs for opportunities to live lives as normal as possible (see the Tips for Teachers box).

Tips for Teachers

DETERMINING LEAST RESTRICTIVE ENVIRONMENT

- Determine if a student's individual learning needs require special education services.
- Determine what types of special education services are necessary.
- Determine the intensity of appropriate special educational services.
- Determine the instructional considerations for the individual student.
- Determine the amount of time the special education services are needed.
- Determine which personnel can deliver the special education services.
- Determine where the services should be provided.
- Evaluate all dimensions of the student's physical environment.
- Evaluate all dimensions of the student's human environment.
- Evaluate all dimensions of a student's affective environment.
- Evaluate all dimensions of a student's geographic environment.

As you can see, the issue of LRE is complicated. Educators sometimes make blanket statements about what is or is not least restrictive. Some educators have suggested that a regular classroom is always the least restrictive educational placement for all students with special needs. Others have suggested that a special education classroom is always the least restrictive placement for all students with special needs. In each chapter in this book, you will read of the issues of LRE that arise in the various disability categories. The important point to remember is that special education choices must be individualized and based on the particular needs of each individual.

Americans with Disabilities Act (ADA). Federal disability antidiscrimination legislation passed in 1990.

Amendments to PL 94–142

Since its initial passage in 1975, Congress has passed amendments to PL 94–142, now IDEA. These amendments have expanded the age range of children who are entitled to special education. For example, PL 99–457 (discussed in detail in chapter 3) added infants and toddlers, provided Individualized Family Services Plans (IFSPs), and suggested Individualized Transition Plans (ITPs). Other amendments, such as the Handicapped Children's Protection Act of 1986, have guaranteed legal fees to parents who win their special education disputes and made similar changes. But the substance of the law remains faithful to its original form.

PL 101–476, the Education of the Handicapped Act (EHA) Amendments of 1990, was signed into law by President George Bush on October 30, 1990. Congress made a number of changes, including

- changing the title of the special education law to Individuals with Disabilities Education Act (IDEA)
- changing the language in the law from "handicapped children" to "children with disabilities"
- specifying two additional categories: autism and traumatic brain injury
- requiring transition services no later than age sixteen
- requiring further public comments on defining "attention deficit disorder" in the law
- clarifying that states may be sued in federal courts for violating the law

Americans with Disabilities Act (ADA)

Section 504 of the Rehabilitation Act of 1973 prohibits discrimination by federally funded programs against otherwise qualified individuals with disabilities. This includes protecting the rights of students with handicaps to a free appropriate public education. Although critically important in guaranteeing basic civil rights to people with disabilities, it did not address many important aspects of American society.

On July 26, 1990, President Bush signed the **Americans with Disabilities Act (ADA)**, which bars discrimination in employment, transportation, public accommodations, and telecommunications. He said, "Let the shameful walls of exclusion finally come tumbling down." This law guarantees access to all aspects of life—not just those that are federally funded—to people with disabilities and implements the concept of normalization.

The ADA requires that employers not discriminate against qualified applicants or employees with disabilities; that new buses, trains, and subways be accessible to persons with disabilities; that new or remodeled public accommodations such as

Sometimes litigation is required to clarify the education rights of children with disabilities. Like his client Amy Rowley, the lawyer in her case before the United States Supreme Court also had a hearing impairment.

The United States Supreme Court first interpreted the requirement for an appropriate public education for a child with a disability in the case of Amy Rowley, a young girl with a hearing impairment.

hotels, stores, restaurants, banks, theaters, and so on, be accessible; and that telephone companies provide relay services so that individuals with hearing impairments and voice impairments can use ordinary telephones. Although the protections are delayed for several years, this long overdue landmark law should help put an end to discrimination against people with disabilities.

> **clean intermittent catheterization (CIC).** Inserting a clean tube (catheter) through the urethra to empty the bladder on a regular schedule, usually every three to four hours.

LITIGATION TO INTERPRET AND DEFINE THE LAW

Since 1975, when PL 94–142, the Education for All Handicapped Children Act, became law, less than 1 percent of all children served have been involved in formal disputes (Hill, 1982). The disputes that have arisen concern the identification of children with handicaps, evaluations, educational placements, and the provision of a free appropriate public education (FAPE). Many of these disputes are resolved in the noncourt proceedings called due process hearings.

Some disputes, however, must be settled in the courts of law. A few of these lawsuits have made it all the way to the U.S. Supreme Court. From this litigation the Supreme Court has addressed many different questions about special education. Once the final decision is made, these cases become the law of the land, because an interpretation by the Supreme Court applies to the entire United States. A few of the more important cases that the Supreme Court has decided are listed in Table 1.4.

TABLE 1.4. U.S. Supreme Court Cases Interpreting IDEA			
Case	Date	Issue	Finding
Rowley v. Hendrick Hudson School	1982	Free Appropriate Public Education (FAPE)	School districts must provide those services that permit a student with disabilities to benefit from instruction.
Irving Independent School District v. Tatro	1984	Defined "related services"	**Clean intermittent catheterization** (CIC) is a related service when necessary to allow a student to stay in school.
Smith v. Robinson	1984	Attorneys' fees	IDEA does not provide for attorneys' fees for special education litigation. Congress objected to this interpretation and passed a law authorizing fees to parents who win the case.
Burlington School Committee v. Department of Education	1984	Private school placements	In some cases, public schools may be required to pay for private school placements when an appropriate education is not provided by the district.
Honig v. Doe	1988	Exclusion from school	Students whose misbehavior is related to their disability cannot be denied education.

IN THIS BOOK

Children and youth with handicaps are presented so you understand their different abilities and disabilities. The prevalence of each exceptionality is explained so you will know approximately how many individuals can be expected to have multicultural and bilingual special education needs, mental retardation, communicative disorders, learning disabilities, giftedness and creative abilities, behavioral disorders, visual impairments, hearing impairments, and physical disabilities and health impairments. You will learn about the causes of disabilities and some strategies to prevent or limit the handicapping effects of disabilities. We will also discuss the range of severity of disabilities, from mild, which is the most common, to severe, which is less common, for each category of special education.

In each chapter, we present information about young children—their educational needs and how to support their families during their preschool years. You will learn that early childhood services make tremendous differences in children's learning and the ability of their families to help them achieve their potential.

We discuss students with exceptionalities—learning characteristics that students with each disability might have, teaching tactics that can enhance their learning, tips for teachers as they address the needs of students in their classrooms, and explanations about possible learning environments. We also discuss adults with exceptionalities—what happens after children grow up, and the challenges these adults face, such as achieving integration into society, obtaining work commensurate with their abilities, living independently, and developing personal relationships.

This book emphasizes the many factors professionals and families must consider when determining the least restrictive environment for each individual. The diagram Considerations for Individualized Determination of LRE, in chapter 3, demonstrates how the individual child is the focus of this determination. This diagram considers the following aspects of each individual's needs: the intensity of services required, the expected duration of the services, the types of personnel needed to implement the services, the location of services, and instructional considerations.

To make professional judgments, special educators must know the history of the development of this field, current research findings in each disability area, available technology that assists people with disabilities, and the future trends. Each chapter in this text reviews these topics for each exceptionality.

To help you prepare for teaching and providing other special education services, we have also included lists of resources at the end of each chapter. People with disabilities have been included in many popular books and films. At the end of each chapter about specific disabilities we have provided a listing of books and videos you might find of interest, and in the References for this chapter, found at the end of the text, you will find general resource books about people with disabilities in literature and film. It is important to know that the portrayals of people with disabilities are often fascinating but frequently inaccurate and stereotypical. You should be critical. Do they reflect media and societal attitudes about the disability? Do they present people with disabilities in exaggerated ways? Are the people with disabilities presented as characters of a single dimension—the disability—or are they complex human beings with the full range of emotions and motivations? You may find it interesting to compare portrayals created in earlier periods to more recent ones, particularly those in films. It is also interesting to consider films in the context of the social, political, and economic climate of the time.

This book provides many hints and techniques for *applying* what you learn to real children, classrooms, and situations. Each chapter also includes a section on families, emphasizing the importance of families in the educational partnership, and their importance in the lives of their children. In addition we discuss the critical roles of individuals with disabilities themselves in advocating for their rights and controlling their own lives.

People with exceptionalities, their families, and society face complex social policy issues. At the end of each chapter, trends and issues are presented in sections called Concepts and Controversies. These focus on one issue currently being debated by professionals, families, and persons with disabilities.

The future is promising. The lives of individuals with exceptionalities look bright. But the role of professionals in the field is changing. The complex needs of many students with exceptionalities (which change, of course, over the course of their lives) require a cadre of well-trained, committed, enthusiastic, and supportive professionals to help fulfill the future's promise.

Concepts and Controversies

Educability

Are there children with disabilities so severe that they are uneducable? You will remember that one of the major battles throughout the history of special education has been to get special education school services for children whose needs are different, who do not learn the way typical children do, or who require specialized materials and methods in order to learn effectively. Sometimes the argument has been made that a certain child is so disabled that learning is impossible.

The case of Timothy W. demonstrates some of the concerns. Timothy is a child with severe handicaps. He is legally blind and deaf, has quadriplegia, cannot move, has severe spasticity (muscle incoordination), contacted joints, dislocated hips, scoliosis (curvature of the spine), brain damage, and frequent seizures. The school district argued that Timothy was uneducable and thus not entitled to special education. Although the district stated that Timothy lacked the capacity to learn, his mother argued that he could smile in response to her voice and music, that he reacted to light and noise, and that he could sometimes show a preference by turning his head or attempting to reach.

When the mother pursued a due process hearing in order to get special education services for Timothy, the hearing officer ruled that *all* children are entitled to special education services, regardless of their "capacity to learn." The district court judge who reviewed the decision disagreed, and stated that Timothy could not benefit from school and that "Surely, Congress would not legislate futility!" (*Timothy W. v. Rochester, New Hampshire, School District*, 1987–1988 EHLR DEC. 559:480, p. 482).

The First Circuit Court of Appeals (*Timothy W. v. Rochester, New Hampshire, School District*, 1989) reversed the district court, ruling that Timothy was entitled to a free appropriate public education:

Indeed . . . the Act gives priority to the most severely handicapped . . . [and] speaks of the *state's* responsibility to design a special education and related services program that will meet the unique "needs" of all handicapped children. (p. 960)

The Supreme Court refused a request to hear this case, so the opinion of the First Circuit Court of Appeals is the highest. Do you think the court is correct in its interpretation of the law? Attempts to exclude certain children from school as uneducable have failed. Why do you think these attempts have failed? Think of some reasons why a child, even with a severe disability, might not want to stay home all day.

SUMMARY

After many years of neglect and exclusion, children and youth with handicaps today have a right to receive a free appropriate public school education. For many children this means they will receive special education services for at least part of their school career.

1. Special education is, first, and foremost, individualized education. It is designed to address the unique needs of children with handicaps and to help them achieve their maximum potential. The primary vehicle for designing the program is the Individualized Education Plan, the IEP. All children with handicaps also have rights to appropriate identification and educational services, necessary related services, least restrictive environments, and notification and procedural rights to parents on behalf of their children.

2. The history of special education is relatively short. It is less than 200 years ago that Itard worked with Victor, the wild boy of Aveyron. This history has included periods of optimism, periods of neglect, periods of fear, and finally acceptance of exceptionalities in children.

3. The federal law guaranteeing special education and related services to all children with handicaps, the Individuals with Disabilities Education Act, IDEA (originally the Education for All Handicapped Children Act, EHA), is less than twenty years old. During the time since the law's passage, American schools and teachers have made tremendous gains in integrating all children into education and providing appropriate services to children of widely varying abilities.

4. The principles of least restrictive environment and normalization mean more than mere physical classroom placement. They describe a philosophical commitment to assure that children with handicaps have opportunities for living normal lives, integrated into the flow and pattern of our society.

5. Schools must assure an array of services so that the individual needs of children can be accommodated. A variety of professional opportunities are available for special educators to help educate and provide related services to all children with handicaps.

6. The U.S. Supreme Court has upheld the rights of children and their families to free appropriate public education for all children with handicaps. Other legal issues (such as payment of legal fees, payment for unauthorized educational placements, exclusion of students with behavioral disorders) have also been addressed by the Court, clarifying and defining the federal law.

DISCUSSION QUESTIONS

1. How did Itard influence special education?

2. What do you think Congress intended to accomplish when it passed the Education for All Handicapped Children Act in 1975?

3. Using Table 1.1, from the report to Congress on implementation of EHA, compare the percentage of children in your state receiving special education services for learning disabilities and mental retardation with other states. Why do you think the percentages vary? In what types of classrooms (regular, resource, separate, residential, and so on) do they receive their services?

4. What factors should you consider when thinking about least restrictive environment for a particular student with special needs?

5. Imagine that you teach a class that includes children with physical handicaps. Think of ways in which you might put the principle of normalization into practice in your classroom.

MICHAEL NARANJO, 43, realized he wanted to make a career of sculpting during the Vietnam War while recovering from a wound that left him blind. In the hospital, he was given clay and became determined to succeed as a sculptor. Since that time, he has become a leading sculptor in his home of Espanola, New Mexico, and across the nation. Michael draws on his childhood memories of the Santa Clara Canyon meadows and his native Pueblo culture to create the harmonious forms for which he has won numerous awards, including the New Mexico Governor's Award for Excellence in the Arts.

Chapter Two

MULTICULTURAL AND BILINGUAL SPECIAL EDUCATION

*L*earning

Objectives

After studying this chapter, you should be able to:

- **Define multicultural and bilingual special education**

- **Describe some ways in which a school can integrate children's home cultures and languages into the educational environment and curriculum**

- **Explain four points at which testing bias may occur**

- **List and discuss four basic bilingual education instructional approaches**

A MULTICULTURAL BILINGUAL CHILD GROWS UP

bilingual. Capable of using two languages, but usually with differing levels of skill.

multicultural. Reflecting more than one culture.

*E*loy Gonzales, Professor of Special Education and an educational diagnostician, grew up in the 1940s speaking both English and Spanish. He was raised in Santa Fe, New Mexico, which was at that time approximately 85 percent Hispanic.* His family had lived in Northern New Mexico for almost two hundred years. His ancestors came from Spain to the United States with Catholic missionaries in the early 1800s. Although Gonzales was **bilingual,** as were many of his school friends, he attended a school that forbade the children to speak Spanish at school. All the teachers were nonbilingual. Children who were caught speaking Spanish were reprimanded. His experiences led him to understand the need for **multicultural** bilingual education and helped shape his choice of career. His childhood experiences led him to believe if children's language and culture are denied, they receive the message that they are inferior. This affects their self-esteem and ability to succeed in school.

For nearly twenty-five years, Dr. Gonzales has tested over 800 Hispanic children and approximately 250 Native American children, mostly in rural areas. Regarded as an expert in bilingual assessment, he developed the national normative data for the widely used Human Figure Drawing Test. Before he did so, major ethnic groups in the United States were not properly represented in the scoring of this test. He also helped establish the Spanish normative data for several intelligence tests. Dr. Gonzales shares some thoughts about testing children who are bilingual or multicultural:

Why are you committed to multicultural bilingual assessment procedures?

We cannot accurately determine the strengths and weaknesses of a child who is multicultural or bilingual unless the multicultural and bilingual aspects are specifically taken into account. This is necessary not only for an accurate assessment of the child but also in order to develop an effective individualized education program.

How do your testing procedures change when you test a child who speaks Spanish?

My approach is to test bilingually. Before you do any testing you inform the child that all questions on the test will be asked in English, and the child can answer in either language. If the child does not understand the question in English, it can be repeated in Spanish. The big issue here is that tests often test information learned in school. If the child has been taught in English, the school learning will have been communicated through English and that is the vocabulary the child will have

*The nouns designating particular cultural and linguistic populations in this chapter were selected in an attempt to reflect nondiscriminatory terminology. There is as yet, however, no universal agreement on specific terms for specific populations, especially in light of increasing sensitivity and identity issues. The reader is referred to sources in the bibliography that address these terminology issues in greater depth.

for school-type questions. On the other hand, home and community learning will often have been in Spanish, so that is the language the child might prefer for questions about life outside of school.

When you first meet a child for testing, what is the child's reaction when he or she discovers that you speak Spanish?

At first the children are very quiet, basically not speaking at all. I think that they feel threatened by a stranger coming to do something to them. In order to establish rapport, so that I can validly test the child, I usually go the class to meet the child, then sit in the class for a while. The child then begins to feel at ease. I walk with the child out of the classroom to the testing area. If the child is Spanish dominant, I immediately start speaking Spanish. Usually the child gets a big smile on his face and starts conversing. Not only does the child begin to communicate, but the child is willing to talk about home and family and brothers and sisters, not just school things. You're speaking the *home* language.

Do you feel that an evaluation of a Spanish-speaking child by a Spanish-speaking educational diagnostician is more accurate than an evaluation by a diagnostician who is not bilingually trained?

Without a doubt. And I think it all goes back to that school language/home language difference. Once I evaluated a boy whose parents were migrant workers. He spoke only Spanish. The family moved so frequently that the boy had missed a lot of school and he read about four years below his grade level. The boy had earlier been tested and labeled mentally retarded, based on an IQ test that was administered by a nonbilingual evaluator. But when I tested him bilingually, he scored 15 to 20 points higher. I also discovered, when I interviewed his family in Spanish, that his adaptive behavior at home was very high. He helped his parents move to each new farm job and helped them settle in each new community. Since both his mother and father worked in the fields all day, he cared for the younger children, cooked the evening meal for the family, and was responsible for bathing and dressing the other children.

Clearly the mental retardation label was incorrect. He wasn't mentally retarded, but his opportunity and exposure to school-learned material had been severely limited. Unfortunately, the school did not provide a bilingual education program. As an interim measure, I recommended that the child be allowed to spend time with the Hispanic school counselor, who could act as a model for the child and who could communicate with the child and his parents. I stressed to the school that the parents be encouraged to participate in school activities. But he continued to have problems at school. Before the problems could be remedied, it was time for the family to move again to the next agricultural job. I don't know whether he was ever able to get the help he needed.

1. Imagine a child who is bicultural, bilingual, and having problems in school being tested by someone who is not bicultural or bilingual. What feelings might the child experience during those first few minutes?

2. If a child uses one language at home and another at school, what steps might a teacher take so parents feel comfortable helping the child with homework?

The rich diversity of culture and language found in communities across this country also finds expression in special education classes. Many children with exceptionalities have diverse cultural backgrounds and may be bilingual. This combination of exceptionality and different cultural background or language presents many issues as schools attempt to assure special education services. In addition to the issues and techniques we describe in the other chapters for each exceptionality, there are considerations based on the child's multicultural background and bilingualism.

Exceptional students who are culturally and linguistically diverse require a variety of educational services. They need special education by individuals who speak both English and the child's language, they need nonbiased assessment so that their strengths and weaknesses can be identified in a nondiscriminatory way, and they need learning materials and strategies that address their disabilities and also are sensitive to their culture.

MULTICULTURAL AND BILINGUAL SPECIAL EDUCATION DEFINED

Multicultural bilingual special education is a combination of the fields of multicultural education, bilingual education, and special education. According to Baca and Cervantes (1989),

> Bilingual Special Education may be defined as the use of the home language and the home culture along with English in an individually designed program of special instruction for the student. Bilingual Special Education considers the child's language and culture as foundations upon which an appropriate education may be built. The primary purpose of a Bilingual Special Education program is to help each individual student achieve a maximum potential for learning. Above all the program is concerned with the child's cognitive and affective development. It would be misleading to assume such a program is primarily concerned with teaching or maintaining a second language or culture. Here, language and culture are used as appropriate means rather than as ends in themselves. (p. 18)

You can see that this definition stresses the acquisition of academic and social skills in culturally and linguistically diverse children with exceptionalities. It is the child's special education needs that are primary, but language and culture are the means through which appropriate special education intervention is provided.

Multicultural bilingual special education has not received sufficient attention in the schools. A recent study (Salend and Fradd, 1986) revealed that only five states had even established a definition for bilingual special education. The survey requested other information. The states were also asked whether there was a position in the state agency addressing the needs of bilingual students with handicaps, whether the state had a funding category for these students, whether language dominance and proficiency were determined before placement, whether there were certification requirements for teachers in this area, and whether a bilingual special education training program existed in the state. The results indicate that there is a great deal of work to be done in this area. See Table 2.1 for the results of the survey.

Measurement

In recent years we have come to understand that standardized tests in our schools discriminated against multicultural and bilingual students. In the early 1970s, it became apparent that the standard methods of testing and evaluation were identify-

TABLE 2.1. Nationwide Availability of Services for Bilingual Handicapped Students

Question No.	1 Definition for Bilingual Handicapped	2 State Position	3 Specific Funding	4 Recommended Assessment Instruments	5 Language Dominance & Proficiency	6 Curriculum for Bilingual Handicapped	7 Bilingual/S.E.[a] Certification	8 Bilingual/S.E.[a] Training at IHE
1. Alabama	no	no	no	no	no	no	no	no
2. Alaska	no	no	no	no	yes	no	no	no
3. Arizona	no	no	no	no	yes	no	no	yes
4. Arkansas	no	no	no	no	yes	no	no	yes
5. California	no	yes	no	developing	yes	no	yes	yes
6. Colorado	no	no	no	no	yes	no	no	yes
7. Connecticut	no	yes	no	no	yes	no	no	yes
8. Delaware	no	yes	no	no	yes	no	no	yes
9. Florida	no	yes	no	no	no	no	no	no
10. Georgia	no	no	no	no	yes	no	no	yes
11. Hawaii	yes	no	no	yes	yes	no	no	no
12. Idaho	no	no	no	no	yes	no	no	no
13. Illinois	no	yes	no	no	no	no	no	yes
14. Indiana	no	no	no	no	yes	no	no	no
15. Iowa	no	no	no	yes	no	no	no	no
16. Kansas	no	no	no	no	yes	no	no	no
17. Kentucky	no	no	no	no	no	no	no	no
18. Louisiana	no	yes	no	no	no	no	no	no
19. Maine	no	no	no	no	no	no	no	no
20. Maryland	yes	yes	yes	no	yes	no	no	yes
21. Massachusetts	no	no	no	yes	yes	no	no	yes
22. Michigan	no	yes	no	no	yes	no	no	yes
23. Minnesota	yes	yes	no	no	yes	no	no	no
24. Missouri	no	no	no	no	yes	no	no	no
25. Montana	no	no	no	no	yes	no	no	no
26. Nebraska	no	no	no	no	yes	no	no	no
27. Nevada	no	no	no	no	yes	no	no	no
28. New Hampshire	no	no	no	no	yes	no	no	no
29. New Jersey	no	no	no	no	yes	no	no	yes
30. New Mexico	no	no	no	yes	yes	no	no	no
31. New York	no	yes	no	no	yes	no	no	yes
32. North Carolina	no	yes	no	no	yes	no	no	no
33. North Dakota	no	no	no	no	no	no	no	no
34. Ohio	no	no	no	no	no	no	no	no
35. Oklahoma	no	no	no	no	yes	no	no	no
36. Oregon	no	no	no	developing	no	no	no	yes
37. Pennsylvania	no	no	no	no	no	no	no	yes
38. Rhode Island	no	yes	no	yes	yes	no	no	no
39. South Carolina	yes	no	no	no	yes	no	no	no
40. South Dakota	no	no	no	no	yes	no	no	no
41. Tennessee	no	no	no	no	yes	no	no	no
42. Texas	yes	yes	no	no	yes	no	no	yes
43. Utah	no	no	no	no	no	no	no	no
44. Vermont	no	no	no	no	yes	no	no	no
45. Virginia	no	no	no	no	yes	no	no	no
46. Washington	yes	no	no	no	no	no	no	no
47. West Virginia	no	no	no	no	no	no	no	no
48. Wisconsin	no	no	no	no	yes	no	no	yes
49. Wyoming	no	no	no	no	yes	no	no	no
50. Washington, DC	no	yes	yes	no	yes	no	no	no

[a]S.E. = special education.

Source: S. J. Salend and S. Fradd, *The Journal of Special Education*, Vol. 20, No. 1, pp. 130–131 (1986). Reprinted by permission

nondiscriminatory testing. Assessment that properly takes into account a child's cultural and linguistic diversity.

ing too many multicultural bilingual children as handicapped and two few as gifted. Were IQ tests discriminating against multicultural bilingual students?

In California, the case of *Larry P. v. Riles* (1971) dramatically illustrated the problem. This case brought to the attention of the courts and schools the overrepresentation of African-American children in classes for mental retardation and the possibility of discrimination in intelligence testing. Over the last twenty years, the case has continued in courts, and schools and families have attempted to overcome these problems (MacMillan, Hendrick, and Watkins, 1988).

We can contrast the *Larry P.* case with the case of *Parents in Action on Special Education (PASE) v. Hannon* (1980). An Illinois federal district court judge ruled that even though African-American students were overrepresented in mental retardation classes in Chicago, the standard IQ tests used to place them were not discriminatory. The judge reached this conclusion primarily on the basis of his own examination of individual test items.

How does discrimination in testing occur? Jones (1988) observes that testing bias may occur at four junctures. It may occur at (1) the content level, when items are selected for a test; (2) the standardization level, when minority groups are not represented in the standardization population; (3) the administration level, when an individual untrained in multicultural bilingual techniques conducts the evaluation; and (4) the validation level, when the test is misused for purposes for which it is not valid.

The first systematic attempt to measure and interpret sociocultural variables was the System of Multicultural Pluralistic Assessment (SOMPA) developed by Mercer and Lewis (1978). The test has had a significant effect, decreasing the number of African-American and Hispanic children placed in special education (Gonzales, 1989).

Some exceptionalities are especially difficult to diagnose when the child has difficulty with English. For example, the diagnosis of a learning disability usually depends on a significant point discrepancy between the IQ score and academic achievement. The first problem is that children with a genuine learning disability may not be identified because they do not have the necessary discrepancy between potential and achievement to qualify for services (see chapter 6, Learning Disabilities). These children may get an artificially low IQ score because of discriminatory testing.

The second problem is that some children may be wrongly identified as having a learning disability when, in fact, it is their difficulty with English, mere underachievement in a second language, that is the problem (Bozinou-Doukas, 1983). Underachievement, language differences, or differences in cultural experiences can cause children to score so low on an achievement test that it artificially creates an IQ/achievement discrepancy that is then misinterpreted as a learning disability.

The law requires that testing be **nondiscriminatory.** IDEA requires that each state establish

> procedures to assure that testing and evaluation materials and procedures utilized for the purpose of evaluation and placement of handicapped children will be selected and administered so as not to be racially or culturally discriminatory. Such materials or procedures shall be provided and administered in the child's native language or mode of communication, unless it is clearly not feasible to do so, and no single procedure shall be the sole criterion for determining an appropriate educational program for a child. (20 U.S.C. section 1412(5)(C))

One example of an assessment process developed in an attempt to address some of

Sometimes tests or school environments may discriminate against culturally and linguistically diverse students with giftedness. Every attempt must be made to help all children reach their potential.

these problems can be found at the Southwest High School in California. Students who are referred to special education at that school are first assessed with a screening test developed and normed within that particular school district. Further evaluation is conducted by Spanish-speaking school psychologists who have training in bilingual education and nonbiased assessment procedures (Cegelka, MacDonald, and Gaeta, 1987).

Significance

Even though professionals have recognized that some tests are probably discriminatory, the problem of overrepresentation of minorities in special education continues. Chinn and Hughes (1987) reported that in analyzing four Office of Civil Rights surveys from 1978 to 1984, some minority groups continued to be disproportionately high in certain categories. African-Americans continued to be overrepresented in programs for mental retardation and serious emotional disturbance. Fewer Hispanics were entering mental retardation classes than at the time of the *Larry P.* case and the work of Jane Mercer, but Hispanics were overrepresented in learning disabilities classes. Disproportionately low numbers of African-Americans, Hispanics, and Native Americans were placed in programs for the gifted and talented.

HISTORY OF THE FIELD

Education in the United States has, throughout its history, been faced with issues of bilingualism and multiculturalism. In the late nineteenth and early twentieth centuries, total exclusion (or separate language schools) began to give way to a new era

cultural pluralism. All cultural groups are valued components of the society, and the language and traditions of each group are maintained.

limited English proficiency (LEP). Limited ability to read, write, or speak English.

of "Americanization." Antiforeign feelings were on the rise. The guiding principle during the new period was the "melting pot" model, in which individuals were expected to abandon their home languages and cultures as soon as possible for a new, homogenized American language and culture. The melting pot model failed. Instead of creating a harmonious new culture, it led to racism, segregation, poverty, and aggression toward individuals in each new immigrant group. It also led to a loss of the richness that can result when a country welcomes many cultures and languages to the society.

Cultural pluralism began to be the accepted model in the 1960s. Cultural pluralism involves "mutual appreciation and understanding of the various cultures in our society; peaceful co-existence of diverse lifestyles, folkways, manners, language patterns, religious beliefs, and family structures; and autonomy for each group to work out its own social future as long as it does not interfere with the same rights of other groups" (Poplin and Wright, 1983, p. 367). Cultural pluralism does not require abandoning one's home culture as did the melting pot model.

In the field of special education, systematic recognition of multicultural and bilingual special education issues occurred relatively recently. Two major pieces of federal legislation, the Bilingual Education Act of 1968 (PL 90–247) and the Education for All Handicapped Children Act of 1975 (PL 94–142) helped educators begin to understand the connection between bilingualism and special education (Baca and Cervantes, 1984). By the 1970s research projects on this topic were underway in earnest.

A fact disturbing to educators was that multicultural bilingual children seemed to be overrepresented in special education. This issue was brought to national attention in a variety of ways. First, in 1968 Dunn wrote an important article in which he estimated that "about 60 to 80 percent of the pupils [in special education classes for mental retardation] are children from low status backgrounds—including Afro-Americans, American Indians, Mexicans, and Puerto Rican Americans, those from nonstandard English-speaking, broken, disorganized, and inadequate homes; and children from other nonmiddle class environments" (p. 6). Then, in 1970, the President's Committee on Mental Retardation (PCMR) published the Six Hour Retarded Child (President's Committee on Mental Retardation, 1970) which exposed dramatically the ways in which cultural differences were causing some children to be inappropriately labeled as having mental retardation. The work of Mercer (1973) analyzed in greater detail the extent of the problem and proposed solutions to such inappropriate labeling.

In California in 1970, the case of *Diana v. State Board of Education* brought these assessment issues into focus. This was a class action suit on behalf of Hispanic children placed in mental retardation classrooms on the basis of IQ tests that were argued to be discriminatory. The case of *Larry P. v. Riles* (1971) in California brought to the attention of the courts and schools the overrepresentation of African-American children in classes for mental retardation and the possibility of discrimination in intelligence testing. In 1974 the U.S. Supreme Court ruled in a case brought in San Francisco on behalf of students with **limited English proficiency (LEP)** who were Chinese speaking (*Lau v. Nichols*, 1974). Following the favorable decision in *Lau*, Congress enacted legislation that incorporated the Court's rationale.

Finally, *Exceptional Children,* the journal of the Council for Exceptional Children, published a special issue on cultural diversity in 1974 (Bransford, Baca, and Lane, 1974) that brought together many authors to begin to discuss multicultural bilingual special education issues. Baca and Cervantes's textbook, *The Bilingual Special Educa-*

tion Interface, first published in 1984, continued to bring this question to the attention of students and teachers in the field of multicultural bilingual special education.

Today, multicultural and bilingual special education is recognized as a critical component in any special education program. Throughout this text you will find that special education is individualized, and true individualization must take into account the culture and language of the student. Unless education takes into account the language and culture of children, access to education is being denied and the education cannot be said to be appropriate.

PREVALENCE

It is clear that the number of multicultural and bilingual students in the United States is increasing rapidly. By the year 2000, it is estimated that approximately one-third of public school children will be from culturally diverse backgrounds, with Hispanics being the largest minority group (American Council on Education, 1988). Today, in twenty-five of the country's largest cities and metropolitan areas, at least half of the student population is from culturally and linguistically diverse groups (American Council on Education, 1988). The states with the largest LEP populations are California, Texas, New York, and Florida. In two states—New Mexico and Mississippi—minority students are the majority, and California and Texas will soon join them (Quality Education for Minorities Project, 1990). The largest group and the fastest growing group is Hispanic, currently with 75 percent of all children of limited English proficiency.

Still it is difficult to determine the precise number of multicultural and bilingual children or the number of them who require special education services. We can make some estimates, however, based on census information and a few studies.

Baca and Cervantes (1989) report that approximately 8.8 percent of the population of the United States are native speakers of a language other than English and that they are most highly concentrated in large urban areas in the southwest and northeast. How many of these children also have special education needs? Even if we use the Department of Education figure of 6.7 percent of the general population between the ages of three and twenty-one being served in special education (U.S. Department of Education, 1990), we can predict conservatively that at least 0.59 percent of children are non-native-English speakers and have special education needs. If one adds culturally diverse children, the percentage will be much larger.

Let us give you an example of how difficult it can be to determine how many culturally and linguistically diverse children require special education services. California alone has more than ninety different language groups. A statewide study was conducted to learn about special education for children with limited English proficiency (LEP) who had handicaps (Cegelka, Lewis, and Rodriguez, 1987). The researchers found that more LEP students were identified as handicapped compared to the rate in the total school population. While approximately 8 percent of the total school population were identified as handicapped, 11 percent of the LEP students were identified as handicapped. Two handicapping conditions, severe emotional disturbance and other health impairments, were, however, underrepresented in the LEP students. The Council of Chief State School Officers also reports that many children with limited English proficiency are not receiving the benefits of special education (1990).

Clearly, the number of students who are multicultural and bilingual in American schools is rapidly increasing. This means that the number of children with special education needs who are multicultural and bilingual is increasing as well. If the needs of these children are to be met, the field must devote more attention and resources to the area of multicultural and bilingual special education.

CAUSES AND PREVENTION

Multiculturalism and bilingualism do not cause handicaps, but poverty can cause a variety of handicaps. The impact of multiculturalism must be separated from the effects of poverty (Chan and Rueda, 1979). Many culturally and linguistically diverse students do not live in poverty, but for those who do, the effects of poverty are sometimes confused with the effects of cultural and linguistic diversity.

Social and economic inequities hit hard on children in this country (Reed and Sautter, 1990; Schorr, 1989). Multicultural and bilingual children are not spared. The Children's Defense Fund (1988) reported that more than half (53 percent) of all young African-American families with children live in poverty, and 40 percent of all young Hispanic families with children live in poverty. Although 24 percent of all Native Americans live in poverty, for Native Americans on reservations, the rate of poverty is 42 percent (Quality Education for Minorities Project, 1990).

Some recent groups of immigrants have additional burdens. For example, many Indochinese refugees (Vietnamese, Laotian, Khmer, Hmong) in addition to the culture and language differences, have experienced great disruption in their lives through war. Some children face the new culture without parents or guardians because they were separated or orphaned in their homeland or while seeking refuge.

The consequences of poverty and family and social disruption are momentous for all children, including children from multicultural and poor backgrounds, and can place them at great risk for handicaps. As we discuss throughout this text, the absence of prenatal care for mothers can result in premature births and handicaps

The individual life circumstances of some children create special challenges for their teachers and schools. School performance can be greatly affected by burdens such as poverty, family and social disruption, lack of sufficient nutrition, and disease.

TABLE 2.2. Beliefs of Parents as to Causes of Handicaps ($N = 27$)

Cause of Handicaps	Frequency	Percentage
Mother has a big fright	25	93
Mother has an X-ray	23	85
Mother smokes	24	89
Someone casts spells	15	56
Mother drinks alcohol	26	96
Mother has high fever	27	100
Mother has an accident	25	93
Mother takes drugs	27	100
There is an earthquake	11	41
Child exposed to toxic chemicals	27	100
God's Will	25	93
Mother too old	22	82
There is an eclipse	9	33
Mother is too young	9	33
Punishment for bad behavior	23	85
Evil eye	4	15
Mother has had too many children	16	60
Other[a,b]	2	7

[a]"Bad air" entered the uterus at birth.

[b]The first wife was cheating on the husband. The baby was born normal; but when the mother breast-fed the baby, evil spirits entered the baby's body (reported by the second wife).

Source: Mexican Immigrant Parents and the Education of Their Handicapped Children: Factors That Influence Parent Involvement, Unpublished PhD Dissertation, by A. Gault, 1989, p. 115, Urbana-Champaign: University of Illinois at Urbana-Champaign.

for children. The absence of medical care for children leads to infections, disease, and crippling that could have been prevented. The number of nonwhite infants who have been properly immunized against diseases such as polio, diphtheria, pertussis, and tetanus has substantially decreased compared to white infants (Education Commission of the States, 1988). Lead poisoning, encephalitis, fetal alcohol syndrome (FAS) and fetal alcohol effects (FAE), and malnutrition, are more prevalent among poor families. Poor families typically have less formal education and as a result may not provide the "educational legacy" (Quality Education for Minorities Project, 1990) that can set the stage for a child's learning. Violence, war, torture, and other trauma suffered by many refugee children lead to physical and mental disabilities. Homelessness and high mobility plague the lives of poor children and disrupt their education. It is important for us to repeat here that although not all culturally and linguistically diverse families live in poverty, a large percentage do.

Causation should be viewed within its cultural context. Different cultures sometimes view the causes of handicaps in children differently. The view of the dominant American culture concerning causation seems to favor a direct scientific cause-and-effect relationship between a biological problem and the developing baby. The views of other cultures may, however, place a strong emphasis on fate, bad luck, sins of a parent, food the mother ate, or evil spirits (Hanson, Lynch, and Wayman, 1990). These alternative views affect the way in which a child with a disability is viewed within the culture and the types of intervention services a family might be willing to pursue to address the child's handicaps. Gault (1989), for example, interviewed some Mexican immigrant parents about their beliefs as to the cause of handicap in their child. See Table 2.2 for a list of reasons they gave.

dialect. Words and pronunciation from a particular area, different from the form of the language used by the normative group.

Inappropriate Referrals

Related to the issue of discriminatory testing is the issue of inappropriate overreferral and underreferral of multicultural bilingual students to special education. Too many children may be referred to special education, as in the situation we described for Larry P., or too few multicultural and bilingual children may be referred.

Some have suggested that discrimination is a double-edged sword and that too many *and* too few children who are culturally and linguistically diverse are referred to special education. For example, children who are multicultural or bilingual must exhibit much greater disability than their peers in order to receive special education services (MacMillan, Hendrick, and Watkins, 1988). The problem of underidentification appears to be worst in the exceptionalities of behavior disorder and emotional disturbance (see chapter 8), other health impaired (see chapter 11), and gifted (see chapter 7).

It is clear that referring multicultural bilingual children to special education and evaluating them requires great skill and sensitivity, and that the field of special education must continue to improve in this area. Garcia and Ortiz (1988) identify a schema for preventing inappropriate referrals of language minority students to special education (see Figure 2.1).

PROFILE OF CULTURALLY AND LINGUISTICALLY DIVERSE CHILDREN WITH EXCEPTIONALITIES

Children who are multicultural and bilingual and who have special education needs have special problems in several unique areas. First, language and communication differences may cause challenges for the child and for special education personnel; and second, cultural differences may raise questions about the behavior of the child and family and about the appropriateness of interventions. In addition, mobility, such as homelessness, migrant agricultural traveling, or refugee circumstances may add stress and logistical difficulties to educating some children.

Language and Communication

By definition, children who are culturally and linguistically diverse have language and communication differences that raise educational issues. Some children may speak forms of a language that vary from its literate or standard form. For example, the spoken Spanish used in South Texas usually varies from the spoken Spanish used in New Mexico, both of which may vary from the standard form of Spanish. These variations are dialects. Dialects should not automatically be considered language deficiencies (Dubois and Valdes, 1980).

Some languages do not have certain sounds or grammatical structures found in English. For example, the *f, r, th, v,* and *z* sounds do not exist in Korean. Many English consonant sounds do not exist in Chinese (Chan, 1986). Therefore, a Chinese-speaking child's difficulty with some English sounds may be a result of the child's inexperience with the sounds rather than a communicative disorder. Although many of these children are referred for speech therapy for an articulation disorder, the distinctive speech is simply an accent and therapy is unnecessary (see chapter 5, Communicative Disorders).

In order to find a communicative disorder in a bilingual child, the disorder must be found in the dominant language. For example, a Spanish-speaking child who

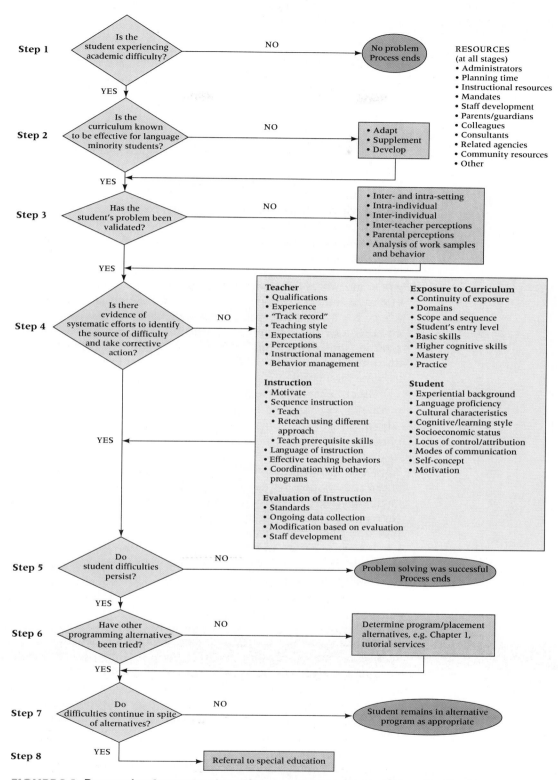

FIGURE 2.1 Preventing Inappropriate Placements of Language Minority Students in Special Education: A Prereferral Process

SOURCE: S. B. Garcia and A. A. Ortiz, 1988, *Preventing Inappropriate Referrals of Language Minority Students to Special Education,* New Focus Series, No. 5 (Wheaton, MD: National Clearinghouse for Bilingual Education). Reprinted by permission.

converses perfectly in Spanish with his brothers on the playground but who has limited ability to discuss academic subjects in English in the classroom certainly has a problem—however, it is due to a communication difference not a communicative disorder. Caution is advised, however, when the child is being tested using native language instruments. When the child's school instruction has not been in the native language, the child may appear disordered because diagnostic instruments primarily assess school language. Eloy Gonzales provides a vivid description of this problem in his interview at the beginning of this chapter.

Cultural Differences and Behavior

Facts in the lives of some multicultural bilingual children may be related to behavioral disorders (Cummins, 1984). Behaviors perceived as problems in the school setting might be related to differences between the standards of behavior in the home and standards of behavior in school, or differences between the behavior demands of parents and the behavior demands of the new peer group. They might also be related to embarrassment about the student's level of language ability, speaking with an accent, or discouragement about the slow acquisition of the second language. Additionally, coping with the social problems of refugee status, immigration, or other disruption, and discrimination and hostility by the dominant culture might be related to behavioral problems.

Other behavioral issues arise when behavior that is appropriate in one environment, for example, at home, is inappropriate in another environment, such as school. A silent child might be behaving in a desirable way according to the standards of his home culture, but be characterized as "withdrawn" and "anxious" according to mainstream American standards for teenagers in high school. Think about the American focus on individual competitiveness compared to the standard of cooperation and cooperative learning in cultures such as the Native American. Intense competitiveness might be interpreted as a behavioral disorder if the standards of Native American culture are the norm, while the refusal to compete might be interpreted as a behavioral disorder in a school that is not sensitive to cultural differences.

Parents who use traditional healing methods such as folk medicine or magical medicine may appear abusive or neglectful of their children in the eyes of social workers unfamiliar with the home culture. In a recent California case, a judge overruled the objections of Hmong parents and ordered corrective surgery for clubfeet for a six-year-old Hmong boy. The boy's father carried a plastic bag containing a live chicken, incense, and ceremonial papers to court each day so that he would be able to conduct a ceremony directing blame away from the family and toward the social service agencies (Over protest . . . , 1990). It is interesting to think about society's changing attitude toward the seriousness of some disabilities. Lord Byron, one of the great English romantic poets (1788–1824), limped because he was born with a clubfoot. His limp was often imitated by fans without disabilities in admiration of him! What might account for the differences between attitudes toward Lord Byron's clubfoot and the young Hmong boy's?

Mobility

Some culturally and linguistically diverse children experience great mobility in their lives. Children who are homeless, or live in unstable situations for other reasons, as do migrant workers or political refugees, may experience disruption and dislocation.

These circumstances have tremendous influence on the educational circumstances of the child, often adversely affecting both physical and mental abilities. Many homeless, refugee, or migrant children have little formal experience with school. A special education teacher may need to address years of missed educational opportunities in addition to the language and cultural issues. (Recall from the interview at the beginning of this chapter the story of the son of migrant workers and the effect missed schooling had on his academic achievement.)

Approximately one-half million migrant students live in the United States, about a third in California. Most have limited English abilities. Those culturally and linguistically diverse children who are migrant are very likely to be affected by handicaps because of the poverty and health problems that accompany migrant working. They are, however, underidentified and underserved in special education (Salend, 1990). The high mobility of migrant children aggravates the educational problems of these children. Baca and Harris (1988) summarize a study by Barresi (1984), and list the following problems of migrant special education:

1. only 10.7 percent of mildly handicapped migrant students appear to be identified;
2. identification occurs late in the student's school career;
3. delays occur in transferring special education records;
4. there are duplications of records;
5. gaps in services occur due to differences in the services provided in each school district;
6. inappropriate placements often are made due to language barriers as well as the delay in processing special education referrals; and
7. the efficient identification of and service delivery to handicapped migrant students is impeded by lack of awareness and consistent and purposeful coordination between migrant education and special education agencies.

Refugee and immigrant circumstances also have a tremendous impact on children. Homelessness also raises severe problems. A child with special needs who becomes homeless may have to move from the school where these needs were being met (or in the process of being assessed) to a series of schools wherever the homeless shelters in which the child finds a bed are located. The stress, hunger, disease, and feelings of hopelessness that often accompany homelessness and high mobility can create new special education needs in a child, or make existing special education needs more severe. The ability of the family to implement aspects of an IEP at home are impaired when the family is separated in large dormitories, or when living conditions are so crowded or dangerous that physical survival requires all the family's energy (Kozol, 1988).

The schools in some communities are greatly affected by influx of political refugees. For example, Dade County, Florida, enrolled more than 16,000 Nicaraguan students in 1989. It was projected that by 1990, approximately 50,000 Soviet refugees would be settled in the United States. They are America's fastest growing refugee population (Bilingual education, 1990).

ISSUES IN EDUCATION

Meeting the special education needs of exceptional children from multicultural bilingual backgrounds can be especially challenging. With multicultural bilingual students who have special education needs, meeting the special education needs must be accomplished with consideration for their multicultural and bilingual needs as well (Henderson, 1980). The professional must not only address the academic needs of the child, but also assist the child to acquire English, while continuing to be sensitive to the child's and family's linguistic and cultural background. At the same time the professional must formulate an appropriate educational program in a least restrictive environment.

In each of the following chapters we describe specific exceptionalities and provide suggestions for teaching children with those exceptionalities. Throughout this chapter we offer tips on incorporating multicultural bilingual considerations into the regular and special education classroom. But most special educators who serve multicultural and bilingual exceptional students are monolingual English speakers (Ortiz, Yates, and Garcia, 1990). In 1990 the U.S. Secretary of Education, Lauro Cavazos, called on colleges of education to make proficiency in a second language mandatory for all teachers (Cavazos asks bilingualism among teachers, 1990). Until that happens, how can a teacher who does not speak the child's dominant language provide special education? Here are several ways:

1. The special education teacher incorporates the child's language into the classroom, for example, by learning survival vocabulary, using audio and videotapes that use that language, and including community resource people who speak the language.

2. A bilingual service provider or other professional who speaks the child's language assists with the child's education program.

3. A monolingual special education teacher and a bilingual educator form a team to educate the child.

4. A bilingual educator takes the lead in educating the child, with the special education teacher providing consultation and instructional support.

Positive classrooms are ones in which cultural and linguistic diversity is valued and forms the basis for exciting learning.

5. ESL methodologies are used.

6. Technology such as **distance education** is used.

distance education. The use of telecommunications to deliver live instruction by content experts to remote geographic settings.

Can you think of other ways to provide special education services to a child when the special education teacher does not speak the child's language?

Education and the Preschool Child

Young culturally and linguistically diverse children with exceptionalities benefit from early educational services. With the inception of Head Start programs in 1965, some of these children were served. Not all young children who needed services had access to Head Start, however. Head Start was designed primarily for children from low-income families and was not specifically developed for children with exceptionalities. Since the passage of the Education for All Handicapped Children Act of 1975 (EHA) (PL 94–142) and the early childhood amendments of 1986 (PL 99–457) (see chapter 3, IFSP, IEP, ITP: Planning and Delivering Services), culturally and linguistically diverse young children with exceptionalities are now served, often by public school preschool programs.

Cultural and linguistic diversity issues are especially pronounced in the provision of services to young children. Many of these services are provided in the privacy of the family's home, and often family members work cooperatively with the early childhood specialist to present the early intervention services to the child with handicaps. In addition, language issues are particularly important during the early developmental years when children are still acquiring their home language.

Hanson, Lynch, and Wayman (1990) describe the unique intimacy that arises from providing preschool services to culturally and linguistically diverse young children.

> What and how families eat, the kind of furniture they own and its arrangement, rituals of religious significance, the ways children and other family members are treated and cared for, and the interactional patterns that comprise the family's communication system become apparent as the interventionist spends time in the home. For instance, early intervention professionals are often able to discuss issues and practices related to health care and medical treatment. These conversations may raise a number of differences in the ways that various cultures view health, prevention of illness or disability, and the causation and treatment of disability. Because one's cultural values are often unrecognized until they are challenged by exposure to different values, early interventionists and families alike may expect reactions that range from suspicion to surprise, from disbelief to delight, and from acceptance to appreciation. The roles of early interventionists include acknowledging different cultural perspectives and learning how to work effectively within the boundaries that are comfortable for the family, while sharing the views of the larger culture to increase the family's understanding and improve their ability to negotiate the new culture. (pp. 116–117)

Preschool education for culturally and linguistically diverse children with exceptionalities has sometimes failed to value the richness of the lives of these children, referring to them erroneously as "culturally deprived" or "culturally disadvantaged." This deficit view, suggesting that the children have no culture or have an inferior culture, was insensitive to the diversity of children and their families. Today, good preschool education values the cultural and linguistic diversity of children and their families. It is important to incorporate that reality of children's lives into special educational services addressing handicaps and giftedness.

The cultural reality of children's lives is an important component in their school experiences. Creative teachers incorporate this reality into school learning experiences.

Education and the School-Age Child

There are several critical issues for the school-age culturally and linguistically diverse child with exceptionalities. We will discuss here cultural diversity, language and instruction, and who is served.

Research has shown that culturally and linguistically diverse students will gain benefits from or be disabled by their experiences with teachers. What kind of school can make the difference? Schools that empower minority students tend to do the following:

1. Incorporate minority students' language and culture into the school program.
2. Encourage minority community participation as an integral component of children's education.
3. Establish a curriculum that promotes intrinsic motivation for students to use language actively to generate their own knowledge.
4. Understand, with help from assessment professionals, the ways in which minority students' academic difficulty is a function of interactions within the school context rather than legitimizing the location of the "problem" within students. (Adapted from Cummins, 1989, p. 112–113)

Cultural Diversity

How can a teacher incorporate multicultural and bilingual aspects in a classroom? Instructional materials should reflect the cultural diversity of students. Textbooks, computer software, and learning materials should reflect the cultural diversity in language and pictures of the students. One California high school with an exemplary multicultural bilingual special education program celebrates Mexican holidays, offers *Ballet Folklorico* as a physical education class and *Estudiansa* as a choral class, and has an ESL club and a Movimiento Estudiantil Chicano de Aztlan (MEChA) club (Cegelka, MacDonald, and Gaeta, 1987). In attempting to incorporate cultural diversity into the day-to-day activities of a school, teachers must be careful not to use stereotyped images of the students' culture. Teachers should also select content that reflects central aspects of the culture.

criteria

Language and Instruction

What language does the teacher use to teach culturally and linguistically diverse students? As you learned when you read the history section, this question was easily answered for most of our history—English. One early belief was that bilingualism caused academic problems and that bilingual children would suffer unless they were transformed into monolingual children. Educators believed that children's learning problems would be aggravated if they were required to deal with two languages of instruction. Some argued that this situation would lead to confusion, language interference, or further academic problems. As a result, many schools established rules that only English could be spoken and many children were severely punished—by, for example, having their mouths washed out with soap or being kept after school—for speaking their home language at school. Even teachers were prosecuted. (See the interview, in the chapter opening, where Gonzales describes being punished at school for speaking Spanish.) Professional educators now know this is a much more complex question.

Today, many educators view bilingualism as a positive force in children's academic development (Cummins, 1984). Most bilingual educators agree that children learn better and maintain pride and comfort with their home language and culture when the language of instruction is bilingual, provided in both English and their home language, and when teaching is accompanied by specially designed English instruction that facilitates the learning of English as a second language. It appears that, as a group, bilingual children have more cognitive flexibility and better divergent and creative thinking abilities. Some studies have reported that bilingual children show more advanced general intellectual ability and greater skill in analyzing linguistic meaning.

Three **mediational strategies** have been found to be effective for students with limited English proficiency: (a) use both English and students' native language for instructional purposes, (b) integrate English language development with instruction in the content areas, and (c) use information from students' native cultures to enhance instruction (Tikunoff, 1987). Although these strategies were developed for students in regular education classes, they are equally effective for children with exceptionalities as well as multicultural bilingual backgrounds.

Bilingual education uses four basic instructional approaches.

1. **English as a second language (ESL).** Children are given English instruction in their classrooms or in special classes until English proficiency is achieved.

2. The **bilingual transitional approach.** Students are taught partly in English using ESL strategies (especially math and science) and partly in their home language (especially reading and writing) until they learn enough English to be able to get by without instruction in the home language.

mediational strategies. The means for transmitting or communicating information.

English as a second language (ESL). Children are given English instruction in their classrooms or in special classes until English proficiency is achieved.

bilingual transitional approach. Students are taught primarily in English and partly in their home language until they learn enough English to learn academic subjects.

L1. Dominant or home language.

L2. Language learned second.

EMPOWERING LANGUAGE MINORITY STUDENTS

- Reflect the various cultural groups in the school district by providing signs in the main office and elsewhere that welcome people in the different languages of the community.
- Encourage students to use their primary language (**L1,** the home or dominant language) around the school.
- Provide opportunities for students from the same ethnic group to communicate with one another in their primary language where possible (for example, in cooperative learning groups on at least some occasions).
- Recruit people who can tutor students in their primary language.
- Provide books written in the various languages in both classrooms and the school library.
- Incorporate greetings and information in the various languages in newsletters and other official school communications.
- Provide bilingual and multilingual signs.
- Display pictures and objects of the various cultures represented at the school.
- Display pictures of culturally diverse individuals in the professions and high-status occupations.
- Create units of work that incorporate other languages in addition to the school language.
- Encourage students to write contributions in their primary language for school newspapers and magazines.
- Provide opportunities for students to study their primary language in elective subjects and in extracurricular clubs.
- Encourage parents to help in the classroom, library, playground, and in clubs.
- Invite second-language (**L2**) learners to use their dominant language during assemblies, award ceremonies, and other official functions.
- Invite people from ethnic minority communities to act as resource people and to speak to students in both formal and informal settings.
- Take into account students' sociocultural backgrounds and their effects on oral langauge, reading and writing, and second-language learning.
- Take into account students' possible learning handicaps and their effects on oral language, reading and writing, and second-language learning.
- Follow developmental processes in literacy acquisition.
- Locate curriculum in a meaningful context where the communicative purpose is clear and authentic.
- Connect curriculum with the students' personal experiences.
- Incorporate children's literature into reading, writing, and English as a second language (ESL) lessons.
- Involve parents as active partners in the instruction of their children.
- Give students experience with whole texts in reading, writing, and ESL lessons.
- Incorporate collaborative learning whenever possible.

SOURCE: Compiled from *New Voices: Second Language Learning and Teaching: A Handbook for Primary Teachers* by New Zealand Department of Education, 1988, Wellington: Department of Education, cited in "A Theoretical Framework for Bilingual Special Education" by J. Cummings, 1989, *Exceptional Children, 56,* p. 113–114; and "An Optimal Learning Environment for Rosemary" by N.T. Ruiz, 1989, *Exceptional Children, 56,* p. 134.

3. The **bilingual maintenance approach.** Students are taught partly in English and partly in their home language so that they maintain proficiency in the home language but also gain proficiency in English.

4. **Total immersion.** The student is taught entirely in English and no English instruction or home language instruction is provided. All the other students are also non-native-English speakers, and the teacher speaks the students' home language. (This approach should not be confused with **submersion,** placement in an all-English classroom with no assistance.)

Although use of total immersion is rare in the United States, the other three approaches are used in different combinations across the country.

We still have many vocal critics of bilingual education. Some people argue that teaching a child in the home language wastes time because the child will need to be retaught everything again later in English. However, research suggests that students who first learned skills in their home language in their home country before changing to instruction in a second language did better in school than children who received all of their instruction in the second language in the new country (Cummins, 1984; Baral, 1979; Skutnabb-Kangas and Toukomaa, 1976). Many skills first acquired and mastered in the home language, arithmetic facts, for example, or reading, are easily transferred to English after English is learned. Some educators believe that unless mastery of the home language occurs, a child who is forced to attempt to function in the second language might develop significant language limitations or fail to communicate effectively in either language.

Professionals in the field of bilingual education also disagree on the appropriate time to move a child from the bilingual class to the all-English class. The proper timing for such a move is critical. Research conducted by Cummins (1984) highlights the issues. The early level of language proficiency is conversational fluency, the mastery of pronunciation, vocabulary, and grammar. Only later does the individual develop the more complex conceptual linguistic ability, the deeper functions of language necessary for competent participation in academic settings. (See Figure 2.2,

bilingual maintenance approach. Students are taught partly in English using ESL strategies and partly in their home language so they maintain proficiency.

total immersion. The student is taught entirely in English. All the other students are also non-native-English speakers and the teacher can speak the students' home language.

submersion. The child is placed with native English speakers in all-English classrooms with no special language assistance. Also known as the "sink or swim" method.

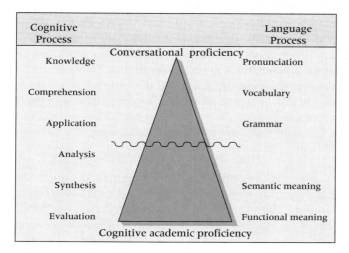

FIGURE 2.2 Surface and Deeper Levels of Language Proficiency

SOURCE: *Bilingualism and Special Education: Issues in Assessment and Pedagogy* (p. 138) by J. Cummins, 1984, Austin, TX: Pro-Ed. Copyright 1984 Jim Cummins. Reprinted by permission.

basic interpersonal communicative skills (BICS). Face-to-face conversational language.

cognitive/academic linguistic proficiency (CALP). The abstract language abilities required for academic work.

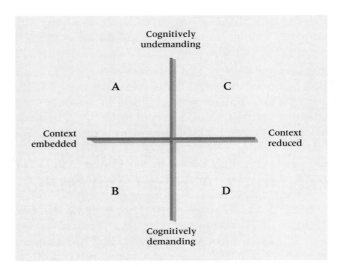

FIGURE 2.3 Range of Contextual Support and Degree of Cognitive Involvement in Communicative Activities

SOURCE: *Bilingualism and Special Education: Issues in Assessment and Pedagogy* (p. 139) by J. Cummins, 1984, Austin, TX: Pro-Ed. Copyright 1984 Jim Cummins. Reprinted by permission.

which shows the surface as well as the deeper levels of language proficiency.) Cummins cautions that children first develop face-to-face conversational skills. Because they then appear to have English proficiency, they are too quickly transferred to all-English instruction. They then fall further and further behind academically because they do not have the more complex linguistic abilities required for academic success. Their **basic interpersonal communicative skills (BICS)** are more developed than their **cognitive/academic language proficiency (CALP).** Conversational skills in a second language can be acquired within about two to three years, but the more complex language abilities required for academic work require about five to seven years of meaningful exposure and practice.

The student's understanding is also affected by how many contextual clues accompany the language, for example, explanatory pictures, specific people speaking, particular tone of voice. Understanding is also affected by how demanding the activity is—if the task is not very demanding, it is easier to understand than if it is quite demanding. Figure 2.3 illustrates these principles.

Controversy over multicultural bilingual education has spread beyond the field of education and into local and national politics. The choice of instructional method sometimes becomes a political issue, with communities objecting to non-English instruction. In fact, some communities and states have even attempted to declare English the "official" language. (See Concepts and Controversies later in this chapter.)

How does the discussion of multicultural bilingual education affect special education? Certainly the approaches suggested for regular classes can be equally effective in special education classes. The models for multicultural bilingual education work in concert with the methods developed to teach children with specific exceptionalities.

As we all know, whether children are able to attend school and what experiences they have in school have a profound effect on the way they grow to adulthood and the manner in which they can fulfill their potential. Some states have attempted to

MAKING A BOOK

Teachers can help multicultural and bilingual exceptional students to create books in their home language that reflect their culture. Here is an example from Cuba Independent Schools, Cuba, New Mexico.

Níléí Ya'niilzhiindi t'óó ahayóí dahooghan, diné łahgóó kéédahat'į. Áko baa shił hózhǫ́.

limit the right to education and to exclude children who are not citizens. The problem concerns children who are undocumented, that is, children who do not have the proper immigration papers. How are they to be educated? This issue has gone all the way to the Supreme Court. In 1982 the Supreme Court decided a Texas case in which the question was whether undocumented children, the children of Mexican nationals residing in Texas without proper documentation, had a right to free public school education (*Plyler v. Doe,* 1982). Many of the immigrant children had special education needs. The Supreme Court ruled that the children had a right to free education and eloquently addressed the importance of education.

> Public education is not a "right" granted to individuals by the Constitution. But neither is it merely some governmental "benefit" indistinguishable from other forms of social welfare legislation. Both the importance of education in maintaining

community-based instruction (CBI). A strategy of teaching functional skills in the environments they occur in; for example, shopping skills should be taught in the local market rather than a classroom "store."

our basic institutions, and the lasting impact of its deprivation on the life of the child, mark the distinction. The American people have always regarded education and the acquisition of knowledge as matters of supreme importance. We have recognized the public school as a most vital civic institution for the preservation of a democratic system of government, and as the primary vehicle for transmitting the values on which our society rests. As noted early in our history, some degree of education is necessary to prepare citizens to participate effectively and intelligently in our open political system if we are to preserve freedom and independence. And these historic perceptions of the public schools as inculcating fundamental values necessary to the maintenance of a democratic political system have been confirmed by the observations of social scientists. In addition, education provides the basic tools by which individuals might lead economically productive lives to the benefit of us all. In sum, education has a fundamental role in maintaining the fabric of our society. We cannot ignore the significant social costs borne by our Nation when select groups are denied the means to absorb the values and skills upon which our social order rests. (Citations omitted; p. 2397)

The Court's ruling in this Texas case has implications for undocumented children all over the country. It seems clear that no state may prohibit children within its borders from attending public school.

Educational Environments

As we have mentioned earlier, special education environments for students who are multicultural and bilingual should be responsive to the cultural and language needs of the students. At the same time the environments need to be directed toward the child's special educational needs. Depending on the students' specific needs, schedules, classrooms, staff, and appropriate supports vary.

For example, at Southwest High School in San Diego County, California, all students choose from a continuum of placement options in the regular school program. All classes are presented in at least three ways: English, bilingual transitional, and Spanish. English and Spanish courses are also offered. Additionally, for the special education students there are special courses in math and social studies, a Spanish section of English, and an English section of English. The special education program stresses the development of learning strategies and provides tutorial support for students with handicaps in regular classes. The special education program includes bilingual concept development, Spanish and English language development, social and personal development, and acculturation (Cegelka, MacDonald, and Gaeta, 1987).

Paramount Elementary School in the Azusa United School District, California, provides another example of how a school provides multicultural bilingual special education. Students spend approximately one and a half hours per school day in special education and are grouped by both academic level and language fluency level. Students may also be receiving English as a second language (ESL) instruction each day. Hispanic cultural values are emphasized in the program and family members are incorporated into the education. Parents are colearners, receiving specific instruction with the students and serving as tutors in the classroom and at home (Cegelka, MacDonald, and Gaeta, 1987).

The elements of **community-based instruction (CBI)** (see chapter 4) can be effectively applied to multicultural and bilingual special education. Using the community as a primary educational environment can have several important benefits.

Teaching skills in the children's home community can help them learn functional skills that are useful in their daily lives, can help them maintain cultural ties to their families and neighbors, and can keep them integrated in their home communities. Think about the advantages of taking a group of Hispanic children with special education needs shopping in the neighborhood *bodega* (grocery store) instead of giving them an arithmetic lecture in the classroom on adding a column of numbers with decimal points and dollar signs. Can you think of other community-based instruction teaching activities that build the child's academic skills but also take into account the child's cultural and language needs? What about community festivals, museum exhibits, or home language movies?

By now you have an understanding of the commitment that is needed for a teacher of multicultural bilingual special education students. Below we list the characteristics you will need to work as an effective teacher of these students:

1. The desire to work with the culturally and linguistically different child with exceptionalities
2. The ability to work effectively with parents of these students
3. The ability to develop appropriate individual educational plans (IEPs) for these students
4. Knowledge and sensitivity toward the language and the culture of the group to be served
5. The ability to teach English as a second language to the students
6. The ability to conduct nonbiased assessment with culturally and linguistically different exceptional students
7. The ability to use appropriate methods and materials when working with these students (Baca and Amato, 1989, p. 169)

FAMILIES OF CULTURALLY AND LINGUISTICALLY DIVERSE CHILDREN WITH EXCEPTIONALITIES

Some children who are culturally and linguistically diverse are the first generation in their family to enter an educational system that is basically English. Their parents and families may speak little, if any, English. The culture of their homes may be different from the culture represented by the teacher and the school. A significant risk under these circumstances is that the family might feel excluded, rejected, or even offended by their child's school. The child is put in the unfortunate position of feeling he or she must choose between the world of school and the world of family. Or the child may feel that the school is irrelevant to real life. The teacher must be aware of this potential conflict when dealing with the student in the classroom and with the family at conferences.

In addition, a child from a multicultural background may have a family constellation that is different than other children's. The family of a multicultural bilingual child may include many extended family members, and each family member may have special responsibilities or restrictions dictated by the culture (Miller and Abu-darham, 1984). Often these extended family members play a crucial role in the family. The educational system must be sensitive to this. Other members of the child's home community may also have important roles in the life of the family. For example, tribal elders may play a significant role in the lives of many Native American children. Parents may feel it necessary to consult with tribal elders before making any decisions about treatments or educational strategies. In some cultures, grandparents, aunts and uncles, and older brothers and sisters provide much of the child care. When working with the families of these children, teachers should encourage and anticipate the participation of extended family members.

How does the teacher help the child and family have a positive school experience? The teacher must plan for communication and cooperation with the child's parents and family. If the teacher does not speak the home language of the family, an interpreter who is not a family member should be available to facilitate each communication. When planning home visits, the teacher may need to bring along an interpreter so that communication will be comfortable. School personnel should make certain that all written communication is in the language that the family understands and reads. What do you do if you teach in a rural area where families live great distances from school or where there is no telephone? A creative teacher might be able to use videocassettes to communicate with these families—video recorders are found in many geographically isolated homes, even areas where telephone service is not available.

In part, a child's success in school depends on respect between the school and the family. Parents and families are important to children's success at school, and must feel confident that their cultural heritage and language are valued by the teacher and school. A teacher can bring the strengths, contributions, culture, and

Parents, family members, and community leaders are a valuable resource in children's education.

language of the family directly into the school experience in many ways. For example, the grandfather of a multicultural child might teach the class a special skill like making silver jewelry. A grandmother who is an artist and creates pottery following the ancient techniques might demonstrate that art. A mother who programs computers might tutor the class. A parent who is a migrant agricultural worker might sing folk songs or tell fairy tales in the home language. An aunt who has recently emigrated from the country of origin might have photos, musical instruments, examples of clothing, or other items to help the students dramatize a myth and better understand the customs of the country. A tribal leader might be asked to officiate at a school awards ceremony.

A FATHER DESCRIBES HIS ADOPTIVE SON WHO IS DISABLED BY FETAL ALCOHOL SYNDROME

Fetal alcohol syndrome (FAS) is found around the world in all cultures in which alcohol is found. Disabilities caused by fetal alcohol syndrome are disturbingly high among Native Americans living on reservations (Streissguth, LaDue, and Randels, 1988). These disabilities compound the challenges faced by culturally and linguistically diverse children in American society. As many as 25 percent of all children on some reservations are reportedly affected. The rate of fetal alcohol syndrome may be 30 times higher in Native Americans than in whites (Rosenthal, 1990). Alaska has the highest fetal alcohol syndrome rate reported in the world (Quality Education for Minorities Project, 1990).

Michael Dorris, a member of the Modoc tribe, adopted a son, Adam, who is Sioux. We now know that a pregnant woman should eliminate all alcohol consumption. Many people today also know that on many reservations a high percentage of Native American children are harmed before they are born by the alcohol consumed by their mothers. However, it was many years before Dorris understood that the school failures and disabilities of his beloved son, Adam, were the result of fetal alcohol syndrome. Dorris wrote *The Broken Cord* (1989) about his son, now an adult, who has severe disabilities as a result of his biological mother's drinking.

> My son will forever travel through a moonless night with only the roar of wind for company. Don't talk to him of mountains, of tropical beaches. Don't ask him to swoon at sunrises or marvel at the filter of light through leaves. He's never had time for such things, and he does not believe in them. He may pass by them close enough to touch on either side, but his hands are stretched forward, grasping for balance instead of pleasure. He doesn't wonder where he came from, where he's going. He doesn't ask who he is, or why. Questions are a luxury, the province of those at a distance from the periodic shock of rain. Gravity presses Adam so hard against reality that he doesn't feel the points at which he touches it. A drowning man is not separated from the lust for air by a bridge of thought—he is one with it—and my son, conceived and grown in an ethanol bath, lives each day in the act of drowning. For him there is no shore. (p. 264)

At Southwest High School (Cegelka, MacDonald, and Gaeta, 1987), there is extensive parent and community involvement. The special education program holds monthly meetings. A "parent facilitator" provides services to enhance the ability of parents to be involved with their children's special education. The facilitator acts as a parent contact and advocate as well as a translator, provides transportation to meetings, meets with parents in their homes concerning special education referral and assessment procedures, and accompanies parents to IEP meetings. The program makes sure that all written communications, including IEP forms, newsletters, memoranda, and so forth, are sent in both English and Spanish, and the district has developed a special handbook for bilingual special educators.

CULTURALLY AND LINGUISTICALLY DIVERSE ADULTS WITH EXCEPTIONALITIES

The statistics show that low-income and minority students, many of whom are culturally and linguistically diverse, tend to drop out of school at a higher rate than others. Although there has been improvement in the last twenty years, the dropout rate remains troubling. High school dropouts suffer more unemployment than all other groups.

Fewer minority individuals complete college (see Figure 2.4), which contributes to the low employment of multicultural and bilingual adults (see Figure 2.5).

The unemployment rate for African-Americans is more than twice the national average, for African-American teenagers it is an astoundingly high rate of 34.2 percent. Although African-American men are only 6 percent of the total population, they make up nearly 46 percent of the prison population (Quality Education for Minorities Project, 1990).

As in all exceptionalities, job training and preparation is an important component of special education transition services for students with handicaps who are multicultural and bilingual. Vocational programs for individuals with limited English

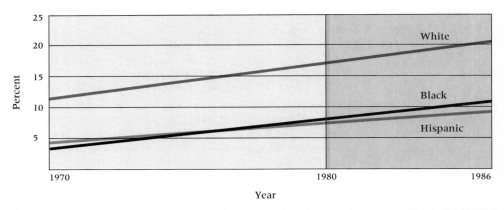

FIGURE 2.4 Percent of Persons 25 Years Old and Over Completing Four or More Years of College, by Race and Ethnicity

SOURCE: U.S. Bureau of the Census, *Statistical Abstract of the United States: 1988* (Washington, D.C.: 1987), Table 202: 125.

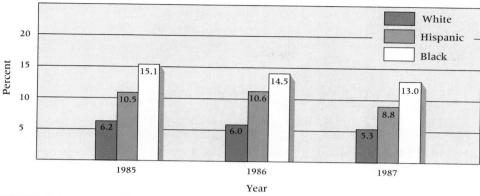

FIGURE 2.5 **Unemployment Rates, by Race and Ethnicity**

SOURCE: U.S. Department of Labor Statistics, "Current Labor Statistics: Employment Data," *Monthly Labor Review* (Washington, D.C.: September 1987), Table 1.6: 91–92.

Migrant Student Record Transfer Service (MSRTS). A nationwide computerized transcript and health record service for migrant students, located in Little Rock, Arkansas.

proficiency require special consideration (Technical Assistance for Special Populations Program, 1989).

TECHNOLOGY AND MULTICULTURAL AND BILINGUAL SPECIAL EDUCATION

Microcomputers

As computerized language translators begin to develop, there may be a significant impact for special education students with a primary language other than English. Imagine if the student could use a computer to write an assignment in his or her primary language, check the spelling and punctuation, then press a button to translate the work into English and transmit it to the teacher. Or perhaps the student wrote the assignment in a dialect, and then the computer was able to translate it into the standard form of that language. Such technology is possible.

One successful use of the microcomputer has been for the students to write their journals and for the teacher to respond via computer (Goldman and Rueda, 1988). Multicultural bilingual special education students were successful in developing their writing skills and their interaction skills with their teacher.

George Earl (1984) created a Spanish-to-English as well as an English-to-Spanish computerized version of the word game "hangman." Hangman is one of the many instructional games used by special education teachers to help improve language skills. Although the program had some difficulty (Zemke, 1985) with dialects (it translates standard Spanish), it demonstrates how technology can be applied to the learning needs of children who are multicultural and bilingual.

Computers have contributed to improved education for migrant children. A nationwide computerized transcript service, the **Migrant Student Record Transfer System (MSRTS)** in Little Rock, Arkansas, serves as a centralized location for transcripts and health records. A special education component contains information on the existence of a disability, assessment results, related services provided, and IEPs.

Microcomputers can be a useful tool when children are gaining confidence in a second language.

Distance Education

One unique form of technological delivery for students in rural settings is distance education (Condon, Zimmerman, and Beane, 1989; Clark and Verduin, 1989). Distance education uses telecommunications to deliver live instruction by content experts to areas where particular expertise is desired (Barker, 1989).

Distance education may become an increasingly important tool for students from different cultures. For example, it is possible to create a nationwide "classroom" for a small number of students with special learning needs who speak a particular language. Imagine having an immigrant student in your class who speaks only Lapp and who has mental retardation. Neither you, nor anyone else in the school or town can yet speak more than a few words of Lapp. The child's aunt and uncle, with whom he is currently living, are eagerly studying Lapp, but even they are not yet sufficiently fluent to explain academic material to the child. Distance education would allow hooking up by satellite to a teacher or even an entire classroom for instruction and assistance in Lapp during the time before you learn Lapp or the child becomes proficient in English.

Television and videocassette technology can be used imaginatively by teachers also. Many families have televisions and videotape players in their homes or can arrange to borrow the equipment from the school. Lessons might be taped and sent home with the child so that the parents can help reinforce skills in the home language. This technique would enhance interaction between the family culture and language and the school. Teachers could prepare videotaped hours of the special education classrooms, and introductions of the personnel and other students to help

VIDEO TECHNOLOGY AND COMMUNICATION WITH FAMILY

The teacher or school might

- tape lessons so parents can reinforce them in the home language.
- tape a tour of the classroom and introduction of teachers.
- tape the child's progress in school.
- tape the child in physical therapy exercises.
- tape the teacher's messages to parents.
- tape the child in all activities as a "report card."
- tape children in excellent levels of performance as an example or model.
- use English captioned TV when children view programs. (See chapter 10, Hearing Impairments.)

The parents/family might:

- tape introductions of members of family, including the extended family.
- tape introductions of important members of the child's community.
- tape the child performing chores and family functions.
- tape significant community events.
- tape messages to teacher.
- tape reading or oral history in home language.
- use English captioned TV when children view programs. (See chapter 10, Hearing Impairments.)

introduce children and their parents to special education. See the Tips for Teachers box for other possible uses of video technology.

CONCEPTS AND CONTROVERSIES

Laws That Mandate Speaking English

Efforts such as "English Only" laws and "English Language" amendments have passed in more than fourteen states and various municipalities (Quality Education for Minorities Project, 1990). Some have argued against these attempts, saying that they discriminate against bilingual individuals and that they create hostility and divisiveness in communities. Speaking more than one language should be regarded as a valued skill, and pluralism is an American strength. Some support an alternative position of "English Plus," asserting that "national interests can best be served when all members of our society have full access to effective opportunities to acquire English-language proficiency plus mastery of a second language or multiple languages" (Quality Education for Minorities Project, 1990, p. 40).

Others argue that English Only laws are necessary to prevent loss of American values—that English is a unifying force in the United States. They fear that the country is being divided along language lines. What do you think? Is a town's effort to pass a measure declaring English the official language discriminatory? Or is it an attempt to unite the people in a community? Perhaps it is fear that if the schools make it too easy, the immigrant children will never learn English at all. Or might it be a political and economic backlash against the new immigrants? See the following article.

IMMIGRANTS' TOWN IS DIVIDED OVER OFFICIAL-LANGUAGE ISSUE*

LOWELL, Mass., November 3—This riverfront city of old textile mills and factories has always drawn immigrants by the thousands. First there were the Irish and the Italians, then the Greeks and Poles. Most recently, Latin Americans and Southeast Asians have migrated here for jobs.

Relations among the various groups have not always been smooth, and a nonbinding measure on Tuesday's ballot that would declare English the city's official language has produced an ugly division between those who back it and those who say its possible later reintroduction as a binding measure could create a tool of oppression.

Mayor Richard P. Howe says the issue has needlessly brought racial and ethnic animosity to the surface in a relatively peaceful period. But the measure's sponsor, George D. Kouloheras, a member of the School Committee, says he does not want to inflict pain on any ethnic group but simply wants to protect a language "under attack."

Nearly 40 percent of Lowell's 100,000 residents are Asian or Hispanic and no one disputes the value of conducting most of the city's affairs in English. But some worry that the move might be a first step toward policies that discriminate against people who cannot speak English, or cannot speak it well.

Divisive, a Cambodian Says

"I feel it is a divisive community strategy," said Boran Reth, president of the Cambodian Mutual Assistance Association here, who came later to the United States in 1981 after his family was killed in the Cambodian civil war. "The Cambodian community feels that they are not welcome in this city, and the purpose of this seems to be to punish the people who cannot speak English or speak English with accents."

Mr. Kouloheras, whose parents emigrated from Greece at the turn of the twentieth century, has joined the Washington-based organization U.S. English, which promotes the use of English in government.

"We have sort of a laissez-faire attitude that English is our language," Mr. Kouloheras said, "and it is best to establish some principles that will guide the courts and policymakers in the future. It's best to take benign action now before the problem reaches a crisis. The minority language population continues to grow."

"These measures are always so vague," said Martha Jimenez, a staff attorney and policy analyst for the Mexican American Legal Defense Fund in Washington, "and no one is really sure what they mean. But the pattern has been for people to interpret them on their own, and it leads to an increase in private discrimination. People try not to be overtly racist, because they don't want to be labeled, so to a great extent language can be used as a proxy for that."

The referendum, coming when Lowell and much of Massachusetts are in an economic slowdown, seems to have prompted ill will toward recent immigrants. Lowell now has 25,000 Cambodians here and several hundred Vietnamese, Thai, and Laotian families.

"This has brought out the anger and resentment and frustration that hadn't seemed to be a problem recently," Mayor Howe said. "People are calling up radio talk shows to express their objections to Southeast Asians in the city. We were well on our way to making this system work when along comes George," a reference to Mr. Kouloheras.

Desegregation of Lowell's schools, begun in 1987, is now all but complete, with busing to classrooms beyond students' neighborhoods for racial balance. The plan had been hotly disputed. Shortly after it went into effect a young Cambodian boy, fighting with another boy as both waited for a bus, was pushed into a canal and drowned.

Most Asians came here in the last five years, and that has strained services, especially the school system. Last year the city spent $10 million of its $51 million budget on bilingual education and busing to keep the schools integrated.

The Influx of Children

About 3400 of the 13,000 students are Asian, and 2000 are Hispanic. Last year, Mayor Howe said, Asian children arrived at the rate of 30 to 50 a week, forcing the school system to rent extra classrooms and hire bilingual teachers. Many Cambodian children spent their earliest years in Thai refugee camps and came here with no formal education, Mr. Boran Reth said.

The superintendent of schools, Henry J. Mroz, said he favored extra Federal aid to help cover the costs of educating children who came with no English. "It's all right to welcome people in," he said, "but you have to provide for them."

Mr. Mroz said he expected the referendum to win approval from most voters. The school committee endorsed it last week. "It's not to divide people," Mr. Kouloheras said. "It's to unite people. *E pluribus unum.*"

SUMMARY

Special education reflects the rich diversity of culture and language found in communities across this country. Many children with exceptionalities have diverse cultural backgrounds and may be bilingual. This combination of exceptionality and cultural and linguistic diversity presents many issues as schools attempt to assure special education services for all children.

1. The definition of multicultural and bilingual special education stresses the acquisition of academic and social skills in culturally and linguistically diverse children with exceptionalities. It is the child's special education needs that are primary, but language and culture are the means through which appropriate special education intervention is provided.

2. One of the risks in testing culturally and linguistically diverse children with exceptionalities is discriminatory testing. Discrimination can occur in testing at four junctures: the content level, when items are selected for a test; the standardization level, when minority groups are not represented in the standardization population;

the administration level, when an individual untrained in multicultural bilingual techniques conducts the evaluation; and the validation level, when the test is misused for purposes for which it is not valid.

3. The number of multicultural and bilingual students in the United States is increasing rapidly. By the year 2000, it is estimated that approximately one-third of public school children will be from culturally diverse backgrounds, with Hispanics being the largest minority group in the United States. Today, in twenty-five of the country's largest cities and metropolitan areas, at least half of the students are from culturally and linguistically diverse groups. The largest group and the fastest growing group is Hispanic, currently with 75 percent of all children of limited English proficiency.

4. Multiculturalism and bilingualism do not cause handicaps. But, poverty can cause a variety of handicaps. Many culturally and linguistically diverse students do not live in poverty, but for those who do, the effects of poverty are sometimes confused with the effects of cultural and linguistic diversity.

5. Culturally and linguistically diverse children with exceptionalities have special problems in several unique areas. Language and communication differences may challenge both the child and special education personnel; and cultural differences may raise questions about the behavior of the child and family and about the appropriateness of interventions. In addition, mobility, such as homelessness, migrant agricultural traveling, or refugee circumstances may add stress and logistical difficulties to educating some children.

6. For those culturally and linguistically diverse children who are migrant, they are very likely to be affected by handicaps because of the poverty and health problems that accompany migrant working. They are, however, underidentified and underserved in special education. The high mobility of migrant children aggravates the educational problems of these children.

7. One of the primary issues is which type of instructional approach to use with students. The four basic instructional approaches in multicultural and bilingual special education are English as a second language (ESL), where children are given English instruction in their classrooms or in special classes until English proficiency is achieved; the bilingual transitional approach, where students are taught partly in English using ESL strategies (especially math and science) and partly in their home language (especially reading and writing) until they learn enough English to be able to get by without home language instruction; the bilingual maintenance approach, where students are taught partly in English and partly in their home language so that they maintain proficiency in their home language but also gain proficiency in English; and total immersion, where the student is taught entirely in English, no English instruction or home language instruction is provided, all the other students are also non-native-English speakers, and the teacher speaks the students' home language.

8. The two levels of language proficiency are BICS and CALP. The early level of language proficiency, basic interpersonal communicative skills, or BICS, is conversational fluency, the mastery of pronunciation, vocabulary, and grammar. Later the individual develops the more complex conceptual linguistic ability, CALP, the deeper functions of language necessary for competent participation in academic settings. Conversational skills in a second language can be acquired within about two to three years, but the more complex language abilities required for academic work require about five to seven years of meaningful exposure and practice.

DISCUSSION QUESTIONS

1. List some advantages of being able to speak more than one language.

2. Develop an outline for an information handbook about one of the cultures represented in a local school. In what ways might an information handbook be useful? Might it help student relationships? What steps would you take to try to develop such a handbook? Do you think a working group that included parents and family members might help?

3. What steps might a school take to move from merely "tolerating" cultural diversity to actually embracing diversity? What might be the benefits for students, teachers, and families in a school that was genuinely multicultural and bilingual?

4. Why does it take longer to learn the language required for cognitive academic tasks (CALP) than the language required for everyday interpersonal communication (BICS)?

5. How might you assure that as a teacher you evaluate learning in ways that do not discriminate against a member of certain cultural or linguistic minority group?

SUPPLEMENTARY BOOKS AND VIDEOS

Over the years, culturally and linguistically diverse individuals have been included in fictional and nonfictional roles in both books and films. (We only included videos that can be rented at many large video stores. Unfortunately, copies of many excellent television shows and movies are not readily available.) Below is a brief listing of such creative works that you might find of interest.

Books

Anaya, R. A. (1979). *Tortuga.* Berkeley, CA: Editorial Justa Publications.

Vonnegut, K. (1961). Harrison Bergeron. In *Welcome to the monkey house.* New York: Delacorte Press/ Seymour Lawrence; excerpted in E. M. Bower, ed. (1980), *The handicapped in literature.* Denver: Love Publishing, pp. 391–406.

Deloria, E. C. (1988). *Waterlily.* Lincoln: University of Nebraska Press.

Kozol, J. (1988). *Rachel and her children: Homeless families in America.* New York: Crown Publishers.

Rodriguez, R. (1982). *Hunger of memory: The education of Richard Rodriguez.* Boston: David R. Godine.

Tan, A. (1989). *The Joy Luck Club.* New York: G. P. Putnam's Sons.

Videos

To Kill a Mockingbird (1960). United Artists.
West Side Story (1961). 20th Century Fox/Mirisch Production.
El Norte (1984). Cinecom International/Island Alive Production
The Milagro Beanfield War (1988). Universal.
Stand and Deliver (1988). Warner Brothers.

*J*OSE VINCENTE ALVARADO, 61, and his wife, Gladys Matilde Dulce, are both self-taught painters who have leprosy and degenerative bone disease. Jose met Gladys eight years ago in a hospital in Agua de Dios, Colombia. Today Jose and his wife live in Colombia and exhibit their paintings all over the world. They attended the 1989 International Very Special Arts Festival and exhibited their paintings in Washington, D.C.

Chapter Three

IFSP, IEP, ITP: PLANNING AND DELIVERING SERVICES

*L*earning Objectives

After studying this chapter, you should be able to:

- List five environments where special education services are delivered

- Compare and contrast three different program plans: Individualized Family Service Plans, Individual Education Programs, Individualized Transition Plans

- List the seven steps used to develop an individualized program

- Describe the roles of the special services committee

- Discuss the factors that must be considered when determining the least restrictive environment for individual students

MULTIDISCIPLINARY TEAM MEMBERS SHARE THEIR THOUGHTS ABOUT THE IEP PROCESS

We asked professionals who have served on many special services committees a set of questions that reveal their perspectives on the individualized planning process required by law for every student receiving special education.

CHRIS ARBUS	Physical therapist
DORA GARCIA	Teacher of students with severe handicaps
CAROL HEARON	Adaptive physical education teacher
MAGGIE BREST	Regular education teacher
PETER SOPS	Special education teacher
JILL WALLITSCH	Special education teacher
ZINA MCLEAN	Speech/language pathologist
MYLA PITTS	Occupational therapist
LEA GETTS	Resource room teacher

From your perspective, what are the benefits of the IEP process?

PETER SOPS *Special Ed.*	"The benefits of the IEP are to aid the teacher in setting realistic and achievable goals for special education students, and provide a plan for reaching these goals."
JILL WALLITSCH *Special Ed.*	"Parents have an opportunity to participate in their child's educational program."
ZINA MCLEAN *SLP*	"One great benefit is the team approach where, working on developing objectives, one team member may observe a behavior no one else on the team has observed."

From your perspective, what are the disadvantages of the IEP process?

MAGGIE BREST *Teacher*	"Finding out that the services a child should have are not available."
MYLA PITTS *OT*	"Sometimes these meetings seem to be a race against time, and merely a process of getting the blanks filled in. Also, parents are sometimes 'talked down' to—not enough care is taken to draw them out, or they are simply ignored. Sometimes even simple courtesies are not extended to them."
LEA GETTS *Resource*	"Often, there is no follow-through or check-up. It is easy to promise the moon in order to look good in front of parents, but frequently the promises or assurances are just words."

How do people representing so many different perspectives work together at these meetings?

CAROL HEARON
Adaptive Phys. Ed.
"We all have one common goal, the *child*. With that in mind, we can help each other since areas of instruction overlap. This is better than having gaps in a child's education."

ZINA MCLEAN
SLP
"By respecting each others' different approaches, we learn from each other and integrate our joint disciplines."

LEA GETTS
Resource
"One person needs to assume the leadership role."

Is the IEP meeting typically the first time you have met the child's parents? If so, how does this affect your interaction with them?

CHRIS ARBUS
PT
"Yes, and I want to listen to them more, and be sure they understand me."

JILL WALLITSCH
Special Ed.
"No, usually I have done some home visits before this meeting."

ZINA MCLEAN
SLP
"Ideally not. I find it helpful to be in contact with parents before the meeting through home visits. I regard parents as members of the IEP team, and this affects the way I interact with them. Also, the fact that I am a parent myself alters my perspective."

Have you ever changed your mind about the needs of a child after participating in an IEP meeting? What caused you to change your mind?

DORA GARCIA
"I remember one time in particular. After working with a little girl, I realized that she was able to do a lot more than we expected or anticipated based on the information we had at the time of the IEP meeting."

CHRIS ARBUS
PT
"It has been not so much a change of mind, as an occasional feeling of "unease" that I have not done my homework sufficiently before the IEP meeting, and haven't presented goals or ways to meet them clearly. Generally, all team members are familiar enough with common goals that there are no "surprises" from my colleagues."

If there are disagreements about the content of a child's IEP, when do they usually occur?

DORA GARCIA
"They sometimes occur during the IEP meeting."

ZINA MCLEAN
SLP
"The only disagreements I have seen have been about the amount of integration that is appropriate for a child or the type of classroom (resource room versus self-contained class) that is best for a particular child, and these have happened during the IEP meeting."

1. Why might people coming from different professions have a different perspective on the individualized educational process?

2. What are some of the common beliefs shared by people across disciplines who are members of individualized education teams?

In this chapter you will learn about the various educational placements and services available to students with special needs. You will also learn about the wide range of professionals who come from a variety of disciplines to offer highly specialized expertise to students with handicaps. Individualized educational programs both set goals and objectives for youngsters with handicaps and bring professionals together to offer an appropriate education. To help you understand the process of planning an individualized educational program, we will discuss and interpret three major plans: one designed for infants, one for students, and one that aids in the transition to adulthood. You will learn about the stages of referral, assessment, and analysis of the youngster that lead to the individualized program plan. Let us begin with a discussion of what special education services comprise.

DELIVERING EDUCATIONAL SERVICES

The law generally referred to as the Individuals with Disabilities Education Act (IDEA) concerns special education. IDEA incorporates Public Law (PL) 94–142, adopted in 1975, and its successors, with amendments, such as PL 99–457, adopted in 1986, and PL 101–476, adopted in 1990. These laws guarantee a free appropriate public education (FAPE) for all youngsters with handicaps through age 21. Although

Members of special services committees represent the many different viewpoints of professionals from a variety of disciplines and the child's parents. By working together, plans are put into place for the balance between FAPE and LRE.

the laws mainly concern educational programs, PL 99–457 and PL 101–476 include incentives and mandates for states to implement services for infants, toddlers, and their families. They also provide guidelines for assisting high school students to make the transition from school to postschool activities. These laws have become very important to the field of special education.

Educational Environments

Special education is always based on the individual needs of the student. This individualized instruction is delivered in a wide range of settings. A variety of service delivery options is available in many schools, almost all school districts, and in all states. These range from **itinerant teachers,** who travel from school to school, to **center schools.** The law requires placement in the least restrictive environment (LRE). While the location or placement of a child alone does not always indicate whether an environment is least restrictive, it serves as a quick and easy measure when research data are collected. The U.S. Department of Education categorizes environments as follows:

- regular class
- resource room
- separate class
- public separate school facility
- private separate school facility
- public residential facility
- private residential facility
- correctional facility
- homebound/hospital environment

We can describe placements used as the location of special education in other ways. Table 3.1 lists and explains the terms schools commonly use to denote service

itinerant teachers. Teachers who teach students or consult with others in more than one setting.

center schools. Separate schools (some residential), typically dedicated to serving students with a particular disability.

TABLE 3.1. Service Delivery Options

Type	Description	Government Category
Itinerant or consultative	Student remains in the regular class. The teacher and/or student receives assistance from a specialist.	Regular class
Resource room	Student attends a regular class most of the day but goes to a special education class several hours per day or for blocks of time each week.	Resource room
Special education class (partially self-contained)	Student attends a special class but is mainstreamed into regular education classes for a considerable amount of time each day.	Separate class
Special education class (self-contained)	Student attends a special class most of the school day and is mainstreamed into regular education activities minimally.	Separate class
Special education schools (center schools)	Schools—some private, others supported by the state—that serve only students with a specific category of disability. Some offer residential services, while others do not.	Public separate school facility Private separate school facility Public residential facility Private residential facility

delivery options, and matches those terms with the environment categories used by the federal government.

It might seem reasonable to presume, since each state has proportionately about the same prevalence of youngsters with handicaps, and since students with handicaps have similar needs for education no matter where they live, that we would see in each state roughly the same percentages of students in each of the types of educational environments listed in Table 3.1. However, inspection of Table 3.2 and Figure 3.1 will show that this is not the case. You can see tremendous variation in the types of placements that states use when teaching children with special needs (Danielson and Bellamy, 1989). For example, New York's rate of segregated day and residential placements is approximately seven times Oregon's rate. Clearly, it is not only students' characteristics that determine their least restrictive environment. What

TABLE 3.2. Percentage of Students Attending Different Types of Special Education Placements According to the Twelfth Annual Report to Congress

State	Regular Classes	Resource Room	Separate Classes	Public Separate Facility	Private Separate Facility	Public Residential Facility	Private Residential Facility	Homebound Hospital Environment
Alabama	8.54	57.54	31.61	1.70	0.07	.	0.17	0.39
Alaska	49.49	33.42	15.77	0.72	0.02	0.22	0.31	0.06
Arizona	0.68	69.54	26.17	0.71	0.98	0.47	0.67	0.79
Arkansas	23.83	58.64	12.49	0.78	2.44	1.26	0.32	0.23
California	28.03	38.53	29.53	2.72	1.19	0.00	.	.
Colorado	25.27	51.05	18.67	2.16	0.75	0.60	0.75	0.77
Connecticut	6.49	52.85	30.12	4.12	3.00	0.61	1.67	1.14
Delaware	29.50	40.52	15.84	12.09	0.09	0.30	0.47	1.20
District of Columbia	20.07	15.50	44.28	11.56	4.32	0.25	3.08	0.95
Florida	32.21	32.57	27.63	5.30	0.50	0.37	0.24	1.17
Georgia	1.09	72.79	23.30	1.38	0.19	1.11	0.10	0.03
Hawaii	39.28	36.26	22.00	1.24	0.18	0.43	0.31	0.30
Idaho	37.16	37.25	18.88	4.21	0.00	0.00	0.24	2.26
Illinois	27.90	32.52	31.09	4.61	2.17	0.66	0.47	0.59
Indiana	38.74	28.68	27.28	4.43	0.00	0.67	0.14	0.06
Iowa	23.81	57.49	15.35	1.97	0.00	0.74	0.13	0.52
Kansas	38.78	30.65	22.26	2.87	1.24	2.00	1.15	1.04
Kentucky	30.61	51.17	14.78	1.82	0.22	0.70	0.11	0.60
Louisiana	39.12	18.17	34.53	5.98	0.40	0.00	0.37	1.43
Maine	51.01	29.11	13.30	1.44	1.79	0.44	1.04	1.87
Maryland	39.13	18.08	32.49	6.25	2.41	0.81	0.47	0.36
Massachusetts	59.69	14.48	18.93	2.10	3.03	0.55	0.53	0.68
Michigan	42.33	21.74	26.65	8.26	0.00	0.43	0.20	0.39
Minnesota	13.45	64.85	16.85	2.81	.	1.78	.	0.26
Mississippi	32.89	41.89	23.76	1.04	0.01	0.03	0.05	0.33
Missouri	41.47	31.38	20.32	5.41	0.62	0.11	0.51	0.17
Montana	56.47	24.46	16.54	0.56	0.09	1.30	0.47	0.11
Nebraska	65.46	19.91	9.83	2.30	0.34	0.67	0.17	1.31
Nevada	30.83	46.08	12.81	7.98	1.48	0.15	0.03	0.64
New Hampshire	54.52	19.39	19.82	0.08	3.97	0.21	1.49	0.51

Data as of October 1, 1989.
Annual.CNTL(LRXXNP1A)

do you think some of the reasons for the differences between states are? As you study this book, the answer to this question will become clearer. We offer some insight into the ways different states define, count, and assist children with special needs and their families. Find your state on both Table 3.2 and Figure 3.1. How does it compare with others?

array of services. A constellation of services, personnel, and educational placements.

Special education services should be flexible and responsive to the needs of the student. Children and youth with special needs should have access to a variety of services, varying by type, intensity, location, personnel, and length of time. An *array,* or wide selection, of services should be readily available. When the term **array of services** is used, it means that students do not have to travel step by step up and down a ladder of services. There are many selections from which to choose. For example, in some cases the regular education classroom can meet the needs of the

TABLE 3.2. Percentage of Students Attending Different Types of Special Education Placements According to the Twelfth Annual Report to Congress (continued)

State	Regular Classes	Resource Room	Separate Classes	Public Separate Facility	Private Separate Facility	Public Residential Facility	Private Residential Facility	Homebound Hospital Environment
New Jersey	38.84	20.79	29.06	5.55	4.86	0.48	0.09	0.33
New Mexico	52.85	29.32	16.43	0.13	0.13	1.08	0.00	0.07
New York	7.97	36.94	39.49	7.94	6.01	0.55	0.43	0.67
North Carolina	44.25	34.93	15.81	2.68	0.29	1.12	0.41	0.51
North Dakota	69.83	10.39	14.49	2.44	0.16	1.07	0.63	0.98
Ohio	35.20	22.82	28.49	6.56	5.74	0.21	0.00	0.98
Oklahoma	50.60	29.04	17.45	1.45	0.40	0.48	0.15	0.44
Oregon	62.69	27.79	7.49	0.97	0.63	0.02	0.10	0.33
Pennsylvania	34.57	24.87	30.87	4.17	3.71	0.38	0.46	0.97
Puerto Rico	12.02	43.40	30.12	4.52	2.34	0.50	0.23	6.87
Rhode Island	51.39	14.72	27.88	1.03	2.97	0.00	1.12	0.89
South Carolina	32.21	42.75	20.79	2.88	0.01	1.11	0.06	0.19
South Dakota	8.58	75.00	11.32	0.23	0.15	1.78	2.33	0.62
Tennessee	35.40	42.76	16.76	2.57	0.51	0.87	0.03	1.10
Texas	3.23	78.26	11.86	2.95	0.17	0.11	0.06	3.36
Utah	40.39	43.31	12.51	2.82	0.07	0.64	0.00	0.25
Vermont	75.36	5.94	12.47	0.85	1.16	0.06	1.71	2.45
Virginia	26.44	38.57	31.32	2.32	0.39	0.05	0.58	0.34
Washington	40.72	32.64	21.21	1.22	2.41	0.99	0.30	0.51
West Virginia	42.32	34.65	20.27	1.60	0.03	0.79	0.01	0.32
Wisconsin	30.37	38.22	28.04	2.48	0.01	0.69	0.01	0.18
Wyoming	27.91	51.81	16.72	1.47	0.01	1.32	0.62	0.13
American Samoa	43.15	21.77	5.24	29.03	0.00	0.00	0.00	0.81
Guam	28.23	30.44	30.77	10.08	0.00	0.11	0.11	0.27
Northern Marianas	.	.	.	.	.	.	.	.
Trust Territories	.	.	.	.	.	.	.	.
Virgin Islands	.	.	.	.	.	.	.	.
Bur. of Indian Affairs	.	.	.	.	.	.	.	.
U.S. and Insular Areas	29.67	38.16	24.98	3.87	1.73	0.49	0.29	0.81
50 States, D.C. & P. R.	29.67	38.17	24.98	3.86	1.73	0.49	0.29	0.81

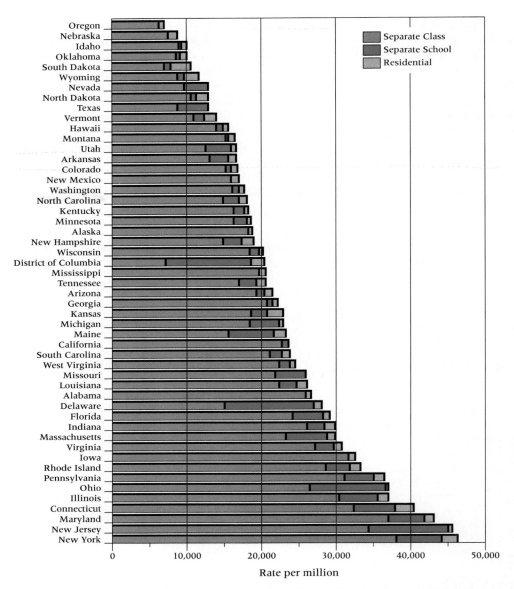

FIGURE 3.1 Placement Rate for Students with Handicaps 6–17 Years Old in Separate Classes, Separate Schools, and Residential Facilities School Year 1986–1987

NOTE: California did not report students in separate school facilities, but included them with students in separate classes.

student with some support from a consulting teacher. At other times, more intense services are required. As long as an array of services is available, students should not be forced to prove themselves at every step of the ladder before finally entering a regular classroom program. The critical point is that the system must respond to the needs of these students rather than force them into a rigid system.

Although we believe that visualizing the range of educational services as an array is preferable, the word *continuum* is often used to describe all the services available. A **continuum of services** is a full range, from most restrictive to least restrictive. For example, a continuum of living arrangements for people with handicaps would probably include a large congregate institution, smaller congregate facilities, foster care, structured group homes, independent group homes, apartments with roommates, and independent apartments and homes. The continuum model has been criticized as being too lock-stepped. Individuals are often required to prove themselves in each successively less restrictive placement before they are allowed to enter the least restrictive placement.

A model for educational services that uses the continuum approach, the **cascade of services** (Deno, 1970), is shown in Figure 3.2. In this model, special education

continuum of services. A graduated range of educational services; one level of service leads directly to the next one.

cascade of services. A linear and sequential model used to describe educational environments from the most to the least restrictive.

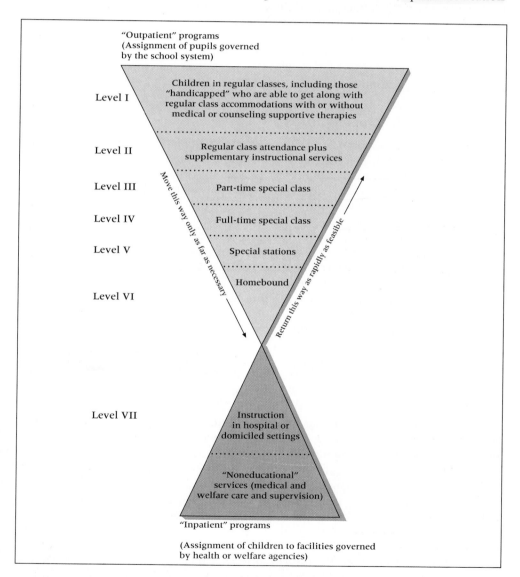

FIGURE 3.2 Deno's Cascade of Special Education Services

SOURCE: *Mental Retardation in School and Society,* 2d ed., p. 456, by D. MacMillan, 1982, Boston: Little, Brown & Co. Reprinted with permission.

services are pictured as an inverted triangle with one level leading to another in a continuous series like a cascade. At the apex, indicating the fewest students, are residential and hospital services. With numbers of students increasing as the triangle widens, other types of special education services are pictured. These include separate special education schools, full-day special education classes in neighborhood schools, part-time special classes, regular classrooms plus resource rooms, regular classrooms plus supplementary treatment, and consulting teachers who assist regular education teachers in selecting intervention procedures and evaluating their results.

A risk in the cascade model of services is that professionals might assume that assignment to a place in this cascade automatically corresponds to a determination of the severity of the student's disability. They might assume that youngsters with the most severe disabilities belong no higher than Level IV on the cascade. But that can be an erroneous assumption. It may be that a particular student with a very severe disability is most appropriately served in the regular classroom, while the needs of a student with a less severe disability might require temporary placement in a full-day special education classroom.

A Model for LRE Considerations

We believe a fluid approach is necessary when determining services and placements for students with handicaps. Figure 3.3 diagrams some of the factors that must be considered when identifying what services an individual requires and where they should be delivered. This diagram shows the student with special needs at the center of factors related to both an appropriate education and the least restrictive environment (factors such as the intensity of the required services, the professionals who have the expertise to deliver the services, the estimated length of time the services will be needed, where services are available). Keep in mind that the arrangement of any specialized service will have an impact on the student's entire educational program. For this reason, all of the factors shown on the diagram must be considered when balancing an appropriate education with the concept of least restrictive environment.

Let us take Becky's case as an example. Eight-year-old Becky is profoundly visually impaired. She lives on a ranch in a sparsely populated rural community and has been attending a regular class at an elementary school in the town nearest to her home. There are not any teachers with special training in visual impairment within 250 miles. Becky needs to learn how to use some special equipment and technology that will assist her with reading and writing, and she needs to begin specialized mobility training. After considerable consultation with Becky's state residential school for the visually impaired, her teacher, principal, and family members, it was decided that Becky would attend the residential school for at least one month. There, the teachers at the school for the visually impaired will continue with the curriculum used at Becky's home school. She will be trained to use a computerized print enlarger and a microcomputer for word processing. In addition, a mobility specialist will initiate an orientation and mobility program (see chapter 9, Visual Impairments). It was also agreed that Becky's third grade teacher, Mrs. Marcus, would visit the center school twice, spending several days on each visit. Mrs. Marcus will be certain that Becky is making progress on her class assignments, but more important, Mrs. Marcus will be learning how to use the special equipment so she can help Becky if Becky has difficulties when she returns home. Also, Mrs. Marcus will learn how to reinforce and continue the program initiated to enhance Becky's independent mobility skills.

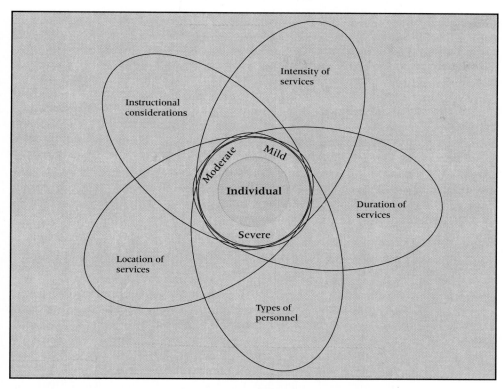

FIGURE 3.3 **Considerations for Individualized Determination of LRE**

Throughout her school years, Becky, her family, and her regular education teachers will make many visits to her state's center school for students with visual impairments. Flexible services that are individually applied can be the best answer for a student. They also show the importance of professionals working together so the educational needs of individual students with special needs can be fully met.

Special Education Professionals

Just as there is an array of services available in special education, there is also an array of special education professionals. Many different types of professionals are needed to provide the services required by individuals who are handicapped. Many professional possibilities exist. A special educator might be a paraprofessional (teacher's aide), a resource teacher, a consultant, an itinerant teacher, a special education classroom teacher, a job coach, a school psychologist or diagnostician, or an administrator. A teacher might choose to assume several of these professional roles during a career in special education. You could also choose to work in related services as a speech/language pathologist, audiologist, occupational therapist, physical therapist, counselor, nurse or physician, transportation specialist, recreational therapist, supported living worker, personal care attendant, job coach, vocational rehabilitation worker, or lawyer.

Special education teachers and others who work with individuals with handicaps must be able to collaborate—work cooperatively—with professionals from a

collaboration. Professionals working cooperatively to provide educational services.

Individualized Family Service Plan. A written plan that identifies and organizes services and resources for infants and toddlers with special needs who are under the age of 3 and their families.

Individualized Educational Program. A management tool used to identify and organize individualized educational and related services for preschoolers and school-age children.

Individual Transition Plan. A statement of the transition services required for coordination and delivery of services as the student moves to adulthood.

variety of disciplines. In many cases, collaboration among professionals is ultimately the key to successful integration for individual students. Students with handicaps require various combinations of services over their school careers. Some services are provided by regular educators, some are provided by special educators, and some are provided by professionals from a variety of related fields.

Special education teachers also collaborate in many other areas that touch a child's life. Collaboration skills are necessary when cooperating with parents and families, performing multidisciplinary assessments, working with a team to develop individualized program plans, coordinating all the components of students' individualized plans, and helping them make the transition from early childhood programs to elementary school, the transition from elementary school to middle school, from middle school to high school, and finally the transition from school to work. Collaborative efforts by all involved smooth these transitions and help the child, adolescent, or young adult move to different types of agencies and services.

INDIVIDUALIZED SPECIAL EDUCATION PROGRAMS

To safeguard the principles contained in the concept of a free appropriate public education, the law requires that an individual program plan must be developed and implemented for every child identified as handicapped and in need of special education. Several kinds of individualized program plans are available for children with special needs. An **Individualized Family Service Plan (IFSP)** serves children under the age of 3. The IFSP addresses both the infant's or toddler's needs and the needs of the family. For preschoolers age 3 and above and school-age students, an **Individualized Educational Program (IEP)** is required. An IEP is a management tool used to ensure that preschoolers and school-age children receive the educational and related services needed to meet their individual special needs in several areas (academic, social, speech and language, motoric, vocational). For youngsters making the transition from school to job placement under the guidance of special education personnel, an **Individual Transition Plan (ITP)** is recommended. An ITP is usually written as part of an adolescent's IEP. These plans list needed transition services for students beginning no later than age 16; however, when appropriate, they can be written for students even younger than 14. These plans prepare individuals for the transition from school to work and adult life, and coordinate various agencies, before they leave school, that will provide services to them after they leave their school settings. We will discuss each of these three program plans later in this chapter.

Federal regulations, such as for Medicaid and Social Security, require that special individualized plans also be developed and implemented for individuals residing in institutions or community-based living arrangements, such as group homes. For example, Individual Written Rehabilitation Plans (IWRPs) are used to provide vocational rehabilitation. People living in Intermediate Care Facilities for the Mentally Retarded and Persons with Related Conditions (ICF/MR) must have Individualized Habilitation Plans (IHPs) developed for them. As you can see, individualized plans cover a range of educational, social, and vocational goals of people with special needs. Although the various types of plans respond to different goals, they all share some basic principles.

To help you understand individualized program planning, we will discuss and analyze three different types of plans that you will most likely encounter: the Individualized Family Service Plan, the Individualized Education Plan, and the Individual Transition Plan. A case study illustrates each plan. Through the case study you will learn how each program is developed and implemented. Before studying the individualized program, however, you need to learn about the process that leads to the development of the plan. What steps lead from concern over a child's performance, to identification of a handicap, to development of a plan to provide special services for that child?

neonatal intensive care. A specialized hospital unit for infants who are in need of intensive medical attention.

The Planning Process

Individualized program plans are the means by which the educational concepts outlined in IDEA are guaranteed to each student and that student's family. Therefore, it is important for you to understand the process followed in their development.

The formation of an individualized program involves seven steps in a comprehensive process, beginning with a referral and ending with a formal plan for a youngster's program. Figure 3.4 highlights the phases of identification and decision making. As you read this section, refer to Figure 3.4 to see how each step fits into the entire process.

Seven Steps to an Individualized Program Plan

1. REFERRAL. In this first step, a child is referred for special education services. For preschoolers, the referral can come from a variety of sources—the parents, a social service agency, a public health nurse, a day care or preschool teacher, or a doctor. For example, parents might be concerned about a child who is not walking by the age of 2 or talking by the age of 3. Also, preschool teachers are trained to notice children who have frequent and excessive bursts of violent behavior. Inappropriate displays of temper often trigger a referral. Pediatricians are concerned about children whose physical or motor development is slow. Delayed language, difficulties in eating, inability to locate the source of sounds, or excessive crying are other signals that normal child development may be delayed. Typically, the more severely handicapped a child is, the sooner the referral process begins. Infants with significant handicaps may be identified at birth or early in infancy. Children who are at risk because of improper prenatal care, low birthweight, accident, or trauma during infancy are also often referred for special services. Infants in need of **neonatal intensive care (NIC)** as a result of prematurity or other health reasons are typically referred to an infant social services agency for assessment and follow-up. In ideal situations, a transition plan is developed in the hospital for medically fragile infants so that a smooth transfer from hospital to home can occur. This plan also addresses consistent early intervention services and communication between different agencies and the family.

Individual states have a special office or function called "child find" to help in the referral process. The professionals who work in this capacity can provide information for parents of very young children. The staff of your state's Department of Education Special Education Division, located in your state capitol, can provide information on child find offices and the procedures for individual states.

For school-age children, referral usually is begun by the regular education teacher concerned about a particular student's behavior or academic achievement. Candidates for referral are students whose academic performance is significantly behind their classmates' or students who continually misbehave and disrupt the

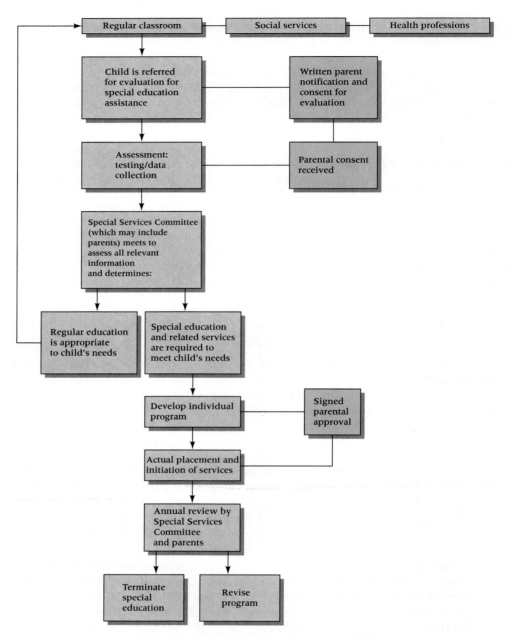

FIGURE 3.4 **Flow Chart for the Individualized Program Process**

Source: Adapted from *Teaching Students with Learning and Behavior Problems*, 2d ed., p. 28, by D. D. Smith, 1989, Englewood Cliffs, NJ: Prentice Hall. Reprinted by permission.

learning environment. Students who are thought to be gifted because of their accelerated academic performance or high levels of creativity may be referred for evaluation. Although gifted education is not included in IDEA, 17 states follow the guidelines outlined in these laws and develop IEPs for those who are identified as gifted (Boyle, 1987). Although teachers are careful in their recommendations for referrals, not all students they refer will qualify for special education services. It is estimated that 75 percent to 81 percent of those children referred actually qualify for special education services (Algozzine, Ysseldyke, and Christenson, 1983; Kroth, 1990).

What is the actual referral process for school-age children? First, the regular classroom teacher notifies the school's principal, counselor, or the special services committee, which can also be called the appraisal and review team or the child study team. Regardless of its name, this committee decides whether a child should be evaluated more thoroughly.

The person who refers a student for special education services must provide clear and specific reasons for the referral. He or she must present data—such as behavioral observations, samples of academic work, or anecdotal notes. For example, a teacher might include the results from an achievement test, scores from weekly quizzes, and samples from a student's writing. If social behavior is of concern, the teacher provides a written description of the child's atypical behavior in the classroom and on the playground. The teacher presents information that he or she has collected. These data can include written notes describing each incident, a record of the frequency (count) of temper tantrums a child had each morning before recess, or the percentage of time each day that the child engaged in disruptive behavior.

Special services committees review the material presented. The permanent members of the committee normally include the school's principal, counselor, school psychologist, and a special education teacher. Rotating members, who change referral by referral, are the student's classroom teacher and the parents. If a social service agency is working with a child and family, a representative from that agency would also be included. In each case of referral, the special services committee meets and decides whether a formal evaluation is needed. If the committee decides to proceed, a written notice of the referral and a request for permission to evaluate is sent to the parents. The parents must consent in writing before formal assessment (diagnosis) can begin.

2. ASSESSMENT.

The assessment (diagnosis) stage is initiated to decide whether a youngster is handicapped, whether special education is required, and what types of special or related services are needed. The information gathered about the child during this stage is used through the rest of the process. An expert in assessment and other specialists are usually called in at this stage to judge abilities and disabilities of the child.

School psychologists (in some states educational diagnosticians or psychometrists) also use standardized, formal tests to determine whether the student is handicapped. A variety of formal tests compose the assessment battery. Usually, students are given tests of intelligence, academic achievement, **acuity** (vision and hearing), and learning style. Many states also request that less formal assessments be used as well. For example, classroom observations of both social and academic behavior may be included with the assessment battery. In some cases, additional tests may be necessary. For students suspected of having mental retardation, for example, an adaptive behavior scale is typically required. According to Grossman (1983), adaptive behavior (see chapter 4, Mental Retardation) is defined as the "effectiveness or degree with which individuals meet the standards of personal independence and social responsibility expected for age and cultural group" (p. 1). **Adaptive behavior** generally refers to a variety of skills required in self-care, domestic abilities, social competence, and the ability to function in one's own community. Adaptive behavior comprises many different behaviors, such as communication, self-care, home living,

why are these under school psychologist?

skills, community use, self-direction, health and safety, functional academics, and work. It also includes inappropriate behaviors (Lambert, Windmiller, Tharinger, and Cole, 1981). As you would expect, the persons best qualified to evaluate an individual's adaptive behavior are those most familiar with the daily demands of living in home, school, work, and community environments.

Assessment must be nondiscriminatory. This means that tests and procedures used must be validated for the purposes for which they are used. Tests must be given in a child's primary language or other mode of communication (for example, sign language) by a school psychologist or diagnostician. The formal and informal tests must not be culturally, linguistically, or ethnically discriminatory. To safeguard against unfair identification of children as handicapped, multidisciplinary teams should be used to assess the child's abilities. Teachers must be careful to avoid referring children for special education assessments solely on the basis of cultural or ethnic differences. Also, school psychologists must give considerable weight to samples of students' classroom work and teachers' descriptions of social behavior. The details of the identification procedure are established by each state. As the state determines the process to be used to identify children with handicaps, teams of professionals must be involved to ensure the procedures adopted represent the points of view of all ethnic groups.

In many cases, various experts participate in the assessment stage. Children suspected of being hearing impaired, for example, are assessed by at least three different specialists. In addition to the school psychologist or educational diagnosti-

This child is responding to questions in one of the subtests of a frequently administered test of intelligence. During the assessment process, she may be tested by several different professionals.

Focus: Issues of Diversity

The fastest growing group of American students comes from homes where the dominant language is not English. There is a shortage of trained school personnel who are culturally and linguistically diverse. This situation can result in reduced participation by parents in individualized program planning meetings, ineffective home–school connections, an inability to explain concepts and provide instruction in the student's primary language, and a lack of understanding of a student's culture. Miramontes (1990) proposes a solution to this problem. She suggests collaboration in multilingual/multiethnic instructional service teams composed of regular education teachers, special education teachers, related services personnel included in the IEP, and at least one paraprofessional. The paraprofessional members of these teams would be trained in assessment and instructional methods and be from the student's cultural and linguistic background. These paraprofessionals would fill three major roles—instruction, home contacts, and assessment—under the supervision of fully trained professionals. Clearly, this might be an excellent way to create a liaison between home and school.

cian who assesses intelligence, academic achievement, and learning style, these children will see an **audiologist** to determine if they have a hearing impairment, and if so, the extent of the hearing loss. A **speech/language pathologist** will assess the impact of the hearing loss upon their speech and language abilities. All of these specialists and the tests that they give help to determine the types and amount of special services required.

3. IDENTIFICATION. The assessment stage can result in a child being identified as having one or more handicaps. Assessment tests, first, identify whether a student is handicapped and, second, classify the handicap (mental retardation, learning disabilities, behavior disorders, visual impairment, hearing impairment, communicative disorder). The test results, observations, and the child's educational and medical history (if available) are then summarized. The results and summary become part of the student's confidential school record.

Confidential school records are private, and sometimes are not even kept at the child's school. They contain all the student's test scores, professional observations about the child's social, academic, and other skills such as motor and language development, and the family's history. The file should also contain a report from the special services committee regarding service and placement recommendations. Although it is sometimes difficult to gain access to this material, special education teachers often find this information useful as they plan specific remediation programs for the child.

What happens next? Slightly less than 25 percent of children tested are ineligible for special services because they do not meet the criteria set by individual states (Algozzine, Ysseldyke, and Christenson, 1983; Kroth, 1990). (Specific criteria for each handicapping condition are discussed in the individual chapters of this text.) These youngsters will continue to be served by regular education. Special education is intended for a relatively small percentage of school-age students. IDEA permits the federal government to reimburse states for no more than 12 percent of all children (ages 5–17) identified as disabled. Most states serve somewhat fewer children, the national average being closer to 11 percent (U.S. Department of Education, 1989).

physical therapist. A professional who treats physical disabilities through many nonmedical means.

occupational therapist. A professional who directs activities that help improve muscular control as well as develop self-help skills.

interpreter. Someone who translates oral speech into sign language for persons who are deaf.

Some children require the services of professionals from different disciplines, such as physical therapy.

For those who are identified as handicapped, the next step requires decisions about appropriate placement and services. The assessment results are used to help make these decisions.

4. ANALYSIS OF SERVICES. Many schools, school districts, and all states offer a variety of options to deliver special services. In many instances, professionals work with students with special needs in areas beyond the expertise of most special education teachers. For example, many students who have learning disabilities also have a language deficit. These students need the services of a speech/language pathologist (SLP) or therapist. Many with mental retardation have motor coordination difficulties requiring the assistance of both a **physical therapist** (PT) and an **occupational therapist** (OT). Individuals who are deaf need the services of an audiologist, an SLP, and possibly an **interpreter.** The special services committee uses the data gathered during the assessment stage to determine which abilities need strengthening and which disabilities need remediating. Once those needs are determined and noted on the individualized plan, the services of experts in specialized areas are made available.

5. PLACEMENT. The fifth step in planning the individual program involves possible placement for the student. Placement encompasses two critical and controversial concepts: least restrictive environment and free appropriate public education. The special services committee must balance these two concepts as it reaches decisions on the programs for a child.

The concept of the least restrictive environment, or LRE, requires that the student be integrated with nonhandicapped children as much as possible and included in the mainstream of society. Under an educational reform movement called the Regular (or General) Education Initiative (REI), some interpret LRE as meaning that students

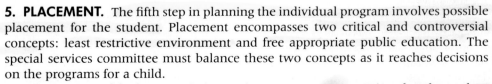

with handicaps should be educated exclusively in regular education classes (Gartner and Lipsky, 1987; Snell, 1988; Stainback and Stainback, 1989). Others find this interpretation too extreme (Council for Children with Behavior Disorders (CCBD), 1988; Keogh, 1988; Smith and Bassett, 1991). For example, Turnbull (1991) interprets the principle of LRE as a legal mandate that ensures the right of those who are handicapped to associate with nondisabled peers and as an educational strategy aimed at enhancing individuals' potential through an appropriate education. LRE focuses on integration, but also allows for some separation when it is in the best educational interests of the child involved. Some professionals (Keogh, 1988; Smith, 1988) point out that the regular education classroom teacher referred the child in the first place, indicating that at least this professional believes that the regular classroom, as it is currently structured, is not the most appropriate placement for the child of concern. In that teacher's view, this child needs additional support in the regular classroom, or supplemental services, or even possibly a separate curriculum to have a successful educational experience. To those (Wang and Reynolds, 1985) who suggest that special and regular education are unnecessary dual systems, others (CCBD, 1988) counter than special education was established because a single system did not meet the needs of students with special needs.

LRE is an important concept. Special educators must be constantly aware of how placement decisions can segregate students by removing them from normal role models, social interactions, and curriculum; and can fragment their daily lives. Placement decisions further identify a student as being different. Finally, removing a child from the regular classroom has serious implications for today and in the future. If, however, the student's needs cannot be met in the regular classroom or that environment impedes learning, then placement there is not appropriate.

The second concept in placement is that each child with a handicap should be provided with a free appropriate public education. The term *education* is broadly defined. It includes all types of supportive services, a curriculum that may be different from that presented in regular education (Edgar, 1987), and a highly individualized educational program. The difficulty is trying to balance FAPE and LRE. Professionals (CCBD, 1988; Wang and Reynolds, 1985), parents, and those who have disabilities are among many who debate this issue. See the Concepts and Controversies sections in this chapter and chapter 10 for detailed discussions on these highly charged issues.

After reviewing and analyzing all the available information, the special services committee must make important suggestions about placement and related services. After they summarize their findings and suggestions, they invite the parents of the child to a meeting and inform them, in their native language, of their child's abilities and disabilities. Adolescents and young adults with disabilities can be invited to participate in this meeting. At this meeting, the committee presents the results of the assessments and discusses their recommendations for the child's education. A major goal of this meeting is to form a partnership between the parents and the agency or professional who will provide the needed services. In most cases, the parents and professionals are in agreement about the types of services and the educational placement a child requires. If the parents do not agree with the special services committee, they have a right to challenge any of the team's decisions. If agreement between the two parties cannot be reached, a due process hearing may be called, in which an impartial, third party settles the dispute. If either party does not agree to the decision made at the due process hearing, they can appeal to the state education agency. If they still do not agree, they may take the matter to the courts.

Parents and teachers can form essential partnerships in the special education of children.

6. INSTRUCTIONAL DECISION MAKING. At this stage, decisions must be made about the educational program the child will receive. Now, the teacher writes the actual program plan. The plan includes a statement of the present abilities of the child as well as a summary of the annual goals and objectives that the teacher and the school hope to attain.

The goals and objectives must be stated in a specific way according to federal law. First, they must center on the child, indicating what is expected of the student after the instructional program is completed. Goals and objectives must be worded precisely and must specify both the task or concept to be taught and the level of performance the student should be able to achieve. For each area of instruction, the team sets overall goals. Each goal comprises many behavioral objectives. Table 3.3 shows part of one teacher's lesson plan for one goal and some related objectives for telling time, a skill that needs to be taught to many students with handicaps. Although not all students require direct instruction on telling time, the table gives you useful information on structuring goals and objectives.

Creating behavioral goal and objective statements for each child can be a daunting task for a teacher. Fortunately, help is readily available. For example, the teachers' manuals accompanying many basal reading and mathematics textbooks provide detailed targets of instruction. Also, many school districts have developed standard goal and objective statements for various curriculum areas, and computer-generated ones are available as well. Although prepared goals and objectives can be a convenient tool for a teacher writing a plan for a student, teachers who use them need to be aware of the danger of failing to truly individualize the program. Materials must match a child's needs. The wise teacher uses the prepared materials as a foundation and tailors them to the individual student. The teacher may often need to prepare supplemental materials to complement commercially available instructional packages. When the individualized program plan is truly individualized—written specifically for one student—it is a useful and reliable management tool that assists the

TABLE 3.3. Behavioral Goals and Objectives for Telling Time

Abbreviated Objective	Behavioral Statement	Criterion	
Clock hand discrimination	2.01 The student is able to point to and name both the hour and minute hands	2.01	with 100% accuracy within 15 seconds
Hour hand	2.02 The student is able to identify all hour hand placements 　2.02.01 The student is able to identify the hour for exact hour hand placements 　2.02.02 The student is able to identify the hour for any hour hand placement	2.02 (.01–.02)	with 100% accuracy within 10 seconds
Minute hand	2.03 The student is able to identify all minute hand placements 　2.03.01 The student is able to identify the minute for minute placements on any interval of five 　2.03.02 The student is able to identify the minute for exact minute hand placements 　2.03.03 The student is able to identify fractions of hours using the minute hand (e.g., quarter after)	2.03 (.01–.03)	with 100% accuracy within 10 seconds
Combination of hour and minute hands	2.04 The student is able to identify the correct time using both the hour and minute hands 　2.04.01 The student is able to identify the time for the "o'clock" times 　2.04.02 The student can identify the time for all intervals of five 　2.04.03 The student is able to identify the exact time 　2.04.04 The student can identify the time for fractions of the hour	2.04 (.01–.04)	with 100% accuracy within 10 seconds

Source: *Teaching Students with Learning and Behavior Problems*, 2d ed., p. 34, by D. D. Smith, 1989, Englewood Cliffs, NJ: Prentice-Hall. Reprinted by permission.

curriculum-based assessment. A method of evaluating children's performance by collecting data on students' daily progress.

teacher by guiding the instructional program, rather than an exercise that merely meets the requirements of the law.

7. PROGRAM EVALUATION. The individualized program—whether an IFSP, an IEP, or an ITP—must contain frequent evaluations of student performance. A student's individualized program is evaluated in three ways.

In the first case, the student's program is evaluated while he or she is actively participating in the plan during the school year. One method that many special educators use is a data collection system. In this system of instruction, often referred to as **curriculum-based assessment (CBA),** teachers collect data about a child's daily progress on each instructional task. For example, a teacher instructing a youngster in math would keep a daily record of the number or percentage of problems the child correctly solved. This helps the teacher judge whether the instructional methods selected are both efficient and effective. CBA allows teachers to know how well their students are learning and whether the chosen instructional methods help the child meet the goals and objectives of the individualized program plan.

Second, every student's individualized program plan must be reevaluated every year. As the student grows and learns, the educational decisions made one year might not be the best for the ensuing years. At the time of the annual review, a new program plan is developed. Decisions about placement, supportive services, and the goals and objectives for the upcoming year are made. In some cases, a child's progress might have been so great that special services are no longer required. In other cases, the degree of special service might change. For example, a child's progress while attending a special education class might have been so great that only periodic attendance in a special education class or resource room is necessary to maintain growth and continued progress. In other cases more special services might be needed. For example, a student who was identified as having a behavioral disorder might have first been placed in a resource room. The special education teacher implemented a behavior management program aimed at reducing excessive outbursts of temper, inappropriate verbal statements, and physical aggression. However, at the end of the school year, the special services committee and the child's parents agreed that sufficient progress had not been made, and a more intensive program was necessary. This student would spend at least part of the upcoming year in a self-contained special education class taught by a teacher trained to work with children with behavioral disorders and emotional disturbances.

Third, the law requires that a full evaluation of every child with special needs be conducted every three years. In other words, three years after a child's initial identification, steps 2 through 6 in the process are repeated. This comprehensive evaluation could be conducted earlier if the child's parents or teachers request it. At this point students who are no longer in need of special services are returned to the regular education system for their education.

Roles and Responsibilities in Planning the Individualized Program

The IFSP, IEP, and ITP guide educators and the educational system to ensure that each child receives an appropriate education. The process of developing these program plans is a tremendous responsibility: guaranteeing that students who are not handicapped are not mistakenly identified, that students who are handicapped are identified and receive the educational and related services they require, and that parents and families are properly involved in decision making. In addition, the process must safeguard students' rights to education in the least restrictive environment. This section has reviewed the steps involved in this process showing you the different people who participate. Table 3.4 summarizes the process and the roles and responsibilities of the participants.

Three Individualized Program Plans

Having discussed the variety of individualized program plans available in special education, let us now turn to a more detailed look at three specific plans. First, we will consider an Individualized Family Service Plan (IFSP) for a preschooler. The second plan is an Individualized Education Program (IEP) for a second grader with learning disabilities. The third is an Individualized Transition Plan (ITP) for a 20-year-old making the transition from school to work. As you read, keep in mind that these plans must show that the school is providing an appropriate education in a setting that is least restrictive.

These program plans are an important part of students' education. If done well, they should guarantee high-quality and comprehensive educational services for exceptional students.

Individualized Family Service Plans (IFSPs)

Infants or toddlers who might be handicapped are guaranteed the right to a professional assessment of their needs by PL 99–457. Once the assessment determines that the child has special needs, or is at risk, an IFSP is drawn up by the special services

TABLE 3.4. Roles and Responsibilities in the Individualized Program/Plan Process

Steps	Responsibility	Action	Process Stopped If:
1. Referral	Parents or teachers or doctors or social services	Request assessment to determine eligibility.	Child's behavior or performance does not indicate a possible handicap.
			Parents do not give approval in writing. Negotiation. Due process/arbitration.

Parents notified in writing of referral

· · · · · · · · · · · · · · ·

Parent consent obtained

2. Assessment	Special services committee	Collects performance data.	
3. Identification	Special services committee	Analysis of performance data.	Child does not have a disability.
4. Service analysis	Special services committee	Listing of special education and related services needed by student.	No special services required.
5. Planning and instructional decision making	Special services committee	Plan/programs developed, including placement recommendations and goals and objectives.	

· · · · · · · · · · · · · · ·

Signed parent approval

			Negotiation. Parent and district disagreement.
6. Implementation	Teacher and/or related services	Placement and initiation of services.	
7. Program Evaluation	Teachers'/related service providers, special service committee	Annual review with recommendation for new program/plan.	

team. Johnson, McGonigel, and Kaufmann (1989) state the purposes and intent of IFSPs well:

> The purpose of the IFSP is to identify and organize formal and informal resources to facilitate families' goals for their children and themselves. The IFSP is a promise to children and families—a promise that their strengths will be recognized and built on, that their needs will be met in a way that is respectful of their beliefs and values, and that their hopes and aspirations will be encouraged and enabled. (p. 1)

Table 3.5 lists the required contents of the IFSP. Like all individualized programs, the plan is evaluated once a year, but the IFSP is also reviewed with the family every six months.

TABLE 3.5. Required Contents of Individualized Family Service Plans

- The child's current functioning levels: physical development, cognitive development, language and speech development, psychosocial development, and self-help skills
- The family's strengths and needs to assist them in enhancing the development of their child
- The major outcomes expected including criteria, procedures, and a timeline, so progress can be evaluated
- The services necessary and a schedule for their delivery
- Projected dates for initiation of services
- The name of the service manager
- Indication of methods for transitioning the child to services available for children ages 3 to 5

service manager. The case manager who oversees the implementation and evaluation of an Individualized Family Service Plan.

service coordinator

To many **service managers** and early childhood specialists, the IFSP is a working document, an ongoing process where parents and specialists work together, continually modifying, expanding, and developing a child's educational program. For this reason, many early childhood specialists do not type the contents of an individual child's IFSP. Instead, they write it in pencil, so parents feel that the goals and objectives suggested by the early childhood specialist are open to modification.

CASE STUDY: A TODDLER'S INDIVIDUALIZED FAMILY SERVICE PLAN. Jason is almost three years old, and has multiple handicaps. He will soon attend a class offered by his local school district for preschoolers who are handicapped. When he was a newborn, Jason did not eat as other infants do; his mother often had to coax him to take a bottle of milk. His breathing was sometimes irregular and difficult, and his sleeping patterns were uneven. His condition was described as "failure to thrive." Jason has cerebral palsy, a condition caused by damage to the brain either before, during, or soon after birth, that affects an individual's neuromotor development. Jason also has been diagnosed as having moderate mental retardation. His language development is delayed, as are other aspects of his development, such as his fine and gross motor skills.

The IFSP shown on pages 96–102 is Jason's second official IFSP. Despite Jason's young age, he has been receiving a full educational program almost since birth, as has his family. His program is managed by Therapy Services Providers, a private agency that is funded with federal and state money. Patti Dominic is Jason's service manager/early childhood specialist, and coordinates all the services Jason receives. Jason attends a preschool for children under the age of 3 two mornings a week. This is a special program integrating children with and without disabilities. Social activities are integrated, and the children learn to interact during play and group activities.

Understanding that education does not happen only at school, Patti Dominic has planned social activities in the organized "toddler play group" that is part of Jason's weekly home activities. Once a week, Jason and several other toddlers, some of whom are disabled, meet at one of the youngster's homes. There, a teacher supervises the play sessions, and provides some structure when necessary. Specialists come to Jason's home twice a week to further the accomplishment of the goals and objectives set for him. At both his home and at his school, Jason receives services from many different people. His motor skills program was developed by both occupational and physical therapists. Not only do these specialists work directly with Jason, but they also collaborate with Jason's teacher and his family. They teach ways to improve Jason's motor development. For example, Jason's family and others know how to sit Jason on the floor and roll a ball to him so he can "catch" it between his legs. They will soon learn how to play different, more complicated ball games with Jason. These games develop Jason's eye–hand coordination and his fine and gross motor skills, as well as teaching him how to play. Jason also receives help from a speech/language pathologist, Juan Gonzales, who works with him directly and who trains his family and friends to help him improve his oral language skills. For example, Juan has taught Jason's grandparents, parents, teacher, and even his babysitter to phrase questions that force Jason to respond by labeling items that he wants. "Jason, don't just point. Tell me what you want. Say cookie, Jason." Jason also receives collaborative (consultation) services from a feeding specialist. Periodically, several times a month, this specialist works with Jason directly and trains his family and his babysitter how to teach Jason to eat more independently.

Jason's family also receives support and education. Besides the training they receive from the specialists who come to Jason's school and home, his parents, Susan and Richard, belong to a parent support group that meets twice a month. Guest speakers often address the support group on topics such as stress management, community resources, language development, and cognitive development. Some sessions are spent sharing victories, problems, concerns, and possible solutions. The Moriaritys have found these meetings to be an important part of their lives.

Now, let us look at Jason's Individualized Family Service Plan. The IFSP was developed for Jason when he was 28 months old. It was reviewed, evaluated, and updated when Jason was 32 months old. The first page is a summary and signature sheet showing some demographic data about Jason and his family. Included on this first page are five goals that Jason, his family, and various specialists have set, are working on, and hope to make progress on over the course of this year. These goals are in the areas of feeding, motor skills development, speech and improved communication among family members. In individualized plans, goals and objectives are worded in language parents and all professionals can understand. Jason's parents signed the IFSP, indicating that they agreed with the plan and with the services to be made available to Jason and his family. At a later time another goal was added, relating to Jason's transition to preschool, and it was written in at the bottom of the page.

On the second page of the IFSP, called the Family Priority Sheet, the family (in this case Jason's parents and grandparents) expressed their concerns about their child's development and progress. This sheet was completed with the help of an early childhood specialist, and lists the family's goals. On this page, the family's functional style is also summarized. In this section important information related to working with the child and family, family strengths, home environment, family resources, and ways family members interact are included. This information is taken into consideration when goals and objectives are written and interventions are planned.

A summary of the child's performance on a norm referenced developmental scale, Hawaii Early Learning Profile (HELP), can be found on page 3 of his IFSP (Furuno et al., 1979). The early childhood specialist, Ms. Dominic, conducted this assessment of Jason's performance. She marked, on the preprinted scale, the range of Jason's performance in each of these six important areas of child development. In the area of gross motor skills, Jason, at the age of 26 months, performed at the level of a child between 10 and 21 months old. His average performance paralleled a 16-month-old child in activities involving gross motor skills. In all six areas, Jason is substantially below the performance levels of peers without handicaps. In the space below the grid, Ms. Dominic wrote brief summaries of Jason's abilities.

Specific goals and objectives for Jason's treatment program are listed on pages 4 and 5 of the IFSP. On September 20, five goals, each with supporting objectives, were developed. These goals and objectives were scheduled to be reviewed twice, once in January and once in May. The HELP developmental scale was administered again in January. New lines were added in the grid on page 6 to show the growth Jason had made on the skills tested, and new summary statements about the progress Jason made in each area tested were also provided by the early childhood specialist. At this time, the family added a sixth goal to Jason's plan. Its purpose was to assist Jason and his family in making the upcoming transition from his current program to a more structured preschool program offered by the local schools for three- to five-year-olds.

A TODDLER'S IFSP

SUMMARY AND
SIGNATURE SHEET

Child's Name: _____*Jason Moriarity*_____   DOB:___*5/9/89*___   Date: ___*9/16/91*___

Name of Parent(s): _____*Susan and Richard Moriarity*_____

Phone #: ___*555-1342*___   Address: ___*1086 Plains Dr.*___

Service Coordinator: ___*Sally Maechlin*___   Program: ___*IND. TM #3*___

Service Manager: ___*Patti Dominic*___

Service Team: ___*#3*___

Other Service Providers: ___*Therapy Services*___   Phone: ___*555-5342*___

Parent comments related to goals:

goals jointly developed by team & parents & family members

Statement of Goals:

1. Improve feeding, especially chewing, and teach Jason to feed himself.
2. Continue to demonstrate and facilitate more challenging motor skills.
3. Continue to explore and develop tolerance to varied textures in his hands.
4. Work on speech to make it more clear so we'll know what he says.
5. Work out time and ways for parents to share info between themselves and other family members in appropriate activities for Jason's development.

Review Dates: Periodic review will be provided at six-month intervals or at the discretion of the family.

Monitoring: After assessment and goal setting is completed, child/family progress will be documented at monthly team meetings and through anecdotal records noting parent and staff comments and satisfaction. Formal evaluations are conducted at mid-year and end-of-the-year and include updating child and family assessment and assessing parent satisfaction.

I/We are in agreement with the goals and objectives/steps in our Individualized Family Service Plan.

Signature of parent/guardian

Susan Moriarity

Richard Moriarity

1/18/92: Help Jason and his family prepare for transition into preschool.

A TODDLER'S IFSP, p. 2

FAMILY PRIORITY SHEET

Child's Name: _Jason_   Date: _9/16/91_

Child Family Needs/Concerns	Date of follow-up	Update comments
1. Improve feeding skills and feed self, chewing seems to be a problem.	11/16/91	Continue to demonstrate and facilitate more challenging gross and fine motor skills.
2. Learn how to use feet on ride-on toys, need to show him new skills to learn.		
3. Continue to explore & develop tolerance to varied textures in his hands, progress from solid to semisolid.	12/16/91	
4. Need to work on speech & make it more clear so we'll know what he says.		
5. Work out ways & times for parents to share information between themselves & other family members on Jason's development.		Improving, but communication seems to be a continuing issue.

Family Functional Style:

Susan (mother) works hard to try to meet Jason's needs & to coordinate his medical & intervention services. Richard (father) would like to be more informed as to ongoing programming. Paternal grandparents often assist taking Jason to therapy when parents are at work. The babysitter & members of the extended family provide child care and various degrees of support to Jason.

A desire to share the joys and challenges of raising a child with disabilities can bring families together into parent support groups.

A TODDLER'S IFSP, p. 3

SUMMARY OF CHILD'S PERFORMANCE

Assessment Tool: HELP   Date: 5-10-91   Chronological Age: 28 months   Service Coordinator: Sally M.

Child's Name: _____Jason_____

Date: _____9/9/91_____

DOB: _____5/9/89_____

Months	6	7	8	9	10	11	12	13	14	15	16	17	18	19	20	21	22	23	24
Gross Motor					←————————————————————→														
Fine Motor												←————→							
Self-help	←————————————————→																		
Social							←————————————→												
Cognitive							←————————————————→												
Language								←————————————————————→											

Summary of Child's Performance and Behavior: Jason continues to make significant progress in all domains. He has responded well to year-round services from Patti D., preschool, therapy services, and from a home program.

Gross Motor: Walks pulling or carrying large toy, also walks independently on 8" balance beam and backward. Stands on 1 foot with legs and nudges a ball with foot. Throws ball with 2-hand thrust. Goes up/down stairs sideways holding on to railing with 2 hands. Balance responses need to be improved.

Fine Motor: Builds 5-block tower and puts 6 pegs in board; uses 1 hand to hold while other manipulates; scribbles and inverts a bottle spontaneously to obtain tiny object.

Self-help: Drinks from a cup and tolerates more food texture. Is beginning to bite crackers & finger feed self, but hypersensitivity around mouth remains a problem. Puts on hat and removes hat and socks.

Social-Emot.: Plays ball cooperatively; has toy preferences; enjoys being center of attention; hugs & kisses parents; desires to control others (age approp.).

Cognitive: Identifies more than 6 body parts; assembles 4 resting blocks; matches 4 sounds to animals; points to clothing items; activates mechanical toys; solves single problem with tools.

Exp. Lang.: Imitates phrases and has vocab. of 15–20 words, but poor articulation makes Jason difficult to understand. Uses elaborate jargon and vocalizes with gesturing to communicate. Names 3 pictures.

Behavioral Observations: Jason's very social and he seeks out interactive activities. He enjoys imitative and turn-taking activities.

A TODDLER'S IFSP, p. 4

IFSP GOALS AND IMPLEMENTATION

Date: _9/20/91_   Scheduled Review Date: _1/92_

Child's Name: _Jason_   Scheduled Review Date: _5/92_

Parent(s): _Susan and Richard Moriarity_

Objectives	Date	Implementation	Date	Evaluation
GOAL A: Improve feeding, especially chewing, and teach Jason to feed himself.				
1. Consult with Pam Marvin, feeding specialist.	9/20/91	Phone contact initiated. Coordinate consultation between school, baby-sitter, and family.	10/7/91	Consultation done.
2. Decrease oral hypersensitivity.	9/20/91	Continue to offer Jason increased textures and solid foods. Re-initiate oral stimulation to decrease hypersensitivity. Work on oral-motor skills to improve oral functioning to decrease hypersensitivity by using straw and oral toys.	1/18/92	Continue this objective.
3. Improve self-feeding with spoon and fingers.	9/20/91	Practice spoon feeding, decreasing assistance as Jason becomes more skilled. Encourage self-feeding with favorite or new foods when Jason is hungry.	1/18/92	Continue this objective. Family has been encouraged to engage Jason in family meals at dinner table in high chair.
GOAL B: Continue to demonstrate and facilitate more challenging motor skills.				
1. Will throw ball overhand within 3 feet of target.	9/20/91	Practice throwing balls at target in game-like activities.	1/18/92	Continue to work on all Goal 2 objectives.
2. Will climb stairs up and down, holding on with one hand.	9/20/91	Practice stair climbing, walk on uneven surfaces to improve balance.		
3. Will jump down from 4-in. step.	9/20/91	Practice bouncing and jumping on trampoline. Practice jumping off 2-in. step.		
4. Will kick ball forward.	9/20/91	Practice kicking and balance activities.	1/18/92	Now kicks ball. Continue to work for improved balance and skill.
5. Will imitate vertical and horizontal strokes with a crayon.	9/20/91	Practice coloring and painting activities.		

A TODDLER'S IFSP, p. 5

6. Will string three 1-inch beads.	9/20/91	Practice stringing beads and 2-handed manipulation.	1/18/92	Now strings beads using pipe cleaners.
7. Will make a 6–8 block tower, a 3-block train.	9/20/91	Practice block-building activities.	1/18/92	Makes 6-block tower.
8. Will fold paper independently.	9/20/91	Practice paper-folding activities.		

GOAL C: Continue to explore and develop tolerances to varied textures in his hand (from solids to semisolids).

1. Expand tolerances to varied, solid textures.	9/20/91	Work with beans, lentils, corn meal, dried leaves, Play-Doh, clay, yarn, fuzzy textures, sandpaper, etc.
2. Expand tolerance to semisolid textures.	9/20/91	Work with cornstarch paste, fingerpaints, paste, puddings, jello, shaving cream.

GOAL D: Work on speech to make it more clear so we'll know that he says.

1. Improve sound distinction and articulation.	9/20/91	Practice imitating sounds through cardboard tube.
2. Improve verbalizations through concept usage.	9/20/91	Support actions and concepts by verbalizing concepts while performing skills like "pouring," "putting in," etc.
3. Improve symbolic language skills.	9/20/91	Play with and care for dolls, utilize environmental objects.
4. Stimulate verbal responses with "who?" "what?" "where?" and "yes" and "no" questions.	9/20/91	Ask appropriate questions in context.
5. Improve participation in finger play songs.	9/20/91	Pair gestures and songs and encourage Jason to join in.

GOAL E: Improve communication skills—regarding Jason and other issues—between parents and among family members.

1. Explore ways and time for parents to communicate.	9/20/91	Work with Susan with modeling and role playing to improve her communication skills. Work with both parents to clarify communication needs and specific issues.	1/18/92	Patti and Sally will continue to work with family on this and other issues.

A TODDLER'S IFSP, p. 6

SUMMARY OF CHILD'S PERFORMANCE

Child's Name: _____ *Jason* _____

Date: _____ *1/18/92* _____

DOB: _____ *5/9/89* _____

Months	6	7	8	9	10	11	12	13	14	15	16	17	18	19	20	21	22	23	24
Gross Motor																			
Fine Motor																			
Self-help																			
Social																			
Cognitive																			
Language																			

Assessment Tool: HELP   Date: 9–10–91   Chronological Age: 28 months   Service Coordinator: Sally M.
              HELP   1–18–92   32 months   Patti D.

Summary of Child's Performance and Behavior: Jason continues to make progress in all domains. He has responded well to intensive intervention from both the preschool (and its family-education model) and from Therapy Services (and its clinical approach).

Gross Motor: 14–22 mo. Jason walks upstairs with 1 hand held; pulls and pushes large toys; kicks ball forward; throws ball into box. Postural and balance problems seem to be factor in his development.

Fine Motor: 18–23 mo. Strings three 1-inch beads; builds 6-block tower.

Self-help: 12–19 mo. Bites food; finger feeds; holds cup handle; feeds self with spoon with some spilling; gives empty dish to adult; gives up bottle; removes shoes (laces undone); sits on potty. Still resists some textures and tastes of food; has difficulty with chewing and swallowing of solids.

Social Emot.: 12–24 mo. Engages in parallel play; has developing sense of self; is appropriately shy with strangers.

Cognitive: 12–24 mo. Is learning color; finds hidden objects; recognizes animal pictures and knows animal sounds, paints, rights upside down picture; enjoys finger plays, sorts objects; matches objects to pictures; recognizes people in photos; places shapes in formboard; ID 6 body parts; engages in simple make-believe play.

Exp. Lang.: 13–24 mo. Uses up to 3-word sentences; vocabulary is about 20 words; refers to self by name; has longer utterances; more parts of words, more imitation and spontaneous use of speech.

A TODDLER'S IFSP, p. 7

NEW GOAL AND IMPLEMENTATION

Date: _____ 1/18/92 _____   Scheduled Review Date: _____ 6/1/92 _____

Child's Name: _____ Jason _____

Parent(s): _____ Susan and Richard Moriarity _____

Objectives	Date	Implementation	Evaluation

GOAL F. Help Jason and his family prepare for transition into the public schools.

1. Patti will work with classroom team to facilitate transition to public schools.	3/22/92	Patti will remain as service manager for the Moriarity family. She will attend monthly team meetings and will stay in touch with family throughout transition process.	
2. Parents will attend transition meetings.	3/22/92	Three transition meetings will be held in coordination with the public schools.	
3. Staff will act as consultants to family to provide appropriate and necessary information regarding transition.	3/22/92	Self-explanatory	
4. Jason will participate in classroom activities to transition.	3/22/92	Circle activities such as simple story-telling and role playing will be used in the classroom to prepare children for transition.	

Individualized Education Program (IEP)

The Individualized Education Program (IEP)is a management tool designed to assure that school-age children who have special needs receive an individualized program that includes special education and the related services appropriate to the child's special learning needs. The IEP was originally required in 1975 by PL 94–142. As it did for the IFSP, Congress delineated the minimal contents of the IEP, and those are found in Table 3.6. The law also requires that the IEP be evaluated at least once a year.

CASE STUDY: A SCHOOLCHILD'S INDIVIDUALIZED EDUCATION PROGRAM. Sara is a second grader who was referred to her school's special services team by her regular education teacher because she was significantly behind her classmates in academic areas. At the time of her referral in November, she was reading at the preprimer level while most of her classmates were able to read comfortably in the second grade basal reader. Her math skills were not as deficient as her reading abilities although she was somewhat behind her classmates. Because she was not progressing at the same rate as her peers, Sara's regular education teacher, Ms. Blackwell, was concerned that she would fall further and further behind in mathematics. Ms. Blackwell also believed that Sara's speech and language skills were delayed as well. Her vocabulary was limited and her grammatical usage was poor. Her social skills were strong, however. She got along well with her peers, acted appropriately in class, and, in general, was a well-behaved and pleasant child. It is probably for these reasons that she was not referred to special education earlier in the year.

The school psychologist and the special services committee confirmed Ms. Blackwell's assessment of Sara's present functioning level. Sara's score on a test of intelligence indicated that she was well within the range of normal intelligence, but her academic achievement was more than two years below what would be expected for a child of her age. Based on the analysis of all the information, the committee determined that she has a learning disability. To improve her academic performance, the special services committee recommended that Sara attend a resource room for eight to ten hours per week and be mainstreamed into regular education. They also found that her language was delayed and she made some consistent and age-inappropriate articulation errors in her speech. Therefore, the committee felt that the services of a speech/language pathologist (SLP) were necessary. Her parents agreed with the assessment and with the plan for educational services. Since her IEP was put into effect in November, it would be operative for the remainder of the school year and a new IEP would be developed for the following academic year.

TABLE 3.6. Required Contents of Individualized Education Program

- The child's present levels of educational performance
- Annual goals and short-term instructional objectives
- Specific educational services to be provided
- The extent to which the child will participate in regular education
- Projected date for initiation of services
- Expected duration of those services
- Objective criteria and evaluation procedures

Sara's IEP requires special instruction in the area of reading. Here she is working on reading comprehension with a small group of peers.

In the resource room, Sara worked with Ms. Nielsen, the special education teacher, on computational arithmetic, problem solving, and reading. Ms. Nielsen is implementing instructional programs to help Sara acquire and become proficient in addition and subtraction. She will continue this work and build on these skills and begin work on multiplication when Sara demonstrates mastery of the easier concepts. In the area of reading, Ms. Nielsen is developing word recognition and phonic skills. Ms. Nielsen uses instructional techniques to improve the number of words and phonic skills Sara knows and also seeks to increase her fluency (proficiency) in their application. Some of these objectives, and the methods, materials, and procedures to be used are listed in Sara's IEP.

Ms. Nielsen and Ms. Blackwell worked together to plan a schedule so Sara would attend the resource room during the time Sara's classmates were assigned reading and math. In this way, Sara is working in the resource room on the same subjects as her classmates. These two teachers worked closely with the SLP, Mr. Keene. Programs initiated by Mr. Keene are reinforced by these two teachers. For example, as Sara works to improve her articulation of the speech sound "s", these two teachers insist that Sara correctly articulate that sound when she speaks to them. Mr. Keene is seeking to increase Sara's ability to label objects. Every week, he gives Sara's teachers a list of the words she has learned, and they help Sara use those words in her classroom conversations. Once her teachers see mastery of these words at school, they inform Sara's family and they encourage their use at home. During the year, Sara's parents have become more and more involved with her school program. They reward her with special dinners or privileges or special events for significant achievements in her academic work at school. They also read with her every night before bedtime, and report their progress to Sara's teachers. Such coordination and collaboration among teachers and specialists and between the school and family provides the best educational programs for children.

Portions of Sara's IEP are presented on pages 105–110. The first page of her IEP is a copy of a special services committee's report, with a summary of Sara's levels of function at the time of assessment. Page 2 shows the portions of her IEP for reading, and pages 3, 4, and 5 show the speech and language component of her IEP.

AN IEP SPECIAL SERVICES COMMITTEE REPORT, p. 1

VALLEY VISTA SCHOOL

STUDENT NUMBER: | 1 | 2 | 3 | 4 | 5 | 6 |

CURRENT GRADE: | 3 |

HOME SCHOOL: | 2 | 1 | 6 |

MEETING DATE: | 11 | 16 | 91 |

NAME: Winter (last) / Sara (first) / (Mi)

PARENTS: John & Leslie Winter
ADDRESS: 125 Arizona NE

Franklin   Utah
City   State   Zip

DOB: | 3 | 19 | 83 |

INDIVIDUAL EVALUATION REPORT DATE: | 10 | 16 | 91 |

PHONE: (H) 877-4382   (W) 291-3648

PURPOSE(S) OF MEETING:

- [X] Review evaluation results to determine exceptionality and eligibility
- [ ] Develop initial IEP
- [ ] Revise IEP
- [ ] Develop Exit/Transition Plan
- [ ] Other: _____

PRESENT LEVELS OF PERFORMANCE:

Reading: knows upper and lower case letters, reads at a preprimer level, knows 100 basic sight words, answers basic recall questions accurately

Mathematics: recognizes and writes number to 100, adds and subtracts without regrouping, computes simple word problems

Social Skills: gets along well with peers and adults, eager to please, likes school

Communication/Speech: follows simple commands and directions, answers simple questions (PLAI Level 2)

EXCEPTIONALITY (IES)   1 - PRIMARY   2 - SECONDARY

(04) _____ Behaviorally Disordered	(07) _____ Gifted
(10) _____ Blind	(09) _____ Hearing Impaired
(17) _____ Communication Disordered (Artic)	(06) _X_ Learning Disabled
(18) _____ Communication Disordered (Fluency)	(12) _____ Multiply Impaired
(05) _____ Communication Disordered (Language)	(21) _____ Other Health Impaired
(19) _____ Communication Disordered (Voice)	(03) _____ Physically Impaired
(08) _____ Deaf	(16) _____ Severely/Profoundly Handicapped
(13) _____ Deaf/Blind	(02) _____ Trainable Mentally Handicapped
(01) _____ Educable Mentally Handicapped	(11) _____ Visually Impaired

STATUS: [X] Eligible   [ ] Not Eligible   [ ] In Exit (see comments)

LONG TERM GOAL(S)   The student will show improvement in the following area(s):

_X_ (02) Reading	_____ (06) Social Adaptation/Behavior	_____ (11) Home Community Living
_X_ (03) Math	_____ (07) Prevocational/Vocational	_____ (12) Sensory Stimulation
_____ (04) Language: Written	_____ (08) Motor Skills	_____ (14) Enrichment/Academic
_X_ (05) Language: Oral	_____ (09) Self Help	_____ (15) Other: _____
_____ (13) Study Skills	_____ (10) Functional Academics	

SE10-1-8/86   Office Copy - White   School Copy - Yellow   Parent Copy - Pink

AN IEP SPECIAL SERVICES COMMITTEE REPORT, p. 2

READING COMPONENT

Reading	Sara Winter	11/28/91
(Area)	(Student's Name)	(Date)

Annual Goal: To increase word recognition by 200 words and demonstrate mastery of 20 phonetic rules.

Short-Term Objectives	Methods, Materials, Procedures	Person Responsible	Start Date	Target Date
1. Sara will demonstrate mastery of 25 words.	Word cards, drill, practice, language master machines, CAI instructional program, points toward a special lunch.	Ms. Nielsen	12/01/91	12/20/91
2. Sara will demonstrate mastery of 175 additional words.	Word cards, drill, practice, language master machines, CAI instructional program, points toward a special lunch.	Resource room teacher	12/15/91	03/15/92
3. Sara will demonstrate mastery of 5 phonics rules by achieving 3 consecutive scores of 100%.	Flash cards. CAI instructional program reinforcement.	Ms. Nielsen	12/05/91	02/25/92
4. Sara will demonstrate mastery of 15 additional phonics rules by obtaining 3 consecutive scores of 95%.	Flash cards. CAI instructional program reinforcement.	Resource room teacher	02/26/92	05/15/92
5. Sara will read at a rate of 30 words per minute correctly with an error rate of less than 5 in a first grade reader.	Pre-primer, primer, and first grade basal readers. Reinforcement for each 10% improvement in correct rate scores.	Resource room teacher	01/03/92	05/15/92

AN IEP SPECIAL SERVICES COMMITTEE REPORT, p. 3

INDIVIDUALIZED EDUCATION PROGRAM
IMPLEMENTATION PLAN

Student: _Sara Winter_ I.D. # _123456_ School: _Valley Vista_ Age: _6-8_ Grade/Level: _3rd_

Speech-Language Pathologist: _Mr. Keene_ Teacher: _Ms. Blackwell_ Date: _11/28/91_

Long-Range Goal: _The student will spontaneously and appropriately use new vocabulary, trained and acquired. The student will increase receptive and expressive vocabulary._

Short Term Objectives	Date Init.	Methods/ Materials	Method of Evaluation	Date Accom.	Comments
The student will: 1. point to objects/pictures or perform an action, following concrete demonstration earlier in session, to represent target vocabulary items named by clinician.	12/91	Peabody Language Development Kits DLM Vocabulary Series Teaching Resources Vocabulary Unit	80% correct, two consecutive sessions		
2. point to previously untrained objects/pictures or perform an action to represent concrete and obvious demonstration target vocabulary items named by clinician.		DLM Photo Library Communication Skill Builders: "Pictures Please"	Same		
3. label objects/object relationships/pictures/actions representing the target vocabulary, following demonstration, in response to clinician's verbal question or fill-in task.		DLM "I Gotta Be Me" Series	Same Mixed presentation		
4. demonstrate ability to discriminate less obvious examples representing the target vocabulary by pointing or performing an action.		Concepts for Communication	Two trials, correct each item; mixed presentation		

AN IEP SPECIAL SERVICES COMMITTEE REPORT, p. 4

INDIVIDUALIZED EDUCATION PROGRAM
IMPLEMENTATION PLAN

Student: _Sara Winter_   School: _Valley Vista_   Implementor: _J. Keene (SLP)_

Long-Term Goal: _CATEGORIES: To increase vocabulary through categorization skills._

Initiated	Short-Term Objectives/Criteria	Methods/ Materials	Date & Method of Evaluation	Comments/Summary
12/91	**1.** Sort cards or objects into two main categories.	Peabody Lang. Dev. Kits	Clinician-designed probes (on-going)	
_____	**2.** Choose the correct object or picture to match one designated category.	Pictures, Please		
_____	**3.** Find the one that does not belong.	Parquetry blocks	Post: Word Test (2/92, 4/92)	
_____	**4.** Match objects or pictures to a description of their category.	Brainstorming	Post: PPVT (5/92)	
_____	**5.** Categorize objects or pictures on the basis of attributes.	MEER		
_____	**6.** Look at a selection of objects or pictures and say the name of the category to which they belong.	Classification Game, CAI		
_____	**7.** Listen to selected words and say the name of the category to which they belong.			
_____	**8.** Listen to a list of four or five objects belonging to two different categories and tell which belong to a designated category.	Same/Diff. Concept		
_____	**9.** Name multiple items of a given category.	Synonym/ Antonym Game M/B		
_____	**10.** Name something that is _____ and _____.	Teaching Vocab.		
_____	**11.** Tell how two objects, events, or pictures are different.	PPC Cards		

AN IEP SPECIAL SERVICES COMMITTEE REPORT, p. 5

SPEECH/LANGUAGE COMPONENT
INDIVIDUALIZED EDUCATION PROGRAM
IMPLEMENTATION PLAN

Student: _Sara Winter #123456_   School: _Valley Vista_   Implementor: _J. Keene (SLP)_

Long-Term Goal: _To improve production speech sounds._

Initiated	Short-Term Objectives/Criteria	Methods/ Materials	Date & Method of Evaluation	Comments/Summary
12/91	**1.** Produce /s/ in isolation: 90% accuracy.	Peabody Artic. Decks	Post: Goldman-Fristoe (5/92) Articulation Test	
12/91	**2.** Imitate the sound in the initial position in words: 90% accuracy.	Goldman-Lynch Sounds & Symbols posters		
12/91	**3.** Produce the sound in the initial position when naming pictures: 90% accuracy.		Clinician-designed probes (on-going)	
12/91	**4.** Imitate the sound in the medial position in words: 90% accuracy.	SPARC		
12/91	**5.** Produce the sound in the medial position in words/naming pictures: 90% accuracy.	The Inter-state Big Book of Sounds		
12/91	**6.** Imitate the sound in the final position in words: 90% accuracy.	Recorder		
12/91	**7.** Produce the sound/final position/naming pictures: 90% accuracy.	Language Master		
_____	**8.** Imitate the sound in the initial position in phrases: 85% accuracy.	Self-monitoring		
_____	**9.** Imitate the sound in the medial position in phrases: 85% accuracy.			
_____	**10.** Imitate the sound in the final position in phrases: 85% accuracy.			
_____	**11.** Produce the sound in the initial position in phrases: 80% accuracy.			
_____	**12.** Produce the sound in the medial position in phrases: 80% accuracy.			
_____	**13.** Produce the sound in the final position in phrases: 80% accuracy.			
_____	**14.** Imitate the sound in sentences: 80%.			
_____	**15.** Produce sound in structured sents: 80%.			

AN IEP SPECIAL SERVICES COMMITTEE REPORT, p. 6

SPEECH/LANGUAGE COMPONENT
INDIVIDUALIZED EDUCATION PROGRAM
IMPLEMENTATION PLAN

Initiated	Short-Term Objectives/Criteria	Methods/ Materials	Date & Method of Evaluation	Comments/Summary
_____	**16.** Imitate blends in words: 80% accuracy.			
_____	**17.** Produce blends in words/naming pictures: 80%.			
_____	**18.** Imitate blends in sentences: 80%.			
_____	**19.** Produce blends in sentences: 75%.			
_____	**20.** Produce the sound in all positions and blends in structured sentences: 75%.			
_____	**21.** Produce the sound in all positions and blends in spontaneous connected speech during speech class: 70%.			
_____	**22.** Produce the sound in all positions and blends in spontaneous connected speech outside speech class: 65–70%.			

Individual Transition Plan

IDEA, through PL 101–476, the Education of the Handicapped Act Amendments of 1990, provides details about the expectations of programs that serve those adolescents and young adults with handicaps through the age of 21 who are in school and those who have recently left school. It stresses the importance of vocational and life skills for these individuals. It ensures that transitional services are provided throughout the school years. This new law states that for students who will need transitional services, the IEP include at least a statement of interagency responsibilities and linkages before the student leaves school. By no later than age sixteen, an Individual Transition Plan (ITP) should be a facet of the IEP. This adds an important component to adolescents' educational programs. In the past, there was little dialogue between special educators and the vocational rehabilitation counselors who assume some responsibility for many of these youngsters after their school years. As a result many young adults with handicaps are ill-prepared for community living or the world of work. This recent effort toward collaboration of special and vocational education is exciting and promises to benefit many individuals who need to be better prepared for independent living and employment.

In most cases, the ITP supplements and complements the school-based IEP process. While the IEP describes the educational goals and objectives to achieve during a school year, the ITP addresses the skills and the supportive services required in the future (being able to shop, make leisure-time choices, and cooperate with co-workers). Many high school students have both an IEP and an ITP developed and active at the same time. For youngsters who are severely handicapped, the ITP can replace the IEP, particularly as they approach the age of twenty-one. A typical ITP should plan instruction that is conducted in the community and referral to appropriate agencies for job placement and on-the-job follow-up evaluations. In some cases, the ITP includes ways for agencies to plan and supervise community-living arrangements for the client and to provide services. Keep in mind that ITPs should reflect the goals and objectives for the individual to function on the job, at home, and in the community. They should cover a variety of topics such as money management, independent travel from home to work, and social interaction with others (Wehman et al., 1988). ITPs are important for many reasons. First, they ensure that school-based personnel set different goals and objectives for their students. These goals and objectives should address the training of skills that will help the student as an adult. Second, they can assist individuals with handicaps make the sometimes difficult transition from the structure of school to the freedom of adulthood. Third, they can help the student get a meaningful job in competitive work. Fourth, ITPs offer a mechanism for the coordination of services available from different agencies and adult service providers (schools, vocational rehabilitation, agencies for community-based living). Finally, they can help students and parents participate more actively in the next phase of their lives.

Many professionals suggest that ITPs be initiated four years before graduation, and that one to two annual goals be included (Wehman et al., 1988; Ludlow, Turnbull, and Luckasson, 1988). Others suggest that ITPs be developed for students as early as age twelve, a time when some students should begin career and vocational education (LaMar and Rosenberg, 1988), and PL 101–476 states that these plans could be developed when a student is age fourteen or younger.

CASE STUDY: A YOUNG ADULT'S INDIVIDUAL TRANSITION PLAN. Tom, twenty years old, is classified as having severe mental retardation and has been attending special education classes since his first day of school. He has been receiving vocational and community-living instruction for several years. For Tom's last year of school, his teachers have planned that he spend most of his time in supported employment in a local business. In this arrangement, Tom will spend a great portion of his school day off-campus, learning on the job. Mike Roberts, Tom's teacher, also known as a job coach, actually comes to the place of employment to provide Tom with instruction about his job and how to work alongside co-workers who are not disabled. He will help Tom learn important social skills such as when to engage in conversations with his co-workers, and when to work. After several trials at various places of work, Tom is being placed at a veterinary clinic where he will be an assistant, and his job coach will also help Tom become an independent worker at the clinic. Throughout the year, Tom will learn to commute and use the city bus for his means of transportation.

If Tom meets the expectations of his employer, he would continue working for the veterinary clinic after completing high school. Tom enjoys working at the clinic, and his potential co-workers get along well with him. Therefore, agreements were eventually made between the employer and the Department of Vocational Rehabilitation to ensure the smooth transition of responsibilities and his continued employment.

On Saturdays, Tom participates in a leisure activities program sponsored by the Parks and Recreation Department. Tom's teachers and family hope that, if he participates in a recreational and leisure program while still under the supervision and guidance of school personnel, he will continue such activities after he has completed school.

Tom's parents would like him to continue living at home after his school years. Like many parents, they are concerned and maybe even a bit overprotective. For many years, Tom's parents have been active in a parent support group. They encouraged other parents to allow their young adult with a disability to move out of the home to a more independent living arrangement. However, as the time approaches for Tom to leave, they have become reluctant. After much thought and considerable discussion between themselves and with Tom, plans are now set for Tom to reside in a group home after high school graduation.

Tom's ITP reflects the coordination of services from the schools, also called local education agencies (LEAs), the Department of Vocational Rehabilitation, and the Association for Retarded Citizens (ARC)—the agency that operates the local group homes. Procedures are in place so that Tom can make a successful transition to adulthood.

A YOUNG ADULT'S ITP, p. 1

INDIVIDUALIZED TRANSITION PLAN GOALS

Name: _Tom Padilla_   Date: _9/15/91_   Date of Graduation: _6/15/92_

Current Age: _20_   D.O.B.: _5/6/71_

Employment: To obtain full-time competitive employment.
 Transition Activity: To obtain supportive competitive employment 6 months prior to graduation.
 Projected Completion Date: 1/20/92
 Agencies Involved: DVR, LEA
 Person Responsible: Vocational Education Teacher

Residential: To live in a group home that offers full-time supervision and residential services support.
 Projected Completion Date: 7/92
 Agencies Involved: ARC
 Person Responsible: ARC Service Manager

Recreation and Leisure: Special Saturday recreation program offered by Parks & Rec.
 Projected Completion Date: 3/15/92
 Agencies Involved: ARC
 Person Responsible: ARC Service Manager

Community Access: Ride city bus to and from work.
 Transition Activity: Training will be part of supported employment.
 Projected Completion Date: 6/15/92
 Agencies Involved: LEA, DVR
 Person Responsible: Vocational Education Teacher

A YOUNG ADULT'S ITP, p. 2

SEQUENCE OF STEPS TO ACCOMPLISH GOALS

Student: *Tom Padilla*

Date: *6/15/92*

	Liaison: School	Comp. Date	Liaison: Rehabilitation	Comp. Date	Liaison: MR/DD	Comp. Date
Employment	1. Monitor student community-based training site.	9/91	1. Attend regularly scheduled ITP meetings.	9/91	1. Introduce the range of available MR adult services in this community.	9/92
	2. Provide an opportunity for the student to experience at least three different types of employment opportunities.	9/91	2. Assist schools with selecting/identifying competitive employment placements.	9/91	2. Assist family with adjustments needed with SSI benefits, notification of employment, etc.	3/92
	3. Implement program to increase social interactions with nondisabled co-workers.	10/91	3. Begin paying for transportation training.	1/92	3. Assign individual responsible for employment management.	5/92
	4. Look for a full-time employment opportunity 6 months prior to graduation.	1/92				
	5. Transportation training program initiated.	1/92				
	6. Meet with student and family prior to accepting job position.	3/92				
	7. Begin full-time job-site training 2 months prior to graduation.	3/92				
	8. Phase out assistance and provide follow-along support.	5/92				
	9. Secure employment.	6/92				

A YOUNG ADULT'S ITP, p. 3

SEQUENCE OF STEPS TO ACCOMPLISH GOALS *(continued)*

	Liaison: School	Comp. Date	Liaison: Rehabilitation	Comp. Date	Liaison: MR/DD	Comp. Date
Residential	1. Review entrance criteria to local group home services.	9/91			1. Assist family with residential services application.	1/92
	2. Assess student ability to meet residential services entrance criteria.	9/91				
	3. Design program to assist student in meeting group home entrance criteria.	10/91				
	4. Implement program to meet all necessary requirements for group home services.	10/91				
Recreation					1. Contact Parks & Rec. and obtain application and schedule specialized programs.	4/92
					2. Select Parks & Rec. Recreation events with student and family.	4/92
Community	1. Provide public transportation training to and from job.	1/91	1. Pay for transportation training to and from work.		1. Assist student in selecting feasible transportation option to recreation event.	4/92
					2. Arrange transportation to Parks & Rec. with family.	4/92

Source: Adapted from and uses the format from *Transition from School to Work* (pp. 80–85) by P. Wehman, M. S. Moon, J. M. Everson, W. Wood, and J. M. Barcus, 1988, Baltimore: Paul Brooks.

Concepts and Controversies

Least Restrictive Environment (LRE): Where Should Children with Special Needs Be Served?

The concept of LRE is at the center of a heated debate within the field of special education, which is often called the Regular (or General) Education Initiative (REI).

The debate concerns the issues of what constitutes a least restrictive environment, and where children with handicaps are best educated. Professionals place themselves along a philosophical continuum. At one end of this continuum, some professionals maintain that even children who are severely handicapped should be placed and educated in regular education classrooms (Stainback and Stainback, 1989). At the other end of the continuum, professionals (Commission on the Education of the Deaf, 1988) maintain that the special needs of many of these students are so great that they can only be met in residential programs that are exclusively designed to meet the needs of that particular group of students. Most special educators find themselves somewhere between these two extremes.

This complex debate has serious ramifications for the field of special education, and the children and families it serves. There are many elements of this debate. For example, some professionals believe that being labeled is not beneficial to children (Will, 1986). They maintain that this process, which often includes placing children in programs outside of the regular classroom, stigmatizes the children and results in their being viewed negatively by their peers, parents, and teachers. Other professionals (Gartner and Lipsky, 1987) conclude that special education is unnecessary and students should not be removed from the regular education classroom. Some advocate that all children, even those with severe handicaps, receive their education in the regular education setting where special education and related services personnel can work alongside the regular education teacher (Stainback and Stainback, 1989). To fulfill their goals, these professionals call for massive educational reform that could dismantle special education.

Other special educators (Anderegg and Vergason, 1988; Dublinske, 1988) believe that the majority of regular education teachers are not able to teach students who have substantial variation in abilities, learning styles, and behavioral patterns. They feel that regular educators' primary responsibility is to teach children who learn in typical ways. Asking teachers to improve the basic skills and academic achievement of regular education students and also individualize and manage students who have disabilities is, in their estimation, unreasonable. The fear is that all students' educational needs would be unmet and the quality of instruction would diminish.

Special educators, regular educators, those who work with individuals with handicaps in a variety of capacities, and the public in general need to develop their own positions about this debate. Many special educators do not adopt an extreme position on this issue. They suggest that an array of services be maintained, yet encourage more integration of students with handicaps into mainstreamed settings (regular education, parks and recreation programs, social clubs). Even if you adopt a middle-of-the-road point of view, what should guide your decisions about how, when, and to what degree individuals with handicaps should be integrated?

SUMMARY

A cornerstone of the federal laws assuring a free appropriate education to all children and youth with handicaps is a mandated process of individualized educational program planning. It is the Individual Family Service Plan (IFSP), Individualized Education Program (IEP), and the optional Individualized Transition Plan (ITP) that guarantee the individual child the educational and related services required. Each of these management tools guides the educational system as it plans for and delivers an appropriate education to these individuals.

1. All children and youth with handicaps, ages birth to twenty-one, are entitled to a free appropriate education (FAPE) in the least restrictive environment (LRE) possible. These rights are guaranteed by the Individuals with Disabilities Act (IDEA).

2. Regardless of the type of program being utilized, a general process is followed in development of individualized program plans. For youngsters first being considered for placement into special education three steps are followed before the program plan is written: referral, assessment, and identification. Not all children referred for special education services qualify. Some referred are not handicapped and do not require special assistance. Others with handicaps do not require special services to meet their educational needs. A wide range of services are available to children with disabilities. Some of these youngsters require only short-term assistance from a specialist, while others require intensive full-time services. Many different professionals are available to children with handicaps: special education teachers, speech/language pathologists, occupational therapists, physical therapists, vocational educators, audiologists, counselors, social workers. Special education placement decisions must be made by balancing an appropriate education with the concept of least restrictive environment. Every student receiving special services must have a program individually tailored to meet his or her needs, and this program must be specified in terms of annual goals and objectives, complete with measurable ways to evaluate their attainment. Evaluation and review of these goals and objectives must occur at least once a year. At the time of the yearly evaluation, a determination about next year's program must be made. For children requiring continuing special services, a new program plan is developed. For those who no longer require special services, transition back to the regular education system is made.

3. For infants and toddlers, PL 99–457 mandates that an Individualized Family Service Plan be developed and implemented. The IFSP must contain information about the child's current functioning levels, the strengths and needs of the family, measurable goals and objectives, the services required and the time of their delivery, and the name of the person responsible for coordination of these services. Developing IFSPs is the responsibility of a multidisciplinary team of professionals, who must address the needs of the child and the family. Usually, services are provided by many different professionals, with some or all of these services provided in the child's home. As a culminating activity, the multidisciplinary team assists the child and the family in making a transition to preschool.

4. Children with handicaps, from age 3 to twenty-one, are served by the public schools. PL 94–142 mandates Individualized Education Programs be prepared for them. The IEP is the management tool that guides the educational program, including related services, for these students. It includes an assessment of the child's present level of educational performance, annual goals and objectives, the extent to which the student will participate in regular education, the specific services to be provided, and the date for initiation of those services.

5. Good educational practice indicates that students with handicaps should have an Individual Transition Plan developed and implemented no later than four years before graduation. The ITP serves to coordinate services from different agencies (the schools, vocational rehabilitation, community services), and helps the student to prepare for employment and community-based independent living. ITPs supplement and complement IEPs. The goals and objectives included in these working documents center on those skills needed for independent living and work. For some, this may mean learning how to use public transportation, maintain an apartment, or shop for food and clothing. Like the IFSP and the IEP, the ITP is designed to address the individual needs of the student.

DISCUSSION QUESTIONS

1. Brainstorm goals and objectives that could be included in students' ITPs.

2. Develop criteria for applying the concept of LRE to the educational placements for students with mild handicaps. Where should these children be served? What are the issues that need to be considered?

3. How would you define an appropriate education?

4. What are the differences between IEPs and IFSPs? Why do you think Congress specified these differences?

5. How might ITPs and the process used to develop them be improved?

*H*ORACE WALKES, 17, is a student at the Pre-Vocational Center in Barbados and has mental retardation, aphasia, and is autistic. Art has become a means of communication for Horace. He particularly enjoys sponge painting and is known for his carefully blended colors.

*C*hapter Four

MENTAL RETARDATION

After studying this chapter, you should be able to:

- Analyze the three-part AAMR definition of mental retardation

- Compare the AAMR definition of mental retardation to the sociological definition

- List five major causes of mental retardation

- Describe how technology can be used to enhance the lives of students with mental retardation

AN OLDER BROTHER WITH MENTAL RETARDATION

group homes. Apartments or homes in which a small number of individuals with mental retardation live together as part of their community with the assistance of service providers.

Maurice Pasternack is over fifty years old. He has Down syndrome and mental retardation. He has actually lived through many of the changes you will read about in this chapter.

When Maurice was born in 1940, the doctors recognized his Down syndrome immediately because of the physical signs in his face. They also diagnosed an obstruction in his intestine (common in infants with Down syndrome) that prevented him from digesting foods properly. The intestinal obstruction could be easily repaired by surgery, but because Maurice had Down syndrome, the doctors made a recommendation to his parents that was typical then: to let Maurice die by not giving him the surgery. They told Maurice's parents that his life, since he would be a "vegetable" and would have to be "put away" in an institution, would be so difficult that they should not agree to the operation that could repair the obstruction and save his life.

Maurice's mother opposed the doctors and rejected the advice they gave. According to Maurice's brother Bob, she later explained her defiant attitude as a simple decision that her firstborn son *was* going to live. This was an unusual action for a parent to take in 1940.

Maurice's childhood was indeed difficult. The 1940s were a long way from the 1970s. It was an era before IDEA, before "normalization," before integration, before community living, before family support, before people with mental retardation were recognized as having the rights of citizens. So Maurice was not permitted to attend his neighborhood school, and no programs existed in his community to give him the services and therapies that he needed. There was not yet even an Association for Retarded Citizens.

Maurice was eventually institutionalized in a large facility a four-hour drive from his home. It was the only place he could live and perhaps get some of the services he needed. Although his family drove to see him on many weekends, he spent most of his time alone. In the facility, he was forced to sleep on a dirty mattress on the floor, never got enough to eat, and received almost none of the programs he needed.

Maurice's younger brother Bob was born ten years after Maurice. Bob did not have a disability and so he lived at home with their mother and father. His only contact with his older brother for many years was on those weekend visits, which he admits frightened him. Later, the family moved to Florida and Maurice was transferred to a private residential facility in Miami. Bob went to college and began working in special education. Bob is now the president of a firm that provides diagnostic services for students with handicaps and directs a summer camp for children with severe handicaps and their families.

Bob speaks about Maurice's life now:

In 1980, after my mother died, I decided to drive to Florida to bring Maurice back to the Southwest to live closer to me. Although he lived in a segregated facility in Florida, he now lives in an eight-person **group home** in our community. For the first time in his life, Maurice has a job—in fact, he has two jobs. He is a janitor at a scientific laboratory and he grows bedding plants at a greenhouse. Maurice loves to go to work and he loves the group home. We go places together. We have a tradition that every year we go to the Dallas Cowboys / Washington Redskins football game. Sometimes on the weekend, we go to a bar or out to dinner at a restaurant. I am his guardian, and I take care of him. I have for a long time and I guess I always will.

When we were young, the thing he used to do that embarrassed me the most was to hug and kiss me in public. It took a long time before I could accept that. The funniest thing I remember was trying to fix the zipper on his pants in the men's room at the New York World's Fair in 1966. The expressions on the faces of the men in that bathroom have stayed with me for twenty-five years!

I wish my mother could have lived long enough to see the way special education has changed. Attitudes toward people with mental retardation have changed so much: She could not have imagined that the day would come when parents would be able to have their sons and daughters with mental retardation live at home; when there would be family support groups, wide availability of services, the trend toward independent living, normalization, and integration.

Maurice has always been a strong influence in my life. He affected my choice of a career in special education. But very early I had to face the fact that he would never be the ideal of the big brother that every boy wants—Maurice would not be able to fight my fights, take care of me, or help me with my homework. But he has done something else for me that an extraordinary big brother can sometimes do: He has helped me learn what things are important in life, and he has loved me unconditionally for my entire life.

1. In what ways might Maurice's life be different if he had been born in 1980 instead of 1940?

2. What do you think would have happened to Maurice if Bob had not moved him from the segregated facility to his home community?

Individuals with mental retardation are ordinary children and adults who happen to have a seriously impaired intellectual ability that affects their learning. Let us look at their "ordinariness" first. Then we will study the impaired learning ability that makes up their mental retardation.

Children and adults with mental retardation are people first. Their mental retardation is only one of many attributes that make up who they are. It is important to remember they are members of families, they have relationships with friends and neighbors, and they have personalities shaped by their innate characteristics as well as by their life experiences. Youngsters with mental retardation go to school, plan for the future, hope for a job, wonder whom they will marry, and anticipate adulthood. They experience joy, sadness, disappointment, pride, love, and all the other emotions that are a part of living.

But mental retardation is a serious disability. The person with this disability must make special efforts to learn and needs the special assistance of teachers and others. The impaired ability to learn creates obstacles in the lives of people who have mental retardation. Frequently these obstacles are aggravated by society's prejudice and discrimination. But through persistence and courage, and with support from their families, friends, teachers, and others, people with mental retardation can overcome some of these obstacles. With appropriate assistance and support, people with mental retardation can lead lives that are rich and satisfying.

MENTAL RETARDATION DEFINED

Over the years, mental retardation has been defined in many different ways. The definitions have had many similarities, however. Most referred in some way to intelligence and the limited ability to learn. Some also referred to limitations in the everyday behaviors necessary to function independently. Still others stressed a certain age by which the mental retardation must have begun, or perhaps even a requirement that the disability be incurable. Some definitions required some physical proof of disability or a physical origin for the mental retardation. Before we look at the

---

TABLE 4.1. Definitions of Intelligence

Binet (in Terman, 1916)	"The tendency to take and maintain a definite direction; the capacity to make adaptations for the purpose of attaining a desired end; and the power of autocriticism" (p. 45).
Binet and Simon (1916)	". . . judgment, otherwise called good sense, practical sense, initiative, the faculty of adapting one's self to circumstances. To judge well, to comprehend well, to reason well, these are the essential activities of intelligence" (pp. 42–43).
Spearman (1923)	". . . everything intellectual can be reduced to some special case . . . of educing either relations or correlates" (p. 300).
	Eduction of relations—"The mentally presenting of any two or more characters . . . tends to evoke immediately a knowing of relation between them" (p. 63).
	Eduction of correlates—"The presenting of any character together with any relation tends to evoke immediately a knowing of the correlative character" (p. 91).
Stoddard (1943)	". . . the ability to undertake activities that are characterized by (1) difficulty, (2) complexity, (3) abstractness, (4) economy, (5) adaptiveness to a goal, (6) social value, and (7) the emergence of originals, and to maintain such activities under conditions that demand a concentration of energy and a resistance to emotional forces" (p. 4).
Freeman (1955)	". . . *adjustment or adaptation of the individual to his total environment,* or limited aspects thereof. . . . the capacity to reorganize one's behavior patterns so as to act more effectively and more appropriately in novel situations. . . . the *ability to learn.* . . . the extent to which [a person] is educable. . . . the *ability to carry on abstract thinking.* . . . the effective use of concepts and symbols in dealing with . . . a problem to be solved" (pp. 60–61).
Wechsler (1958)	"The aggregate or global capacity of the individual to act purposefully, to think rationally and to deal effectively with his environment" (p. 7).
Das (1973)	". . . the ability to plan and structure one's behavior with an end in view" (p. 27).
Humphreys (1979)	". . . the resultant of the processes of acquiring, storing in memory, retrieving, combining, comparing, and using in new contexts information and conceptual skills; it is an abstraction" (p. 115).
Gardner (1983)	". . . a human intellectual competence must entail a set of skills of problem solving—enabling the individual *to resolve genuine problems or difficulties* that he or she encounters, and, when appropriate, to create an effective product—and must also entail the potential for *finding or creating problems*—thereby laying the groundwork for the acquisition of new knowledge" (pp. 60–61).
Sternberg (1986)	". . . mental activity in purposive adaptation to, shaping of, and selection of real-world environments relevant to one's life" (p. 33).

Note. The first five definitions appeared in Snow (1978, p. 234).

Source: From *Assessment of children* (3rd ed.)(p. 45) by J. Sattler, 1988, San Diego: Sattler. Reprinted by permission.

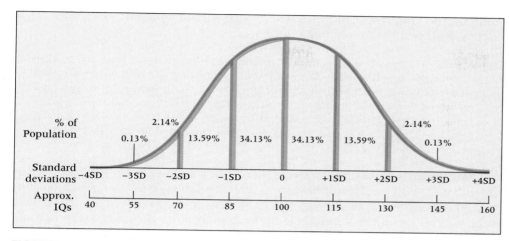

FIGURE 4.1 **The Normal Curve**

theoretical construct. A model based on theory, not practice or experience.

normal curve. A theoretical construct of the normal distribution of human traits such as intelligence.

intellectual functioning. The actual performance of tasks believed to represent intelligence such as observing, problem solving, and communicating.

mental age (MA). An age estimate of an individual's mental ability, derived from a comparison of the individual's IQ score and chronological age.

two most widely recognized definitions, let us think about intelligence and its measurement.

The question of what intelligence is has challenged philosophers, scientists, educators, and others for centuries. Since intelligence is a **theoretical construct,** it has been defined in many ways. Study Table 4.1. Compare and contrast these ten definitions.

On IQ tests, intelligence is regarded as a human trait that is distributed among humans in a predictable manner. This statistical distribution can be represented as a bell-shaped curve, called the **normal curve.** As shown in Figure 4.1, in this curve, the majority of a population fall in the middle of the bell, at or around an intelligence quotient (IQ) score of 100, and fewer and fewer people fall to either end of the distribution, having very low or very high intelligence. IQ level is then determined by the distance a score is from the mean, or average, score.

Mental Age

Sometimes, the concept of mental age is used to describe the **intellectual functioning** of an individual. **Mental age** is calculated as the chronological age of children without mental retardation whose average IQ test performance is equivalent to that of the individual with mental retardation. For example, a man of thirty-five who has an IQ of 57, mild mental retardation, might be said to have a mental age of nine years five months. Such a comparison is imprecise, since adults have the physical attributes, interests, and experiences of their nondisabled adult peers and thus describing them by mental age underestimates these characteristics. At the same time, the mental age comparison can overestimate certain intellectual skills such as the use of logic and foresight in solving problems. Professionals prefer not to refer to mental age, especially when referring to adults with disabilities.

Doll's Definition

In 1941, Edgar Doll proposed a definition of mental retardation that was widely accepted for many years. His definition contained six criteria: (1) social incompetence, (2) due to mental subnormality, (3) mental ability that is developmentally arrested, (4) acquired before maturity, (5) is of constitutional origin, and (6) is essentially incurable. According to Doll:

> Mental deficiency is a state of social incompetence obtaining at maturity, or likely to obtain at maturity, resulting from developmental mental arrest of constitutional (hereditary or acquired) origin; the condition is essentially incurable through treatment and unremediable through training except as treatment and training instill habits which superficially or temporarily compensate for the limitations of the person so affected while under favorable circumstances and for more or less limited periods of time. (p. 217)

Professionals have substantially reworked Doll's ideas. Today, most people believe that an individual might have mental retardation even if there is no "constitutional" or bodily basis for the retardation. We also know that it is becoming possible to cure some cases of mental retardation, for example through prenatal surgery (such as correcting fetal hydrocephaly, repairing an organ, or moving the umbilical cord), and to prevent many more cases, for example through early intervention programs, so that Doll's requirement that mental retardation be "essentially incurable" is no longer true.

The AAMR Definition

The definition of mental retardation now generally accepted comes from the American Association on Mental Retardation (AAMR). Its manual, *Classification in Mental Retardation* (Grossman, 1983), states:

> Mental retardation refers to significantly subaverage general intellectual functioning existing concurrently with deficits in adaptive behavior, and manifested during the developmental period. (p. 1)

Let us examine this definition more closely. The three major themes are intellectual functioning, adaptive behavior, and developmental period.

1. INTELLECTUAL FUNCTIONING. AAMR defines "significantly subaverage general intellectual functioning" as an IQ score below approximately 70–75 on an individually administered intelligence test. The two most frequently used tests to assess students' IQ are the Wechsler Intelligence Scale for Children–Revised (WISC–R) (Wechsler, 1974) and the Stanford-Binet Intelligence Scale (Thorndike, Hagen, and Sattler, 1985).

2. ADAPTIVE BEHAVIOR. Adaptive behavior is defined by AAMR as "the effectiveness or degree with which individuals meet the standards of personal independence and social responsibility expected for age and cultural group" (Grossman, 1983, p. 1). (See also the discussion of adaptive behavior in chapter 3.) Standardized tests have been developed to help assess an individual's adaptive behavior. It is important to understand that assessing an individual's adaptive behavior, even using commercially available adaptive behavior scales, remains imprecise.

Study the AAMR definition of mental retardation displayed previously. You will notice that according to this definition the impaired intellectual functioning and the deficits in adaptive behavior must exist at the same time ("existing concurrently"). What does this mean? As shown in Figure 4.2, if the individual has a subaverage IQ

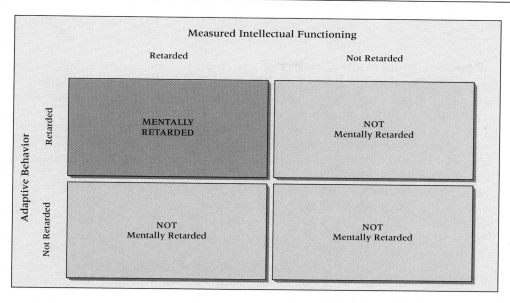

FIGURE 4.2 Possible Combinations of Measured Intellectual Functioning and Adaptive Behavior

SOURCE: *Classification in mental retardation* (p. 12) by H. Grossman (Ed.), 1983, Washington, D.C.: American Association on Mental Retardation. Copyright 1983 by American Association on Mental Retardation. Reprinted by permission.

but functions well in adaptive behavior, mental retardation is not present under this definition. Or, if the individual has a normal IQ but has deficits in adaptive behavior, mental retardation is not considered present.

3. DEVELOPMENTAL PERIOD. The third requirement in the definition is that the impairments in intelligence and adaptive behavior must be "manifested during the developmental period." This means that the disability must have arisen sometime between conception and adulthood, officially the person's eighteenth birthday. For individuals who acquire their disability after their eighteenth birthday, in an automobile accident for example, the label mental retardation is not applied. Such individuals are usually referred to as having a brain injury, dementia (Grossman, 1983), or sometimes a developmental disability.

A Sociological Definition

Although the AAMR definition is widely used in the field, it is not universally accepted. Many sociologists and others believe it is too clinical and does not reflect the significant influence of unique social systems in which each person with mental retardation is identified. Jane Mercer (1973) has written that mental retardation has to be understood as a social role, assigned by a particular social system and assumed by the individual:

> From a social system perspective, "mental retardate" is an achieved social status and mental retardation is the role associated with that status. A mental retardate is one who occupies the status of mental retardate and plays the role of the mental retardate in one or more of the social systems in which he participates. (p. 27)

Mercer suggests that irrespective of a person's IQ score, what is important is whether the individual is assigned the role of being mentally retarded in the particular social system. Under the sociological definition, "normal" means that the individual is achieving role expectations in a satisfactory manner.

How valid is the sociological definition? In 1970 the President's Committee on Mental Retardation (PCMR) published *The Six-Hour Retarded Child*. The title of this influential pamphlet referred to the fact that some children in the United States were labeled mentally retarded only during the six hours they were in school. These children functioned appropriately during the time they spent at home and in their communities. Many of these children performed poorly in school because of language or cultural differences. When they left school at the end of the day and returned to their home communities, they adequately met demands and responsibilities of family and community.

The Six-Hour Retarded Child emphasized the importance of assessing the child's functioning or adaptive behavior in the social system. This study supported the sociological definition of mental retardation and also supported the inclusion of the adaptive behavior component of the AAMR definition.

Subclassifications

As you can see on the normal curve shown in Figure 4.1, approximately 2 to 2.5 percent of the population can be classified as having mental retardation (Zigler and Hodapp, 1986). Professionals (Grossman, 1983) in this field usually subclassify mental retardation into four levels: mild, moderate, severe, and profound (see Table 4.2). These subclassifications are used to compare an individual with others who have mental retardation. Mild mental retardation refers to a disability substantial enough to be classified as mental retardation, but less severe than those at the lower (left) end of the bell-shaped curve.

Professionals have continually worked to refine these subclassifications. Some refinements were successful, some were not. A subclassification method popular among educators in the 1960s and 1970s distinguished educable mental retardation (EMR) from trainable mental retardation (TMR). EMR corresponded roughly to the subclassification mild mental retardation, TMR to moderate mental retardation. The use of EMR and TMR soon came into disfavor probably because educators knew that *all* people can learn, that education and training cannot be separated, and perhaps because suggesting that certain human beings were merely trainable sounded like an unfortunate comparison to animals. Since passage of the Education for All Handicapped Children Act (EHA) in 1975, any distinction between education and training has blurred. Today, we understand that all children are capable of

TABLE 4.2. Subclassifications of Mental Retardation

Severity	IQ Range low → high
Mild	approx. 50–55 to approx. 70–75
Moderate	approx. 35–40 to approx. 50–55
Severe	approx. 20–25 to approx. 35–40
Profound	below approx. 20–25

education and have the right to education. The terms *educable* (EMR) and *trainable* (TMR) are no longer favored.

As children with the most severe disabilities, including **severe** and **profound mental retardation,** have entered schools, and as new techniques have proven successful for teaching these students, a new subclassification, "severe handicaps," has begun to be used. The Association for Persons with Severe Handicaps (TASH) defines severe handicaps in the following manner (*TASH Newsletter,* August 1987):

> These people include individuals of all ages who require extensive ongoing support in more than one major life activity in order to participate in integrated community settings and to enjoy a quality of life that is available to citizens with fewer or no disabilities. Support may be required for life activities such as mobility, communication, self-care, and learning, as necessary for independent living, employment and self-sufficiency. (p. 5)

Other changes in the classification system have occurred as all children with mental retardation have been provided education. It is interesting to note that the children now classified as having mild mental retardation are frequently children who in a previous time would have been classified as having moderate retardation, and that higher functioning children now often fail to meet the eligibility criteria of mental retardation (Polloway and Smith, 1983).

severe mental retardation. The level of mental retardation that usually includes individuals with IQs from approximately 20–25 to 35–40.

profound mental retardation. The level of mental retardation that usually includes individuals with IQs below approximately 20–25.

mild mental retardation. The level of mental retardation that usually includes individuals with IQs from approximately 50–55 to 70–75.

moderate mental retardation. The level of mental retardation that usually includes individuals with IQs from approximately 35–40 to 50–55.

Measurement

Since mental retardation is an impairment of intelligence and the ability to learn socially expected behaviors, measuring the disability centers on attempting to assess intelligence and behavior. Judgment in these areas is often subjective, however, and disagreements over the definition of intelligence and socially expected behaviors have prevented universal acceptance of any one measurement tool. Moreover, these characteristics are interwoven with a child's language and the expectations in his or her cultural group. Therefore, any attempt to measure an individual's "pure" intelligence is risky because intelligence cannot be separated from influences such as home language and the influence of the cultural group.

Mental retardation varies in intensity along a continuum: most individuals have the disability at a mild level, some at a moderate level, and a few have it at a severe or profound level. The measurement of the disability for these subcategories differs.

MILD AND MODERATE MENTAL RETARDATION. Intelligence tests and measures of adaptive behavior are typically used to evaluate the nature of the mental retardation in individuals whose disability is **mild** or **moderate.** Intelligence tests usually attempt to investigate the individual's mental functioning in a variety of intellectual areas such as general information, problem solving, and recall. Measures of adaptive behavior attempt to determine whether the individual actually performs the everyday skills expected of an individual of that age in a typical environment. Often, individuals with mild or moderate mental retardation receive an overall score of intellectual functioning and adaptive behavior.

SEVERE AND PROFOUND MENTAL RETARDATION. Global intelligence scores and global measures of adaptive behavior are usually not appropriate for individuals with more severe mental retardation. And since physical disabilities more frequently

Disputes about discriminatory testing and placement sometimes arise when students who are culturally and linguistically diverse are identified as having mental retardation and placed in segregated classes. Traditionally, these challenges assert that a school or state has used inappropriate IQ tests or procedures and has, as a result, misidentified culturally and linguistically diverse students as having mental retardation. IQ testing to identify culturally and linguistically diverse students is forbidden in at least one state. Recently, however, a few parents have made the opposite argument—that denying their children the right to take an IQ test has deprived the children of identification as having a disability and eligibility for important special educational services.

accompany these levels of mental retardation, accurate measures of intellectual functioning are influenced by the physical impairments. Moreover, whatever the value of IQ scores at the mild and moderate level, they have little use when measuring the abilities and disabilities of individuals who function below the IQs of 35 to 40. Measurement at this level of severity can more usefully focus on determining precisely which essential daily living skills the individual can currently perform, and which learning techniques are most efficient for improving daily functioning and health. Often individuals with severe and profound mental retardation will have functional evaluations specific to the individual and his or her environments and activities.

HISTORY OF THE FIELD

Although mental retardation has always been a part of human history, it was only in the late 1700s that it became the focus of sustained study by professionals. Jean-Marc-Gaspard Itard, the French physician we discussed in chapter 1, began working in 1798 with the boy, Victor, who had lived all his life in the wild with animals. Itard's work and the progress reports he published provided tangible evidence that it was possible to improve mental disability through skilled teaching.

Around 1840, in Switzerland, Johann Guggenbuhl created Abendberg, the first mental retardation residential habilitation program. Built in the mountains, this institution provided fresh mountain air, good diet, baths, massages, physical exercises, sensory stimulation, regular routine, memory exercises, and speech training. Guggenbuhl believed the combined emphasis on education and medical care was important. His beliefs are still valid today. Although favorably received at first, Abendberg and Dr. Guggenbuhl came under fire for alleged financial and medical malpractice. Allegations of mismanagement, misrepresentation of "cures," lack of medical supervision, insufficient teachers, inadequate supplies of necessities, and lack of records ruined the dream (Kanner, 1964; Scheerenberger, 1983, 1987). Abendberg closed by 1867.

Although Guggenbuhl's institution had many problems, the idea of residential institutions had taken root by the midnineteenth century. Residential institutions appeared throughout Europe and Great Britain. In the United States, Samuel Gridley Howe, the first director of the Perkins Institute for the Blind in Boston, developed the first American mental retardation institution in 1848. Initially located in a wing of the Perkins Institute, it later became known as the Walter E. Fernald State School.

Ironically, Howe clearly saw the dangers of residential institutions that isolated people with handicaps both geographically and socially. He wrote that there should be only a few residential institutions and they should remain small in size:

> Grave errors were incorporated into the very organic principles of our institutions, which make them already too much like asylums; which threaten to cause real asylums to grow out of them, and to engender other evils. . . . all such institutions are unnatural, undesirable, and very liable to abuse. We should have as few of them as possible, and those few should be kept as small as possible. (Howe, 1866)

Despite warnings to keep the number down and keep them small, institutions spread over the United States until by 1917, all but four states had institutions for people with mental retardation. Unfortunately, Howe's prophesy proved true. Widespread abuses developed in these residential institutions. The 1970s and 1980s saw many exposés of institutions for people with mental retardation. Citing inhumane conditions and standards far below minimum, the courts ordered many closed because they violated residents' constitutional rights.

At about the same time that residential institutions were started, organizations of professionals and parents sprang up to call attention to the needs of these citizens. The American Association on Mental Retardation (AAMR), founded in 1876, became the largest and oldest interdisciplinary organization of professionals in the field of mental retardation. In 1954 the Association for Retarded Citizens (ARC) was founded by a group of parents. This organization exerted great influence during the years of change that followed. In 1961 President Kennedy founded the President's Committee on Mental Retardation (PCMR), leading the federal government toward a more enlightened view of this disability.

In the 1960s a new philosophy, normalization, appeared in Scandinavia (Nirje, 1969). This philosophy held that people with mental retardation should have available to them "patterns of life and conditions of everyday living which are as close as possible to the regular circumstances and ways of life of society" (Nirje, 1976). The principle of normalization as well as the principle of dignity of risk (Perske, 1972; Wolfensberger, 1972) helped provide a foundation for the civil rights case being brought before the courts. These legal actions brought two important points to the attention of the general public: (1) that people with mental retardation should live as normal a life as possible, and (2) that conditions for people with mental retardation in residential institutions were horrible. These court actions led to widespread **deinstitutionalization** of people with mental retardation. These events coincided with great successes in developing model programs that allowed people with mental retardation to live in their own communities. Today, most people live in **community living arrangements.**

Although residential programs were developed by the middle of the 1800s in the United States, the first American special class for "defective children" was not opened until 1896. This first special class, in Providence, Rhode Island, was soon followed by others in large cities. By the beginning of the 1900s, special classes dotted the country. These early classes were generally segregated: the students spent their entire day with other students with mental retardation. Most communities had no special education classes at all. Some communities permitted only children with the mildest disabilities to attend the special education classes. Only since 1975 has special education been widely available. The passage of the Education for All Handicapped

deinstitutionalization. Decreasing the number of individuals with mental retardation living in large congregate facilities.

community living arrangement. A home in a typical residential neighborhood.

toxin. A poisonous substance that can cause immediate or long-term harm to the body.

Children Act (EHA) in that year allowed all children with mental retardation to attend public schools. Most of these children attend their neighborhood schools and are integrated with their nonhandicapped peers.

PREVALENCE

How many students have mental retardation? Look again at the curve for the normal distribution of intelligence, Figure 4.1. The portion of the curve estimating mental retardation, IQs of 70 to 75 and below, is very small. Estimates of the prevalence of mental retardation vary from approximately 1 percent to 3 percent of the total population. According to the federal government, slightly more than 1 percent (that is, 1 in every 100) of the school-age population is identified as having mental retardation and requiring special education services (U.S. Department of Education, 1990). During the 1988–1989 school year, approximately 502,172 children with mental retardation were served throughout the United States. By far, most of these students have mild mental retardation. In fact, 89 percent of all individuals with mental retardation have mild retardation. Of the remaining levels of mental retardation, 7 percent have moderate retardation, 3 percent have severe mental retardation, and 1 percent have profound mental retardation (Baroff, 1986). While the numbers are rough estimates, this means that a school district of 40,000 students could expect a total of approximately 672 students with mental retardation. Of this total, 598 could be expected to have mild mental retardation, 47 to have moderate mental retardation, 20 to have severe mental retardation, and only 7 to have profound mental retardation.

CAUSES AND PREVENTION OF MENTAL RETARDATION

Causes

Mental retardation can be caused by a variety of factors. Only rarely can any one of these factors be singled out as *the* cause of mental retardation. Typically, the factors interact in complex ways to cause mental retardation. We will identify the major causes of mental retardation. Although these causes are divided into four groups, the dividing lines between the groups are not always clear. For example, lead is a **toxin,** but it is also a socioeconomic and environmental factor. Similarly, malnutrition of a pregnant woman is a socioeconomic factor, but the damage to the baby is also biological. With this complexity in mind, we will attempt to categorize causes into these major categories:

1. Socioeconomic and environmental factors
2. Injury
3. Infections and toxins (poisons)
4. Biological causes

Turn back to the definitions section in this chapter. You will recall that we defined mental retardation as "significantly subaverage general intellectual functioning existing concurrently with deficits in adaptive behavior and manifested during the developmental period." How can socioeconomic conditions cause mental retardation? Well, think about children who do not get adequate nutrition during the early years when their brains should be developing. And injury? What could happen to children who do not use seat belts and whose skulls are fractured against the windshield in automobile accidents? How about the brain damage that can result to infants whose families cannot afford to have them vaccinated and who develop very high fevers during infections?

The retardation may be manifested before a child is born, during the birth process, or after a child is born (but before the eighteenth birthday). It is important to keep in mind that we do not know the precise cause of the disability for the majority of individual children with mental retardation (MacMillan, 1982).

SOCIOECONOMIC AND ENVIRONMENTAL FACTORS. Socioeconomic factors are major causes of mental retardation. Menolascino and Stark (1988) report that poverty is a determinant in 75 percent to 80 percent of people with mild mental retardation where there is no organic basis for the condition. How does poverty cause mental retardation? Unsafe housing (with lead paint, for example), poor sanitation, inadequate nutrition, impure water, inadequate health care, unsafe neighborhoods, and inadequate child care are all facts of poverty and are factors that can lead to disability.

Children living in poverty are at terrible risk for mental retardation and other disabilities.

trauma. An injury.

anoxia. Inadequate supply of oxygen to the body, usually at birth.

asphyxia. Deprivation of oxygen, often through near drowning or smoke inhalation.

fetal alcohol syndrome (FAS). Congenital mental impairments, behavioral problems, and perhaps some physical disabilities, caused by the mother drinking alcohol during pregnancy.

fetal alcohol effects (FAE). A disabling condition in which full fetal alcohol syndrome cannot be documented as caused by the pregnant woman drinking alcohol.

INJURY. Injuries (**trauma**) are another major factor in mental retardation. Many children who suffer brain and head injuries in automobile and cycle accidents, falls, near drownings, and child abuse and other forms of violence, acquire mental retardation. Measures that protect children from traumatic injuries, such as seat belts and child restraint systems in automobiles, protective helmets, water flotation devices, stairway gates, and assistance for parents at risk for abusing their children can reduce the incidence of mental retardation by protecting children from traumatic injuries.

Injuries at birth, including the deprivation of sufficient oxygen (**anoxia** or **asphyxia**), can also lead to mental retardation. The brain requires a certain amount of oxygen in order to function. Deprivation of oxygen will lead to death in a relatively short period of time. An even shorter period of oxygen deprivation or oxygen saturation can cause damage to the brain.

Children who already have mental retardation can develop more severe disabilities as a result of injuries and accidents. If a child with mental retardation sustains brain damage in an automobile accident, the mental retardation might become more severe and physical impairments might be added to the mental disabilities. A child with mild mental retardation who is victimized by child abuse might lose many abilities and become profoundly retarded.

INFECTIONS AND TOXINS. Viruses such as rubella, meningitis, and measles can cause mental retardation. Programs of immunization have decreased the incidence of mental retardation from these infections. However, immunization programs are still not provided for all children. (See Concepts and Controversies at the end of chapter 5.) For example, some families do not have access to immunizations because a health care facility is unavailable or they cannot afford immunization fees. Some families ignore or are uninformed about the risks of skipping vaccinations, and some families avoid immunizations for religious or philosophical reasons. As a result, easily preventable cases of mental retardation due to infection still occur.

Toxins, such as alcohol, cigarettes, and other drugs taken by mothers during pregnancy can also cause mental retardation in infants. Mothers who drink, smoke, inhale secondary smoke, or take drugs place their unborn children at serious risk for premature birth, low birth weight, and mental retardation. **Fetal alcohol syndrome (FAS),** a condition where the baby is born with mental impairments, behavioral problems, and perhaps some physical disabilities is caused by the mother's drinking alcohol during pregnancy (Streissguth, 1986; Streissguth and LaDue, 1987; Dorris, 1989). **Fetal alcohol effects (FAE)** does not include documentation of the full syndrome, but may associate mental retardation with consumption of alcohol during pregnancy. Mental retardation from these causes is simple to prevent—if pregnant mothers abstain from alcohol during pregnancy. No amount of alcohol has been determined to be safe when a woman is pregnant. (See the description of a young Native American boy with FAS in chapter 2.)

Parental use of drugs also places infants at risk for mental retardation in other ways as well. For example, when a pregnant woman uses cocaine, crack, or heroin, the infant she delivers is usually born addicted to the drug and must go through the agony of withdrawal. The baby will likely suffer serious mental, physical, and social problems. In addition, the drug-using parents are often unable to provide the care and nurturing required for healthy infant development after birth. Moreover, the needle sharing that often accompanies drug use is one of the culprits in the spread of AIDS.

Sexually transmitted diseases such as syphilis, gonorrhea, and **HIV infection** (AIDS) can also cause mental retardation. When the mother has, or is at risk for, a sexually transmitted disease, proper medical care and advice are essential. The HIV virus has been found in blood and other bodily fluids, especially semen and vaginal secretions, and in rare instances, in breast milk. HIV infection is transmitted most frequently through needle sharing or unprotected sexual intercourse with an infected person. Many pregnant women who are HIV positive pass the infection on to their unborn children, who are then born with a variety of handicaps, including mental retardation. Parents who carry the AIDS virus can take precautions, such as abstaining from sex or using condoms, to reduce the chance of prenatal AIDS infection. The consequences of HIV infection for infants are devastating (Crocker and Cohen, 1988). The central nervous system is damaged, opportunistic infections cause progressive disability requiring prolonged hospitalization, and psychosocial factors and nutritional deficiencies lead to a chaotic and painful time before early death. (For more information about the disabilities caused by HIV, see chapter 9, Physical Disabilities and Health Impairments.)

Lead poisoning is another significant cause of mental retardation in children. The major source of lead in the environment is exhaust fumes from leaded gasoline. Children who live near freeways and other sources of these fumes are at risk, as are unborn children whose mothers absorb lead (Dietrich et al., 1987). Another source of lead is lead-based paint frequently found in older apartments and houses. Children can breathe lead directly from the air or eat it from a surface where paint is cracked or chipped. For example, children get their fingers dirty from paint chips or household dust that contains lead particles from the air; then, when they put their fingers into their mouths or eat with the dirty hands, they ingest the lead.

Lead poisoning can be controlled by laws banning lead in gasoline and paint and requiring lead paint to be removed from homes, thereby reducing the risk that children will develop mental retardation. If all children were regularly tested for the level of lead in their blood, doctors would be able to monitor and treat those in whom the level has reached a dangerous height.

BIOLOGICAL CAUSES. Down syndrome is an example of retardation with a biological cause (Peuschel and Rynders, 1982). Down syndrome occurs at a rate of about 7.63 per 10,000 births (Evrard and Scola, 1990). This cause accounts for only about 10 percent of all individuals with moderate and severe mental retardation, but it is the most common specifically identified genetic cause of mental retardation (Patterson et al., 1987). Down syndrome is a chromosomal abnormality. Each human cell normally contains twenty-three pairs of **chromosomes** (a total of forty-six) in its nucleus. The most common type of Down syndrome is **trisomy 21,** where the twenty-first pair of chromosomes has three rather than the normal two.

Certain identifiable physical characteristics, such as an extra flap of skin over the innermost corners of the eyes (an **epicanthic fold**), are usually present when the individual has Down syndrome. In Down syndrome, the child's degree of mental retardation varies. As with all types of mental retardation, the resulting degree of disability is greatly influenced by the speed with which the disability is identified, the adequacy of the supporting medical care, how quickly early intervention is provided to the child and family, the appropriateness and intensity of the habilitation, and the adequacy of all the other factors necessary for a child to develop into a healthy and productive person. Since Down syndrome produces physical signs identifiable at birth, early intervention is always possible. The outstanding success with

(HIV). Human immunodeficiency virus. A microorganism that infects the immune system impairing the body's ability to fight infections.

Down syndrome. A chromosomal disorder that causes identifiable physical characteristics and usually causes delays in physical and intellectual development.

chromosome. Microscopic rod-like structure that carries the genes.

trisomy 21. The most common cause of Down syndrome, this genetic anomaly occurs when a third chromosome attaches to the chromosome 21 pair.

epicanthic fold. A flap of skin over the innermost corners of the eye.

sonography. A prenatal diagnostic test that uses sound waves to determine size, position, and possible abnormalities of a fetus.

spina bifida. Failure of the spinal column to close properly.

anencephaly. A condition in which the brain fails to completely develop or is absent.

Early intervention and appropriate education enhance the abilities of students with mental retardation. These early experiences have allowed for this boy's successful integration into a regular educational setting.

early intervention programs with infants with Down syndrome demonstrate that appropriate education can be effective in many cases in reducing the severity of disability (Hanson, 1984). Table 4.3 summarizes some biological causes of mental retardation, including the ones we have just discussed.

Couples can take certain actions before the woman becomes pregnant to reduce the risk of biologically caused mental retardation. Some couples have medical tests before deciding to conceive a child. These tests, combined with genetic counseling, help couples determine whether future children are at risk for certain causes of mental retardation. Tay-Sachs disease is an example of a form of mental retardation that can be predicted through genetic testing.

Other couples seek tests, many of which are listed on Table 4.4, after they find they are pregnant. The tests available include alpha fetoprotein analysis, amniocentesis (analysis of the amniotic fluid), chorionic villus sampling (analysis of the hairlike strands of the placenta), and **sonography** (ultrasound testing). It is possible to determine, in utero, the presence of approximately 270 defects, including Down syndrome, tuberous sclerosis, and neural tube closure defects such as **spina bifida** and **anencephaly.** It is also possible to determine the gender of the fetus and therefore assess the risk in syndromes that are sex-linked.

Screening of newborns after birth can also detect certain disorders that, while not yet causing symptoms, would lead to mental retardation if not treated. Routine

TABLE 4.3. Some Biological Causes of Mental Retardation

Cause	Explanation
Down syndrome	An extra chromosome attaches to the twenty-first pair causing mental retardation, distinctive facial features, and (frequently) physical problems such as heart defects.
Tay-Sachs	A metabolic error in processing fats leads to severe mental retardation and death. Found mainly in people of Ashkenazi Jewish descent.
Phenylketonuria (PKU)	A metabolic error in processing protein leads to toxicity and mental retardation. Can be controlled by diet.
Tuberous sclerosis	A progressive neurological disorder characterized by seizures, mental retardation, tumors, and lesions.

hospital screening for phenylketonuria (PKU) is a good example of prevention after a child is born. Many states require PKU testing for all newborns. A simple blood blot test is conducted on a few drops of the newborn's blood taken from the heel. PKU occurs when a person is unable to metabolize phenylalanine, which builds up in the body to toxic levels that damage the brain. If untreated, PKU eventually causes mental retardation. Changes in diet, eliminating certain amino acid proteins such as milk, can control PKU and prevent the mental retardation (Batshaw and Perret, 1986). By identifying newborns with PKU and helping their families to control the childrens' diets, these infants can be spared mental retardation.

Prevention

As you can see from this discussion of causes, many cases of mental retardation in this country are preventable. The President's Committee on Mental Retardation reports that *more than 50 percent of all cases* of mental retardation could have been

TABLE 4.4. Prenatal Tests

Test	Approx. Cost	Substance Tested	Earliest Time of Test	Approx. Risk of Miscarriage	Abnormalities Tested
Alpha fetoprotein analysis	$125	Woman's blood	16th week	None	Down syndrome Spina bifida
Amniocentesis	$1000	Amniotic fluid	12th week	0.5%	Approx. 270 defects including Down syndrome, sickle-cell anemia, muscular dystrophy, and cystic fibrosis
Chorionic villus sampling	$1000	Hairlike strands on the placenta	9th week	2%	Approx. 270 defects including Down syndrome, sickle-cell anemia, muscular dystrophy, and cystic fibrosis
Genetic counseling	Varies	History of family	Any time	None	Varies
Ultrasound image	$125	Noninvasive view of structure of fetus	Any time	None	Structural abnormalities such as spina bifida

---

TABLE 4.5. Prevention of Mental Retardation

For women who are pregnant:

Obtain prenatal medical care
Maintain good health
Avoid alcohol drinking
Avoid drugs
Avoid smoking (fetal tobacco syndrome)
Obtain good nutrition
Prevent premature births
Precautions against injuries and accidents
Prevent or immediately treat infections
Avoid sexually transmitted diseases
Plan and space pregnancies
Seek genetic counseling and prenatal tests

For children:

Ensure proper nutrition
Place household chemicals out of reach
Use automobile seat belts, safety seats, and cycle helmets
Provide immunizations
Prevent infections
Provide medical care to treat existing infections
Prevent lead intake (from paint and automobile exhaust)
Routinely test lead level
Shunt (drain) excess fluid around the brain
Provide neonatal intensive care services
Guarantee proper medical care for all children
Offer early education programs
Eliminate child abuse
Eliminate child neglect

For society:

Eliminate child poverty
Create appropriate education and habilitation programs for children with retardation
Educate parents and provide support for good parenting skills
Protect children from abuse and neglect
Provide family planning services; support spacing of children
Screen at birth for PKU and other conditions that can lead to retardation if untreated
Provide systematic state prevention programs
Provide public education on fetal alcohol syndrome
Provide public education on HIV prevention
Eliminate environmental toxins such as lead
Assure proper nutrition for pregnant women
Assure proper health care for pregnant women
Assure proper health care for children

---

prevented through known intervention strategies (PCMR, no date). You will see from the list in Table 4.5 that most of these strategies are simple.

Given that many cases of mental retardation are preventable, why have we not taken more aggressive steps to prevent it? Are these prevention strategies too expensive? Is the connection between a prevention strategy and the birth of a healthy baby too obscure? Would the imposition of these strategies put a clamp on many cherished freedoms of our society? What strategies does a government implement to "eliminate child abuse"? (See Concepts and Controversies at the end of chapter 5 for a discussion of the prevention debate.)

PROFILE OF CHILDREN WITH MENTAL RETARDATION

Each person with mental retardation is an individual. We should never rely on stereotypes about them or suggest that they are all alike. But intellectual impairment often is related to certain characteristics of people with the disability. It is useful to summarize some of the effects of intellectual impairments on an individual's functioning. Your teaching will be more effective if you are aware of the possibility of some of these behaviors and characteristics.

Learning Characteristics

COMMUNICATION. Children with mental retardation frequently have problems in communication. Delayed speech is a common problem, and other speech problems also occur more frequently in children with mental retardation than in other children (Lloyd, 1976). Similarly, hearing impairments occur more frequently than among individuals without mental retardation (Lloyd, 1976). All of these affect a child's ability to learn.

For most students with mental retardation, communication problems are of a mild degree and can be corrected with special help. If the child did not begin speaking at the typical age, a speech/language pathologist can assist the family and the school. The specialist identifies the communication problems and uses or suggests techniques to spur the development of communication skills. If the student's speech is not clear, as sometimes is the case in children with Down syndrome, a specialist works to improve articulation. Some corrective surgery, for example, to the tongue, might even be required.

Some children who have mental retardation also have other disabilities that interfere with communication (Bricker, 1983). Children with severe handicaps frequently do not acquire speech at all, or do not acquire speech that can be understood by most of the people around them. This does not mean that these students cannot communicate. Even children without speech are able to use or learn other methods of communication. For example, a student may use eye blinks, touches, movement, posture, or special sounds to indicate needs and desires. The teacher's job is to encourage and shape the communication techniques into a reliable system of communication for the student. With reliable communication, learning and social interaction can take place.

Often, what seems at first to be useless or destructive behavior in a child with mental retardation is an attempt by the child to communicate (Donnellan et al., 1984). Through careful attention and study, a teacher may channel this disruptive behavior into meaningful communication. Let us look at the example of Janie, an eleven-year-old child with severe mental retardation who seems to pound her fists on the table in class at random. Enrolled in her neighborhood school, Janie attends special education classes. Her teacher is determined to eliminate this disruptive behavior. But first, he observes Janie's behavior to see if he can distinguish any pattern. It is important to observe when an incident occurs, and what occurs before and after (antecedent and consequent events) each instance of "fist pounding." From his observations, the teacher discovers the following: the pounding usually occurs when Janie's lunch tray is being removed. The teacher had been told that Janie's appetite is especially hardy for a child of her age. He also recalls being told that Janie's morning medication upset her stomach so that she could not eat much breakfast

augmentative communication systems. Alternative methods of communicating (such as communication boards, communication books, sign language, and computerized voices).

communication board. A flat device on which words, pictures, or other symbols are used to expand the verbal interactions of people with limited vocal abilities.

biased responding. A predisposition to answer in a certain way regardless of the question.

task analysis. Breaking down problems and tasks into smaller, sequenced components.

before the school bus came. The teacher concludes that perhaps Janie has been attempting to express hunger. He arranges for a larger lunch for Janie and a little more time in which to eat it. He also teaches Janie a gesture for "more" so that Janie could communicate the idea in a more functional manner. The gesture is a way for Janie to express herself without speech and without being disruptive. Janie now eats a hearty lunch at a more leisurely pace. When she is still hungry she signals the teacher. Janie is able to communicate her needs more effectively and her disruptive behavior has been eliminated.

Augmentative communication systems create an opportunity for a student to overcome some of the effects of the disability. A good example of such a system is a **communication board,** a flat surface on which words, pictures, or both can be placed, allowing the student to point to the symbols of what he or she wants to communicate. Communication boards are customized to the individual. The words or other symbols on the board must reflect the individual and the needs of the environments in which he or she operates. Some boards are simple homemade projects. Others are quite sophisticated, and can be computerized. Some computerized boards even incorporate an attachment that synthesizes a "voice" for the student. Simple communication books, which function like a board but are more portable, are also popular.

Some students with mental retardation use a system of sign language to assist communication, even if they do not have a hearing impairment. The signs may be simple gestures that are personal to the individual, family, and teacher. The student may use the more versatile American Sign Language (ASL). (See chapter 10, Hearing Impairments.) The selection of a signing system will depend on the abilities of the student and the requirements of the child's environments.

We have seen that mental retardation can affect the way a person communicates. The *content* of a student's communication is also affected by this disability. If the student's understanding is limited, the communication expressing that understanding is also limited. Some students with mental retardation are prone to **biased responding,** for example, answering "yes" more often than "no" (Sigelman et al., 1981). The teacher may ask, "Did you understand what I said?" The student may answer "yes," even though the student did not understand in order to hide his or her confusion or to please the teacher. A teacher can ask the student to explain the topic just covered to learn if the student has truly understood. For example, after giving the class schedule for the afternoon, the teacher could ask, "What will we do first after lunch recess?" Notice that the form of the question will often determine whether a student displays biased responding. Whether the student believes that the behavior asked about is desirable or not may also determine his answers (Rosen, Floor, and Zisfein, 1974).

ATTENTION. Students with mental retardation also often have problems attending to tasks (Zeaman and House, 1963; Mercer and Snell, 1977). A student may have a short attention span for certain tasks. That student needs special help focusing, or selecting the appropriate tasks on which to focus attention. Teachers, by responding to the student's preferences in learning materials, activities, and environments, can enhance students' attention to learning. Task analysis is one teaching strategy that has been successful in this area.

Task analysis is a useful strategy for helping a student with attention problems learn a new skill. In task analysis the job is broken down into components. Each

TABLE 4.6. Task Analysis: Steps in Folding Towels

1. Listen for the buzzer on the dryer signaling that the clothes are dry.
2. Place laundry basket on floor next to dryer door.
3. Open the dryer door.
4. Remove the towels to laundry basket.
5. Carry basket to the folding table.
6. Place basket on the floor next to folding table.
7. Remove one towel.
8. Lay towel on table long side perpendicular to body.
9. Smooth wrinkles from towel.
10. Grip left side of towel with both hands and bring to right side, meeting edges.
11. Smooth wrinkles from towel.
12. Grip upper sides of halved towel and bring to lower sides, meeting edges.
13. Smooth wrinkles from towel.
14. Grip folded towel with one hand on each side holding all layers tightly.
15. Lift towel to stack at left side of table.
16. Repeat steps 7 to 15 until basket is empty.

incidental learning. Knowledge that is gained as a result of other activities and experiences that were not specifically designed to teach the knowledge.

step is taught in sequence and the individual moves on to the next step only after mastering the previous one. To see how task analysis works, let us look at the example of towel folding shown in Table 4.6. For some individuals with severe mental retardation, removing freshly laundered towels from the clothes dryer and folding them may seem impossible, when viewed in its totality. By using task analysis the teacher can change this seemingly impossible job into a set of small jobs leading to success. In the section Education and the School-Age Child, we provide a description of the research on task analysis, additional examples of the task analysis framework, and a more detailed example of how to teach using this instructional framework.

MEMORY. Students who have successfully acquired communication skills must cope with another obstacle to learning—memory deficits. Memory, especially short-term memory, is often impaired in students with mental retardation. The student may also have trouble with long-term memory—correctly remembering events, or the proper sequence of events, particularly when the events are not clearly identified as important. Even when something is remembered, it may be remembered incorrectly, inefficiently, too slowly, or in insufficient detail.

GENERALIZATION (TRANSFER OF LEARNING). One of the limitations of mental retardation is that the individuals with the disability are frequently less able than their peers to acquire knowledge through **incidental learning,** as an unplanned result of their ordinary daily experiences, than their peers. Direct instruction is required. Special care must be taken to assure that learning is carefully structured and designed to address each of the individual's needs.

generalization. The transfer of learning from particular instances to other environments, people, times, and events.

natural setting. The environment in which individuals of comparable age typically live, work, and play.

Children need opportunities to learn and apply skills in natural settings. Generalization must be planned for and can occur in playful situations.

Teachers must plan for **generalization** (transfer of learning) of skills when they are teaching students with mental retardation. All students must be able to transfer the learning or generalize the skill they learn in school to their home or community environment. This does not always happen in special education classes and, as a result, the students' learning time has been wasted on skills that are not yet functional. Students cannot perform needed skills in their normal environment or **natural setting.**

Let us look at a lesson on traffic safety where the teacher did not adequately plan for generalization of learning. Larry is thirteen years old and has moderate mental retardation. He is in a special education class four periods per day at his neighborhood high school. Like his classmates, Larry is eager to get a part-time job. This will require that he be able to walk safely from school to the bus stop several blocks away, then deal with the public bus system in order to get to a job, and then return home alone. Larry's teacher designed a unit on street safety for the class. This was an appropriate skill to teach Larry; it would enable him to travel more independently, and it was a well-designed learning experience. There was one flaw, however. All of the teaching and learning was done in the classroom, with sidewalk lines drawn with chalk on the floor, and with small cardboard "street lights." Larry became very skilled at stopping at the chalk lines and waiting for the red cardboard light to be switched for the green cardboard light. In his neighborhood, however, Larry continued to walk into the street (which had no chalklines, of course) without stopping, and he paid no attention to the streetlights.

What was wrong with this lesson? Larry's teacher failed to plan for generalization. With a few modifications the teacher's unit could have included a plan for generalization so that Larry could use his skills in his community rather than solely in the artificial environment of the classroom. Below we list a number of strategies for helping students with mental retardation to learn and remember skills and generalize those skills to different environments (Kendall, Borkowski, and Cavanaugh, 1980):

1. Students *actively* participate in the learning.
2. Students perform the task repeatedly, **overlearning** or overtraining the strategy.
3. Students "talk themselves through" the activities.
4. Teacher provides effective feedback.
5. Teacher uses many examples so the student can generalize.
6. Teacher systematically introduces the components of the strategy.
7. Teacher gradually phases out and eliminates his or her role.
8. Teacher teaches same task in a variety of environments.

If Larry's teacher had followed this strategy, his lesson would have been more successful and he would have learned to cross the street safely.

MOTIVATION. Frequently, students with mental retardation appear less motivated to solve problems than students who do not have mental retardation (Harter and Zigler, 1974). This is especially apparent with students who have lived in large institutions. Sometimes this is described as **learned helplessness** or outer-directed behavior (DeVellis, 1977; Weisz, 1982). Students who exhibit learned helplessness often seek and even require direction from authority figures, such as their teachers, or from high-status peers, such as the more popular students in class. (For more discussion about learned helplessness and motivation, see chapter 6, Learning Disabilities.) A teacher must be sensitive to students' needs for motivation in order to maximize their learning.

Physical Characteristics

Some students with mental retardation also have accompanying physical disabilities. Students with the most severe forms of mental retardation are the most likely to have additional physical impairments. Some physical disabilities commonly found include cerebral palsy, seizure disorders, spina bifida, hydrocephalus, and generally fragile health. When a child with mental retardation also has a physical disability, the Individualized Education Program (IEP) may include goals and objectives directed toward medications, leg braces, casts, bowel and bladder management, and the like. (See chapter 11, Physical Disabilities and Health Impairments.)

The Stigma of Mental Retardation

Our society places a high value on intelligence. Think about the insults and comments that you hear when someone is being criticized or put down. Many of these insults, for example "stupid," "dummy," "moron," or "the village idiot," accuse the person of not being smart.

overlearning. More or longer practice than necessary for the immediate recall of a task.

learned helplessness. A phenomenon in which individuals gradually, usually as a result of repeated failure or control by others, become less willing to attempt tasks.

at risk. A predisposition or high possibility of mental retardation and other learning problems based on the child's environment, life circumstances, or physical characteristics.

Inclusion in normalized activities allows this girl and her friends to share common experiences of growing up.

It is not surprising, therefore, that some people whose intelligence is impaired suffer severe criticism. They may become the victims of prejudice and discrimination solely because of their limited intelligence. The stigma that often accompanies mental retardation is an additional layer of disability.

Sometimes the fear of rejection and stigma leads individuals with mental retardation to pretend that they are not retarded. Or it may cause them to be shy or especially reserved. Some people have even lied about their stay in a mental retardation institution, claiming to have been in psychiatric institutions or even prisons (Edgerton, 1967). It should give us pause that some would place higher value on prison than institutions for mental retardation.

ISSUES IN EDUCATION

Education and the Preschool Child

Early identification is a key to assuring that intervention services are provided to children with mental retardation. Usually, intervention can limit the severity of the mental retardation. Sometimes, intervention might even prevent the mental retardation, as in the case of PKU. An attentive social worker or teacher might observe possible signs of mental retardation in a child. Table 4.7 provides some possible signs of mental retardation.

Early childhood education programs are essential for young children with handicaps and young children who are **at risk** for developmental delay. Children who are at risk are those whose medical needs or whose environment makes it likely that they will have developmental delays if early intervention is not provided.

Early childhood education can have a profound effect on children and their families (Berrueta-Clement et al., 1984). How does early education help? High-quality education prepares children and helps them gain the skills necessary to

---

TABLE 4.7. Possible Signs of Mental Retardation

- Mother had a difficult delivery.
- Family has history of alcohol and drug abuse.
- Home environment provides limited stimulation.
- Family lives in poverty.
- Child is malnourished.
- Youngster suffered head trauma.
- Child is victim of abuse or neglect.
- Language development is delayed.
- Physical abilities seem immature.
- Student has difficulty following oral directions.
- Child has difficulty understanding the environment.
- Social abilities seem delayed.
- Student seems generally "slower" than age peers.
- Youngster has many difficulties in school.
- Child has physical characteristics of some types of mental retardation.

---

perform well in school. It can limit the effects of an existing handicap and even prevent acquiring a new handicap. Early education can assist and support the children's families so that they can better integrate their children with handicaps into family life and help them learn skills.

An important longitudinal study (Berrueta-Clement et al., 1984), begun in the early 1960s, followed 123 children in Ypsilanti, Michigan, for twenty years. One-half of the children participated in early education and one-half did not. Since the children are now past school age, it is possible to look at real-world indicators of their success. The children who participated in early education showed the following advantages:

- a higher rate of high school graduation,
- a higher rate of employment and training after high school,
- fewer teen pregnancies,
- fewer arrests.

Another important study recently reported that young children born prematurely who received early education and family support had higher IQs at the age of three than those who did not (Infant Health and Development Program, 1990).

Preschools also provide special education to young children. Table 4.8 summarizes the qualities of good preschool programs.

TABLE 4.8. Indicators of High-Quality Preschool Programs

- Emphasis on language development
- Emphasis on social skills development
- Emphasis on motor development
- Opportunities for integration with nonhandicapped peers
- Family support and involvement

Education and the School-Age Child

Most students with mental retardation—approximately 89 percent—have mild mental retardation. Some of these students are mainstreamed in regular classrooms, but most will spend time throughout their school careers in special education programs. Frequently their learning goals are similar to or identical with the goals of their nonhandicapped peers. However, teachers often have to adapt their techniques to accommodate students' learning (Robinson et al., 1989).

Although less than 4 percent of all students with mental retardation have severe handicaps, their learning needs are so complex and intense as to require the most creative efforts (Snell, 1987). Task analysis is one important technique. It is also important to provide community-based instruction, instruction in the ordinary environments of the community, so that the student can generalize the skills learned. Teaching Larry street safety in the community rather than in the classroom, in the earlier example, would be community-based instruction.

For students with mental retardation, one of the most useful skills is the ability to make and express decisions and choices. We all recognize this ability as a vital component of independence and autonomy and as critical to life satisfaction (Williams and Schoultz, 1982). Teachers can help their students get a head start on decision-making skills by assuring that such opportunities exist in the classroom (Shevin and Klein, 1984; Houghton, Broniki, and Guess, 1987).

Merely choosing an option is not enough—one must be able to *express* the choice. How do students with mental retardation express their choices? As do their nonhandicapped peers, most *say* what they want. But students with severe handicaps often cannot express themselves so easily. So they must learn to use other creative means to make their choices known. These techniques range from pointing with a finger or arm, to using different gestures for "yes" and "no," to using certain facial expressions, to pointing with a light or stick attached to a head band.

What happens when a child cannot make choices on his or her own? Look at the case of Lennie, a cheerful four-year-old who has mild mental retardation. He seems happy with the choices that his teacher, other students, parents, and younger brother make for him. Lennie always accepts whatever toys are brought to him at his nursery school. Even though he speaks clearly, he rarely asks his teacher or anyone else for particular toys. His teacher and family wish to develop Lennie's ability to make his own choices. Together they decide that given his age and in his environment, teaching Lennie how to choose toys would be a good place to start. The teacher first placed a variety of toys that she believed Lennie would like on the shelves under the classroom windows. Then she explained to Lennie that he would be allowed to select toys from that area during toy time. The teacher pointed out to Lennie some especially appealing toys that were located in that area. When toy time arrived, Lennie waited at his table for toys to be brought to him. The teacher reminded Lennie that he could go to the shelves to select something to play with. Lennie went to the shelves and looked around but did not reach for any toys. Other children in the class started to choose for him, but the teacher reminded them that Lennie was to choose his own. With reorganization of the classroom and direction, support, and reinforcement for choosing, Lennie began to make more and more of his own choices of toys. Next, the teacher plans to foster Lennie's independent choice making in other areas.

How might a teacher organize the classroom to give students opportunities to make choices? There are many ways. For example, students can choose from an assortment of snacks, they can choose from a variety of activities, and they can choose whether to work alone or with a partner.

Teaching Tactics

TASK ANALYSIS

As we mentioned earlier, teachers often use a task analysis of the skill they wish to teach as a guide for their instruction. When using these systems, teachers may elect to teach a skill in two different orders of **chaining.** In forward chaining, students are taught to perform the first step in the chain first. In the case of zipping a jacket, students would be taught to engage the talon and the tab first. Once that step is mastered, students are taught to slide the talon up the zipper accurately. Each step up the chain of steps is taught and mastered before the next step in the chain is taught and mastered. In other cases, the teacher might elect to teach the steps in reverse order. This is called backward or reverse chaining. Mrs. VanEtten elected to use this approach when teaching Ted how to zip his coat.

Ted is a five-year-old youngster with severe mental retardation. His fine and gross motor skills are not yet well developed, but he does have the ability to use both of his index fingers and thumbs to pinch and grasp with sufficient strength to be able to pull up a talon of a zipper. Winter is coming, and Mrs. VanEtten, his teacher, has decided that Ted must learn to put on and zip up his jacket by himself now. Dressing skills are part of his IEP, but Mrs. VanEtten had planned to target this skill a little later in the school year. Until now, Mrs. VanEtten or the class paraprofessional has prepared Ted to go outside for recess or to go home after school. At home, Ted's mother dresses him.

Mrs. VanEtten decides to use task analysis for zipping, with backward chaining of the instructional sequence. Ten minutes before recess, Mrs. VanEtten schedules time to work with Ted alone on the skill of zipping. On the first day of instruction, Mrs. VanEtten tells Ted that he is going to learn to zip up his jacket by himself. She tells him that for several days she will help him do the task, but fairly soon he will be responsible for doing the job himself. She also tells him that he will learn how to zip in small steps. Each day they will work on a different step. If he can show her that he can do the step being taught that day correctly three times, he can go out to recess early. Mrs. VanEtten stands behind Ted with her arms around him. She slides the talon into the tab, and pulls the zipper up about halfway. She then tells Ted to finish zipping the jacket. He does not respond, so she takes his right hand, helping him grasp the talon, and guides his hand as they finish the zipping task together. Mrs. VanEtten then unzips Ted's jacket. She repeats the process, zips Ted's jacket about halfway up, and asks him to finish zipping his jacket. This time he completes the task. She repeats this step three times. Ted correctly finishes zipping his jacket three times, and leaves for recess early.

On the next day, 10 minutes before recess, Mrs. VanEtten works with Ted again. Standing behind him and putting her arms around him, she tells Ted to watch her as she zips his jacket. Mrs. VanEtten slides the talon into the zipper, and moves it up approximately one inch. She then tells Ted to finish zipping his jacket, which he does. She unzips his jacket, and repeats the process until Ted has completed the task correctly three times. She then dismisses him for recess.

On the third day, Mrs. VanEtten asks Ted if he is ready for the hard part. She repeats the steps she has followed on the two previous days, and for the first time helps Ted slide the talon into the slider. She guides him several times; each time he finishes the last steps by himself. She then asks Ted to zip his coat by himself. She offers him some assistance by holding the sides of his jacket firmly. Ted then zips his jacket. When he does so three times correctly, she praises him for his good work and excuses him to go to recess. Mrs. VanEtten plans to begin instruction on putting on his jacket next week.

chaining. A strategy to teach the steps of skills that have been task analyzed, either first step first (forward chaining) or last step first (backward chaining).

Mimosa Cottage Project. One of the earliest demonstration and research sites, located at a state-funded institution in Kansas, where institutionalized individuals were shown to be able to learn a variety of tasks.

Tips for Teachers

1. Have the student's attention before talking or starting a lesson.
2. Select learning goals and objectives that are functional for the student's life.
3. Teach in the environments in which the student will be required to use the skills.
4. Use actual materials (rather than symbols or representations) when teaching new skills.
5. Repeat the teaching over a period of time.
6. Make certain that students *actively* participate in the learning.
7. Make certain that students practice the new skills.

Task Analysis

Many students with severe or profound mental retardation spend the substance of their time in school learning how to do many of the basic tasks that most people without disabilities learn at home when they are very young. Simple tasks such as buttoning a shirt, zipping a jacket, or tying shoes require direct instruction for some of these children. For these students, learning many self-help skills (housekeeping, cooking, using public transportation) is part of their prescribed Individualized Education Plans (IEPs) and these skills are often topics of instruction for a considerable portion of the school day.

Professionals in the field turned to researchers from special education and psychology to find practical ways to teach life skills (Lent and McLean, 1976; Birnbrauer et al., 1965; Ayllon and Azrin, 1964, 1968). During the 1960s and 1970s professionals worked to develop techniques that would ensure control over a variety of skills by individuals who were very disabled. Their work has had a significant impact on special education and influenced all of education, and various forms of their instructional technology can be found in most classrooms today. What is this system and how does it work? Researchers helped to develop and refine a system, called task analysis, of breaking tasks down into small teachable units. Jim Lent and his colleagues at the **Mimosa Cottage Project** analyzed many complex tasks and skills found in daily life and on the job (Lent and McLean, 1976). In turn they decided to teach these complex skills to their pupils, residents of a state-funded residential school in Kansas, who were moderately and severely retarded. By using the techniques of task analysis they taught their students far more than educators thought they could learn. With task analysis the student learns each step in sequence until he or she masters the whole task. Task analysis is not an instructional procedure, but rather a framework for instruction. The teacher may elect to teach the components of the skill that were identified in the task analysis through several different instructional methods: verbal instructions, demonstrations, verbal feedback, praise, rewards.

The task analysis shown on Table 4.6, Steps in Folding Towels, is merely a listing of the skills that make up this activity. Another way to present the analysis of a task is by using a lattice framework. If you review Figure 4.3, you will see how this framework works in teaching a student to zip a jacket. The skill is broken down into teachable units and the clusters for instruction are shown in groupings. In the case of the subtraction task analysis (see Table 4.9), the operations that need to be mastered are listed and behaviorally defined. As you can see, there are many different

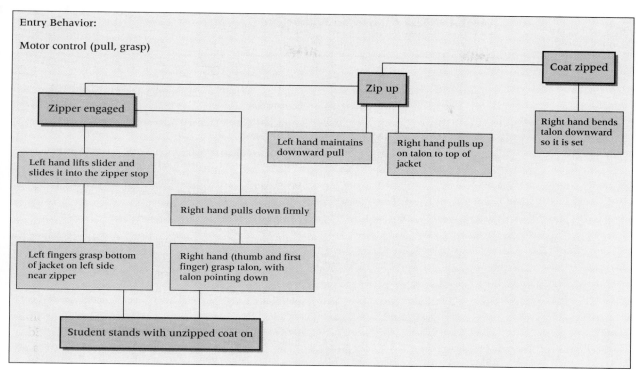

FIGURE 4.3 Lattice for Zipping a Jacket

examples of task analyses. Regardless of the format, they are used to organize instruction.

Educational Environments

We have mentioned community-based instruction (CBI), the strategy to teach functional skills in the environments in which they naturally occur (Snell and Browder, 1987). Like task analysis, CBI is a critical teaching tool for students with mental retardation. For example, learning how to make change is more natural at the neighborhood store than using paper cutouts of coins in the classroom. CBI is appropriate for all ages of students and for all levels of disabilities. It is also convenient— the entire community is the classroom. Rather than addressing a specific curriculum area such as self-help or language, CBI addresses each area in one of at least four domains: vocational, community, recreation and leisure, and home and family.

CBI assists students with mental retardation in overcoming a major learning roadblock—impaired ability to generalize (Horner, McDonnell, and Bellamy, 1986). The process of transferring learning across situations, people, and places can be enhanced by teaching in the environment where the behavior is typically expected (Gaylord-Ross et al., 1987). Students also have the opportunity to learn and practice generalizing from one person to the next. Of what use is it to be able to make change with the teacher if the students forget the skill and cannot make change with the local shopkeeper, a stranger? Generalizing from one place to another is also enhanced by purchasing items in a store rather than from an old refrigerator carton on which the teacher has painted the word *STORE*.

functional skill. A skill or task that will be used in the individual's normal environment.

TABLE 4.9. Task Analysis for Subtraction

Code	Symbol	Sample	Description
SA-1	NN −X	47 −3	Subtracting 1-digit numeral from 2-digit numeral without borrowing
SA-2	NN −XX	78 −24	Subtracting 2-digit numeral from 2-digit numeral without borrowing
SA-3	NNN −XXX	956 −323	Subtracting 3-digit numeral from 3-digit numeral without borrowing
SA-4	ANN −AXX	976 −932	Subtracting 3-digit numeral from 3-digit numeral without borrowing, answer contains zero in the hundred's place
SA-5	ANAN −AXAX	7429 −7225	Subtracting 4-digit numeral from 4-digit numeral without borrowing, answer contains zero in the ten's and thousand's places
Review SA	Mixed		*Subtraction problems mixed from 5 types: SA-1, SA-2, SA-3, SA-4, and SA-5*
SB-1	NB −X	42 −7	Subtracting 1-digit numeral from 2-digit numeral borrowing tens to ones
SB-2	NB −XX	71 −14	Subtracting 2-digit numeral from 2-digit numeral borrowing tens to ones
SB-3	NNB −XXX	365 −127	Subtracting 3-digit numeral from 3-digit numeral borrowing tens to ones
SB-4	NBN −XXX	629 −254	Subtracting 3-digit numeral from 3-digit numeral borrowing hundreds to tens
SB-5	NBB −XXX	721 −497	Subtracting 3-digit numeral from 3-digit numeral borrowing hundreds to tens and tens to ones
Review SB	Mixed		*Subtraction problems mixed from 5 types: SB-1, SB-2, SB-3, SB-4, and SB-5*
SC-1	NO −XX	80 −14	Subtracting 2-digit numeral from 2-digit numeral borrowing tens to ones, minuend contains zero in the one's place
SC-2	NON −XXX	505 −324	Subtracting 3-digit numeral from 3-digit numeral borrowing hundreds to tens, minuend contains zero in the ten's place
SC-3	NOO −XXX	900 −432	Subtracting 3-digit numeral from 3-digit numeral regrouping hundreds to tens, tens to ones, minuend contains zero in the ten's and one's places
Review SC	Mixed		*Subtraction problems mixed from 3 types: SC-1, SC-2, and SC-3*
Subtraction Review	All Mixed		*Subtraction problems mixed from all subtraction types.*

Source: The computational arithmetic program (CAP) (cover sheet) by D. D. Smith and T. C. Lovitt, 1982, Austin, TX: PRO-ED. Reprinted by permission.

Millions of examples of incidental learning occur in natural settings. A trip to the store can include crossing streets, reading road signs, locating the store, finding the items, purchasing them, and interacting politely with the clerk. For those trips outside walking distance, students learn about bus routes, change for the bus, locating the stop, and so on.

FUNCTIONAL ACADEMICS. When academic subjects are taught in the classroom, the educational environment should focus on functionality (Brown et al., 1979). Functionality or **functional skills** refers to those skills which are used in everyday life or which prepare students for life after graduation. Teachers must remember that their lessons should relate to those skills students need for independence.

Many teachers of students with mental retardation have begun to emphasize functional academics. For example, counting can be taught by asking the student to count the number of books in the room rather than by absentmindedly reciting numbers from one to twenty. A unit on measurement is an opportunity to teach cooking rather than having the students measure meaningless lines in a workbook.

INSTRUCTORS. One other important factor influencing the educational environment is who is providing instruction in the classroom. As we discussed in chapters 1 and 3, many professional disciplines contribute to students' special education, including speech and language, occupational therapy, physical therapy, and nursing. Many times these professionals can work together in a single teaching activity at the same time.

The transdisciplinary approach to implementing the IEP reinforces the idea that all disciplines can work on their goals and objectives in relation to the class routine. For example, speech/language pathologists can accompany the class to the grocery store and use that opportunity to teach labeling objects, rather than pointing to pictures in the speech room. Occupational therapists and physical therapists can work on functional mobility skills or on adapting devices to complete a shopping task. Scheduling and coordinating the transdisciplinary approach can be challenging for the teacher, but the benefits to the students are obvious.

FAMILIES OF CHILDREN WITH MENTAL RETARDATION

Every summer, Dr. Bob Pasternack (whom you met in the chapter opening biography) and Dr. Roger Kroth help run a summer camp for children with severe handicaps and their families. The camp demonstrates many of the concepts we have discussed in this chapter. The children are engaged in an experience that is normalized, in that many children of their age attend summer camp; they are having fun with their parents, sisters and brothers, and friends, building a sense of family and community; and they are learning functional skills in the usual environment for those skills that can also be generalized to other recreation environments when they return home.

Welding Together Special Families*

TAOS—With a wide, wobbly swing, four-year-old David Cordova of La Joya cast his fishing line into the small lake and jittered about waiting for the tug.

"David, be careful, you'll pierce my ears a second time," his mother, Sarah Cordova, said with a laugh. David's father, Ernest, fished next to him. On the bank lay David's baby sister, Laura, clutching her bottle. As her mother pushed Laura's curls back from ears usually fitted with tiny hearing aids, the baby turned unfocused brown eyes toward her.

Scattered along the banks and off the dock, others fished and boated, relaxing and laughing in the afternoon sunshine. The lakeside group shared a common identity as families of handicapped children. A few of the children had minor impairments; most were deaf-blind, without expressive language.

Albuquerque Journal, June 26, 1988, p. F–1. Reprinted by permission.

Summer camp provides opportunities to learn new skills, gain confidence and independence, and have fun with family and friends.

All of them—parents, siblings, and disabled children—were participating in a federally funded learning vacation for families of special-needs children in mid-June at Camp Summer Life, a private camp tucked into the pine-covered Sangre de Cristo mountains east of Taos.

Siblings, and many of the handicapped children, headed full-tilt into all the activities that spell camp—games, water play, horseback riding, nights around the campfire. At one point, brothers and sisters as a group discussed the effect of a special-needs child in their lives.

While teachers and volunteers cared for their handicapped children, parents learned and shared and supported, heard speakers address school, insurance, legal and medical issues, coping with the children in the home, stress management, and respite care.

Outdoors, there was beauty and play and rest; inside, a catharsis of sorts.

During an evening session, tears came to the eyes of kindergarten teacher Leslie Cordova of Truchas (no relation to Sarah Cordova), a camper last year, this time a parent advocate, as she related the difficult birth of her second child.

Alfredo, deaf and blind and developmentally delayed, was born with no nasal passages, she said. "At four months he had a heart operation. That's when we learned he was blind. . . . Have you ever cried for two hours? My husband and I did, all the way from Albuquerque to Truchas.

"Next we learned of the hearing thing. It was one thing after another, two years of such painful experiences. At one point, I shouted that I didn't want this child. I said that I *hated* him. There are people who will take him, the pediatrician told me.

"Then," she said, clasping an imaginary child to her, " 'Nobody,' I told him, *'Nobody* is going to take him away from me.' "

She paused, smiled. "And here I am nine years later." The circle of parents nodded in understanding.

Alfredo, who has had eleven surgeries, spent three years in the School for the Visually Handicapped at Alamogordo. "That was the hardest thing I ever had to do," said Cordova, "leaving a child in a residential school. It affects the whole family. In the long run it was the best decision we ever made. He learned to walk, so many things. He'll return this fall; the School for the Deaf will monitor and consult to provide hearing and communication development."

The emotional dimensions of parenting a severely handicapped child emerged again in the staffings each parent had with a doctor, audiologist, occupational therapist, physical therapist, and speech and hearing therapist. All had reviewed the child's records beforehand. The group included a professional who works with the child, a person parents were asked to bring along so new knowledge could be applied back home.

Leau Phillips of Albuquerque is in the process of adopting two boys. One is multi-handicapped. "When I first got him," she told staffers in her session, "he was all ooze from infections in his ears, eyes, nose. His hair was matted, his hands wrapped to keep him from pummeling his bruised face.

"I picked him up and zap, he did the Velcro thing, head right down against my shoulder. 'I want this child,' I said."

The son she is adopting has had two mastoidectomies (surgery to remove the mastoid, a projection of the temporal bone behind the ear) and an adenoidectomy (surgical removal of the adenoids) and is plagued with ear and sinus infections, she said.

"He still doesn't know how to eat—he doesn't like to feel things in his mouth and I always have to force-feed the first bite. But he has stopped throwing things. He's become ambulatory. He's lost a lot of the tactical defense he had, especially around the mouth.

"He didn't want you to touch him, and any change in activity brought a tantrum. He still doesn't like change, but he's much better. Mostly at home he's a pleasant little boy. He's developed a sense of humor, he rides horses, he loves to sing, well, hum sort of—on key. He learned to say 'happy' at camp after we sang Happy Birthday to Rol Blauwkamp, one of the fathers, and I cry every time he says it."

Patrika Griego, a teacher at the New Mexico Preschool for the Visually Handicapped in Albuquerque, the professional-from-home for Phillips' adoptive son and two others at camp, added to the progress report.

"During the last field trip to Uncle Cliff's, instead of the tantrums he went from ride to ride to ride, standing in line with others."

At the end of the session, Phillips, parent-liaison for Parents Reaching Out, a nonprofit organization helping parents raise a child with any kind of disability, talked about her organization setting priorities for deaf, blind and multi-impaired children. "The two big ones (priorities) we came up with were creative living alternatives—where is the child going to live when he's twenty-one—and family subsidies," she said.

Medicaid waivers in some counties pay many costs, including respite care, she noted. "It never covers enough but it's a good start. Now twenty-seven states have family subsidies for severely handicapped children in institutions or at risk of institutionalization so families can keep them at home."

Blauwkamp of Albuquerque, father of severely/profoundly handicapped Bria, reflected parental attitudes against institutionalization. "As long as we're capable of taking care of her, Bria will stay with us," he said.

On one panel, Bria's mother, Sharon, talked about the effects of a severely handicapped child on brothers and sisters. Her strapping sixteen-year-old son loves seven-year-old Bria. "He holds her up, dances with her, raps with her," she said with a laugh. "Our nine-year-old didn't have anything to with her for a time but now is like a mother to her. Our five-year-old lets me know how Bria takes my time away from him."

Asked for advice to parents, Blauwkamp said, "Learn everything possible. Don't let anyone talk you out of something you don't think should be done, even if it's not the norm. Stick with it, follow your own intuition."

Chuck Fisher of Lovington—who with his wife is raising a special-needs granddaughter, urged parents to "just hang in there. Love makes the world go around; you're going to be a better person."

And Leslie Cordova, who said she tried to be a supermom, thought if she had it to do over again, she would know what to tell friends or family who asked what they could do. " 'Make supper,' I'd say. 'Vacuum, watch Alfredo while I take a bath.' And I'd be a little more forward with professionals, telling them instead of them telling me."

Cordova said parents get more out of the camp than they would from dozens of conferences.

"It's hands on, talking directly with professionals not necessarily involved with your child," she said. "That's important if you're not sure of the relationship between a professional and your child or of some therapy or procedure being used."

"And I think the sharing that goes on between parents is invaluable."

Some were foster parents like Cindy Smith of Rio Rancho, a former social worker at Carrie Tingley Hospital in the process of adopting two handicapped children.

Another grandparent, Helen Hubbell of Albuquerque who is raising a granddaughter, really appreciated the camp, she said. "There are not too many places you can go where everyone around accepts us. It's hard. We used to go the park all the time but when we go now, there'll be ten kids standing around staring at us."

Camp ended on a Sunday with an awards ceremony in which, campers stressed, everyone wins something. "Last year," said Leslie Cordova, "Alfredo won an award as the camper who enjoyed horseback riding most."

ADULTS WITH MENTAL RETARDATION

Only a short time ago, many adults with mental retardation were shut away from the world in isolated institutions. Today, most individuals with mental retardation live in their own homes, in apartments with roommates with or without mental retardation, or live with their families. Fewer and fewer remain in large state institutions (Braddock et al., 1990).

Remember that all individuals with mental retardation can lead satisfying lives as adults. They can work in jobs, establish close relationships with friends and family, live in their home communities, and pursue desired activities. Adults with a mild disability may require assistance only from time to time during their lives. Other individuals with mental retardation will always need assistance and supportive services.

But how can these adults support themselves? Must they always depend on government or family aid? Jobs have become an ever more important issue for these people living in their communities. Jobs are important for many reasons including the opportunity to earn money, the opportunity for friendships, the opportunity to engage in the social activities of the community, and to develop the individual's sense of self-satisfaction and feelings of making a contribution. According to Hasazi et al. (1985), factors such as whether the individual worked while still in school, and whether the individual has a network of people willing to help locate a job increase the likelihood that an individual with mental retardation will have a job after completing secondary school. Many students with mental retardation may need the help of a **job developer** to develop—discover or even design—work that the individual can accomplish. A **job coach** might also be necessary to work alongside the individual helping her to learn all parts of the job.

The **transition** from the school years to young adulthood is a critical time for those with mental retardation. Most students require planned and coordinated services in order to move from student life to adult life (Ludlow, Turnbull, and Luckasson, 1988). While the student is still in school, Individual Transition Plans (ITPs), discussed in chapter 3, should be developed that address issues such as entering the work force, moving from the family home to a community living arrangement and assuming the other roles that go with being an adult in our society.

Many adults with mental retardation, particularly those who were not trained as young children to make choices, continue to find that they need help in making decisions for themselves and assuming control of their own lives. In order to learn to make decisions and to develop choice and autonomy in their lives, many adults with mental retardation participate in self-help groups such as **self-advocacy** to support one another in these efforts.

Why is it so critical for adults with mental retardation to learn to make independent decisions? We can find the answer as we consider the case of Kari. Kari is twenty years old. Cerebral palsy and mental retardation cause her speech to be ineffective. But she has learned to express choices in many areas of her daily life by pointing her head wand to words and letters on her communication board. Kari also uses a wheelchair. At this time she is ready to move from her family home to an apartment. A young woman without disabilities would ordinarily spend some time visiting various types of apartments before making a choice, viewing a range of apartments from a quiet duplex on a residential street to a place in a large apartment complex with many social and sports activities. Do you think it is important for Kari to visit some apartments? Why or why not?

Let us assume that Kari has visited a range of apartments in her city. How might she express her choices about an apartment? Perhaps Kari should keep a notebook listing the pros and cons of each apartment. Kari could indicate her opinion on her communication board and ask a friend to come along and keep notes. Perhaps Kari will need a roommate in order to meet the expenses of her apartment. Do you think she will need to meet the possible roommates? What attributes might be important for Kari to consider when selecting a roommate?

What if Kari makes choices that she later wishes to change? For example, Kari might decide that she would prefer a smaller apartment or an apartment in a complex with a swimming pool. How should Kari proceed if she wishes to make some

job developer. An individual who seeks out, shapes, and designs employment opportunities in the community for people with disabilities.

job coach. An individual who works alongside people with disabilities, helping them to learn all parts of a job.

transition. Often refers to the process of moving from adolescence to adulthood, within the context of social, cultural, economic, and legal considerations.

self-advocacy. A social and political movement started by and for people with mental retardation to speak for themselves on important issues such as housing, employment, legal rights, and personal relationships.

SELF-ADVOCACY

Many adults with mental retardation have difficulty assuming control of their lives. This difficulty arises not only from their disabilities but also from society's attitudes toward them. In order to help themselves learn to make decisions and take control of their own lives, a consumer-directed movement called self-advocacy was begun in Oregon in 1974 by a group of individuals who themselves had disabilities.

People with mental retardation want the opportunity to speak for themselves. They can teach others a great deal about how best to assist them. Self-advocates, at a conference in New Jersey in 1986, had this to say about what it is like to strive toward adult status as a person with mental retardation: It takes skill to make decisions. It takes practice—lots of practice.

Travel decisions served as an example.

"How can we control where we want to go?" a man asked.
"Get somebody to teach us bus routes," Michael Kennedy said.
"But what if they don't want to help?" a person answered.
"Get somebody else," came an answer.
"But sometimes they get angry; they don't cooperate."
"*Get somebody else,*" came the answer again.
"Keep looking until you find someone who will teach you."
"That's what you have to do if you want to make decisions."

Some felt staff members hindered decision making.

"But they help us, too," a woman said.
"But if you don't do what they want, they get angry," someone said.
"They treat you like a student."
"It's as if you aren't an equal person."
"Some staff are just out of college with no background," a man said.
"*You* might even be older and more experienced."

"Get on the board," Lisa Obrist said.
"Teach them to be sensitive."
"But we're afraid of staff," someone said.
"What's the worst they might do?" a person asked.
"They'll yell at you," came the answer.
"If that's the worst, that's not so bad," someone added.

It became obvious, voicing such fears in self-advocate groups can help. Some group members felt their parents held them back.

"But what if they retire and move away?" someone said.
"That's why we have to make our own decisions," another answered.
"Sometimes they don't let us decide."
"Let's face it," Steve Dorsey said. "I love my mom."
"And Mom is learning."

The group members came to an eye-opening conclusion:

"Parents weren't born with the skill of letting you decide."
"They must be taught to let you do it."

Source: How we lived and grew together, 1986, pp. 8–9. Reprinted by permission.

changes? The decision-making process we described is natural for any adult contemplating a move to a new apartment. Kari may need special assistance and extra time to make a decision, and like everyone, she may change her mind later about her choice, but the important fact is that she is developing some control in her life and she is learning to be an independent adult.

TECHNOLOGY AND MENTAL RETARDATION

Medicine

Modern technology can make a tremendous difference in the lives of individuals with mental retardation. Medical technology has provided interventions and techniques that lessen the impact of certain handicaps, and, in fact, *prevent* some handicaps.

Advances in the area of medical technology permit surgeries that could not have been possible previously: surgeries to correct the blockage that prevents some infants with Down syndrome from digesting food, shunting (draining) the excess fluid around the brain when an infant has hydrocephalus, and closing the spinal sac and thus reducing the harmful effects of infection in infants born with spina bifida. Children born with myelomeningocele who receive medically indicated shunts and do not get infections can have average IQs (McLone et al., 1982). Developments in modern cardiac surgery make it possible to correct many of the heart defects that often accompany Down syndrome. Some of these medical techniques can be performed in utero, before the baby is born.

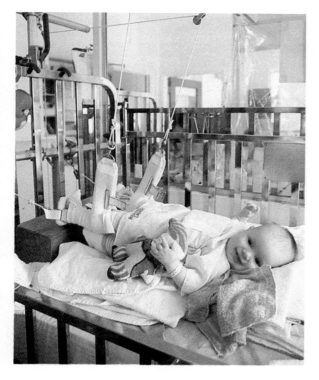

Advances in medical technology can save the lives of infants who previously might not have survived, can prevent disabilities, or lessen the impact of disabilities.

Advances in medical technology have also made it possible to save the lives of very premature infants who in the past might not have survived. Sometimes these children already had handicaps or developed handicaps as a result of their prematurity.

Computers

Ready availability of computer technology has opened up communication possibilities for many students with mental retardation. Computer technology has also empowered individuals with handicaps by putting their environment within their control. In what ways has modern technology assisted people with mental retardation?

The ability to communicate is essential to life satisfaction. It can make the difference between a sad, depressed, isolated child and a child who is an enthusiastic participant in the world. Computer technology allows many individuals with severe handicaps to communicate. Computers can be used as communication boards, to synthesize speech, to write, and to communicate with others who have computers. Modern computers can also drive gadgets and toys. In these ways a person with serious physical handicaps or inadequate strength and energy can control his or her environment.

Let us look at the example of Jerry, a six-year-old with severe physical handicaps and mild mental retardation. He is unable to move except for a weak grip in his left hand. Jerry is in an integrated first grade classroom. He used to spend his days reclining in a seat, staring at the wall. Other children in the class rarely spoke to him because he could not respond effectively and they got bored. Then Jerry's teachers arranged for him to use a computer in class. He can now use the grip of his hand to

Computers can be used to individualize instruction and give students an opportunity for more active involvement in their classrooms.

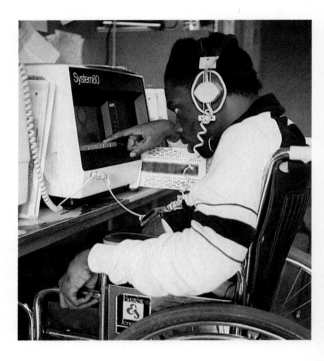

control many things in the class. His computer can control the switch that turns a corner reading lamp on and off or operate a number of mechanical toys and games. Now Jerry is "in charge" of the reading lamp and when his classmates want to spend time reading in the special corner, they ask Jerry to turn on the light. He also has collected some intriguing computerized learning games, which makes him quite a sought-after math partner!

Sue is fourteen and in high school. She has Down syndrome, moderate mental retardation, and speech problems. Although she has received good speech and language therapy for several years, Sue continues to have great difficulty making herself understood in conversations with others. Sue's teacher felt that somewhere, deep inside, Sue had many ideas she wanted to express. If only a way could be found to allow Sue to express herself! After careful analysis and a few false starts, Sue's teacher found creative writing was Sue's best outlet. A modified word processor enables Sue to express herself with more ease and skill than she has ever been able to accomplish without her computer. The computer supplies the words she can recognize, rather than requiring her to type or spell the word. This has made a big difference for Sue. Her classmates are impressed with her skill on the computer and, more important, with her writing. Sue's self-esteem has improved dramatically.

Concepts and Controversies

Poverty is a serious problem for an increasing number of American children. Children have the highest rate of poverty of all Americans. Today, one in five American children live in homes where the family's income is below the poverty line. Twelve million American children live in poverty. Many of these children live in single-parent families headed by women, which doubles their chances of living in poverty. Many of these children are members of minority language or ethnic groups, which also makes it more likely that they will live in poverty.

The poverty suffered by children in the United States is directly related to problems such as the high mortality rate of infants (the infant mortality rate is higher than in 19 other countries, including Singapore and the former East Germany). Poverty leads to poor nutrition which, in pregnant women, causes low birth weight and disabilities such as mental retardation and cerebral palsy. In growing children, poor nutrition can retard brain development and compromise the child's ability to learn and to fight diseases and infections.

Poverty limits access to prenatal care for pregnant women and access to vaccinations and medical care that would protect children from health problems that lead to disabilities.

The social and familial disruption caused by poverty, including homelessness, frequent moves, unemployment, and increased stress and fear can create mental health problems for children in addition to the physical problems. The fastest growing segment of the homeless population is families with children. The widespread poverty of children and its effects on their physical and mental development seem to be particularly related to the prevalence of mild mental retardation. Some researchers assert that poverty of children is *the* major mental retardation issue for the 1990s.

Why has the poverty of children become so widespread in this country? What can be done to prevent it?

The Children's Defense Fund (1990) argues that the federal government must invest in this country's children through programs such as nutritional programs for women, infants, and children; screening, diagnosis, and treatment services for children; childhood immunization programs; increased special education services for all handicapped children; increased minimum wage levels so that working parents can support their families; job training programs for youth and disadvantaged people; quality child care; preschool programs; and compensatory education programs.

Others argue that the country cannot afford the cost of these programs, that taxes are already too high, that states and charitable organizations should respond rather than the federal government, and that social services such as those described cause dependence, laziness, and ever-increasing numbers of poor people. What is your analysis of these problems? How can these children avoid disabilities such as mild mental retardation?

SUMMARY

People with mental retardation have significantly impaired intellectual abilities and deficits in adaptive behavior. The disability must have been manifested during the developmental period, from birth to age eighteen. But people with mental retardation are people first, with all of the emotions, motivations, and complexities of any human being. All attempts to provide education and habilitation to students with mental retardation must be based on the realization of the fundamental similarities of all people.

1. Most students with mental retardation have mild mental retardation. Approximately 89 percent of all people with mental retardation function within the mild level. Some of these students are not in special education at all, although most will spend time throughout their school careers in special education programs. While less than 4 percent of all students with mental retardation have severe handicaps, students with severe handicaps have complex and intense learning needs that require the most creative efforts from families and educators.

2. Early identification and early intervention are critical. When children are identified early, it is possible to provide assistance and support to their parents and education and therapy to the children so that the effects of the retardation can be lessened, or in some cases, prevented.

3. Mental retardation is caused by many factors including socioeconomic causes, injury and trauma, environmental problems, poisons, and biological causes. The incidence of mental retardation could be cut dramatically by simple prevention techniques.

4. Public school education for students with mental retardation must, by law, address the individual child's learning needs. For some children that will mean merely specialized academic instruction in reading, spelling, and mathematics. For other children, it will mean instruction in functional skills of daily living. For a small number of students, it will mean many therapeutic services, an extended school year, and a duration of perhaps years after the typical graduation date.

5. Successful transition from school to work and adult status requires planning and the cooperative work of school personnel, vocational rehabilitation workers, family members, friends, employers, independent living facilitators, and others who can assist youth with mental retardation to assume their roles as contributing adults in their communities.

6. The primary goals for most adults with mental retardation are to achieve lives of autonomy and self-direction. Opportunities to live in normalized living arrangements in communities, to work, and to have satisfying personal relationships are extremely important. Education can provide the foundation for achieving these goals.

DISCUSSION QUESTIONS

1. Think about the various types of definitions: Doll's incurability definition, the AAMR three-part definition, and the sociological definition. Compare the AAMR definition to the sociological definition. Under what conditions could a child be considered as having mental retardation under the AAMR definition but be considered normal under Mercer's definition? Would it be possible for a child to have mental retardation under Mercer's social systems definition but not under the AAMR definition? What are the advantages of each approach?

2. Some children are "retarded" only at school but not in their homes and communities. What is the advantage of labeling such children as having mental retardation? What are the disadvantages? Does labeling allow some children special services? Does labeling affect the way they think of themselves and the way they are regarded by their peers? Does labeling stigmatize them as "different?"

3. You are a guest speaker in a high school health class. What would be important to teach the students about the prevention of mental retardation?

4. Many cases of mental retardation are preventable. Why might a state choose not to take the steps necessary to prevent mental retardation?

5. What kinds of assistance might a student with mental retardation require that a student without mental retardation probably would not need?

SUPPLEMENTARY BOOKS AND VIDEOS

Over the years, people with mental retardation have been included in fictional and nonfictional roles in both books and films. Below is a brief listing of such creative works that you might find of interest.

Books

Blatt, B. (1976). *Revolt of the idiots.* Glen Ridge, NJ: Exceptional Press.

Hunt, N. (1967). *The world of Nigel Hunt: The diary of a mongoloid youth.* New York: Garrett Publications.

Kaufman, S.Z. (1988). *Retarded isn't stupid, Mom.* Baltimore: Paul H. Brooks.

Keyes, D. (1966). *Flowers for Algernon.* New York: Bantam Books.

Menashe, A. (1980). *Inner grace.* New York: Alfred A. Knopf.

Meyers, R. (1978). *Like normal people.* New York: McGraw-Hill.

Perske, R. (1986). *Don't stop the music.* Nashville: Abingdon Press.

Sachs, O. (1987). *The man who mistook his wife for a hat and other clinical tales.* New York: Harper & Row.

Steinbeck, J. (1937). *Of mice and men.* New York: Viking Press.

Videos

Of mice and men. (1939). Hal Roach/United Artists

Charly. (1968). ABC-Selmur Pictures-CBS/Fox

L'Enfant Sauvage (The wild child). (1969). Traffaut, F. (Director).

Being there. (1979). Lorimar/CBS/Fox.

Best boy (documentary). (1979). International Film Exchange.

Bill. (1981). CBS-TV.

*Y*OUNG DUK CHO, 17, *is hearing impaired and a student at the Jordan Vocational High School in Columbus, Georgia. His artwork has won several awards and has been exhibited at Very Special Arts Festivals as well as the University of Georgia School Art Symposium.*

Chapter Five

COMMUNICATIVE DISORDERS

After studying this chapter, you should be able to:

- **Describe the communication process**

- **Differentiate between speech and oral language disorders**

- **Suggest two instructional methods that enhance language development or remediate a language disorder**

- **Explain the roles of technology in the area of communicative disorders**

Our society places a high value on oral communication, and, for most of us, it is the primary method of interacting with others. We talk with each other to share knowledge, information, and feelings. It is clear that most of us prefer talk to other forms of communication such as writing. Notice the intensity of conversations in cafeterias, college dining halls, and restaurants. Think about how often we choose to use the telephone instead of writing a letter. Oral communication allows us to interact with others on many dimensions. Through communication, we socialize, learn from teachers, and function as human beings. Researchers believe that people who can communicate effectively are better adjusted, possess better social skills, and are more likely to perform to their potential in school and as adults (Van Hattum, 1985). Clearly, communication is a critical part of life.

This chapter will help you understand people who have difficulty communicating with others because they have either a speech or oral language disorder. We will discuss the different types of communicative disorders, what causes them, and how they might be prevented or corrected. You will learn how this handicap affects children during their school years. You will also learn how speech and language specialists and classroom teachers can improve children's communicative abilities.

You will learn what problems these individuals face as adults and what hope there is in technological advances. You will come away with a clearer understanding of communicative disorders and the role professionals play in ameliorating them.

COMMUNICATIVE DISORDERS DEFINED

The Communication Process

In order to understand communicative disorders we must first understand the communication process people use to interact with others. Think of communication in terms of a game with at least two players (the sender and the receiver) and a message (the purpose of the interaction) (Marvin, 1989). Communication occurs only when the message intended by the sender is understood by the receiver. The sender may have an idea or thought to share with someone else, but the sender's idea needs to be translated from thought to some code the other person can understand. Coding thoughts into signals or symbols is an important part of the communication game. **Communication signals** announce some immediate event, person, action, or emotion. Signals can be gestures, a social formality, or a vocal pattern such as a gasp or groan. The U.S. Marine band playing "Hail to the Chief" signals the appearance of the President of the United States. A teacher rapping on a desk announces an important message. Symbols are used to relay a more complex message. **Communication symbols** refer to something; a past, present, or future event, person, object, action, concept, or emotion. Speech sounds are **vocal symbols.** Letters of the alphabet are **written symbols. Sign language** uses gestural symbols. Symbols

communication signals. A variety of messages that announce some immediate event, person, action, or emotion.

communication symbols. Voice, letters of the alphabet, or gestures used to relay communication messages.

vocal symbols. Oral means of relaying messages, such as speech sounds.

written symbols. Graphic means, such as the written alphabet, used to relay messages.

sign language. An organized established system of manual gestures used for communication.

These children are engaged in the communication process. They are taking turns being receivers and senders.

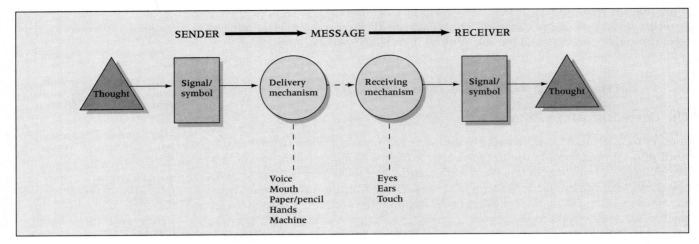

FIGURE 5.1 **The Communication Process**

SOURCE: *Teaching Students with Learning and Behavior Problems*, p. 148, by C. Marvin in D. D. Smith, 1989, Englewood Cliffs, NJ: Prentice-Hall. Reprinted by permission.

communication. The transfer of knowledge, ideas, opinions, and feelings.

language. The formalized method of communication by which ideas are transmitted to others.

are used in combination with each other, and are governed by rules. Signals, symbols, and the rules that must be followed constitute language and allow for language to have meaning.

Once thought is coded, the sender must select a mechanism for delivering the message. The sender chooses from a number of mechanisms: voice, sign language, gestures, writing tools. The delivery system must be useful to the receiver. For example, selecting voice via telephone to transmit a message to someone who is deaf is useless (unless the deaf person has technology for voice decoding telephone device). Sending a written message to someone who cannot read also results in ineffective communication.

Communication messages require the receiver to use eyes, ears, or even tactile (touch) senses (for example, those who use braille) to take the message to the brain where it is understood. Receivers must understand the code the sender uses and be able to interpret the code so it has meaning. Figure 5.1 illustrates the communication process. As you review this diagram, think about how even a simple message, such as an order at a fast food restaurant, follows the steps outlined in the diagram.

Communication cannot be initiated if there is no thought to share. It is either impaired or unsuccessful if the sender or receiver cannot use the signals or symbols adequately. And, if either person has a defective mechanism for sending or receiving the information, the communication process is inefficient or ineffective. As you can see, all the steps in the process must be effective for communication to be successful.

At this point, it might be helpful for us to distinguish three terms—communication, language, and speech—that are different, but related to each other. **Communication** is the transfer of knowledge, ideas, opinions, and feelings (Oyer, Crowe, and Haas, 1987). This transfer is usually accomplished through the use of language. Sometimes, however, communication can occur with the glance of an eye, a gesture, or some other nonverbal behavior. Language is a formalized method of communication. **Language** is the comprehension and use of the signs and symbols by which ideas are represented. Language also uses rules that govern the use of signs and symbols so the intended message has the correct meaning.

Speech is the vocal production of language. In most instances, it is the fastest and most efficient means of communicating. Understanding how we produce speech requires knowledge of the neurological, respiratory, vocal, and speech mechanisms that work together in our bodies to produce speech and language. Refer to the diagram of the head and chest cavity, shown in Figure 5.2, as you read the following description of the process of generating speech.

When we want to speak, the brain sends messages that activate the other mechanisms. The **respiratory system's** primary function is to take in oxygen and expel gases from our bodies. We must breathe to live. However, the diaphragm, chest, and throat muscles of the respiratory system that work to expel air also activate the **vocal system.** Voice is produced in the larynx, which sits on top of the trachea and houses the vocal folds. As air is expelled from the lungs, the flow of air causes the vocal folds to vibrate and produce sounds. The vocal folds lengthen or shorten to cause changes in pitch. The larynx and vocal folds are referred to as the **vibrating system.** As the sounds travel through the throat, mouth, and nasal cavities (the **resonating system**), the voice is shaped into speech sounds by the articulation or **speech mechanisms,** which include the tongue, soft and hard palates, teeth, lips, and jaw. The resonance system consists of the oral and nasal cavities and shapes voice sounds into speech.

We have discussed, in general terms, the communication process. Let us turn now to a discussion of disorders in communication.

speech. The vocal production of language.

respiratory system. The system of organs whose primary function is to take in oxygen and expel gases.

vocal system. Parts of the respiratory system used to create voice.

vibrating system. The orderly function of the larynx and vocal folds to vibrate and produce sounds and pitch.

resonating system. Oral and nasal cavities where speech sounds are formed.

speech mechanisms. Includes the various parts of the body— tongue, lips, teeth, mandible, and palate—required for oral speech.

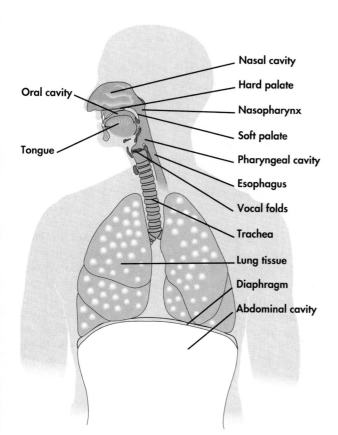

Oral cavity

Tongue

Nasal cavity

Hard palate

Nasopharynx

Soft palate

Pharyngeal cavity

Esophagus

Vocal folds

Trachea

Lung tissue

Diaphragm

Abdominal cavity

FIGURE 5.2 The Body's Systems for Generating Voice and Speech

speech disorders. Abnormal speech that is unintelligible, unpleasant, or interferes with communication.

language disorders. Difficulty or inability to master the various systems of rules in language, which then interferes with communication.

voice disorder. An abnormal spoken language production, characterized by unusual pitch, loudness, or quality of sounds.

pitch. An aspect of voice; its perceived high or low sound quality.

TABLE 5.1. Types of Communicative Disorders

Disorder	Explanation
Speech	Impairment in the production of oral or spoken language
Voice	Absence or abnormal production of vocal quality, pitch, loudness, resonance, and/or duration
Articulation	Abnormal production of speech sounds
Fluency	Interruptions in the flow, rate, and/or rhythm of verbal expression
Language	Delayed or deviant development of comprehension and/or use of the signs and symbols used to express or receive ideas in a spoken, written, or other symbol system
Form	Lack of knowledge or inappropriate application of the rule systems that govern the sounds of language, word structures, and word forms that provide the basic elements of meaning, and the order and combination of words to form sentences
Content	Inability to understand or correctly transmit the intent and meaning of words and sentences
Use	Inability to apply language appropriately in social context and discourse

Types of Communicative Disorders

People with communicative disorders have difficulty using the communication process efficiently. The American Speech-Language-Hearing Association (ASHA), the professional organization of specialists in communicative disorders, has categorized communicative disorders into two major types: **speech disorders** and **language disorders** (Committee on Language-Speech and Hearing Services in the Schools, 1982). Each of these major types are broken down into more specific problems as shown in Table 5.1.

Let us look at each type of disorder to better understand how a problem with any of the areas listed in the table influences the effectiveness of communication.

Speech Disorders

Speech is abnormal when it is unintelligible, unpleasant, or interferes with communication (Van Riper and Emerick, 1984). The three major types of speech disorders are voice, articulation, and fluency (for example, stuttering). Any one of these three speech disorders is distracting to the listener and can negatively affect the communication process.

VOICE DISORDERS. Voice is a measure of self; it is part of one's identity (Oyer, Crowe, and Haas, 1987). We can identify many of our friends simply by hearing their voices. A relative calls on the phone and does not have to tell you who is calling. The voice distinguishes each person from others, and we typically do not think about how it functions. When it does not function as usual, such as during laryngitis, we find it frustrating. Many famous personalities are recognized by their unique voices. Think of how impressionists such as Rich Little create mental images of famous people through voice and gesture. Our voices also mirror our emotions. When you are nervous, doesn't your voice change pitch and sound more tense? We often can tell when people we know well are happy, sad, angry, or scared merely by hearing their voices.

Two aspects of voice are important: pitch and loudness. **Pitch** is the perceived high or low quality of voice. Men typically have lower voice pitch than women. A

loudness. An aspect of voice, referring to the intensity of the sound produced while speaking.

articulation disorders. Abnormal production of speech sounds.

Children with communicative disorders may require extra encouragement to practice their newly acquired skills in front of their peers.

man's voice whose pitch is high, or a woman's pitch that is low, attracts attention. If the receiver of communication pays more attention to the voice than to the message, communication is impaired. When young boys' voice pitch changes during puberty, attention is drawn to the boys and their unintentional changes in voice. Classmates often laugh at a young boy's cracking voice if his voice suddenly changes pitch while he is speaking. Of course, this pitch change is a normal part of development, and the distraction disappears as the boy's body grows and his voice pitch becomes stabilized. This is one example of how different voice pitch can affect communication. **Loudness** is the other main aspect of voice. In some cases, people are labeled with certain personality traits because of the loudness of their voices. "She is such a soft spoken individual." "He is loud and brash." Voice can communicate much of the intended message for delivery. In some cases the quality of voice is so distracting that the message is misunderstood or lost. In these instances, speech therapy is probably necessary.

ARTICULATION DISORDERS. Articulation is the process of producing speech sounds. The receiver of communication must understand the sounds of the words spoken to understand the full message being delivered. If speech sounds are incorrectly produced, one sound might be confused with another, changing the meaning of the message. A child who substitutes a "w" for an "r" sound might say "wed wagon" instead of "red wagon." A child who substitutes "t" for "k" would say "titty tat" instead of "kitty cat." If the words are different or unintelligible, the message has no meaning.

Articulation problems are the most common speech disorder (McReynolds, 1986). Professionals, speech/language pathologists (SLPs), who specialize in correcting communicative disorders spend a considerable portion of their time remediating articulation errors. They also work with language, voice, and fluency disorders.

Articulation is related to the speaker's age, culture, and environment (Oyer, Crowe and Haas, 1987). Compare the speech of a 3-year-old child, a 10-year-old, and an adult. Some of the most common articulation errors young children make are substitutions and distortions of the "s" and "z" sounds and substituting a "w" for "l" and a "w" for the "r" sound (Boone, 1987). A 3-year-old might say, "Thee Thuzi thwim" for "See Suzi swim," and is perceived by adults as being "cute" and acceptable. However, the same articulation behavior in a 10-year-old child or an adult is not developmentally correct or acceptable. Articulation behavior that is developmentally normal at one age is not acceptable at another. If we look at the chart in Figure 5.3 we can see the ages when various speech sounds develop. For example most children learn to articulate "p," "m," "h," "n," "w," "b" sounds from age 2 to 3. But the range for learning to articulate "t" and "ng" can be from age 2 to 6 (Sander, 1972). Some children are able to correctly articulate particular speech sounds earlier than the ages shown in Figure 5.3, and others develop them later.

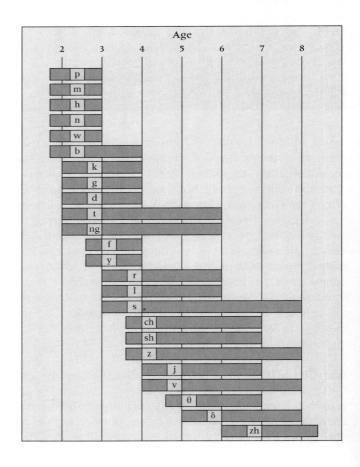

FIGURE 5.3 Sander's Chart, Which Indicates When 90 Percent of All Children Typically Produce a Specific Sound Correctly

Average age estimates and upper age limits of customary consonant production. The solid bar corresponding to each sound starts at the median age of customary articulation; it stops at an age level at which 90 percent of all children are customarily producing the sound.

NOTE: At the bottom of Sander's chart you will find two speech symbols. The θ symbol stands for the breathed "th" sound, as found in the word, bathroom. The ∂ symbol stands for the voiced "th" sound found in words like feather.

SOURCE: "When are speech sounds learned?" by E. K. Sander, 1972, *Journal of Speech and Hearing Disorders, 37,* p. 62. Reprinted by permission.

About 2 to 3 percent of all children require professional help to overcome or compensate for their articulation disorders. Teachers and others working with young children should be aware that young children, age 2 to 6, generally make certain articulation errors as they go through a normal sequence of speech sound development. Adults should not pay too much attention to misarticulations in young children, for they are a normal part of the developmental process. However, if they become concerned that the child is not acquiring articulation skills in a normal manner, as shown on the chart, the child should be referred to an SLP for a speech evaluation.

Articulation also is related to the geographical region in which a person lives. For example, some people from certain sections of New York substitute a "d" for the "th" sound, resulting in "dese, dem, and dose." Bostonians often use an "er" sound for an "a" ("idear" for *idea*), and many Southerners draw out vowels. Although these different articulations are apparent to people who do not reside in a particular locale, they are normal in those regions. Differences in articulation due to regional dialects are *not* considered disordered. Teachers should be careful not to refer children who have moved from one area of the country to another to a SLP solely because of dialectal differences in their speech.

FLUENCY DISORDERS. Fluency is the rate and flow pattern of a person's speech. **Stuttering** is one type of fluency disorder. Some young children (ages 3–5) often demonstrate **dysfluencies** (nonfluencies) in the course of normal speech development. These are not usually indicative of a fluency disorder. Adult speech is not always smooth and fluent either. Even the best of speakers find times when they are dysfluent—when they hesitate in the middle of sentences, break the flow of their speech with unmeaningful sounds, repeat parts of words, or speak very quickly. It is also common to hear people insert fillers such as "you know," "like," or "umm" in their speech. Dysfluencies are more likely to occur in exciting, stressful, or different situations. As young children search for words or the rules to apply to their messages, they may become nonfluent in a manner that suggests stuttering. Four of every five children recover spontaneously from these dysfluencies, usually by age 5 (Sheehan and Martyn, 1970). As with articulation, too much attention paid to a perceived problem early in a child's development can exaggerate rather than eliminate the problem. Individuals who have a true stuttering disorder frequently experience some difficulty in speaking throughout their childhood and adult lives. (Refer to the opening vignette on John Casey.) Their ability to communicate, their interactions with other people, and their own self-concepts are affected, but their speech generally can be improved with professional help.

Language Disorders

Language is the second major area of communicative disorders. It is the complex system we use to communicate our thoughts to others. Oral language is expressed through the use of speech sounds that are combined to produce words and sentences, while other language systems, such as manual communication or sign language, use gestures or other means of communication without using speech sounds. These are the three aspects of language: form, content, and use.

FORM. Form includes the rule systems used in oral language. Three different rule systems characterize form in language: phonology, morphology, and syntax. **Phonology** is the sound system of language; it includes the rules that govern various

fluency disorders. Hesitations or repetitions of sounds or words that interrupt a person's flow of speech.

stuttering. The lack of fluency in an individual's speech pattern, often characterized by hesitations or repetitions of sounds or words.

dysfluencies. Aspects of speech that interrupt the pattern of speech; typical of normal speech development in young children.

form. The rule system of language, it is comprised of phonology, morphology, and syntax.

phonology. The rules within a language used to govern the combination of speech sounds to form words and sentences.

morphology. Rules that govern the structure and form of words, comprise the basic meaning of words.

syntax. Rules that govern word endings and order of words in phrases and sentences.

content. An aspect of language that governs the intent and meaning of the message delivered in a communication; includes semantics.

semantics. The system within a language that governs content, intent, and meanings of spoken and written language.

sound combinations. The phonology of language varies according to language. For example, the speech sounds of German are different from those of Spanish, and different from those we use in speaking English. The English language, for example, uses 45 different speech sound combinations; the Hawaiian language uses only half that number (Marvin, 1989). Swahili and some Native American languages use "clicking" sounds not found in European languages. Rules govern how vowels, consonants, their combinations, and words are used. The rules that govern the parts of words that form the basic elements of meanings and various structures of words are called **morphology.** For example, various prefixes and suffixes change the meanings of the roots of specific words. An "ed" at the end of a verb changes the tense to past, an "un" at the beginning of a word means that something is not. Notice the difference in the meanings in the following words: *cover, uncover, covered, uncovered, covers, discovered, discovering, discover, discovery, recover.* We understand the changes in these words' meanings because we understand the rules governing the structure of words and how that structure influences words' meanings.

Syntax determines where a word is placed in a sentence. As with phonology, syntax rules vary in different languages. Compare how a sentence is made negative in the English language, in Spanish, and in French. The rules within a language determine the meaning of the communication. In English, nouns generally precede verbs in a sentence, but when they do not it might imply a question. Notice the difference in meaning between these two sentences: *It is one o'clock. Is it one o'clock?* The placement of the words in the sentences changed their meaning. For example, *The car hit the boy* has a very different meaning from *The boy hit the car.* Such rules also structure our placement of adverbs and other parts of speech. *I hardly studied this chapter* and *I studied this chapter hard* show different understandings of how the elements of the English language are put together. Many of these subtleties can be difficult to master.

Form is important in all language (oral, written, and sign); form comprises the rules of language where not all combinations are acceptable. In oral and written language, letters and letter combinations are used to produce the words and word combinations (sentences) of language. The use of these letters (symbols) and words is governed by the rules of language. Knowing the speech sounds, letters, words (or vocabulary), and the rules of language influences the way we speak, read, write, and spell (Lindfors, 1987). Games like "Scrabble," "Wheel of Fortune," and "Hangman" require knowledge about letters and their rules for combinations. Those who play such games well have mastered these rules of language.

CONTENT. The rules and form of language are important, but for communication to be effective, words must become meaningful. The second aspect of language, **content,** relates to the intent and meanings of spoken or written statements. **Semantics** is the system that patterns the intent and meanings of words and sentences to comprise the content of the communication. The key words in a statement, the direct and implied referents to these words, and the order of the words used all affect the meaning of the message. Often, we are not clear and precise in our use of words. We use words like "these" and "those," "here" and "there" without being clear about their exact meaning. When senders of messages use indirect or implied references, the receiver might not understand the message that is intended. When a child comes home and tells his mother that he "left it at school," she might be unclear about what the child left at school, unless he is answering a direct question like, "Where is your jacket?"

USE. Use, the third aspect of language, concerns the application of language in various communications according to the social context of the situation. Use includes **pragmatics,** which is the study of language in context. Use, in part, focuses on the intention of the communication. For example, an individual may request, order, or give an action or some information through a communication. The communication is different depending on the intent. It may also be different depending on the social context of the communication. For example, the context of discussion between two children talking to each other during free play is quite different from the context of discussion between a teacher and a child.

The relationships among language, perception, and cognition are key factors in the development of communicative competence. Blank, Rose, and Berlin (1978) make the point that language cannot be considered separately from children's overall development. They point out that a child must know what an object is before he can label it meaningfully, describe it, or refer to it in communications. For example, a child must know what a cup is—an object that holds liquid, is picked up, used to drink from—before that child can develop a concept about cups or use it in conversation. Blank and her colleagues' pragmatics approach to language and its development provides yet another perspective of language and how children develop an ability to gain meaning from oral communication. Although developed to describe preschoolers' discourses and communicative interactions with their teacher, Table 5.2, created by Blank, Rose, and Berlin, clearly illustrates how teachers must match

use. An aspect of language; applying language appropriately; includes pragmatics.

pragmatics. A key element of communication; the relationship among language, perception, and cognition.

TABLE 5.2. A Model and a Scale of Abstraction for Preschool Discourse

A Model of Discourse for the Preschool Age Child

Component[a]	Constituents
1. Speaker-listener dyad	Teacher↔child
2. Topic of discussion	Perceptually based experiences that are within the young child's level of comprehension
3. Level of discussion	I Matching perception II Selective analysis of perception III Reordering perception IV Reasoning about perception

An Overview of the Scale of Abstraction for Preschool Discourse

I Matching perception	Reporting and responding to salient information	What things do you see on table?
II Selective analysis of perception	Reporting and responding to delineated and less salient cues	What shape is the bowl?
III Reordering perception	Using language to restructure perceptual input and inhibit predisposing responses	Show me the part of the egg that we don't eat.
IV Reasoning about perception	Using language to predict, reflect on, and integrate ideas and relationships	What will happen to the cookies when we put them in the oven?

[a]These categories have been adopted from Moffett's model (1968), as described in the preceding text, but represent the modifications that we have introduced to make the model appropriate for use with the preschool age range.

Source: The Language of Learning: The Preschool Years, pp. 18 and 20, by M. Blank, S. A. Rose, and L. J. Berlin, 1978, New York: Grune & Stratton. Reprinted by permission.

their language to the language, cognitive, and perceptual abilities of their students. By showing how communication abilities develop sequentially through expanded understanding of the concepts being discussed, they illustrate that as the child's understanding of the concept develops, the meaning of the concept becomes fuller and more complex. This pragmatic approach to language and its development is becoming widely adopted by professionals in the field.

To achieve competence in communication, a person must be able to use language correctly in a social context. Social conventions or rules are used to initiate conversations and communicate with others. The way we use language at home or with our friends in a casual conversation is probably different from the way we speak to an employer, a school principal, or people in authority. Not understanding the social rules of language can have serious consequences. Not following the appropriate social language rules when speaking to a policeman might lead to arrest. Perceived rudeness to a teacher can result in a trip to the principal's office. Mastering the rules and the nuances of language and communication can be difficult for some children. These children require specific intervention from highly trained professionals so their communicative competence is sufficient to allow them to function in social situations and to achieve maximally.

Measurement

Although most people can tell that someone has a speech or language disorder by listening to that person's oral communications, the formal assessment of speech and language disorders is complicated. Usually, the professionals who conduct these assessments are speech/language pathologists (SLPs) who have considerable skill, knowledge, and training in normal and abnormal speech and language development.

SPEECH DISORDERS. Each of the three aspects of speech—articulation, voice, and fluency—requires a different type of assessment to determine whether the child has a speech disorder. Let us look at each separately.

Articulation. Children learn to articulate the sounds of our language throughout their early childhood. (Refer again to Figure 5.3, Sander's Chart, for a review of the age groupings for when speech sounds are typically mastered.) The last sound most American children master at 90 percent accuracy is the "z" sound (as in wa*s*), and they do this when they are about eight and a half years old. The judgment about whether a child has an articulation disorder or not must be made by considering when children typically master various speech sounds. For example, a six-year-old who cannot produce the "z" sound correctly probably does not have a speech disorder, but a child of age twelve who is still making many articulation errors probably does have an articulation disorder.

When considering whether children have a speech disorder, both their age and the situation must be evaluated. Professionals understand that children tend to simplify speech and make more articulation errors when they are excited (Boone, 1987). For example, a child eager for a freshly baked cupcake might say, "I dan a tutay," when under normal situations the child would articulate the specific sounds correctly, and say, "I want a cupcake." Articulation errors like these, even when made in nonstressful situations, might not represent a speech disorder for a young child, but certainly would for an older child or adolescent.

Some children make articulation errors because they do not use the right motor

TABLE 5.3. The Four Kinds of Articulation Errors

Error Type	Definition	Example
Substitution	Replace one sound with another sound.	Standard: The ball is red Substitution: The ball is wed
Distortion	A sound is produced in an unfamiliar manner.	Standard: Give the pencil to Sally Distortion: Give the pencil to Sally (the /p/ is nasalized)
Omission	A sound is omitted in a word.	Standard: Play the piano Omission: P_ay the piano
Addition	An extra sound is inserted within a word.	Standard: I have a black horse Addition: I have a balack horse

Source: Functional articulation disorders, p. 147, by L. McReynolds, in G. H. Sames and E. H. Wiig (Eds.) *Human Communication Disorders: An Introduction* (2d ed.), 1986, Columbus: Charles E. Merrill. Reprinted by permission.

cleft palate. An opening in the roof of the mouth, causing too much air to pass through the nasal cavity when the individual is speaking.

responses to form the sounds correctly. This may be due to a physical problem, such as a **cleft palate,** where the roof of the mouth is not joined together, or an injury to the mouth. It may also be caused by errors in the way the individual uses the speech mechanisms—tongue, lips, teeth, mandible (jaw), or palate—to form the speech sounds.

SLPs find that people make four different kinds of articulation errors: substitutions, distortions, omissions, and additions. Table 5.3 defines and provides an example of each of these types of errors. Any one of these articulation errors can affect or change the meaning of a communication. Of course, more than one articulation error must occur before a child is diagnosed as having an articulation disorder. However, no hard-and-fast rules exist regarding the number and types of articulation errors a child must make before a referral for speech therapy is made. SLPs use their professional judgment and weigh a number of factors when identifying children as having an articulation disorder. For example, they consider how seriously communication is negatively affected by poor articulation. They also consider the frequency, type, and consistency of errors made by a child.

Voice Disorders. Voice disorders are not common in young children. However, a significant change in voice or a voice quality that deviates substantially from one's peers can be a sign of a serious laryngeal disease. For this reason, even very young children with an abnormal voice quality should have a medical examination. Overall there are two general reasons for a voice disorder in children: an organic cause (such as a tumor) and a functional cause. Although functional causes of voice disorders in children are not common, they are usually due to individuals using their voices inappropriately. For example, screaming for long periods of time puts undue stress on the vocal folds and larynx causing damage to the voice mechanisms and a voice disorder. This disorder can manifest itself through a voice that sounds hoarse, too low or high in pitch, or breathy. As they do with articulation disorders, SLPs measure voice disorders by using their clinical judgment—their knowledge and experience— to determine when children's voice is actually disordered and in need of therapy.

Fluency Disorders. The third kind of speech disorder is a fluency disorder. In this situation, the flow of speech breaks down because syllables are repeated, or a communication includes many hesitations, or extraneous words or sounds. Stuttering is a fluency disorder, but there are important distinctions between stuttering and dysfluent speech. All of us, particularly young children mastering language, are dysfluent sometimes, and this is normal. Adults can distinguish between normal dysfluency and stuttering in children by looking carefully at what aspects of speech are repeated (Boone, 1987). Children with normal speech often repeat whole words or phrases, like "Give me the, give me the, give me the ball." Children who stutter are more likely to say, "Gi-gi-gi-give m-m-m-me the b-b-b-ball." These children are more likely to repeat specific sounds or syllables. Children who stutter also have a higher frequency of repetitions than children who are dysfluent. For example, children with normal speech do not repeat more than 3 percent of what they say, while children who stutter repeat syllables in 7 to 14 percent of what they say (Wingate, 1962). They also tend to show nonverbal signs of struggling with their speech by blinking, grimacing, or becoming tense. How does a professional measure a fluency disorder? SLPs analyze the frequency and type of an individual's involuntary dysfluencies by taking samples of oral language in various situations, such as free play and answering direct questions, to determine whether a fluency disorder exists or not.

LANGUAGE DISORDERS.   The second major category of communicative disorders can for many children result in more serious learning problems than the speech disorders we discussed above. The lack of language competence apparent in these children influences their ability to learn to read and write at the pace of their classmates, as well as their ability to communicate orally with others. An SLP assesses an individual's language competence through a thorough evaluation, which usually includes assessment of the three aspects of language: form, content, and use. To assess the first aspect of language competence, the *form* or structure of an individual's language, the SLP determines how well the child uses the rules of language. Problems with form cause errors in letter or sound formation, in using correct grammatical structures, or in sentence formation. Many children who have difficulty with the rules of language also have problems recognizing sounds, understanding the meaning of different grammatical constructions, sentence types, and sentence complexities. For example, a child who has not mastered the rules of language might not be able to tell the difference between these two sentences: *Go to the store. Did you go to the store?* The second aspect of language that SLPs assess to determine language competence is *content*. Children whose language content is insufficient often do not understand the meaning of what is said to them and often choose inappropriate words to use in their oral language communications. These children might also have difficulty comprehending the written material presented in textbooks. The third aspect of language competence, *use* (sometimes called pragmatics), is assessed to determine how appropriately a child uses language in social contexts and conversations.

SLPs evaluate children's language competence to determine if the child actually has a language disorder. One part of this evaluation or assessment is a case history which documents the child's birth, development, and cognitive and physical growth. Usually, the child's doctor and the parents complete a case history form before the SLP actually sees the child. When the parents bring their child to the clinic for the evaluation, they are interviewed and the child's language is evaluated in several different situations: free play, informal testing, and formal testing. When the child's use of language in a free play setting is evaluated, the parents are often asked to play with their child in a room equipped with many toys and objects to describe and interact with, a one-way mirror (for the SLP to observe without distracting the child or parents), and an audio system. The SLP might take data by using a standardized evaluation scale, or might take informal notes about the child's language. Some SLPs tape the child's language, and transcribe it at a later time so they can conduct a

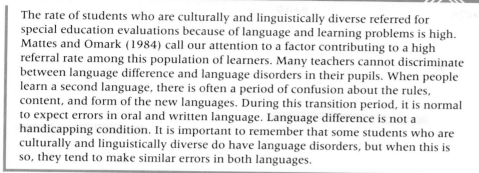

The rate of students who are culturally and linguistically diverse referred for special education evaluations because of language and learning problems is high. Mattes and Omark (1984) call our attention to a factor contributing to a high referral rate among this population of learners. Many teachers cannot discriminate between language difference and language disorders in their pupils. When people learn a second language, there is often a period of confusion about the rules, content, and form of the new languages. During this transition period, it is normal to expect errors in oral and written language. Language difference is not a handicapping condition. It is important to remember that some students who are culturally and linguistically diverse do have language disorders, but when this is so, they tend to make similar errors in both languages.

formal and detailed evaluation of the form, content, and use of language. The SLP uses both formal and informal methods of testing the child's language competence. The SLP will set up play situations where particular language behaviors can be assessed. For example, the SLP might ask a series of questions to see how well a child understands what is said. The SLP might show the child some pictures, asking the child to name and describe what is in a picture or make up a story about several pictures. Audiotaping or videotaping the language evaluation allows the SLP to thoroughly analyze the child's speech and language competence at a later time. The child's language is also evaluated formally by using standardized tests. The number and types of tests used vary depending on the speech and language difficulties the SLP identified in the less formal evaluations.

Finally, the SLP prepares an evaluation report that becomes part of the child's permanent record if the evaluation was conducted by or paid for by the school district the child attends. This report presents the status of the child's speech and language and includes a statement about whether the child has a speech or language disorder. It also presents a summary of the child's strengths and weaknesses in speech and language, and an overall assessment of the child's language competence. In addition, the report usually includes a suggested remediation plan, a list of the services the child requires, and a statement about the predicted outcome of treatment and remediation. The SLP reviews this report with the parents so they understand which specific services are being recommended and why. For children diagnosed as having a speech or language disorder, this process is the beginning of a partnership of parents and professionals working together to remediate what can be a very significant disability.

Significance

Understanding and being able to use speech and language well influences an individual's success in school, social situations, and employment. A speech disorder affects how a person interacts with others in all kinds of settings. The story of John Casey, in the opening vignette, tells how his stuttering influences his career choices and even his social life. A language disorder has the potential of being even more serious, for it can have an impact on all aspects of a child's classroom experiences, including the abilities to speak, write, as well as comprehend what is written and spoken.

Language is a complex system to master. Its rules are not consistent, and there are many subtle conventions to learn and follow. Language is an important foundation to the skills children learn at school. We know of the relationship between the knowledge of language and the ability to learn to read and write easily. (We discuss the relationship between language disorders and learning disabilities in several sections in this chapter and in chapter 6, Learning Disabilities.) The histories of many children with learning disabilities reveal that they were identified as having a significant language delay or disorder as preschoolers. There are many reasons for a relationship between learning disabilities and language disorders. For example, children who do not understand what is said to them do not develop language at the same rate as children who do understand and benefit from communicative interchanges. Some children who have delayed language also do not develop cognitive or thinking skills at the same pace as their nonhandicapped peers. This can influence all levels of academic achievement, particularly in reading and writing.

In addition researchers have recently been drawn to study the relationship between communicative competence and individuals' ability to interact socially (Mathinos, 1988). Communication occurs in a social context, and many children with learning disabilities seem less effective than their nonhandicapped peers in communicative interactions. Although learning disabilities are primarily academic problems, it now appears that many persons with learning disabilities also have difficulties in social interactions with others. For such individuals, academic *and* social programs must be carefully planned, and included in their IEPs.

It is clear that people who cannot communicate well find that this inability affects the way they interact with others and how efficiently they communicate and learn. Ultimately, this influences employment options. For example, a receptionist in an office must be able to talk on the phone, take and deliver messages to the public and the other workers in the office, and provide directions to visitors. If you take a moment to reflect, you will see that the ability to communicate successfully with others is a requirement of many jobs.

HISTORY OF THE FIELD

Speech and language problems have been a part of the human condition since our ancestors began to speak. From the writings of people who lived thousands of years ago, we know that often people with disabilities were thought to be funny. Even before 1000 B.C., individuals with disabilities were considered fools or buffoons, and sources of entertainment. During Roman times, cages were placed along the Appian Way to display individuals with disabilities. There, Balbus Balaesus the Stutterer would attempt to talk when a coin was thrown into his cage (Van Riper and Emerick, 1984).

Although there are documented cases of communicative disorders, treatment programs were not based in schools, and met with mixed results. In the United States, speech correction was not available in the public schools until the twentieth century. In 1910 the Chicago public schools hired an itinerant teacher to help children who "stammered" (Moore and Kester, 1953). In 1913 the superintendent of the New York City schools began a program for speech training which was offered to children who had speech disorders. The first speech clinic was opened in 1914, by Smiley Blanton at the University of Wisconsin. In 1925 the American Academy for Speech Correction (later called the American Speech and Hearing Association and

Robert West, one of the founders of what is now the American Speech-Language-Hearing Association, is considered by many to be the father of this field.

now called American Speech-Language-Hearing Association) was formed by a small group of professionals to share their ideas and research. A leader in the formation of the academy, Robert West, is credited by some (Van Riper, 1981) as being the father of his field. Two other pioneers—Lee Travis and Wendell Johnson—developed the program at the University of Iowa, and guided this emerging field at the organizational and national level. Through their guidance, the field of communicative disorders became independent from medicine, psychology, and speech and debate.

During the early part of the twentieth century, some public schools hired speech clinicians to work with children who had speech problems, but services were limited. World War II saw the military develop screening procedures to identify persons with speech and hearing difficulties and begin their own clinical and research programs. These efforts demonstrated that speech therapy can be effective, and after the war university programs to train speech/language pathologists increased in size and number. Correspondingly, public school programs expanded. By 1959, thirty-nine states had laws allowing or requiring school districts to provide services for students with handicaps, including those with communicative disorders, and to receive state funding.

Throughout the history of the field, professionals who work to remediate children's speech and language problems have been referred to by different titles. These title changes partly reflect changing roles. At first, they were called speech correctionists or speech teachers. These early professionals centered their efforts on remediating stuttering, voice, and articulation difficulties. During the late 1950s and 1960s, speech correctionists began to be called speech therapists and speech clinicians. During this time, they saw more than 200 children per week, primarily in small groups for as little as thirty minutes per day. Many children with significant language problems, with moderate to severe disabilities, or with mental retardation, did not receive speech therapy because they were not thought to be developmentally able to profit from therapy. During the early 1970s, professionals were called speech pathologists. By the end of the decade, ASHA coined the term speech/language pathologist to reflect the broader view of the services they provide.

The 1970s was a period of transition. ASHA and the professionals it represents sought to further improve the quality of services provided to children. Research data indicated that many articulation problems were developmental in nature, and were corrected naturally with age. Therefore, this period of time also saw a shift in the priorities of speech therapy in the schools. SLPs began to work with fewer children with mild articulation problems, and concentrated on youngsters with severe speech and language problems.

Today, SLPs often consult with regular classroom teachers to work together to remediate minor speech or language problems. SLPs can then work intensively with twenty or thirty children who have significant speech and language disorders. Although articulation deficits are still a large part of SLPs' caseloads, they are interested in language and learning. They serve in a variety of roles ranging from consulting to self-contained classroom teaching. They work with children, their teachers, and their parents.

PREVALENCE

Many professionals believe that children with communicative disorders form the largest population of students with handicaps in the schools (Garbee, 1985). However, as you will see when you read chapter 6, Learning Disabilities, official reports show that the largest single category of exceptional learners are those identified as having learning disabilities (U.S. Department of Education, 1987, 1990). How can we account for these differing opinions? Remember, children are reported by their primary handicapping condition. For a large proportion of children with communicative disorders their primary handicapping condition is learning disabilities, mental retardation, hearing impairments, or health impairments. When the children have *only* a communicative disorder, they are counted in this group. But when we look closely at the caseloads of SLPs, we see that 42 percent of all the children with a communicative disorder they serve have another primary handicapping condition (Dublinski, 1981).

Data from the Twelfth Annual Report to Congress, reported by the U.S. Department of Education (1990), indicate that during the 1988–1989 school years, 2.3 percent of the entire school-age population were identified as handicapped because of speech or language impairments or both. This means that about 2 of every 100 schoolchildren, or a total of 968,908 students received services for communicative disorders as their primary handicapping condition. If this comprises 58 percent of those school-age youngsters SLPs serve, then an additional 701,623 students whose primary handicapping condition was not communicative disorders received supportive services because of speech or language difficulties or both.

As many as 5 percent of all school-age children receive services for communicative disorders, whether this category represents their primary handicapping condition or not (Rice, 1988). This figure includes all students who require speech and language therapy, regardless of their primary handicap. What type of communicative disorder do these children possess? Estimates indicate that 53 percent of the students seen by SLPs have speech disorders, and 47 percent have language disorders (Dublinski, 1981). Of those with speech disorders, the most common problem is articu-

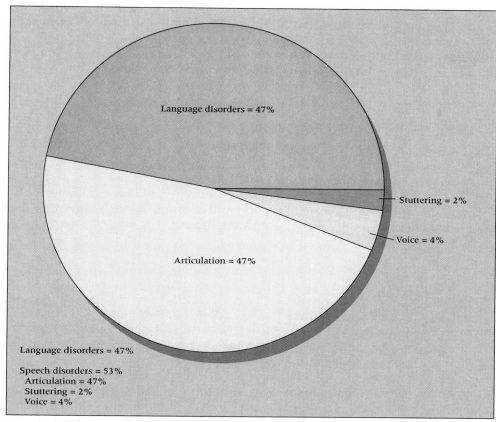

FIGURE 5.4 The Percentage of Students Having Different Types of Communicative Disorders

lation (89 percent). Voice and stuttering are much less common disorders (4 percent and 8 percent of those with speech disorders, respectively). (These data are displayed in Figure 5.4.) Of interest to professionals in the field is the relationship between a student's age and these disabilities. Articulation problems, for example, are more common during the preschool and elementary years. The American Speech-Language-Hearing Association's Committee on Prevention of Speech-Language and Hearing Problems (1984) estimates that 71 percent of all preschoolers with handicaps are diagnosed as having a speech or language disorder as their primary handicapping condition, but this percentage does not continue throughout the school years. Do these problems disappear with age? Are early remediation efforts so successful that these disorders are corrected and do not persist through childhood? Or, are these youngsters reclassified into another handicapping group (such as learning disabilities) as they become older? Although we do not have the answers to all these questions, evidence is mounting of a strong relationship between early language difficulties and a diagnosis of learning disabilities during a child's school years (Mallory and Kerns, 1988).

The foundation for academic learning begins early in a child's life, and many of the skills needed to succeed at various academic tasks are rooted in a strong background in the use of language. The relationship between language and cognition allows individuals to think, problem solve, and generalize their learning to new and novel tasks and situations. Children who are delayed in their use of language or whose language development is incomplete often do not communicate well with others, whether the task is to understand information received orally (spoken language) or visually (written language) or to express their thoughts orally or by writing.

CAUSES AND PREVENTION OF COMMUNICATIVE DISORDERS

It is useful to know what factors cause certain disabilities so they might be prevented. In this section, you will learn that although there are various theories, professionals do not know what causes many different types of speech and language disorders. You will also find that some communicative disorders are preventable, while others are not.

Causes

For the great majority of those who do have a speech disorder, the cause of a speech or language disability is unknown. They are referred to as having functional causes for their communicative disorders. The known causes of communicative disorders are varied and include brain damage, malfunction of the respiratory or speech mechanisms, or malformation of the articulators. Some types of communicative disorders have an organic cause. That means there is a physical reason for the disability. For example, many individuals with severely misaligned teeth cannot articulate well. Think of the speech of the young girl who is missing her front teeth and the old song, "All I want for Christmas is my two front teeth." Once her adult teeth grow in, her articulation will probably be fine. She does not have a speech disorder, but this case serves as an example of how a problem with one of our articulators can affect speech. Other organic causes of communicative disorders are more serious. For example, a cleft lip or palate affects the ability to produce oral speech. Cleft lip or palate occurs in about 1 of every 750 live births (McWilliams, Morris, and Shelton, 1984). Of those, about 25 percent only involve the lip, 50 percent involve the lip and the palate, and the remaining 25 percent have clefts of the palate (Boone, 1987). Most cleft lips can be repaired through plastic surgery and do not result in a long-term or permanent effect on articulation. A cleft palate, however, can present continual problems because the opening of the palate and the roof of the mouth allows excessive air and sound waves to flow through the nasal cavities. This can result in a very nasal-sounding voice and difficulties in producing some speech sounds, such as the "s" and "z." Having a cleft palate is one physical reason for having a speech disorder, and requires the intensive work of many specialists (plastic surgeons, orthodontists, and SLPs) to help the individual overcome the resulting speech disorders.

Figure 5.3, Sander's Chart, shows the ages when children typically acquire various speech sounds. Remember, the ability to articulate speech sounds comes at different times for individual children. Many children "outgrow" their inability to properly articulate sounds. Children who make consistent articulation errors that are not developmental are less likely to learn to make speech sounds correctly without therapy than those who make inconsistent errors (Oyer, Crowe, and Haas, 1987). Therefore, all children who are quite late in acquiring correct production of specific speech sounds and make consistent articulation errors should be referred to an SLP for assessment.

Voice problems are not as common in school-age children. They can be, however, symptomatic of a medical problem. For example, conditions that interfere with muscular activity, such as juvenile arthritis, can result in a vocal disturbance. Voice problems also can be caused by the way we use our voices. Undue abuse of the voice by screaming, shouting, and straining can cause damage to the vocal folds and result in a voice disorder. Rock music singers frequently strain their voices so much that they develop nodules (callouses) on the vocal folds, become chronically hoarse, and must stop singing or have the nodules removed surgically. Teachers who notice changes in children's voices that are not associated with puberty should refer the student to an SLP.

Stuttering, a lack of fluency speaking may be characterized by severe hesitations or the repetition of sounds and words. Although professionals can describe stuttering, they are unable to explain the cause. There are many different theories about the causes of stuttering, but no explanation for its origins is agreed upon by the experts. Gregory (1986) believes that stuttering could be caused by any one of many situations, some of which might be family history, a faulty auditory system for monitoring speech, physiology, language, or environment.

Language disorders also are caused by a variety of situations. Language disorders can result from brain injury or disease that damages the central nervous system and result in **aphasia,** the loss or impairment of language ability. There is a relationship between the inability to hear well at the time language should be developing and language disorders. For example, children with chronic **otitis media,** ear infections, often have associated difficulties with language development. More often, poor language development is caused by various environmental factors, including the lack of stimulation and proper experiences for mental development and learning language.

As we know, language develops throughout childhood. The ability to use language and follow its rules increases with a child's age. Although individual children acquire language skills at different times, there are ranges of development within which most normal children fit. This is similar to children's development of speech sounds. Look at Table 5.4 for a comparison of a child whose language is developing normally and a child whose language is not. Note that most children after the age of three can use some fairly sophisticated language. The language-disordered child, at the same age of forty months, is speaking in only two-word combinations. Compare the differences in language abilities of these two children.

Differences between children whose language is delayed and those whose language is disordered are apparent to those who analyze children's language development. Children with delayed language generally acquire language in the same sequence as their peers, but do so more slowly. Many of these children are not language disordered, and may or may not catch up with their peers. For example, most children with mental retardation have **language delays.** Their language development will remain below that of their peers who have normal intelligence and are developing at expected rates. Leonard claims that children with language disorders tend to follow a common pattern of language acquisition. They develop slowly *and* differently. Review Table 5.4 again. Notice that the language-disordered child uses the word ending "ing" after her mean sentence length is two words. The normally developing child is using "ing" at the same time she is using two-word combinations. Find another instance on the table that the two children are not developing in exactly the same sequence.

aphasia. Loss or impairment of language ability due to brain injury.

otitis media. Middle ear infection which can result in hearing impairments, communication disorders, or learning disabilities if it becomes a chronic condition.

language delay. Slower development of language skills than in the majority of peers; may signal language disorder that will require assistance of a specialist to use language proficiently.

TABLE 5.4. Pattern of Development Shown by a Language-Disordered Child and a Normally Developing Child

Language-Disordered Child			Normally Developing Child		
Age	Attainment	Example	Age	Attainment	Example
27 months	First words	*this, mama, bye bye, doggie*	13 months	First words	*here, mama, bye bye, kitty*
38 months	50-word vocabulary		17 months	50-word vocabulary	
40 months	First two-word combinations	*this doggie more apple this mama more play*	18 months	First two-word combinations	*more juice here ball more T.V. here kitty*
48 months	Later two-word combinations	*Mimi purse Daddy coat block chair dolly table*	22 months	Later two-word combinations	*Andy shoe Mommy ring cup floor keys chair*
52 months	Mean sentence length of 2.00 words		24 months	Mean sentence length of 2.00 words	
55 months	First appearance of -*ing*	*Mommy eating*		First appearance of -*ing*	*Andy sleeping*
63 months	Mean sentence length of 3.10 words		30 months	Mean sentence length 3.10 words	
66 months	First appearance of *"is"*	*The doggie's mad*		First appearance of *"is"*	*My car's gone!*
73 months	Mean sentence length of 4.10 words		37 months	Mean sentence length 4.10 words	
79 months	Mean sentence length of 4.50 words			First appearance of indirect requests	*Can I have some cookies?*
	First appearance of indirect requests	*Can I get the ball?*	40 months	Mean sentence length of 4.50 words	

Source: Reprinted with permission of Merrill, an imprint of Macmillan Publishing Company, from Laurence Leonard, "Language Disorders in Preschool Children" from *Human Communication Disorders: An Introduction* (2d ed.) by G. H. Shames and E. H. Wiig (Eds). © 1990 Macmillan Publishing Company.

Environmental factors also affect children's abilities to acquire language and become proficient in its use. Some children do not develop language because they have no appropriate role models. Some are left alone too often, while others are not spoken to frequently. Some are punished for speaking or ignored when they try to communicate. Many of these children have no reason to speak. They have nothing to talk about, few experiences to share. For these reasons, the number of preschool programs for such children is increasing. To be effective, preschool programs must be enriched with a well-trained staff, appropriate child-use materials, and must provide a variety of experiences for the children.

Prevention

Some types of speech and language disorders can be prevented today. Chapter 10, Hearing Impairments, discusses the prevention of hearing disabilities, and, in turn, the prevention of accompanying speech and language problems.

Table 5.5 lists preventable and unpreventable causes of communicative disorders. As you can see from the table, many disorders have a medical basis. Preventive measures often are needed prior to the birth of a baby. For example, polio and rubella can have devastating effects on an unborn baby. Proper immunization protects adults and children from these and other diseases.

Proper prenatal care is also important to the health of babies. Good nutrition influences the strength and early development of very young children. Also, the

TABLE 5.5. Marge's Examples of Preventable and Nonpreventable Causes of Communicative Disorders

Disorder	Preventable Causes	Nonpreventable Causes
Articulation	Hearing loss Dental abnormalities Chronic infections, especially upper respiratory infections Most types of mental retardation Injuries Infectious diseases (mumps, measles, encephalitis)	Developmental immaturity Neuromuscular disorders associated with unknown etiologies Some types of genetic disorders
Voice	Vocal abuse Upper respiratory infections Allergies Airborne irritants Smoking Hearing loss Trauma and injury Faulty respiration due to allergies, infections, and emphysema Drug and alcohol abuse Some genetic disorders	Constitutional factors Some cancers Viral infections Some genetic disorders
Language	Familial factors Cultural factors Some types of mental retardation Some types of hearing loss Some genetic disorders Brain damage due to prematurity, anoxia, physical trauma, Rh blood factor, infections Malnutrition Low birth weight Fetal alcohol syndrome Prenatal drugs and smoking Strokes Environmental pollutants (lead poisoning)	Some types of hearing loss Some genetic disorders Developmental immaturity Autism Progressive neurological deficits Suspected constitutional factors resulting in psychosis (schizophrenia) Some types of mental retardation

Fluency (Stuttering)	Environmental factors:
	  General stress
	  Communicative stress
	Adverse reactions by others
	Cultural factors
		Suspected genetic factors
		Suspected neurophysiological problems

Source: "The prevention of communication disorders" by M. Marge, 1984, *American Speech-Language-Hearing Association, 26,* pp. 29–33. Reprinted by permission.

availability at birth of proper medical care is crucial so conditions like viral encephalitis can be avoided or treated early. Although encephalitis is no longer common in the general population, it is more prevalent in poorer communities of our society. If left untreated, encephalitis causes brain damage, which, in turn, can result in cognitive and language disabilities. The link between poverty and language disabilities is clear. Those who are poor are less likely to have access to information and medical programs, which puts them at risk for disease. Better public education programs available to the entire population inform people of the necessity of good prenatal care, nutrition, and medical care. These services are expensive, but the positive impact on preventing and overcoming disorders could be even more significant. (See Concepts and Controversies at the end of this chapter.)

One of the most important ways of reducing the impact of any disability is

> **TABLE 5.6. Possible Signs or Characteristics of Communicative Disorders**
>
> *Speech*
>   Makes consistent and age-inappropriate articulation errors
>   Exhibits dysfluencies (repetitions, prolongations, interruptions) in the flow or rhythm of speech
>   Has poor voice quality, such as distracting pitch
>   Is excessively loud or soft
> *Language*
>   Is unable to follow oral directions
>   Is unable to match letters with sounds
>   Has an inadequate vocabulary
>   Demonstrates poor concept formation
>   Has difficulty conveying messages or conversing with others
>   Has difficulty expressing personal needs

through early identification, so treatment can begin as soon as possible. With communicative disorders, children who receive the help and support from highly trained experts can learn to either correct or compensate for their disability. For many of these youngsters, referrals and identification will not occur until their school years, when speech and language is reaching its final stages of development. Alert teachers can be most helpful, by referring youngsters who might have either a speech or language disorder to an SLP. Table 5.6 lists some of the signs of possible communicative disorders. It is important for teachers to remember that many signs of a communicative disorder are part of the normal developmental process. Teachers must balance their concern about a possible disorder with the child's need to work through problems that may just be developmental and can be corrected with age. Paying too much attention to a normally developing speech or language skill can cause problems.

PROFILE OF CHILDREN WITH COMMUNICATIVE DISORDERS

Children with communicative disorders comprise a large and diverse group of youngsters. Some have a particular speech disorder, while others have a language disorder, and yet others have both a speech and language disorder. Naturally, these children have different learning needs. For example, a child with a voice disorder will have a different remediation program from a child who has difficulty articulating speech sounds correctly. Certainly, those with speech disorders have entirely different remediation programs than children with language difficulties. It is important for teachers to understand the differences among these types of communicative disorders so they can make better referrals and more effectively assist with treatment programs.

Speech Disorders

Most children whose primary handicapping condition is a speech disorder (articulation, voice, or fluency impairment) attend regular education classes and function well academically with their peers. Usually, their handicap does not influence their academic learning. If, however, their speech handicap is severe and sustained, they might have some difficulty with their peers in social interactions. Depending on how the peer group reacts to an individual's handicap, the person with a severe handicap might have long-term difficulties with self-concept and independence. This situation is common for those who stutter (Shames, 1986). Stuttering can negatively affect a person's sense of adequacy and confidence. To avoid embarrassment, many people who stutter avoid situations where they have to talk to others. This influences the types of jobs they seek, the friends they make, their relationships with others, and their overall quality of life. Think about how you react to people who have severe speech disorders. Do you look away from them? Do you try to be helpful to the stutterer by finishing his or her sentence? Do you try to avoid the person? Now think about how young children treat their peers who use different speech sounds or have a different voice quality or who stutter. Facing these reactions is an everyday reality for individuals with speech disorders. It is understandable that some would withdraw from society that treats them as different.

Language Disorders

Unlike children with speech disorders, children with language disorders often have related academic difficulties in school. Aram, Ekelman, and Nation (1984) studied twenty youngsters who had attended a preschool for children with language disorders. Ten years after their preschool attendance, 20 percent of the total attended classes for students with mild mental retardation. The largest group—69 percent—required special academic tutoring, were retained a grade, or attended classes for those with learning disabilities. Most of these students were judged to have poor language and academic skills and to be socially less competent than their peers. Only 25 percent of the research group studied scored above the 50th percentile in academic achievement in reading and spelling. Well over half of the group scored below the 25th percentile. Their math achievement scores were even worse. To be sure, children who are attending special preschool programs have been identified early because their language disorders are severe. The children in this study were among the more severely affected children with communicative disorders. Those children with mild language disabilities are typically not identified until they are attending elementary school.

It is important to remember that there is a correlation between poor language development and learning disabilities (Cantwell and Baker, 1987a; Carrow-Woolfolk and Lynch, 1982; Wallach and Butler, 1984), because of the relationship between language development and cognition. For example, students who have difficulty remembering, solving problems, and using language do not function well academically in regular education classes without specialized assistance. In this regard, some data might be misleading. The prevalence of preschoolers identified as having a language disorder is slightly more than 3 percent, while this prevalence in elementary school is approximately 1 percent (Snyder, 1984). Although it would be nice to believe that early remediation has reduced the prevalence of language disorders by school age, it is more likely that these children are relabeled or identified as learning disabled (Mallory and Kerns, 1988; Reichman and Healey, 1983; Snyder, 1984). No doubt some of these youngsters will need continuing and intensive instruction in special education classes for children with language and learning disabilities (discussed in chapter 6).

ISSUES IN EDUCATION

There are a variety of issues in education for children with communicative disorders. Table 5.7 presents the "Bill of Rights for Children with Communicative Disorders,"

TABLE 5.7. Bill of Rights for Children with Communicative Disorders

Every school-aged child should have her or his communication evaluated early in the educational experience.

Each child with a speech-language-hearing difference should have that difference evaluated further to determine the potential impact on the child's social, emotional, and educational future. In this process, the importance of differentiating between the severity of symptoms and the potential effect of the problem must be recognized. It is likely that there is no such thing as a *mild* communication disorder.

Each child with a speech-language-hearing difference should have a plan developed for the handling of that difference. The least action appropriate for each child should be recommendations to classroom teachers and parents and an evaluation scheduled for a specific later time to note the child's progress and for additional recommendations.

Each child in need of speech-language-hearing therapy should have such therapy. The exact type and amount of therapy must be left to the professional discretion of the appropriate specialist, speech-language pathologist (SLP), or audiologist, as should all decisions regarding the child's communication abilities.

Efforts should be made to extend downward to the earliest possible age the evaluation of speech-language-hearing so that preventative measures can be initiated at the earliest possible time, rather than allowing the ravishes of communication disorders to take their toll.

Source: Organization of Speech-Language Services in the Schools: A Manual, p. 3, by R. J. Van Hattum, 1985, Austin, Tx, PRO-ED. Reprinted by permission.

which was devised by Rolland Van Hattum to ensure that the educational system would be more responsive to children with communicative disorders.

Education and the Preschool Child

There are two types of programs for preschool children with communicative disorders. The first are programs for children who have been identified as having speech or language disorders and who need therapy to correct the problem. The second type of program is the early intervention program for preschool children who are at risk for communicative disorders. Many researchers believe early intervention programs enhance the development of at risk children and help them escape the problems that can lead to communicative disorders (Casto and Mastropieri, 1986; Liebergott, Bashir, and Shultz, 1984).

Researchers have identified three categories of children at risk:

1. those with an established risk,
2. those whose environment places them at risk,
3. those with a history that might place them at risk.

Many children with an established risk have a diagnosed medical disorder with a known cause. For example, a medical disorder, like Down syndrome, strongly suggests they will have a communicative disorder. Because the production of speech requires motor skills, many children with cerebral palsy also have an established risk for communicative disorders. Children in this first category should be enrolled in preschool programs.

Children who are environmentally at risk, the second category, are born well and healthy, but are at risk for a communicative disorder because they were abused, neglected, became ill, or failed to thrive as infants. The third category of at risk children comprises infants who have a history (pre- or postnatal) that might lead to

Families are children's first language teachers. Home environments rich in language opportunities help children develop concepts and vocabulary necessary for communicative competence.

a communicative disorder. For example, babies born prematurely or with very low birth weight are more likely to have a communicative disorder than the rest of the population. These children are good candidates for preschool programs.

How should an early intervention program for children at risk be organized? Preschool programs for children with or at risk for communicative disorders should be highly accepting and responsive environments where children are motivated to communicate (Fey, 1986). One national example of early intervention programs is Head Start. Head Start preschool programs were started to assist disadvantaged children. Among the many things children learn in these preschool programs are better thinking and language skills. Early intervention programs need to be directed and supervised by professionals who have expertise in the areas of speech and language. Such programs should foster cooperative play, encourage spontaneous talking, facilitate positive social interactions with peers, and develop responsiveness with conversational partners. Free-play settings should approximate real places where children are free to interact and explore (Wilcox, 1984). Children need to develop language skills that are useful in real settings (Paul, 1985). Because language does not occur in isolation, the social interaction aspects of language and the generalization of those skills must be part of the instructional program (Stremmel-Campbell and Campbell, 1985). In these "play" settings, children need to learn to attend to important cues in the environment, learn about social language functions, and expand their verbal skills. We point out in chapters 2 and 4 that the families of children with special needs also need to facilitate and reinforce the use of newly learned language skills at home. For this reason, most preschool programs include a strong family component.

Professionals who work in preschool programs for children with handicaps or those at risk should help parents implement language learning lessons at home. They also help these children transfer (or generalize) their learning from school to home. The team effort of teachers and parents enriches the child's learning experience. This rich learning experience enhances communication skills in children at risk or with handicaps. Finally, these programs need to be carefully planned, implemented, and evaluated so that they become appropriate educational experiences for the children who need them.

Education and the School-Age Child

Teachers and parents need to be alert to substantial differences in children's speech and language use and development. All communicative skills develop at different rates. Before becoming overly concerned about an individual's speech or language abilities several factors—age, setting, stress—must be considered. When judging the adequacy of children's speech and language, teachers and parents should pay careful attention to the consistency of the speech or language errors before calling in an SLP.

Still, many children do have a serious speech or language disability or both and need special help. The federal government estimates that almost 3 percent of the school-age population are communicatively disordered. Therefore, in a class of thirty children, teachers might expect to find at least one child with a speech or language problem. Of course, children with other handicaps, such as learning disabilities or mental retardation, who are mainstreamed into that class may have difficulties with speech and language. Therefore, it is probable that regular education teachers may also have several students with a speech or language handicap attending their classes.

not necessarily

Today, almost every school in the United States has access to a speech/language pathologist, or SLP. In some cases the SLP is a permanent part of the faculty. In other cases the SLP works part-time at several schools, or may even be an itinerant teacher, traveling from one school to another. In all cases the SLP is available to receive referrals, provide therapy, and consult with teachers concerned about a student's communicative abilities. Regular education teachers play a critical role in the child's life. Teachers should create a rich language learning environment by providing a stimulating instructional setting that encourages oral language (Dudley-Marling and Searle, 1988). How does a teacher make this happen? For one, teachers can include activity centers in their classrooms. One center might contain a set of electrical components to create circuits where children can discover cause-and-effect relationships; another center might contain magnets and containers of different types of materials. Then, some time during the day could be set aside for children to talk about their exploration of the materials found at the activity centers. Teachers can also use this discussion time to talk about other topics of interest to the children, such as current affairs, environmental issues, or sports.

Alert teachers will refer students who *consistently* exhibit poor communication skills for special help. Once a child is identified as communicatively disordered and receives special services from a SLP, the teacher must work closely with the SLP to implement individualized programs for that child. SLPs can offer guidance and practical tips to use in the regular class. For example, an SLP might suggest ways that the teacher can encourage children to expand oral language production (for example, be an attentive listener, provide more opportunities for children to talk about what they are interested in, ask open-ended questions that encourage children to talk more). Many SLPs and teachers also team teach special units that integrate language instruction into the regular curriculum. An example is a unit about a local environmental

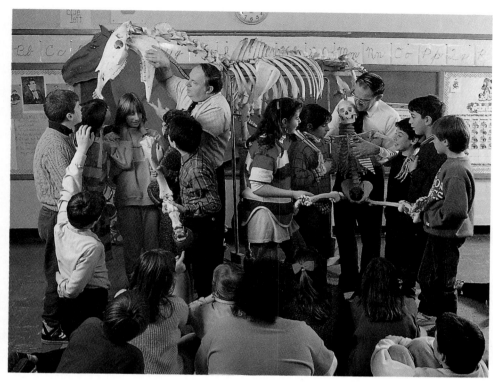

Exciting classroom environments stimulate children's language and learning.

issue culminating in students preparing short position papers, "letters to the editor" of the local newspaper, oral presentations by a "panel of experts," or a debate. SLPs and teachers find that such collaborative efforts greatly improve students' speech and language disabilities. In addition, teachers often see improvement in the language skills of their other students.

TEACHER'S LANGUAGE. The responsibility for creating and fostering a positive learning environment rests with the teacher. Gruenewald and Pollack (1984) illustrate the relationship that exists among the student, the teacher, and the curriculum in all academic settings. Students interact with one another, the teacher, and the curriculum as they participate in classroom activities. The interaction diagrammed in Figure 5.5 is controlled by the teacher. By planning both the content and the manner of delivering the instruction, the teacher can match language with the understanding abilities of the students. The teacher delivering a lecture is the sender; the students are the receivers of the message.

Effective teachers understand the role language plays in learning. Teachers use language as they instruct their pupils about academic subjects. They adjust their language and adapt written materials so students understand the message being delivered. How can teachers make these adjustments? Teachers can facilitate learning by moderating their rate of speech, the complexity of their sentences, and their choice of questions (Gruenewald and Pollack, 1984). Almost naturally, teachers adjust their rate of speech depending on the age and level of their students (Cuda and Nelson, 1976). For instance, first grade teachers speak slower than fifth grade

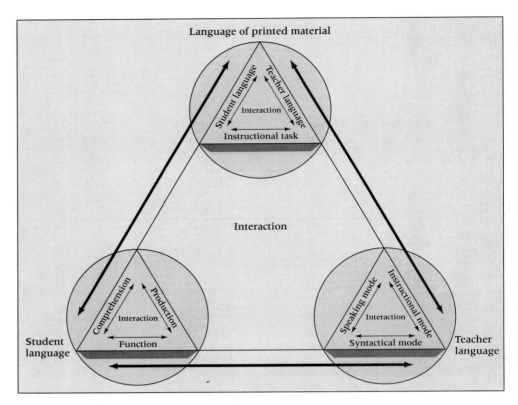

FIGURE 5.5 The Triad of Classroom Language

SOURCE: *Language Interaction in Teaching and Learning*, p. 15, by L. Gruenewald and S. Pollack, 1984, Austin, TX: PRO-ED. Adapted by permission.

teachers. Effective teachers are also careful in their use of referents. They systematically show students the relationships among items and concepts. They expand discussions about new concepts and ideas. They demonstrate to show children how concepts relate. They also ask questions of graduated levels of difficulty to help students test the accuracy of their new knowledge. All of these simple techniques facilitate teaching and learning. These good teaching techniques can be helpful to all professionals working with children with special needs, and they can be particularly helpful to children with disabilities receiving their instruction in regular education settings.

LANGUAGE INSTRUCTION. Students who have a language disability need to be taught how to use language effectively. Language teaching should be part of the curriculum throughout the elementary school years. Unfortunately, in many schools time is not devoted specifically to language development. Language instruction is part of the early school years, but this instruction should continue through at least the upper elementary grades. Just as time is devoted to mathematics, reading, spelling, social studies, and other traditional academic subjects, time should be allocated to teaching the language skills that underlie these subjects. This is particularly true at the elementary level. During these times, children should be encouraged to listen, talk, and understand the language of instruction as well as the language of social interactions. All students benefit from this instruction. For students with communicative disorders, it is essential.

Tips for Teachers

1. Be alert to the presence of speech or language disorders.

2. Refer children suspected of having a communicative disorder to an SLP.

3. Remember that children with speech or language disorders have difficulty communicating with others.

4. Work with the SLP to integrate appropriate language development activities in all academic instruction.

5. Incorporate activities in class that allow children to practice skills mastered in therapy.

6. Always consider the developmental stage of the child suspected of having a communicative disorder before making a referral.

7. Create a supportive environment where children are encouraged to communicate with each other.

8. Create a section of the classroom where the physical environment—perhaps a large, round table—encourages sharing and discussion.

9. Provide opportunities where children feel free to exchange ideas and discuss what they are learning in different subjects.

10. Arrange for activities where children use oral language for different purposes (making a speech, leading a discussion) with different audiences (classmates, children in different classes).

11. Build self-confidence in all children, particularly those with communicative disorders.

barrier games. Games that encourage language development by having children describe objects while others guess what they are describing.

But what if you are not trained in oral language development? For teachers who are not comfortable developing units on language independently, a number of excellent instructional materials are commercially available. For example, the Peabody Language Development Kits (PLDK-Revised), Levels P–3, Developing Understanding of Self and Others (DUSO-Revised), and Classroom Listening and Speaking (CLAS) all include useful activities to increase language and cognitive skills for students in primary grades. Let's Talk, Conversations, Communicative Competence, and Directing Discourse provide ideas for adolescents.

Teachers can use a variety of classroom activities, including games, that encourage children's use of language (Dudley-Marling and Searle, 1988; Fey, 1986; Marvin, 1989). **Barrier games** require children to describe objects while the other players guess what they are describing. In a simple version of this game the teacher creates a card game out of picture cards, such as those found in the Peabody Picture Collection (PPC). The teacher asks the children to tell about a recent experience or make up stories from a set of sequential pictures.

Remember, classrooms should be rich in language experiences for children. In the Tips for Teachers box in this chapter, we provide other suggestions. Learning is not merely listening to lectures, but also mastering the communication game.

Children who have a language disorder typically have difficulties with both written and oral language. These children also have problems mastering other related skills. For example, such students need direct instruction in how to organize their thoughts, so others can better understand their communicative messages. Providing

THE ELEVEN-SENTENCE PARAGRAPH

Children in the upper elementary and middle school grades are often asked to write short paragraphs on specific topics. The topics range from what they did on vacations, to current events, to book reports. Many children with mild handicaps, particularly those with language disorders, find it very difficult to write even one coherent paragraph. They seem unable to develop their thoughts about a topic or an issue from a beginning point to a logical conclusion. The eleven-sentence paragraph method has proved effective in helping these students. How does it work? First, it teaches students to begin a paragraph with a topic sentence. Within the body of the paragraph, students give three reasons that justify or explain the opening sentence. After each reason, the students write one sentence that gives an example of the stated reason and another sentence that supports the example. The paragraph concludes with a summary or rephrasing of the opening sentence. This tactic helps students approach the task of writing paragraphs in a purposeful manner. It provides them with some structure and a way to organize their thoughts and words. Let us see how this works in a classroom:

Henry Pierce is a middle school resource room teacher. His second period students were not receiving passing grades on the homework assignments in their regular education language arts class. He met with the language arts teacher, Beth Sandoval, who showed him a sample of writing from one of his students, Josh. Both teachers agreed that the work was unsatisfactory. The paragraph did not make a point. It was disorganized, and did not lead the reader to a logical conclusion. Ms. Sandoval and Mr. Pierce discussed the paragraph writing abilities of his other six second period students, whose writing skills were comparable to Josh's. Except for one girl, Emily, the other students in Ms. Sandoval's regular education class did not need to spend class time learning how to write cogent paragraphs.

The two teachers agreed that the students might benefit from learning the eleven-sentence paragraph technique. Mr. Pierce rearranged some schedules so he

TABLE 5.8. The Steps to Follow to Write an Eleven-Sentence Paragraph

Sentence	Wording and Punctuation
1. Write topic sentence.	There are three reasons why . . .
2. State the first of the three reasons. (Be sure to include comma in structure.)	First, . . .
3. Give an example.	For example, . . .
4. Support the example.	
5. State the second reason.	Second, . . .
6. Give an example.	For example, . . .
7. Support the example.	
8. State the third reason.	Third, . . .
9. Give an example.	For example, . . .
10. Support the example.	
11. Conclude with a summary or restate topic sentence.	

Source: "The Eleven-sentence paragraph" by R. A. Ray, 1986, unpublished manuscript, University of New Mexico, Albuquerque. Reprinted by permission.

(continued)

Teaching Tactics

(continued)

could spend extra time with his students and Emily helping them improve their writing skills. First, he discussed with the group the importance of being able to write a logical paragraph. He reminded the students that they were not receiving passing grades on Ms. Sandoval's homework assignments, and he explained that the technique he was about to teach the group would help them write better paragraphs.

He then handed out a written description of the steps to follow when using the eleven-sentence paragraph, and explained the handout to the students. On this first day of instruction, Mr. Pierce had the students, as a group, write a paragraph using the steps described in the handout. As the class agreed upon each sentence, Mr. Pierce wrote it on the blackboard. After they were finished, the group corrected the errors with Mr. Pierce's guidance.

On the next day of class, Mr. Pierce divided his class into smaller groups. He assigned each group a different topic, and had them write a paragraph using the eleven-sentence paragraph technique. After the groups finished their paragraphs, he had them switch papers and correct another group's work. When the papers were returned, the correcting group had to explain why they had changed the other group's paragraph. He continued this procedure until he was certain that all of the children understood each step of the technique.

Then, Mr. Pierce had the children write paragraphs by themselves. They could use the handout as they wrote and self-checked (proofread) their paragraphs. On some days, he had the children suggest topics to write about. On other days, he gave the students a list of topics to choose from, and sometimes he assigned the same topic to each student. During this time, Ms. Sandoval reinforced the lessons by encouraging these students to use the eleven-sentence paragraph technique when completing homework assignments for her class.

Does the technique work? Look at Figure 5.6, a sample of Josh's writing after he learned the eleven-sentence paragraph technique. You can see that in only five weeks Josh's writing moved from unacceptable to adequate. This method is easy to teach children, provides them with a structured approach to writing, and does not take long to master.

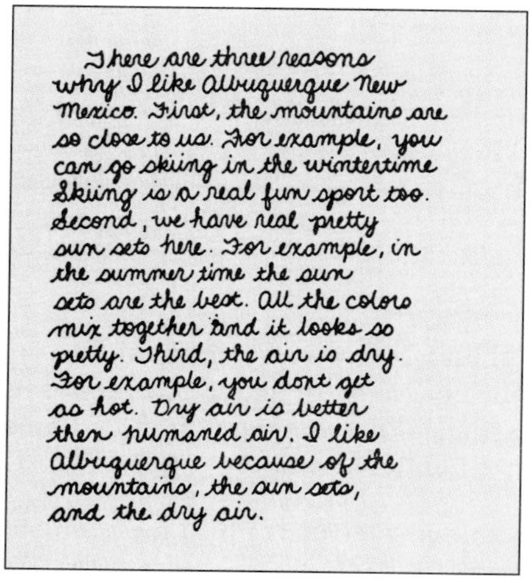

> There are three reasons why I like Albuquerque New Mexico. First, the mountains are so close to us. For example, you can go skiing in the wintertime. Skiing is a real fun sport too. Second, we have real pretty sun sets here. For example, in the summer time the sun sets are the best. All the colors mix together and it looks so pretty. Third, the air is dry. For example, you dont get as hot. Dry air is better then humaned air. I like Albuquerque because of the mountains, the sun sets, and the dry air.

FIGURE 5.6 Josh's Story of Albuquerque Using the Eleven-sentence Paragraph Technique

them with a structure or a systematic way to approach the task is often helpful. Many teachers have found that students who have language disorders can improve their written communications by using a standard format (Smith, 1989). The eleven-sentence paragraph format devised by Ray (1986) is one such technique. You can find an illustrative example of this technique in the Teaching Tactics box. As you read the example, note how this technique helped the middle school student write well-organized, structured paragraphs. The technique is easily adapted to many subject areas in upper elementary and middle schools.

Educational Environments

Children with communicative disorders must have a full array of services available to them (see chapter 3). Most of these children receive therapy in small groups rather than individually. In 1981, 67 percent of children with communicative disorders received therapy from an SLP in some group arrangement, 26 percent received individual therapy, 3 percent received assistance through their classroom teachers with consultative help from an SLP, and 4 percent attended a self-contained or resource class (Dublinski, 1981). Today, self-contained classes for students with communicative disorders, particularly at the early elementary grades, are becoming more available (Rice, 1988). School districts in several states (for example, Arizona, Maryland, New Mexico, and California) are now serving students with severe language disorders in classes designed especially for them. In part, this reflects the need to provide intensive, specialized instruction for those children who have severe language disorders affecting all other aspects of their academic development. It also is an attempt to reduce the number of students classified and served as learning disabled.

Increasingly, SLPs work as consultants with the classroom teachers who implement the remediation programs. The SLP becomes part of a team including regular teacher, parents, and the child. This professional guides and supervises the speech and language program for a particular child but does not work with the child directly. This arrangement is becoming more common in rural areas, where the number of SLPs is limited and the distance between schools is great.

FAMILIES OF CHILDREN WITH COMMUNICATIVE DISORDERS

A PARENT'S PERSPECTIVE ON COMMUNICATIVE DISORDERS

Gloria E. Enlow is the mother of two daughters, now ages twenty and twenty-five. Divorced when the children were five and ten years of age, Ms. Enlow raised them on her own for five years until her remarriage. The younger daughter, Samantha Reid, has cerebral palsy. Ms. Enlow tells her family's story:

Communication is not something that I was thinking about as I held my adorable baby daughter in my arms for the first time. As she looked at me with those big, bright brown eyes, though, I knew there was something different about her. She cried a lot, had trouble sucking and chewing, was quite stiff, and startled easily. As time went on and she was not able to sit unassisted or hold objects by herself, my anxiety heightened. Finally, at eighteen months of age she was diagnosed as having cerebral palsy. Samantha's condition is the result of lack of oxygen at birth, causing brain damage which, for her, means lack of muscle control including the larynx and tongue. The latter translates into labored and, often, unintelligible speech.

Relieved to know just what the problem was, we launched into a regimen of physical, occupational, and speech therapy, which continued through high school. Even though Samantha had special problems, we always treated her as just another member of the family and she fully participated in everything from sledding to religious ceremonies. She was beautiful, happy, well adjusted, and developed a positive self-image. Her own personal desire to be involved in as many normal activities as possible prompted me, her teachers, and school administrators to act as advocates to maximize her potential and tap that obvious intelligence, which was masked by her lack of spontaneous, articulate speech.

We were fortunate that stable and well-established special education programs were already in place by the time Samantha was ready for first grade. Even so, I had to search constantly for the proper care, services, equipment to help Samantha. A major goal was to enhance her speaking capability. As a result, an administrator and speech therapist identified her first augmentative communication device. By age ten, she had learned to program and use the Autocom, which had a digital display and printout capability. This aid made it easier for her to be integrated into her first regular academic class, a major accomplishment for all of us. Although Samantha liked and appreciated her special education classmates and teachers, she did not want to operate in an isolated environment. As Samantha's integration increased, people realized that she had academic ability. This set the stage for her introduction to newer and more sophisticated communication aids and word processors. This strong support from me, classroom aides, assistive devices, and clearly, Samantha's sheer determination all contributed to her ability to accomplish work. Samantha's long-term academic goal was to attend college and through her ability and will she earned an academic scholarship at the University of New Mexico.

As mentioned earlier, Samantha refused to be restricted by her physical disability even as a young child. I remember when she announced one day in elementary school that she was going to learn to write with a pencil. This comment elicited raised eyebrows from teachers, who informed me that her inability to hold *anything* would make that impossible. It took several years, but she did learn to write legibly enough to pen her own letters and address envelopes. It is true she can only do this if she is in just the right position, and the process is very slow, but she writes nevertheless.

Samantha is very concerned about personal appearance and she had resisted the idea of accumulating contraptions to carry around on her wheelchair. However, by the time she was completing high school she knew that an electronic device would be necessary once she was on her own in college. She was introduced to the Touchtalker, a computer with a digital display and synthesized voice. She knew it could be of great assistance to her for communicating her own thoughts in the larger, more unfamiliar environment of the university. It has taken tremendous effort and time for her to learn to use the Touchtalker effectively, but she has mastered it well enough to work it herself and to teach others how to use the equipment. .

From reading this story you may have the impression that Samantha's life and my life were ordered. But that is not the case. I have not discussed my sustained efforts to identify sources of support and necessary resources. I joined committees, councils, and advocacy groups to learn what options and programs were available and to take part in influencing their direction. For many years I wrote Samantha's dictated answers to homework assignments, spent countless hours at the library, and was intimately involved in her progression of study to assure that she would meet college enrollment requirements. A full-time aide was authorized for high school only after many sessions with numerous levels of school officials to justify the need. Similarly, justifying her eligibility for services from state agencies has required numerous evaluations and endless justification. Samantha is considered to be a unique case because of her intelligence and accomplishments despite multiple disabilities. She is determined to earn her degree, live independently, and earn a living. She does not intend to stay dependent on federal or state support. She will require substantial support until she earns a college degree, but the return on investment will be a self-sustaining, accomplished adult who will benefit society.

Today, after completing her first year in college, Samantha works as a paid consultant, on a part-time basis, for the State of Texas teaching children of all ages, teachers, and administrators how to use augmentative communication devices. Parents, teachers, and administrators are anxious to see Samantha demonstrate her Touchtalker and other devices, and to learn how their own children and students can overcome similar disabilities.

Samantha has maintained very high expectations for herself and has been able to achieve most things except for developing close friendships with peers. She has had to grow up faster than a nonhandicapped child and has coped extremely well with the reality of not fitting in with people her age. Most of her friendships continue to be with former teachers, therapists, and administrators because they appreciate her intelligence and look beyond her physical limitations to experience the incredible energy and enthusiasm for sharing information. She looks forward to summers when her two stepsisters visit. It is a time when she and all her sisters can chatter and laugh late into the night catching up on all that has happened during the year.

I only hope that the future holds a reward for her in the way of acceptance for all that she has to offer. She is a wonder and an inspiration to me and those who give her the opportunity to let the real Samantha Reid shine through. She has proven that there are no permanent limits to what she will be able to accomplish as an adult. I am sure we will hear more from and about Samantha in the future.

In this family section we focus on two topics: the home environment as a necessary and critical ingredient for language development in young children and parents as consumers of technology. As you will see, these two topics are critical to children with communicative disorders.

Language and the Home

Throughout this book, in the sections titled Education and the Preschool Child, we stress the importance of the early childhood years for children with exceptionalities. It is at this stage of development that young children begin to develop the motor, social, cognitive, and speech and language skills they will use the rest of their lives. Even for children who spend a great portion of their day out of the home at nursery schools or day care centers, the child's parents and the home environment provide the foundation for these skills. Children whose home environment is rich in language, where parents talk to their children, where children are provided the opportunity to explore using language, and where experiences are broad usually develop fine speech and language skills. When children do not have appropriate language models, when they do not hear a considerable amount of language used, when they do not have experiences to share or a reason to talk, their language is often delayed in its development. Children are individuals; so too are parents and the language environments they provide at home.

Language is normally acquired in a rather orderly fashion (Boone, 1987). During the first year of life, infants hear language spoken around them and organize what they hear so they can gain meaning from it. Toward the end of their first year, infants are able to respond to some of the language they hear. For example, they know their names, respond to greetings, respond to some simple verbal commands, and use objects in their immediate environment. At this time, infants also seem to copy the voice patterns they hear by babbling, and this occurs regardless of the language they hear. Babies begin to talk by first using one- and two-word utterances that are easy to say and have meaning to them (*mama, cookie, doggie*). Throughout their second year of life, children speak using a growing vocabulary, longer sentences, and more complexity. They are learning the form (the rules) of language and how to apply language rules to give meaning to their oral communications. Regardless of the language heard, children seem to develop language in much the same way across cultures, and they do so by interacting with their environment.

To make sense of the language they hear, and ultimately to learn how to use that language, children seem to use various strategies (Lindfors, 1987). They do not all use the same ones, but children who develop language normally apply some structure so they can make sense of what they are hearing. For example, some young children, who do not yet understand oral language, might come to understand an adult's intentions by watching nonverbal clues and comprehending the context of the situation. Through such repeated experiences, they come to learn language as well. Some children attend more selectively and learn more vocabulary for objects they can act on or interact with (*ball, key, sock*), or objects that change or move (*clock, car*). Others focus on specific characteristics of objects (*size, shape, sound*). These children are learning to categorize and organize objects and their thoughts; skills necessary to learn academic and other tasks as well later.

When children do not develop language at the expected rate (refer to Table 5.4 for a comparison of children's language gains), intervention is needed. In almost every community, speech and language specialists are available to provide therapy and instruction to children and to assist parents as they more directly help their children acquire language. With training and guidance from SLPs, parents can be excellent language teachers for children with language disorders. In fact, when home-based intervention is provided by parents, children's language scores improve more than when only clinic-based instruction is provided by professionals (Casto and White, 1987). What kinds of strategies can parents use at home to improve language skills? Specialists might suggest that family members, during their normal interactions with the child, specifically label or name objects in the home. They also suggest that simple words be used more often to describe the objects the child is playing with: "This ball is red. It is round. It is soft." Specialists also suggest that the family include the child in more activities outside of the home, such as visits to the zoo, the market, or a shopping center, so the child has more to talk about. Family members should model language and have the child imitate good language models. For example, a parent might say, "This pencil is blue. What color is this pencil?" and the child should be encouraged to respond that the pencil is blue. Children need a reason to talk, and the home environment can foster children's oral expression by

assistive technology. Technological equipment designed to help individuals function in their environment.

speech synthesizers. Equipment that creates voice.

providing many rich and diverse experiences for children to talk about and by providing excellent language models for children to imitate.

Parents as Consumers of Technology

Some children are unable to develop understandable speech. For example, some children with cerebral palsy have difficulty communicating (see chapter 11, Physical Disabilities and Health Impairments, and Gloria Enlow's comments at the beginning of this section). Many of these children understand and use language, but cannot produce speech sounds correctly. Individuals can benefit from the use of **assistive technology** to communicate with others. An example of such technology is **speech synthesizers,** the development of which has advanced rapidly over the past years. Most certainly, these and other devices will become a part of these individuals' lives, even during their preschool years. As more and more equipment and technology become available, parents of the children who need it will have to become more sophisticated consumers. They will need to judge the worth of a piece of equipment, its cost for purchase and maintenance, and the family budget.

Parents must resist the temptation to acquire every new version of electronic communication devices in the hopes of making their child's speech seem normal. Fishman (1987) makes an important point: "Just as an individual who is a paraplegic and given a wheelchair cannot be equal in physical ability to a person who is able to walk, a speech-impaired individual with a communication aid cannot be equal in speech ability to a person who is able to speak" (p. 13). Parents will need to obtain objective evaluations of new equipment. How can the parents make these technical judgments? In some cases, the SLP and the teacher can assist the family and the student. These professionals can help parents evaluate hardware and software, and help parents find knowledgeable experts who can help them decide what equipment will be beneficial to these youngsters and their special needs. This is a treacherous area for parents who must juggle their desire to give their child the best with their need to be objective.

ADULTS WITH COMMUNICATIVE DISORDERS

"Most communicative disorders in adults are acquired after a lifetime of using normal communicative skills" (Boone, 1987, p. 129). Typically, communicative disorders in adults are caused by disease, accidents, or aging. Those who had some kinds of communicative disorder during childhood represent a small percentage of this adult group. To date, very little is known about how children with communicative disorders fare when they become adults. King, Jones, and Lasky (1982) followed up fifty individuals who had attended one university speech and hearing clinic when they were preschoolers. At the time of the study, most of their subjects were still in high school, so we do not know anything about this group as independent adults. According to their parents, 42 percent still had some communicative difficulties; the highest percentage of those were originally diagnosed as having language, not articulation, disorders. Almost half of the entire group studied intended to attend college, with an additional 14 percent planning to attend vocational schools. In another follow-up study (Hall and Tomblin, 1978), parents of adults in their early 20s were surveyed. Their children had also attended a university speech and hearing clinic as young children. Again, there appears to be a substantial difference between the group identified as language disordered and the group identified as articulation disordered. According to their parents, 50 percent of the group with language impairments still had communicative difficulties, while only one member of the group with articulation disorders was reported as having communicative difficulties. All members of both groups completed high school, but a small proportion of those with language impairments completed college. This is probably related to their performance in elementary and secondary schools. The group with language impairments had poorer academic records, and had a special difficulty with reading. According to these researchers, there seems to be a relationship between language disorders and the ability to acquire and become proficient in reading, a basic skill needed for academic success. Much more research in this area is needed. However, these two studies indicate that continued and extensive remediation efforts for individuals with language impairments are probably necessary into adulthood.

In addition to these few **follow-up** studies, a few individual case reports also indicate that individuals with communicative disorders have continued difficulties as adults. For example, Shames (1986) reports about a young woman who stuttered throughout her childhood and young adult life. This person avoided social interactions with others and remained dependent on her family. Her feelings of inadequacy permeated her life. Although prepared for a professional job, she did not seek employment because she was embarrassed by her speech. Such situations are probably very common for people with severe speech or language disabilities. Unfortunately, we do not know the number of persons nor the degree to which their lives are affected. We do know that the number is substantial.

Other studies of children with communicative disorders provide troubling clues for their futures as adults. For example, in Cantwell and Baker's research (Cantwell and Baker, 1987b), 600 children who had speech and language disorders were included in their sample. Of that group, 45 were language disordered, 203 were speech disordered, and 352 were speech and language handicapped. Over half of the group studied had a psychiatric disorder as well as a communicative disorder. Of those with only a speech disorder, 31 percent had a psychiatric disorder; of those with a language disorder, 73 percent had psychiatric difficulties. These data indicate that more attention needs to be paid to this possible relationship between communicative and psychiatric disorders, and remediation programs should include components that assist these individuals in their relationships with others and their own personal adjustment.

Another study indicates that language disabilities continue throughout the adolescent years (Prather, 1984). The high school students with communicative disorders who participated in this study made little additional progress through their later years in school. Either tests are insensitive to language changes, or these youngsters stop improving in the area of communication. It appears that they make little improvement in areas related to grammar, and make only some improvement in increasing their vocabularies. Remember the earlier discussion of Blank's concept of communicative competence (Blank, Rose, and Berlin, 1978), and its importance in all aspects of individuals' lives. Apparently, if people do not master pragmatic aspects of language (for example, topic maintenance, sensitivity to misunderstandings, strategies for problem solving) during their school years, they probably will not do so as adults. Without these skills, they could have difficulties in social interactions and job performance. Prather also points out that many adults who had communicative disorders that were persistent throughout childhood do not seek professional help when they are adults. They do not have the motivation to seek assistance or profit from therapy. Their prevailing attitude seems to be, "Therapy did not work before, why should it now?" Clearly, we need more follow-up studies of this population. Educators need to know whether this group does have significant problems in adulthood. They need to know what those problems are so they can plan better instructional programs for these children.

follow up. To provide later evaluation, diagnosis, or treatment of a condition.

TECHNOLOGY AND COMMUNICATIVE DISORDERS

obturator. A device that creates a closure between the oral and nasal cavities when the soft palate is missing or damaged.

Technology has had an impact on rehabilitation and the instructional programs of some children with communicative disorders. For example, an **obturator** is used to help create a closure between the oral and nasal cavities when the soft palate is

SAMANTHA REID TELLS US WHAT TECHNOLOGY MEANS TO HER

Earlier, Gloria Enlow shared her experiences as a parent of a child with a severe communicative disorder. Below, Samantha Reid, her daughter, explains to us what technology means to her. Samantha was born with cerebral palsy, which affected her speech. Samantha has used and demonstrated different types of communication boards and devices since she began elementary school. Now twenty years old, Samantha is a student at the University of New Mexico. She is currently using a device called a Touchtalker, which has a synthesized voice. This device allows her greater opportunity to interact with others.

Until I started school I used my own speech, but my speech was not clear, and I was becoming frustrated having to repeat myself. Eventually, I started using an electric typewriter for classwork and to communicate when people could not understand me. My speech pathologist, Claudia Pacini, also drew symbols and letters on a piece of cardboard which I used as a communication board by pointing to symbols or spelling out words with my thumb. Then, during the late seventies and early eighties, Mrs. Pacini took me to workshops with her to view and demonstrate adaptive/assistive devices. The Autocom was one of the first major breakthroughs in adaptive devices. It helped me tremendously at school. My seventh-grade English teacher grew to hate the Autocom because it tended to break down in the middle of her English class.

When I was ready for college, I learned about two other adaptive communication devices. One of them, the Speech Pac, is simple to operate, but it is usually used by people who understand fewer words. The Touchtalker was more sophisticated, but takes much more time to learn to use effectively. I have always loved challenges, but I thought college was enough of a challenge without having to learn this difficult technology. However, I soon discovered that the Speech Pac although easy to learn was too limited. Also, the Touchtalker has a female voice, and I really did not want to use a speech synthesizer that had a man's voice. Before I knew it, I had taken on another challenge—learning how to use the Touchtalker.

Today, I use the Touchtalker not only when speaking to strangers and taking tests, but also when I act in my capacity as a consultant in the State of Texas. As a consultant I am paid to demonstrate the usefulness of augmentative communication devices for parents, teachers, and administrators who work with children with speech disorders.

Assistive devices have helped me greatly in sharing my own thoughts and ideas with people, and will be a major contributor to my growing independence.

missing or has been damaged by a congenital cleft. An artificial larynx can be implanted when the vocal folds become paralyzed or have been removed because of a disease. >?

Communication boards have long been available to persons who are unable to speak. A person wishing to communicate merely points to pictures or words that have been placed on the board. These communication devices will probably be replaced almost entirely by computerized communication devices. As discussed in chapter 10, Hearing Impairments, advances in computer technology, particularly in the area of voice synthesis, have changed and will continue to change the mode of communication for many of these individuals. With a computer a person can type in the message to be conveyed and the computer converts that message to voice or print. Some computers allow the individual to select the voice qualities the machine uses. Some are solely dedicated to speech production, while others have a voice capability as one of its many functions. Some computerized communicative devices are even small enough to be worn on the person's wrist. *not necessarily*

Many individuals who are severely speech impaired, their families, and the professionals who work with them resist using electronic communication aids (Fishman, 1987). These people fear that the individual will lose the motivation to continue to develop speech. Many practitioners, however, have found the opposite to be the case: speech often improves as the individual masters a communication aid. They believe the person becomes more eager to communicate with others when communication is easier. Perhaps this is why technology, in the form of electronic communication devices, is now being used in many preschool settings. It is clear the availability of these machines, allowing nonverbal people to express their thoughts orally, will revolutionize children's educational programs. Individuals who have mastered the use of such sophisticated equipment should be able to attend and participate more fully in regular education programs during their school years.

Learning to use electronic communication devices can enable even a student with severe communicative disorders to engage in complex interchange of ideas with others.

Technology is also influencing professionals' work in this area. A survey of all members of the American Speech-Language-Hearing Association showed that in 1982, only 28 percent of the members used computers in their work. In 1984 that number jumped to 38 percent (Hyman, 1985). Computer use is an especially important part of SLPs work today. Because of the amount of paperwork and information to manage, ASHA developed a computerized management package for SLPs (Clymer, 1988). This package organizes all the administrative tasks such as report writing, correspondence regarding individual program plans, management of clients' assessment data, attendance records, developing daily and weekly schedules, grade books, mileage records, and quantification of services provided. Computer packages have also been developed to assist in analyses of speech samples from children. SLPs can now get more detailed information about children's speech and language production as well (Rice, 1988). These data assist SLPs in understanding a child's communicative disorder, and help them plan more efficient remediation programs. Numerous therapy exercises are also available in a computerized learning format to use in school and home if a computer is available.

Concepts and Controversies

Can We Afford Not To?

"When the Great Plague was devastating Russia many years ago, someone asked what was being done about it. The answer was that another thousand coffins had been ordered! To my mind, the tens of billions of tax dollars allocated to various government agencies concerned with our chronic social problems have accomplished little more than buying those coffins." (Anderson, 1972, p. 1)

Two decades ago, Camilla May Anderson called for our government to address the problems of health care. Her special concern was the prevention of diseases causing lifelong disabilities and death. In her book, *Society Pays: The High Costs of Minimal Brain Damage in America,* she pointed out that diseases affecting pregnant women and young children can result in brain damage, which even if minimal, can profoundly influence children's abilities to learn. The health care issue is still a topic of debate today.

The measles virus is an example. Measles is a very dangerous disease that can easily be prevented. The airborne virus can cause death and serious handicapping conditions in children (visual impairments, hearing impairments, brain damage, language disorders) especially if contracted by a pregnant woman or a young child. A vaccine that prevents measles has been available in this country since 1963. During the 1960s approximately 400,000 cases of measles were reported each year. This number dropped to 1497 in 1983, and predictions were made that the disease would soon be eradicated. However, a new epidemic of measles is raging in the United States today. Why is this so? Two major causes are that free vaccinations were no longer available for those who were poor, and that many parents failed to make sure that their children are properly vaccinated. Nationally, 45 children died of measles in 1989; 40 died during the first four months of 1990. In Los Angeles County, the number of measles cases in 1986 was 42, in 1989 it was 1202, and in the first four months of 1990 it reached 2000 (Hilts, 1990). The epidemic is predominantly affecting unvaccinated African-American and Hispanic preschoolers living in inner cities, but the disease also struck secondary school students, college students, migrant workers, and other adults (Bradley, 1990). It is estimated that while 95 percent of school-age children are vaccinated because it is required, only 50 percent of inner city preschoolers are vaccinated. Remember, the disease is most devastating when it strikes young children.

Should the federal government take on the responsibility of a national immunization program? How much does it cost? The cost for an individual child is small, but for all children is quite high. But what are the costs of not preventing diseases like measles and rubella? ASHA's Committee on the Prevention of Speech-Language and Hearing Disorders (1984) cites an excellent example of how preventative measures are cost effective. In 1969 the Bureau for the Education of the Handicapped (BEH) conducted a study of the impact of the rubella epidemic that hit this country during the early 1960s. The findings of this study show that if, in 1963, all young females had been vaccinated for rubella, the epidemic would not have occurred. The cost of a national immunization program in the 1960s would have been $10 million. Although considered, the program was not implemented. The rubella epidemic left between 20,000 to 30,000 children handicapped. BEH estimated that the projected total expenditure for special education and related services for all the children who became handicapped because of the rubella epidemic would approach $1 billion. This staggering amount is probably an underestimation of the financial costs. Wisconsin's Department of Health and Social Services developed a series of comparative cost figures for prevention versus treatment of mental retardation, mental illness, and alcoholism. They projected that $1 million could be saved for each individual whose retardation was prevented (ASHA, 1984).

Currently, people mainly pay private health care providers to immunize themselves and their children. Those who cannot afford health care are doing without. It is this group that is suffering the most. Should the federal government step in? Can we afford it? Can we afford not to have it?

SUMMARY

Communication does not occur in isolation. It requires at least two parties and a message. Communication is impaired when either the sender or receiver of the message cannot use the signs, symbols, or rules of language effectively. There are two general kinds of communicative disorders: speech and language. A speech disorder is present when the sender's articulation, voice, or fluency patterns impair the receiver's attending to or understanding the message. When either the sender or the receiver of the message cannot use the signs, symbols, or rules of language, a language disorder might exist.

1. The field of communicative disorders has grown and changed over the years. In the past, remediating speech disorders filled the large caseloads of SLPs. More recently, professionals in the field are concerned about children's abilities to communicate with others. For most of us, oral language is the primary mode of socializing, learning, and performing on the job. Therefore, communicative competence is the most important goal that SLPs have for many of their students. Clearly, language needs to become a topic of substantial interest for all educators.

2. Articulation problems are the most common type of speech disorder in children. Children with articulation problems make consistent errors in producing speech sounds. Articulation errors are part of the normal developmental sequence, with most children able to correctly produce individual speech sounds at various ages. Teachers should be careful not to confuse dialect (regional) differences in speech. They should also be careful not to refer young children whose speech is developing normally but is not yet correct.

3. About half of the children seen by SLPs have language disorders. Although the cause of most language disorders is unknown, the relationship between language disorders and delays in cognitive development is clear.

4. Communicative disorders is not the single largest category of exceptionalities. However, 5 percent of the school-age population is estimated to have communicative disorders, and 42 percent of the youngsters seen by SLPs have another primary handicapping condition (mental retardation, learning disabilities, hearing impairments). Most certainly, the size of the group of students who have a communicative disorder—whether it is or is not their primary handicapping condition—is substantial.

5. Early intervention programs are important and can reduce the impact of a communicative disorder. Unfortunately, relatively few of these children receive services as young children. Those who do are usually those children who are very severely impaired or those who have an accompanying handicapping condition (in addition to their communicative disorder). There are a number of reasons for this situation. Language does not emerge until about the age of 3, and many youngsters who are not talking by this age might well be late in language development. Some of these youngsters go unrecognized until their school years, and others are not referred because professionals are uncomfortable labeling very young children. For many children at risk, there are no services available because states are not mandated to serve preschoolers (age three to five) at risk of having a handicapping condition. (By age three, they must be identified as having a specific handicapping condition.) Certainly, criterion need to be developed to assist in the identification and referral of these youngsters at an earlier age.

6. The role of the family is crucial to the development of strong language skills. During the first few years of life, children learn how to gain meaning from the language they hear, and learn to express themselves using oral language. The relationship between language development and cognition (thinking skills) is clear, and it is during infancy that these skills begin to develop. The family and the home environment impact on language acquisition and development in many ways; it is during this developmental period that children develop reasons to communicate with others, as well as the beginnings of communicative competence.

7. Little is known about adults who had a communicative disorder as children. Unlike many other groups of people with handicaps, few services are available to them. Scant data are available to indicate how they function in mainstream society.

8. The role of the teacher is important in the educational programs available to students with communicative disorders. Teachers need to integrate language development into the entire curriculum, as well as provide direct instruction about oral language to their students. Teachers should try to match the language they use to the language comprehension skills of their students. They must create a language-rich environment for *all* students. Because of their role in the referral process, teachers also have a critical role to ensure that children with communicative disorders are identified and receive the specialized services they require. They also assist in remediation programs, collaborate with SLPs, as well as work to foster maintenance and generalization of skills mastered in therapy.

9. Speech/language pathologists, experts in the field of communicative disorders, serve youngsters whose speech or language impairs their ability to communicate effectively with others. Professional SLPs work in a variety of roles. Depending on the individual's difficulties, SLPs assess and remediate deficits that prevent efficient and effective participation in communication. The most common problems they address are speech disorders. The second most common problem involves language development. SLPs provide both supportive and direct services. They work not only with students whose primary handicapping condition is either a speech or language deficit, but also with individuals who have a primary handicapping condition other than communicative disorders. These professionals serve in a variety of roles ranging from consultative services to classroom instruction. They work with families, teachers, small groups of children, and individuals.

DISCUSSION QUESTIONS

1. Develop three examples of teachers' language use that would not match the communicative competence of second grade students.

2. What strategies might be implemented to assure that Van Hattum's Bill of Rights for Children with Communication Disorders be guaranteed to the students for whom it was intended?

3. What accommodations might regular classroom teachers need to make for children with speech disorders? language disorders?

4. Provide some rationales for early intervention programs for children at risk for communicative disorders.

5. Explain why follow-up studies need to be conducted for individuals with communicative disorders.

SUPPLEMENTARY BOOKS AND VIDEOS

People with communicative disorders have not been included in as many fictional and nonfictional roles in either books or films as people with other disabilities. A few we were able to identify are listed below.

Books

Butler, S. (1936). *The way of all flesh.* New York: The Limited Editions Club.

Byars, B. (1970). *The summer of the swans.* New York: Viking.

Caldwell, E. (1948). *Tobacco Road.* New York: Grosset and Dunlap.

Johnson, W. (1930). *Because I stutter.* New York: Appleton.

Melville, H. (1962). *Billy Budd.* Chicago: University of Chicago.

Videos

World according to Garp. (1982). Twentieth Century Fox.

This side is good. (1983). Filmmakers Library.

The pain of shyness. (1985). ABC News 20/20—Filmmakers Library.

Life is but a dream. (1985). Filmmakers Library.

LARRY RUSSELL'S teacher reports that the 17-year-old artist from Richmond, Virginia, has just begun to blossom into his own individuality. Larry, who has emotional and learning challenges, is also skilled at woodworking and creating designs for blue jeans. He recently held a one-man show for Very Special Arts Virginia.

*C*hapter Six

LEARNING DISABILITIES

*L*earning Objectives

After studying this chapter, you should be able to:

- **Describe two major definitions of learning disabilities and list the differences between them**

- **Provide reasons why students identified as having learning disabilities in one state or school district might not qualify for special education services elsewhere**

- **Discuss how learning disabilities can result in a life long handicapping condition**

- **Explain the debates being held among professionals about what constitutes an appropriate education for these students and in what setting it should be provided**

COLLEGE STUDENTS WITH LEARNING DISABILITIES SPEAK OUT

College students with learning disabilities were asked a set of questions that reveal their feelings and some of the challenges they face as young adults.

ANDRA ARWOOD
Twenty-year-old freshman
First identified as having a learning disability in first grade
Major: considering elementary education

KYLE MORGAN
Twenty-two-year-old sophomore
First identified in second grade
Major: considering athletic training

JACK GELFAND
Twenty-six-year-old freshman
First identified in eleventh grade
Major: plans on business

TIMOTHY DANIEL HERRON
Twenty-year-old freshman
Identified in eighth grade
Major: undecided

TANLEY GRESS
Twenty-nine-year-old sophomore
Identified when she was ten years old
Major: preparing for economics

DAVID BARRINGTON CONRAD
Twenty-six-year-old junior
Identified last summer
Major: mechanical engineering

CHRIS BACA
Twenty-three-year-old junior
Identified in middle school
Major: fine arts

SHAWN MURRAY
Twenty-four-year-old junior
Identified during college
Major: pre-law

ALLAN GROSS
Thirty-five-year-old senior
Identified last summer
Major: geography
Minor: special education

PETER HAINES
Twenty-three-year-old junior
Identified while in college
Major: history

Why did you decide to come to college?

ANDRA: "So I could help others, better than I was helped."

KYLE: "I want to receive a better education to pursue a better job. Both of my parents are college graduates. This gave me the incentive and push to succeed."

TIMOTHY: "I wanted to play college golf. Also, I know I need a four-year degree to succeed and achieve the standard of income I am used to right now."

DAVID: "To earn a degree so my engineering designs will have credibility when viewed by others."

CHRIS: "I used to go with my mother to her classes when she attended college when I was ten years old until I was fifteen, and this experience fueled my desire to go to college. I enjoyed the atmosphere of learning. I could see my mother bettering herself through learning, and she was happy. So, to me, college was a good place that I eagerly awaited."

What are your goals?

ANDRA: "To help other children, and make me a better person also."

KYLE: "To finish college, get a good job in my field, and to have a family."

JACK: "To graduate from college, and proceed to a well-paying job or, I hope, start my own business."

TIMOTHY: "Play four years of golf and become an All American, and to get a four-year degree within five and a half years."

TANLEY: "To be the world's greatest economist. (You think I'm joking. I can do it. No problem now.)"

CHRIS: "I have always enjoyed art, and I am now working toward a bachelor's degree in fine arts. And, then, the sky's the limit!"

SHAWN: "To attend law school and then enter politics."

ALLAN: "First, to finish this semester with passing grades; second, to graduate from college during May of next year; and third, to teach or get into some career by getting a useful degree."

PETER:	"Improve my grades, play lacrosse better, travel, teach history, and raise a family."

What accommodations/support do you need and use from the university?

ANDRA:	"I get help from a tutoring service at the university and help at home."
KYLE:	"Tutoring, extended time for test-taking, talking books, counseling, and support group."
TANLEY:	"Special Services: It has lots of things. I did use a tape recorder, but this semester I don't need it. I take advantage of extended test time and tutoring in math."
DAVID:	"Very few. I am still learning what is available, but I do use a word processor for English."
CHRIS:	"The most important accommodation, one I feel has been the most helpful to me, is the support and understanding of others. For example, the people who devote their careers to educate, understand, and support me because they understand how I can overcome my learning disabilities make a difference."
SHAWN:	"Books on tape and adjustments to class tests."
ALLAN:	"People who read some of the difficult parts of my textbooks to me, and proctored testing through Special Services that allows me extra time on exams."
PETER:	"Extended time on tests, special LD tutors, and books on tape."

What social aspects of college do you participate in?

KYLE:	"I am a member of Resident Hall Student Senate, and a representative for Coronado Hall Student Government."
JACK:	"Karate, and I swim."
TIMOTHY:	"I am on the varsity golf team; we practice three to six hours a day."
CHRIS:	"I have always participated by going to theatrical and musical events like plays, movies, and concerts. But recently, I have been participating in the political aspects of college life. I am also president of MEChA (a Chicano student group)."

SHAWN: "I participate in College Republicans, Rodeo Western Club, and Western Dance Club."

What would you like to say about your disability to other college students who are not learning disabled?

KYLE: "We may have disabilities, but we are just like you. We walk, talk, feel, and dream just the same."

TIMOTHY: "I am not dumb, but not highly intelligent. My disabilities give me a hard time in remembering almost everything, like reading, taking notes, and listening. It is not a cop-out. I know that I take twice as long as some of my friends to study the same subject."

CHRIS: "I would like to say that no obstacle is too big. It just requires that we learn more than the average person in order to overcome the disability. They too should learn more so maybe they can understand why some people learn differently. We are not dumb or slow, we just learn differently. Moreover, the learning process for a LD student sometimes requires special accommodations, which is *not* a way to take the easy road, but a necessity."

ALLAN: "It is not something that I'll ever be cured of, but I am always learning new ways to adapt to my disabilities."

PETER: "Everybody is different. Some people have blue eyes, some brown. Some people learn differently than others. Just because I'm learning disabled doesn't mean I'm stupid. College is a place to seek knowledge and an understanding of the world around us. *Always* keep an open mind."

1. Why do you think so many of these people were identified as having learning disabilities while they were attending college?

2. What support systems do these students need (that are different from your needs) to succeed in college?

3. How are these students like you?

learning disabilities (LD). A handicapping condition where the individual possesses average intelligence but is substantially delayed in academic achievement.

heterogeneity. Variation among members in a group.

We have all had experiences where no matter how hard we try it is difficult to understand the information presented. In school we might sit through lectures and not understand the messages the instructor was trying to deliver. We may not understand the reading material for a particular class. We find it impossible to organize our thoughts to write a coherent essay or report. Sometimes, we stumble over words and are unable to convey our thoughts, feelings, or knowledge. And, occasionally, we are uneasy and uncomfortable with other people. For most of us, these situations are the rare exception. For people with **learning disabilities,** however, one or more of these situations is commonplace.

People who have learning disabilities belong to a group of very diverse individuals, but they do share a common problem: They do not learn in the same way or as efficiently as their nonhandicapped peers. Although most possess normal intelligence, their academic performance is significantly behind their classmates'. Some have great difficulty learning mathematics, but most find the mastery of reading and writing to be their most difficult challenge (Mercer, 1987).

In this chapter you will come to understand learning disabilities. This exceptionality presents many puzzling questions to individuals with this handicap, their families, their teachers, and the researchers who have specialized in this area. You will learn that because of this group's diversity **(heterogeneity),** there is no single answer about why such otherwise normal individuals have problems learning at the same rate and in the same style as their nondisabled classmates. You will learn that professionals in this area do not agree about how best to teach these individuals. You will also learn that many individuals overcome their learning disabilities through highly specialized, intensive, individualized instructional programs. Unfortunately, for many others a learning disability will last a lifetime.

LEARNING DISABILITIES DEFINED

Students who qualify for special education services because of a learning disability must meet specific criteria established by the state and school district in which they live. These criteria are based on federal or professionally adopted definitions, or their combination. However, the way the definition of learning disabilities is interpreted and students are identified varies considerably from state to state (Mercer, King-Sears, and Mercer, 1990). Most state and local school districts have detailed and complex eligibility requirements for educational programs designed for students with learning disabilities. Many use complicated formulas combining a student's age, intelligence quotient, achievement test results, behavioral observations, and other performance data (Forness, Sinclair, and Guthrie, 1983). Some states also require a test revealing the student's perceptual abilities be included in the diagnostic battery. All states use a general definition as the basis for their specific criteria for identification of these students. Nationally, two definitions of learning disabilities are used most often. One is included in IDEA; the other was adopted by a coalition of professional and parent organizations concerned with learning disabilities. Let us look at these two major definitions.

The first is the federal government's definition: IDEA

"Specific learning disability" means a disorder *in one or more of the basic psychological processes* involved in understanding or in using *language, spoken or written,* which may manifest itself in an imperfect ability to *listen, think, speak, read, write or do mathematical calculations.* The term includes such conditions as *perceptual handicaps, brain injury, minimal brain dysfunction, dyslexia and developmental aphasia.* The term *does not include* children who have learning problems which are primarily the result of visual, hearing or motor handicaps of mental retardation, or emotional disturbance, or of environmental, cultural or economic disadvantage. (U.S. Office of Education, 1977, p. 65083; emphasis added)

The National Joint Committee on Learning Disabilities' definition is as follows:

"Learning disabilities is a general term that refers to a *heterogeneous group of disorders* manifested by significant difficulties in the acquisition and use of *listening, speaking, reading, writing, reasoning or mathematical abilities.* These disorders are intrinsic to the individual, *presumed to be due to central nervous system dysfunction,* and may occur across the *life span.* Problems in *self-regulatory behaviors, social perception, and social interaction* may exist with learning disabilities but do not by themselves constitute a learning disability. Although learning disabilities *may occur concomitantly* with other handicapping conditions (for example, sensory impairment, mental retardation, serious emotional disturbance) or with extrinsic influences (such as cultural differences or insufficient or inappropriate instruction), they are not the result of those conditions or influences. (National Joint Committee on Learning Disabilities, 1988, p. 1; emphasis added)

Basically, the difference between these two definitions rests in orientation about the causes of the disability. The federal definition is older, and reflects a more medical orientation. The medical orientation in turn reflects the earliest work done in this field by doctors working with individuals who suffered injuries to the brain. (See the history section in this chapter). Notice that terms like brain injury and **dyslexia** are included in the federal definition, but not in the more recent National Joint Committee's definition. The Joint Committee's definition states that an individual's learning disability may be due to a **central nervous system dysfunction,** but allows for the inclusion of individuals who do not have such a dysfunction. There are other differences between these two definitions; see if you can identify several more.

The more recent definition requires that the primary reason for a student's handicap be learning disabilities, but allows for another disability as well. Therefore, we now see educational records indicating that a student is deaf and has a learning disability or is gifted and has a learning disability. Some states insist that students be classified and served by their primary disability; that is, they will not "serve a student twice." In those states, a student is eligible for services for either those who are hearing impaired or learning disabled, but not both. Other states have taken a different approach. For example, they have created classroom programs for students who are both gifted and learning disabled (see chapter 7).

There has been considerable debate about the definition of learning disabilities. Many definitions have been developed and are being used; Cartwright, Cartwright, and Ward (1989) identified thirty-eight different definitions of learning disabilities. Some differences among these definitions are due to philosophical orientations about what causes the disability and how it should be treated. Some definitions are more medically oriented; others are more educationally based, while others seek to limit the size of this population of learners. The common features in definitions of learning disabilities are summarized in Table 6.1.

Although the federal and the National Joint Committee definitions are most commonly used, many professionals and parents are not satisfied with them and continue to work toward a more precise definition of learning disabilities. Precisely identifying individuals with this handicap is often difficult because learning disabilities is not a single condition. Some suggest that if we can develop a classification

dyslexia. Severely impaired ability to read, presumed to be caused by a central nervous system dysfunction.

central nervous system dysfunction. Some brain or neurological damage that impedes individuals' motor and/or learning abilities.

disgraphia. Severely impaired ability to write, presumed to be caused by central nervous system dysfunction.

discalculia. Severely impaired ability to calculate or perform mathematical functions presumed to be caused by central nervous system dysfunction.

hyperactivity. Impaired ability to sit or concentrate for long periods of time.

impulsive. Impaired ability to control own behavior.

TABLE 6.1. Common Features of Definitions of Learning Disabilities

1. Using individually administered standardized tests, students with learning disabilities have intelligence scores within the normal range.
2. These students have substantial academic difficulties, resulting in a significant discrepancy between their academic achievement and how well they are expected to perform.
3. This disability is the primary cause of learning difficulties and school-related problems.

---

system that identifies the vast range of learning and behavioral characteristics possessed by people called learning disabled, we would be able to more precisely identify and serve them (Keogh, 1987).

Types of Learning Disabilities

There is no uniform classification system for students with learning disabilities. This is because learning disabilities are manifested in different ways with different individuals. Although these students have normal intelligence, they do not achieve academically as well as they are expected to achieve. Some individuals' academic problems occur in only one area, while others' academic difficulties are more pervasive. Results from achievement tests allow teachers and diagnosticians to talk about how far behind a particular student is in a certain academic area. However, information about an individual's social skills, learning style, and other characteristics that might be interfering with efficient learning is usually discovered only by working individually with the person of concern.

Practitioners typically do not further divide this diverse group of learners into specific types. Research (Hooper and Willis, 1989; McKinney, 1987) aimed at identifying subgroups of individuals with learning disabilities is still in its formative stage, and so far cannot give teachers useful information about how to work effectively with specific groups.

Despite the diversity in types of learning disabilities, professionals have observed some characteristics that seem to cluster some of these individuals. One example is their difficulty reading and writing. Their academic achievement in these areas is significantly below the levels of their nonhandicapped classmates. In school, students must be able to read information from a variety of texts (social studies, science, literature), and write in varying formats (essays, reports, creative writing, notes). As the complexity of academic tasks increases, students who are not proficient in reading and writing cannot keep pace with the academic expectations of school settings. A small percentage of students with learning disabilities have difficulties only in mathematics; however, most find all areas of academics challenging. In the past, students with specific academic difficulties were classified or grouped together. For example, those with severe reading problems were called dyslexic. Students with writing disorders were said to have **disgraphia,** and those unable to learn mathematics readily had **discalculia.** These terms imply that the individual has experienced brain injury that resulted in the disorder. Since very few students with learning disabilities have documented brain damage, such terms should be applied cautiously.

Some youngsters with learning disabilities display behavioral problems, along with poor academic performance. For example, many are **hyperactive** or **impulsive,** seem unable to control their behavior, and display excessive movement. These children seem unable to sit or concentrate for very long. Their parents and teachers comment that they are in constant motion. Some psychologists and educators call

Focus: Issues of Diversity

The overrepresentation of culturally and linguistically diverse students in programs for students with learning disabilities has raised the concerns of parents and educators across the nation. This problem is particularly acute for those Hispanic students who have limited English proficiency. Evidently, some school districts have placed 100 percent of their limited English proficient students in special education (Dew, 1984). Rosas (1990) suggests that this situation occurs for a number of reasons: the imprecise definition of learning disabilities and the lack of specific criterion for identification of students, no commonly accepted definition of limited English proficiency, and primitive assessment procedures. However, another critical factor is the lack of appropriate, alternative educational options for some students who are culturally and linguistically diverse. It appears that a range of educational programs, outside of special education options, need to be developed and made available to students whose dominant language is not English.

attention deficit disorder (ADD). A condition that refers to students who are hyperactive, have an impaired ability to control their own behavior, and display constant movement.

discrepancy scores. The scores used in some states to determine eligibility for services designed for students with learning disabilities.

discrepancy formulas. Formulas developed by state educational agencies or local districts to determine the difference between a child's actual achievement and expected achievement based on student's IQ scores.

this condition Attention-Deficit/Hyperactivity Disorder (ADHD), and suggest carefully planned educational procedures, such as rewards and teaching students to use self-control, to reduce inappropriate behaviors (Ellenwood and Felt, 1990). Some physicians use the term **Attention Deficit Disorder (ADD)** to describe the same condition, and prescribe drugs, such as Ritalin, to help these children focus their attention on assigned tasks. Controversy surrounds the usefulness of behavior-control drugs for some youngsters with ADD. However, considerable clinical evidence indicates that behavior-control drugs are effective in reducing the hyperactivity for some children. (See Casey's story in the concepts and controversies at the end of this chapter.) Regardless of the issues surrounding treatment, the youngsters who can be clustered together and labeled as having ADD are *not* all learning disabled or handicapped. Some researchers (Tarnowski and Nay, 1989) maintain that from 30 to 60 percent of children with ADD are learning disabled, and the remaining percentage are hyperactive but do not have learning difficulties.

Teachers of students with learning disabilities must devise remediation plans on an individual basis. This, of course, is a time-consuming process for the teacher. Throughout this chapter we offer some teaching tips and tactics to help you formulate an effective plan.

Measurement

While some researchers wrestle with issues of identification and definition, others are trying to refine the criteria for inclusion in this group. Many school districts and states rely on quantitative data such as **discrepancy scores.** Others put more stock on classroom observations, input from parents and teachers, and evaluations of children's academic performance on their daily schoolwork. To date, a measurable, nationally consistent method of determining whether a student has a learning disability has not been agreed upon. Many different methods for identifying these youngsters are used across the country; Ysseldyke, Algozzine, and Epps (1983) found seventeen different methods when they analyzed different states' practices.

Many states and school districts have developed **discrepancy formulas** to help in the identification of students with learning disabilities (Forness, Sinclair, and Guthrie, 1983). These formulas measure the difference between a child's potential,

standard scores. Converted test scores that equalize scores from different tests to allow comparison.

as measured by a standardized intelligence test, and that student's actual academic achievement, as determined by a standardized achievement test. Many discrepancy formulas are very complicated, with some even requiring a computer program to calculate the discrepancy score. Some states have developed tables for diagnosticians to use as they evaluate students' scores, and other states use a minimum discrepancy that must be present for identification. For example, the state of New Mexico uses standard scores to classify students as having a learning disability. **Standard scores** represent a measure common to all tests so that the results can be compared. If students have a discrepancy or difference of twenty-three or more standard scores points between the scores they received on an intelligence test and on an achievement test, they qualify for special education. Let us use Suzi, a ten-year-old fourth grader, as an example. Suzi is reading at the first grade level, she is able to solve third-grade arithmetic problems, and she has difficulty writing an organized, coherent paragraph. Her intelligence quotient (IQ) or standard score on an intelligence test is 100, which is considered average. However, her standard achievement score on an achievement test is 72. Because the difference between the two scores is greater than twenty-three points, Suzi has been classified as learning disabled, and she qualifies for special education.

There is great controversy in the field of learning disabilities about the use of discrepancy formulas. First, they are complicated to calculate, taking much time and effort. They tend to focus solely on academic achievement and do not consider other factors such as cognitive or social abilities. Professionals know that discrepancies between intelligence and achievement are not exclusively characteristic of students with learning disabilities (McKinney, 1987). Second, the identification process is also criticized because available tests lack precision and accuracy. Finally, because these

One way to determine whether a child's academic achievement is equal to her overall intellectual abilities is by using standardized achievement tests. Another method is to collect data on her daily academic performance.

individuals show unique learning patterns, more rigid requirements for identifying students as learning disabled remain difficult to accomplish. As Robinson and Deshler (1988) point out, a student can be identified and served as learning disabled in one school district, but may not be considered learning disabled in another school district just a few miles away.

Professionals are attempting to employ alternative methods of assessment for identification purposes. Some use a standard score cut-off as an identification measure. This means that a student may be identified as learning disabled if a standard score on an achievement test falls below a certain number. Other professionals may compare the subtest scores on an IQ test. Great variability between the scores on different subtests may be evidence of a learning disability. Also, a growing movement of professionals carefully considers observational data and input from parents, teachers, and other professionals acquainted with the student. Despite their inherent subjectivity such data can provide valuable information. Clearly, professional debate will continue on these issues.

Significance

As with other groups of individuals who have handicaps, those with learning disabilities range in abilities. Some children with learning disabilities have a mild handicap. With assistance, they profit from the standard curriculum offered in regular education, and are college-bound. Others, however, are severely disabled, requiring intensive remediation and support throughout their school years and into adulthood. (See Scott's story later in this chapter.)

Most children with learning disabilities are not identified as handicapped until they have attended school for several years. (Compare the ages at which the students in the opening vignette were identified as having a learning disability.) Many are identified around third grade, when reading and writing take on greater importance. It is at this time that students begin to read textbooks to gain information, and are required to write reports and themes. Teachers expect students at this age to work at their desks independently for longer periods of time. For many students with learning disabilities, being able to work independently and concentrate on one task is a difficult, seemingly impossible requirement. As the demands of school increase, many of these students fall further and further behind their classmates' academic achievement. Some develop behavioral problems as well. It is at this point—when they are several years behind their classmates' academic achievement levels and when they do not behave according to teachers' expectations—that they are referred for special education services. Even intensive efforts from special educators do not enable some students with learning disabilities to learn at the same rate as their normal peers. Without special assistance, they usually find the increasing academic demands of school impossible to cope with. According to Schumaker et al. (1983), by the time students with learning disabilities reach seventh grade, their average achievement in reading and written language is at the high third grade level. By their senior year in high school, their average academic achievement in these two areas is at the fifth grade level with mathematics scores slightly higher.

Another concern of educators is whether all those identified as having learning disabilities actually have this handicap. Some professionals believe that services designed for those with learning disabilities are being provided to low-achieving students who are not handicapped. Unfortunately, it is fairly easy for this error to occur

(Algozzine and Ysseldyke, 1987). Most students with normal intelligence quotients who are several years behind in academic achievement meet the criteria for learning disabilities. Therefore, it is quite probable that low-achieving students, who are not handicapped, are placed in special education under this category of students with special needs. Because of public pressure to raise the achievement levels of America's students, the demands of regular education settings are increasing. Some educators (Algozzine and Ysseldyke, 1986) believe that programs for children with learning disabilities are serving many unmotivated and low-achieving students. They maintain that these classes serve as a means for regular education teachers to rid themselves of their most difficult students. How can we resolve this issue? More stringent criteria, better identification procedures, and a regular education system more tolerant of individual differences should bring about a reduction in the number of low-achieving students referred and ultimately incorrectly identified as disabled.

As mentioned earlier, most individuals with learning disabilities have a lifelong disability. Table 6.2 shows that students' learning difficulties can be present from the preschool years through adulthood, and recommends some remedial procedures. Notice that some challenges these individuals confront exist across their life span.

TABLE 6.2. Life-span View of Learning Disabilities

	Preschool	Grades K–1	Grades 2–6	Grades 7–12	Adult
Problem Areas	Delay in developmental milestones (e.g., walking) Receptive language Expressive language Visual perception Auditory perception Short attention span Hyperactivity	Academic readiness skills (e.g., alphabet knowledge, quantitative concepts, directional concepts, etc.) Receptive language Expressive language Visual perception Auditory perception Gross and fine motor Attention Hyperactivity Social skills	Reading skills Arithmetic skills Written expression Verbal expression Receptive language Attention span Hyperactivity Social-emotional	Reading skills Arithmetic skills Written expression Verbal expression Listening skills Study skills (metacognition) Social-emotional-delinquency	Reading skills Arithmetic skills Written expression Verbal expression Listening skills Study skills Social-emotional
Assessment	Prediction of high risk for later learning problems	Prediction of high risk for later learning problems	Identification of learning disabilities	Identification of learning disabilities	Identification of learning disabilities
Treatment Types	Preventative	Preventative	Remedial Corrective	Remedial Corrective Compensatory Learning strategies	Remedial Corrective Compensatory Learning strategies
Treatments with Most Research and/or Expert Support	Direct instruction in language skills Behavioral management Parent training	Direct instruction in academic and language areas Behavioral management Parent training	Direct instruction in academic areas Behavioral management Self-control training Parent training	Direct instruction in academic areas Tutoring in subject areas Direct instruction in learning strategies (study skills) Self-control training Curriculum alternatives	Direct instruction in academic areas Tutoring in subject (college) or job area Compensatory instruction (i.e., using aids such as tape recorder, calculator, computer, dictionary) Direct instruction in learning strategies

Source: Students with Learning Disabilities, 3d ed., p. 44, by C. Mercer, 1987, Columbus: Merrill Publishing. Reprinted by permission.

HISTORY OF THE FIELD

The field of learning disabilities is relatively new. The term *learning disabilities* was coined on April 6, 1963 by Professor Sam Kirk and others at a meeting of parents and professionals in Chicago. From this date, public school programs were started for children of elementary school age who had learning disabilities. The past twenty-five years have seen an explosion in the number of pupils identified, teachers trained, and classroom programs offered. Services continue to expand, as we provide programs for **postsecondary** students and adults.

Investigation of learning disabilities, however, has its roots long before 1963. In 1919, Kurt Goldstein began working with young men with brain injuries who had returned to the United States from World War I. He found many of them distractible, unable to attend to relevant cues, confused, and hyperactive. Many could no longer read or write well. Some years later, Alfred Strauss and Heinz Werner, two immigrants who came to the United States after Hitler's rise to power in Germany, expanded upon Goldstein's work. Strauss and Werner worked at the Wayne County Training Center in Michigan with pupils who were thought to be brain injured. They found many similarities to the group of World War I veterans that Goldstein had studied earlier. However, there was one important difference between these two groups. Goldstein's group *lost* their abilities to read, write, and speak well. Strauss and Werner's group had *never developed* these abilities in the first place. Regardless, study of learning disabilities originated in the work of these pioneers, and their concentration on brain injury continues to affect the field today.

During the 1920s and 1930s, Samuel Orton, a specialist in neurology, developed a number of theories and remedial reading techniques for children with severe reading problems, whom he called "dyslexic" and believed to be brain damaged. He emphasized the importance of **lateral dominance.** In the late 1930s, Newell Kephart worked with Strauss at the Wayne County School, and further studied a group of children who were considered retarded but behaved like Goldstein's brain-injured subjects. Both Kephart and Laura Lehtinen developed teaching methods for what they thought were a distinct subgroup of children with disabilities. Kephart's approach was more motoric. He sought to remediate these children's difficulties through physical exercises. Lehtinen developed a set of instructional procedures similar to those used by some classroom teachers today. At about the same time, Sam Kirk also worked at the Wayne County School, and helped to develop a set of word drills and other teaching procedures he referred to throughout his career. In 1961 the Illinois Test of Psycholinguistic Abilities (ITPA) was published; it was used for many years to identify students as learning disabled. The ITPA was intended to identify individuals' strengths and weaknesses and their learning styles and preferences (whether they learned better by seeing or hearing information presented). This test was used for many years as an instrument for identification as well as instructional planning, but it is not used very much today because of serious flaws in its conceptualization and development (Swanson and Watson, 1989).

During the early years of learning disabilities programs, professionals supported approaches that were perceptual in orientation. In the 1960s Marianne Frostig, for example, developed materials that were used to improve students' visual perceptual performance. The thought was that students with learning disabilities were unable to process information accurately through the visual channel. If their visual perceptual skills were enhanced, their reading abilities would also show improvement. This approach was popular for many years, but little research evidence was offered to support its value.

postsecondary. Education that comes after high school (e.g., community college, technical vocational school, college, university, continuing education).

lateral dominance. A preference for using either the right or left side of the body for one's motoric responses; some believe that mixed dominance or lateral confusion is associated with poor reading performance.

direct instruction. Specifically focusing instruction on the desired, targeted behavior.

process/product debate. Argument that either perceptual training or direct instruction was more effective for instruction.

information processing theory. Suggests that learning disabilities are caused by an inability to organize thinking and approach learning tasks systematically.

metacognition. Understanding one's own learning process.

cognitive behavior modification (CBM). Instructional strategies that teach internal control methods (such as self-talk) in structured ways to help students learn how to learn.

self-management technique. A set of instructional procedures where the individual uses self-instruction, self-monitoring, or self-reinforcement to change behavior.

During the 1970s, the field of learning disabilities was embroiled in heated debate about the best approaches to use in the remediation of students' academic deficits. One camp advocated the use of perceptual training, or process, approaches. The other camp advocated **direct instruction** and behavior modification approaches. This debate, which raged for years, seriously divided the field and was known as the **process/product debate.** In the end, an analysis of the research data showed that perceptual approaches were seldom effective in teaching academic skills (Hammill and Larsen, 1974).

Throughout the history of learning disabilities, various fads have become popular with the press and the public. One such notion suggested teaching students with learning disabilities to crawl again, regardless of their age. Others have claimed that various diets improve students' academic and behavioral performances. Fluorescent lighting has been blamed as the cause of learning disabilities. Plants placed on students' desks have been given credit for improving academic skills. In most of these instances, people have made claims about students' improvement, but little if any research data are available to support the method being advocated. In many cases, parents spend considerable money, time, and resources chasing one cure after another. In almost all of these cases, the problems do not disappear. The best tool we have for evaluating recommended programs is professional research. To be better consumers, parents, and advocates, we must consistently and persistently ask for research data that prove the benefits of such treatments.

The 1980s saw a number of different approaches developed and researched. Learning strategies are now being taught to students to help them learn to learn. Other research explored how individuals who are learning disabled acquire, retain, and transfer knowledge. This line of research, which is studying the **information processing theory,** is described later in this chapter. **Metacognition,** or **cognitive behavior modification** (see Table 6.4), has students use **self-management techniques** as they learn, and is proving to help students remember what they are taught, to think, to organize their study, and to solve other problems. The research of the 1980s has provided promising preliminary results that may universally change the way these students are taught and how successful they are in school and later life.

PREVALENCE

Learning disabilities has grown to be the largest category of exceptional learners in the United States. In 1976–1977, 22 percent of the school-age handicapped population was learning disabled. In 1988–1989, according to the *Twelfth Annual Report to Congress on the Implementation of the Education for the Handicapped Act* (U.S. Department of Education, 1990), 47 percent of all children with handicaps were identified as having learning disabilities as their primary handicapping condition, an increase of 2 percent over the previous school year. (At the same time, the number of students identified as having mental retardation decreased by 3 percent.) Figure 6.1 shows the growth in the number of students identified as having a learning disability across a 13-year period.

Today, there are some 1,917,935 children served by our nation's schools as learning disabled, indicating that 4.4 percent of America's children are identified and served within this special education category. This means that more than 4 of every 100 school-aged children has a learning disability. As we mentioned earlier, some

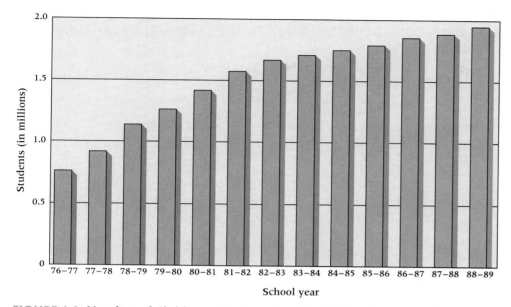

FIGURE 6.1 Number of Children with Learning Disabilities Served under EHA–B, Age Six to Twenty-One: School Years 1976–1977 through 1988–1989

SOURCE: *Twelfth Annual Report to Congress on the Implementation on the Education for Handicapped Act,* p. 15, by the U.S. Department of Education, 1990, Washington, DC: U.S. Government Printing Office.

states have reported excessive numbers of students with learning disabilities. The number and percentage varies state by state, and even school district by school district. In some states, more than 5 percent of the school-age population is identified as learning disabled, with more than 50 percent of the handicapped population belonging to this category (Gerber, 1984).

Recall the discussion about the different ways students are identified as learning disabled. Different identification systems produce different numbers of students. Some states have stricter requirements for eligibility. States that require a greater discrepancy between intelligence and achievement identify fewer students. States that define normal intelligence by using a narrower range of intelligence quotients (for example, IQ scores must be greater than 90, or IQ scores must be between 95 and 110) also identify and serve fewer students as learning disabled. Table 6.3 shows the number of students served as learning disabled in each state. Find how many students your state considers to be learning disabled.

Many teachers and administrators, as well as many state directors of special education, are concerned about the growing number of those identified as learning disabled. Here are some of the questions they have raised:

1. Are some of these children not disabled, but rather low achievers?

2. Because it might be harmful to some individuals to be identified and, therefore, labeled as disabled, should fewer students now considered learning disabled be included in special education?

3. Can the states and the nation afford to serve so many students in special programs?

4. Why are so many students not succeeding in regular education programs?

TABLE 6.3. Number of Children Six to Twenty-One Years Old Served in Different Educational Environments during School Year 1987–1988: Learning Disabled

	Learning Disabled							
	Number							
State	Regular Classes	Resource Room	Separate Classes	Public Separate Facility	Private Separate Facility	Public Residential Facility	Private Residential Facility	Homebound Hospital Environment
Alabama	2,883	25,315	1,458	2	0	·	0	9
Alaska	3,089	2,400	720	2	0	1	17	5
Arizona	141	22,629	5,512	0	13	0	3	0
Arkansas	2,644	18,638	1,314	60	36	1	27	24
California	5,440	154,147	65,273	6,021	769	0	·	·
Colorado	3,406	18,267	1,462	12	0	5	11	9
Connecticut	1,704	21,228	6,581	304	304	41	58	43
Delaware	1,645	3,651	1,078	240	5	0	1	6
District of Columbia	20	1,003	1,789	164	117	0	5	0
Florida	10,424	43,206	21,421	583	15	0	0	24
Georgia	317	17,203	7,724	57	21	65	11	0
Hawaii	2,455	3,919	837	0	2	2	0	0
Idaho	5,105	4,464	23	165	0	0	0	140
Illinois	3,495	66,875	29,473	407	156	7	26	21
Indiana	1,154	26,577	8,782	24	0	0	0	3
Iowa	217	21,477	622	13	0	0	0	6
Kansas	6,007	6,937	1,404	46	0	3	30	12
Kentucky	1,514	17,323	2,236	73	2	0	3	29
Louisiana	6,093	9,831	10,371	397	27	0	7	115
Maine	5,030	4,841	569	24	6	1	6	6
Maryland	13,231	12,195	18,119	423	275	3	15	49
Massachusetts	27,331	6,970	8,130	996	1,443	265	259	282
Michigan	26,140	25,314	12,634	761	0	6	20	27
Minnesota	5,125	27,564	2,758	124	·	92	·	11
Mississippi	4,448	15,280	5,888	29	0	0	0	20
Missouri	12,762	17,396	4,962	522	8	0	20	34
Montana	3,679	3,094	776	0	0	1	6	0
Nebraska	8,322	3,450	406	7	0	0	7	14
								(continued)

Data as of October 1, 1989.
Annual. Cntl (LRXXNP1A)

Source: Twelfth Annual Report to Congress on the Implementation of the Education for the Handicapped Act, p. A 56, by the U.S. Department of Education, 1990, Washington, DC: U.S. Department of Education.

5. Is the label *learning disabled* not as stigmatizing as other handicapping labels and, therefore, used for students who have mild mental retardation or behavioral disorders?

These are serious questions that the professionals, parents, state legislators, educators, and the federal government need to answer. Answers to these questions are far reaching, for they will affect the lives of many students and their families. They will also affect entire school systems because they influence who regular educators have in their classes. These answers will determine the range of students' abilities for which regular educators have to plan educational programs, and could alter the depth of content covered and the instructional methods used.

TABLE 6.3. Number of Children Six to Twenty-One Years Old Served in Different Educational Environments during School Year 1987–1988: Learning Disabled (continued)

Learning Disabled

State	Regular Classes	Resource Room	Separate Classes	Public Separate Facility	Private Separate Facility	Public Residential Facility	Private Residential Facility	Homebound Hospital Environment
Nevada	1,636	5,966	744	57	2	4	0	5
New Hampshire	5,706	2,319	1,473	0	120	4	49	6
New Jersey	9,693	31,254	33,883	1,380	1,277	16	12	98
New Mexico	7,848	4,956	716	0	22	0	0	0
New York	2,146	81,146	66,946	2,323	418	0	0	524
North Carolina	17,491	22,276	3,441	22	2	9	1	68
North Dakota	4,429	710	108	30	1	0	3	4
Ohio	22,415	38,501	10,449	45	1,753	0	0	27
Oklahoma	12,431	12,806	1,912	33	24	2	7	36
Oregon	13,836	9,235	1,074	17	85	0	6	39
Pennsylvania	15,626	34,703	26,634	500	1,064	42	72	23
Puerto Rico	621	7,518	960	120	86	6	3	40
Rhode Island	6,294	2,365	3,257	64	48	0	53	15
South Carolina	1,492	19,795	4,385	103	3	0	1	9
South Dakota	603	4,951	70	4	0	8	4	1
Tennessee	5,580	31,688	5,983	171	14	2	2	32
Texas	4,657	143,939	9,401	1,000	7	196	1	306
Utah	3,162	5,391	732	11	0	0	0	12
Vermont	4,371	388	51	5	36	0	33	5
Virginia	7,965	25,697	11,692	116	103	2	59	21
Washington	12,033	16,283	3,879	38	29	16	82	134
West Virginia	5,401	11,392	2,109	0	0	0	0	11
Wisconsin	6,628	14,013	2,305	23	0	1	0	11
Wyoming	386	2,434	508	1	0	0	5	1
American Samoa	0	0	0	0	0	0	0	0
Guam	266	260	229	0	0	0	0	0
Northern Marianas	.	.	.	.	.	.	.	.
Trust Territories	.	.	.	.	.	.	.	.
Virgin Islands	.	.	.	.	.	.	.	.
Bur. of Indian Affairs	.	.	.	.	.	.	.	.
U.S. and insular areas	336,537	1,131,182	415,263	17,519	8,293	801	925	2,317
50 states, D.C. & P.R.	336,271	1,130,922	415,034	17,519	8,293	801	925	2,317

CAUSES AND PREVENTION

You have learned that people with learning disabilities comprise a heterogeneous group of individuals. Their learning disabilities are manifested in different ways and at different levels of severity. Unfortunately, researchers do not have much concrete information about the causes of learning disabilities. Unlike some other groups of individuals with handicaps (hearing impairments, visual impairments), knowing the cause of an individual's learning disabilities does not necessarily influence the selection of instructional procedures. Of course, some general guidelines can be useful to teachers.

Causes

As the field has wrestled with definitions of learning disabilities, so too has it argued over the causes of the problem. As we discussed earlier, some professionals have maintained that learning disabilities result from some injury to the brain or central nervous system. If you review the two definitions presented under Learning Disabilities Defined, you will notice that both discuss damage or presumed damage to the central nervous system. In the majority of cases of learning disabilities, however, there is no physical evidence or actual medical diagnosis of brain injury or damage to the central nervous system.

For this reason, many special educators oppose the use of medical terms associated with brain injury. They believe that using terms like *assumed brain injury* or *presumed central nervous system dysfunction* leads to a conclusion that cannot be proven and may be misleading. Many special educators believe that the use of the term *brain injury* gives the impression that nothing can be done about the condition. This impression can lead parents, educators, and the individuals concerned to give up or not try to remediate or compensate for identified educational difficulties. They might also set expectations too low. We know from research on education that when expectations and goals are set low, they are usually met but not exceeded. This can be a critical problem for a child with a learning disability. If goals are set too low the child may never reach his or her potential.

a bad sign for those students who have actually sustained TBI's

Although we know little about the causes of learning disabilities, we can presume that students who have them are diverse as are the types. Some of these students may have some central nervous system dysfunction that inhibits their learning. Some of these students do have proven brain damage that has resulted in neurological difficulties that affect their ability to learn. Brain injury can be caused by influences such as an accident or lack of oxygen before, during, or after birth. Also, some researchers have observed that learning disabilities tend to be hereditary (Decker and Defries, 1980, 1981; Owen et al., 1971). Diet and various environmental factors have also been suggested as causes of learning disabilities. Although not proposing that ear infections cause learning disabilities, Reichman and Healey (1983) did find an interesting connection between otitis media and children identified as learning disabled. They found that chronic and early incidence of otitis media was twice as common in children identified as learning disabled than those without learning disabilities. They maintain that mild hearing losses could make these children at risk for developing delays in auditory, language, and academic skills. There does seem to be a connection between communicative disorders and learning disabilities. Gibbs and Cooper (1989) found that 96 percent of the learning disabled sample they studied had either a speech, language, or hearing problem. Yet others (Englemann, 1977; Lovitt, 1977, 1989) maintain that some of these children may have serious difficulties learning academic material because they were poorly taught in the first place.

By definition, students with learning disabilities typically display poor performance in at least one area of academic achievement. Some maintain that poor academic achievement is due to poor cognitive (thinking) abilities (Meichenbaum, 1985). Swanson (1987), through his information processing theory, suggests that these students' learning difficulties are caused by their inability to organize their thinking skills and systematically approach learning tasks. He maintains that future research might determine that these students are different from others in their abilities to self-regulate (check, plan, monitor, test, revise, and evaluate) their attempts to learn and to solve problems, and that these factors are the cause of many of these youngsters' learning problems.

Teachers can help children focus on instructional tasks by selecting materials and activities that are interesting and appropriate for the child's level of ability.

Why do children with learning disabilities not learn as efficiently or in the same way their classmates do? Some professionals (Hallahan and Bryan, 1981) believe that individuals with one type of deficit are unable to focus their attention constructively: Their **selective attention,** or ability to attend to relevant rather than irrelevant features of a task, is faulty. Such children might have difficulty dealing with distractors in arithmetic word problems. (An example word problem is the following: Twelve children went to the beach. Each child brought five dollars spending money. David bought three hot dogs at $1.50 each and a coke for 50 cents. Kathryn bought a bag of popcorn for 75 cents. How much money did David have left?) Some children with a selective attention deficit might have difficulty gaining information from the teacher when others are talking at the same time. Others might have trouble distinguishing important from unimportant facts presented in a lecture and remembering them. Children with such difficulties (such as those described in Table 6.4) seem to benefit greatly from the use of strategies that use verbal rehearsal.

Despite many hypotheses about the causes of learning disabilities, for most of these students, the cause of their handicap is unknown. Expert after expert tends to concur: There is no single cause of this handicapping condition, and we know very little about why this disability occurs (Hallahan, Kauffman, and Lloyd, 1985; Wallace and McLoughlin, 1988).

Prevention

Providing guidelines about preventing learning disabilities is difficult because we cannot pinpoint causes. Ways to prevent or reduce the *effects* of this disability do exist, however. There seems to be a strong relationship between poor language development and learning disabilities (Cantwell and Baker, 1987; Wallach and Butler, 1984). Young children who do not develop good language skills (see chapter 5, Communicative Disorders) during their early childhood years tend to be at risk for academic problems during their later school years. Children who develop language very late tend to have poor cognition: They do not reason or solve problems well. Therefore, children who do not develop adequate language skills early in their lives are at risk for learning disabilities. There is strong evidence that early intervention programs, such as Head Start and other well-structured preschool programs, positively influence children's language and thinking skills (Casto and Mastropieri, 1986) and their later success in school (Lazar et al., 1977). Children who are at risk or show definite developmental lags in these areas should be referred to an early intervention program, even if they are not yet identified as handicapped or learning disabled.

In the previous section, a brief overview of Swanson's research on the information processing theory was presented. This promising research states that students with learning disabilities need to learn *how to learn.* Data already exist showing students who are learning disabled profit from instruction that centers on helping them learn how to learn (Deshler and Schumaker, 1986). One such approach, cognitive behavior modification (CBM), was developed by Meichenbaum (1985) to help students improve their general learning abilities while remediating specific deficits. Lovitt (1989) helps us understand this approach by breaking it down into five steps, which are explained in Table 6.4.

As we mentioned earlier, some professionals believe that some learning disabilities are caused by poor teaching. Englemann (1977) claims that 90 percent of the learning disabled population is handicapped because of faulty instruction during the early years at school. Of course, this claim is hard to prove, but a closer look at the educational system is warranted. Traditional instruction is not always sensitive enough to individual differences in learning rates and styles. We know that not all children learn at the same pace. Individual children require different amounts of drill, practice, and review, and those who do not receive enough repetition to master the skills being taught will be left behind. Since the concept currently being taught

---

TABLE 6.4. Steps Used in Cognitive Behavior Modification

1. The teacher models or shows the student how to correctly complete a task, and also verbalizes the process being followed.
    "John, watch and listen as I solve this addition problem that requires carrying." Teacher then demonstrates how to compute a sample addition problem.

2. The student completes a task similar to the one the teacher just solved following the teacher's instructions.
    "John, add the two numbers in the unit's column. Write the answer for the unit's column in that column, and write the part of the number that belongs in the ten's column above the ten's column. Add the numbers in the ten's column. Write the answer."

3. The student performs a similar task while verbalizing the steps to be followed.
    John solves an addition problem that requires carrying and instructs himself aloud while he does so.

4. The student whispers the steps to follow when performing a similar task.
    John speaks quietly as he provides himself with the steps to follow to solve a similar addition problem.

5. The student performs the task independently.
    John solves a similar addition problem while thinking through the steps to follow to arrive at the correct solution.

TABLE 6.5. Possible Signs or Characteristics of Learning Disabilities

Significant discrepancy between potential and academic achievement
Distractibility or inability to pay attention for as long as peers do
Hyperactive behavior, exhibited through excessive movement
Inattentiveness during lectures or class discussions
Impulsiveness
Poor motor coordination and spatial relation skills
Inability to solve problems
Poor motivation and little active involvement in learning tasks
Overreliance on teacher and peers for class assignments
Evidence of poor language and/or cognitive development
Immature social skills
Disorganized approach to learning
Substantial delays in academic achievement

often builds upon one that was just previously presented, the lack of mastery of basic concepts could result in children falling further and further behind their peers' academic achievement. In learning environments that do not follow a mastery approach to education, it is possible that some children will not profit from the instruction presented. It is clear that a closer look at teaching methods can help all children but especially those at risk.

To prevent the compounding effects of learning disabilities, children with this disability need special assistance, either from a special educator or their regular education teacher as soon as possible. Attentive teachers, who observe characteristics such as those found in Table 6.5, can help through timely referral and provision of special services. Remember, not all students with learning disabilities have all of these characteristics listed in this table; in fact, some have only one.

PROFILE OF CHILDREN WITH LEARNING DISABILITIES

It is difficult to provide a profile for children with learning disabilities. The most cited characteristic of this group is their individual differences. Time after time, reference is made to the group's heterogeneity (Mercer, 1987). Wallace and McLoughlin (1988) believe that the term *learning disabilities* refers to a variety of specific disorders with no two individuals possessing the same patterns of skills and behaviors. Recent research has also found that, for many children with learning disabilities, social skills are deficient as well. We can make some general statements in areas of learning characteristics and social skills.

Learning Characteristics

Those with learning disabilities have difficulties learning academic material. Although they might differ in their strengths and weaknesses, learning styles, and personalities, their learning difficulties result in poor academic performance. For most, the learning impairment is so severe that by the time they are in high school, they are many years behind their classmates in achievement. Many researchers feel

motivation. Internal incentives that are influenced by previous success or failure.

Motivation and attribution are directly related to success in school. Many students with learning disabilities become poorly motivated to accomplish educational tasks and may attribute their difficulties to external factors.

that the following learning characteristics impede these students' abilities to learn efficiently: lack of motivation, inattention, an inability to generalize, and insufficient problem-solving and thinking skills (Smith, 1989; Robinson and Deshler, 1988). Depending on a student's learning style, altering these characteristics can lead to substantial improvement in achievement.

MOTIVATION AND ATTRIBUTION. Motivation is usually defined as the inner stimulus that causes people to be energized and directed in their behavior. Motivation can be explained in many different ways. It can be explained as a person's traits (a need to succeed, a need not to fail, a great interest in a topic), and it can be explained as a temporary state of mind (a test or class presentation tomorrow, a passing interest in the topic). Differences in motivation may account for differences in the ways people approach tasks and differences in their success with those tasks.

By the time most students are identified as having a learning disability, they have experienced many years of failure. School failure can result in both academic and motivational deficits. Therefore, students are afraid to respond, take risks, or actively engage in learning. They come to believe that their failure is a result of lack of ability, rather than a signal to work harder or ask for help. They lower their expectations and believe that success is an unattainable goal. They do not believe in themselves, and do not try to learn. When people expect to fail, they become dependent on others—the situation referred to as learned helplessness. They come to believe they are not responsible for their achievements, that luck is the reason for their successes and failures, not effort (Pearl, 1982). To overcome this pattern, students need to be shown the relationship between effort and accomplishment. How can adults help them?

Many individuals who are learning disabled need structure; they need to work in an environment that is systematic and predictable. Teachers and parents can provide more structure and organize the day more carefully as well as help these students learn to structure their lives themselves. Such skills are important in later life when, as adults, they need to be able to allocate time to a variety of activities including work and leisure time.

Children with learning disabilities also must learn to handle failure. They know that they are not performing as well as the other students in their classes. Some have problems in one academic area, while others have problems in almost all their classes. These students need more careful instruction. For example, they need to be told how to solve a problem, when others seem just to know how instinctively. Tutoring by a classmate or extra assistance from the teacher often helps these students.

Attributions are the internal justifications that individuals use to explain why they succeed or fail at particular tasks. Attributions affect people's motivation. After many and repeated experiences with failure, individuals come to expect failure. This expectation becomes outwardly directed, viewed as something beyond one's control (Pearl, 1982; Switzky and Schultz, 1988).

Students who expect academic failure tend to be more passive. Many students who are learning disabled are said to be **inactive learners** (Torgesen and Licht, 1983). They do not approach the learning task purposefully, and are not actively involved in their learning. They do not ask questions, seek help, or read other related material to learn more. They often attribute their success to luck rather than to their abilities or effort (Pearl, Bryan, and Donahue, 1980). **High achievers** tend to expect success and view it as an incentive to work harder, while **low achievers** expect failure and see no use in expending more effort. In fact, some researchers (Kleinhammer-Tramill et al., 1983) believe that many teachers contribute to their students' learned helplessness. Many teachers plan the entire school day, select rewards for accomplishment, make tasks too easy, and offer too much assistance. This can lead to students not persisting on tasks, not following them through to completion. When students give up, they do not learn that their efforts contribute to success. How can teachers help students become more self-directed and confident? Teachers can praise students for completing assignments, reward students when they go to extra lengths to produce high-quality work, and point out how their efforts are the reasons for their success.

By thinking about low-achieving students' motivation and attributions and comparing those with high-achieving students, we can better understand the concept of attribution and learned helplessness. Let us look at a classroom situation, such as writing a social studies term paper to see how a student's motivation affects the way he or she approaches the task as an example. High achievers, when given the assignment of writing a term paper on the Revolutionary War, approach the task with confidence, knowing they are capable of producing a thorough and well-written paper. They also know that if they read their textbook and other materials available in the class and at the library, they will know enough about the topic to prepare the paper. Because of past successes, they also know that putting forth effort results in success. Therefore, these students will probably proofread their term papers, and even add extras (such as maps and diagrams) to their final products. The low-achieving students do not approach this assignment with much vigor. They seem overwhelmed by the assignment, and complain that it is too difficult. These children believe that it is useless to ask for assistance, spend time in the library, or read extra

attributions. The explanations individuals give themselves for their successes or failures.

inactive learners. Students who do not become involved in learning situations, do not approach the learning task purposefully, do not ask questions, seek help, or initiate learning.

high achievers. Students who expect success and view it as an incentive to work harder.

low achievers. Students who expect failure and see little use in expending effort to learn.

attention deficits. A characteristic often associated with learning disabilities where students do not pay attention to the task or the correct features of a task to learn how to perform it well.

problem solving. Finding answers or solutions to situations.

classifying. The ability to categorize items or concepts together by their common characteristics.

materials. Instead, they write a short and incomplete term paper that was probably not developed with care or proofread.

Attributions and motivation can be altered (Borkowski, Weyhing, and Turner, 1986). With intensive efforts from teachers and parents, youngsters can learn that their efforts do lead to success and accomplishments. Adults need to discuss actual performance and how it can be improved. Students need to be helped to approach learning strategically. They need to be taught strategies for approaching the learning task. As one suggestion, Aponik and Dembo (1983) taught students to break tasks down into smaller units to master them more easily. Using such techniques can help students realize that many tasks are not as difficult as they are originally perceived. This can lead them to realize that more effort and greater persistence on tasks can lead to success.

ATTENTION. Another learning characteristic commonly observed by teachers and researchers is inattention or **attention deficits** (Hallahan, Kauffman, and Lloyd, 1985). Children who do not focus on the task to be learned or who pay attention to the wrong features of the task are often said to be distractible. Several researchers (Lenz, Alley, and Schumaker, 1987) have found that using advance organizers (described at more length in chapter 9) helps to focus students' attention by providing an introductory overview of the material to be presented. Teachers present advance organizers to preview the lecture students are about to hear. These introductory statements explain why the information is important, and provide a key to the critical elements of the presentation.

GENERALIZATION. Most students with learning disabilities also have difficulties transferring or generalizing their learning to different skills or situations (Rivera and Smith, 1988). They might apply a newly learned study skill in history class, but not use it when studying English. A child might have mastered borrowing in subtraction with a zero in the units column, but not apply that rule when borrowing with two zeros. (See also the discussion of generalization in chapter 4.) Again, some research has shown that some teaching methods can actually interfere with students learning the concept of generalization (Ellis, 1986). The overuse of feedback on performance (knowledge of results), reinforces dependency, learned helplessness, and learning inactivity. How can teachers help students learn to generalize? Having students take more responsibility for managing their own instructional programs is one way to facilitate generalization. For example, a special education teacher who is concerned about a student who is not applying a recently learned study skill to a regular education science class might do several things. This teacher might first remind the student to use the study skill when preparing for the next science test. Second, the teacher might collaborate with the science teacher by explaining the strategy and asking that teacher to remind this student to apply the strategy while studying. Third, the special education teacher can ask the student to keep a record of the times the strategy was used, and, finally, can reward the student for improved performance in science class.

PROBLEM SOLVING AND THINKING SKILLS. Many researchers also feel that students with learning disabilities have poor **problem solving** and thinking skills (Smith, 1989). They are not strategic learners. To study efficiently and remember content, one must be proficient in the following thinking skills: classifying, associating, and sequencing. **Classifying** allows the learner to categorize and group items or concepts together by common characteristics. Usually, people will remember more items in the list because they approached the task by **chunking,** or clustering, the information presented. For example, if you forget your grocery list, and are already at the store, you might try to remember what items you needed by thinking about groups of items. You might recall that potatoes and corn were on the list when you think of vegetables and that ice cream, pizza, and TV dinners were on the list when you think of frozen foods.

People are more strategic in their learning and remembering when they relate information by some common denominators (for example, softness or hardness, styles of painting). **Association** also helps individuals see the relationships that exist among and between different knowledge bases. By associating facts or ideas, the mind is able to find the relationships and connections that units of information possess. By using this thinking skill, people can relate information on different dimensions. **Sequencing** information also facilitates memory and learning. Items can be sequenced in many ways. For example, physical items can be sorted and sequenced by size, weight, or volume. Facts, events, and ideas can be sequenced by time, importance, or complexity. These thinking skills—classifying, associating, and sequencing—help students approach learning tasks more purposefully. With guided practice, these abstract skills can be learned and developed into useful tools for learning.

> **chunking.** Grouping information into smaller pieces so it can be more easily remembered.
>
> **association.** In thinking, the ability to see relationships among different concepts or knowledge bases.
>
> **sequencing.** Mentally categorizing and putting items, facts, or ideas in order according to various dimensions.

Social Skills Characteristics

Many students with learning disabilities also exhibit behavioral characteristics that interfere with good school performance. Some are distractible and hyperactive. They seem to have boundless energy that is undirected. Some seem to be in constant motion, unable to stay in their seats for any reasonable length of time. These problems become more serious as these children get older. In the early primary years, children are allowed to move around. Activities are short in duration, and instructions are concise and direct. Teachers provide more assistance. In the later school years, children are expected to work independently, and sit at their desks for an entire 40-minute period. For many children with learning disabilities, short attention spans and distractibility make meeting the expectations of teachers difficult.

These behavioral problems also interfere with their relationships with teachers and parents. When confronted with failure day after day, many students begin to rebel and act out at school. It is at this point that teachers typically refer them for special education services. Before referral, these children are often misunderstood by their parents and teachers. Because they do have normal intelligence, they are frequently accused of being lazy or not trying hard enough to succeed at school. Many are inconsistent in their learning patterns, which leads to more misunderstanding. "If you can do well in mathematics, why are you having trouble writing a social studies paper?" parents ask the child.

The social status of children identified as learning disabled is a concern to many educators and parents. Teachers often note that these children seem to be less accepted by their classmates and have difficulties making friends. These concerns are borne out by research that shows that children with learning disabilities are rejected by their classmates without learning disabilities, and have more difficulty accurately perceiving their social status (Hoyle and Serafica, 1988). This may contribute to their relative inability to make and sustain friendships. (See Scott's story later in the chapter.) Another study found that peer rejection was related to classroom behavior:

These students are learning important science concepts together. By pairing a student with learning disabilities with another student, a teacher can enhance learning and limit social rejection.

Those children who exhibit either acting out or withdrawn behavior were more likely to be rejected by their nonhandicapped classmates (Kistner and Gatlin, 1989). However, most students with learning disabilities who did not display either behavioral excesses or deficits do not experience rejection from their peers. Teachers can play an instrumental role in reducing peer rejection by pairing these students with nonhandicapped classmates in areas of mutual interest (Fox, 1989). For example, teachers might plan activities where students with common interests (sports, music, hobbies) are assigned to work together on an academic assignment such as a social studies report.

Researchers have identified a number of areas of social behavior where the behavior of many youngsters with learning disabilities is inferior to that of their normal classmates (Bryan and Bryan, 1986; Schumaker and Hazel, 1984a, b). For example, these youngsters tend to:

1. choose less socially acceptable behaviors;
2. be unable to predict the consequences of their behaviors;
3. misinterpret social, nonverbal cues;
4. make poor decisions;
5. be unable to solve social problems;
6. use social conventions (manners) improperly; and
7. adapt to the characteristics of the person they are interacting with incorrectly (do not defer or assert themselves when appropriate).

In sum, the challenge that students with learning disabilities present to their teachers is great. These individuals are far behind their classmates' levels of academic achievement and many are less competent socially as well. However, the outcome of carefully planned educational programs presented by well-prepared educators can be productive, achieving members of society who have overcome or compensated for their negative learning characteristics.

reversals. Letters, words, or numbers written or read backward.

ISSUES IN EDUCATION

You have already learned that considerable debate surrounds the issues of properly identifying students with learning disabilities. Professionals also debate over what their educational programs should include and where they are best educated. In this section, you will learn about the controversies that surround educational programs for students with learning disabilities, programs that span preschool through young adulthood. You will learn about the successes, the failures, and the work that still needs to be done. Students with learning disabilities represent a substantial challenge to our educational system. You will also learn of some alarming data about the dropout rate of students with learning disabilities. The issues presented here have not been resolved, and certainly require the attention of current and future special education professionals.

Education and the Preschool Child

Because learning disabilities primarily involve academic accomplishment, the condition is usually not diagnosed until children are eight or nine years old. Some are identified as late as high school or even college. Therefore, not many preschool programs are designed specifically for these students. As discussed in chapter 5, Communicative Disorders, many children who are identified during their preschool years as having a language disorder are later identified as learning disabled. But, many professionals are reluctant to identify children as learning disabled in kindergarten or even first grade. Why is this the case? As we all know, young children do not develop at exactly the same rate. Some youngsters are not as ready for school as their classmates in kindergarten. For example, a child who has been in structured day care and preschool programs appears to many kindergarten teachers more ready for school than a child who has been at home for five years. Other children have not developed as quickly as their peers, but are not handicapped and will catch up. Still others are the youngest in their class, and have not and should not be developmentally equal to their classmates (Kroth, 1989).

Many characteristics of learning disabilities are similar to normal developmental patterns shown in young children. For example, it is normal to observe **reversals** of letters, numbers, or words (letters or a word written or read backward) by young children. If a child is still reversing many letters and words by third grade, then there might be cause for concern. Most young children have difficulty paying attention for long periods of time. Young children also fidget and need to move around a lot. As we have noted before, these are common characteristics of many students with learning disabilities, but these characteristics are also *typical* of young children in general. Therefore, most educators do not want to identify preschoolers as learning disabled. Many educators are also concerned that labeling a young child as handicapped could become a self-fulfilling prophecy, lowering adults' expectations of the child and resulting in damage to the child's self-concept and possibly his or her cognitive and social development (Smith and Schakel, 1986).

Many states offer preschool programs to children at risk, particularly those students below the age of three. Many of these programs are noncategorical, and do not require participants to have been identified as having a specific handicapping condition. However, most states require that children between the ages of three and five be identified as disabled and as having a particular handicapping condition to be eligible for special preschool programs. New Hampshire is an example. Researchers in that state found that when children moved from noncategorical preschool programs to categorical ones at the age of three, 69 percent were identified as speech and language impaired, and by the age of five 76 percent of these children were so identified (Mallory and Kerns, 1988). Less than 2 percent of the preschool children between the ages of three and five were identified as learning disabled. However, a major change occurred when these children became school age. At the age of ten, less than 20 percent of the handicapped population in New Hampshire were served as speech and language impaired and over 60 percent were said to be learning disabled. Another research study found that 91 percent of eight- to twelve-year-old students with learning disabilities had a language disorder (Gibbs and Cooper, 1989). These research studies show a strong relationship between language development and learning disabilities. The line between being identified as learning disabled or communicatively disordered is a fine one indeed.

Of course, children who can be definitely identified as having learning disabilities at an early age should receive specialized services as soon as possible. However, only a small number of children can be identified as learning disabled during the preschool years. For example, children who received injury to the brain during birth or infancy or children who are not talking by the age of three would be candidates for special services. Data about the influence of early intervention programs (Casto and Mastropieri, 1986; Lazar et al., 1977) indicate positive, long-term effects of these programs for those who are disadvantaged, at risk, and disabled. It is clear that early intervention preschool programs do result in improved IQ, motor, language, and academic achievement. Considering the benefits of such programs, it seems apparent that every child—whether labeled or not—who is not developing at an expected or normal rate should be involved in a planned early intervention program.

Education and the School-Age Child

As we have discussed, most students who are learning disabled are not well organized and do not approach learning situations strategically. How does a teacher help these students succeed in class? Teachers need to help them structure their learning. Teachers can use simple techniques to assist these students: advance organizers—telling students what they are going to learn before a lecture begins (see chapter 9 for a detailed example of advance organizers); demonstrations—showing students how to solve a sample problem, or task analysis—breaking instruction into smaller units (see chapter 4 for detailed examples of task analysis). Using overhead transparencies, teachers can emphasize the important points of an instructional unit. They can teach children proper note-taking skills—separating the main ideas from details in either texts or lectures. Teachers can use concrete examples to help students remember important information. They can encourage children to become more actively involved in their learning by selecting in-class and homework activities that are interesting and novel (for example, writing a class play about a historical event,

Tips for Teachers

1. Use instructional tactics that actively involve the child in learning activities.

2. Teach students strategies to help them comprehend and remember difficult reading assignments.

3. Include activities in the instructional day that teach youngsters how to think and solve problems.

4. Help children focus their attention on the relevant features of a task.

5. Allow children to manage some part of their instructional day (decide when they will do an academic task, pick the instructional technique you will use, determine a reward for achieving a goal).

6. Individualize instruction, allowing children to master basic academic skills at their own rate.

7. Help children understand the connection between effort and success.

8. Have children predict the consequences of their behavior.

9. Use concrete examples, often demonstrating how to correctly perform the instructional task.

10. Refer children who are unable to keep pace with the academic demands of your classroom, do not have the communicative competence of their peers, or have inappropriate or immature social skills (withdrawn, hyperactive) to members of your school-based IEP Team.

writing an essay about a historical figure transferred to present day). Teachers should give specific feedback about the quality of students' work, and show them where their work was in error or where and how it can be improved. Most important, teachers should tell students what is expected of them, and keep data about students' progress toward accomplishing that goal. These methods are helpful for all students. For students who have learning disabilities, these methods can be critical to their academic survival.

Teachers can use a variety of specific tactics, such as those just mentioned, with some general approaches to the education of children with learning disabilities. For example, many teachers have found curriculum-based instruction or curriculum-based assessment (CBA) to provide the necessary structure to their instruction, while having a built-in evaluation system that allows them to determine whether the instructional tactics they have scheduled are effective with specific students. In this approach, evaluation of children's progress in achieving these goals and objectives on their IEPs is measured each school day on the materials presented to the children in class. For example, Ryan's resource room teacher, Ms. Tuttle, works with him every day to improve his reading skills. Ryan is a fourth grader who is reading about at the second grade level. At the moment, Ms. Tuttle is increasing Ryan's sight word vocabulary by using a computer game and individualized flash card drill. Every day that Ryan comes to the resource room, he works with the computer for ten minutes and individually with the teacher's instructional assistant. Then, Ms. Tuttle has Ryan read aloud to her from a second grade basal reader for five minutes. As he reads, Ms. Tuttle keeps a record of the number of correctly and incorrectly read words, and the types of reading errors he made that day. This information is used to monitor Ryan's

learning strategies. Instructional methods to help students read, comprehend, and study better by helping them organize and collect information strategically.

mnemonics. A learning strategy that promotes the remembering of names by associating the first letters of items in a list with a word, sentence, or picture.

progress, determine whether he has met an instructional objective, or whether it is time to select a new instructional tactic.

Specialists working with middle school and secondary students with learning disabilities recommend using a **learning strategies** approach. For example, researchers at the Kansas University Institute for Research in Learning Disabilities advocate direct instruction to learning *how* to learn (Deshler and Schumaker, 1986). Their learning strategy helps students learn and remember information better. For many years, teachers of these students "crisis taught." That is, they tutored their students with learning disabilities to prepare for imminent crisis—so they might have a better chance of receiving a passing grade on tomorrow's test or term paper. The approach developed by the Kansas University group—learning strategies—goes beyond crisis teaching and helps students meet the demands of the regular education secondary curriculum. The approach teaches students how to learn more efficiently, rather than spending all of the special education teacher's instructional time on teaching students specific instructional content.

Teachers who use the strategies developed at Kansas University receive intensive, specialized training using the materials and the theories produced from years of research and application. The materials are highly structured and have been successfully used by efficient learners. These all use advance organizers and mnemonics. For example, many people remember the names of the Great Lakes by associating them with the mnemonic HOMES—Huron, Ontario, Michigan, Erie, and Superior. Using and developing **mnemonics** helps people remember information. Other strategies have individuals group activities by main ideas and details. Taking class notes or developing study notes that organize information in this way also helps students

This boy has been learning how to learn. His teacher has been using a learning strategies approach with him. She is reminding him to apply his recently learned strategies to his reading assignment.

FIGURE 6.2 An Example of a Pictorial Mnemonic

SOURCE: "Mnemonic social studies instruction: Classroom application," by M. A. Mastropieri and T. E. Scruggs, 1989, *Remedial and Special Education, 10,* p. 43. Copyright 1989 by PRO-ED. Reprinted by permission.

remember a great amount of information. Using the learning strategies approach, youngsters are taught how to read difficult passages in high school social studies and science texts. They are taught how to write themes and reports in systematic ways. Strategies have been developed that help students study more efficiently and take tests more effectively.

Although the learning strategies approach has proven to be very effective with many middle and high school students with learning disabilities, it might not be the best approach for all of these students. Other researchers are developing different kinds of strategies to help youngsters better comprehend and remember material presented in middle and high school texts (Mastropieri and Scruggs, 1988, 1989). An example of a pictorial mnemonic is shown in Figure 6.2. This one depicts the pioneers' difficulties in traveling in covered wagons and is used to help children understand and remember information of some complexity. The data from the research about these instructional procedures are impressive, and show that many students with significant learning difficulties can learn and master the content presented in traditional high school curricula.

The purpose of teaching youngsters learning strategies is to have them succeed in the traditional regular education curriculum (for example, history, science, literature). But is the traditional education curriculum appropriate for all students with learning disabilities? Using data gathered in the state of Washington, Edgar (1987) found that 42 percent of students with learning disabilities dropped out of high school. Only 30 percent of the total dropout group was employed. Of the entire group of young adults with learning disabilities studied, the ones who completed school and those who dropped out, 61 percent were not engaged in either work or school. A study of young adults with learning disabilities who live in rural settings basically supports Edgar's findings. De Bettencourt, Zigmond, and Thornton (1989)

Teaching Tactics

THE DEMONSTRATION PLUS PERMANENT MODEL TECHNIQUE

The Demonstration Plus Permanent Model Technique has proven to be a very effective instructional method when applied to assist children in the mastery of computational arithmetic problems (Blankenship, 1978; Rivera and Smith, 1987). The technique has several key features. First, the teacher models (demonstrates) the skill being taught before the student solves arithmetic problems assigned from one class or group. Second, the student can refer back to a recently solved problem when completing the assigned worksheet. This technique works best with individuals, although it has proved effective with small groups of children who need to learn exactly the same type of problem at the same time. Of course, this use of individualized instruction does require some teacher-time, but experience indicates that no more than two minutes of a teacher's or instructional assistant's time is required each day during the instructional phase.

One key to this technique's success is the precise pinpointing of exactly what the student does and does not know. For example, a student should demonstrate mastery of simple addition problems before receiving instruction about how to compute more complex addition problems that require carrying. Teachers must either use materials that are already task analyzed or analyze the task themselves. The instructional materials and worksheets given to the child should also be carefully constructed. Students learning how to solve addition problems that require carrying should receive worksheets on which only problems of that type are represented. Of course, the child may receive other mathematics worksheets that contain different types of problems on the same school day. However, the worksheet upon which instruction is to be delivered should be carefully constructed.

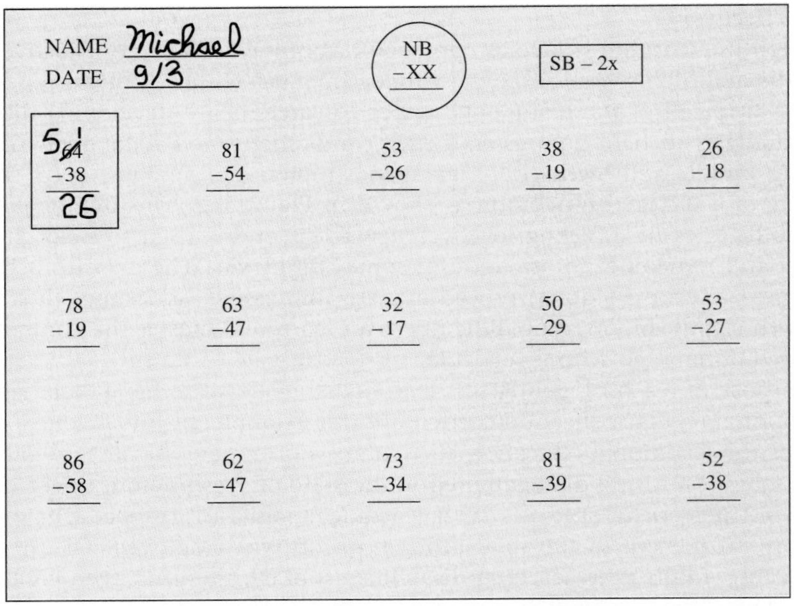

FIGURE 6.3 Sample of a Child's Arithmetic Worksheet

(continued)

Teaching Tactics

(continued)

Michael has a severe learning disability and has great difficulties learning academic subjects. He is eleven years old and spends a great deal of his day working with a special education teacher. Michael's IEP indicates that mathematics and, in particular, computational arithmetic is one of several areas that need very special attention. Michael has recently demonstrated mastery of all of the subtraction facts $\left(\genfrac{}{}{0pt}{}{9}{-5}\right)$, of two- and three-digit subtraction problems that do not require borrowing (or regrouping) $\left(\genfrac{}{}{0pt}{}{479}{-125}\right)$, but he does not know how to solve problems that require borrowing $\left(\genfrac{}{}{0pt}{}{611}{-429}\right)$. For several days, Mrs. Bassett, Michael's teacher, has assigned him subtraction worksheets that contain fifteen problems all of the same type: two-digit problems that required borrowing in the unit's column.

Mrs. Bassett had assigned Michael a different version of these worksheets each day for several days. This way she could assess the types of errors Michael was making and be certain that she really needed to spend instructional time teaching Michael how to solve this kind of subtraction problem. After several days it became clear that Michael did not know how to solve this type of problem and needed direct instruction in problem solving. Mrs. Bassett decided to implement the Demonstration Plus Permanent Model Technique.

Using this technique, each day before Michael solves the problems on his worksheet, Mrs. Bassett comes to his desk, and solves the first problem on his worksheet for him. As she does so, she verbalizes the steps she is following to arrive at the correct solution. Then, she asks Michael to solve another problem on the worksheet. She asks him to tell her the steps he followed to solve the problem. On the first day, he cannot correctly solve the problem, and Mrs. Bassett redemonstrates the correct process to use on another problem. Each day of the instructional phase, she reminds Michael that, if he forgets how to compute these problems, he is to look at the problems on his worksheet they have just solved.

Before leaving to work with another student, Mrs. Bassett tells Michael to do the best he can, not to make careless errors, to use her answer key to correct his worksheet when he is done, and to calculate a correct percentage score for this part of the day's arithmetic assignment. This instructional phase lasts for five days; it concludes after Michael receives three consecutive correct percentage scores above 90 percent.

For the next three school days, Mrs. Bassett assigns Michael the same types of worksheets, but she does not provide any instruction before Michael solves the problems. She wants to be certain that Michael has mastered problems of this type hand can calculate them accurately while working independently. She finds, however, that Michael cannot correctly answer problems where a zero appears in the minuend $\left(\genfrac{}{}{0pt}{}{70}{-27}\right)$. This type of problem becomes the next target for instruction.

found an alarming high school dropout rate (36 percent) for their sample of students with learning disabilities. However, their employment rates were close to their non-handicapped peers', probably because of the high overall employment rate in the rural setting they studied. Given these discouraging data, should educators consider different curricular options—such as career and vocational education, educational programs that stress daily living skills—for these students?

Educational Environments

Services for students with learning disabilities are typically available at every elementary, middle, and high school. In some states and local school districts, these classes are organized to serve only those identified as learning disabled. This is called a categorical service delivery system. In other places, students with learning disabilities are grouped with students having a variety of handicaps, according to level of severity. This system is referred to as noncategorical. Regardless of the placement system used, usually almost every local public school has special education classes that serve students with learning disabilities.

The kind of services available depend to a large extent on the severity of the disability (see the chapter 3 discussion of least restrictive environment for a more thorough review). Some have a learning disability in only one academic area, and that disability can be either remediated or compensated for with short-term assistance from a special education teacher. These students are usually served in a resource room. Other students with learning disabilities have more difficulty learning and succeeding in the regular education program. They require more intensive assistance. Some of these students are served for longer periods of time each day in a resource room or in a partially self-contained classroom. Yet others, although a much smaller number, require full-time special education services, attend self-contained classrooms, and return to regular education for only limited periods of time. The various classroom arrangements represent the array of services used to educate students with learning disabilities. Unfortunately, these services were not available to many of the adults with learning disabilities when they were children.

During the 1960s, many educators thought that a learning disability could be resolved during the elementary school years. They believed that, if the learning problems were caught early enough, the individual's specific learning problem(s) could be remediated. For this reason for many years classes for these students were available only at the elementary school level. Over time, however, it became apparent that in most cases, students' difficulties with school only intensified across the school years. Today, services for students with learning disabilities are available in every public school system from elementary through high school. However, educators still debate where these children should be educated. It is how the concept of least restrictive environment (LRE) should be interpreted that is at the heart of the question. (See Concepts and Controversies in chapter 3 for a summary of this debate.) Some educators believe that education for students with learning disabilities should be provided exclusively in regular education classrooms, while others maintain that a full array of services should be available. The wise option is for school systems to develop a variety of well-researched model programs that can respond to the individual needs of students with learning disabilities.

Some students with learning disabilities choose to go to college. In an attempt to be more responsive to the needs of their student bodies, many universities and colleges are now providing additional services for adults with learning disabilities. If you refer back to the college student interviews in the beginning of this chapter, you will see the variety of students with learning disabilities and the range of services needed at the college level. An example of such a response comes from the state of Connecticut.

The governor of Connecticut sponsored a bill that became law to benefit postsecondary students with handicaps (Chronicle of Higher Education, 1988). This law now requires Connecticut's state (public) universities and colleges to determine the number of students with handicaps who are enrolled. They must also provide career counseling and job placement services for such students. In addition, faculty members are being prepared to teach college students with disabilities. Plans are being drawn up so each campus, regardless of when the building was constructed, will be accessible to individuals with physical handicaps. This precedent has far-reaching implications not only for students with learning disabilities, but with all handicaps. In Connecticut, at least, a serious commitment is being made that not only makes postsecondary education available but also maximizes the possibilities for successful college experiences for others with disabilities.

FAMILIES OF CHILDREN WITH LEARNING DISABILITIES

A PARENT SHARES SCOTT'S STORY

Judy Zanotti is the mother of three sons. Divorced when the children were nine, eight, and six years old, she raised the children on her own. Her middle son, Scott, has a learning disability. This is her story.

When my middle son, Scott, was only about eighteen months old, I began to worry that he might not be developing normally. His motor coordination was good, but his speech and language were obviously delayed. It was difficult to believe that anything could be wrong with Scott, because he was such a healthy and absolutely beautiful child. While others offered advice such as "Second children always talk later," "He's not talking because his older brother says everything for him," I became more frightened, desperate, and frustrated. Several years, many doctors, and a lot of sleepless nights later, Scott was diagnosed as having "minimal cerebral dysfunction." That only began the long search for answers and for help.

No one really had heard of learning disabilities when Scott was three, four, and five years old. School personnel did their best to place him, but no one really knew exactly what type of placement he needed, exactly what his disabilities were, or how they would affect his life—and mine.

Scott was always an adorable, lovable little boy with no behavioral problems. Teachers, friends, and family loved him dearly, and everyone wanted to believe that he would eventually begin to talk and "grow out" of his perceived disability. However, as he grew older it became apparent that he would not grow out of the problem and that it would be something that he would have to deal with the rest of his life.

He had severe communicative disorders, which meant that his speech and receptive and expressive language were greatly delayed and he would probably never learn to read and write. Scott attended special schools, participated in speech and language therapy, physical therapy, and many other special training programs. Every year it was a different program; every year it was a different struggle just to find the teacher, the school, and the therapist who would accept this child and work with him. And it seems that the kind of programs Scott needed developed right behind him. As he moved on and grew older, the types of programs he had needed when he was younger began to exist. I found myself in the role of having to push

(continued)

and be an advocate—often a very aggressive advocate—when that was really the last thing I wanted to be doing.

As I struggled to learn more about Scott's disabilities and to decide how I might better assist his growth, I returned to the university and obtained a master's degree in special education. As a result of that education and my goals I became the founding executive director of a local chapter of the Association for Children with Learning Disabilities. As part of the Association, I and other parents advocated for programs for our children and supported one another in our own development.

Scott, his brothers, and I grew as a family. We learned to appreciate individual differences. We learned to rejoice in individual accomplishments, although the magnitude of those accomplishments might vary greatly. And we learned how to cope with and support one another in the pain, disappointments, and fears of having a family member with severe disabilities.

From a very early age Scott has known that he was different in an "invisible" way. This awareness caused him pain and also led him to develop a repertoire of ways to cope and, sometimes, ways to hide.

Scott grew magnificently in his social skills. He and his brothers grew close and Scott shared their friends. It was difficult for him to make friends of his own. On the whole his brothers' friends liked Scott and readily accepted him into their activities.

Scott has never mastered reading, writing, or math skills, but he has learned to drive a car and has a good job. He has worked on an assembly line in a computer facility, bused tables at restaurants, and currently works as the person who makes all the photocopies for the special education office in our school system. He continues to be liked by those who work with him. He is a thoughtful, considerate, caring, capable human being.

Scott is a good-looking young man in his mid-twenties, loves to date, but has difficulties sustaining a relationship once the young woman learns of his difficulties. Scott's older brother is married and beginning his family. His younger brother is getting married in the near future, and I have worried so much about how Scott would feel when this happened, because Scott said after his older brother's wedding that it was now his turn. He wants so much to have a romantic relationship in his life and be with someone who will love and accept him and someone whom he can love. I am not sure this will ever happen for Scott, but I continue to hope and pray it will.

Scott has taught his family, teachers, friends, and co-workers a lot about living. He has taught us about persevering when there seems to be no possibility of success; he has taught us how to feel the incredible joy of a task accomplished that no one thought he could do; he has taught us that we all have disabilities—and abilities; he has taught us that it is okay to feel pain, embarrassment, and failure; and he has taught us more about compassion, love, sensitivity, and caring than one could ever have imagined. Most of all, Scott has given us a different vision of the meaning of "success."

I still worry about Scott and always will; but when I worry I draw from what is perhaps the thing we have all learned the most from him: to trust, to love, to have faith, and never to give up.

He has changed our lives!!

As discussed earlier in this chapter, most children with learning disabilities are not identified until they are school age, and some are not identified until they are in college. Most children who are deaf or blind or severely handicapped are diagnosed when they are very young by medical professionals (such as doctors and nurses). These parents are aware of their children's handicaps during their early years of life. Most have prepared themselves to cope with the day-to-day challenges a disability can present, and many have become active participants in their children's educational programs during the preschool years. Many parents of children with learning disabilities, however, do not suspect that their children have a disability until difficulties at school become apparent, and it is often school personnel who have to deliver the bad news to parents that their child has a disability. This is a critical time for parents and for the children who are diagnosed as having a learning disability. It is a time of confusion and concern—and, often, a time of anger and frustration. The issues for the family are complex. They must learn to face this challenge as a family unit. The parents have to help the child with the learning disability to understand and to grow to his or her potential. Because learning disabilities is an academically related handicap, parents must learn to make the connections with teachers, school administrators, special education teachers, and whoever else can help their children accomplish realistic goals in school.

Parents and Teachers

Let us turn first to the relationship between parents and teachers. This is an instance when the schools and the parents and family should become partners who work collaboratively to design the best educational program possible for the child of concern.

One key in developing a good relationship with parents is for educators to use good conferencing skills when they meet with parents. Four factors contribute to successful meetings with parents (Kroth, 1978). First, an area should be selected that is comfortable and free from interruptions. A desk or table between the parents and the teacher or service provider acts as a barrier to discussion. Talking while all are seated at a round table might get better results. Second, the professional must be a good listener. By listening carefully, the professional can help parents solve problems, and parents can come to a better understanding of how the family and the school can develop a partnership. Third, teachers should write down significant information shared by the parents. This helps the teacher remember, and stresses to the parent the importance of the meeting. And, finally, parents should know how many and how long the meetings are to last. Time periods should be adhered to, for having limits to both the number and length of the meetings seems to enhance their effectiveness.

Brower and Wright (1986) interviewed many families about the impact their child's disability had on them. They asked them to comment on the role of the school and teachers. The responses below are enlightening. By studying these, teachers can be more helpful and develop better working relationships with families.

> [The teachers were] not listening to me about my son's problem. I always thought Brad was hyperactive. No one would admit that; instead they would call his behavior everything else, but not hyperactive. No one believed me.

> The least helpful experience was refusal on the part of school and others to acknowledge his problems.

Being ignored simply because we are parents of a child with a handicap—this nonacceptance is one of my most frustrating problems.

The least helpful were people who tried to tell us: (1) how bad we have it and, (2) how it could be worse . . . (p. 10)

Parents as Partners in Teaching

What role can parents play in helping their child with learning disabilities? Many parents of children with learning disabilities become active participants in their children's educational programs. Some tutor their children on the skills being learned at school. For example, each day a parent may review and practice the week's spelling words and set a reading time where parent and child read to each other each evening. Parents can learn to observe and take notes on their children's behavior so they can share with the teacher information about progress made at home. If both parents and teachers note data on a target behavior they will be able to compare performance at school and home and determine whether sufficient progress is being made or whether new tactics should be selected.

An example of such parent–teacher cooperation is helping Tara, a third grader with learning disabilities who has great difficulties interacting positively with other children. Her mother and father are keeping a record of the number of times Tara fights with her sister, and Tara's teacher, Ms. Navarrete, is keeping similar data at school for fights with classmates. Both at home and at school, Tara gets a mark for each fighting incident. Each day, the teacher sends home a daily report card about Tara's behavior at school. Among other notes about Tara's daily accomplishments to her parents, Ms. Navarrete includes the number of times Tara fought at school. At eight o'clock each evening, the points from school and from home are added together, and Tara is allowed to watch a half hour of television, minus the number of fights she had during the day. So, on a day that Tara had ten marks, she would be allowed to watch only twenty minutes of evening television. By working together, Ms. Navarrete and Tara's parents are providing the continuity in the educational program that Tara requires. Although not always achievable, such collaboration between school and home is a goal whose attainment should be sought. In some cases, it is the first meeting between school personnel and parents that sets the tone for their relationship for the rest of the child's school career.

Although learning disabilities are most recognized as a school-related problem, they can affect all aspects of a person's life. This disability can also affect family interaction. Scott Zanotti (see part of his story at the beginning of this section) was invited to the junior prom by a young woman at his school. His mother, Judy, immediately began to make plans. She told Scott to ask his friend what color dress she would be wearing, so he could order a corsage. She told him that he would need to rent a tuxedo, arrange for a car to borrow, and decide where to take his friend to dine. Because Scott cannot read or make change, Judy even suggested that she could go to the restaurant and get a copy of the menu so she could review it with Scott, help him decide what to order, and estimate how much the dinner would cost so they could determine how much of a tip he would need to leave. Scott let Judy review the entire plan with him, and then said very calmly, "Paula knows I don't know how to read. She'll read the menu for me and help me pay the tab and get the right change. I have already asked her the color of her dress, and she is going to order the corsage since her parents own a flower shop. My brother has taken me to be fitted for the tux, and her grandparents are going to let us use their car for the

Parents and teachers can form important partnerships. Here, the teacher is showing the child's mother how to teach a sequencing activity, so extra practice on this important thinking skill can occur both at home and at school.

evening." This experience shows that Scott was more comfortable with his disability than his mother was and had developed far more coping skills than she had recognized or admitted; it also demonstrates the possibility that some parents of children with special needs might be overprotective. The struggle to find a realistic balance is difficult.

ADULTS WITH LEARNING DISABILITIES

Some research studies have been conducted that follow students identified as learning disabled into their adult lives. These longitudinal studies provide valuable information on how adults with learning disabilities fare. At the same time, we must be cautious in interpreting the findings, asking: Do they reflect the unavailability of educational programs in many locales some fifteen or twenty years ago? Do they indicate a deficit in our educational programming during these individuals' school years? Or, do they indicate disturbing patterns that demand drastic changes in our service delivery approaches for adults with learning disabilities? Longitudinal studies provide insight into the nature of learning disabilities, the adults with this disability, and the services they need throughout their lives.

Many highly successful adults such as Hans Christian Andersen, Leonardo da Vinci, Thomas Edison, Nelson Rockefeller, and Woodrow Wilson had a learning

socioeconomic status. The status an individual or family unit holds in society, usually determined by job, level of education, and the amount of money available to spend.

disability, and some present-day celebrities such as Cher, Magic Johnson, Brook Theiss, Bruce Jenner, Neil Bush, and Greg Louganis have acknowledged being learning disabled. These public cases show the gains an individual with a learning disability can make in his or her life. Such cases are not typical, however. Follow-up studies indicate that many adults with learning disabilities are unemployed or underemployed (Blalock, 1989), do not possess the basic mathematical skills necessary for daily living (Johnson and Blalock, 1987), and are extremely dependent upon their families (Fafard and Haubrich, 1981). Regardless of their abilities, most work in jobs that do not require them to read or write (Haring, Lovett, and Smith, 1990). Many work in fast food and service-related jobs—and most are not satisfied with their jobs. A substantial number of young adults with learning disabilities (in their twenties) live at home, seldom participate in social activities, and do not seek or obtain assistance from vocational rehabilitation services. Possibly because of their failure in employment settings, a majority (67 percent) of these adults indicated future plans to go back to school (White et al., 1982).

A recent study in the state of Washington (Edgar et al., 1988), provides useful information about the lives of individuals with learning disabilities after graduation from high school. These researchers followed a large group of high school graduates periodically for two years. Six months after graduation almost 30 percent of the group with learning disabilities were attending postsecondary schools, but after two years about only 15 percent of that group was still in school. About 45 percent of the nonhandicapped group was still living at home two years after graduation, while over 60 percent of the group with learning disabilities was still living with their parents. Six months after graduation almost 70 percent of the group with learning disabilities was employed, and that percentage rose to almost 80 percent two years after graduation. In Table 6.6, you see the kinds of jobs these individuals with learning disabilities held, and can also compare those jobs to those held by their nonhandicapped peers.

One important factor in the success of adults with learning disabilities is their parents' **socioeconomic status** and educational status. In fact, O'Connor and Spreen (1988) believe that these are the most important factors. Children with learning disabilities who come from wealthier families tend to complete more schooling than individuals with learning disabilities who come from less advantaged families. The individuals from more advantaged families earn higher salaries and hold better jobs than their classmates with learning disabilities who come from poorer, less educated families. Unfortunately, socioeconomic status is not a variable controlled for in most studies about individuals with learning disabilities, despite the fact that this variable influences the results of research studies.

Today, another variable is also critical to the occupational success of many of these individuals: Vocational education and on-the-job training is beneficial to individuals with learning disabilities. Neubert, Tilson, and Ianacone (1989) found that such high school programs improve their employability, but they also found that these individuals require additional support during their first few years of employment.

The results from such studies should help educators plan better educational programs for students with handicaps. In the case of those with learning disabilities, students who are college-bound need to be prepared to compete academically in postsecondary school settings. Like the college students interviewed at the beginning of this chapter, many young adults with learning disabilities who attend college need supportive services (academic tutoring, readers, assistance with note-taking). The

TABLE 6.6. Job Names at 18 Months Following Graduation for the 1983–1986 Graduates Statewide

Learning Disabled N = 340		Nonhandicapped N = 345	
37 Military	9 Skilled Trade	44 Military	4 Driver
26 Retail	8 Boxperson	41 Clerical	4 Mgr.—Retail, Rest.
25 Janitor	7 Driver	36 Retail	4 Computer Operator
25 Construction	6 Waitperson	26 Fast Food	3 Farmer
20 Manufacturing	4 Landscape	22 Cashier	3 Childcare
19 Fast Food	4 Gas Sta. Attd.	21 Construction	2 Adult Home Care
19 Clerical	4 Semi-Skilled	21 Manufacturing	2 Animal Care
18 Engine Repair	3 Fisher	14 Engine Repair	2 Landscape
15 Cashier	3 Security Guard	10 Hairdresser	2 Fisher
13 Cook	3 Job Corps	10 Janitor	1 Tutor, Teacher
13 Dishwasher	3 Mgr.—Retail	9 Boxperson	1 Busperson
11 Loader	2 Adult Home Care	9 Cook	1 Gas Sta. Attd.
11 Childcare	1 Sanitation Engr.	9 Healthcare Aide	1 Lifeguard, Coach
10 Healthcare Aide	1 News Delivery	8 Waitperson	1 Tel. Solicitor
9 Busperson	1 Tel. Solicitor	6 Dishwasher	1 Clergy
9 Odd Jobs	1 Clergy	6 Loader	1 Commercial Artist
		6 Odd Jobs	1 Apprentice
		6 Semi-Skilled	1 Security Guard
		5 Skilled Trade	1 Musician, Actor, Artist

Source: Washington State Follow-along Studies 1983–1987 Students in Transition: Final Report, p. 26, by E. Edgar, P. Levine, R. Levine, and M. Dubey. Seattle: University of Washington. Unpublished manuscript. Reprinted by permission.

case of Amy Shimm is a good example (Van Ness, 1989). Ms. Shimm was able to complete her education with a B⁺ average at Brown University despite her learning difficulties. Ms. Shimm claims that she could not have attained this goal if Brown University officials had not made special accommodations for her, such as allowing her extra time to complete examinations and papers, and to take a reduced load (it took her five years to finish her studies). Special accommodations are sometimes hard to arrange, however. William Koeppel's request of the New York Board for permission to give oral (rather than written) answers to the New York State bar examination was denied. When he sued on the basis of discrimination, his case was denied by an appellate court (Green, 1988).

It is clear that college students with learning disabilities need to learn to be more assertive and to advocate for themselves and the supplemental services they need to succeed. Also, postsecondary schools—colleges and universities—need to follow the examples of the state of Connecticut (Chronicle of Higher Education, 1988) and Brown University in Rhode Island and provide assistance for those with learning disablties on their campuses. Also, a different curriculum should be available to high school students with learning disabilities who are not college-bound. An alternative career education curriculum covering information about vocations, job skills, home budgeting, home management, and leisure pursuits would better prepare them for adult life and employment.

Support services are not readily available for adults who have learning disabilities. The notion of providing transition services for this group of individuals has only been discussed by professionals and parents since the 1980s. It is clear, however, that

computer-assisted instruction (CAI). Self-contained instructional software programs that students use to supplement or replace traditional teacher-directed instructional methods.

computer-enhanced instruction. Software programs that students use to supplement traditional instruction, used primarily for drill and practice.

Hypertext. A computer program that can be used to modify textbook materials through rewording, defining vocabulary, and providing further explanations.

for many, learning disabilities is a lifelong disability that influences both the social and occupational adjustment of individuals with this condition (Kavale, 1987; Mercer, 1987).

TECHNOLOGY AND LEARNING DISABILITIES

Today, it is common to find microcomputers in classrooms or computer labs in almost every school (Cosden and Semmel, 1987). Microcomputer technology is changing the quality of education for students with handicaps. Most certainly the way instruction is being delivered is changing. For example, 88 percent of all schools use microcomputers in the instruction of students who have learning disabilities and behavioral disorders (Mokros and Russell, 1986). Both regular and special education students use computers to assist them as they study, learn new information, and write essays and reports. For students with learning disabilities advances in software will produce the most changes in their learning and their abilities to function in society. The effectiveness of either **computer-assisted instruction (CAI),** to supplement or replace traditional instruction, or **computer-enhanced instruction,** for drill and practice, depends on the quality of the software available and selected (Kolich, 1985). Breakthroughs and improvements in both hardware and software are occurring almost daily. If the future holds the promises of today, tomorrow's teachers might use the computer to keep track of student progress, to prepare individualized instruction, to manage students' learning presented via the microcomputer, and spend less time providing direct instruction to groups or individuals.

Research has shown that individuals who have learning disabilities can make great gains in academic achievement through the use of microcomputer programs (Moore and Carnine, 1989). For example, in one study, Trifiletti, Frith, and Armstrong (1984) found that children receiving instruction by only using a microcomputer learned more mathematics and problem-solving skills than children who received instruction from experienced resource room teachers. Microcomputers have also been used to teach traditional academic tasks such as spelling (Cohen, Torgesen, and Torgesen, 1988) and geography (Horton et al., 1989), as well as more abstract targets such as reasoning (Collins, Carnine, and Gersten, 1987) and problem-solving skills (Stearns, 1986). However, many teachers are most excited about the outstanding improvements they see in students' written language performance. Students with learning disabilities often have great difficulty writing. Their inability to organize thoughts is often compounded by poor handwriting. Many teachers report that it is easier for them to teach composition skills when students type their compositions on a computer. They also report that the quality of compositions is enhanced when the computer is used (Messerer and Lerner, 1989). Why? First, some students seem less resistant to rewriting texts when they can do it on a word processing program which erases and replaces text quickly. Second, they can more easily read and proof neatly typed drafts. Third, teachers can read typed material more easily, and, therefore, can offer better critiques. Fourth, spelling checkers, built into many word processing programs, assist those who cannot spell many words correctly. When regular and special education students are encouraged to use microcomputers and word processing programs, the quality and quantity of their written work may well improve.

One exciting development in the area of microcomputer software is the program **Hypertext.** This program allows for further explanation of usual textbook material. For example, definitions for difficult vocabulary words, rewording of confusing or complicated text, additional detailed maps, further explanation of concepts being introduced in the text can be made available to the student with a simple press of a key on the computer keyboard. This feature of computer programming has many possibilities for teachers who plan instructional units for individuals who have learning disabilities. It allows teachers to create instructional units where students can participate in the individualization of their course content. For example, students read what would usually be printed in a textbook, but now is presented on a computer screen. They simply highlight on the screen words that they do not know, concepts they do not understand, or material they would like more information about in order to obtain explanations. Higgins (1988) studied the effectiveness of this approach, and found that students with learning disabilities learned the content required for a course in Washington state history quickly and efficiently. As with all software, even Hypertext programs vary in quality. But those that are well done do assist these students in mastering even difficult course content.

For students who have grown up with sophisticated technology in their homes, advanced hardware and software capabilities and the importance of making instruction dynamic will continue to influence education and the presentation of information. For example, Carnine (1989) reports the successful use of laser videodisk equipment in the teaching of earth sciences. He used an interactive format where students can see experiments conducted or text content demonstrated in video segments. Such a mode of instruction should add an exciting dimension to classroom instruction where students can learn at their own pace, yet experience activities that cannot be made available in most classroom settings.

Concepts and Controversies

Casey's Story

Casey was nine years old when the administrators from his school district and his parents came to an impasse. Casey was diagnosed as hyperactive when he was six years old, and throughout his time in school, he was highly disruptive. Frustrated by the situation, the school superintendent suspended Casey and insisted that the state Department of Education hear this case, arguing that this child's behavior was so disruptive that neither he nor his classmates could benefit from school. The Department ruled that Casey be excluded from school unless he took Ritalin, a drug prescribed to reduce disruptive behavior. Casey's parents refused to put their child on drugs. During the twenty months he had been on the medication, it had made him depressed and destructive (Becker, 1988).

The story about Casey could be a story about many children with learning disabilities. Since the late 1930s, it was observed that stimulant drugs can cause a reduction in the excessive behavior patterns of hyperactive children (Bradley, 1937). Beginning in the 1960s, many children with learning disabilities have been prescribed either Ritalin or Dexadrine by doctors to control their hyperactivity. These two drugs tend to work as depressants for children and stimulants for adults. Drug therapy is controversial and seems to gain and lose popularity across time. During the 1960s and 1970s, it was a common treatment method for hyperactivity. During early 1980s, doctors were more conservative in their prescription of these drugs, but in the 1990s the prescriptions of these drugs is on the rise.

During the 1970s, considerable research about the influence of medication on children's school performance was conducted. Relatively few studies about drug therapy and school performance were conducted during the 1980s. The findings of these older studies tend to support cautious use of prescription drugs to control behavior or school-related problems. For example, in one comprehensive study (Whalen et al., 1979), the classroom performance of hyperactive children was studied while they were on and off medication. Their performances were compared to those of nonhandicapped peers. The hyperactive subjects, when unmedicated, were less attentive, more mobile, less predictable, more energetic, and made disruptive noises and verbalizations. When on medication, these students acted more like their nonhandicapped peers, and the classroom environment was more conducive to learning. However, other studies indicate that the effects of behavior-control drugs are idiosyncratic, affecting different children in different ways (Axelrod and Bailey, 1979; Sulzbacher, 1972). Some children experience unpleasant side-effects from the medication (Eaton, Sells, and Lucas, 1976; Shafto and Sulzbacher, 1977). Aman (1980), at the conclusion of his comprehensive review of the influence of behavior-control drugs, stated that there is little proof that such drug therapy treats learning problems and educational treatment should be used in conjunction with medication. Also, many educators feel that drug therapy is not necessary for the majority of youngsters who are hyperactive, because drugs merely mask the symptoms of the problems and do not cure the underlying problems. In addition, research has shown that inappropriate behavior patterns can be modified without the use of drug therapy (Patterson, 1965).

In Casey's story, the officials and teachers at his school insisted that his behavior was so serious and distracting to him and his classmates that the learning environment for everyone was negatively affected. They maintained that he could not function at school when he was not medicated. Casey and his parents have said "No" to drugs. They insisted he not be medicated. Can you think of ways to resolve such disagreements between parents and school officials?

SUMMARY

Individuals with learning disabilities have great capacities. They do not learn in the same way or at the same pace as many of their classmates. The future is promising for students with learning disabilities, and the field is most interesting and exciting for those who dedicate their careers to these individuals. Current research is finding better methods of instruction resulting in greater improvements in academic performance. When taught by teachers who are well trained and knowledgeable about the newest research findings, most of these individuals should be able to overcome their handicaps. However, without the best that education can offer, the likelihood that individuals with learning disabilities will succeed is small.

1. Learning disabilities, a recent category of handicapping conditions, is currently the largest category in special education. Although the field can be traced historically to the turn of the century, learning disabilities gained national prominence in 1963 at a meeting of the Association for Children with Learning Disabilities (ACLD), now called Learning Disability Association of America (LDAA). Since that time, public school services for this group of students have grown and expanded.

Regardless of the service delivery option used by a school district—whether categorical or noncategorical—services for students with learning disabilities are available across the nation. Programs, specially designed to meet the learning needs of these individuals, range from elementary to high school with many postsecondary educational options being developed today. Many local communities are now developing services for adults with learning disabilities as well.

2. Debate about the best definition of learning disabilities has raged since this field was begun in the 1960s. Since then, almost forty different definitions have been proposed, each with a slightly different orientation, philosophy, and thrust. Some definitions, particularly the older ones, are more medical in nature. Some definitions address the fact that this is a lifelong disability and might result in deficits in academic as well as social skills. Regardless of the definition, there are some common characteristics. For example, most people with learning disabilities do have normal intelligence, but for some reason are significantly behind in academic achievement.

3. There is concern among special educators about the definition of learning disabilities and the criteria for identification. Nationally, there has been a tendency to identify a large number of students as learning disabled. Some estimates about the size of this group have ranged from 3 to 30 percent of the school population. Without stringent controls over the number of students served as having learning disabilities, this group of learners seems to grow in numbers every year. Educators fear that children who are not succeeding at school are being misdiagnosed. Naturally, teachers are concerned about students who cannot keep up with others in their classes. In many regular education classes, teachers must plan for students who have a great range of abilities. It is not uncommon for these teachers to have over a five-year achievement spread among their students. This makes teaching more difficult. Social studies textbooks written on grade level might present an impossible reading task for at least one-third of the students in a class.

4. Learning disabilities is a complex handicapping condition. These students have normal intelligence but perform significantly below their expected academic achievement. Many of these individuals have difficulties in the social arena as well; they seem unable to understand the social contexts of various situations. Because of their relatively poor abilities to communicate well, reason, or solve problems, they tend to have difficulties in social situations. This can result in peer rejection, an inability to make and sustain friendships, and their falling victim to more sophisticated peers. However, with specific instruction in the area of social skills, such deficits can be remediated.

5. Recent research findings tell us that many of these learners do not approach learning tasks as others do. Many seem to be passive (inactive) learners. Possibly, because of a history of failure, they attribute success with academic tasks to luck or chance rather than effort and ability. These attributions are not innate personality traits, but are learned characteristics that can be altered through systematic instruction. Also, exciting research breakthroughs are being made in the instructional area. As one example, the development of learning strategies and other teaching techniques are proving to help many of these youngsters compete successfully in basic high school courses such as history, science, and literature.

6. Debate has and will continue to rage about where these students should be educated. The use of different options—consulting teachers, resource rooms, self-contained special education classes—varies state by state. These practices reflect professionals' philosophies about the concept of LRE, the segregation of students, the most appropriate curriculum for these students, and the roles of regular and special education with students who learn differently.

7. The school dropout rate of students with learning disabilities is alarming. This has led some professionals to question the curricular options available to these students. Possibly, various and different curricular options need to be developed for these students. College-bound students might receive a supportive curriculum that includes learning strategies, social interaction targets, study skills, and the content academic subjects needed for college preparation. Those who do not elect a college preparatory curriculum might be better prepared for work and adult life through vocational training.

8. The future will be different for adults with learning disabilities. They will find more services and resources available to them. Those in college will have supportive assistance to help them cope with the increased academic demands of college course-work. Those in the workplace will have, when needed, assistance from vocational rehabilitation and community agencies to help them train for and find jobs. Of course, considerable effort and funding from community agencies will be required to meet these individuals' needs throughout adulthood.

9. Advances in technology continue to shape and change the way in which these students are taught. Computer-assisted instruction (CAI) allows students to learn many basic academic skills at their own pace in a tutorial fashion. New developments in computer software capability, such as Hypertext, will allow students to gain more from traditionally prepared textbooks by providing students with definitions of words and explanations of difficult concepts when they indicate they are confused by the material presented. The use of interactive video technology will allow students to see video demonstrations of the material presented in printed texts. All of these advances will certainly change the way in which students are taught, and the roles that teachers assume as they plan and deliver classroom instruction.

DISCUSSION QUESTIONS

1. In Table 6.2, Mercer (1987) presents learning disabilities as a lifelong handicap. What aspects of this disability seem to persist across a person's lifetime? Why do you suppose some of these problem areas seem related?

2. Are there different types of learning disabilities? Do you think educators should attempt to cluster and label children labeled as learning disabled into smaller categories?

3. Many educators have questions and concerns about the size of the learning disabled population in American schools. Develop your own positions on these issues.

4. You have been selected as the student representative on a university-wide or college-wide committee to develop services for students with learning disabilities on your campus. Outline a proposal to submit to your administration that describes the services you would provide.

5. Refer back to Table 6.3. It shows the number of students identified and receiving services for learning disabilities. Find your state. Calculate the percentage of those students in your state who participate in each different type of classroom arrange-

ment. What percentage are served in resource rooms? What percentage are served in self-contained classes? How does that differ from other states? If you were a special education policymaker, would you alter this pattern? Why?

SUPPLEMENTARY BOOKS AND VIDEOS

People with learning disabilities have not been included in as many fictional and nonfictional roles, particularly in films, as people with other types of disabilities. This may be because learning disabilities is one of the newer categories in special education; it may also be that this disability is not as visible as some others.

Books

Brown, C. (1965). *Manchild in the promised land.* New York: Macmillan.

MacCracken, M. (1986). *Turnabout children.* Boston: Little, Brown, & Co.

Moss, P. B. (1990). *An autobiography: P. Buckley Moss: The people's artist.* Waynesboro, VA: Shenandoah Heritage Publishing Co.

Sacks, O. (1985). *The man who mistook his wife for a hat.* New York: Summit Books.

Smith, S. (1986). *No easy answers.* Cambridge, MA: Winthrop Publishers.

Videos

The hero who couldn't read (1984). ABC–TV.

When words don't mean a thing (1987). ABC.

Read between the lines (1989). ABC Video Enterprises.

*T*IM BALEY, *a resident of Anaheim, California, is an accomplished musician as well as a visual artist, and his extensive work often features musical themes. A self-taught pianist with mental challenges, Tim has performed in over 30 states, numerous foreign countries, and at the White House. He is 38 years old.*

*C*hapter Seven

GIFTEDNESS AND CREATIVITY

*L*earning

Objectives

After studying this chapter, you should be able to:

- Compare two major definitions of giftedness—Terman's and Marland's

- Provide a definition for creativity

- Discuss reasons for the lack of continuity in educational programs for children who are gifted across the years

- List five factors that can inhibit giftedness or creativity

- Describe and explain the purposes of two educational approaches—acceleration and enrichment—used with children who are gifted

STUDENTS ATTENDING A CLASS FOR CHILDREN WHO ARE GIFTED SHARE THEIR THOUGHTS

Middle school students who are gifted were interviewed by their teacher. Their responses reveal their feelings about their education and what it is like to be identified as gifted. These children are sixth and seventh graders, attend the same school, and have the same teacher of the gifted for their special education classes.

How does it make you feel to be called gifted?

ROBERT MONTANO: "It doesn't really feel any different than how I used to feel, but it makes me feel like good and happy when people say I'm smart and gifted."

KIMBERLY SILVER: "It feels strange because I'm the same as everybody else—like everybody's gifted somehow."

JOSHUA BARNARD: "Kinda funny because the other kids make fun of you. I guess they are kinda jealous."

ROY BERNALES: "I don't know—normal. Just feels like when someone calls me by my name—no different too."

MICHELLE GOMEZ: "It feels neat because you're in higher classes and sometimes you have more fun than in regular classes."

DECTRA DIXON: "Sometimes it makes you feel like you're ahead of other students. Sometimes they call you nerds, but I like the word *gifted* even if they do call me a nerd."

MARTY FREDRICKSON: "I feel singled out. I feel pressured."

JESSICA LUCERO: "It feels nice because you have a gift and you should be proud of it."

CHRISTY OLLOWAY: "Like everybody thinks you're smart and they ask you to do stuff. Sometimes it bugs me because you don't want to answer the questions, but you're expected to."

What do you like best about your time in gifted class?

GUADALUPE VELASQUEZ: "I like it because we dissect things, and it's fun in here, and I think that they teach you more."

KIMBERLY SILVER: "I can get more help if I need it, and the teacher explains better."

JOSHUA BARNARD: "I like being with only a few people, and I like the teacher. It's nice to be with other people who understand you."

ALIMA MILLS:	"Things you do in this class are interesting and fun, but still learning."
ROY BERNALES:	"I like it because there aren't a lot of people—it's not noisy."
DECTRA DIXON:	"You learn more stuff than in your regular classes because in the other one they mess around and in the gifted you have to be serious about what you're doing."
JEREMY CORDOVA:	"Work is challenging, but more fun. Also, I like working in a small group."
CHRISTY OLLOWAY:	"You have to try to work extra hard and you feel good about being here."

What does it mean to you to be gifted?

GUADALUPE VELASQUEZ:	"It means you're more educated. You know more in that subject."
KIMBERLY SILVER:	"Smart in a different way. Like a different way of learning."
ALIMA MILLS:	"It's easier for you to learn things and you are a little smarter than others."
ROY BERNALES:	"You're special. People think you're all smart and stuff."
MICHELLE GOMEZ:	"It's like you're smarter in some sections than other people, and you get to show it in higher classes instead of hiding it."
DECTRA DIXON:	"That you have a faster learning ability than other students."
MARTY FREDRICKSON:	"Being smarter. Being able to do more. Being singled out."

1. What are the differences between what the children think the term "gifted" means and what it feels like to them to be called gifted?

2. What do these children perceive to be the differences between regular and special education?

3. What do you think being called gifted means?

Across time, people living in different periods of history have sometimes exhibited extraordinary levels of particular skills, abilities, or talents. For example, the Indus civilization in North Africa between 2400 and 1800 B.C. demonstrated advanced concepts of city planning and architecture. Indus cities were built on a regular grid with major streets running north and south. A drainage system served an entire city, and each home had a bathroom and toilet connected to a sewer system. During the time of the ancient Greeks, athletic prowess and excellence in the fine arts reached peak levels, obvious in the legacies of their civilization: their philosophical writings, dramas, architecture, and sculpture. During the time of the ancient Chinese, literary works, architecture, music, and art far surpassed the standards of other cultures. During the second century B.C. the Chinese wrote books, using silk for paper, on topics such as astronomy, medicine, and pharmacology. By the first century B.C., books on mathematics and other topics were produced on paper. Similarly, the temples of the ancient Egyptians stand as testimony to the skills of architects, engineers, and artisans.

A concentration of particular abilities and outstanding achievement can be observed during other segments of history as well. During the height of the Roman civilization, the number of great orators far surpassed the numbers found in many other periods of history. Another example of a culture advanced for its time is Teotihuacan in Mexico. Between 300 and 750 A.D., this civilization had developed a sophisticated craft industry that produced figurines, pottery, and tools for export throughout the region. During the Renaissance in Europe, a great number of fine artists—Michelangelo, Leonardo da Vinci, Raphael, and others—created beautiful paintings, sculpture, scientific inventions, homes, palaces, churches, and public buildings. Almost two hundred years ago a concentration of musical protégés (Handel, Haydn, Mozart, Chopin, Liszt) created work that is still valued and enjoyed. Today, computer developers amaze us with their brilliance and technical aptitude.

Why have there been periods in history when particular talents are displayed in abundance? Pressey (1964) believed that such periods of brilliance result from a combination of excellent early opportunities, early and continuing guidance, and instruction for the individual. This must be coupled with a major interest of society in that particular ability, opportunities provided by society to continually practice and progress, close association and interchange with others with similar abilities, and strong success experiences. Certainly, those individuals who demonstrate superiority in a particular area must also have innate talent, but it seems that traits valued by the culture emerge with some frequency when importance is placed upon them. The discussions in this chapter will lead to a better understanding of gifted and creative individuals and the conditions necessary for them to make significant contributions to society.

GIFTEDNESS AND CREATIVITY DEFINED

Individuals who have high levels of intelligence, are high achievers academically, have unique talents, or are extremely creative are not handicapped in the sense of having a disability. Certainly, these people do not face the limitations or some of the difficulties that most children who receive special education services do. However, many of these individuals, because of their differences, are handicapped by society and our educational systems. They can be stifled by traditional educational approaches. Sometimes directly, and often indirectly, their peers, teachers, and parents discourage them from developing their abilities maximally. This situation creates a significant loss to these individuals and to society in general (Gallagher, 1985).

> Failure to help handicapped children reach their potential is a personal tragedy for them and their families; failure to help gifted children reach their potential is a societal tragedy, the extent of which is difficult to measure but which is surely great. How can we measure the loss of the sonata unwritten, the curative drug undiscovered, the absence of political insight? They are the difference between what we are and what we could be as a society. (p. 4)

Although giftedness and creativity are probably not mutually exclusive, some highly creative people do not obtain high scores on tests of intelligence. Likewise, many individuals who are very bright do not show comparable levels of creativity. In the next two sections, giftedness and creativity are described and defined. But first, let us define some important terms and develop some concepts about giftedness, creativity, and different forms of thinking. Table 7.1 provides some frequently used terms and the way they are usually interpreted. Use this helpful reference as you read the rest of this chapter and learn who these individuals are and what they are like.

TABLE 7.1. Terms Relating to Giftedness and Creativity

Term	Definition	Explanation
High intelligence	A composite of human traits, including a capacity for insight into complex relationships, an ability to think abstractly, solve problems, and the capacity to develop more capacity.	Children with high intelligence typically master academic tasks more quickly than their classmates. It is not unusual for them to come to kindergarten already knowing how to read, write, and calculate. These students grasp concepts presented in class faster than most other children, and they can use that knowledge to extend discussions beyond the levels of their classmates.
High IQ	High = 1.5–2 standard deviations above the mean.	IQ scores are obtained by taking tests of intelligence. Children who are gifted are often said to have a high IQ because they receive a high score on these tests. School districts and state education agencies set arbitrary cut-off scores that allow youngsters to qualify for education of the gifted. Many districts set their cut-off score at somewhere between 1.5 and 2 standard deviations above the mean. The mean or average IQ score is approximately 100. Children with an IQ score above 130, on an individually administered IQ test, are usually considered gifted.
Gifted	A term used to describe children who exhibit evidence of having high levels of intelligence.	Children who meet their state's or school district's eligibility requirements for education of the gifted. To be considered "gifted," most states require that students score above a specified IQ score (such as 130) and also exhibit above average academic achievement or potential. High academic achievement is often measured by the scores on an achievement test where the student scores at least two grade levels above his or her peers.
Creativity	A form of intelligence that results in advanced divergent thought, unique products, high levels of intuition, or being able to solve complex problems.	Creative individuals are able to arrive at novel solutions to problems. For example, some creative children can generate unusual stories that are either more unique, complex, or otherwise more detailed, or more humorous than their peers'.
Convergent thinking	Taking apparently unrelated information, and moving it toward a common conclusion; requires memory, classification, and reasoning abilities.	Convergent thinking abilities are useful in completing academic tasks required at school. For example, most individuals who are high academic achievers tend to be able to organize thoughts by categorizing information into meaningful groups (size, length, type). High academic achievers also have good memory skills. Good organizational skills, such as categorizing, assist in being able to remember large amounts of information and draw useful comparisons and conclusions.
Divergent thinking	Extending information in different directions from a common point; critical for creative behavior (fluency, flexibility, originality, elaboration).	Creative individuals engage in high levels of divergent thinking. They are able to act upon information by breaking it apart and extending it in an unstructured manner that results in unique and original products.
Evaluative thinking	Thinking skills used to make decisions, allow for comparisons and contrasts between and among items and concepts.	Another type of thinking ability that is often attributed to people who are gifted or creative and allows them to evaluate information at an advanced level. Evaluative thinking allows individuals to compare, contrast, judge, and arrive at solutions to complex problems, anticipate consequences, predict results, and analyze effects.
Talented	A term that refers to persons who have superior skills or abilities in just one or a few areas.	Individuals with specific talents demonstrate specific and superior skills in fields of activities (math, or art, or art and music, or performing arts). One way to understand the difference between giftedness and talents is to make a distinction between ability and performance.

gifted. A term describing individuals with high levels of intelligence, outstanding abilities, and capacity for high performance.

Giftedness

Who are individuals with giftedness? That question has been asked throughout this century and continues to be unresolved today. Three of the various definitions proposed are contrasted in this section. One major issue professionals in the education of the gifted face is the underrepresentation of various groups of students (see the discussion of subgroups of gifted learners). This problem is also discussed in this chapter's Concepts and Controversies section, which presents an alternative definition designed to be more inclusive of students who are culturally and linguistically diverse. The relationship between a definition adopted and a specific student qualifying for services is significant.

TERMAN'S DEFINITION. Terman, in 1925, considered as **gifted** only those children who scored in the highest 1 percent (having IQ scores over 140) on an intelligence test. There are a number of things wrong with this definition. Terman held a narrow view of giftedness, writing that intelligence is fixed and determined by heredity. Over the years, experts have questioned this view and, in the process, have expanded our notions about giftedness. Sternberg (1985), for example, asserts that an IQ score provides too narrow a view of individuals and their capabilities and therefore does not accurately represent an individual's capacity to learn and achieve.

Professional educators are much less confident in the results from standardized tests, believing such tests can bias against individuals who are not from the dominant American culture. Some tests identify as gifted only persons who have received a

Individuals who are gifted, talented, and creative often find many avenues to express their special abilities. It is important to consider the whole child when planning educational programs.

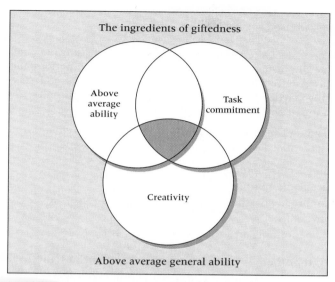

The ingredients of giftedness

Above average ability

Task commitment

Creativity

Above average general ability

FIGURE 7.1 Renzulli's Three-Ring Concept of Giftedness

Source: "What makes giftedness: Reexamining a definition," by J. S. Renzulli, 1978, *Phi Delta Kappan, 60,* p. 182. Reprinted by permission.

talented. A term that describes individuals who show natural aptitude or superior ability in a specific area without necessarily implying a high or superior degree of intelligence.

creativity. A form of intelligence characterized by advanced divergent thought, the production of many original ideas, and the ability to develop flexible and detailed responses and ideas.

strong educational foundation, the basic information upon which these tests are constructed. They also have limited ability to identify students with handicaps who are also gifted, **talented,** or creative. Our understanding of intelligence has changed since Terman's time. In contrast to Terman's view that intelligence is fixed across an individual's lifetime (barring accident or illness) and is genetically determined, researchers now believe that intelligence is influenced by genetics and environment (Gallagher, 1985). The literature about individuals with handicaps also shows that intelligence can be diminished or enhanced by environmental influences. Even though his definition is often criticized, Terman's work with individuals who are gifted continues to be respected and often referred to in the professional literature.

RENZULLI'S DEFINITION.   Other researchers believe that giftedness is multidimensional, with high academic aptitude or intelligence being only one factor to be considered. For example, Renzulli (1978) suggests that those who have three clusters of characteristics—above average intelligence, high **creativity,** and substantial task commitment—should be considered gifted. Certainly, Renzulli's view of giftedness is broader than Terman's. As you can see from Renzulli's graphic illustration shown in Figure 7.1, some individuals who have obtained high scores on tests of intelligence might not meet his other qualifications for giftedness. However, Renzulli's approach to education of the gifted is more inclusive than most others, for he advocates that 15 to 20 percent of America's schoolchildren should receive enhanced educational services that include many opportunities to develop creativity, critical thinking, and problem-solving skills.

Notice that in his definition, Renzulli does not include special talents, such as an unusual artistic or musical ability, in his illustration. Because most school districts that offer programs for students who are gifted do not specially serve those with unique talents, discussion in this chapter is primarily limited to those who are gifted and/or creative.

MARLAND'S DEFINITION. In 1972, Sidney Marland, then U.S. Commissioner of Education, offered the nation a definition of the gifted and talented to supplant the Terman definition. The Marland definition, with minor variations, is still the most widely accepted and used.

> Gifted and talented children are those identified by professionally qualified persons who by virtue of outstanding abilities are capable of high performance. These are children who require differentiated educational programs and services beyond those normally provided by the regular school program in order to realize their contribution to self and society.
>
> Children capable of high performance include those with demonstrated achievement and/or potential ability in any of the following areas singly or in combination:
>
> 1. General intellectual aptitude
> 2. Specific academic aptitude
> 3. Creative or productive thinking
> 4. Leadership ability
> 5. Visual and performing arts. (Marland 1972, p. 10)

Notice, also, that there is no reference to a minimal IQ score to be identified as gifted. This definition, unlike those presented in other chapters of this book, includes a statement that these youngsters should be educated differently from their classmates. The assumption is that under the right conditions (good instructional programs, student motivation, and interest) these students will show overall accelerated performance. This suggests a difference between potential and performance. What other features set this definition apart from those used to identify students with handicaps? What differences do you see among Terman's, Renzulli's, and Marland's views of giftedness? A few of the differences are outlined in Table 7.2, but the less obvious differences are about two issues: (1) who should receive special education services, and (2) what that education should comprise.

Definitions aside for the moment, let us identify some characteristics ascribed to individuals with superior abilities. The most traditional view of children qualifying for educational services for the gifted are those who achieve in school at high academic levels. They master academic subjects quickly, and excel significantly beyond their classmates. Their superior academic ability is accompanied by a high score (above an IQ score of 130) on a standardized test of intelligence. Excellence in academic ability might not result in outstanding grades in academic courses taken at school, for the motivation to demonstrate the ability to achieve is not always or uniformly stimulated in these learners. However, many experts (Clark, 1988; Laycock, 1979; Terman, 1925) have observed other characteristics among this group of youngsters. We discuss many of these characteristics later in this chapter, but you will better understand who these individuals are by studying this simple listing of

TABLE 7.2. Differences among Three Definitions of Giftedness

Criterion	Terman	Renzulli	Marland
Minimum IQ score	140	Above average	Not specified
Percentage of population	1%	10–15%	Not specified
Specific talent	—	—	High performance
Creativity	—	High	High potential or performance
Academic performance	—	High	High potential or performance

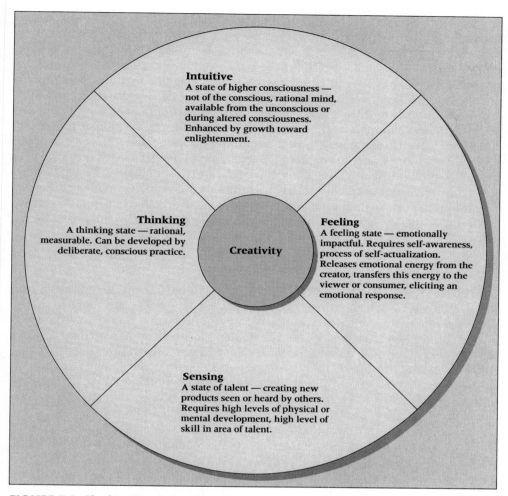

Intuitive
A state of higher consciousness —
not of the conscious, rational mind,
available from the unconscious or
during altered consciousness.
Enhanced by growth toward
enlightenment.

Thinking
A thinking state — rational,
measurable. Can be developed by
deliberate, conscious practice.

Creativity

Feeling
A feeling state — emotionally
impactful. Requires self-awareness,
process of self-actualization.
Releases emotional energy from the
creator, transfers this energy to the
viewer or consumer, eliciting an
emotional response.

Sensing
A state of talent — creating new
products seen or heard by others.
Requires high levels of physical or
mental development, high level of
skill in area of talent.

conceptualize. Generate a mental impression or formulate abstract ideas.

reason abstractly. Think about ideas and concepts; draw inferences or conclusions from known or assumed facts.

divergent thinking. Using thinking skills related to creative behavior such as fluency, flexibility, originality, and elaboration; usually, conclusions are reached by reorganizing information and developing a variety of responses.

convergent thinking. Reaching conclusions by using known facts; using thinking skills associated with academic learning such as memory, classification, and reasoning.

FIGURE 7.2 Clark's Creativity Graphic

SOURCE: *Growing Up Gifted,* p. 47, by B. Clark, 1988, Columbus: Merrill Publishing. Reprinted by permission.

some of these characteristics. These individuals are, to an exceptional degree, able to generalize, **conceptualize, reason abstractly,** solve problems, and lead others.

Creativity

Professionals disagree on a common definition of creativity. Some, like Renzulli, integrate creativity into the definition of giftedness, while others (Treffinger, 1986a) believe creativity is a characteristic distinctly separate from superior intelligence or high academic achievement. Many authorities believe that no single test can reliably distinguish highly creative individuals. Creativity is not correlated to high intelligence. Although there is no unifying theory about creativity accepted by the professionals who work in this field, we can make some statements. Creativity is a complex human function that requires extreme abilities to think **divergently** and **convergently** and to solve problems (Treffinger, 1986a). To some (Clark, 1988), creativity is the highest form of giftedness. Clark developed a graphic, shown in Figure 7.2, to better explain her views of creativity and the characteristics it comprises.

standard deviation (SD). A statistical measure that expresses the variability and the distribution from the mean of a set of scores.

So, who are the gifted and creative individuals in our schools and society? Renzulli (1973a) believes strongly that they are represented in all communities in our society. Although ethnicity is not a limiting factor, traditional perspectives of giftedness can discriminate against those who are not in the dominant American culture. Renzulli cites Terman's early work to show that giftedness, even in a traditional or narrow sense, is not restricted to the "advantaged" members of society, for Terman found that twice as many gifted children came from families of nonprofessional workers. Whitmore and Maker (1985) also challenge a common stereotype and remind us that many people with handicaps are also gifted. (For an example, see Paul Longmore's story in chapter 11.) Regardless of the definition used, sensitive teachers who work with gifted learners recognize their uniqueness. Students who are highly intelligent or creative stand apart from their classmates on many different dimensions because of their unique abilities to learn quickly, draw inferences, reason abstractly, generalize, and generate novel solutions to the problems put before them.

Measurement

GIFTEDNESS. Many definitions of giftedness do not include precise criteria to use when determining which specific children are eligible for special programs. Marland's definition, for example, lacks precision in the sense that considerable latitude is left to professionals as they decide who qualifies for services. As stated earlier, the number of children who are eligible for special programs depends on the definition of giftedness and the criteria used for inclusion. To better understand this point, let us look at how intelligence scores are distributed. The assumption is that, if measurements of intelligence were given to a large sample of people, the scores obtained would approximate a normal (bell) curve. (See also chapter 4 for a discussion of the normal curve.) The scores would cluster around the mean or average in a predictable way. Two commonly used tests of intelligence, the Stanford-Binet and the Wechsler Intelligence Scale for Children—Revised (WISC–R), use the score of 100 as the mean. Each of these tests break scores into groups called a **standard deviation (SD).** On the Stanford-Binet, 16 points away from the mean equals one standard deviation. On the WISC–R, 15 points away from the mean equals one SD. So, a score of 130 on the WISC–R is two SDs away from the mean. Figure 7.3 shows a normal curve that has been divided by SDs. It also shows the percentage of the population that falls within each SD grouping. Notice that slightly more than 68 percent of the population fall within one SD below and above the mean (of 100). By using a criteria of two SDs higher than the mean, slightly more than 2 percent of the population should fall above the score of 130 on the WISC–R. This is why you often hear that students who are gifted have IQ scores above 130.

Although Marland's definition is used in many states, it is not universally accepted because it does not provide specific criteria for identifying students who are gifted. Some educators believe the definition must clearly define which children should receive additional or different educational services and which should not. Let us review the definition currently being used in the state of New Mexico (New Mexico State Board of Education, 1988). This definition attempts to provide the specificity needed to identify those who should receive special services for children who are gifted and/or creative and who should not.

"Gifted child" means a school-age person whose measured intelligence quotient, either verbal or nonverbal, measures at least two standard deviations above the

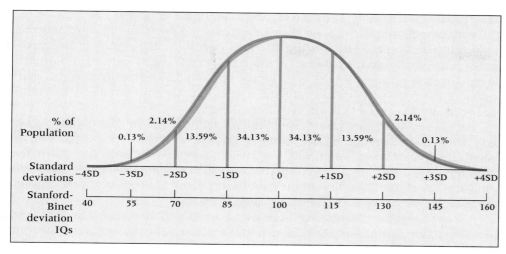

FIGURE 7.3 **Distribution of Intelligence Scores**

mean (a minimum IQ score of 130) on an intelligence test approved by the State Board and who meet at least one of the following additional criteria:

a. Score of at least the ninety-fifth percentile and above on the total battery score on a standardized achievement test approved by the State Board

b. Outstanding creativity or divergent thinking . . . as indicated by a test score at or above 1.5 standard deviations from the mean, above the ninety-sixth percentile, or three grade placements above the student's age-grade placement . . .

c. Outstanding critical thinking or problem-solving ability on a test as defined in a manner established by the test author based on the normative data available on the instrument. . . . Reports from observation of the child's performance should be used to supplement these scores. (pp. B31–32)

States that are concerned about how many children they either desire to serve or can afford to serve in special programs often use specific cut-off scores when they identify and qualify students. As we discuss throughout this chapter, this technique often excludes many children, particularly members of certain subgroups who would qualify if more flexible criteria were applied.

CREATIVITY. Some standardized tests of creativity, such as the Torrance Tests of Creative Thinking (Torrance and Ball, 1984), do exist and are used to identify children who are uniquely creative. However, since there is no widely accepted definition of creativity and most formal tests of creativity are criticized, it is difficult to apply standardized criteria to the identification of children who are creative, but not gifted. Quite possibly, this is one reason why classes for children who are creative do not exist in most parts of this country. It is also probably why so many educators advocate including more than 3 percent of all children in special programs and for more flexible ways of qualifying children, such as teacher nominations.

Significance

Individuals who are gifted or creative are not handicapped by any lack of ability. Rather, the challenge to educators is to provide a stimulating educational environment and a broad curriculum to help these individuals reach their full potential. As

eminence. Superiority in ability.

mentioned under History of the Field, education of the gifted has not received the full commitment of policymakers across this century. Education of the gifted is not funded by IDEA, as is education for those who have handicaps. Funding for school-based programs for gifted children comes from states' funds. Americans' attitudes about giftedness place this field in a precarious position. Their attitude is that education of the gifted is an unnecessary frill, a series of programs that can be discontinued when budgets need to be cut (Silverman, 1988).

Americans' negative attitudes about the education of the gifted most likely stem from some myths about the field and the individuals it serves. For example, many people think that these children will thrive without special programs. They can make it on their own; they do not need special assistance. Other people think that these programs are elitist. Regardless of the reasons, the result has been that programs for the gifted have been sporadic over the last three decades.

Of course, some children who are gifted achieve their potential without the benefits of special education. Silverman points out that "giftedness does not occur in a vacuum" (p. 246). Even the development of a talent, like playing a musical instrument, requires considerable fostering, guidance, and practice. Children who have the potential for creativity can strengthen their creative abilities. This occurs when the educational environment encourages and rewards creativity, where even wild ideas are valued and can be safely proposed. All children need to develop the motivation to grow and expand. For many children who are gifted or creative, the regular classroom alone cannot provide the challenges they require to remain motivated or learn at an accelerated and comfortable pace.

HISTORY OF THE FIELD

Emphasis on the education of the gifted has been sporadic in human history. Confucius, a famous Chinese philosopher who lived around 500 B.C., believed that all children should be educated, but that education should be tailored to their abilities. His views evidently were implemented during the Tang dynasty in 618 A.D., when gifted and talented children were brought to the imperial court, where they received special education and attention. Because the Chinese valued literacy, leadership, imagination, memory, and reasoning, these topics were part of the curriculum offered to children. The Japanese also provided differential educational opportunities to their children. For example, during the Tokugawa society (1604–1868), children born of the Samarai nobility were educated in Confucian classics, martial arts, history, moral values, calligraphy, and composition. The children of the poor, however, were educated about the value of loyalty, obedience, humility, and diligence (Davis and Rimm, 1989).

Attention to innate and superior abilities in people in Western cultures can be attributed to the work of Charles Darwin and Sir Francis Galton, in the middle of the 1800s. Charles Darwin is most famous for his theories about natural selection and the evolution of all species. Before that time no one had on a broad scale studied individual differences among people or issues relating to intelligence and heredity (Clark, 1988). In 1869 Galton proposed some reasons for individuals displaying superior abilities. He believed that genius is solely attributed to heredity, and that **eminence** was due to two factors: (1) an internal motivation to excel and (2) intellect, both of which were thought to be genetically inherited (Callahan, 1981). The notion that genetic factors contribute greatly to giftedness is still adhered to today, but the important contributions of the environment are recognized.

In the United States, our wavering commitment to the education of the gifted reflects our national philosophy about equity and social justice. During the eighteenth century the leaders of the country leaned toward the view that education was best for the elite. However, during the nineteenth century egalitarianism—the view that no one should get special treatment—became popular. Our national hesitation in providing distinctly different educational experiences for gifted students may reflect American attitudes formed when this country was founded. Thomas Jefferson argued against elitism in this country and believed that the purpose of education was to foster democracy, a notion of equality of citizens. Since the early nineteenth century, the American people have been offered different models for creating a better society. For example, egalitarianism became very popular during the Jacksonian era (around 1830). This egalitarian position was extreme, holding that no individual will be considered "better" than anyone else regardless of innate abilities, status, or education. Gardner (1984) suggests that it is from this social philosophy that the concept of equal opportunity was developed. One legacy of egalitarianism is the attitude that special education for gifted children is undemocratic, elitist, unnecessary, and wasteful. Some researchers believe that special programs for gifted youngsters in this country were not advocated "for fear that any attention to their abilities would give rise to a dangerous aristocracy" (Silverman, 1988, p. 136). A position of support for gifted education risks criticism as alien to democracy and equality.

Most chroniclers of gifted education in the United States (Clark, 1988; Gallagher, 1988; Tannenbaum, 1983) stress the importance of the development of the Binet Intelligence Test in 1905. Not originally developed to identify students who are gifted, this test nonetheless marks the beginning of real interest in this country about individuals who are gifted. Although there were some programs for the gifted established as early as 1866, real development and growth in educational services for these individuals did not occur until the 1920s (Maker, 1986a).

A classic study of individuals who were gifted, both as children and adults, was conducted by Lewis Terman in 1925. Although dated, it still might be the most comprehensive work on the topic. This study stimulated interest in gifted education, but efforts were halted by the Great Depression of the 1930s and World War II in the 1940s. The 1960s saw a renewed interest in children who are gifted. The promotion of unique educational services can be linked to one specific historical event: the 1957 Russian launching of **Sputnik,** a space satellite. America feared losing the space race. The launch was viewed as a risk to national security, and a blow to national pride. The United States vowed to catch up and surpass the competition. Federal funding became available to establish programs, develop ways to identify students with high academic achievement particularly in math and science, and conduct research to find effective methods for providing excellent educational experiences. These students were seen as a great national resource, the persons who would make America the leader once again.

During the late 1960s and 1970s, the nation turned its attention to the civil rights movement and the needs of the culturally and linguistically diverse and poor, and interest in the education of the gifted waned. Education of the gifted was thought to be one more advantage for the already advantaged youth of our society, and the nation's policymakers adopted a position that these youngsters could make it on their own (Maker, 1986a). Continuing the cycle, it appears that today, once again, there is a renewed interest in education of the gifted. In 1988 more than $200 million was being spent by the fifty states for special programs for students who are gifted (Gallagher, 1988). Why the renewed interest? We have become concerned about the quality of education and the place of the United States in the world. For example,

Sputnik. The name of the Russian spaceship that was launched in 1957 and caused a renewed interest in the education of the gifted in this country.

comparisons of the mathematics scores for eighth graders across many nations show that America's students are ranked near the bottom (Stern, 1988). Japan and other countries are more competitive in the world's marketplaces. We are concerned about America's position in the newly emerging, technologically based, competitive world. This might well generate into a national commitment to education of the gifted.

PREVALENCE

The number of children identified as gifted in the United States depends on the definition and concept of giftedness used. For example, if we consider that only those who score in the highest 1 percent on an intelligence test can qualify for special services, the number served would be 1 in every 100 children. If we consider those who score in the highest 2 percent as the criterion, giftedness should occur twice in every group of 100 children. Some estimate that as many as 3 to 5 percent of the school-age population should receive specialized services for the gifted (Mitchell and Erickson, 1978; Sisk, 1981, 1987), while others place the percentage higher, at 10 to 15 percent (Renzulli, 1978). It is important to know that when a score from a test of intelligence is the sole means for identifying students who are gifted, the number who qualify for services is much smaller than when other unique and exceptional characteristics are also considered. If the criterion used is more flexible, then children with other outstanding traits could receive these special educational services. For example, children whose primary language is not English who obtain an IQ score of 120 but demonstrate outstanding creative and leadership skills would not qualify for services under the more restrictive definitions.

Students who are gifted or creative are not funded by IDEA (for a review of IDEA, see chapter 1); therefore, the number receiving services is not reported by the states to the federal government, and no other national reporting system is used to indicate how many of these students actually receive different educational services. Moreover, not all states or local school systems provide services for these youngsters. Therefore, estimates of the total number of students with IQ scores above a certain level probably overrepresent the number of children actually being served. Table 7.3 shows how many children should be identified per units of children by bands of IQ scores. This table estimates approximate numbers of children who might qualify for gifted services in a school or school district. Using this table you can identify how many children might be provided special services in a school district of 50,000 students, in an elementary school of 400, and in a high school of 2000. These calculations are based solely on the criterion of the scores obtained in an intelligence test. If other factors, such as leadership or creative abilities, were considered, more children might be identified. It is also important to know that giftedness is not evenly distributed across locales. For example, some communities, particularly those with a high proportion of highly educated parents, have more children with IQ scores above 130 attending their schools.

It is clear that the number of students who are gifted or creative receiving specialized educational services is much lower than it should be. This is a long-standing problem in the education of the gifted. Marland, in 1972, found a relatively small percentage of the estimated 1.5 to 2 million children who should qualify for services actually receiving special services. The situation, ten years later, had improved, and only two states did not have programs for these children (Mitchell, 1982). Another study, conducted in 1987, found that forty-seven states have special programs for

TABLE 7.3. Prevalence of Individuals Who Are Gifted, Depending on the IQ Cut-off Score Used

IQ Score	Approximate Incidence
130	2 in 100
140	1 in 1,000
150	1 in 10,000
160 and above	1 in 100,000

Source: *Educating Special Learners*, 3d ed., p. 322, by G. P. Cartwright, C. A. Cartwright, and M. A. Ward, 1988, Belmont, CA: Belmont Publishing. Reprinted by permission.

children who are gifted (Houseman, 1987). Of those states, twenty-five mandate services, while twenty-two permit special programs but do not require them. So, not all school districts in these forty-seven states actually provide special education for students who are gifted. Only nineteen states of the total require specific training or certification of teachers involved in programs for gifted children (Kutner, 1989). In addition, even if all states and school districts were providing services, they would still not serve all of the children they should. Considerably less than 3 percent of American children receive education for the gifted (Kirschenbaum, 1988). In particular, culturally and linguistically diverse students are underrepresented. These youngsters have a 1 in 200 chance of being identified as either creative or gifted (Branscomb, 1980). In Kirschenbaum's study, many more white children (2.9 percent) received gifted education when compared to African-Americans (1.5 percent), Hispanics (1.5 percent), and Native Americans (1.1 percent). How can this situation be changed? One solution is not to rely as much on results from standardized tests (Callahan, 1981). Other methods, such as teacher nominations and behavioral observations that draw upon the experiences and environment of the child, have been used to successfully identify youngsters who are gifted.

CAUSES—HEREDITY AND ENVIRONMENT

Throughout the history of the field of education for the gifted and creative, people have believed that genetics was the primary cause of giftedness. (Refer to the History of the Field for Galton's views from the mid-nineteenth century.) In the 1920s Terman, the leader in the field, also reflected the view that genetic factors are responsible for giftedness. However, today, researchers recognize the important role the environment plays in the development of the intellect (Laycock, 1979).

Research has shown that factors such as the values and expectations of the culture, the socioeconomic level of the family, one's birth-position in the family (e.g., first born), and the number of children in the family are related to giftedness (Terman, 1925). So, too, does environmental stimulation correlate to the probability of excelling and developing gifted or creative abilities. Environmental factors can also diminish giftedness. For example, children whose early experiences are not rich or diverse often do not develop outstanding cognitive skills, and children who are not challenged in school do not develop their potential. Today, superior abilities are generally recognized as resulting from the interrelationship between heredity and the environment. Therefore, special programs that help gifted individuals achieve to their potential need to be available.

Factors That Enhance or Inhibit Giftedness and Creativity

Many factors enhance or inhibit giftedness and creativity. Boredom can inhibit giftedness. This point is well made by a nine-year-old child who is gifted:

> Oh what a bore to sit and listen,
> To stuff we already know.
> Do everything we've done and done again,
> But we still must sit and listen.
> Over and over read one more page
> Oh bore, oh bore, oh bore.
> Sometimes I feel if we do one more page
> My head will explode with boreness rage
> I wish I could get up right there and march right out the door.*

Let us keep in mind that intelligence and creativity are not fixed. Although heredity plays a critical role, an individual's intellectual and creative abilities are also influenced by the environment, an individual's life experiences, and by others' expectations. Intelligence can be both enhanced and inhibited by the environment. "Patterns of high and low achievement during various historical eras provide considerable post hoc evidence of the effects of the environment on giftedness" (Callahan, 1981, p. 63). Creativity, or possibly how we measure it, is also influenced by environment and culture. For example, Native Americans residing in urban areas show a greater degree of creativity on typical measures than those living on reservations (Bradley, 1990). Major environmental factors—wars, famines, social upheavals—can affect the potential of any individual. Certainly, prenatal malnutrition, isolation, neglect, abuse, insufficient infant stimulation, and poor medical treatment can have devastating effects upon the development of the intellect. (Refer to prevention sections in other chapters in this text, in particular in chapter 4, Mental Retardation.)

Another factor that can inhibit giftedness and creativity is the way children grow up. Renzulli (1973a) has observed that many young children are inherently creative, but he notes that relatively few adults are creative. What happens to children thought to be creative during their preschool and early elementary years? Were they really not very creative in the first place? Or, is creativity discouraged and not fostered by our society?

It appears that certain cultures are unable or unwilling to tolerate creativity or extreme differences, while other cultures are more receptive to certain talents or types of creativity. This can be demonstrated by different periods in history. For example, the Renaissance was a period when extraordinary creativity was recognized, as demonstrated in the unique architectural, artistic, and literary achievements of the day. Likewise, the excavations at Pompeii revealed an advanced, rich culture and life-style that thrived more than 1300 years before the Renaissance, complete with many conveniences like water transported to homes through pipes. Such features were common in the ancient Roman Empire, but not found in later civilizations. What was it about these societies and cultures that fostered and encouraged the development of such creativity?

Krippner (1967) argues that the values of the dominant American culture inhibit creativity. He believes that "the creative individual—to some extent—must stand

---

*J. R. Delisle, 1984. *Gifted Children Speak Out*, p. 72. New York: Walker and Company. Reprinted by permission.

Enthusiasm and creativity should never be discouraged.

apart from his culture in order to produce a new idea, a novel image, or an original product" (p. 144). He maintains that for society to advance, education must transmit cultural heritage as well as encourage innovation. Unfortunately, these goals are often in conflict. Krippner makes the case that creativity is often punished both at home and at school. Children are encouraged to fit into a mold. Teachers favor highly intelligent students who do well academically but are not creative. Even children's peer groups criticize divergent, independent, and imaginative behavior among their creative friends. To further demonstrate his points, Krippner created a set of "ten commandments," or expected norms, that he believes inhibit the development of creativity and are both directly and indirectly communicated to children. Krippner's first commandment, "Everything thou doest must be useful," points out the practical and pragmatic nature of Americans. We, as Americans, place a high premium on the usefulness of our education. Examples used in classrooms and at home are realistic instead of imaginative. Toys, the curriculum, and classroom experiences leave little for imagination: Dolls that talk and act like real children; computerized toys that teach children the correct answers to arithmetic problems and the correct way to spell words. Think of other examples of toys that might enhance or inhibit imaginary play. College students are often guided by parents and others to select majors that will lead to high-paying jobs. Krippner also makes the point that America is an achievement-oriented society where individuals are reinforced for being competent and adequate in all possible respects. Qualities valued are getting along with others, ability to work toward a goal, and adjustment. He believes that these individual characteristics are valued more than creativity and individual differences. Also, the need for acceptance causes many people to repress creativity. Review Krippner's "ten

TABLE 7.4. Krippner's Ten Commandments That Impede Creativity

Everything thou doest must be useful.
Everything thou doest must be successful.
Everything thou doest must be perfect.
Everyone thou knowest must like thee.
Thou shalt not prefer solitude to togetherness.
Remember to concentrate attention and keep it holy.
Thou shalt not diverge from culturally imposed sex norms.
Thou shalt not express excessive emotional feelings.
Thou shalt not be ambiguous.
Thou shalt not rock the cultural boat.

Source: S. Krippner, 1967, "The ten commandments that block creativity," *Gifted Child Quarterly, 11,* p. 144.

commandments," found in Table 7.4, and provide examples of situations that might inhibit creativity for each of his proposed commandments of American society.

PROFILE OF CHILDREN WHO ARE GIFTED OR CREATIVE

As with any group of people, it is unfair to any specific member to generalize group characteristics to individual members. On the other hand, it is easier to understand a group if some commonly observed features are described. Research findings presented in Table 7.5 provide us with some common characteristics of people who are gifted (Clark, 1988; Laycock, 1979; Maker, 1986a; Maker and Schiever, 1989).

Another way to learn about characteristics that members of a group share is to study the tests used to identify them. In 1970 the Commission on Tests analyzed the Scholastic Aptitude Tests (SAT), and found this test too narrow in judging the probability of students' success in college. The Commission determined that the SAT tests students' verbal, mathematical, and reasoning abilities well. However, this team of experts concluded that high potential comprises more skills and abilities than these

TABLE 7.5. Common Characteristics of the Gifted Child

Intellectual	Social/Emotional
Reasons abstractly	Criticizes self
Conceptualizes	Empathizes
Processes information well	Plays with older friends
Solves problems	Persists
Learns quickly	Is sensitive to others' feelings
Shows intellectual curiosity	Exhibits individualism
Has wide interests	Has strength of character
Dislikes drill and routine	Demonstrates leadership abilities
May show unevenness	
Generalizes learning	
Remembers great amount of material	
Displays high level of verbal ability	

three. Although not meant to be a description of students who are gifted, thinking about the skills and abilities related to high potential can broaden our understanding of what these learners are like. Renzulli (1973) endorses the Commission's views of human abilities, and suggests that if a test could be constructed that measures the following characteristics, it would be more equitable to students who come from less enriched educational backgrounds. Gifted students

1. adapt to new learning situations;
2. solve problems in situations that require varied reasoning and thinking skills;
3. demonstrate abilities to search out, analyze, and synthesize information;
4. manage, process, and use information meaningfully;
5. use nonstandard pools of information;
6. comprehend the meaning of information gathered in different ways (experiencing, listening, looking, as well as reading);
7. are able to express themselves in many different ways (artistically, orally, nonverbally, graphically, as well as in writing);
8. are highly motivated;
9. have good work habits and a high degree of task involvement under varying conditions.

To further our understanding of individuals who are creative, Renzulli lists characteristics that occur frequently among those who are creative and come from disadvantaged backgrounds (Renzulli, 1973):

"1. high nonverbal fluency and originality;
2. high creative productivity in small groups;
3. adeptness in visual art activities;
4. high creativity in movement, dance, and other physical activities;
5. ability to be highly motivated by games, music, sports, humor, and concrete objects;
6. language rich in imagery." (p. 440)

Gifted learners are victims of stereotypes, and sometimes negative descriptors are ascribed to this group: "thin, nervous, brash, snobbish, difficult to tolerate, and concerned only with books, ideas, and self" (Laycock, 1979, p. 57). Hollingworth (1942) popularized the belief that gifted individuals are likely to develop personality problems. However, research has consistently shown that these negative characteristics do not exist for the group. Individuals who are gifted are not necessarily anxious, nor do they exhibit discipline problems. In fact, it appears that those who are gifted are better adjusted than the general population (Grossberg and Cornell, 1988; Terman, 1925).

Subgroups Requiring Special Attention

As with any group of people, there are subgroups of people who are highly intelligent or highly creative who face unique or specific problems. We discuss in this section four subgroups: females who are gifted, students who are culturally and linguistically diverse, persons with handicaps who are gifted, and underachievers who are gifted. Throughout these discussions, remember how society's values and expectations can influence all of us.

We might all agree that it is important to identify and serve all children who are gifted. However, many subgroups in this category are not currently served, or even identified as gifted or uniquely creative. This represents a significant loss to these individuals and to the nation.

> If we do not provide for these underserved children, we will never know how many Franklin D. Roosevelts or Helen Kellers, or George Shearings or Nelson Rockefellers, or Count Basies are hiding, never to be discovered in the next generation. If we do not start in the beginning of their school career, we may lose in them the fragile desire to do well in school and to pursue knowledge vigorously. (Gallagher, 1988, p. 110)

FEMALES WHO ARE GIFTED. Terman, during the 1920s, studied many individuals identified as gifted. The number of men identified in his study far outnumbered the women. Even today, it appears that the number of men considered gifted or creative far exceeds the number of women who have achieved such status (Callahan, 1981). This is the case even though the number of preschool boys and girls who are gifted is about equal (Silverman, 1988). What are the reasons for this? Are there innate differences between the genders that cause giftedness to occur more frequently in men than in women? This has never been proven in research. Are society's expectations for people and the roles they assume the critical factors in the achievement levels of either gender (Kerr, 1985; Reis and Callahan, 1989)? Will the changing roles of women affect the number of school-age girls identified as being gifted and their ultimate career choices? Silverman (1986b) observed that young girls who are gifted were more likely to hide their abilities so they would not be viewed by their peers as different.

Some researchers (Eccles, 1985; Rand and Gibb, 1989) believe that females who are gifted need a different kind of educational programming to achieve to their potential, especially in the hard sciences. It is not yet clear whether differences between the genders are related to innate abilities, differences in personalities, interests, and values, or differences in achievement motivation. Regardless, in the past, women faced bias and discrimination that affected the opportunities available to them. Today, they still face barriers and stereotypes that restrict the development of their abilities. These barriers and stereotypes in society influence choices young women make throughout their school years (Callahan, 1981). Silverman (1988) suggests that girls who are gifted must be identified early in their schooling, provided with a challenging curriculum, counseled to achieve in areas not traditionally pursued by women, and be given many examples and role models to follow.

GIFTED STUDENTS WHO ARE CULTURALLY AND LINGUISTICALLY DIVERSE. Students who are culturally and linguistically diverse face many challenges (see chapter 2), particularly the subgroup who are gifted. These youngsters frequently do not qualify for special services because some do not meet stringently applied cut-off scores on standardized tests. One reason for lower scores may be families' different cultural values and different emphasis on cognitive development (Gallagher, 1988; Maker and Schiever, 1989a). (Also see this chapter's Concepts and Controversies.) Table 7.6 compares the absolute characteristics of giftedness with those generally

TABLE 7.6. Characteristics of Giftedness and Cultural Values of Hispanics, and the Behaviors Resulting from Their Interactive Influence

Absolute Aspects of Giftedness	Cultural Values Often Characteristic of Hispanics	Behavioral Differences
High level of verbal ability	Traditional language of family	Communicates fluently with peers and within community, even if using nonstandard English
Emotional depth and intensity	*Abrazo*, a physical or spiritual index of personal support	Requires touching, eye contact, feeling of support to achieve maximum academic productivity
Unusual sensitivity to feelings and expectations of others	Family structure and dynamic-male dominance	Personal initiative, independent thought, and verbal aggressiveness often inhibited in females
Conceptualize solutions to social and environmental problems	Nuclear and extended family closeness valued	Often assumes responsibility for family and/or younger siblings
Unusual retentiveness; unusual capacity for processing information	Traditional culture	Adapts to successful functioning in two cultures
Leadership	Collaborative rather than competitive dynamic	Accomplishes more, works better in small groups than individually

Source: "Defining the Hispanic Population," p. 4, by C. J. Maker and S. W. Schiever (Eds.), 1989, in *Critical Issues in Gifted Education: Defensible Programs for Cultural and Ethnic Minorities* (Vol. II). Copyright 1989 by PRO-ED. Reprinted by permission.

found and valued by the Hispanic culture. This table helps us understand the dynamic relationship between culture and individuals' performance. These differences in characteristics should be considered not only when identifying youngsters for services, but also when planning their educational programs. How might these differences shown in this table affect selection of students and educational program planning?

For gifted learners who are culturally and linguistically diverse, more flexible identification procedures may be required (Mistry and Rogoff, 1985). Baldwin (1987) proposes that a multidimensional identification system be adopted for culturally and linguistically diverse children. She proposes that scores from intelligence, achievement, cognitive processing, creativity, *and* rating scales completed by parents, the children's peers, and teachers all be used. Once selected for special programs, these students also need educational programs that continue to foster their cultural diversity while developing their intellectual and creative abilities.

INDIVIDUALS WHO ARE GIFTED AND ALSO HAVE A DISABILITY. Another group of students not typically chosen for inclusion in programs for the gifted are those students who also have a handicapping condition. These individuals' disabilities often mask their potential, and frequently the scores they receive on ability and achievement tests are falsely low (Silverman, 1986a, 1988). Whitmore and Maker (1985) estimate that 2 percent of persons with disabilities are also mentally gifted. Despite often inadequate and frustrating educational experiences, many gifted adults

---

Focus: Issues of Diversity

Over the past three decades Americans have made considerable progress improving race relations; however, the belief that we are approaching a color and creed-blind society is disabused by the ethnic image data collected by Smith in 1990. Smith studied the ethnic images—the general beliefs about group characteristics and attributes—Americans have about six cultural groups. His findings indicate that the majority of Americans see most minority groups in a decidedly negative light, with images that are neither benign nor trivial. Such attitudes help shape local and national policies about civil rights, affirmative action, school desegregation, and access to educational programs. Perhaps negative ethnic images are in part responsible for the underrepresentation of students who are culturally and linguistically diverse in programs for the gifted. Certainly, educators must become conscious of such images and advocate that all students who demonstrate gifted or creative abilities receive an appropriate education.

---

with disabilities have distinguished themselves as leaders in their communities, and have made significant contributions to the professions in which they work. This is exceptional given the fact that few people with disabilities receive education designed for students who are gifted. Why is this so? People with disabilities are seldom perceived by their families or teachers as possessing gifted abilities. Society's biases about people with handicaps can overshadow these individuals' strengths. For example, a student with a severe physical disability might require more time to answer questions on a timed, standardized test. Students with handicaps might need to use special equipment such as a print enlarger or a computer to function in a traditional testing situation. Modifications to the testing situation are seldom provided when qualifying a youngster for classes for the gifted. In the 1970s, Maker (1977) began to raise the awareness of educators about the needs of gifted learners with disabilities. In her research, Maker (1986a) found one of the key variables leading to these individuals' success: motivation to succeed. She maintains that, in addition to providing the educational content usually found in programs for the gifted, these students need additional guidance to become more self-confident and develop a strong, internally driven motivation to achieve.

One underserved group of gifted students who are handicapped are those individuals who are both gifted and learning disabled. These students are extremely bright, but because of their learning disability many do not achieve to their potential. Often, these students are caught in the middle, and receive no special services, despite their obvious uniqueness. In many states, because of their high IQ scores they do not qualify for educational programs for the learning disabled, and because of their low achievement test scores, they do not qualify for educational programs for the gifted.

UNDERACHIEVERS WHO ARE GIFTED. Finally, our attention is drawn to children who are gifted but are underachievers. These students demonstrate high intelligence, but also demonstrate low academic achievement. Depending on the discrepancy between these individuals' scores on intelligence and achievement tests, in some states these students are confused with students who are gifted/learning disabled. Teachers and parents often recognize these students' true capabilities, but these students do not do well in school or perform up to their abilities, sometimes for unexplainable reasons. These students have been described as disorganized, unmotivated, lacking interest in school, having poor study skills, and lacking in self-confidence (Rimm, 1986). Some of these children are hyperactive, while others are passive. Some present discipline problems to their teachers and families, while others do not. Some are bored with school; others are frustrated by the experience. Clearly, these students, like those who are handicapped and gifted, need a strong motivation to succeed. These youngsters need specialized educational services to teach them how to achieve in school, how to approach learning tasks more meaningfully, and how to use their talents in a directed fashion.

ISSUES IN EDUCATION

Enhanced educational opportunities for those who are gifted or creative have been available inconsistently across time and across the nation. Education of the gifted is part of special education in many states, but not all, since no federal law requires these students be guaranteed instructional programs tailored for gifted and creative students. Education of the gifted is not part of IDEA, and, therefore, does not receive federal funding for school-based programs. In 1980 Branscomb noted, "although gifted and talented students comprise 3–5 percent of the school-age population, they receive only 0.003 of the federal funds for education" (p. 37). The federal Office of Gifted and Talented closed in 1981, and was not reopened until 1989 under the auspices of the U.S. Department of Education. After years of no funding for national research, demonstration, or teacher preparation programs, today a relatively small amount of federal money is being allocated for these purposes.

This inconsistent commitment to the education of the gifted stems from differing philosophical beliefs about society, elitism, and educational opportunities rooted in our national history. One argument centers on the notion that these children are already advantaged and do not need more benefits. But, as you have learned in this chapter, youngsters who are gifted are atypical learners. They need specialized services to make full use of their extraordinary talents. Their potential, if wasted, represents a significant loss. Educators for many years have discussed the educational options that could be made available to students who are gifted. For example, over sixty years ago, Scheidemann in her 1931 text about exceptional children wrote:

> Enrichment of curriculum, rapid progress, or segregation in special classes for only gifted children are advocated by modern educators. The arguments extended by early objectors for these special methods, namely, that attainments of the bright children are needed to stimulate the progress of normal children, or that an I.Q. aristocracy would be encouraged among school children, are groundless. Even the objections on the basis of the discrepancy between physical and intellectual maturity that would result in permitting the superior child to progress at his individual rate are no longer tenable. . . . Some specialists urge time-saving by rapid promotions in pre-college education, and regular or longer attendance in professional schools, because the gifted mind can spend unlimited time in specialization.

> Rapid promotion is urged by many educators because it is easy and inexpensive. The more thoughtful are more inclined to encourage an enrichment of program for gifted children, thus keeping their intellectual powers active in association with

children who are mentally and physically their equal. Social ostracism, which is the usual fate of the very young high-school child, is thus avoided. Many suggestions in regard to the specific ways in which the curriculum may be enriched are offered. (pp. 261–262)

Education and the Preschool Child

What can we do for the preschool child who is gifted? As we know, early stimulation is critical to the development of *all* young children. Certainly, the American public is aware of the value of early childhood education and has been pushing for more and better day care centers and preschool programs. Research has shown that early childhood programs are helpful for children who are gifted. In studies of eminent people (Terman, 1925; Goertzel and Goertzel, 1962), evidence is presented that these individuals had enriched experiences early in their lives. In many instances, parents shared a talent or aptitude with their precocious offspring, and provided role models as well as substantial encouragement as the child began to develop (Bloom and Sosniak, 1981). As we all know, with the rise of the two-parent working family and the single-parent household, more and more children attend day care and preschool programs. For a variety of reasons, children sometimes receive their primary stimulation from these programs. Throughout this text, we present evidence that shows the importance of early childhood educational experience for children with exceptionalities. Early education is also important for children who are gifted. The quality of early education programs must be consistently of the highest level.

This young preschooler is already demonstrating advanced reading and conceptual abilities. Many youngsters who are gifted come to school possessing skills beyond their peers. Teachers must be alert to continually challenge and support children with giftedness and creativity.

CRITICAL THINKING SKILLS

The development of critical thinking skills can begin early in children's education. Units specifically aimed at developing critical thinking can be incorporated as enrichment activities. McDowell (1989) demonstrates that critical thinking can be taught to very young children through an experiential approach. She used an apple as the basis for lessons designed to develop vocabulary, oral language, reading, as well as thinking abilities (cognition). The following example, using the apple model, illustrates how critical thinking skills can be integrated into educational programs for even very young children. It involves a slight modification of typical teaching routines, more involvement of the children, and some good question-asking from the teacher.

Mrs. Peterson, a preschool teacher, teaches a group of bright children. Because of their young age, their experiential backgrounds are still very limited. On the first day of her unit about apples, she reads the story of Johnny Appleseed to her class. During her reading, she stresses important concepts and language (words) presented in the story. After reading the story, she engages the children in a discussion about the story and their own experiences with apples. How do you get apples? Where do they come from? Are they all alike? What do you do with them?

On ensuing days, Mrs. Peterson creates different lessons to help the children to think and experience more about a food they have all eaten. She has the children reenact the story of Johnny Appleseed, with each child taking a turn playing the main character. Then, she rereads the story. She stops several times, and asks the children to predict what is going to happen next. On another day, the children discuss where apples come from, how they grow on trees, and when they are picked.

Later, the class takes a trip to the store. One by one, Mrs. Peterson tells them to go find the apples. The children meet in the vegetable section, compare different types of apples, and discuss how they differ (in color, size, texture, taste). The class then goes to find other products in the store that are made of apples. Instructed to find different products, the children identify the following items: cereal, pies, cookies, applesauce, and juice. Before leaving the store, the children and Mrs. Peterson buy several sacks of apples to use at school later in the week.

At school the next day, the class studies the apples they had purchased. They slice one open and talk about the various parts (seeds, stem, peel). The children create a story about apples through a language experience approach and then role-play their story.

One day Mrs. Peterson writes, "Foods with Apples" on the board. The children have to think of all the foods they can that are made with apples. They talk about how these foods were packaged (in boxes, bottles, jars). They discuss how many apples it would take to make these foods. Since the children seem to have no concept of the number of apples it takes to make various foods, the next day Mrs. Peterson helps them to make applesauce. Beforehand the children take turns guessing how many apples it will take to fill the two jars that Mrs. Peterson has brought to school. They all participate fully in making the applesauce, and enjoy eating their culinary creation the next day during snack time.

In one of the few demonstration preschools for gifted youngsters, researchers made some interesting observations about these children, even in their very early years (Karnes, Shwedel, and Linnemeyer, 1982). These children were healthier, quicker to learn, larger for their age, emotionally better adjusted, socially more mature, had longer attention spans, persisted in tasks longer, had a keen sense of humor, enjoyed independence, resisted rigid rules, and enjoyed competition. These researchers maintain that children, particularly those who show signs of accelerated development, must be challenged so their motivation to learn is not dulled. They caution that no child should be forced to relearn what is already mastered. Time after time, stories are told about children who come to kindergarten already reading but are not allowed to continue developing their reading skills. Instead, they are forced to engage in readiness activities with classmates. Instructional time might well be better spent on different instructional activities like teaching students to classify and organize information or to think critically. The example provided in the Teaching Tactics box demonstrates how teachers can foster critical thinking skills even in very young children.

Education and the School-Age Child

Today, a variety of educational programs are available to gifted students. These programs vary by locale and differ in philosophy and orientation. Unfortunately, some "have not been developed on the basis of research or theoretical design, but often by a seat-of-the-pants style that has been heavily influenced by a few leading educators in this special field" (Gallagher, 1988, p. 109). No nationally adopted curriculum or standardized set of instructional procedures exists for the education of the gifted. So, how should we judge the quality of programs for these students if there is no uniformity? Maker (1989) suggests that the "curriculum content designed for gifted learners must be qualitatively different from that usually included in the basic curriculum for all children" (p. 34). She (1986b) also reminds teachers that they must teach students *how* to think *and* also *what* to think about. In many programs for students who are gifted, content is disregarded for instruction on critical thinking skills.

In this section, we discuss different approaches to education for the gifted and several techniques for teaching creativity. Some approaches are comprehensive models and influence the entire school day; others modify a portion of the school day; still others are instructional procedures that can be easily integrated into any ongoing instructional program. Regardless, all seek to develop the unique talents possessed by gifted individuals, and serve as illustrative examples of educational systems that are responsive to individuals' needs by altering traditional educational programs.

Approaches to Education of the Gifted

Although no one agrees on what is the best educational approach for students who are gifted and/or creative, generally, one of two approaches—enrichment or acceleration—or their combination, is used. Within each approach many different versions and a variety of instructional methods can be applied to each. Table 7.7 summarizes the approaches we discuss in this chapter.

TABLE 7.7. Approaches to Education of the Gifted

Approach	Explanation
1. Enrichment	
a. Interdisciplinary instruction	Teaching a topic by presenting different disciplines' perspectives about the issues involved.
b. Independent study	Examining a topic in more depth than is usual in a regular education class.
c. Mentorship	Pairing students with adults who guide them in applying knowledge to real-life situations.
d. Internship programs	Programs that allow gifted students, usually during their senior year in high school, to be placed in a job setting that matches their career goals.
e. Enrichment Triad/Revolving Door Model	An inclusive and flexible model for gifted education that changes the entire educational system. Students are exposed to planned activities that seek to develop thinking skills, problem solving, and creativity.
2. Acceleration	
a. Advanced placement	Courses that students take during their high school years resulting in college credit.
b. Honors sections	A form of ability grouping where gifted and nongifted students who demonstrate high achievement in a particular subject are placed together in advanced classes.
c. Ability grouping	Clustering students in courses where all classmates have comparable achievement and skill levels.
d. Individualized instruction	Instruction delivered on a one-to-one basis, with students moving through the curriculum at their own pace independently.
3. Combination	
Purdue Secondary Model for Gifted and Talented Youth	A comprehensive high school curriculum for gifted students that incorporates counseling into the standard program for all students.

enrichment. Adding topics or skills to the traditional curriculum or presenting a particular topic in more depth.

interdisciplinary instruction. An approach to the education of the gifted that involves studying a topic and its issues in the context of several different disciplines.

1. ENRICHMENT. Enrichment can include the addition of curricular topics or the development of skills not usually included in the traditional curriculum. For example, a group of students might spend a small portion of time each week working with instructional materials that enhance creativity or critical thinking skills. Or, enrichment may be the study of a particular academic subject in more depth and detail. Some teachers, when using enrichment in this way, guide students to select a character or an event for research and study. The student's product might be an oral or written report that could become part of a class play or short story, or a nonverbal product such as a painting, construction, or model.

The enrichment approach is often used in regular classroom settings to meet the needs of advanced learners without having them leave the regular classroom for their education. To use this approach successfully, however, teachers must be well prepared to guide children as they learn and apply skills like critical thinking, problem solving, advanced reasoning, and research.

To better understand the enrichment process, let us look at an example from a history lesson. This lesson involves **interdisciplinary instruction,** allowing for the further development of traditional subjects by encouraging students to study a subject using different perspectives. Students studying the historical figure of King Richard III through an inquiry method would study the king both as a historical figure

independent study. A common approach to the education of the gifted which allows a student to pursue and study a topic in depth on an individual basis.

mentorship. A gifted student is paired with an adult in order to learn to apply knowledge in real-life situations.

and as the central character in Shakespeare's play, "The Life and Death of King Richard III" (see Hubbard, 1983). The students are encouraged to question the guilt or innocence of Richard. Did he murder his young nephews or not? To arrive at their conclusions, students study the historical background, analyze conflicting sources of information, assess the believability of their sources, synthesize conflicting information, develop hypotheses, and defend their positions. Students must study and understand the political realities and key concepts of King Richard's day (feudalism, homage, chivalry, dower rights, Divine Right of the monarch). Throughout this process, students learn to be "historical detectives." They advance their knowledge of a particular historical period while sharpening their critical thinking skills. This integrative approach to learning can be applied to many different topics of instruction. Think of some similar topics that might be studied in this way and provide an exciting learning environment for students with high abilities.

Another option used in some schools is **independent study** (Sisk, 1987). As with the enrichment option, independent study is usually used within a traditional course. It allows a student to study a topic in more depth to enrich the traditional curriculum or explore a topic not part of the regular program. Independent study does not mean working alone, but rather learning to be self-directed, to work on problems in which the individual has an interest and can assume ownership (Treffinger, 1986b). Such a program, if well guided by the teacher, can provide youngsters with experiences that stress independence, problem solving, critical analysis of a topic, research skills, and the development of a product. Table 7.8 shows a sample independent study project for a ninth grade English honors student.

Educators of the gifted and creative have developed other approaches to enrich youngsters' growth and development. In **mentorship programs,** students with special interests are paired with adults who have expertise in that special area. For example, a student who is interested in engineering might be matched with an engineer who will help with a special project or invite the student to participate in some activity at work. Mentors can be college students, retired persons, or professionals in the community, and the experiences and knowledge they share can include

---

TABLE 7.8. Sisk's Independent Study Worksheet

Content to Be Studied	Resources/Materials	Learning Process/Product
1. Charles Dickens: personality, beliefs, attitudes	1. *A Tale of Two Cities,* Charles Dickens	1. Prepare videotape discussion on findings
2. People's relationship to time	2. Interview English professor at UCLA, a specialist in Dickens	2. Conduct short session on Dickens with Pi Lambda Theta
3. Our inhumanity to one another	3. Examine history of French revolution through history text	3. Write article for school literary magazine
	4. Attend *A Tale of Two Cities* play in Los Angeles	
	5. Examine history books for history of England during Dickens's life	

Source: Creative Teaching of the Gifted, p. 43, by D. Sisk, 1987, New York: McGraw-Hill. Reprinted with permission.

internships. Programs that place gifted students, usually high school seniors, in job settings related to their career goals in order to challenge them and apply knowledge in real-life skills.

Mentorship programs pair adults in the community with students who are gifted. These programs allow students to experience focused and advanced learning in real-life situations.

almost any topic (ecology, medicine, psychology, archeology, farming, management of endangered species).

Internship is an option used with many gifted high school students who have expressed interest in a particular career. The Illinois Government Internship Program allows high school students to explore careers in law or government (Cox, Daniel, and Boston, 1985). In this program students spend a semester at the state capitol in one of many offices: the U.S. Attorney's Office, the Governor's Office, the Department of Conservation, Department of Transportation, the State Board of Education, the Auditor General's Office, and the Attorney General's Office and its legislative support staff. Professionals in the office serve as sponsors helping students to learn about careers associated with that office. Although credit is given for the internship assignment, students who qualify for the program typically have all the credits necessary to graduate from high school at midterm. This program is part of a national internship program, the Executive High School Internship Association. These programs generally follow a standard schedule where students report to work during business hours four days per week. On the fifth day, all students in the program located in a particular city meet for an internship seminar. Many different students can benefit from an internship experience. For example, Hirsch (1979), the developer of the national internship program, found that students who were both gifted

Enrichment Triad/Revolving Door Model. A model for gifted education where 15 to 20 percent rather than 3 percent of a school's students periodically participate in advanced activities planned to develop thinking skills, problem solving, and creativity.

infused. The incorporation of enrichment activities into the regular education curriculum.

curriculum compacting. Reducing instructional time spent on typical academic subjects so enrichment activities can be included in the curriculum.

acceleration. Moving students through a curriculum or years of schooling in a shorter period of time than usual.

advanced placement. High school courses that carry college credit.

and disabled participated successfully in internships. Some needed additional support to overcome barriers caused by their physical disabilities, but these students performed as well as their peers without handicaps.

The **Enrichment Triad/Revolving Door Model** seeks to modify the entire educational system (Renzulli and Reis, 1986). This model offers a different view of education for all children by allowing students to move into advanced level activities on the basis of their performance in general enrichment offerings. (Refer to Renzulli's concept of giftedness under the section Giftedness and Creativity Defined.) Remember, he believes three traits—above average ability, creativity, and task commitment—constitute giftedness. In support of this flexible definition, Renzulli and Reis developed a model for the education of the gifted where enrichment activities are **infused** into the regular education classroom. In addition to providing some enrichment for all students, the Enrichment Triad Model more directly serves from 15 to 20 percent of the school population, rather than limiting it to the top 2 to 3 percent. This highly successful program has been adopted in many school districts across the country, and its supporters maintain that it includes students with high potential for creative production. They also believe this larger pool will include more students from culturally and linguistically diverse backgrounds. How does the program work? Students "revolve" into and out of different levels of their program. In step 1, enrichment activities expose students to new and exciting topics of study, and are carried out through a variety of instructional approaches (speakers, field trips, demonstrations, use of videotapes and films, and interest centers). For many of these enrichment activities, the entire regular class is encouraged to participate. In step 2, enrichment activities center on the development of cognitive and affective abilities, and are also available to the entire regular education class. In step 3, enrichment activities seek to develop advanced investigative and creative skills. At this point, students who are motivated and show great interest are provided with more specialized instruction and activities to explore particular topics, issues, or ideas. Time in the weekly schedule for these enrichment activities is made available by compressing traditional elements of the curriculum. Using what is sometimes referred to as **curriculum compacting,** time spent on three or four subjects (spelling, social studies, mathematics, reading), for example, might be reduced by ten minutes each week. Such recaptured instructional time then becomes available for enrichment activities.

2. ACCELERATION. Through **acceleration,** which comes in many different forms, students move through several years of school in a shorter period of time. An accelerated student might complete three years of school in two years. It could mean skipping a grade or taking advanced placement courses. A student could also move through academic material more quickly, for example completing a traditional sixth grade mathematics book in one semester instead of two. Researchers see many positive aspects of acceleration for students who are gifted (Kulik and Kulik, 1984). First, these students are able to handle the academic challenges of acceleration. Second, when grouped with students of comparable abilities, they make greater achievement gains. Third, they develop better self-concepts and more positive attitudes about course content and school in general. Also, the acceleration approach is cost effective, saving parents millions of dollars in college tuition. A study done about **advanced placement** courses, courses students take while in high school that earn college credit, showed that in ten states more than $19 million in college costs was saved in one year alone (Gallagher et al., 1983).

Another form of acceleration, individualized instruction, provides one-to-one instruction (Bloom and Sosniak, 1981). In this approach, teachers serve in tutorial roles, monitor student progress, provide corrective feedback, and reward students as they move through the curriculum at their own pace.

Another option, **ability grouping,** has gained considerable support from educators of the gifted. In this approach, youngsters are grouped together for specific activities or courses where they excel. These are easily arranged in middle and high schools, where most students travel from class to class. Gifted students can attend more advanced classes. For example, a ninth grader might attend sophomore or junior level mathematics classes; a high school senior might take several classes at a local college. Many high schools provide **honors sections** of academic courses as a form of ability grouping. The criterion for entrance into these classes is outstanding academic achievement in specific subject matter. The requirements for inclusion are not based on a score from an intelligence test, but rather on achievement. Ability grouping and honors sections are approaches that allow students to attend classes with other students, not all of whom are gifted.

Renzulli, Reis, and Smith (1981) believe that ability grouping can be too rigid. They recommend instead flexible ability grouping, allowing a student to participate when that individual shows specific creative or productive performance in a particular area. Ability grouping can be used in elementary, middle, and high schools. It has many advantages, for it allows children who have demonstrated exceptional capabilities to excel in some areas, yet remain with their regular education classmates, in areas where they are closer to grade level. This allows for acceleration part of the school day and integration with their age-peers for part of the school day as well. Although it is used today in many schools as one option available to gifted students, Tannenbaum (1983) reminds us that ability tracking was struck down in a decision by the D.C. District Court in 1967. Ability tracking was deemed discriminatory and a form of racial segregation because so few students from minority groups were included in those programs (*Hobson v. Hansen,* 1967).

3. COMBINATION OF ENRICHMENT AND ACCELERATION. Other approaches to the education of students who are gifted are broader. One example is the **Purdue Secondary Model for Gifted and Talented Youth** (Feldhusen and Robinson, 1986). This comprehensive program, intended to meet all the educational needs of high school youngsters who are gifted, has many components. This program combines enrichment as well as accelerated features into students' educational programs, and includes counseling services. A summary of the model is shown in Figure 7.4. Feldhusen and Robinson believe that counseling is critical to students who are gifted. Because of their superior abilities, some of these youngsters are too challenging to their teachers and classmates; others exhibit adjustment problems because they are bored with school. The school districts that have adopted this approach have found that counseling helps these students cope with the often difficult situations adolescents face at school, and also guides students toward particular areas of study and careers, develops self-awareness, and promotes self-acceptance of their abilities, interests, and needs. Another unique feature of the Purdue Model is the use of seminars to allow for expansion of discussions and topics studied in other classes or the development of library and research skills.

ability grouping. Placing students with comparable achievement and skill levels in the same classes or courses.

honors sections. Advanced classes for any student who shows high achievement in specific subject areas.

Purdue Secondary Model for Gifted and Talented Youth. A high school curriculum for gifted students that combines enrichment and acceleration.

1. Counseling Services

1. Talent identification
2. Education counseling
3. Career counseling
4. Personal counseling

2. Seminar

1. In-depth study
2. Self-selected topics
3. Career education
4. Affective activities
5. Thinking, research, and library skills
6 Presentations

3. Advanced Placement Classes

Open to students in grades 9 – 12
All subject matter areas

4. Honors Classes

1. English
2. Social Studies
3. Biology
4. Language
5. Humanities

5. Math-Science Acceleration

1. Begin algebra in 7th grade
2. Continue acceleration and fast-paced math
3. Open science courses to earlier admission

6. Foreign Languages

1. Latin or Greek
2. French or Spanish
3. German or Oriental
4. Russian

7. The Arts

1. Art
2. Drama
3. Music
4. Dance

8. Cultural Experiences

1. Concepts, plays, exhibits
2. Field trips
3. Tours abroad
4. Museum program

9. Career Education

1. Mentors
2. Seminar experience
   a) study of careers
   b) study of self
   c) educational planning

10. Vocational Programs

1. Home economics
2. Agriculture
3. Business
4. Industrial arts

11. Extra-school Instruction

1. Saturday school
2. Summer classes
3. Correspondence study
4. College classes

FIGURE 7.4 Components of the *Purdue Secondary Model for Gifted and Talented Youth*

SOURCE: *The Purdue Secondary Model for Gifted and Talented Youth*, p. 158, by J. Feldhusen and A. Robinson, 1986, Mansfield Center, CT: Creative Learning Press. Reprinted by permission.

Techniques for Teaching Creativity

To a certain degree, creativity can be taught and encouraged in those who have potential for growth in this area. Some important factors, however, must be in place before effective instruction can occur (Davis and Rimm, 1989). First, an environment must be prepared where students feel safe and free to explore their creative natures. The learning environment developed must be noncritical, nonevaluative, and receptive to novel and even "wild" ideas. Students must be made aware of different types of blocks to creative thinking. For example, the way individuals are accustomed to perceiving things can become a barrier to thinking in new or different ways. Societal barriers can also inhibit creativity. For example, traditions, pressures to conform, and social expectations can inhibit creativity. Read the following phrases. How would you counteract these blocks in order to develop a new program for children who are gifted?

> It won't work . . .
>
> It's not in the budget . . .
>
> We've never done it before . . .
>
> We're not ready for it yet . . .
>
> What will parents think . . .
>
> We're too small for that . . .
>
> We have too many projects now . . .
>
> Somebody would have suggested it before if it were any good . . .*

We have discussed how easy it is to inhibit creativity. Let us now discuss the factors that can facilitate creativity. Many creative people draw upon the work of others for their own creative work. For example, George Lucas wanted to develop an epic story, and when he was creating the film *Star Wars,* he read books on Greek and Roman mythology. *Star Wars* uses mythological themes (transition from childhood to adulthood, struggle between good and evil, a daring and courageous rescue) in a very successful story. What other means can we use to stimulate creative thinking? Davis and Rimm (1989) make the following suggestions:

1. Deliberately seeking inspiration from analogically related situations, innovations, and ideas.

2. Adapting solutions from similar types of problems, which also is analogical thinking.

3. Modifying, combining, and improving present ideas.

4. Starting with the goal and working backward to deduce what is required to reach that goal.

5. Beginning with an "ideal" or "perfect" solution—such as having the problem solve itself—and again working backward to design a creative solution.

6. Asking yourself how the problem will be solved 25, 100, or 200 years from now.

Other methods of enhancing creativity are available. One example is the **Future Problem Solving Program,** a national project that was developed by Torrance and his colleagues during the late 1970s and continues today (Torrance and Torrance, 1978). In this program students are asked to solve global problems—the nuclear arms race, the destruction of rain forests, and predicted future shortages of safe

Future Problem Solving Program. A national competition and instructional program to teach creative problem solving, in which students attempt to find positive solutions to real issues such as the nuclear arms race and water conservation.

*G. A. Davis and S. B. Rimm, 1989, *Education of the Gifted and Talented,* 2d ed., p. 236. Reprinted by permission.

brainstorming. An instructional technique where students quickly generate as many ideas as they can.

attributes. Common characteristics or features of a group.

inferences. Incomplete decisions or opinions, based on assumptions or reasoning.

deduction. Coming to a logical conclusion from facts or general principles that are known to be true.

categorizing. Classifying or grouping concepts or items; a thinking skill.

Teachers need to be bold and take some risks when challenging creative students.

drinking water. Each year in a national competition, classes of students are presented with three problems to study and solve, submitting their solutions for evaluation by a panel of judges. Through this program students learn many critical thinking skills and are encouraged to develop positive solutions to real world problems. In another approach students are provided instruction and experiences at different levels (Treffinger, 1986b). Regardless of the topic, students first are given basic experiences that encourage them to generalize their knowledge and analyze concepts and ideas. Next, they learn to develop divergent (or creative) thinking skills by exercises that include **brainstorming** (how many different ways can a brick be used, what changes can be made to eliminate litter on the playground, identify ways that the amount of garbage being sent to landfills can be reduced), listing **attributes** (what are the characteristics of plants, of animals, of people), and determining the relationships or associations among items and concepts (what are the common features of houses and school buildings, plants and animals, Mayan and Polynesian cultures). Students' convergent (or critical) thinking skills can be enhanced by having them make **inferences** and **deductions,** decide what information is relevant, practice with analogies, use evidence to come to conclusions, and **categorize** information.

Educational Environments

Because of inconsistent educational opportunities for students who are gifted and creative, there is no uniformity in the types of educational services available. While some districts provide a vast range of educational services, others do not offer either enhanced or even different curricular options. Regular classroom teachers must and

Tips for Teachers

1. Teach a full range of content areas in considerable depth.
2. Vary your instructional approaches.
3. Encourage students to become independent learners.
4. Enrich topics of study with additional activities such as guest speakers, field trips, demonstrations, videotapes, and interest centers.
5. Allow students to move through the curriculum at their own pace.
6. Watch for signs of boredom.
7. Encourage lively class discussions.
8. Create a safe environment where novel ideas are accepted.
9. Pose important problems to solve so that thinking about present and future dilemmas is considered.
10. Teach and foster the use of library and research skills.
11. Develop instructional activities and use questions that generate the application of different types of thinking skills.
12. Integrate the use of technology into your instruction.

cluster programs. A plan whereby a group of gifted students spend a part of their day in the regular classroom on enriched or accelerated activities.

pull-out programs. The most common educational placement for gifted students, who spend part of the school day in a special class.

do provide educational experiences that are at grade level or at the average achievement level of their students. (See the Tips for Teachers box for some suggestions.) However, giftedness is fostered through unique offerings and experiences. Some school districts offer a variety of educational placements (ability grouping, resource rooms, special classes, special schools), some only have a few, while others provide no differential services. Enrichment and acceleration can occur in a variety of settings and administrative arrangements. Let us look more closely at some possible settings for these approaches.

Cluster programs use the regular classroom and the regular classroom teacher for the delivery of special instructional opportunities. Under this plan, gifted students spend some portion of their school day engaged in enriched or accelerated activities, but in the regular education classroom setting. For example, these students might be assigned special independent study activities that support and extend topics that are part of the regular education curriculum. Sixth graders, studying state history in social studies, might prepare a "Who's Who" book of the historical figures in their state's history. Or, they might prepare a position paper on a current issue, like water rights, including the historical reasons for the controversy and concluding with solutions to the problem.

The most common settings and administrative arrangements for gifted students are **pull-out programs,** where students leave the regular class for a portion of their school day to attend a special class. Some estimate that over 70 percent of programs for gifted students use this option (Cox, Daniels, and Boston, 1985). Such programs provide services for either several days per week or for an hour or so each day. They operate much like the special education resource room described in chapter 3. Some schools combine the cluster and pull-out programs.

Some researchers believe that cluster and pull-out programs can be successful if instruction delivered during the time allotted is high quality (Renzulli, 1987). Any administrative arrangement (cluster, pull-out, special classes, special schools) can be inferior or superior depending on the administrator, the teacher, the curriculum, and

magnet school. A center school that serves children who do not live in the immediate neighborhood; some magnet schools are designed to serve children whose parents work in a nearby area; other magnet schools emphasize a particular theme (such as theater arts, math, and science).

the instructional methods used. Both the cluster and the pull-out options have been criticized, however. Some researchers (Baldwin, 1987; Cox, Daniel, and Boston, 1985; Van Tassel-Baska, 1987) assert that they are only part-time solutions to full-time problems. Their position is that these students need full-time, separate educational programs where they can interact for most of the day with other gifted students in a different and accelerated curriculum.

As we mentioned earlier, in some programs, such as ability grouping, students who are gifted or creative spend a substantial portion of the school day with classmates who do not share their accelerated skills. Some educators maintain that regular classroom placement for these students represents the most restrictive, rather than the least restrictive, educational environment (Whitmore, 1980). They believe that when students with specialized, high abilities are grouped together, they behave differently: They challenge each other, do not hide their special abilities from others, and profit maximally from specially trained teachers and a unique curriculum. In fact, many school districts do provide special classes for gifted students. Such classes are typically used for students who are moderately or highly gifted (IQ scores over 140), and who are at the elementary school level. These classes are self-contained. For the major part of the school day, these students attend classes where the teacher is specially trained, the curriculum is different from that used in the regular education classroom, and all of the students participating are of comparable ability. Self-contained classes for the gifted are usually not available at high schools, where honors sections, advanced placement courses, and other options are more easily employed. Sometimes, however, the number of students with comparable, advanced abilities in a particular school is small. This is common in sparsely populated areas of our country. In cases where the number of students who are gifted is insufficient to warrant forming a special class, Clark (1988) suggests that all classes be individualized, so that all students can learn at their own pace.

Special or center schools, although much less common, are available in some locales. These schools are usually at the high school level and stress special areas of emphasis. In New York and other cities, for example, schools specializing in the performing arts, math, or science are available to students who pass qualifying exams or auditions. Students attending these programs have outstanding skills and potential in particular areas that their school district administrators have decided to further develop. Such special schools have been implemented in several states, often as **magnet schools** emphasizing a theme (such as the arts, science, technology). Unfortunately, a full range of programs is not consistently available in school districts across the nation.

FAMILIES OF CHILDREN WHO ARE GIFTED OR CREATIVE

Many parents of children who are gifted, not unlike most parents, do not have a realistic perspective on their children's abilities. Some of these parents deny their child's special abilities in an attempt to keep them normal or "well adjusted." Others take the opposite tack, and magnify their children's abilities and put excessive pressure on them to achieve and excel in all areas. All parents need to learn what is realistic for their child, and develop appropriate standards and expectations. This is particularly true for children who are gifted or creative.

GIFTED STUDENTS CAN CAUSE DILEMMAS FOR THEIR FAMILIES AND TEACHERS

Ellie Ferguson said "ink" for "drink" at four months old. She spoke in complete sentences before she was a year old. She was reading books like "Little House on the Prairie" before she went to kindergarten. Clearly, Ellie is not like most other children for her IQ is over 170. But at age five, Ellie was like most preschoolers, waiting with anticipation for the first day of school. However, her excitement soon waned. After a few weeks of coloring the letters of the alphabet and circling triangles with color markers, she became bored and disillusioned with school. Her mother had to force her to go to school each morning. So, the following year, Ellie's mother taught her at home. The next year, her family moved to another community where Ellie entered third grade. Now at age ten, instead of attending a fifth grade class, she is placed with sixth graders for most of her subjects and studies pre-algebra with seventh graders. Although some teachers and school administrators are concerned that such acceleration leads to social difficulties, Ellie reports that she is now happy at school and has many friends even though they are older than she (Wernick, 1990).

When Bala Krishna Ambati was 12 years old, he was a third-year pre-med student at New York University. When he was ten, he scored 750 on the mathematics section of the Scholastic Aptitude Test and 620 on the verbal test (a score of 500 is average for most twelfth graders intending to attend college). Bala prefers solving algorithms to playing Nintendo, but he also likes to play chess and basketball. He has set a goal for himself: to be the youngest person to graduate from medical school. According to the *Guinness Book of World Records,* the record is held by an Israeli who graduated at age eighteen. If Bala continues with his studies at this pace, he could finish two months before his eighteenth birthday. Although not the best student in all of his classes, he does well on his examinations and is considered a better than average student. However, his professors are afraid that his parents are pushing him too much, and that he needs to learn about life and become a well-rounded person. Bala counters that if he were in seventh grade now, "my mind would be rotting." (Stanley, 1990)

Both of these children are studying in accelerated programs and have the support of their families. Decisions about these children's education and what is the best for them are difficult, and subject to considerable criticism by professionals who are also concerned about what is best for gifted children.

Many gifted children are extremely verbal and have unusual abstract thinking skills. In many instances, they seem to be more mature than other children of their age (Davis and Rimm, 1989). Such characteristics can be deceptive. These children, like others of their age, are not capable of making complex decisions or setting their own goals and directions. Of course, their interests and feelings should be considered, but parents and teachers must not abdicate responsibility for guidance. According to Davis and Rimm, successful gifted achievers felt confident throughout their school years that adults were concerned about them, and made appropriate decisions about their education. They also feel that it was a wise decision to follow the lead of these significant adults.

Parents of children who are gifted need to have positive expectations of their children, and send clear and consistent messages about their expectations. Children who are expected to achieve and engage in constructive activities, and are rewarded for those actions, tend to internalize these expectations for themselves. Research that studied successful gifted and talented adults found that their parents stressed achievement, doing one's best all of the time, and the importance of success. These parents were models of the work ethic who emphasized working hard, excelling, and spending time constructively (Bloom, 1985). However, these children also need to learn how to balance school work with other activities. They need to learn how to deal with situations when they are not successful. Parents must guide their children so they will not give up or lose interest in a subject when they are not immediately successful, and they must also help their children resist the temptation to always have to be "Number 1" in everything attempted.

ADULTS WHO ARE GIFTED OR CREATIVE

The most comprehensive study of adults who were gifted was conducted by Terman (1925), and is still considered a classic follow-up study in the field of the education of the gifted. Of course, there have been many criticisms of Terman's work (Hughes and Converse, 1962). First, the sample represented only a small proportion of individuals with IQ scores over 140 who might have qualified for inclusion. Second, Terman used a criterion of those who scored in the highest 1 percent on a standardized test of intelligence as the subjects in his study. Third, Terman used teacher nominations as part of his subject selection and that could have biased or limited his sample. Finally, the study is over sixty years old. Changes in cultural values, different concepts of giftedness, and the times can all influence who is considered gifted, what educational options are selected for them, and their ultimate career choices.

Although a college education is one key to entering many professions, many individuals who are gifted, particularly women, do not avail themselves of higher education. In a study conducted in the mid-1960s, a far greater number of men, identified as gifted during their elementary school years, entered graduate or professional schools than women who were also identified as being gifted during their childhood (Nichols and Astin, 1966). Most likely, some gender differences are a function of role expectations of earlier times, and the results from such a study would be somewhat different today. Regardless, high school and college counselors need to assist students who are gifted and creative in choosing careers and being aware of the educational requirements of those jobs.

Unfortunately, many of the follow-up studies of individuals who are gifted are dated, but there are some findings that hold up regardless of the age of the study. Highly intelligent children tend to excel as adults (Terman and Oden, 1959; Oden, 1968). At midlife, 77 of the 800 men in Terman's survey were listed in *American Men of Science* and 33 were found in *Who's Who of America*. These men were also highly productive, producing 67 books, more than 400 short stories and plays, and over 1400 professional and scientific papers. Of Terman's sample, 47 percent of the men were in professional occupations with another 40 percent in office, managerial, and semiprofessional work. Of the women, 45 percent were housewives.

Individuals identified as creative during their school years became productive, creative adults (Torrance, 1972). They tend to select unusual occupations that in-

Children who are gifted when challenged by the educational system grow up to be successful adults.

volve various combinations of training and experience, including work or study in foreign countries. The creative, more often than less creative persons, select careers in categories like the following: explorer, inventor, writer, entertainer, artist, dancer, and product designer.

The probability for success is great for individuals who are gifted (Tannenbaum, 1983). These individuals tend to be well-adjusted and happy with their occupations, family, and friends. In greater proportions, they are productive and contributing members of society. However, as Laycock (1979) argues, society needs more productive and contributing members; therefore, as children gifted individuals need to be fostered and developed. Gifted people are not only needed to lead society and our culture, but also to keep America competitive in the business, technological, and scientific communities. For this to occur, more individuals who are gifted need to be accurately identified, educated well, encouraged to attend and complete post-secondary and graduate schools, and, ultimately, assume leadership roles.

TECHNOLOGY AND THE EDUCATION OF THE GIFTED

Technology for many groups of people with disabilities can change the quality of their lives, improve the chances for more successful integration in the community, and enhance employment opportunities. Those who are gifted can contribute to technology, as well as have technology contribute to them. One advantage of micro-computer technology in the schools is that it allows for more and more applications

desktop publishing. Using a microcomputer and special software to prepare written and graphic material in publication format and quality.

telecommunications network. Various electronic devices that allow students and teachers to access and send materials and information using a computer network system.

of individualized instruction (Yin and White, 1984). A class of students can work on a variety of instructional tasks at the same time. For example, one student can work on a tutorial in chemistry or physics, while a classmate can be learning how to program the computer to develop an environmental monitoring and control system. As more and more software becomes available, the opportunities multiply for children to master academic tasks more quickly, practice problem-solving skills, and work independently. Students who are gifted can master required subjects more efficiently. Such technological advancements could also be used in the development of new kinds of acceleration programs. For example, a required subject for graduation—a state history course—if available in courseware materials, could be mastered independently by an individual in a shorter period of time than usually allocated for mastery by the class. Frequently, teachers of the gifted comment that their students are bored by traditional instructional topics and methods; too much instructional time is spent on already mastered units or courses. As more and more courses become available in computerized software formats, content mastery can be relegated to the computer and class time can be spent on more in-depth study of a topic being mastered independently or reallocated to another curriculum target. The time saved can be spent on further developing problem-solving skills, creativity, or on computer use and programming.

Computer technology has almost unlimited applications. For example, even very young children can learn and apply word processing to their writing assignments. As they become more sophisticated in its use, they can use **desktop publishing** to produce a variety of written products. They can also use telecommunications to send simple and complex materials to others miles away. Youngsters who have never met can work together on joint projects. Students who live in remote areas can access major library facilities and major computers that have capabilities to analyze complicated sets of data. In one state, a computer-based **telecommunications network** called, CISCONET, links up teachers, students, and research laboratories. A student, for example, could ask for help solving a scientific or mathematical question by requesting assistance from a scientist based at the Los Alamos National Laboratories. The use of this system is free to those residing in rural areas, and encourages dialogue between students and practitioners on real issues and problems.

Tisone and Wismar (1985) believe that the microcomputer can also be used to teach thinking skills, such as solving problems. They suggest that at least one aspect of creativity, risk taking, is encouraged through computer use. Students can try many different solutions to problems without embarrassment. Students can practice divergent thinking skills by guessing at different ways to solve problems. In chapter 6, Learning Disabilities, we discuss microcomputer games and other instructional programs available that help children practice a variety of thinking skills: categorizing, sequencing, classifying, and making analogies. Such instructional programs allow children rare opportunities to practice use of different types of thinking skills, and can be beneficial to youngsters who are gifted as well.

Jenkins-Friedman and Nielsen (1990) provide guidelines about how different technology (calculators, microcomputers, mainframe computers, networks, telecommunication, and interactive video) can be used with the standard curriculum from regular education classes, and how they can help extend beyond that curriculum. Study Table 7.9. See if you can think of other applications of technology that might be used in educational programs for children who are gifted.

TABLE 7.9. Potential Uses of Information Technologies by Gifted Students

Technology	Uses Within Standard Curriculum	Uses Beyond Standard Curriculum
Hand-held (lap) computer	• To individualize and accelerate learning • To do word processing, data management, and temporary storage • To move students rapidly through the basic curriculum	• To immediately record information obtained in libraries, interviews, conferences, and so on • To temporarily store information for use in advanced research and projects
Microcomputer	• To practice and review basic skills briefly and rapidly • To develop critical thinking, problem-solving, and decision-making skills when appropriate software is used • To create and rapidly edit written material through use of word processing • To reduce students' anxiety over written assignments through word processing features such as spelling and grammar checks	• To store, retrieve, manage, and analyze vast amounts of information for special projects and research • To enhance creativity through use of special music, drawing, or desktop publishing software • To learn basic programming skills • To integrate word processing, data bases, and spreadsheets
Mainframe computer	• To conduct on-line searches for library materials • To access and search national and international data banks	• To expand students' knowledge base • To access, where possible, university or business mainframe data courses
Computer network system	• To connect students with network users at other school systems or buildings	• To communicate beyond the classroom and the home • To reduce restrictions imposed by distance • To enable itinerant teachers to communicate with G/T students • To collect special research and project information by surveying network bulletin boards
Telecommunication	(Until this technology makes its way to the classroom, use will be only beyond the standard curriculum.)	• To access televised, interactive instruction • To establish easy, rapid communication between students and professionals • To connect groups of G/T students with a mentor
Interactive video	• To individualize and accelerate learning by enabling students to control the pace and direction of knowledge acquisition • To provide opportunities to learn and use decision-making skills	• To practice higher level decision-making and problem-solving skills when more advanced interactive videos are utilized

Source: "Gifts and talents," by R. Jenkins-Friedman and M. E. Nielsen in *Exceptional Children in Today's Schools: An Alternative Resource Book* (2d ed.), p. 481, by E. L. Meyen (Ed.), 1990, Denver: Love Publishing. Reprinted by permission.

Concepts and Controversies

**Do we need a different way to identify and provide
education for the gifted to Native American students?**

Although somewhere between 3 and 5 percent of America's school-age children
should qualify for education of the gifted, children from culturally and linguistically
diverse groups are not proportionally represented in classes for the gifted. As we
mentioned, most states determine eligibility for programs for students who are gifted
by using a score on a test of intelligence—the most common method used to identify
children as gifted (Alvino, McDonnel, and Richert, 1981). Typically, to be eligible for
education of the gifted, a child must score at least 130 on a test of intelligence and
demonstrate excellence in academics as well. Unfortunately, adhering to these criteria means that proportionally fewer children from culturally and linguistically diverse
groups qualify for education of the gifted.

In particular, the intelligence tests have been criticized by many political and
social leaders as being culturally biased, and fostering discrimination practices. Children from African-American, Native American, and Hispanic communities tend not
to score well on these tests. In other words, proportionally fewer of these students
obtain scores over 130 on these tests than their white counterparts. It is argued that
such tests tend to favor the experiential backgrounds of the dominant culture (Tannenbaum, 1983).

Relatively little attention has been paid to Native American children who might
be eligible for educational programs for gifted students. How should eligibility criteria
be modified? Can one identification system be used for all Native American children?
Standard systems are used to determine whether youngsters are handicapped, and,
thereby, qualify for special education. Should nationally normed standardized tests
of intelligence and achievement not be included in the assessment batteries for Native
American children? One problem with developing a uniform criterion for these
youngsters is that they do not come from a homogeneous group. The U.S. government recognizes 177 different tribes in this country. Also, it is estimated that there
are over 3000 distinctively different cultures and languages spoken by Native Americans in North America (Poppe, 1989). Cultural and language differences are compounded by the critical levels of poverty found among some groups of people. The
average annual income of Native Americans in this country is about $2000 (Waka-
bayashi et al., 1978). The unemployment rate for Native Americans is approximately
40 percent. Of the Native American children included in one study (Chinn and
Hughes, 1987), proportionally very few of these children were identified as gifted.
Only 1.1 percent of Native American students participate in programs for the gifted,
while 2.9 percent of white students and 1.5 percent of African-American and Hispanic students are enrolled (Kirschenbaum, 1988).

Are there really fewer children who should receive specialized educational services for the gifted who come from Native American groups? Or, should the criterion
for entrance in such programs be different for Native Americans? Poppe (1989)
proposes that the definition of giftedness and the criterion for inclusion into education of the gifted be changed. He suggests that for these children we adopt George's

(1987) definition of gifted, and leave identification as the prerogative of the local community. George defines giftedness in this way:

> Gifted children shall be defined as those children who consistently excel, or consistently show potential to excel, beyond their age and the expectations of their cultural community in the following areas:
>
> 1. Cognitive, high level thinking skills.
> 2. Creative and performing skills.
> 3. Social helping and leadership skills.
> 4. Those skills which the cultural community may deem important to the well-being of its members. (p. 5)

The adoption of such a definition of giftedness leaves the criterion for selection to the local community. It does not limit the number of students who would be included. It might exclude some children who would be considered gifted by the dominant culture and include others who would not be typically identified as gifted but possess certain traits valued by the local culture. Since the use of standardized tests yields questionable results, Poppe suggests that a nomination system, using parents, community members, and teachers would have to be implemented.

A different plan for Native American students leaves us with many questions. For example, should the size of these programs be limited to some percentage of the school population? Should a consistent way of identifying students be used across all tribes or should each local community devise its own system for qualifying youngsters? What would the content taught in these classes be? If a local community decided to emphasize its culture in these classes rather than academic achievement, creativity, and problem solving, would that be acceptable to the professional community of educators of the gifted? Who should pay for these programs? Would reimbursement (possibly from the Bureau of Indian Affairs or the State Educational Agency in the state where the tribe is located) be contingent on a curriculum deemed acceptable by an outside community or agency?

Certainly, these issues leave us with considerable room for debate and discussion. How would you assist a Native American community in identifying students who should participate in specialized programs for the gifted?

SUMMARY

Individuals who are gifted and creative are not handicapped in the sense of having a disability that presents obstacles to their learning and participating in society. However, they can be handicapped by our social and educational systems, which present barriers to achieving to their potential. Gifted individuals possess unique intellectual and creative abilities that need to be fostered and developed. One challenge facing American educators is to develop and put into place a consistent array of educational options throughout the century that will facilitate these individuals' development.

1. Education of the gifted has experienced periods of great interest and periods of neglect across American history. When the nation's leaders sense threats to the country's national security, education of the gifted becomes a priority. For example, education of the gifted flourished after the Russians launched the space satellite, Sputnik in 1957. Therefore, the 1960s were a time when programs for the gifted were developed and expanded. The 1970s were marked by a diminishing of educational services for students who were gifted or creative. Today, America's leaders see external threats to our nation's economy. Standardized test scores reveal that our nation's students do not achieve at levels of students from other nations. It appears that a national interest in the education of the gifted is being renewed. Partly because programs for those who are gifted and creative are not mandated by the federal laws that ensure educational programs for those who have disabilities, education of the gifted is subject to these changes in priorities.

2. Many characteristics are ascribed to the group of learners who are called gifted or creative. Although each person is an individual, possessing unique abilities, some common descriptors apply to this group. Under the most common definitions, these individuals are very bright and demonstrate their high intellectual abilities by scoring well on tests of intelligence, learning more quickly than their peers, and applying complex thinking skills. Their academic achievement is significantly higher than their classmates'. These individuals also tend to become leaders.

3. The nation serves fewer children who are gifted than it should. Estimates indicate that between 3 and 5 percent of America's children should qualify for gifted education. Kirschenbaum's work (1988) showed that there is an inequality in the receipt of educational services for those who are gifted, with substantially less than 3 percent of children from culturally and linguistically diverse groups in this country receiving services. Programs for those who are gifted are not equally available to all those students who demonstrate unique and outstanding abilities. Because standardized tests of intelligence and achievement tend to favor children who come from the dominant culture, fewer African-American, Hispanic, and Native American children receive educational services for gifted students. Also, individuals from other subgroups—those with handicaps, underachievers, and females—have less access to these programs. Programs need to be put into place that support these subgroups and are designed to meet their individual needs. There are many proposals that aim to correct these situations. But in all cases, educators seem uncertain about how many children should be specially served and how best to identify these children.

4. Unlike other groups of youngsters with special educational needs, concern about them does not center on causation and prevention. Rather, educators are interested in identifying the factors that enhance and inhibit giftedness and creativity. For example, environmental variables, such as deprivation and lack of stimulation, can impede normal child development. More educational and social service programs might be developed that would enable these youngsters to achieve their potential.

5. A number of different educational programs are available for these students. Some school districts provide a variety of different options, while others provide no special programs. Few early education programs are specifically designed or available for these children. At the school level, enrichment, acceleration, or a combination of these two approaches is being explored. A number of educational options—mentorships, honors programs, advanced placement, internships—are particularly attractive at the middle and high school level.

6. As with children with disabilities, there is some debate about where gifted students should be educated. Some educators maintain that they should remain in the regular education class and be offered enriched instruction by the regular education teachers. Others (Renzulli and Reis, 1986) suggest that the entire regular education curriculum be enriched, and students who show interest and ability to learn beyond this enriched program receive additional educational experiences in a resource room or pull-out program. Yet others (Whitmore, 1980) believe that these students should spend their entire school day with others of comparable abilities engaged in an accelerated and enriched program that cannot be available in regular education classes.

7. It is clear that these individuals, as adults, tend to be very successful, productive members of our society. If they, as children, are considered a national resource to be protected and fostered, then it is important that they receive the best education possible. It is also important that the size of this national resource be substantial. As many children as possible who can profit from accelerated and enriched educational experiences should participate. Children who are bored with school and lose interest in educational goals are a loss to the nation. The area of education of the gifted is exciting. It offers challenges and opportunities for educational innovation and reform to those who become professionals devoted to youngsters who are gifted and creative.

DISCUSSION QUESTIONS

1. Why do you think Marland included the need for "differentiated educational programs" in his definition of giftedness? Using his definition, how would you qualify children for specialized services? Would you limit the number of children receiving services?

2. Compare New Mexico's definition with Marland's. How are these definitions similar, and how do they differ? Why do you think that the State Board of Education in New Mexico adopted a different definition? What are the limitations of the Marland definition? What are the limitations of the New Mexico definition?

3. Devise an educational program for a hypothetical individual from one of the underrepresented subgroups of gifted learners.

4. List five internships that could be developed in your city.

5. Brainstorm five topics that can be studied using the interdisciplinary instructional method.

SUPPLEMENTARY BOOKS AND VIDEOS

Over the years, people who are gifted have been included in fictional and nonfictional roles in both books and films. Below is a listing of such creative works that you might find of interest.

Books

Fitzgerald, J. D. (1985). *The great brain.* New York: Dell.

Galbraith, J. (1983). *The gifted kids survival guide.* Minneapolis: Free Spirit Publishing.

Kerr, B. A. (1985). *Smart girls, gifted women.* Columbus: Ohio Psychology Publishing Co.

L'Engle, M. (1962). *A wrinkle in time.* New York: Farrar, Straus, & Giroux.

Meir, G. (1975). *My life: by Golda Meir.* New York: Putnam.

Videos

Charly (1968). ABC–Selmur Productions.

Paper moon (1973). Paramount–1.

The black stallion (1979). Omni–Zeotrope/UA.

Goonies (1985). Warner Brothers/Amblin Entertainment

Weird science (1985). Universal Pictures.

ALEXANDER REUVEN WEISZ, 45, experiences recurring severe depression. He was born in Hawaii and has lived in Israel. A resident of Minneapolis, Minnesota, since 1967, he is an active member of the 26th Street Project, an art therapy group. Alexander began drawing with primitive pencil sketches and now works in pen and ink.

Chapter Eight

BEHAVIORAL DISORDERS AND EMOTIONAL DISTURBANCE

Learning

Objectives

After studying this chapter, you should be able to:

- Define the term *seriously emotionally disturbed* according to IDEA, listing the characteristics of this disability

- Compare externalizing behavioral disorders to internalizing behavioral disorders

- Analyze the ways an individual's age and environment can contribute to a diagnosis of behavioral disorder or emotional disturbance

- List and define the seven major conceptual models for the education and treatment of children and youth with behavioral disorders and emotional disturbance

- Discuss the arguments for and against the exclusion of children with social maladjustment in the definition of seriously emotionally disturbed

"THE ONES WHO ALWAYS GET THE BLAME": THE WRITINGS OF CHILDREN WITH EMOTIONAL AND BEHAVIORAL HANDICAPS*

Children with behavioral disorders and emotional disturbance wrote the pieces below. When you read them, you can hear their frustration, confusion, and anger with their environments and themselves.

THE ONES WHO ALWAYS GET THE BLAME

I got Rosado, Woody, Francis, and James.
The ones who always get the blame.
Nathan is bad, Joanna is a lion.
She bites, kicks, and never gives up cryin!
James comes to my house, what do I do?
Kick 'em in the butt with a big combat shoe.
by Michael

HOW I FEEL

When I get angry I can't control my temper. I get hand crazy. I hit when I don't mean to hit anyone. See Juanito got something he shouldn't had got but he got it anyway. Now Juanito acts like he's a big shot but he isn't. Now he's using me, Kevin and James because he gots that watch. He thinks he can get into a fight and let us stick up for him and cleanup his mess. And we're going to get beat up when we try to stick up for that no good botherful brat. Juanito gets me sick. Sometimes I feel sorry for Juanito. Sometimes because he's poor. But he can be a little cute boy.
The End

Juanito you're all right.

MY CLASS BY MR. MR. MR. FRESH

I do not have to like anybody. But I love my reading. Joanna was in my reading group. I read and I read but I can not get away from it.

KEVIN GO TO READING BY MR. GOODMAN

I'm mad because JoAnna go to a different classroom.

THE TRACHODON

This story is about the trachodon. When a girl was alking down the street TRACHODON came to her. TRACHODON said, "I want something to eat and I fount it, it is you!" The girl ran fast as a dog, so TRACHODON won't get her. He felt sad.

Mrs. D'Alessandro came to the rescue, and Mrs. D'Alessandro came to the rescue, and Mrs. D'Alessandro said, "How is that girl going to be a food? She is a person. A person is not a food. And Mrs. D'Alessandro was walking away.

*" 'The ones who always get the blame': Emotionally handicapped children writing" by M. E. D'Alessandro, 1987, *Language Arts, 64,* pp. 516–522. Copyright 1987 by the National Council of Teachers of English. Reprinted with permission.

Creative expression, through writings or drawings, can help children communicate their feelings and understand the world.

MY FEELINGS

When I wake up in The morning I feel like yelling. Once my day starts I forget all about my feelings. Sometimes I feel like crying because my friends tease me. I hate that. When I watch my favorite show my brother turns the T.V. channel. I feel hurt. I don't want to hit him, he is bigger than me. When we eat dinner my brother throws food at me and laughs at me. I feel embarrassed but today my feelings are in control.

1. What are the advantages of encouraging children with behavioral disorders and emotional disturbance to regularly write about the things that they feel strongly about?

2. What did you learn about the children's feelings from their writing?

Children in our society—in schools, in their communities, and in their homes—are expected to conform to certain standards of behavior. These standards are rooted in the long history of what society has determined to be normal in certain environments.

Standards of normal behavior change as children grow up and move through the stages of their lives. Infants, for example, are expected to be messy, dependent, and to communicate through gurgles, facial expressions, and crying. Toddlers, in turn, go through routine stages when temper tantrums and resistance are tolerantly interpreted as the predictable "terrible twos." As children progress through childhood

behavioral disorders. A condition of disruptive or inappropriate behaviors that interferes with a student's learning, relationships with others, or personal satisfaction to such a degree that intervention is required.

emotional disturbance. A term used interchangeably with behavioral disorder.

and adolescence, accepted stages of development, including even rebelliousness, are usually viewed as predictable and appropriate for the age of the child.

But some children behave contrary to the predicted stages of child development in our society. An eight-year-old who suddenly begins to wet the bed, cling to his mother, and stop talking creates great concern about his behavior. Even though almost identical behavior would be totally accepted in an infant, an eight-year-old who acts in that way is perceived as having a problem. We can cite many examples of behavior that raise concern in children of one age, but if demonstrated by a child of a different age, do not raise questions at all. Think of Christy, a teenager who throws "kicking and screaming" temper tantrums. If she were two years old instead of sixteen, she would probably be regarded as normal—but because she is now at an age when such behavior is no longer developmentally appropriate, her behavior is seen as a serious problem.

Just as society provides norms of behavior for different stages of development, it also provides norms of behavior for specific environments. Children in school, for example, are expected to be generally quiet, orderly, cooperative with other children, and attentive to learning. Children at home are expected to be cheerful, loving, helpful, and obedient to their parents. In their communities, children are expected to respect their neighbors' property, abide by curfews and traffic rules, and generally to grow into their roles as the new generation of adult leaders of society. Children whose behavior is inconsistent with expectations of normal behavior in these environments are regarded as having problems.

Complicating this issue further, behavioral expectations differ in different environments. For example, what behavior is expected of Richie, a football player, during a hotly contested game with a rival team? He will be regarded as a hero if he physically overpowers team members with tackles and body blocks to stop them from scoring touchdowns. But if he behaves in the same way off the playing field, he will probably be arrested for criminal battery. Or consider a young girl who, during the time she is being sexually abused by an older brother, withdraws into an imaginary world. This tactic, which may help her endure the abuse, will cause her many problems if she continues the emotional withdrawal at school or in her social relations with nonabusive adults.

As you can readily see, we have highlighted behavior problems that in rather obvious ways do not fit with societal standards for the age and environment of the child. Sometimes, however, the problems are not so obvious. Perhaps the individual's behaviors are hidden. Perhaps the behaviors appear at first glance to conform but actually exaggerate certain societal standards. What of the teenage girl who constantly diets, starving herself to the point of endangering her health, in an exaggerated effort to be fashion model slim? Or the boy who hides his suicidal depression behind a facade of perfect behavior? These hidden disorders are also serious problems.

Some behavior problems are expressed in obviously behavioral ways, while others are primarily emotional or psychological. For example, a child may not appear to have normal feelings toward others, or may not interact emotionally with others in the expected ways. Consider the child who is withdrawn—who refuses to leave his bedroom, who spends entire days in a fantasy world, and who constantly uses a fantasy language that prevents communication. The terms **behavioral disorders** and **emotional disturbance** have come to be used interchangeably for these handicaps. It is usually the training and philosophy of the speaker rather than any genuine differences in the children that determine usage. The problems of these children cannot be so precisely interpreted as either emotional or behavioral. This issue has been the subject of ongoing discussion in the field. In this chapter we will consider some of the issues in this debate because particular orientations have implications for causes, prevention, treatment, and teaching.

We do not want to leave you with the impression that all disorders are simple violations of age or societal norms. Some behavioral disorders and emotional disturbance appear to be unrelated to age and societal norms. These disorders would be obvious at any age or in any society. For example, **psychosis,** a major departure from normal acting, thinking, and feeling, sometimes expressed in unprovoked physical aggression toward self or toward others, would be considered disordered behavior at any age or in any society.

But the fact that many behavioral and emotional problems can be described, and even defined, in terms of differences from developmental stages and societal norms does not diminish the problems. When these problems reach a certain level of severity and when they persist, they are undeniably serious problems—for the child, for the family, for the school, and for the community. Teachers and other professionals can play an important part in helping children with behavioral or emotional disturbance learn in school, have more satisfying relationships with friends and family and assume adult responsibilities in their communities. The purpose of this chapter is to review the major issues concerning children with behavior problems and emotional disturbance.

psychosis. A generic term for severe major departure from normal acting, thinking, and feeling that interferes with everyday adaptation.

BEHAVIORAL DISORDERS AND EMOTIONAL DISTURBANCE DEFINED

As the introduction makes clear, behavioral disorders and emotional disturbance are difficult to define. In fact, some have argued that disordered behavior is "whatever we choose to make it" (Kauffman, 1980, p. 524). The definition that, however, has gained the most support was developed by Bower (1960, 1982). The Bower definition, with some modification (see the Concepts and Controversies section at the end of this chapter), has been adopted in the Individuals with Disabilities Education Act (IDEA).

IDEA uses the term *seriously emotionally disturbed* to describe children with behavioral disorders and emotional disturbance, defining it as follows:

(i) The term means a condition exhibiting one or more of the following characteristics over a long period of time and to a marked degree, which adversely affects educational performance:

(A) An inability to learn which cannot be explained by intellectual, sensory, or health factors;

(B) An inability to build or maintain satisfactory interpersonal relationships with peers and teachers;

(C) Inappropriate types of behavior or feelings under normal circumstances;

(D) A general pervasive mood of unhappiness or depression; or

(E) A tendency to develop physical symptoms or fears associated with personal or school problems.

(ii) The term includes children who are schizophrenic. The term does not include children who are socially maladjusted, unless it is determined that they are seriously emotionally disturbed.

(34 C.F.R. 300.5(b)(8)(1990)

seriously emotionally disturbed. The term used in IDEA to categorize students with behavioral disorders and emotional disturbance.

socially maladjusted. A category of children who are excluded from the definition of "severely emotionally disturbed."

The IDEA definition requires only one of the characteristics mentioned above to be present. However, the definition requires that the behavior or behaviors adversely affect educational performance for the child to be eligible for special education.

This definition has other important requirements. The person must exhibit the characteristic over a long period of time and "to a marked degree," that is, with a degree of intensity. These two requirements are designed to exclude children and youth whose problem behaviors are of short duration, since many (perhaps all) individuals exhibit these maladaptive behaviors at some point in their lives for short periods. The requirements are also so designed to exclude children who exhibit merely mild forms of these behaviors. Only the extreme forms of these behaviors should cause the individual to be identified as **seriously emotionally disturbed.**

Children who are **socially maladjusted** are not included in this definition. Although social maladjustment is a widely recognized disorder, there is no generally agreed upon definition of social maladjustment. This exclusion of a category of children by IDEA, coupled with a lack of definition of this particular disorder, raises many troubling issues (see Concepts and Controversies). It is a major area that the field of special education continues to need to address.

Let us review the list of characteristics of children with behavioral disorders and emotional disturbance:

1. inability in interpersonal relationships
2. inappropriate behavior or feelings
3. pervasive unhappiness or depression
4. physical symptoms or fears associated with problems
5. schizophrenia

We will focus on the educational needs of these children and the ways teachers and other professionals can enhance their success in school. But we must keep in mind that peers and adults frequently respond negatively to students who have these characteristics. It is clear that the potential for psychological pain is always present for these children and their families. Therefore, their needs almost always extend into other areas of their lives and require the team efforts of many professionals, including psychologists, psychiatrists, physicians, social workers, family counselors, and others.

Other definitions of behavioral disorders and emotional disturbance are available. The American Psychiatric Association's publication the *Diagnostic and Statistical Manual of Mental Disorders* (DSM III-R)(1987) contains the diagnostic categories and definitions used to classify mental disorders. This manual is used by psychiatrists and

---

TABLE 8.1. A Comparison of Sample DSM III-R Psychiatric Categories with Possible Educational Categories

Psychiatric Categories	Educational Categories
1. Developmental Language Disorder	1. Communicative Disorder
2. Schizophrenic Disorders	2. Severe Emotional Disturbance
3. Post Traumatic Stress Disorder	3. Behavioral Disorder
4. Developmental Reading Disorder	4. Learning Disability

psychologists who treat children with behavioral disorders and emotional disturbance. Teachers should be familiar with these psychiatric categories as well as the educational categories listed in IDEA (Forness and Cantwell, 1982). Psychiatrists and psychologists often serve on Individualized Education Plan (IEP) teams. Table 8.1 shows a comparison between the terminology used in the psychiatric categories and the educational categories.

Types of Behavioral Disorders—Internalizing and Externalizing

Behavioral disorders and emotional disturbance are generally categorized by whether they are primarily externalizing or internalizing. **Externalizing behaviors** are generally aggressive behaviors expressed outwardly toward other persons. Some typical examples are hyperactivity, a high level of irritating behavior that is impulsive and distractible, and persistent **aggression. Internalizing behaviors** are those expressed in a more socially withdrawn fashion. **Anorexia** and **bulimia** are two examples of internalizing behaviors. Table 8.2 lists other examples of common internalizing and externalizing behaviors. Various researchers have other ways of differentiating disorders; for example, Achenbach and Edelbrock (1978) categorize them as either "environmental conflict" or "personal disturbance."

Since the externalizing behavioral disorders are so obviously disruptive to other people in the environment, they are often identified more quickly in schools than disorders that are more internalizing (Brophy and Evertson, 1981; Cullinan, Epstein, and Kauffman, 1984; Gerber and Semmel, 1984). As a result children with internalizing disorders are not always identified and, therefore, do not always receive appropriate special educational services. School personnel must be alert not only to externalizing disorders but also to the equally serious, although less disruptive to the classroom, internalizing disorders. Children whose internalizing disorders are less challenging to the rules of the school are not always as easy to spot as those with externalizing disorders.

Measurement

Quantifying behavioral disorders is one of the most difficult measurement issues in special education. We can list several reasons for this difficulty:

1. No true standardized assessment instruments exist to measure behavioral disorders and emotional disturbance.
2. No clear line exists to separate normal from abnormal behavior or feelings.

externalizing behaviors. Behaviors, especially aggressive behaviors, that seem to be directed toward others.

aggression. Hostile and attacking behavior, which can include verbal communication, directed toward self, others, or the physical environment.

internalizing behaviors. Behavior that is withdrawn, into the individual.

anorexia. Intense fear of gaining weight, disturbed body image, chronic absence or refusal of appetite for food, causing severe weight loss (25 percent of body weight).

bulimia. Chronically causing oneself to vomit, limiting weight gain.

TABLE 8.2. Examples of Externalizing and Internalizing Behaviors	
Externalizing	Internalizing
Hitting other children	Depression
Cursing at a teacher	Withdrawal
Hyperactivity	Fears and phobias
Stealing	Anorexia and bulimia
Arson	Elective mutism

psychodynamic. Exploring sub-conscious emotions, motivations, and feelings.

projective test. A psychological test in which ambiguous stimuli are presented in order to elicit unconscious thoughts or feelings.

ecological assessment. Taking into consideration all dimensions of the individual's environment, including the individual.

3. Professionals offer many different theoretical models to view behavior.

4. The judgment of appropriate behavior is closely linked to the child's developmental stage and the environment.

Since we cannot use standardized tests to measure behavioral disorders and emotional disturbance, we must use other, less precise methods. Measurement usually takes one or more of the following forms: collection of behavioral data, **psychodynamic** analysis such as on a **projective test** or self-report, or **ecological assessment.** In the case of an individual child, some or all of the following might be used:

behavior rating scales completed by parents or teachers;

rating scales completed by the child;

ratings of peer acceptance or rejection;

projective tests, in which a clinician uses clinical judgment to attempt to determine (project) the individual's thoughts from pictures or an interview;

Appropriate services help students with behavioral disorders and emotional disturbance enjoy improved self-concepts and satisfying school experiences.

intelligence tests;

neurological evaluations;

psychiatric analysis (for example, Freudian analysis);

social work evaluations of the individual's environments; and
physical evaluations.

As you can see, these methods can be used by parents, teachers, psychologists, psychiatrists, and other professionals.

Research continues in the effort to develop more precise assessment instruments. One such possibility is the Systematic Screening for Behavior Disorders (SSBD) (Walker et al., 1990). This instrument is designed to assist regular and systematic screening of *all* students in an elementary school. Professionals in the field believe that one reason students with behavioral disorders and emotional disturbance are underidentified is because of the heavy reliance on teacher referrals alone. An instrument that screens all students should ensure improved identification of students.

Significance

Obviously, behavioral disorders and emotional disturbance have grave impacts on the life of the individual, whether a child or adult, who has the disability. However, this disability affects relationships with family members, friendships with peers, and the individual's academic success. Without intervention, the person is likely to live with emotional pain and isolation, perhaps even drop out of school and engage in ever-increasing antisocial activity. Research has shown that school intervention, however, can have a positive impact. Once students with behavioral and emotional problems are identified and receive appropriate services, they generally improve their academic skills, enhance their personal relations, and enjoy more satisfying relations with their families.

HISTORY OF THE FIELD

Throughout history people have recognized behavioral disorders and emotional disturbance in children and adults (Kauffman, 1976). However, societies have often been confused about the causes of these disorders. In the past people believed individuals who had behavioral disorders or emotional disturbance were possessed by the devil, or had participated in what was then considered deviant sexual behavior (excessive masturbation), or were just lazy. Societies also believed these disorders were contagious. Treatments reflected these beliefs, and commonly included excessive punishment, imprisonment, placement in poorhouses, beatings, chainings, straitjacketing, and other cruel actions.

The first institution for people with mental illness was established in London in 1547. Officially known as St. Mary of Bethlehem, it became known as Bedlam, a term that now means a place of noise and uproar. Individuals were chained, starved, and beaten. A popular form of London entertainment was to take the family, including children, for an outing to view the "lunatics" at Bedlam.

By the eighteenth century, changes began to occur through the efforts of reform-minded individuals. Philippe Pinel, a French psychiatrist, in 1792 ordered humani-

Philippe Pinel, chief physician at Salpêtrière, freeing patients with mental disorders from their chains.

tarian reform, including unchaining, for mental patients at the Salpêtrière, a Paris asylum for the "insane" (Brigham, 1847).

In the United States, major reform in the identification and treatment of children and adults with behavioral disorders and emotional disturbance began with the efforts of reformers in the 1800s. Benjamin Rush (1745–1813), considered the father of American psychiatry, proposed more humane methods of caring for children with these problems. Rush, a signer of the Declaration of Independence, was also a leader in the American independence movement and a founder of the first American anti-slavery society.

In the nineteenth century, Samuel Gridley Howe, in addition to his work in blindness (see chapter 9) and mental retardation (see chapter 4), worked to improve the treatment of people with mental illness. Dorothea Dix influenced the founding of state institutions for people with mental illness. By 1844 many states had institutions for people with mental illness and the Association of Medical Superintendents of American Institutions for the Insane (now the American Psychiatric Association) was founded. But the hope with which early institutions were founded soon gave way to pessimism as the institutions became primarily custodial.

Nonetheless, it was not until the late 1800s that public school classes for children with behavioral disorders appeared. Before that time, the children received no services at all. In 1871 a class for students who were regarded as troublemakers was opened in New Haven, Connecticut. In 1909 William Healy founded the Juvenile

Dorothea Dix, the social policy activist, changed the course of treatment for people with mental disorders across the United States.

Psychopathic Institute in Chicago where he and Augusta Bronner conducted important studies about juvenile offenders (Healy and Bronner, 1926). The theoretical work of Sigmund Freud (1856–1939), the founder of psychoanalysis, and his daughter Anna Freud greatly influenced the education and treatment of children with behavioral disorders and emotional disturbance.

By the twentieth century, professionals realized that children needed special programs, teachers, and teaching techniques. Lauretta Bender pioneered the development of educational services for children with behavioral disorders and emotional disturbance. Meanwhile, Karl Menninger and his father and brother revolutionized American psychiatry by stressing a "total environment" of kindness and treatment for patients with mental illness. Bruno Bettelheim began his work with severely disturbed children at the University of Chicago in 1944. His ideas about the value of a "therapeutic milieu" continue to be used in many classrooms. Residential treatment centers for troubled youth (Redl and Wineman, 1957) began to appear around the country in the 1940s and 1950s. In 1947 Strauss and Lehtinen published the groundbreaking book, *Psychopathology and Education of the Brain-Injured Child,* in which they recommended highly structured educational approaches for children with behavioral disorders. (See also the History of the Field section in Chapter 7, Learning Disabilities.)

During the 1960s and 1970s many new textbooks, publications, and results from research projects about educating children with behavioral disorders and emotional disturbance were available. William Cruickshank and his colleagues, drawing on the earlier work of Strauss and Lehtinen, developed specific classroom procedures (Cruickshank et al., 1961). In 1962 Norris Haring and Lakin Phillips published *Educating Emotionally Disturbed Children*, stressing behavioral principles, a structured environment, and interactions between the child and home and school environments. Pearl Berkowitz and Esther Rothman, building on the work of Lauretta Bender at Bellevue Hospital and others, wrote many influential publications including *The Disturbed Child* (1960) and *Public Education for Disturbed Children in New York City* (1967) based on their pioneering teaching with students with behavioral disorders and emotional disturbance in New York.

Meanwhile, Eli Bower, working in California, developed a definition of behavioral disorders that is still widely used (Bower and Lambert, 1962). Nicholas Hobbs headed Project Re-Ed in 1960, developing an ecological approach stressing that children must function in the whole society. Frank Hewett developed the "engineered classroom" model, a totally structured classroom based on behavior management principles. The classic text, *Conflict in the Classroom*, was published by Long, Morse, and Newman in 1965. This book presented many different views on how to educate these students and was used in many college classes to train teachers.

Classic work on the conceptual models of educating disturbed youngsters was conducted in the 1970s by William Rhodes and his colleagues (Rhodes and Tracy, 1972a, b; Rhodes and Head, 1974). Their work helped to clarify and synthesize the diverse opinions and practices that had developed in the field. Since the 1970s, progress has continued in efforts to educate children and youth with behavioral disorders and emotional disturbance. But a great deal of work remains to be done. We need a more refined definition. The field of special education must also resolve the issues surrounding social maladjustment as well as the low number of these students who receive school services. Continuing educational, psychological, medical, and technological advances should enable more children, youth, and adults to benefit from education and lead satisfying lives.

PREVALENCE

It is difficult to estimate the prevalence of behavioral disorders and emotional disturbance for two major reasons. First, as the definition of behavioral disorders and emotional disturbance remains unclear, the identification is necessarily subjective. Second, schools have many disincentives for identifying these children. Some conservatively estimate that approximately 3 to 6 percent of students have behavioral disorders (Kauffman, 1989). It is clear that the number of students with behavioral disorders and emotional disturbance who receive special education services in the schools is smaller than the total number of children with behavioral disorders and emotional disturbance in this country (Center and Obringer, 1987).

Various research studies support this assertion. Costello and her colleagues found a much higher rate when investigating psychiatric problems in children, estimating that approximately 22 percent had a psychiatric problem during the previous year (Costello et al., 1988). She found that only one in five of these children had ever been referred for help. Similar results were found by Whitaker and her colleagues;

they estimated prevalence of approximately 19 percent of selected psychiatric disorders in young people (Whitaker et al., 1990).

The *Twelfth Annual Report to Congress on the Implementation of the Education of the Handicapped Act* (U.S. Department of Education, 1990) indicates that during the 1988–89 school year, less than 1 percent of all students received special education for behavioral disorders and emotional disturbance. Only about 9 percent of all students receiving special education services have behavioral disorders and emotional disturbance. You can readily see that these government figures are far below what professionals expect. Our ability to accurately define, measure, and assess is part of the problem. Professionals also question whether schools try to get rid of disruptive students and thus have fewer to be identified. Also, students with behavioral and emotional disorders are still stigmatized by the label and thus educators may be especially reluctant to label them.

What about figures for the various disorders? We do have estimates of the prevalence of certain disorders. For example, we know that approximately 4 to 10 percent of all children are reported as having a **conduct disorder,** one of the most common behavioral problems (Kauffman, 1989).

Another important factor we must consider is gender. We can note clear gender differences in the identification of this exceptionality. Most children who are identified as having behavioral disorders and emotional disturbance are male (Edgar, 1987). In fact, some estimate that the ratio in special classes is approximately 8 boys to 1 girl (Coleman, 1986). Why is this the case? Researchers believe that teachers often perceive female students as having more acceptable behavior than male students (Center and Wascom, 1987). Researchers have not yet answered the critical question in gender. That is, do boys have greater difficulty with behavioral disorders and emotional disturbance? Do boys exhibit more externalizing behavior disorders while girls exhibit less disruptive or more internalizing behavior disorders? Or, do attitudes toward the problems of boys versus girls account for this difference?

Finally, any student may develop behavioral disorders or emotional disturbance, including one who already has been identified as having another disability such as mental retardation (Epstein, Cullinan, and Polloway, 1986; Reiss, Levitan, and McNally, 1982). Bower (1982) reported that 50 percent of the students in special education classes diagnosed with other disabilities also had behavioral disorders and emotional disturbance.

CAUSES AND PREVENTION OF BEHAVIORAL DISORDERS AND EMOTIONAL DISTURBANCE

Causes

The causes of behavioral disorders and emotional disturbance in an individual are usually unknown. Children are so unique, our scientific study of biological causes so young, the interactions of children and youth with their families and environments so complex, and the interactions with society so individual that we can almost never point to any one variable with certainty as the cause of the behavioral disorder and emotional disturbance. We can, however, identify four general areas where we can find possible reasons for behavioral disorders and emotional disturbance: (1) biology, (2) environment or family, (3) school, and (4) society (see Figure 8.1). If the reasons

> **conduct disorder.** A type of behavioral disorder in which persistent negative, hostile, antisocial behavior impairs daily life functioning.

schizophrenia. A type of psychosis, a severe emotional disorder in which the individual becomes irrational, and often delusional and socially withdrawn.

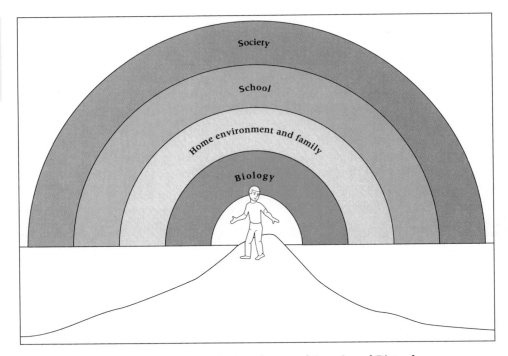

FIGURE 8.1 **Causes of Behavioral Disorders and Emotional Disturbance**

for behavior problems in a particular child can be pinpointed at all, they are likely to be the result of multiple and overlapping factors.

BIOLOGY. Today, researchers are discovering biological causes for some types of disorders with some children. Children born with fetal alcohol syndrome (FAS), for example, exhibit problems in impulse control and interpersonal relations that result from the brain damage caused them by their mothers' drinking alcohol during pregnancy. Malnutrition can cause problems in reasoning and thinking (Ashem and Janes, 1978). Also, researchers believe that there may be a biological dimension to a psychological disorder such as anorexia or bulimia. Disorders such as **schizophrenia** may have a genetic foundation.

Biology also plays a role in treatment. For example, although we do not always know if depression has a biological cause, medications such as antidepressants are often an important component of a treatment program for depression. As researchers continue to work in this area, we will see more treatments based in biology.

ENVIRONMENT OR FAMILY. Families are important in the healthy development of children. Behavioral disorders and emotional disturbance can occur in any family. This does not necessarily mean that the family caused the disorder. Nonetheless, unhealthy interactions can create disorders in some youngsters as well as aggravate existing problems. Examples of harmful family interactions are abuse and neglect, lack of supervision, erratic and punitive discipline, low rate of positive interactions, high rate of negative interactions, lack of interest and concern, and poor adult role models. On the other hand, healthy interactions, such as warmth and responsiveness, consistent discipline, demand for responsible behavior, and modeling, teaching, and rewarding desired behaviors can promote positive behaviors in children (Anderson, 1981).

SCHOOL. Teachers themselves have tremendous influence in their interactions with students. Teachers' expectations influence the questions they ask students, the feedback they give, and the number and character of interactions with students (Brophy and Good, 1970). Teachers sometimes cause or aggravate behavioral disorders and emotional disturbance. This may occur if a teacher who is unskilled in managing the classroom or insensitive to students' individual differences creates an environment where aggression, frustration, or withdrawal are common responses to the environment or teacher. Keep in mind that behavioral disorders cannot be separated from the environment in which they appear. Some academic environments are simply unhealthy for some children. Children might also be using a behavioral disorder to cover up another disability such as a learning disability. Good teachers must be able to analyze their relationships with their students and the learning environment, and keep close watch on problems and potential problems.

SOCIETY. Societal problems can also cause or aggravate behavioral disorders and emotional disturbance. The extreme poverty in which some children live, usually accompanied by poor nutrition, disrupted families, feelings of hopelessness, and violent neighborhoods, can lead to or aggravate behavioral disorders. Many children who might otherwise be able to avoid behavioral disorders and emotional disturbance become vulnerable when faced with stressors such as family disruption, poverty, death, illness, and violence.

But we all know of examples of youngsters who have survived horrible situations and grown into healthy adults. These especially resilient individuals teach us that adverse circumstances do not lead inevitably to behavioral disorders and emotional disturbance. Other children, however, seem especially vulnerable to life problems, and develop disorders under circumstances that do not seem so serious by comparison. Each child is an individual; there are no general cause-and-effect explanations for why a particular person develops a particular disorder at a particular time.

Prevention

Prevention of behavioral disorders and emotional disturbance can be accomplished in two ways. In some cases techniques can be directed toward eliminating the major causes of these disorders. For example, the behavioral effects of fetal alcohol syndrome can be prevented if pregnant women do not drink. In other cases, prevention consists of eliminating or ameliorating the symptoms of the behavioral disorder or emotional disturbance.

The choice of prevention strategies often depends on the theoretical orientation of the teacher or therapist. As an example, let us take the problem of Tod, who is beginning to disrupt his fourth grade classroom immediately before school dismisses. How might his teacher, Ellen Brudos, prevent this from developing into a serious problem? The answer to that question depends, in part, on the theoretical orientation of the teacher. Teachers who are trained to think about behavioral disorders and emotional disturbance in strictly behavioral terms would likely select prevention strategies that are based on a model of antecedent, behavior, and consequence (the

ABC model. An analysis of behavior considering three events: Antecedent, Behavior, and Consequence.

TABLE 8.3. Prevention Strategies for Behavioral Disorders and Emotional Disturbance

Behavior management techniques (ABC model)
Individual and family therapy
Teaching the family new ways of interaction
Character training
Moral education
Medical interventions

ABC model). Using the ABC model, Ms. Brudos analyzes three stages: the circumstances prior to the behavior, the behavior itself, and the circumstances after the behavior. She then intervenes prior or subsequent to the target behavior. Ms. Brudos might decide to institute a more structured and predictable class dismissal or might arrange for Tod to receive verbal praise when he remained orderly during dismissal. A teacher with a strong background in clinical psychology would address the problem differently. If she used this strategy, Ms. Brudos might determine that Tod and his family need therapy and urge the school to assist with arranging that therapy. Alternatively she might institute a teaching program for the family to help them improve their interactions with Tod. She might also specifically teach Tod to monitor his own behavior and to control himself better when he anticipated the disrupting behaviors. If her theoretical orientation was in moral education, Ms. Brudos might emphasize the moral aspects of Tod's behavior, and help him learn to consider the consequences of his behavior on others. Medical intervention, perhaps in the form of medication to calm Tod, represents yet another orientation.

Usually, prevention strategies are not as sharply differentiated as those just described. In practice, many other variables contribute to the selection of a strategy including the cause of the behavior, the educator's experience with strategies that succeeded in the past, recommendations from other professionals, the preferences of

---

TABLE 8.4. Possible Signs or Characteristics of Behavioral Disorders and Emotional Disturbance

Few or no friends
Problems with family relations
Problems with relationships with teachers
Hyperactive behavior, exhibited by excessive movement
Aggression toward self or others
Impulsivity
Immature social skills
Feelings of depression and unhappiness
Withdrawal into self
Anxiety or fearfulness
Ideas of suicide expressed
Distractibility or inability to pay attention for a length of time comparable to peers

the child and family, and the overall orientation of the program. Sometimes a combination of strategies are used. Table 8.3 summarizes major prevention strategies, and Table 8.4 lists typical signs or characteristics associated with the disability.

PROFILE OF CHILDREN WITH BEHAVIORAL DISORDERS AND EMOTIONAL DISTURBANCE

Behavioral disorders and emotional disturbance can affect a student's functioning beyond simply behavior problems or inappropriate emotional expression. The student will likely exhibit learning impairments that affect both academic performance and social interactions with peers and the teacher.

Learning Characteristics

LOWER ACADEMIC PERFORMANCE. Students with behavioral disorders and emotional disturbance typically have low academic performance for their age (Kauffman, 1989). Gottlieb, Alter, and Gottlieb (1991) report that 74 percent of youth classified as behaviorally handicapped also have academic difficulties. Thus a teacher must, in addition to helping the child with behavior, teach academic skills.

SOCIAL SKILLS DEFICITS. Students with behavioral disorders and emotional disturbance also typically have deficits in social skills. These social skills deficits negatively affect their ability to cooperate with their teachers, function in classrooms, and get along with other students (Williams et al., 1989). The social skills deficits rather than academic difficulties may, in fact, be the reason the student is removed from the academic mainstream.

"Sam, neither your father nor I consider your response appropriate."
Drawing by Ziegler; © 1983 The New Yorker Magazine, Inc.

Behavioral Characteristics

We can identify three general types of disorders in students: externalizing behavior problems, internalizing behavior problems, and low-incidence disorders. We discuss each of the general types below as well as the most common disorders within each type.

EXTERNALIZING BEHAVIOR PROBLEMS.   You recall that Table 8.2 lists five externalizing behavior problems. Here we discuss three general problems: hyperactivity, aggression, and delinquency.

Hyperactivity is probably one of the most common complaints about children referred for evaluations as behaviorally disordered and emotionally disturbed. (You will remember from chapter 6 that it is also a frequent complaint about students with learning disabilities.) Hyperactivity is difficult to define because any definition must consider both the nature of the activity as well as the type of activity. The judgment of whether a certain level of a specific activity is "too much" or "hyper" is often subjective. If, for example, the activity is admired, the child might be described as "energetic" or "enthusiastic" rather than hyperactive. Nevertheless, we can arrive at a working definition. A hyperactive child engages in too much activity that is troublesome. According to Ross and Ross (1982), hyperactivity is "a class of hetero-

Children need to learn appropriate ways of dealing with feelings of frustration and anger. Externalizing behavior problems disrupt interactions with peers, family, and other important people in the child's life.

Internalizing behavior problems such as depression, anxiety, and withdrawal are often difficult to recognize in children. Sometimes adults overlook the pain children are experiencing.

geneous behavioral disorders in which a high level of activity is exhibited at inappropriate times and cannot be inhibited upon command" (p. 14).

Aggression, or aggressive acts, have been found to occur in many settings serving children with behavioral disorders (Ruhl and Hughes, 1985). The aggression may be turned toward objects, toward the self, or toward others. The use of control techniques such as punishment usually only increases the child's aggression. Professionals have been more successful teaching children healthy ways of dealing with frustration, such as recognizing feelings of frustration, accepting those feelings, tolerating frustrating experiences, and building coping resources. Teachers can help aggressive students by teaching the following concepts:

1. Frustration results from inevitable blocks in trying to achieve important goals.
2. Frustration is upsetting, uncomfortable, and tension-arousing.
3. Strong and different feelings are aroused by frustration.
4. Upset is a normal and common result of frustration.
5. Frustration can occur without fault or wrongdoing.
6. It is OK to feel bad about not reaching a goal.
7. A person can feel bad and not be bad. (Fagen and Hill, 1987, p. 50)

Delinquency, or juvenile delinquency, is a category of behavioral disorder that is defined by the criminal justice system rather than the medical or educational systems (Berdine and Blackhurst, 1985). **Delinquency** refers to illegal acts committed by juveniles. The acts include crimes such as theft that would also be illegal if committed

depression. A state of despair and dejected mood.

anxiety. A state of painful uneasiness, emotional tension, or emotional confusion.

low-incidence disability. A disability that occurs infrequently, the number of new cases is very low.

autism. A severe disorder of thinking, communication, interpersonal relationships, and behavior.

by adults, and truancy, which would not. Some children who are delinquent have behavioral disorders and emotional disturbance, but some do not—just as some children with behavioral disorders and emotional disturbance are delinquent and some are not.

INTERNALIZING BEHAVIORAL PROBLEMS. Table 8.2 lists five examples of internalizing behavioral problems. We will discuss depression and anxiety/withdrawal here.

Depression is often difficult to recognize in children. Its components, such as guilt, self-blame, feelings of rejection, lethargy, low self-esteem, and negative self-image, are often overlooked or may be expressed by behaviors that look like a different problem entirely. Children's behavior when they are depressed may appear so different from the depressed behavior of adults that teachers and parents may have difficulty recognizing the **depression.** For example, a severely depressed child might attempt to harm himself by running into a busy street or hurling herself off of a ledge. An adult might assume the behavior was normal because many children accidentally do those things. Adults, who often misinterpret or undervalue the pain of children, believe that children have easy lives and should always be happy. In addition, children usually do not have the vocabulary or personal insight or experience to be able to recognize and label feelings of depression.

Anxiety disorders may be demonstrated as intense **anxiety** on separation from family and friends or familiar environment, excessive shrinking from contact with strangers, or unfocused excessive worry and fear. *Withdrawn* children engage in very low levels of positive interactions with their peers; therefore peer rating scales may help with identification. Because anxiety disorders are difficult to recognize in children, many remain untreated.

LOW-INCIDENCE BEHAVIORAL DISORDERS. Two behavioral disorders that occur very infrequently, but are quite serious when they do occur, are schizophrenia and autism.

Schizophrenia, a form of psychosis, is an extremely rare disorder, but when it occurs it places great demands on service systems. It usually involves bizarre delusions (such as believing thoughts are controlled by the police), hallucinations (such as voices telling the child what to think), "loosening" of associations (disconnected thoughts), and incoherence. Children with schizophrenia have serious difficulties with schoolwork and often live in special hospital and educational settings during part of their childhood. Their IEPs are complex and require the collaboration of team members from a variety of disciplines.

Autism is also extremely rare, with an incidence of about 4 for every 10,000 (Batshaw and Perret, 1986). It is a disorder in which thinking, communication, and behavior are severely disordered. Individuals with autism seem isolated and have severely dysfunctional interpersonal relationships, abnormal language or no language, absorbing ritualistic movements, and frequently self-injurious behaviors. When autism was first identified in the 1940s (Kanner, 1943), it was thought to be a psychosocial problem caused by parents' aloof or hostile behavior. Now researchers understand that **autism** is a severe language disorder associated with brain damage.

The classification of autism has had a varied history. It was traditionally believed to be a mental illness. Earlier in PL 94–142, autism was classified with the physical impairments. In the IDEA 1990 amendments it was designated a category of its own. Because many of the identification and service issues are similar, we discuss it with behavioral disorders and emotional disturbance.

The treatment for children with autism includes appropriate education, speech and language services, behavior modification, counseling, family support, and sometimes medication. Children with autism have, in the past, frequently been subject to extremely punitive **aversive treatments** such as electric shock. But new behavioral therapies that emphasize positive interactions show promise (LaVigna and Donnellan, 1986; McGee et al., 1987).

aversive treatment. A noxious and sometimes painful consequence that would usually be avoided, for example electric shock.

ISSUES IN EDUCATION

Education is extremely important for children with behavioral and emotional disorders. In addition to helping them to acquire necessary academic skills, education can provide opportunities for improvements in other areas. Self-image improves as their skills increase, emotional outlets are created when opportunities to learn artistic and creative expression are provided, and interpersonal interactions improve when they have environments in which specially trained people guide their efforts and role models whose healthy behavior they can attempt to copy.

Education and the Preschool Child

It is often difficult to identify behavioral disorders and emotional disturbance in young children unless it is a severe disability such as a psychosis. Young children normally go through great changes in their behavior as they mature, they do not yet have the verbal language abilities to express possible disorders, and the environmental stresses that might eventually cause them problems have probably only begun to affect them.

It is advantageous, however, to identify a child's behavioral disorder and emotional disturbance as early as possible. The early identification and management of young children with disorders can significantly affect their adult adjustment (Cass and Thomas, 1979). If children's disorders can be identified early, it might be possible to intervene with family therapy at an early stage, or assist these children with environmental stresses such as extreme poverty, or help them in other ways without necessarily removing them from the natural environment. Children identified and provided with appropriate services early in their lives may be spared the years of pain that can accompany serious problems. Bower (1982) suggests that it is more costly in terms of money and lost education when children are not served early.

Let us look at the example of Susan, who is three years old. She began speaking at about 1½ years, which is a normal age to begin to speak. When Susan was 2½ years old, however, she stopped speaking to everyone except her pet cat and her grandmother. At first the family ignored this situation, hoping that she would "get over it," but it has continued for six months. The last time Susan's father took her to the pediatrician, the doctor asked about her speech and language. When the father explained how Susan had begun to speak normally but then suddenly stopped six months before, the doctor recommended they have Susan evaluated by the speech/language therapist and the child psychiatric social worker in the medical office. The team determined that the problem was significant and developed an individualized plan to address it. Susan is now enrolled in a preschool program for children with behavioral disorders and emotional disturbance. It is hoped that with counseling for Susan and for her family, together with the special preschool environment and support services, that Susan's elective mutism (which means silence by choice) can be understood and addressed before it becomes even more serious. If the family had waited two more years, until Susan began school, it is likely that the problem would have become more severe and more difficult to address, Susan and her family would have suffered for those additional years, and Susan's opportunity for success in school would have been harmed.

Education and the School-Age Child

The education and treatment of school-age children with behavioral disorders and emotional disturbance can take many forms. A good deal depends on the conceptual model of treatment and education a professional uses for teaching children with behavioral disorders. Table 8.5 lists seven major conceptual models of treatment and education. You can see at a glance that the basis for each model is grounded in a different approach to behavioral disorders. Some take a clinical approach to treatment, others concentrate on the behavioral management of the individual, while others view the child as a part of the whole community. These seven models are the most widely used in the field. One or more have been popular at different times as researchers and philosophers have urged support for their ideas. A good deal of controversy exists in the field over which is most effective and if any one model *alone* can be effective. Generally, educators incorporate parts of several models for the benefit of the children. Since a major focus of school programs is to increase the child's academic success in school, many teachers find the behavioral approach in combination with one or two other approaches most useful for educating these children.

MEASURING PROGRESS. Teachers often use curriculum-based assessment (CBA) to measure whether a child is making academic gains. With CBA teachers measure percentage of spelling words correct, number of new arithmetic facts memorized, reading speed, and ability to write a topic sentence, and they use other techniques in order to report a child's progress. But how can teachers adequately measure additional personal problems that cause children and youth with behavioral disorders and emotional disturbance to be identified as handicapped?

Tips for Teachers

1. Establish clear rules for the class.
2. Role play and practice the rules with the students.
3. Reinforce individual students when they follow a rule.
4. Be sure that the consequences for following and not following the rules are fair and realistic.
5. Foster cooperation and friendship by teaching students how to work in small groups.
6. Communicate regularly with the students' families.
7. Teach students how to negotiate and mediate conflict.
8. Keep accurate records on behavior changes during changes in medication.
9. Find at least one thing each day to praise a child for.
10. Listen.

> **TABLE 8.5. Conceptual Models in the Treatment of Children with Behavioral Disorders and Emotional Disturbance**
>
> 1. *Behavioral approach.* Based on the work of B. F. Skinner (1953) and other behaviorists, this model focuses on providing children with highly structured learning environments and teaching materials. The student's behaviors are precisely measured, interventions are designed to increase or decrease behaviors, and progress toward goals is measured carefully and frequently.
>
> 2. *Psychoanalytic view.* Based on the work of Sigmund Freud and other psychoanalysts, this model views the problems of the child as having a basis in unconscious conflicts and motivations. Treatment is generally individual psychotherapy, long term, and designed to uncover and resolve these deep-seated problems.
>
> 3. *Psychoeducational approach.* The psychoanalytic view is combined with principles of teaching, with treatment measured primarily in terms of learning. Meeting the individual needs of the youngster is emphasized, often through projects and creative arts.
>
> 4. *Ecological approach.* The problems of the child are seen as a result of interactions with the family, the school, and the community. The child or youth is not the sole focus of treatment, but the family, school, neighborhood, and community also are changed in order to improve the interactions.
>
> 5. *Social cognitive approach.* The interaction between the effects of the environment and the youngster's behavior are taught to the child.
>
> 6. *Humanistic education.* Love and trust, in teaching and learning, are emphasized and children are encouraged to be open and free individuals. A nonauthoritarian atmosphere in a nontraditional educational setting is developed.
>
> 7. *Biogenic approach.* Physiological interventions such as diet, medications, and biofeedback are used, based on biological theories of causation and treatment.
>
> Adapted from Kauffman, 1989, *Characteristics of Behavioral Disorders of Children and Youth* (4th ed.), Columbus: Charles E. Merrill.

One useful way for teachers to measure progress in complex personal areas is to break down those areas into precise behaviors, collect data on the current frequency, duration, or rate of those behaviors, and measure gains by taking periodic data on the behaviors after remedial techniques have been implemented. Let us take Shirley as an example. Shirley is a second grader who has been diagnosed by her psychiatrist as psychotic. She is described as "withdrawn" and "in her own world most of the time." The IEP team included the psychiatrist, a psychologist, a family therapist, a social worker, the school nurse, Shirley's teacher, and Shirley's family. Working together, the team developed a comprehensive plan that included individual therapy and family counseling. The team members all agree that Shirley's withdrawal in school is a serious problem and they discuss possible techniques to improve her interactions at school with other people and her surroundings.

The teacher's responsibility, in addition to coordinating with the other aspects of Shirley's therapy, is to improve her school performance. But what can she do to improve "withdrawal"? Can the team come to an agreement on the concrete meaning of such subjective terms as "withdrawn" and "in her own world" in the academic setting? What techniques should the teacher use? After selecting a technique, how will the team know whether the program really works? And how will they know whether Shirley is actually improving at school?

As we discussed in chapter 3, a problem that multidisciplinary teams planning individualized educational programs often face is that the team members represent different perspectives. In this case each member of the team has a different view of Shirley's withdrawal. To the teacher it may mean she does not make eye contact with the teacher during the morning opening exercises. To the parents it may mean she refuses to come out of her bedroom after supper. To the social worker it may

behavior modification. Systematic use of the principles of learning, including rewards and punishment, to increase desired behaviors and decrease undesired behaviors.

mean that she does not look at other children during playground games. Unless the team members can agree on what Shirley needs to change, it will be difficult to focus the resources of the team and to determine the success or failure of various strategies.

Let us assume that the team, after discussion, decides that a **behavior modification** program should be implemented. The behavior they wish to target is eye contact. They decide that Shirley should increase the amount of eye contact she has with others and that the classroom is the first environment in which they will attempt the intervention.

Shirley's teacher must now select an intervention program. Since the agreed upon behavior is eye contact, the teacher first collects data on the number of times that Shirley meets her eyes during the opening exercises. For one school week, during the opening ten-minute morning exercises, the teacher marks with a pencil on a simple chart the number of times Shirley's eyes meet her eyes. Shirley's average eye contact during these morning exercises is one time. Some days she looks at the teacher twice, but some days she never does. The teacher now has a baseline data against which to evaluate future improvement for the targeted behavior. For the first intervention, Shirley's teacher decides that she will praise Shirley each time she achieves eye contact during the morning exercises. The teacher continues to collect data each morning. Shirley responds well to the praise and her rate of eye contact quadruples, to an average of four, from the baseline data.

At the next team meeting, Shirley's teacher can demonstrate in a concrete way that the target behavior has improved. She can show what technique is causing an

This teacher is modeling and directing the social aspects of the boys' participation in a team sport. The teacher's interaction is directly related to his student with a behavioral disorder and emotional disturbance being able to successfully integrate with his teammates. As the student learns important social skills, the teacher will be able to withdraw from such intense teaching.

Focus: Issues of Diversity

Correcting the behavior of students in schools that are culturally or linguistically different from the students' home communities can raise challenging issues for teachers. Fresno Public Schools, for example, has the largest Hmong community in the United States, and the second largest in the world. The Hmong fled Communist repression in Laos, and settled in Fresno County in the last decade. Many efforts have been made to make connections between the cultures, including hiring Hmong primary language tutors, home-school liaisons, and cultural specialists, but the learning never stops. An example of a routine discipline problem may illustrate one of the challenges diversity brings. A principal who needed to discipline a newly arrived student for fighting asked a Hmong translator to call the boy's parents for permission. The translator burst into tears when the parents gave their permission because they added, "Please do not break his legs or blind him." (Snider, 1990)

discipline. Training for self-control or self-management of behavior; training to follow the rules of proper conduct.

setting demands. The behavioral requirements, both obvious and subtle, of an environment.

improvement, and that genuine improvement occurred. With this clear information, it is much easier for the team to decide what areas to work on next, what interventions to use, and determine whether progress continues. Compare a meeting based on this information with a meeting where the teacher comes with no targeted behaviors, no data, and announces simply, "Shirley is a lot less withdrawn than she used to be."

TEACHING SOCIAL SKILLS. A teacher may improve the social skills of students through several strategies: (1) implement a commercially available social skills curriculum such as the Walker Social Skills Curriculum, called the ACCEPTS Program (Walker et al., 1988); (2) develop and implement an individualized program of teaching and reinforcement for a student; (3) set up cooperative learning situations such as peer tutoring; and (4) post rule statements related to specific skills (Fad, 1990). In addition to helping the child improve social skills in the immediate environment, Hollinger (1987) suggests that improving a student's social skills will improve his or her chances for later life satisfaction.

DISCIPLINE. If schools are to be safe and predictable environments for all students and teachers, **discipline** must be maintained. Discipline means training to follow the rules of proper conduct. The critical aspects of maintaining discipline are (1) to make clear the expectations for proper behavior; (2) to teach the students how to achieve the expected behavior; and (3) to implement a system of responses to violations of the rules. Discipline does not necessarily mean punishment.

Many students with behavioral disorders and emotional disturbance need special help to maintain self-discipline. For example, the teacher may have to spend much more time discussing the school and classroom rules so that students have a clear idea of the behaviors required. The teacher may also need to explicitly teach the proper behaviors and personal strategies for the individual to use to control the behaviors. The teacher may also have to help the student understand the consequences of any actions that violate the rules.

Some of the requirements students must meet in academic environments are obvious, such as keeping quiet when the teacher is talking or joining the other students in the line to go to the lunchroom. But some **setting demands** are more

Teaching Tactics

BEHAVIOR GAMES

Behavior games, created by Barrish, Saunders, and Wolf in 1969, have gained in popularity throughout the years. There are many variations. Behavior games allow teachers to deal with negative behavior in a positive way that emphasizes peer cooperation and friendship. Because the other team members want to win, they assist their teammates to control their own behavior. Let us look at an example of a behavior game in action.

Mr. Gonzales's seventh-grade social studies period, scheduled right after lunch, has always been a bit rowdy. The boys have a difficult time settling down to work. Mr. Gonzales is beginning a unit on Central America and wants their full attention for lectures and their work in small groups.

Mr. Gonzales arranges the class in six groups at six tables so they can have small group discussions, sharing maps and other information. This social studies class comprises twenty-four students. Four are students with special needs, and one of the four, Paul, has a great deal of difficulty controlling his behavior. Sitting still for over seven minutes, listening when he is supposed to, and generally following directions are all difficult for Paul. The other children with special needs do not present behavior problems. They do, however, need some additional assistance with the academic tasks. Mr. Gonzales pairs each of these students with a classmate who is doing well in the class. These students help the others take notes, read maps and tables, and understand the homework assignments. Paul's tutor-friend has an extra assignment. He is to help Paul with the academic work, but he is also to assist Paul's efforts to control his behavior. He is to gently remind Paul about what is necessary in order to accomplish the work throughout class time.

Although these arrangements work well, the class still has problems changing from one activity to another. They are too noisy and many do not pay attention while the teacher presents important information. They are not all working on their assignments during group time.

Mr. Gonzales decides to try a timer behavior game to improve class behavior. He explains the rules of the game to the students. Whenever the kitchen timer he has on his desk rings, each group working quietly on task receives a point on the blackboard. Every member of the group has to be meeting this behavioral standard if the group is to receive a point. The trick is that no one knows when the bell will ring. Sometimes it is almost five minutes between rings; other times only a few seconds. Mr. Gonzales does arrange it so the bell rings, on the average, about every five minutes. At the end of the period, all teams with over six points win for the day. (If Mr. Gonzales feels that Paul needs some practice by himself before joining a team, he can make Paul a team of one, with a goal of earning fewer points in order to qualify as winning for the day.)

Mr. Gonzales is pleased with the results of the timer game. He does not have to constantly remind the class about the behavior he expects, or reprimand students who are not following the rules. The outcome is that the class enjoys the game and behaves according to the teacher's expectations.

subtle. For example, the student is expected to make eye contact with the teacher when speaking in the hallway, take turns in group games, or sit with good posture when school administrators visit the classroom. Violations of setting demands such as these can lead to students being perceived as lacking in discipline. All this can be prevented by specifically teaching the child to meet the demands of the environment.

PUNISHMENT. At one time or another, most teachers find themselves faced with the question of whether to use **punishment** with a student. For example, the parents of a child might urge that it is "the only way to get Sam's attention" or "the only way to show Sam who is boss." Even other teachers or administrators might urge that punishment is needed to "keep control of the classroom." But teachers of students with behavior problems should resist these judgments. Excessive use of harsh punishment by a teacher can change the classroom to a battleground where the theme is power and coercion. The theme should instead be a safe, orderly environment where students can feel secure to attempt the difficult tasks of learning.

> **punishment.** Any consequence that results in a decline in the rate or strength of the behavior being punished.

Punishment is a tool that must be used only with great caution and full understanding. Even though punishment may temporarily stop undesired behaviors, it does not teach new behaviors that students can use to achieve their goals. Punishment should always be accompanied by teaching a new behavior. Punishment may also cause the teacher to become engaged in a power struggle with the student, an unhealthy negative interaction that the youngster has in effect dictated. When a teacher uses punishment, the teacher is modeling a negative style of interaction that the other students, as well as the one being punished, may copy in their interactions with others. There is also considerable risk that punishment will be used in a discriminatory way. For example, even though African-American students make up only 16 percent of the student population, they comprise 31 percent of all corporal punishment cases (Quality Education for Minorities Project, 1990).

What is punishment? Many people mistakenly believe that punishment must necessarily involve physical hitting, or screaming, or embarrassment for the child. But punishment is correctly defined as any consequence that reduces the rate or strength of the behavior being punished. Therefore, punishment should always be accompanied by teaching a new behavior. Some teachers find that certain forms of punishment can be an important part of an effective teaching plan to change unwanted behaviors. But even when necessary, the punishment should be limited to mild reprimands, temporary withdrawal of attention, or the loss of certain privileges (Kauffman, 1989). Some general guidelines for the use of punishment are found in Table 8.6.

Educational Environments

Educational environments for children with behavioral disorders and emotional disturbance range from the regular classroom, to special education classrooms, to special schools, to community-based residential group homes and halfway houses, to institutions and hospitals. It is clear, however, that the majority of children with behavioral disorders and emotional disturbance are never officially identified. They are in regular classrooms if they are in school at all.

Many students identified as having behavioral disorders and emotional disturbance have problems that extend beyond the school door. Many are involved with other service delivery agencies such as the foster family care system, the corrections system, or the state mental health agency. This means that schools and teachers will

response cost. Loss of privileges or rewards or withdrawal of attention contingent upon inappropriate behavior.

TABLE 8.6. General Guidelines for Humane and Effective Use of Punishment

- Use only after positive correction methods have failed and when allowing the behavior to continue will result in more serious negative consequences than the proposed level of punishment.

- Institute only in the context of ongoing classroom management and instructional programs that emphasize positive consequences for appropriate conduct and achievement.

- Punishment should be used only by people who are warm and loving toward the individual when his or her behavior is acceptable and who offer ample positive reinforcement for nonaggressive behavior.

- Administer matter-of-factly, without anger, threats, or moralizing.

- Punishment should be fair, consistent, and immediate.

- Punishment should be of reasonable intensity. Relatively minor misbehavior should mean mild punishment.

- Whenever possible, punishment should involve **response cost** (loss of privileges or rewards or withdrawal of attention) rather than aversive treatment.

- Whenever possible, punishment should be related directly to the misbehavior, enabling the youngster to make restitution and/or practice a more adaptive alternative behavior.

- Do not give positive reinforcement immediately after punishment; the child may learn to misbehave and endure the punishment to obtain reinforcement.

- Discontinue punishment if it is not immediately effective.

- Written guidelines for using specific punishment procedures should be known to all—students, parents, teachers, and school administrators.

- All punishment procedures should be approved by school authorities.

Adapted from Kauffman, 1989, pp. 279–280, referring to Braaten et al., 1988 and Wood and Braaten, 1983.

---

be asked to develop, or at least communicate with, multiagency teams to serve the needs of a particular student with behavioral disorders and emotional disturbance. Although this may require complicated and time-consuming efforts, collaboration with other service providers is an important part of providing education to these children and youth (Huntze, 1988; Knitzer, Steinberg, and Fleisch, 1990).

Some students with behavioral disorders and emotional disturbance may find that their disorders bring them to the attention of the legal and criminal justice system. During this time it is especially important that their educational needs not be neglected. Students have a right to receive appropriate and individualized special education even if they are in correctional settings such as halfway houses, jails, or prisons. Unfortunately, children in these situations often do not receive the education they need. Nelson, Rutherford, and Wolford (1987) recommend techniques to address the special needs of this group of students.

Keep in mind that children who return to school after a long absence will need special attention. When students return to their schools and classrooms after a stay in a hospital, residential facility, or correctional setting, the teacher and other school personnel will need to be especially sensitive to these students' and their family's attempts to reintegrate into the school setting. By coordinating with the teachers and therapists at the facility from which the student is returning schoolteachers and administrators can ensure a smooth transition.

FAMILIES OF CHILDREN WITH BEHAVIORAL DISORDERS AND EMOTIONAL DISTURBANCE

COMMUNICATION: AN INTEGRAL PART OF TREATMENT PROGRAMS

Communication problems between children and their families and other adults frequently accompany behavioral disorders and emotional disturbance. A major goal in the IEPs of most students with behavioral disorders and emotional disturbance is to improve these personal interactions. One school developed a unique program for using computers to help children establish better communication with their parents. Virginia Cavalluzzo, principal of the Mimbres School at the Children's Psychiatric Hospital, a facility for children with severe disorders, created a project where the students were taught computer skills and, more important, were taught how to teach these skills to adults. The children showed therapeutic gains as well as academic gains. Dr. Cavalluzzo reviews the project.

The children clearly expressed their enthusiasm for the project. Some of the younger children skipped back to their cottages after their computer session, others hugged the project teacher, and all asked for more time with the computer activities. The children were eager to share the software programs that they had learned with their peers as well as with the classroom and cottage staff. The positive reactions of these children were especially significant because their emotional problems often included a profound lack of self-confidence and very poor interpersonal relationships.

Using the computer and the various software programs, the children improved their skills in basic academic areas, problem solving, and interpersonal communications. All of the software programs required the users to read and follow instructions sequentially. Some software programs focused on mathematics, some on history and geography. All required some aspect of problem solving. Word processing was an important activity for the older children. Some of these children, with extremely poor self concepts, discovered that the computer gave them a sense of privacy. They were able to explore concepts, practice skills, and make mistakes without embarrassment. They gained self-confidence as they processed information and ideas from concrete to abstract conceptualizations.

An unanticipated positive outcome was the increased opportunity for the children to use oral expression. The children were quite verbal about their computer activities. They were self-motivated to explain to others how the game was played or how to solve a problem. As the children became more proficient, they became more articulate in discussing what they were doing. They also gained skills in interpersonal relationships as they developed some team work and in constructively debating strategies in problem solving.

Parents, Children, and Home Passes with the Computer

The parents who participated in the project were very enthusiastic about the opportunity to do something with their children which was new, nonthreatening, and

For children with severe behavioral disorders and emotional disturbance, using a computer may allow them to communicate competently and begin to control their environment positively.

fun for everyone. The families who took the computer home reported that they had fun and positive interactions with each other as they worked together on the computer activities. The parents and the children felt secure when they took the computer home because they could call the project teacher for help if they needed it. The project teacher was able to visit the family at home to assist with problem solving if necessary. Parents and children did call to ask for assistance from the project teacher. In all instances, she was able to respond and the home activities were successfully completed.

Another significant factor that affected the project's progress was the children's serious mental health problems. Many children successfully participated in the project's first phase, which involved working directly with the project teacher and the staff person who was to be the adult learner. Fewer children participated in the second phase, which involved working with their parents as the learners, and still fewer participated in the third phase, in which they would take the computer home. As many children were wards of the state, the parent-child relationships were tenuous or nonexistent. Although the children, parents, and staff were enthusiastic and eager to participate, there were also enormous scheduling problems. It was difficult to find times for the parents and cottage staff or the therapists to work together at the hospital. Many unanticipated difficulties arose in phase three.

But we had success stories. One child, who dreaded going on a home pass because family tensions were so difficult, was able to face the visit more easily when he knew that he would be able to take the computer home. The computer and the software program that the child selected served as a catalyst in fostering positive interactions between himself and his parents.

One parent who owned a computer, but not an Apple, bought the same software program in a format that would function on her home computer so that she and her daughter could continue to share computer learning experiences together.

ADULTS WITH BEHAVIORAL DISORDERS AND EMOTIONAL DISTURBANCE

We have noted throughout this text that special education students drop out of school at a higher rate than their nondisabled peers. Students with behavioral disorders and emotional disturbance drop out at the rate of 40 percent, the highest proportion of dropouts for all exceptionalities (U.S. Department of Education, 1990). Figure 8.2 shows a pie chart. One part displays how all students with disabilities use

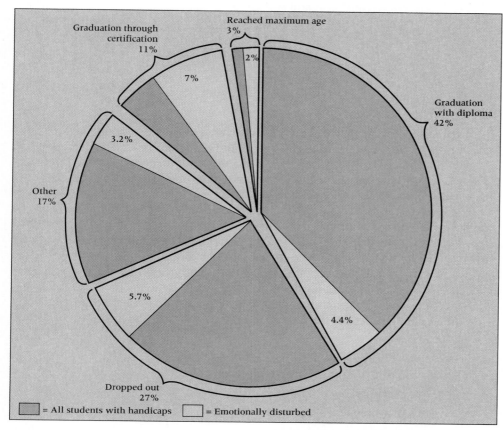

FIGURE 8.2 Students with Disabilities and Children with Behavioral Disorders Exiting School

the five different ways to exit school. The other part illustrates the proportion of students with behavioral disorders and emotional disturbance using each of these ways to leave school. In fact, more students with behavioral disorders and emotional disturbance drop out than graduate. We can, therefore, assume that many adults with behavioral disorders and emotional disturbance will not have the necessary education to enter the job market or make a living wage (Edgar, 1987). Without community mental health services and job training, these adults will probably face poverty and marginal living conditions.

Some students with behavioral disorders and emotional disturbance do graduate from high school and go on to higher education. However, not all of these students will have developed the skills to manage their behavior independently. Other students may not have had severe problems when they were young children, or may not have received intervention at the beginning of their problems, but develop more severe problems as young adults. What happens to them? Colleges report an increased number of students with aggressive behavior and psychological disturbance on their campuses (Carmody, 1990). These colleges are responding with formal codes of student conduct, tightened disciplinary procedures, and special counseling services. However, many adults who had behavioral disorders and emotional disturbance as children do overcome their disabilities and lead satisfying lives after receiving appropriate education and services.

TECHNOLOGY AND BEHAVIORAL DISORDERS AND EMOTIONAL DISTURBANCE

Computers

Throughout this text we have shown how advancements in computerized technology augment and expand students' physical and academic skills. The computer can be especially helpful to a student with behavioral disorders and emotional disturbance. It serves as an emotionally neutral system with which to interact, have fun, achieve success, and even develop job skills.

Used to assist learning without the pressure of subjective judgments by teachers, families, or friends, a computer does not criticize or impose feelings about the child who is using it. Answers are simply right or wrong. A computer serves as a safe environment in which to practice and improve skills. We have discussed in the section on families the positive effect computers can have on children with behavioral disorders and emotional disturbance.

When a teacher incorporates computer-assisted instruction for an individualized learning activity for a child, the computer mirrors many of the attributes of a good teacher by

- providing immediate attention and feedback,
- individualizing to the particular skill level,
- allowing students to work at their own pace,
- making corrections quickly,
- producing a professional-looking product,
- keeping accurate records on correct and error rates,
- ignoring inappropriate behavior,

- focusing on the particular response,
- being nonjudgmental.

Using a computer is not a substitute for learning to interact appropriately with other people, and a teacher should not rely solely on computer interaction with children with behavioral disorders and emotional disturbance. In arithmetic, for example, a teacher might introduce the instruction, allow drill and practice on the computer, and return periodically to monitor the student's progress.

One challenge for the teacher is to carefully monitor progress in specific skills to make sure that when students have mastered a particular level, the computer is used to help them progress to the next level. Many computer learning programs are available at different levels. By consulting with computer specialists, the teachers can ensure that their judgments about the learning needs of the students are translated into the appropriate computer materials. The computer offers yet another strategy for creative teachers to reach their students.

Computer games can help some children with behavioral disorders and emotional disturbance. Even when played alone, the games are rewarding leisure activity. When played with family members or friends, the games can help build relationships.

Medical Technology

Some behavioral disorders and emotional disturbance can be effectively treated with biochemical or drug therapies in addition to educational and psychological or psychiatric therapies. The use of drug stimulants to help control hyperactivity with certain children, for example, has gained acceptance since it began in the 1960s. Yet it is controversial, and pharmacologic therapy is far from universally accepted (Campbell, Green, and Deutsch, 1985; see also Concepts and Controversies in chapter 6, Learning Disabilities). Some disputes about the use of drugs have even been taken to court (Moss, 1988). The variety of issues raised in these cases is summarized in the box on the next page.

MEDICAL RESEARCH. As we discussed in the introduction to this chapter, it is difficult to determine what causes most behavioral disorders and emotional disturbance. Medical researchers are discovering some important clues, however. Genetic researchers, for example, recently suggested a statistical link between schizophrenia and abnormalities in chromosome 5 (Sherrington et al., 1988). Abnormalities in the brain structure of people with schizophrenia have also been identified (Suddath et al., 1990). This research and similar research with other disorders emphasize the role that medical research will play in unraveling some of the mystery of mental disorders. This type of research can take many years before definitive answers are discovered. But finding a cause can be a first step to finding a cure.

Behavior Management Technology

An obvious use of technology in the education and treatment of children with behavioral disorders and emotional disturbance is **behavior management** technology. This chapter contains several examples, such as the Timer Game, and increasing eye contact with the teacher, for implementing behavior management technology. The systematic use of this technology can effect changes in the skills and behaviors of children with disorders.

behavior management. Systematic use of behavioral technologies such as behavior modification to control or direct responses.

Ritalin Under Fire

Two attorneys have filed at least sixteen lawsuits alleging that Ritalin, a drug used to calm hyperactive children, was wrongly prescribed.

Meanwhile, the New Hampshire Civil Liberties Union plans to appeal a decision forcing a boy to take the drug in order to attend public school. And, in Canton, Mass., the attorney for a youth convicted of second-degree murder contended at trial that Ritalin exacerbated the boy's mental illness.

Ritalin, a stimulant, is prescribed for hyperactive children to calm them, help them tolerate frustration and become less distractible, says Dr. Jerry Wiener, president of the American Academy of Child and Adolescent Psychiatry.

Side effects from the drug can include loss of appetite, insomnia, and feelings of sadness or irritability, says Wiener. However, he says, the drawbacks can usually be controlled by adjusting the dosage.

The drug should be prescribed by doctors who are trained in treating hyperactive children, and should be combined with counseling for the child and the parents, he says. Before prescribing Ritalin, doctors should ask about the child's past behavior, require parents and teachers to fill out standardized assessments about the child, and test for learning disabilities, he adds.

Washington, D.C., attorney John Coale filed lawsuits in Minneapolis, Washington, D.C., and Atlanta contending that Ritalin was prescribed without sufficient examination or diagnosis. The suits claim the children suffered side effects such as loss of sleep and appetite, stunted growth, tics, depression, psychotic episodes, and aggressive and erratic behavior.

The Atlanta lawsuit also targets four psychiatrists who defined "hyperactivity" in a psychiatric manual, *Diagnostic and Statistical Manual of Mental Disorders III-R*.

"The definition uses criteria which, using a legal phrase, are void for vagueness," said Coale, a personal-injury lawyer who also represents some of those injured in the Puerto Rican hotel fire. He says the criteria include having difficulty remaining seated or playing quietly.

"This to me is ludicrous because it describes a 6- to 8-year-old," he says. "That's the way they are."

The suit accuses the doctors and the American Psychiatric Association of fraud, the doctors who prescribed Ritalin of malpractice, the Gwinnett County (Ga.) Board of Education and various educators who advocated use of Ritalin of depriving the children of their due process rights and of fraud, and all the defendants with negligent misrepresentation about the drug. *Parker v. The American Psychiatric Association*, No. C87–2444A.

Boston attorney Lawrence Lafferty has filed nine lawsuits in Massachusetts and four in Washington charging the prescribing doctors with medical malpractice.

The suits allege that the doctors failed to diagnose and monitor the children properly, failed to explain to parents the risks of taking the drug, and failed to explain other alternatives.

SOURCE: "Ritalin under fire" by D. C. Moss, November 1988, *American Bar Association Journal*, p. 19. Reprinted by permission.

Concepts and Controversies

Who Should Receive Special Education Services?

IDEA's definition of seriously emotionally disturbed excludes children who are socially maladjusted and does not allow them to receive special education. Therefore, children who are socially maladjusted do not qualify as handicapped for special education. IDEA does not provide a definition of socially maladjusted. As a matter of fact, we have no definition that everyone agrees with. However, most professionals agree that the term socially maladjusted is used to distinguish children and youth who are delinquent and socially deviant from those with emotional disturbance. Should delinquent and socially deviant children receive special services? Some researchers argue that the exclusion is a good idea (Kauffman, 1980). Others argue that the attempt to exclude these children with problems is simply an attempt to reduce costs (Bower, 1982).

What is the issue? Is every youngster with behavior problems disabled (Wood, 1990)? Are some delinquents simply naughty or bad and therefore the responsibility of regular education and their families? What about those who present difficult management problems for schools and their families? Should students be labeled as disordered or disturbed because schools have difficulty with them? Perhaps special education has nothing special to offer these students, and perhaps special education cannot be expected to succeed with them. It is also possible that including these students broadens the role of special education too much. Special education is already serving over 11 percent of the school-age population. Should more children be included in special education? If so, how many more? What criteria should be used for these additional children?

What of incarcerated youth and "delinquents"? Should they receive special education services? Certainly some incarcerated children have behavioral disorders and emotional disturbance, but is the number high or low? Many children and youth in jails and juvenile corrections institutions are currently classified as socially maladjusted and therefore ineligible for special education services in those facilities. Critics argue that these youngsters are handicapped and are being unfairly denied special education services for which they are eligible. A few special educators are beginning to address the problems of incarcerated youth (Nelson, Rutherford, and Wolford, 1987).

Some special educators assert that any student who is socially maladjusted is also seriously emotionally disturbed under IDEA's definition. They argue that the child must be exhibiting at least one of the other indicators in the definition, that is, an inability to learn that cannot be explained by intellectual, sensory, or health factors; inability to build or maintain relationships; inappropriate behavior or feelings; mood of unhappiness or depression; or symptoms or fears associated with problems. Some critics of the socially maladjusted exclusion assert that it is designed to push certain students with aggressive or hostile behaviors out of the school environment. This issue remains difficult for many special educators. We have provided many questions and few answers. But the way in which the issue is resolved has grave consequences for children and youth with serious problems and their families and communities.

SUMMARY

1. The precise definitions of behavioral disorders and emotional disturbance remain unclear. These disorders reflect societal standards for behavior and expectations about the development of children. Many of the behaviors that are labeled disordered in a particular individual might be acceptable if that person were a different age, lived in a different society, or exhibited the behaviors under different circumstances.

2. Behavioral disorders and emotional disturbance may be divided into externalizing behaviors and internalizing behaviors. Some have argued that schools dwell too much on externalizing disruptive behaviors, ignoring the equally serious problems of children and youth with internalizing problems such as depression.

3. The causes of a behavioral disorder or emotional disturbance in a particular individual are almost always unknown. Possibilities include biological causes, such as fetal alcohol syndrome; familial causes, such as abuse and neglect; environmental causes, such as poorly managed classrooms; and societal causes such as the effects of homelessness and violence on children.

4. Students with behavioral disorders and emotional disturbance usually have academic problems as well. In addition to assistance with academic skills, they need individualized programming in learning social skills, improved communication with peers and adults, assistance with family relations, and strategies for dealing with specific emotional problems such as depression, frustration, or aggression.

5. Although it is difficult to identify most behavioral disorders and emotional disturbance in young children, it is advantageous to do so. Early identification can catch problems before they become more serious, can facilitate interventions in the home, and can improve adult adjustment.

6. Educational treatment of students with behavioral disorders and emotional disturbance is usually based in one or several of the following models: behavioral, psychoanalytic, psychoeducational, ecological, social cognitive, humanistic education, or biogenic.

7. Education for children and youth with behavioral disorders and emotional disturbance may be provided in a variety of environments, including the regular classroom, a special education classroom, a community-based residential group home or halfway house, and an institution or hospital. It is important to remember that even when a student is receiving therapeutic services in a facility such as a psychiatric hospital, education remains a critical component of the child's services. Education services will help the child keep up with peers in the neighborhood school, and success in school can build self-esteem and feelings of worth.

DISCUSSION QUESTIONS

1. How might a teacher's choice of intervention strategy be affected by the choice of a conceptual model of behavioral disorders and emotional disturbance and beliefs about human nature?

2. Why might a teacher want to use nonbiological intervention strategies even if a student's behavioral disorder or emotional disturbance has a biological cause?

3. From the perspective of the behavioral model, why is it important to collect precise data on the target behaviors?

4. Outline some activities that a neighborhood might engage in to encourage socially appropriate behavior in the neighborhood children.

5. How might cultural differences affect a child's diagnosis of behavioral disorders or emotional disturbance? How might gender differences affect a diagnosis of behavioral disorders and emotional disturbance?

SUPPLEMENTARY BOOKS AND VIDEOS

People with behavioral disorders or emotional disturbance have been portrayed in fictional and nonfictional roles in books and films. The lists of creative works found below might be of interest.

Books

Greenan, R. (1949). *The secret life of Algernon Pendleton.* New York: Alfred A. Knopf.

Greenfeld, J. (1970). *A child called Noah.* New York: Harcourt Brace Jovanovich.

Kesey, K. (1977). *One flew over the cuckoo's nest.* New York: Penguin.

Paris, R-M. (1984). *Camille: The life of Camille Claudel, Rodin's muse and mistress.* New York: Seaver Books/Henry Holt & Co.

Plath, S. (1971). *The bell jar.* New York: Harper.

Sheehan, S. (1982). *Is there no place on earth for me?* Boston: Houghton Mifflin.

Styron, W. (1990). *Darkness visible: A memoir of madness.* New York: Random House.

Videos

Bedlam (1946). RKO.

Titicut follies (1967). Zipporah Films.

One flew over the cuckoo's nest (1975). United Artists.

Sybil (1977). Lorimar.

Zelly and me (1988). Columbia.

Camille Claudel (1989). Orion.

Rainman (1991). United Artists.

*N*INA HOOPER, 86, from Johnson, Vermont, has glaucoma. Nina lives alone on her farm and spends her time painting. She is involved in Very Special Arts Vermont's Out and About program for senior citizens. Nina has exhibited her work in Vermont and one of her paintings hangs in her Congressman's office in Washington, D.C.

Chapter Nine

VISUAL IMPAIRMENTS

Learning Objectives

After studying this chapter, you should be able to:

- Define two subgroups of visual impairments: low vision and blindness

- List types, causes, and ways to prevent visual impairments

- Provide examples of educational materials and learning environments that accommodate students with visual impairments

- Discuss how technological advances can assist people with visual impairments at school, in the workplace, and in independent living

*B*ill Henderson was a teacher of seventh and eighth grade students, and now is an assistant principal. He had to struggle with a visible sign of blindness, having to use a mobility cane, as his vision deteriorated. When he discussed his disability with his colleagues and students, he found, to his surprise, that they continue to accept him, and he was freed from attempting to hide his handicap.

The first time I used a white cane was one of the most frightening moments of my life. What would my seventh and eighth grade students say? How would my colleagues react?

My vision had not changed radically during the seven years I'd been teaching, but the retinitis pigmentosa was progressing. It was getting harder to pretend I could see like everybody else. I was tired of worrying about what I would say when I next bumped into somebody or couldn't find something. People I'd recently met in the low-vision self-help group assured me that using it would be liberating—that I'd get around and get along more comfortably.

Being in my early 30s, having 3 children and living in Boston at the beginning of the post-504 era was not the time nor the place to fade away—although perhaps many people would have expected just that. No, it was time to come out—not drop out.

When I started using a folding cane in 1980, I found I'd stumbled onto a new world. Students and staffmembers who weren't uptight about it started asking questions about my own and others' disabilities. I was as ignorant as they, holding most of the stereotypes and negative attitudes about people with disabilities non-disabled people held.

So I started to educate myself. What I learned was mind opening. I learned not only that as many as 30% of Americans could probably be considered "handicapped"; I also learned the histories and struggles of persons with disabilities.

We—I no longer said "they"—deserved access. For the first time I began to consider my disability irrelevant in determining my effectiveness as an educator.

Although my vision has decreased some since 1980, I've increased my activities. In addition to working in the public schools—I'm now assistant principal at a Boston "magnet" school—I've served on a number of community boards and disability groups; I've coached soccer, softball, and track and have earned a doctorate in education and taught in community college. I couldn't have attempted these activities without being open about my visual impairment.

Living with a visual impairment has made me a better educator. I've developed a particular sensitivity to "at risk" children, and I know how crucial it is to encourage students to help them succeed.

That long white stick which for a long time represented inadequacy and bondage now serves me as more than a radar for upcoming opportunities. It serves as a symbol and means of freedom.*

*Views of Ourselves, by B. Henderson. This article appeared in the July/August 1989 issue of *The Disability Rag,* p. 26. Copyright 1989 by the Avocado Press. Reprinted by permission.

1. Why do you think Bill was so concerned about revealing his disability?

2. Do you think his disability impacts negatively on his work?

3. What are the benefits of Bill's revealing his disability?

Although we act on information we gain through our sight, we seldom give much thought to the process of seeing. Sometimes, we stop to reflect on the beauty of a particular sunset, the stars at night, a flower in bloom, or the landscape after a snowstorm. We use our sense of sight all of our waking hours, yet we do not think about vision and how it functions. Most of us use vision in our work. For example, secretaries use sight when they type letters, write memos, look up telephone numbers, or direct other people to various offices. At the zoo, animal caretakers use their vision to be certain that the animals are not acting differently by changing their typical patterns of behavior and are not injured. We use our vision for recreation when we watch a movie, view television, or read a book. Some of us actually prefer learning by reading or looking at information, rather than listening to a lecture or instructions. These people are known as visual learners. We also use our vision for self-defense; for example, we look in all directions before crossing the street by foot or crossing an intersection when driving a car. Unlike touch and taste, vision and hearing are **distance senses,** senses that provide us with information outside our bodies. These senses developed to alert us to the presence of helpful as well as dangerous elements in the environment.

Clearly, those of us with unimpaired vision profit from this sense. We learn by observing events, we use our vision to move freely in our environment, and we are alert to danger by using our sight. People with visual impairments have limited use of their sight, but with systematic instruction and advances in technology, most can lead fully integrated lives.

This chapter will help you understand visual impairments and the people who are affected by them. For example, you will learn that the great majority of people who are visually impaired are able to use their sight to function in society. However, their handicap does affect the ease with which they can cope with daily life. You will also learn about one of the biggest challenges for those who are severely impaired—learning to be independently mobile. You will become aware of the obstacles these people often confront, and come to understand that people with visual impairments can assume places alongside others who do not share their disability. Finally, you will learn of the stereotypes and barriers that are uniquely centered on this group of people.

distance senses. Senses—hearing and vision—that provide us with information external to our bodies, developed to help alert us to danger.

visual efficiency. How well a person can use sight.

visual acuity. How well a person can see at various distances.

peripheral vision. The outer area of a person's visual field.

VISUAL IMPAIRMENTS DEFINED

How well people can use their sight, their **visual efficiency,** is influenced by two factors: acuity and peripheral vision. **Visual acuity** describes how well a person can see at various distances. The width of a person's field of vision or the ability to perceive objects outside the direct line of vision is called **peripheral vision.** This aspect of vision helps people move freely through their environment. It helps them

tunnel vision. Severe limitation in peripheral vision.

low vision. Visual acuity between 20/70 and 20/200.

partially sighted. Another term for low vision.

legally blind. Visual acuity measured as 20/200 or worse in the better eye with correction, or peripheral vision no greater than 20 degrees.

central vision. The main field of vision in the eye, usually greater than 20 degrees.

cornea. The transparent, curved part of the front of the eye.

iris. The colored part of the eye.

pupil. Hole in the center of the iris that expands and contracts, admitting light to the eye.

lens. Located behind the iris, brings objects seen into focus.

accommodation. The focusing process of the lens of the eye.

retina. Inside lining of the eye.

optic nerve. The nerve that carries messages from the eye to the visual center of the brain.

see large objects and movement. Severe limitation in peripheral vision is sometimes called **tunnel vision.**

Many professionals in the field of visual impairments divide persons with visual handicaps into two subgroups: those with mild-to-moderate losses and those with severe-to-profound losses. Formerly, those with mild-to-moderate losses were referred to as partially seeing. Today, this group is said to have **low vision** or be **partially sighted.** They use sight to learn, but their low vision may interfere with daily functioning. Individuals classified as **legally blind** have severe limitations with visual acuity or **central vision** (not being able to see a wide area).

To better understand visual impairments, it is helpful to understand how vision normally occurs. For people to see, four elements must be present and operating. The first is light. The second is something that reflects light. Third, that reflected image must be processed by the eye into electric impulses. Fourth, those impulses must be sent to the brain where they are understood. Use the picture of the eye (see Figure 9.1) to trace how the normal visual process works.

Light rays enter the front of the eye through the **cornea.** The cornea is transparent and curved. The **iris** is the colored part of the eye. In the center of the iris is the **pupil,** which is a hole. Light rays pass through the pupil which expands and contracts in response to the intensity of light it receives. The lens is behind the iris. The **lens** brings objects seen into focus by changing its thickness. The process of the lens adjusting to focus things that are close and those that are far away is called **accommodation.** The lens focuses light rays onto the **retina,** which is the inside lining of the eye. It is made up of photosensitive cells that react to light rays and send messages along the **optic nerve** to the visual center of the brain.

Within the category of visual impairments there is great variety. Some persons who are visually impaired have little functional use of sight, while the great majority have substantial use of their vision, particularly with correction (glasses or contact lenses). Although many people do not realize it, the vast majority of people with visual impairments use vision as their primary method of learning, and for many the

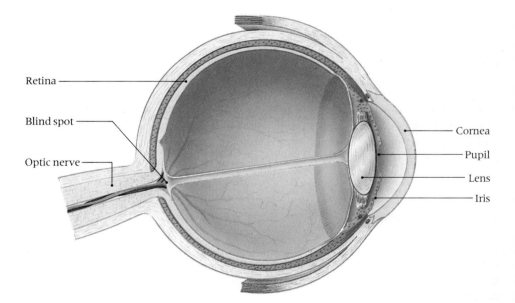

FIGURE 9.1 Cross Section of the Eye

SOURCE: M. L. Hardman, C. J. Drew, M. W. Egan, and B. Wolf, *Human Exceptionality*, 3rd ed., 1990, Needham Heights, MA. Allyn & Bacon. Reprinted with permission.

amount of vision they have left, **residual vision,** can be further developed (Genensky et al., 1979). The vision of some is static, remaining the same from day to day, while others find their ability to see varying by the day, time of day, or setting (Tuttle, 1988). For some, higher or lower levels of illumination (amount of light) affect how well they can see, but for others, it makes little difference. For some individuals distance and contrast are important factors affecting how well they can process information presented through the visual channel. Some are color blind; others are not. For most, optical aids, such as glasses, have a positive effect.

Visual impairment can occur at any age. Persons born with a severe impairment are referred to as **congenitally visually impaired.** Those who acquire a severe visual impairment sometime after birth (usually after the age of two) are called **adventitiously blind** (Barraga, 1976). As with those who are hearing impaired, the **age of onset** (when the handicap occurs) is important. People who lose their sight after the age of two retain some memory of what they had seen. They remember what some objects look like. The later the handicap occurs, the more is remembered. Visual memory is an important factor in learning, for it can influence one's development of concepts and other aspects important to learning.

Two different definitions are commonly used to describe persons with severe visual impairments (Kirchner, 1988a). The first was adopted by the Model Reporting Area for Statistics on Blindness (MRA) to develop a registry of persons who are legally blind. Being legally blind qualifies people to receive some free materials and equipment. It also makes an individual eligible for some special tax deductions, state and federal services, and financial aid. Unfortunately, the MRA group is no longer active, but the definition they used is still commonly applied.

To be eligible for MRA register, persons had to meet the following definition of legal blindness (Kirchner, 1988a):

1. central visual acuity of 20/200 or less in the better eye, with best correction, or

2. the widest diameter of the visual field does not subtend to an angle greater than 20 degrees.

The second definition was developed by the National Center for Health Statistics (NCHS-HIS) for their annual census. Used to classify individuals as **severely visually impaired,** and more functional in nature, it applies to persons

1. who are unable to read ordinary newspaper print even with the aid of corrective lenses, or

2. who, if under six years of age, are blind in both eyes or have no useful vision in either eye. (Kirchner and Lowman, 1985, pp. 5–6)

Types of Visual Impairments

The eye is a very complicated mechanism. Damage to any part of the eye can result in serious limitations in one's abilities to see and process information through the visual channel. Table 9.1 lists disorders of various parts of the eye by using an organizational system suggested by Tuttle (1988). These disorders can result in blindness or severe visual impairments. Many can be corrected or reduced through medical technology. Unfortunately, not all can be resolved by medical treatment at the present time.

residual vision. The amount and degree of vision that one has functional use of despite a visual handicap.

congenitally visually impaired. Severe visual impairment present at birth.

adventitiously blind. Those who acquired a severe visual impairment after the age of two.

age of onset. The age at which a disability occurs.

severely visually impaired. Another term for legally blind.

TABLE 9.1. Types of Visual Impairments

Type	Definition
Disorders of the eye	
Myopia	Nearsightedness; condition allows focus on objects close but not at a distance.
Hyperopia	Farsightedness; condition allows focus on objects at a distance but not close.
Astigmatism	An eye disorder that produces images on the retina that are not equally in focus.
Disorders of the eye muscles	
Strabismus	Improper alignment of the two eyes causes two images being received by the brain, with the possible result of one eye becoming nonfunctional.
Nystagmus	Rapid, involuntary movements of the eye that interfere with bringing objects into focus.
Disorders of the cornea, iris, and lens	
Glaucoma	Fluid in the eye is restricted, causing pressure to build up and damage the retina.
Aniridia	Undeveloped iris, due to lack of pigment (albinism), results in extreme sensitivity to light.
Cataract	A cloudy film over the lens of the eye.
Disorders of the retina	
Diabetic retinopathy	Changes in the eye's blood vessels are caused by diabetes.
Macular degeneration	Damage to a small area near the center of the retina results in restricted fine central vision and difficulties in reading and writing.
Retinopathy of prematurity (ROP)	Excess oxygen to infants causes retinal damage; was called retrolental fibroplasia.
Retinal detachment	Detachment of the retina interrupts transmission of visual information to the brain.
Retinitis pigmentosa	Genetic eye disease leads progressively to blindness; night blindness is the first symptom.
Retinoblastoma	Tumor.
Optic Nerve	
Atrophy	Reduced function of the optic nerve.

Measurement

Normal visual acuity is measured by how accurately a person can see an object or image twenty feet away. Therefore, normal vision is said to be 20/20. A person whose vision is measured at 20/40 can see at twenty feet what people who do not need visual correction (glasses or contact lenses) can see at forty feet away. Field of vision is measured in degrees. Those whose visual field is restricted to no more than 20 degrees are classified as legally blind.

All states require all school-age children to have a visual screening test (Harley and Lawrence, 1984). Vision can be measured in different ways. Children's visual acuity can be tested in the school nurse's office or by a pediatrician using the **Snellen chart.** The Snellen chart was originally developed by a Dutch ophthalmologist in 1862 and comes in two versions. One uses the letter "E" placed in various positions in different sizes and the other uses alphabetic letters in different sizes. To screen substantial numbers of people, a more efficient adaptation of the Snellen chart uses

The photo on the right shows what a person without a visual impairment sees; the one on the left shows what a person with a limited visual field might be able to see.

the "E" version projected on a television monitor placed ten to twenty feet away from the viewer and a computer. The viewer matches a key on the computer with the direction or placement of the "E" on the screen allowing the computer to analyze the data. Although not a requirement, each visual screening of a schoolchild should include teachers' observations about the child's classroom behaviors and performance. For example, teachers should indicate whether a particular child complains about scratchy or itchy eyes or headaches, rubs the eyes excessively, or has difficulty discriminating letters or symbols when completing classroom assignments. Such information is helpful especially when the special services committee (see chapter 3) makes recommendations about placement and the types of special assistance a child should receive.

Two types of eye specialists provide diagnosis and treatment. **Ophthalmologists** are medical doctors who specialize in eye disorders. They can conduct physical examinations of the eye, prescribe corrective lenses and medicines, and perform surgery. **Optometrists** are professionals who measure vision and can prescribe corrective lenses. They cannot prescribe drugs or perform surgery. An **optician** fills either the ophthalmologists' or optometrists' prescriptions for glasses or corrective lenses.

ophthalmologist. Medical doctor who specializes in eye disorders.

optometrist. Professional who measures vision and can prescribe corrective lenses (eyeglasses or contact lenses).

optician. A person who fills either the ophthalmologist's or optometrist's prescriptions for glasses or corrective lenses.

Significance

People suffer visual loss due to damage to the eye. As with other exceptionalities, it is difficult to arrive at one clear definition of visual impairment. One reason is that those with visual impairments range greatly in their abilities. Also, some with visual impairments have multiple handicaps. As mentioned earlier, visual efficiency is an important concept to understand. Interestingly, individuals with the same visual acuity or amount of peripheral vision may differ in their abilities to use their sight. A person's visual efficiency determines the kinds and numbers of aids needed. It also affects how that individual learns primarily (through the visual or auditory channels), and the modifications to instructional methods that teachers must make. For example, a child's visual efficiency could affect how the classroom is organized, where this child must be seated, whether additional equipment (microcomputers, braillers) is required, or if adapted materials (texts with enlarged print) are necessary.

Although different states and school districts vary in the criteria used to determine eligibility for special services, typically people with visual acuity measuring between 20/70 and 20/200 in the better eye with correction are considered to have a visual handicap (Rogow, 1988). These individuals have a moderate visual impairment or low vision. These individuals are able to use their residual vision and may use it as their primary means of gaining information.

HISTORY OF THE FIELD

Our knowledge of people with visual impairments in Western civilization dates back to the days of Homer in ancient Greece. Records from ancient Egypt confirm that people with visual impairments were accepted in society. Despite these indications of attention and acceptance in early societies of Western civilization, there was no systematic attempt to educate and integrate people who were blind into Western society until the eighteenth century.

The first school for the blind, the Institution for Blind Youth, was founded in Paris in 1784 by Valentin Haüy, who also conceived a system of raised letters on the printed page. Unfortunately, his developmental efforts ended when the French Revolution began in 1789. In the early 1800s, Louis Braille, a Frenchman who was blind, developed a tactile system for reading and writing that uses an embossed dot code. This system is still used today.

The first center school for the blind in this country, the New England Asylum for the Blind (now called the Perkins School for the Blind), which was directed by Samuel Gridley Howe, did not open until 1829. Around 1832 the New York Institute for the Blind and the Pennsylvania Institution for the Instruction of the Blind were begun. Following the norm of the time, these nineteenth-century schools were privately supported boarding schools usually attended by children from wealthy families.

The first day classes began in Scotland in 1872. The Scottish Education Act called for children who were blind to be integrated with their sighted classmates and to attend schools in their local communities. Note, our "mainstreaming movement" is not a new concept: its roots are deep in the history of education of children with handicaps. In this country, the first concentrated attempts to integrate students who were blind into local public schools was in Chicago. Frank Hall, the superintendent for the Illinois School for the Blind, came to Chicago in 1900, and convinced people to allow students who were blind to live at home. Hall developed a plan that divided Chicago into several regions. One local school in each region served students with severe visual impairments. The students attended regular classes, but also had a special education teacher who taught them to use braille and encouraged them to participate fully in regular education programs. To help his students use braille more efficiently, Hall developed a mechanical braille writer, a machine that helps individuals take notes and complete other written tasks.

Edward Allen began the first American class for the partially sighted in 1913 in Boston, and later that year Robert Irwin started a class in Cleveland for students who were partially sighted. These programs were modeled after classes in England where schoolwork was exclusively oral. Reading and writing tasks were kept to a minimum, but students attending these classes participated in regular education as much as possible. Classes that followed this model and limited students use of their vision were generally called "sight saving classes." This method was popular for almost fifty years (from about 1915 to 1965), until Natalie Barraga's research on visual efficiency in 1964 changed the field. She proved that people do not have only so much sight, which can be used up; rather, vision can become more limited when it is not used.

Many advances the general population use and enjoy have provided great benefits for people with visual impairments. For example, the telephone, developed by Alexander Graham Bell in 1876, and the phonograph, invented by Thomas Edison in 1877, have proven to be important technologies for those who are visually impaired. This equipment, developed in part to assist people with disabilities, is so available and inexpensive because of its popular appeal. The first radio show was broadcast in 1906 in the United States, and marked access to a form of entertainment and ready access to information for those with visual handicaps.

Although reading and writing present difficult tasks to many individuals who are visually impaired, another major area of difficulty is movement. Between 1918 and 1925, dog guides were trained to help French and German veterans of World War I. Guide dogs (seeing eye dogs) were introduced into this country in 1928, but this is not a popular method of assisting mobility. Less than 2 percent of people with visual impairments use seeing eye dogs (Hill, 1986). Long canes were developed around 1860, but Richard Hoover, after whom the **Hoover cane** is named, is credited with developing a mobility and orientation system in 1944. Before this time, there was no systematic method for teaching individuals to move freely in their environments.

During the 1950s, medical advances that helped save the lives of infants born prematurely ironically caused the disease retinopathy of prematurity (ROP; retrolental fibroplasia) in surviving infants. ROP results in visual impairments that range from mild visual impairments to blindness. During the 1960s, the rubella (German measles) epidemic left many children with visual impairments. The dramatic increase in children with visual impairments strained the capacity of residential schools, which before World War II served 85 percent of all school-age children with visual impairments (Sacks, Rosen, and Gaylord-Ross, 1990). At the same time parents began to call for mainstreaming rather than sending their children away. The result was increased comprehensive programs for children with visual impairments in local communities. Today, the majority of children with visual impairments live at home and attend local public schools.

PREVALENCE

According to the *Twelfth Annual Report to Congress on the Implementation of the Education for the Handicapped Act,* 4 of every 10,000 school-age children are visually handicapped and receive special services (United States Department of Education, 1990). It is difficult to get an accurate count of students with visual impairments (Packer and Kirchner, 1985; Kirchner, 1988a). For example, in the 1984–85 school year, 30,375 students were identified as visually handicapped, in the 1987–88 school year, 22,864 students were so reported, and in 1988–89 17,116 students were classified as visually impaired. A primary reason for differences in such counts is that different states use different definitions and criteria in determining who is eligible for special services. Also, more than half of those identified as having severe visual impairments

Hoover cane. Long, white cane used in the mobility and orientation system developed in 1944 by Richard Hoover to help people with visual impairments move through the environment independently.

multiply handicapped. Possessing more than one handicapping condition.

have an additional disability (Kirchner and Peterson, 1988b). Many of these students are counted in the **multiply handicapped** category rather than in the visual impairment category, even if visual impairment is their primary handicapping condition. Others have their vision corrected with glasses or through surgery. No longer requiring special services, these students do not remain on the special education rolls. Finally, some students with mild to moderate visual impairments are never identified throughout their school years. It is possible that many students with mild and even moderate visual impairments are not identified and do not receive services for which they are eligible (Kirchner, 1983).

The proportion of children who are visually impaired is much smaller than the proportion in the general population. In 1979, 1.8 million persons in the United States had low vision (were partially sighted) or were legally (functionally) blind. Of those, only 111,000 were legally blind (Genensky et al., 1979). The vast majority, over 50 percent of people with severe visual impairments, are over the age of 65; only approximately 1 percent are of school age. Visual impairments are clearly associated with increasing age.

One might think that, because of advances in medical technology, and preventive techniques (for example, vaccinations for rubella), the number of students with visual impairments should be on the decline. However, according to Kirchner, Peterson, and Suhr (1988), the prevalence of severe visual impairments among schoolchildren, which was stable across the fifteen-year period from 1963 to 1978, has continued to remain stable because of the high rate of visual impairments in children being caused by hereditary factors.

CAUSES AND PREVENTION OF VISUAL IMPAIRMENTS

The prevalence of visual impairments, particularly in children, varies country by country. For example, the incidence of blindness in developing countries is much greater than it is in more advanced nations, where access to medical treatment is readily available. In developing nations such as India and countries in Africa, the major causes of blindness are infectious diseases, malnutrition, and vitamin A deficiency (Vaughan and Asbury, 1986). Worldwide, childhood blindness is usually caused by poor nutrition or infections; most of these situations can be prevented.

However, professionals who try to improve health care in these countries often battle on two fronts—improving health and disproving local myths. Many people in developing countries cling to superstitions about handicaps. "In parts of Latin America, villagers believe that bats' urine fell in the baby's eyes, or that a 'black witch moth' flew in the baby's face" (Werner, 1987, p. 244).

Advances in medical technology have helped decrease the number of cases of visual impairment among children. Laser treatment, surgery, and corneal implants all help to reduce the incidence or lessen the severity of some visual impairments. Medical technology can cause increases in this disability as well. As we mentioned earlier, many years ago the hospital care of premature infants actually caused blindness or severe visual handicaps. Once this relationship was understood, care was taken to prevent this form of visual impairment. Today, because of medical advances more infants survive birth. Premature babies with very low birth weights, even some who weigh less than two pounds, are now surviving. Many of these infants have multiple handicaps, some of which are visual impairments. The incidence of retinopathy of prematurity (ROP) (see Table 9.1 for a definition and the section on History of the Field for a discussion) is on the increase once again. New experimental preventive treatments, like freezing parts of the eyes of some premature infants, are being tried to avoid this handicap (Leary, 1988). We should keep in mind that the advances in medical technology that have reduced the prevalence of visual impairment in children outnumber those that contribute to its increase.

We have also seen an increase in the number of babies born with visual impairments (and other handicapping conditions as well) because of substances used by and diseases contracted by their mothers during pregnancy. Most certainly, the rise of drug addiction, the spread of human immunodeficiency virus (HIV—AIDS), and the increase of other diseases among children in this country will result in a rise in the number of children with handicaps who attend school during the 1990s. It is important to remember the complexity of an infant's development during pregnancy and the harmful effects that drugs and diseases can have on the fetus. These harmful effects often result in a lifelong disability.

Causes

Visual impairments may be **congenital** (present at birth) or **acquired.** Almost half of the children who are blind are disabled because of prenatal factors, mostly hereditary in nature (Cartwright, Cartwright, and Ward, 1989). Researchers are beginning to identify genes that cause some forms of blindness. This identification can be the first step leading to a cure. For example, the gene that causes retinitis pigmentosa has now been located and will soon be isolated (*New York Times*, July 18, 1989). Tumors are another cause of blindness or severe visual impairments in school-age children. Such tumors may be in the retinal layer or may be along the optic nerve. Fortunately, two causes of visual impairments have been reduced dramatically over the last ten years. Today, precautions are being taken to prevent retinopathy of prematurity. Rubella was also a significant cause of visual impairments in the past. When this type of measles is contracted by a pregnant woman, it has disastrous effects upon the fetus. Many of these children are born with multiple handicaps; often a vision and/or hearing disability is present. A vaccine can prevent this disease but unfortunately not everyone is immunized (see Concepts and Controversies in chapter 5 for more discussion of this issue).

congenital. Present at birth.

acquired. Having onset sometime after birth.

TABLE 9.2. Common Causes and Some Preventive Measures of Blindness in Children

Causes	Preventions
Dry eye (xerophthalmia or nutritional blindness)	Increase the intake of fruits, vegetables, milk, meat, and eggs in the child's diet, or supplement with vitamin A.
Trachoma	Keep the child's eyes clean, keep flies away from the child's eyes, and have a doctor treat the condition early.
Gonorrhea (a venereal disease communicated from the mother to the infant's eyes at birth)	Treat the baby's eyes with 1 percent silver nitrate solution to prevent blindness.
Chlamydia (a venereal disease caused by the same virus as trachoma)	Doctors can prescribe a tetracycline ointment to put in a baby's eyes three times a day for three days to prevent eye damage.
River blindness (onchocerciasis, spread by the black fly)	No cure.
Measles	Better childhood nutrition and vaccinations.
Eye injuries	Safety precautions.

Source: Disabled Village Children, pp. 244–245, by D. Werner, 1987, Palo Alto, CA: Hesperian Foundation. Adapted by permission.

As we have mentioned, many youngsters who are visually handicapped are multiply handicapped as well (Kirchner and Peterson, 1988a; Packer and Kirchner, 1985). Gates (1985) estimates that between one-half and two-thirds of these individuals are multiply handicapped. Having multiple handicaps depends on the cause of the disability. For example, premature babies with very low birth weights are at high risk for mental retardation. Rubella babies are often multiply handicapped, but those who are visually impaired because of a tumor around the eye are not.

Table 9.2 lists the major, worldwide causes and some measures that can prevent blindness or severe visual impairments.

Prevention

As we mentioned earlier, medical advances have helped reduce the incidence and prevalence of severe visual impairments. For many, medical treatments can also reduce the severity of their visual impairment. Medical treatment is most effective when it is provided as early as possible. In the case of progressive diseases treatment—like improving children's diet or supplementing their diets with vitamins—might halt damage before it is too serious. For example, adding a vitamin A supplement to some children's diet might prevent dry eye. Limiting sugar intake for children prone for diabetes might prevent the blindness that is often associated with this disease.

Education is a critical element in the prevention of visual impairments and especially important in cases when medical technology cannot prevent or reduce the impact of the handicap. Part of the process of education is early identification of those with visual impairments. If children with visual impairments and their families

TABLE 9.3. Possible Signs of Visual Impairments

Eyes water excessively.
Eyes are red or continually inflamed.
Eyes are crusty in appearance.
Eyes look dull, wrinkled, or cloudy.
One or both pupils (black center of the eye) looks gray or white.
One or both eyes cross, turns in or out, or moves differently from the other.
Child bumps into or trips over things.
Child has difficulty seeing after the sun sets (night blindness).
Child has difficulty reading small print.
Child has difficulty identifying details in pictures.
Child is unable to discriminate letters.
Child rubs eyes often.
Child complains of dizziness or headaches after a reading assignment.
Child often tilts head.
Child uses one eye, possibly shutting or covering the other eye when reading.

receive professional help early, they all adjust more quickly to the handicap and the child is able to move quickly to the tasks of learning.

Visual screenings can identify children with visual impairments. However, teachers and parents, attentive to possible signs of a visual problem, might be able to identify such students even sooner. Table 9.3 lists some common characteristics of children with visual impairments. Any child who exhibits one or more of these characteristics should be checked by a professional (school nurse, pediatrician, or ophthalmologist). Alert teachers and parents can help identify students with visual impairments at the earliest stages and ultimately reduce the impact of the disability.

SAFETY. Safety measures can also prevent visual impairments caused by accidents. It is estimated that in one school year alone, over 175,000 children nationally had eye injuries. It was also estimated that over 90 percent of these cases could have been avoided with better safety measures (Benton and Truelove, 1978). In many of these cases, wearing safety goggles and other protective devices would have prevented damage to the eyes.

Public education needs to go beyond the school and the playground (Poirier, 1984). In the mid-1980s, the National Society to Prevent Blindness launched a public education program to inform many professional groups (educators, doctors, nurses) and the general public about eye safety and the importance of early medical treatment. It is encouraging to note that most states have a variety of referral and information networks, as well as public information messages on television and radio providing information to the general public on vision and safety precautions.

Unfortunately, many people try so-called home cures that are thought to prevent or cure eye problems. For example, in Mexico, some villagers place a wet chia seed under a person's eyelid to remove dirt or other particles from the eye. However, dirt sticks to the seed because of the seed's sticky surface layer and causes more problems. Other home cures are dangerous and can cause blindness. For example, lemon juice, urine, feces, pieces of shell, and some topical ointments are desperate cures in some cultures, but they are not safe and can injure the eye. Without education and access to medical care, people continue to suggest and use these techniques or cures in an effort to treat blindness.

blindisms. Inappropriate social behaviors probably due to under-stimulation of infants with low vision.

PROFILE OF CHILDREN WHO ARE VISUALLY IMPAIRED

You may be surprised to learn that over 80 percent of individuals who are legally blind use print as their primary mode of learning (Jones, 1961; Kirchner, Peterson, and Suhr, 1988). When low vision students are included in the statistics, that percentage rises to 90 percent. The great majority of students with visual impairments learn to read and write, watch television, and use their vision to function in society. For many of these students, their visual efficiency can be improved with careful guidance and instruction (Barraga and Collins, 1979). Certainly, they have less information to act upon when compared to individuals who have all of their senses intact.

Behavioral Characteristics

Many individuals with severe visual impairments exhibit inappropriate mannerisms. These mannerisms are sometimes called **blindisms.** Examples of blindisms are rocking, moving their hands strangely in space, or poking at their eyes. Many professionals believe that these behaviors are due to understimulation (Stratton, 1977). Such behaviors probably begin in infancy as these babies try to stimulate themselves. By increasing early infant stimulation, these mannerisms might be eliminated or reduced. In early childhood, children who are blind need to be discouraged from engaging in such behaviors, and be more actively engaged in learning.

In addition to blindisms, the following characteristics are often attributed to people with severe visual impairments: social immaturity, being self-conscious, isolated, passive, withdrawn, and dependent (Tuttle, 1981). Why are these behavioral characteristics exhibited by some individuals with visual impairments? Some of these behaviors might be a function of the disability, but it is probable that some are caused by the way people treat individuals with visual impairments. For example, people with visual impairments tend to be overprotected. They are not encouraged to take risks, participate in sports, and move around as others do (Ferrell, 1986a). This situation often begins in early infancy, and can result in patterns of behavior that reduce social integration. Many sighted people seem uncomfortable with those who are visually impaired (Jernigan, 1983). They do not know how to interact with a person who cannot see well and may feel uncomfortable because some people with visual impairments look different as well. Overprotection by well-meaning family and friends and the aversion and fear of the general population causes some individuals with visual impairments to become dependent and withdrawn.

Academic Performance

Today, most students with visual handicaps are mainstreamed into the general student population. They attend local public schools and participate in the regular education curriculum with their sighted classmates. Data indicate that students with visual impairments, who are not also multiply handicapped, perform well academically (Hodges, 1983). Many use various aids such as glasses, technology, or machines that enlarge type to help them use their vision for learning. Some accommodations in the classroom can help these students function better. Remember that the degree of visual efficiency varies for each person. While most require a few accommodations, some require many. We discuss such modifications to the learning environment later in this chapter.

braille. A system of reading and writing that uses dot codes that are embossed on paper, developed by Louis Braille in 1929.

Easily available adaptions, like baseballs with beepers, allow people with severe visual impairments to have active lives and participate in normalized activities.

METHODS OF READING AND WRITING

"I'm a lawyer—I'm supposed to read the fine print. I can't even read the large print." Mark Leeds, who is legally blind and appreciates new equipment that reads aloud, enlarges text, translates copy into braille and types telephone communication for the deaf, at the law library of the City Bar Association in New York. (Mangrum, 1989, p. 30)

Students with very severe visual impairments may need to learn to read and write using different methods. **Braille** is one reading method used by people who are blind that uses a coded system of dots embossed on paper so individuals can feel a page of text to read. This method has become less popular over the years (Nolan, 1967; Kirchner, Peterson, and Suhr, 1989). In 1963, over 50 percent of persons with severe visual impairments used braille, while in 1978 less than 20 percent did. In 1988, it was estimated that only 12 percent of students who were blind used braille (Diesenhouse, 1989).

As a reading method braille is a very cumbersome and slow. Tuttle (1988) reports that good braille readers read at a rate of only 100 words per minute, while others (Ethington, 1956; Nolan, 1967) have found that the average high school student who is blind reads even fewer words per minute—around 86-90. Try to read that slowly. You will find it quite difficult and laborious. Becoming even minimally proficient at the braille method of reading takes extensive training and practice. Braille

Although fewer people use braille today, it remains an important method of reading and writing for many people who are blind.

also uses different codes for different types of reading. For example, different codes are used for literature and newspapers. Braille editions of many books can still be obtained through regional materials centers, the American Printing House for the Blind, Library of Congress, and Recordings for the Blind. Microcomputers, using special software, can translate standard print to braille.

What other methods do these people use for reading? The majority read print, and some use recorded text. In 1978 approximately 40 percent used reading materials with enlarged type. This percentage has remained constant over a fifteen-year period. The trend, however, was clear; by 1978 more and more students used neither enlarged type nor braille. Most individuals with visual impairments read from the same material as everyone else. As mentioned in the History of the Field, Natalie Barraga's work in visual efficiency (Barraga, 1964; Barraga and Collins, 1979) clearly demonstrated that people do not have only so much sight that can be used up. Rather, using sight can improve an individual's visual efficiency. The methods Barraga developed helps people with visual impairments make better use of their residual vision. Probably because of her efforts, better optical corrections are available, and more of these individuals use their own vision as they read and write.

Many students with severe visual impairments need specially adapted versions of the texts used in their classes. Many texts have been produced on microcomputer disks, and are available from various materials centers. An advantage of many computers is that when students either print out or view this material on a microcomputer screen, they can adjust the size of the type. Future technology (discussed later in this chapter) will add other methods for reading and writing. For example, in the future speech synthesizers will become less expensive and more commonly available. This will allow for instant voice-to-print and print-to-voice translations of documents.

For some, no matter what visual aid they use, the size of print in typical school textbooks is too small. What options do these students have? Many states and school districts have materials centers for students who are visually handicapped. These centers often have modified materials for students to use. For example, texts with enlarged print size allow some students to read the same material as their sighted classmates. Versions using enlarged type are available for many commonly adopted texts. Book of the Month Club now maintains a Large Print Library; competitively priced books are available in 16-point (¼-inch-high) type (*The Disability Rag,* 1989), and some bookstores are finding that the sales of large-print books increased 30 percent from 1989 to 1990 (McDowell, 1990). The print in standard text can also be enlarged through a special piece of equipment using closed-circuit television and a camera with a zoom lens. Such modification is essential for most students with glaucoma, congenital cataracts, or nystagmus. However, for those with good central vision, but a limited visual field, enlargements may be a hindrance. It is important to determine the reading method and material adaptation to be used on an individual basis. Sometimes, audiocassette versions of textbooks are available, and in some instances personal readers are used (these are people who read aloud to students and other individuals who are blind). With the new capabilities of computer-generated print-to-voice systems there will be greater and easier access to classroom materials for students with severe visual impairments.

Some students must adjust or vary the way they hold texts to read print. For example, many students with nystagmic eye movements minimize the distracting movement by pulling their eyes to the right or left corner to read. This lessens the movement of the eye itself. Other students find that they can see reading material better if they hold it in a particular position. A reading stand or easel might be helpful to some of these students. Others have difficulties with thick books that do not remain open or flat. To reduce this problem, pages of sections of a book can be clipped together. Many students with visual impairments find that reading (and other classroom work that places demands on their vision) causes considerable fatigue, particularly if the reading passage is long. Consider this factor when planning the student's school day.

Regardless of the method used, many students with visual impairments have substantial difficulties learning to read (Harley, Truan, and Sanford, 1987). These students require more repetition, more drill, and more practice whether they are learning to read using print or braille. Teachers must find creative ways to keep students' attention and prevent boredom and loss of interest. For students with severe visual impairments, the amount of additional drill and practice is typically significant. Games, computer-assisted instruction, and peer tutoring are fun alternatives to the flashcards and mimeographed worksheets teachers generally (over)use.

LISTENING. All students can benefit from improving their listening skills; however, for students who are visually impaired, good listening skills are imperative. Many of these individuals must rely heavily on their hearing. Mack (1984) found that most adults who were blind used readers and recordings for most of their reading because of the inconvenience of the braille method. As the use of audiotaped versions of books and microcomputers that convert print to voice becomes more commonly available, the importance of listening skills gains even more importance.

Listening is part of the communication process and is a critical skill for all students who are visually impaired. Using hearing rather than vision is the primary mode of gaining information for many individuals whose visual impairment is severe. They listen to teachers, friends, and family; to recorded books and magazines; and to television, radio, and sounds from computers and other electronic devices.

Listening skills can be divided into five categories: attentive, analytic, marginal, appreciative, and selective (Smith, 1972). **Attentive listening** occurs when a person focuses on one form of communication as in a telephone call. **Analytical listening** requires the individual to think about and analyze what a speaker is saying, possibly even drawing inferences about the content of the other person's message. When we listen to music, poetry, or stories being read, we are using **appreciative listening;** and when we are listening to background music when studying or writing, it is called **marginal listening.** In **selective listening,** we eliminate all background noise and listen only to certain sounds or a certain speaker. It is important for all students to develop good listening skills. Teachers should include activities in the school day that aim at developing better listening skills in their students, and through direct instruction listening skills can be enhanced. Many aspects of listening can be improved (Robinson and Smith, 1981). For example, specific tactics—such as peer coaching—used to remind classmates to listen carefully to a particular part of a lesson can help improve the listening skills of children with attention problems. The relationship between language development and listening skills is strong, and children's listening can be improved through instruction to increase vocabulary, knowledge of multiple meanings, and syntax.

Table 9.4 shows a listening hierarchy teachers can use to develop listening skills for their students. Devised for students who have visual impairments, this sequential skill listing is helpful to all students. The questions serve as a guide for the teacher.

attentive listening. Focusing on one form or source of communication.

analytic listening. Listening that includes analysis and possibly interpretation of another person's communication message.

appreciative listening. Listening for the sake of enjoyment, such as to music.

marginal listening. Listening in which part of the auditory content, such as background music, is not the primary focus of attention.

selective listening. Focusing attention on only one sound in the environment, such as the speaker's voice in a lecture.

TABLE 9.4. Listening Skills Hierarchy

Sound awareness
  Does the child change behavior by the presence or absence of sound? (Startle reaction)
Auditory attending
  Can the child interpret different sounds to have different meanings? (The sound of a dog barking, doorbell ringing)
Auditory attention span
  Can the child attend to sounds for some length of time?
Sound localization
  Can the child tell the location or direction of sound?
Auditory discrimination
  Can the child recognize the similarities and differences between sounds?
Auditory memory
  Can the child store and recall a series of sounds?
Auditory memory span
  Can the child associate an event with a sound or remember verbal commands over some period of time?
Auditory sequencing
  Can the child remember the order of items named in a sequence?
Auditory projection
  Can the child attend to and interpret sounds at a distance?
Auditory figure–ground discrimination
  Can the child attend to a particular sound even though there are competing sounds in the environment?
Auditory blending
  Can the child put sounds together to make whole words?
Auditory closure
  Can the child complete a word when only a part is presented?
Re-auditorization
  Can the child remember inflection patterns?

Source: Adapted from R. K. Harley, M. B. Truan, and L. D. Sanford, *Communication Skills for Visually Impaired Learners,* p. 204, 1987. Courtesy of Charles C Thomas, Publisher, Springfield, Ill. Reprinted by permission.

ISSUES IN EDUCATION

sound localization. Being able to locate the source of sounds.

The vast majority of students with visual impairments live at home and attend regular elementary and secondary schools in their local communities. Many receive the same education as their classmates who do not share their disability. They may receive extra assistance from resource room teachers and other specialists, particularly in the area of basic skills. Other students who are visually impaired receive the regular education curriculum, but, in addition, their programs include more instructional topics than their classmates. Students whose functional use of vision is extremely limited require specialized instruction on additional topics such as orientation and mobility.

For those with visual impairments, preschool education is vital. What is a good educational program for a preschooler? What role does this early intervention play in the future lives of persons who are visually impaired?

Education and the Preschool Child

Preschool programs are very important for individuals with severe visual impairments (Moore, 1984; Warren, 1977). These programs help infants and their families from the onset of their visual loss. Remember, those who are congenitally blind (born blind) or adventitiously visually handicapped at a very young age have little or no memory of how the world looks. These infants are not stimulated like sighted infants and have limited opportunities for learning. They do not see their mother's smile or the toys in their cribs. When not stimulated directly, they often withdraw and do not explore their environments like sighted infants do. Many infants who are blind experience a prolonged period of inactivity during their first year of life, which inhibits their exploration and discovery of their environment (ERIC, 1987). Many develop inappropriate behaviors we discussed earlier in this chapter, such as rocking or other "blindisms." Babies may develop other social problems as a result of insufficient interpersonal interactions early in life. It is important to assist babies with visual impairments as they develop relationships, particularly during the first two years of life (Klein et al., 1988). For example, they may need to be taught how to smile and how to make eye contact. These are skills that parents can teach their children with the help of early childhood specialists. Infants and toddlers who are visually impaired do, however, act like sighted babies in other ways. There is no difference in the way that these and sighted babies babble. With some extra guidance from family members their vocabulary development can be the same as sighted babies (Ferrell, 1986b).

Infants who are visually impaired need more stimulation than their nonhandicapped peers (Harley et al., 1986; Stratton, 1977). For example, development of the senses of touch and hearing needs to begin in the early weeks of life and continue on through childhood. These babies should touch their toys and other objects with purpose. They need to learn to feel for shape, size, and other dimensions. Their orientation and mobility can be greatly improved through early intervention techniques that teach locomotion and orientation in space. The development of good listening skills needs to begin early, and one of the first skills to learn is how to judge where sounds are coming from (**sound localization**). These goals are only part of a first-rate instructional program for preschoolers who are visually impaired.

Of course, the involvement of parents is critical. Parents need to learn the effects of visual impairments, the importance of early stimulation, and strategies to cope

life skills. Those skills used to manage a home, cook, shop, and organize personal living environments.

with their baby (Klein et al., 1988; Moore, 1984). Because the home is the most natural setting for the infant, home-based instruction is preferred. One of the most important lessons parents learn is to allow their baby to explore his or her environment. Research shows that parents can help their infants become more mobile and independent through direct efforts by teaching them to crawl and walk in a structured program (Joffee, 1988). Some parents of infants who are visually impaired, fearful that their baby will fall or be hurt, are overly protective. As we have discussed earlier, this attitude fosters dependency and makes it difficult for children and adults with visual impairments to participate fully in society.

Most infants and young children learn through imitation. They see what others are doing and they try to copy it. Imitation is restricted for those who are visually handicapped. Parents, therefore, need to supplement what the infant touches with a verbal description of the activity or object. Simple statements like, "I am washing your hands," help the baby associate the meaning of what is felt and the activity. The child's ability to think in terms of concepts is enhanced when someone communicates and describes in words objects the baby touches but cannot see. Naming concrete objects and describing their physical characteristics (long, soft, hard, heavy, rough) helps develop vocabulary and improve language development.

A wide variety of programs are available for preschoolers with visual impairments. In some cities, teachers work with these children and their families at their homes (Moore, 1984). Some preschool and day care teachers are assisted by special education teachers who travel from school to school (itinerant specialists). In many cities, special preschool programs are available for these children. Sometimes, these programs are segregated (only attended by preschoolers with visual impairments). Some cities offer integrated preschool programs that include both sighted children and those with visual impairments. Many special preschool programs are supervised and managed by staff from a state center or residential school. No matter what program is chosen, it is important for preschoolers to receive the most intensive early educational experiences possible. To provide the fullest attention to the child, the teacher of a preschooler who is visually impaired should coordinate a team of specialists to work with the child and the family. This team might include an ophthalmologist, occupational therapist, physical therapist, orientation and mobility instructor, and social worker. The makeup of the team depends on the needs of each child and family.

Education and the School-Age Child

The educational needs of students with mild or moderate visual impairments differ from those of students who are blind. Students with low vision might require some extra tutorial assistance to learn the same number of phonetic rules as their classmates or additional time to read their history assignment. Students who are blind might require the inclusion of entirely different curriculum topics. For example, they might need to learn independent **life skills** so they can manage an apartment, pay their bills, shop for food, and cook their meals without assistance from others. Or, they might need to be taught how to get from place to place by themselves. Below we discuss some methods of teaching and specific curriculum suggestions for students with mild to moderate visual impairments and those who are blind. It is important for you to keep in mind that these two groups are not truly distinct; suggestions for teachers of students with low vision might well apply to many students who are blind and those made for students who are blind will apply to some students with low vision.

CHILDREN WITH MILD TO MODERATE VISUAL IMPAIRMENTS (LOW VISION). Some minor modifications in teaching style can help students with visual impairments gain more from the learning environment. In many cases, these suggestions are appropriate for all children. One such modification is the careful use of oral language (see also the section on teachers' use of language in chapter 5). For example, many of us, when speaking, do not use words that refer to other words (referents) well. We use words like "this," "that," and "there" without naming the topic we are discussing. Often, teachers write terms on the blackboard without stating them aloud or explaining their meanings. Table 9.5 lists ten steps for devising advance organizers (Lenz, 1989). The Teaching Tactics on this method exemplifies use of advance organizers in a classroom. To assist all students to gain more information the teacher can use both written and oral forms of communication more precisely. The following suggestions can easily be incorporated into classroom situations:

1. Repeat orally information written on a board or an overhead projector.

2. Use an overhead projector to display and enlarge information being presented, if it is helpful to the students (some have difficulty seeing information displayed in this manner).

TABLE 9.5. Steps for Advance Organizers

1. Inform students of advance organizers.
   a. Announce advance organizer.
   b. State benefits of advance organizer.
   c. Suggest that students take notes on the advance organizer.
2. Identify topics or tasks.
   a. Identify major topics or activities.
   b. Identify subtopics or components.
3. Provide an organizational framework.
   a. Present an outline, list, or narrative of the lesson's content.
4. Clarify action to be taken.
   a. State teacher's actions.
   b. State student's actions.
5. Provide background information.
   a. Relate topic to the course or previous lesson.
   b. Relate topic to new information.
6. State the concepts to be learned.
   a. State specific concepts or ideas from the lesson.
   b. State general concepts or ideas broader than the lesson's content.
7. Clarify the concepts to be learned.
   a. Clarify by examples.
   b. Clarify by non-example.
   c. Caution students of possible misunderstandings.
8. Motivate students to learn.
   a. Point out relevance to students.
   b. Be specific, short-term, personalized, and believable.
9. Introduce vocabulary.
   a. Identify new terms and define.
   b. Repeat difficult terms and define.
10. State the general outcome desired.
    a. State objectives of instruction/learning.
    b. Relate outcomes to test performance.

Source: "Setting the Stage for Learning—Use Advance Organizers," by B. K. Lenz, 1989, *Strategram, 1,* pp. 3 and 4. Reprinted by permission.

> ## TEACHING TACTICS
>
> ### ADVANCE ORGANIZERS
>
> As students get older and move into middle and senior high school settings, the demands upon them increase. Teachers require students to be more independent. Students are expected to listen to lectures, read independently from textbooks, and do more homework. In class, students are given less assistance, praised less frequently for their accomplishments, and are required to pay attention for longer periods of time. At the same time, they do not have the background information necessary to put the content of a particular lecture into some context. Using advance organizers can solve these problems by preparing the student for the lesson and the information about to be delivered. Helpful to all students, advance organizers are especially beneficial for students who are visually impaired. Below is a classroom scenario for an American History class. Note how the teacher previews the material. The advance organizers are printed in italics.
>
> Mr. Roberts teaches American History to several sections of high school students. In his fifth period class he has a student, Peter, who has a moderate visual impairment. Today's lecture concerns the American Revolutionary War. The subtopics include a discussion of why some colonists tried to convince England that changes in the relationship between England and the colonies were necessary. Mr. Roberts begins fifth period by welcoming the students to class, and saying,
>
> *First, I am going to tell you what we will cover today to help you better understand my lecture.* Today, we will talk some more about the conditions in America before the Revolutionary War. Last week, we learned about who lived in the American colonies, and what they did for a living. For the next several days, we will be discussing control of the government, taxation, and the growing desire for independence among some colonists. Today, we will talk about the English government in London and the colonies' local governments.
>
> Mr. Roberts *next puts an outline of the day's lecture on an overhead projector.* He

3. Prepare handouts, using enlarged print, that summarize the important information presented in lectures (an easy task for teachers who use computers that can vary print size).

4. Address students by using their names first to get their attention.

5. Audiotape lectures so students can use tapes as study aids at home.

Students with visual impairments must participate actively in the class, and should complete assignments independently and turn them in at an assigned time. Many of these students need more time to complete typical assignments given in regular education classes. The teacher can set a different due date but must enforce this deadline and follow through with contingencies if the assignment is not completed on time. Because reading and writing may be physically fatiguing to these students, some researchers suggest abbreviating their assignments or giving more time to complete assignments (Harley, Truan, and Sanford, 1987). Regardless of these accommodations, teachers should not lower their expectations for students with

TEACHING TACTICS

(continued)

also *hands out a copy of the outline to each student; Peter's version is printed in enlarged type.* Mr. Roberts *reminds the class to listen to his lecture,* to *take notes,* and to *participate in today's discussion.* As his next step, Mr. Roberts spends a few moments *reviewing yesterday's lecture* by asking the class the following questions.

> *Yesterday, we discussed the people who lived in Boston during the time of the Revolutionary War.* Where did these people come from originally? What did they do to earn a living? What were some of their complaints about the government in England? How did they feel about the government in England? Was England listening to their complaints?

Mr. Roberts goes on to explain that part of the day's discussion concerns people's need to feel involved in their own destiny; how they want to participate in decision making that is important to them. He then asks the class to *provide some examples of current affairs* that reflect a similar situation to the period before the American Revolution. Mr. Roberts has prepared several examples beforehand and uses a few to get the discussion started but is careful to allow the students to express their ideas. For this day's lecture and discussion, Mr. Roberts has selected Peter to be class recorder. *Peter will take notes for the class and use them to summarize the day's class at the end of the session.*

Mr. Roberts then explains the importance of this information to the students. He reminds them that they are citizens of the United States and need to know the history of their country. He talks about mistakes of the past and how those mistakes are less likely to be repeated by an informed public. He then *reviews three vocabulary words* ("parliamentary," "participatory," "representation") that he thinks might be difficult for the students. Finally, Mr. Roberts *reminds the students that the content of this lecture will be included in the test* he will give on the entire unit. This reminder is an important motivational tool for some students with exceptionalities.

disabilities. Teachers must keep in mind that students with visual impairments, like everyone else, have the right to try to succeed—or to fail. They need to be encouraged to be full class members who share their work and thoughts with others.

Research has shown that people learn more efficiently when they have been given previews of the lesson about to be taught. Unfortunately, few teachers, particularly at middle and secondary schools, provide students with these previews or advance organizers (Deshler et al., 1983; Lenz, Alley, and Schumaker, 1987). Advance organizers are especially useful for students with visual impairments.

CHILDREN WITH SEVERE TO PROFOUND VISUAL IMPAIRMENTS (BLINDNESS). The Tips for Teachers box provides helpful points for accommodating students who are visually impaired (Barraga and Morris, 1980; Harley and Lawrence, 1984; Harley, Truan, and Sanford, 1987; Orlansky, 1977; Scott, 1982), especially those who attend regular education classes. Teachers can obtain good results by following some simple procedures. Let us look at the example of Elizabeth, a third

career education. A curriculum designed to teach individuals the skills and knowledge necessary to have a career.

grader, who has a severe visual impairment. On the first day of school, Mr. Munroe took the time to show Elizabeth the classroom. He made certain that the furniture and materials were in a consistent pattern and placement, but warned Elizabeth that the classroom would be reorganized periodically. Reorganizing the room every month or so would help Elizabeth learn to adjust to changes in her environment. Many professionals who work with those who are visually impaired recommend that teachers use a consistent daily and weekly schedule so that students will know what is expected at various times of the day (math after morning recess) and across the week (spelling tests on Friday). Also, a teacher can hand out a weekly schedule (see Figure 9.2) to assist students in planning their time and study schedule (Harley, Truan, and Sanford, 1987).

Other modifications to the classroom can help students who are blind. Some of these students use bulky equipment and aids (for example, optical aids, magnifiers, tape recorders) that facilitate their learning. Some use brailling equipment; others use portable microcomputers. These students might need a larger desk or a small table, near an electrical outlet. They might even need cabinet space to store their belongings. Some simple, commonsense accommodations such as those just described can be as beneficial to the student's learning as high-powered technologically advanced equipment.

Many students with visual impairments receive tremendous benefits from regular education classrooms. They are taught the same subjects as other children and, generally, in the same manner. They interact socially with a variety of other individuals and are prepared to take their places in society when schooling is completed. However, many students with visual impairments needed intensive education in addition to the instruction they receive in the regular classroom.

These students also need **career education** and life skills training (Simpson, 1986). They need to learn how to manage a home, cook, shop, and organize their living environments. In some respects, these curricular targets are just as important for people with severe visual limitations as those presented in the typical academic

Week _____	Name _____	
	Class	Homework
Monday	English Grammar p. 46, comma review	Read "Ole Yeller," p. 146 Answer question, p. 151
Tuesday	Turn in questions Quiz over "Ole Yeller"	Write draft 1 on topic "Once I was chased by . . . ."
Wednesday	Turn in draft 1 Review "Ole Yeller" questions	English Grammar, p. 48 Commas
Thursday	Turn in p. 48 Go over draft 1	Write draft 2
Friday	Turn in draft 2 Quiz over commas	None

Weeklong assignment sheet

FIGURE 9.2 An Example of a Week-Long Student Schedule

SOURCE: R. K. Harley, M. Truan, and L. D. Sanford, *Communication Skills for Visually Impaired Learners*, p. 171, 1987. Courtesy of Charles C Thomas, Publisher, Springfield, Ill. Reprinted by permission.

*T*IPS FOR TEACHERS

1. Place the child's desk close to the teacher's desk, the blackboard, and the classroom door.

2. To reduce distracting glare, arrange the child's desk away from a light source, but in a well-lighted area.

3. For special demonstrations or detailed notes written on chalkboards, allow the child to move closer to the presentation to enhance opportunities to see and hear.

4. Free the classroom from dangerous obstacles; remove clutter and litter on the floor.

5. Open or close doors fully (a half-open door can be a dangerous obstacle).

6. Eliminate as much unnecessary noise from the learning environment as possible.

7. Do not speak too loudly, for this tends to increase the volume level in a classroom, including the background noise.

8. Consider the individual's handicap (possibly extending a due date or reducing homework assignments), but do not let the handicap be an excuse for poor or unacceptable performance.

9. Always place materials in the same places so students know where particular items are located.

10. Do not leave the room without telling the student.

11. Seek assistance of a specialist in the area of visual impairments.

12. HAVE HIGH EXPECTATIONS.

curriculum. Also, teachers of students with visual impairments, particularly at high school, should be knowledgeable about the services available to their students after graduation (Irwin and MacDonell, 1988). To better assist their students in making the transition from school to adult life, teachers of students with visual impairments need to be familiar with a number of different agencies and facts. For example, they need to know how students can become eligible for services from the state office of vocational rehabilitation. They should know about the range of jobs available. Teachers should know that there is a strong correlation between the degree of an individual's visual impairment and occupational choices. Bush-Latrance (1988) argues that while people with severe visual impairments are unable to perform some types of jobs, particularly those that are considered semi- or unskilled (such as driving heavy equipment like a fork lift), they can succeed at jobs where technical aids are available to compensate for skills like reading. For these reasons, he believes that whenever possible, people with visual impairments should attend college and earn the qualifications for skilled work. Clearly, teachers' awareness of postsecondary school options for these individuals will help them prepare their students for life after graduation.

ORIENTATION AND MOBILITY/INDEPENDENCE. Children with very low visual efficiencies need special training to increase their independence. Orientation and mobility training helps those with severe visual impairments move around independently. **Orientation** can be described as the mental map people have about their

mobility. The ability to travel safely and efficiently from one place to another.

Independent mobility and orientation remains one of the greatest challenges that people with severe visual impairments face. Direct instruction in mobility training is necessary.

surroundings (Hill, 1986). Most of us use landmarks and other cues to know how to get from one place to another. Think about how you get from your house to a friend's home or from one class to another on campus. What cues or landmarks do you use? These cues or landmarks make up our mental maps and orientation to our environments. **Mobility** is the ability to travel safely and efficiently from one place to another.

It appears that males who have low vision have better spatial orientation than females who have low vision (Edwards et al., 1985). Researchers suggest that because, in general, girls are more sheltered during childhood than boys, they do not explore their environments as fully. They found that all individuals blinded before age three had greater difficulty with mobility and orientation than those who lost their vision later in life. This research also indicates that orientation and mobility is a problem area for many people with visual impairments. Research reinforces the need for direct and early instruction on mobility and orientation for most individuals who are visually impaired.

What methods are used to orient people with visual impairments to their surroundings and increase their mobility? A few adults who are legally blind (less than 4 percent) use guide dogs to help them move about independently (Tuttle, 1988).

Some with very limited vision use canes. These canes make a sound and allow for the use of touch as they are tapped on the ground as a person is walking. They help the person know when the hallway ends, stairs begin and end, and doors are reached. However, there are many obstacles in our world for which a cane is not helpful. Many cities have not yet installed beeper traffic signals. Silent traffic signals can be very dangerous to persons who are visually impaired. Escalators, elevators, and public transportation can present problems. How do people who are visually impaired cope with these? Intensive effort and specialized training help them. Sometimes people with a severe visual impairment need assistance from a sighted person. For example, when people with little or no vision are crossing a busy street or entering an unfamiliar building, their mobility is often reduced. In such situations, a sighted person can help. But the sighted person must be sensitive. First, be certain that the individual wants assistance. Ask. If the answer is yes, guide the individual by offering your arm, holding it in a relaxed position. People with a visual impairment usually will gently grasp your arm at or above your elbow, and will walk slightly behind or to your side. Never push or pull them as you walk. After a few moments, you will find this a rather comfortable system that leaves you free to converse and walk with ease.

Sports and recreation programs and activities can have many benefits to children with severe visual impairments. They not only contribute to better orientation and mobility skills, they also help students become more involved socially. Because many

With creative supports, is there any sport or recreation program in which a person with a severe visual impairment cannot participate?

individuals who are visually impaired tend not to participate in social, recreational, and leisure activities (Kelley, 1981), others need to help involve them in such leisure activities. Many special sports programs are available (for example, skiing, sailing, hiking, baseball, bowling, bicycling, horseback riding), and there are even opportunities to learn various dance forms, such as ballet (*New York Times*, March 18, 1989). People with visual impairments need to learn how to participate in appropriate sports and leisure pastimes, and be encouraged to do so. There are many examples of individuals with severe visual impairments excelling in sports. For example, Lawrence Otero is a member of a university wrestling team and jogs around campus with the help of a teammate (Snouffer, 1989). Clifton Miller is captain of the Minneapolis North High School's cross country track team. He runs with a buddy who helps by warning him of hills, obstacles, and other runners in the path (*Albuquerque Tribune*, 1989). And Tony Candela, a psychologist who is blind, participated in the New York Central Park Triathlon, which consists of a quarter-mile swim, a twelve-mile bicycle ride, and a five-mile run (Martin, 1989).

Educational Environments

Before the 1940s, it was estimated that only 10 percent of students with severe visual impairments attended local public schools. In the 1980s, over 80 percent attended a local school (Lowenfeld, 1982). As we have mentioned earlier, the advantages of attending a local school are substantial. Children who do so live at home with their families and grow up in an environment where home management (cooking, shopping, cleaning) is part of the daily routine.

Those who attend their local public schools also do so with their brothers and sisters and neighborhood friends. They have access to many extracurricular activities, and they are expected to socialize with diverse individuals. They can achieve greater independence throughout their childhood and adult lives. It is important to remember, however, that merely attending a local public school does not guarantee socialization and true integration. These are goals still to be achieved. The case of Olivia Norman demonstrates how full social integration can be accomplished successfully. The parents of Olivia, an eight-year-old who attends first grade, decided that attending regular education classes was her best option for education and development. Olivia is the only student who is blind attending her Washington, D.C. elementary school. She is helped by many people each day. Her teacher, Lissa Cohen, makes sure the classroom environment (from the schedule to the furniture arrangement) is consistent so Olivia can know what is expected and move freely in the room. Olivia uses some extra equipment like an abacus for mathematics, a typewriter, a computer, and a tape recorder so she can listen to textbooks on tape. Her classmates serve as helpers during lunch and recess (although sometimes they are too helpful). Olivia is an active girl who is a member of many clubs (Brownies and the French and science clubs). Certainly, Olivia's case shows that social integration can be a successful experience (Viadero, 1989).

Most children who have a visual impairment attend regular public school classes and also receive the educational services of specially trained teachers. In large cities, many teachers of those who are visually impaired serve as itinerant teachers. These special education teachers move from school to school, sometimes spending only part of any school day at one school. Traditionally, their primary function was to be an academic tutor. They, as many resource room teachers do, helped their students with the assignments from regular education classes. Today, many of these teachers are experiencing a change in their roles, in part because of data indicating adults with visual impairments have difficulties coping with daily life. Many adults with severe visual impairments experience problems managing their homes. Some cannot manage time well. Others have difficulties locating and keeping jobs. Such life skills are necessary for independent living. Without mastery of these important skills, successful academic learning means little. Therefore, many teachers of students who are visually impaired now spend a substantial portion of their time working on these practical life and career education skills.

Many special education teachers who work in rural areas serve in more of a consulting role. Their students participate in the regular education program. The teachers advise and assist regular education teachers who work with these students. They obtain adapted materials and special equipment for those with visual impairments. These itinerant teachers rarely work directly with the students. Rather, they serve students and their regular education teachers in a large geographic area. They spend a considerable amount of time traveling from one school to another, which are often in different towns.

Despite the nation's movement toward integration of students with visual impairments into regular education classes and curricula, some (Gallagher, 1988) advocate categorical classes for these students. Under this arrangement, students with visual impairments would be taught by teachers with very specialized preparation and possibly attend self-contained classes designed specifically for students with this disability. Many experts (Silverstein, 1985) believe that center or residential schools are the best educational option available for some children with moderate to severe visual impairments. This might be particularly true for children who live in rural or remote areas where comprehensive services are not available, or those for whom mainstreaming has failed.

Residential schools for students who are visually impaired can be found in almost every state. In many cases, these schools are serving fewer full-time, residential students. These students tend to come from rural areas, where services and the availability of special equipment are limited, and more and more of these students have multiple handicaps. As more students with visual impairments are mainstreamed, the roles of many of these residential schools have changed. In addition to serving residential students, these schools serve as statewide resource and materials centers. Personnel from center schools consult with teachers at the local schools. Many center schools also offer short courses and summer programs for students and teachers. The specialized staff, materials, and equipment, enable these schools to provide short courses on mobility and orientation, career education, independent living, and technology instruction not available locally. They also offer **outreach programs** across their state or region. For example, in many cities, preschool programs for children with visual impairments and their families are supervised and operated by these center schools. However, some large cities provide services independent of such center operations.

outreach programs. Specialized programs offered in local communities by residential schools or centralized agencies serving students with special needs.

FAMILIES OF CHILDREN WITH VISUAL IMPAIRMENTS

Until the mid-1970s, parental involvement in the educational programs of their children was not commonplace. Education was the teacher's domain. The role of the family in the educational process has changed, partly due to the work of some activist professionals and, substantially, due to parents' involvement in the IEP process as

*J*UST A REGULAR FAMILY

Christine Boone only teaches part-time now that she has two very small children. Edward, her son, is a year old, and Katherine is seven weeks old. Like most moms, Chris cooks the meals, shares the housework with her husband, feeds her children, takes them on walks, reads to them every night, and takes care that her toddler does not get into trouble. But to do this, Chris has had to modify her environment.

Chris uses a lightweight cane when she goes on a walk with her children, and a specially notched needle-less syringe to help measure out the proper dosages of medicines for her children. Edward wears bells on his shoes, so Chris can hear where he is. She says that when she can no longer hear the bells, she knows that he's up to something. Edward follows along with pictures and printed words, while Chris reads children's stories, such as Peter the Rabbit, written in braille.

Chris is congenitally blind, but her children and husband are sighted. Chris and her husband, Doug, were married in 1985, several years after they met. Doug was a teacher of students who were blind, and now teaches adults who are blind. Chris does not want people to feel sorry for her, nor does she want people to think that she is a superwoman who has an extrasensory touch. Chris and Doug want a normal family life, and they live much like everyone else. (Gullett, 1990)

mandated by IDEA. Parents and families should not be viewed as either enemies or friends; they should be considered colleagues in the process of finding ways to fulfill the special needs of their children (Ferrell, 1986; Kroth, 1985).

Unfortunately, there is still friction between those who care for the child in school and those who care for the child at home. Many teachers have high expectations of parents. They sometimes complain that some parents do not follow through with school programs at sufficient levels. Let us look at examples of children with visual impairments. When a program is established at school to eliminate rocking or eye poking, many teachers expect parents to carry out the same educational procedures at home that educators follow at school. Or, when self-care or independent mobility skills are being taught at school, educators hope that parents will expect their children to use these newly learned skills in the home setting. Not all parents are able to meet such expectations. Educators must recognize the stresses and demands on the American family today. The composition of the American family has changed drastically over the last twenty years. Single-parent families are common, and in many families both parents work. This means that educators must be flexible and adjust to the needs of each family. For example, parent conferences may have to be scheduled after work hours. Programs developed to foster transfer of learning (generalization) might have to involve many more individuals (grandparents, siblings, babysitters) in addition to the parents. Also, educators cannot assume that all parents can be effective teachers without considerable training and guidance. For this reason, some school districts offer special training courses for parents of children with special needs.

Educators must also understand the stress that is often associated with a family member with special needs. Parents and siblings of any child with a handicap are at risk for emotional difficulties if their support systems or coping skills are inadequate. An insufficient support system or poor coping skills can affect the entire family, including the child with special needs. For example, such parents often report a feeling of helplessness, which can result in their being more controlling and directive in their young child's play, which, in turn, can result in the child becoming more dependent (St. Peter and Sexton, 1987). As we discussed earlier, this is a particular problem for children with visual impairments. Educators can help these parents to find organized family support groups or introduce them to parents who are successfully coping with their child's disability. They can also teach families how to work more effectively with their child with special needs. For example, they can teach parents some simple behavior modification techniques and some strategies to assist in time management. This can result in fewer behavior problems and a more organized home environment.

A major frustration for parents is finding and gaining access to services for their children. There is a lack of coordination among the many agencies that work with people with disabilities. This makes information about what is available fragmented, incomplete, and sometimes inaccurate. Unfortunately, this situation often occurs throughout these individuals' lives from early intervention through transitional services for adults. When a child has multiple handicaps (for example, both visual impairment and mental retardation), the lack of coordinated services is more obvious (Rogow, 1988). Fortunately, some of these problems are now being addressed. Some state-funded residential schools for the visually impaired, such as the Arizona School for the Blind, are beginning to offer family support services, and even provide educational diagnostic services to better match an individual to the services available in the home community.

The targets for parents to address with their children are many, particularly for children with moderate or with severe to profound visual impairment. These parents must help their children develop many skills across a range of areas: communication, independent living, mobility, sensory development, fine and gross motor skills, cognition, and social skills. Parents also find themselves in a variety of roles. For example, they should provide the support system and continuity needed in their child's life. They are advocates, teachers, and nurturers. Usually, it is for them to provide the most normalized experiences for their children, for they are the ultimate managers of the children's growth and development.

Parents can help educators by keeping records of their child's progress across time, for such information is useful to the many individuals who will work and interact with this child across the school years. For example, knowing the cause and the age of onset of a student's disability can save valuable time as an educational program is put into place. Other information is helpful as well: the age the child began to walk, speak, read, as well as preferences in learning style and instructional delivery. It is also useful to know when certain training programs or therapies occurred. Educators can assist parents in learning how to keep records that will be helpful in the development of future educational programs.

No resource is more important to a child than his or her parents. While teachers are transitory, most parents are the major, consistent factor in children's lives. Parents must provide the consistent, sustained, and systematic support their children require. For parents of children with visual impairments, this demands having information and strategies. They need to understand the nature of visual impairments, their own child's abilities and disabilities, and that child's learning style. Parents need to learn how to set limits, and how to allow for the development of independence. It is for them to guide, reinforce, reassure, and build confidence in their child. The demands and stress on parents of children with special needs are great, but with educators as partners their tasks are more manageable.

ADULTS WITH VISUAL IMPAIRMENTS

As we discussed earlier, some young adults with visual impairments often have a difficult time adjusting to independence and the world of work. They are less experienced in the job world than many of their sighted peers. During high school, many of their classmates held jobs after school or during the summer. They learned about finding and keeping jobs, and also about salaries, wages, and benefits. Students with severe visual impairments often spend their summers attending specialized summer schools while they learn important skills needed for independence, such as further developing their orientation and mobility abilities. Often, they do not have time to apply various life skills to the world of work before graduation. Rochlin (1985) makes the case that these individuals need to be able to earn a living. He maintains that it is expensive for the nation and the individuals themselves not to be productive members of society, and extends his case by stating his feeling that rather than being the receivers of funds, these people need to be contributing taxpayers. Rochlin argues that careers, not just jobs, must be developed for individuals who are severely visually impaired.

Adults with visual impairments hold jobs at every level (Kirchner and Peterson, 1988c). For example, they are scientists, engineers, teachers, office workers, managers of business, and laborers. Unfortunately, despite individual successes and achievements, as a group, people with visual impairments are generally underemployed and discriminated against in the workplace and in society. Many individuals who are blind or severely visually impaired face negative traditions and stereotypes as they attempt to live and work in American society. As an example, two New York police officers mistakenly thought that a folded white mobility cane in the pocket of a man, David St. John, was a set of nunchakus, an illegal martial arts weapon. The police approached Mr. St. John, but did not identify themselves, and asked him to empty the contents of his pockets. Mr. St. John thought he was about to be mugged and defended himself, while the police hit him on the legs and arms. The struggle continued until a witness yelled to the police officers that the man was blind (*New York Times*, May 17, 1989).

Although students with visual impairments are mainstreamed at school, many have difficulties succeeding in the workplace as adults because of poor social interaction skills (Simpson, 1986). This problem is exacerbated by a society that holds a protective view of adults with severe visual impairments which is even expressed in our language system. We refer to agencies that are "responsible" for or "serve" the blind. Often attempts are made to overadapt environments for those who are visually impaired. With proper preparation, many of these individuals can attend college, live in apartments, and hold jobs just like anyone else. Adults with severe visual impairments are calling for their acceptance as individuals who can function well in modern society (Rochlin, 1985). They understand that the protective view of them stems from good intentions, but it severely limits their abilities to be contributing members of society.

A good example of the obstacles individuals who are blind face in an overly protective society is in the story of Kristen Knouse (Lederman, 1988). An excellent horsewoman who wanted to compete at the Intercollegiate Horse Shows Association's national competition, she has been blind since birth. As a freshman at Rutgers University, she had competed all year, and had qualified to compete nationally by winning the regional championship. Despite her previous successes, the association's board of directors attempted to bar her from the competition. They were afraid that she would hurt herself or others. After protests from the American Civil Liberties Union, Rutgers University, and many individuals, Kristen was allowed to participate and finished fourth in the competition. In this case, people made an assumption about a disability that was unfair and biased. Kristen's case is not an isolated example of individuals with visual impairments being barred from competitive athletics. Tim Willis, a senior at Shamrock High School in DeKalb County, Georgia, and the holder of records in national competitions for athletes who are blind, was declared ineligible to compete in high school track competitions because he used a tether and a non-student guide. After deliberations with the state's school association, the school's principal and track coach, Tim was once again allowed to compete (*Education Week,* 1989). It will take more cases like Kristen Knouse's and Tim Willis's to change public opinion.

Many adults with visual impairments feel that their access to recreational, leisure, and cultural activities is also limited. We are beginning to see some positive changes, however. For example, Irma Shore has helped make access to art easier for people with disabilities. Because of her efforts, people with visual impairments can enjoy the permanent exhibit at the Museum of American Folk Art in New York entitled, "Bringing Folk Art Close," which opened September 21, 1989, and is

At the Folk Art Museum in New York, a special tactile exhibit makes art accessible to people with visual impairments.

funded by the Xerox Foundation. This tactile exhibit shows twenty-eight works of art, including items such as a wooden carousel horse, quilts, rocking chairs, and bird and fish decoys. The museum provides labels and a catalogue in braille, an audiotaped guided tour, and even disposable water bowls for seeing eye dogs (Seligman, 1989). Other cultural events are becoming more accessible as well. Now, at the New York Philharmonic concert programs, and the Chamber Music Society and the Great Performers at the Lincoln Center, music programs are available in different versions: braille, large-type, and audiotape (Yarrow, 1989).

What kind of job can a person with a moderate or a severe to profound visual impairment expect? Employment has been a concern of experts in the area of visually handicapped for many years (Johnson and Hafer, 1985; Scholl, Bauman, and Crissey, 1969). Despite having normal intelligence and high school diplomas, individuals with visual impairments have limited job opportunities that are far below the national average in pay and opportunities for advancement (Kirchner and Peterson, 1988c). Although this situation has improved in recent years, much more progress needs to be made for these adults to break out of job stereotypes that limit their earning. Regardless of their abilities, people who are blind are denied access to various types of jobs. For example, until 1988 the U.S. State Department would not consider individuals who are blind suitable as diplomats (*New York Times,* Nov. 29, 1988). After more than ten years of effort, Avraham Raby was able to get the State Department to change this policy that dated back to the eighteenth century. Advances in technology, particularly print-to-voice conversions by new equipment, make it easy for qualified persons who are blind to have a successful career in diplomatic service.

Even when they hold jobs comparable to nonhandicapped adults, adults with visual impairments have incomes that lag far behind the general population (Edwards, 1986). Unfortunately, most of these adults do not work in private industry. They work in sheltered workshops that often do work similar to that done in private industry (Jernigan, 1983). Besides inferior wages and benefits, these workshops have many disadvantages, among them outdated equipment and techniques. Many of the individuals who work in these settings have the skills needed for work in industry, but not the opportunity.

Fortunately, changes are occurring in laws and businesses. Federal antidiscrimination legislation such as the Americans with Disabilities Act (ADA) (see chapter 1) forbids discrimination against job applicants who are disabled. This results in a humanitarian benefit to the individual and a benefit to the company who hires persons with disabilities. Sperry Corporation's Information Group in Blue Bell, Pennsylvania, understood these concepts. Jim Drumheller, who is congenitally blind, works as a computer systems analyst, and uses a voice display device to communicate with the Sperry computer (Losey, 1985). Although individuals with severe visual impairments are beginning to find jobs in private industry, considerable improvement in employers' attitudes still must occur so qualified people with visual impairments can have an equal opportunity.

TECHNOLOGY

For many years, people with visual impairments have used various kinds of technologies to help them learn and function in society. For example, people have used various types of canes, some electronic, to assist in orientation and mobility. Advances in microcomputer technology are providing access to printed information for many people with visual impairments. Because of the popularity of the personal microcomputer, books will soon be readily available on computer disks, allowing for various outputs (voice, enlarged print, braille) (*Disability Rag*, 1988). Organizations such as the Visually Impaired and Blind User Group (VIBUG) of the Boston Computer Society are exchanging information to expand computer literacy among persons with visual impairments.

Computer technology is beneficial in the field of education also. Computer-assisted instruction (CAI) has helped in teaching many useful skills. For example, CAI has been used to teach marketable, up-to-date vocational skills (computer programming, telecommunications) to persons with visual impairments. (CAI is discussed more fully in chapter 6, Learning Disabilities.)

The advantages of microcomputer technology are most apparent in the area of writing. The written products of many students are greatly improved when they use the word processing features available with the microcomputer. Those with severe visual limitations benefit not only because their written assignments are neatly prepared, but also because they can print a version in large type, which they can easily see. Being able to produce versions in different type sizes allow the student with a visual impairment to keep a copy printed in enlarged type and give teachers and classmates copies printed in a standard type size.

Further technological advances are forthcoming. For example, a newly developed machine, The Personal Companion, can respond to human voice and answer with synthesized voice (Feinsilber, 1989). This machine can look up someone's telephone number from an internal directory and dial the telephone. It can balance a checkbook (but cannot write a check). It can "read" aloud sections from a morning newspaper delivered through telecommunications over telephone lines. It can keep a daily appointment book, and turn on and off appliances such as radio or lights. This simple-to-use machine costs about $6,500 and can be leased by those who are blind and cannot afford to purchase it.

Technology allows for rapid dissemination of information. The American Foundation for the Blind (AFB) has established the AFB Information Network, which provides details about regulations and legislation of concern to individuals with visual impairments, their families, advocates, and professionals in the field. The telecommunication network publishes information about issues that these individuals should be aware of and might wish to become involved in by indicating concern and interest to government officials. Clearly, computer technology will affect many aspects (reading, mobility) of life for persons with visual impairments. The systems developed use different means of input: visual, auditory, and tactile.

Visual Aids

Closed-circuit television (CCTV) can be used to enlarge the print found in printed texts and books. By using a small television camera with a zoom lens and a sliding reading stand upon which the printed materials are placed, a person can view printed material greatly enlarged on a television monitor. Such equipment provides immediate access to all types of printed materials such as magazines, textbooks, and mimeographed or photocopied handouts. However, the CCTV is large, cumbersome, not particularly mobile, and expensive (costing about $2,000). Overhead projectors can also enlarge printed materials, but are most useful in the classroom, and are not useful to all individuals with visual impairments. Microcomputers using special word

closed-circuit television (CCTV). A television used for transmissions not accessible to the general public; sometimes only one camera and television monitor is used.

talking books. Books available in auditory format.

Closed-circuit television allows this student to read popular magazines by enlarging the size of the print. Using this method, she does not have to wait for a reader or the availability of a braille edition.

processing programs can produce large-print displays that allow persons with low vision to adjust the size of print to match their own visual efficiencies. Some programs display print on the microcomputer screen at various sizes, allowing the user to select the type size and style that best permits efficient readability.

Most microcomputers also allow the user to select different sizes of print for hard copy printout or visual display on the monitor. This allows individuals who can only read enlarged print to modify materials to various sizes. It also allows teachers who prepare handouts on a microcomputer to prepare different size print for their students with visual impairments and their nonhandicapped students, while still covering the same material.

Audio Aids

Audio access devices allow persons with visual impairments to hear what others can read. **Talking books** have been available through the Library of Congress since 1934, and specially designed record players and tape cassette machines that allow for compressed speech (eliminating natural pauses and accelerating speech) have been developed by the American Printing House for the Blind. A substantial amount of material is available in these forms, but usually it must be ordered from either a regional resource and materials center or from a national center. Audiotape versions of many classics and current best-sellers are now available in most bookstores. Although developed for sale to the general public, this allows greater access to current books for people with visual impairments. The U.S. Department of Education has produced a set of audiocassettes that provide information about federal student aid programs. First available in 1989, these cassettes give information about eligibility requirements, application procedures for federal grants, loans, and work/study programs, and they list scholarships available only to persons who are visually impaired (NASDE, 1989). The introduction of another audio system also gives people who cannot read print immediate access to information. Newsline for the Blind, available in New Mexico and other states, allows people who are blind to hear text from their local newspapers over the telephone line each morning (Sorber, 1990).

The first version of the **Kurzweil Reader,** no longer used much today because of further technological advances, became available about ten years ago. This machine changes printed material into synthesized speech, but this early version of synthesized speech had its limitations. The large and cumbersome equipment was very expensive, so not everyone could afford it. The original Kurzweil Reader cannot recognize all words. The speech it produces is fairly difficult to understand because it does not always provide the correct speech sound for the printed letters it "sees." For example, it sometimes produces a "s" sound for a letter "c" when it should have made an "k" sound. The word "cat" might be produced as the word "sat."

New systems that allow printed material to be synthesized into speech are now available and are becoming rather inexpensive. One of these systems uses a small sensor attached to a microcomputer. When a person moves this sensor along a line of type, information is passed to the computer, which in turn translates the print to speech. The person listening can select the rate of speech (how fast it is delivered), the pitch, and gender of the voice/sound the computer generates. This system has many advantages for individuals who cannot read print. Students can use the same books and materials as their sighted classmates. They are not dependent on the availability of materials at a regional materials center. Individuals using this system do not have to order special materials or wait for their delivery. Even those who are able to read print find benefits in this system. Those who need to use enlarged type do not have to wait for special versions to be prepared. Of course, there is concern that those who can read print will prefer this audio system and will not develop proficient reading skills. For those who can read print, educators should still emphasize proficiency with reading.

Other technology is being developed that benefits people with visual impairments. For example, Norman Coombs, a professor at the Rochester Institute of Technology who is blind, needed a way to work with a student who is deaf. Coombs developed a system whereby he types his messages so they can be read, and his student types his responses, which a speech synthesizer turns into sound. Coombs won an award for his innovation (Turner, 1989). Another development will soon be available to more people with visual impairments. Many of these people listen to a considerable amount of television (approximately six hours per day), but cannot see what is happening. By using the added sound track available in stereo televisions, descriptive videos tell the listener the nonverbal messages others see on the screen. This new system is being piloted in ten cities (*New York Times*, Jan. 28, 1990).

Kurzweil Reader. One of the first computerized systems designed for people with visual handicaps that translates print into synthesized speech.

Tactile Aids

Some persons who are blind use braille as their preferred reading method. The Perkins brailler is a compact and portable machine that uses keys that when pressed down emboss special paper with the braille code. It is inexpensive, but not as efficient as newer electronic versions which use microprocessors that store and retrieve

Optacon. Provides a light sense of printed materials on a person's finger.

information. Also, microcomputer systems, even those designed for sighted users, can support various types of braille and can even be networked so many people can use the braille adaptation simultaneously. As with audiocassettes and talking books, a wealth of materials is available in braille. Remember, enlarged print, audiocassettes, and braille versions of printed materials are not always available for every text or supplemental material used in the regular class. This was and still is a severe limitation for those who cannot read print. A number of years ago, the **Optacon** was developed. It is not used much today, but it allowed individuals to read from texts that had not been adapted or modified. The Optacon provides a light sense of the printed materials on a person's finger. Unfortunately, it was a difficult system to master or use efficiently.

Other tactile advances have made life a bit easier. For example, a braille version of a telephone credit card stores the user's access number so he or she can charge the toll and call on any phone (*New York Times,* Aug. 12, 1989). Personal computers with special printers transform print to braille (*New York Times,* May 9, 1990). By attaching a specially designed braille printer to a microcomputer, standard text can be translated into braille, allowing a teacher who does not know how to use braille to produce braille copies of handouts, tests, maps, charts, and other class materials. This newly available printer costs less than $6,000.

Concepts and Controversies

Another Interpretation of Equal Access

We know that people with handicaps can profit from the use of various kinds of equipment and technology. However, the cost of adaptive equipment can be high. In some cases, a federal agency, such as the Veteran's Administration or the Social Security Administration will reimburse a person with a disability for purchase of equipment. In other cases, loans can be arranged from state or private agencies. Most often, federal reimbursements are not available, and loans must be repaid and add a burden to already limited budgets. It is also difficult for people to keep up with technological advances and the criteria with which to judge the quality and appropriateness of these devices. Many do not even know what devices are currently available. For these reasons, some persons with disabilities maintain that equipment benefiting persons with handicaps should be made available free of cost.

Section 504 of the Vocational Rehabilitation Act was passed in 1973 requiring that all public buildings, built since the act was passed, be accessible to those with handicaps. The intent of the act was that all buildings with more than one floor have elevators. Ramps should be available so that those who use wheelchairs can enter these buildings, and lavatories should be constructed to accommodate wheelchairs. Building accommodations are critically important to those who are physically handicapped. For those with severe visual limitations, aids and other devices allow them better access to the community, society, and greater independence.

In the late 1980s, adults with disabilities, particularly those with visual and hearing impairments, offered a different and broader definition of the term "accessibility." These adults would like the definition of accessibility to include equipment. They maintain that, for them, the availability of equipment and the access to technology is necessary to benefit from and participate in American society. For them, physical accessibility to buildings is not the limiting factor. They need equipment to make them more competitive at school and in the workplace. Equipment such as optical scanners and microcomputers with voice synthesizers will allow individuals who cannot read print immediate access to printed information. Such equipment will allow them a greater choice of jobs. This could possibly lead to higher wages and greater contributions to the tax base in greater ways.

Many of these individuals learn to use a variety of equipment at school. Unfortunately, when they leave school they must return the equipment, and cannot afford to purchase equipment that can assist them in postsecondary schools, at home, at work, or while participating in recreational activities. Also, as new advances are developed, they have no coordinated way of becoming aware of their existence or in being trained in their use.

The Technology-Related Assistance for Individuals with Disabilities Act of 1988 is the first attempt to develop a "consumer-responsive statewide, comprehensive program for the selection and delivery of assistive technology devices and services" (Committee on Education and Labor, p. 16). The Act makes available to states competitive grant funds to develop a coordinated system of technological services. Although this act will greatly enhance the availability of and access to assistive devices, many who are disabled believe that they should be provided with this equipment at no cost to them or their families. Clearly, this would be an expensive program to implement, and leaves many questions. Who should decide what equipment should be provided at public expense? How much equipment would an individual be entitled to? Should the definition of accessibility be broadened to include technology and equipment?

SUMMARY

For most of us, the primary way we learn is through vision. Often, when we are in the process of learning how to perform a new skill, we are shown how to do the task. We observe the actions of others, and imitate their behaviors. We gain information by watching television or reading a newspaper, book, or magazine. People with visual impairments have a restricted ability to use their sight, and that can affect how they function as independent adults.

1. School-age youngsters with visual impairments comprise two general groups: those who are blind and those who have low vision. These distinctions relate to the severity of the handicap or the amount of functional use of sight an individual has. There are two other groups within the category of visually impaired. This distinction is based on the age of the person when his or her handicap occurred. Those who are congenitally blind have been blind since birth or infancy, while those who are adventitiously blind became profoundly visually impaired sometime after the age of two. This latter group comprises persons who usually remember what things in their environment look like, a mental image that can influence how well they learn about concepts during their school years.

2. The great majority of persons with visual impairments use sight to learn and gain information. Although most read print, some require that the print be enlarged. A small number read and write using braille, a system of raised dot codes that requires considerable training and practice to become proficient in its use. With advances in computer technology, and the availability and relatively low price of personal computers, persons with severe visual impairments will use technology-based machines to read and write in the near future.

3. For school-age children, visual impairment is one of the smallest categories of exceptionalities. The incidence of visual impairment increases with age: the older a person, the higher the likelihood of that person having some visual impairment.

4. More than half of school-age children with visual impairment are multiply handicapped. Those who are not multiply handicapped tend to perform well in school. Their achievement tests scores are much like their sighted classmates'.

5. Since World War II, most students with visual impairments have attended their neighborhood schools. They participate in the regular education curriculum, and receive supplemental services from specially trained teachers. The severity of their handicap determines the amount of extra training they need. Some require special courses in orientation and mobility so they can move independently in their environments or in life skills so they can live independently as adults.

6. Almost every state has a residential center school for the visually impaired. In the early part of the twentieth century, this was the only school available for most children who were blind. Today, these schools serve fewer full-time students. Those who attend center schools generally tend to either be multiply handicapped or reside in rural, remote areas of their states. Some center schools now provide consultative services statewide. They often manage and direct locally operated infant and pre-school programs. Many serve as a materials depository for their state, and their teachers consult with regular education teachers who are educating students with visual impairments. Some center schools also offer a variety of short courses, many during the summer. These schools are usually staffed by experts in the area of vision. They are able to provide services not typically found elsewhere. Therefore, topics like orientation and mobility, life skills, career education, braille, and technology use are often offered during the summer and on weekends.

7. Although these students have been successfully mainstreamed for many years, they do not find integration the norm when they are adults. Many have not found competitive employment, but rather work in sheltered workshops. They are not included in the mainstream of American society. In fact, stereotypes and old traditions impede their participation in normal activities as adults. Most clearly, this is an area that will require the concerted efforts of adults with this handicap, their families, and their advocates. With changed attitudes, this group will be able to participate more fully in society.

DISCUSSION QUESTIONS

1. Discuss the importance of early intervention programs for students with severe visual impairments.

2. What services can center schools provide that are not typically available at local public schools? In your view, what should the role of center schools be?

3. Draw a diagram of a regular education classroom that you have adapted for a student with severe visual impairments.

4. List some visual, audio, and tactile technological advances that have helped improve the opportunities for persons who have visual impairments. Brainstorm other advances that might be developed in the future.

5. What are some strategies that could be implemented that would allow persons who are blind greater access to jobs in the competitive workplace?

SUPPLEMENTARY BOOKS AND VIDEOS

Over the years people with visual impairments have been included in fictional and nonfictional roles in both books and films. The books listed below can be found in most major public libraries, and the films are available as videocassettes at many video rental stores.

Books

Bickel, L. (1988). *Triumph over darkness.* London: Unwin Hyman.

Greenberg, J. (1988). *Of such small differences.* New York: Holt.

Hall, R. K. (1983). *A place of her own: The story of Elizabeth Garrett.* Santa Fe: Sunstone Press.

Keller, H. (1988). *The story of my life.* New York: Sig Classics.

Kipling, R. (1969). *The light that failed.* New York: Airmont.

Wagner, S. (1986). *How do you kiss a blind girl?* Springfield, IL: Charles C Thomas.

Videos

The miracle worker (1962). United Artists.

A patch of blue (1965). MGM.

Butterflies are free (1972). Columbia Pictures.

Places in the heart (1984). Tri-Star Pictures.

Mask (1985). Universal Films.

See no evil, hear no evil (1989). Tri-Star.

DJAMIN WAGINO, *a 26-year-old from Suriname, is hearing impaired. He has spent time at the Kennedy Institute for the hearing impaired in Paramaribo, Suriname, and now works as an art designer. Djamin participated in the 1989 International Very Special Arts Festival where he exhibited his paintings at the John F. Kennedy Center for the Performing Arts in Washington, D.C.*

*C*hapter Ten

HEARING IMPAIRMENTS

*L*earning
Objectives

After studying this chapter, you should be able to:

- **Explain the two different types of hearing losses and how the ability to hear is influenced by each type**

- **Describe how hearing is assessed**

- **Discuss four major causes of hearing impairments and describe how to prevent or lessen the impact of each**

- **Discuss the advantages and disadvantages of various educational placement options available to students who are deaf**

EVEN LAW SCHOOL IS NOT BEYOND REACH*

Jamie MacAllister is a law student facing the challenges of graduate study. In the National Bioethics Moot Court, her brief tied for fifth place and her oral argument stood undefeated. Not bad for a first year law student who plans to become a litigator. Jamie is deaf, uses oral speech, but needs an interpreter to sign what is spoken by others. American Sign Language (ASL) is used by many deaf adults, but has no signs for legal vocabulary. This is one of the challenges she and her interpreter face as Jamie studies and participates in moot court. So, she is developing and expanding the sign language system to include legal terminology. Some of her professors worry that when she is in court, she will not be able to tell if a witness is telling the truth. Jamie does not believe this will be an obstacle because interpreters are trained to mime with their body language the voice inflections and other subtle clues about what someone is saying. She believes that people who are deaf are flawless at interpreting body language.

When Jamie graduates and becomes a lawyer, she will join a small number of people who are deaf and practicing law. She will become a role model, showing others that people who are deaf can aspire to many different professions. She is also making an important contribution to the deaf community and the legal profession by creating new signs for legal terminology.

1. Why do you think Jamie is so confident about her future success in law school?

2. What kinds of challenges do you expect Jamie to face once she is a lawyer?

3. How do you think legal sign vocabulary will become nationally understood by lawyers, clients, and interpreters?

The process of hearing is quite remarkable. Sound waves pass through the air, water, or some other medium. The sound waves cause the eardrum to vibrate and the vibrations are carried to the inner ear. There the vibrations pass through receptor cells that send impulses to the brain. The brain translates these impulses into sound. The content or associations of sound affect us in different ways. We are warmed by the sound of an old friend's voice. We are startled by a loud clap of thunder, fascinated by the sound of the wind rushing through trees, lulled by the ocean, excited by the roar of a crowd, consumed by the music of a rock group, and relaxed by the soothing sounds of a symphony. A critical way that most of us learn about the thoughts, ideas, and feelings of others is by listening to people tell us their experiences. We often communicate with others by telling and listening. Through this exchange we expand our knowledge, share ideas, express emotions, and function in

*Adapted from "First Year Student Challenges Stereotypes," by M. Haederle, 1990, *UNM/Law: A Newsletter for Alumni and Friends, 3,* pp. 8–9. Reprinted by permission.

People who are deaf are asserting their rights to equal access and participation in American society.

hearing impairments. An overall term that includes all levels of hearing loss, both deaf and hard of hearing.

deaf. Unable to usefully perceive sounds in the environment with or without the use of a hearing aid; unable to use hearing as the primary way to gain information.

typical workplaces and social settings. Many people who are hearing impaired participate fully and independently in mainstream society in part because of advances in education and technology, such as hearing aids. However, some people who have hearing impairments cannot be helped by hearing aids and thus have a much more restricted ability to communicate than their nonhandicapped counterparts do.

This chapter will help you understand hearing impairments and the people who are affected by them. We will discuss the causes of hearing impairments and the steps being taken to prevent them. You will learn about the major issues in the education of children with hearing impairments and the ways this disability affects these individuals as adults. You will learn about the effect technology has had on this group of people. We will also consider some controversial topics in this field. We present all of this information to stimulate your imagination and challenge you as prospective educators or service providers.

HEARING IMPAIRMENTS DEFINED

People with **hearing impairments** can be divided into two groups: the deaf and the hard of hearing. Those who are **deaf,** or profoundly hard of hearing, have a hearing disability so severe that they have little useful hearing even if they use hearing aids. Although almost all persons who are deaf perceive some sound,

hard of hearing. Having sufficient residual hearing to be able, with a hearing aid, to comprehend others' speech and oral communication.

prelingually deaf. Having lost the ability to hear before developing language.

postlingually deaf. Having lost the ability to hear after developing language.

total communication approach. A system of instruction for students who are deaf that employs both oral speech and manual communication together.

ear drum (tympanic membrane). Part of the ear upon which sound waves and their vibrations fall and cause the ossicles to move; separates the outer and middle ear.

ossicles. Three tiny bones in the middle ear that transmit sound waves from the eardrum through the middle ear to the cochlea.

malleus (hammer). One of the three tiny bones (ossicles) in the middle ear.

incus (anvil). One of the three tiny bones (ossicles) in the middle ear.

stapes (stirrup). One of the three tiny bones (ossicles) in the middle ear.

cochlea. Part of the inner ear that contains fluid and hairlike nerve cells that transmit information to the brain.

auditory nerve (eighth cranial nerve). Nerve that carries messages received through the ear to the brain. Known in neurology as the eighth cranial nerve.

they cannot use hearing as their primary way to gain information. People who are **hard of hearing** can process information from sound, usually with the help of a hearing aid.

Although the degree of hearing loss is important, the age when the hearing loss occurs is also important. Individuals who become deaf *before* they learn to speak and understand language are referred to as **prelingually deaf.** They either are born deaf or lose their hearing as infants. According to data gathered by the Commission on the Education of the Deaf (1988) approximately 95 percent of all children and youth who are deaf are prelingually deaf. Those whose hearing impairment occurs after they have learned to speak and understand language are called **postlingually deaf.** Many are able to retain their abilities to use speech and communicate with others orally. The challenges facing all those who are deaf, and particularly those who are prelingually deaf, are great.

Nonhandicapped preschoolers learn language effortlessly by imitating their parents and other children. In contrast, young children who are deaf may understand only 5 percent of what is said to them (Liben, 1978). Their inability to hear speech and language seriously affects their abilities to communicate with others and to learn academic subjects taught later in school. One in ten of those who are prelingually deaf have at least one parent who is deaf. Children in this group typically learn to communicate during early childhood through manual communication (sign language) or a combination of sign language and oral language. Some learn English as a second language at school. Nine in ten of the prelingually deaf have normally hearing parents. Interestingly enough, these children may have more difficulty acquiring speech and language because their parents do not use a **total communication approach** (using both sign and oral language) as early as possible.

What makes learning even more difficult for many students who are hearing impaired is that 30 percent of the total are multiply handicapped (Karchmer, 1985; Wolff and Harkins, 1986). Additional disabilities may include visual impairments, mental retardation, learning disabilities, behavioral disorders, or cerebral palsy. These accompanying disabilities are often caused by the same disease or accident that causes hearing impairments. For example, rubella (German measles), blood type (Rh) incompatibility between mother and child, and trauma at birth often result in more than one handicap. Students whose hearing impairment is inherited tend *not* to be multiply handicapped.

What is hearing loss? Hearing loss results when the ear and hearing mechanism is damaged. In order to better understand a definition of hearing loss we need to understand the process of hearing. Refer to Figure 10.1, a picture of the ear, to trace how sound moves through the ear to produce normal hearing. A person speaks and the sound waves from the words pass through the air, or some other medium, falling upon the **ear drum (tympanic membrane)** of the listener. The sound waves vibrate the ear drum, which in turn moves the **ossicles** of the middle ear. The ossicles are tiny bones: the **hammer (malleus), anvil (incus),** and **stirrup (stapes).** The last small bone in the chain, the stirrup, is sealed into a small window of the **cochlea.** The sound vibrations transmitted through these bones move fluid inside the cochlea. This stimulates the hairlike cells inside the cochlea. These hairlike cells are part of the **auditory nerve,** which carries messages to the brain. (Neurologists call this the eighth cranial nerve.)

Hearing losses range in severity, differ in type, and influence each person differently. First, let us look at the various aspects of hearing losses and the way they affect the individual.

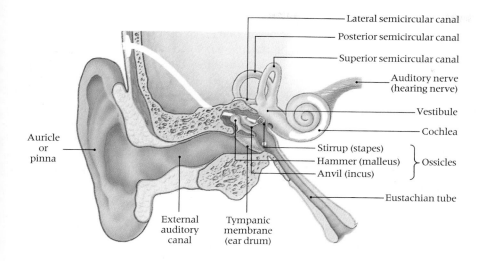

Lateral semicircular canal
Posterior semicircular canal
Superior semicircular canal
Auditory nerve (hearing nerve)
Vestibule
Cochlea
Stirrup (stapes)
Hammer (malleus)
Anvil (incus)
} Ossicles
Eustachian tube
Auricle or pinna
External auditory canal
Tympanic membrane (ear drum)

FIGURE 10.1 **The Structure of the Human Ear**

SOURCE: M. L. Hardman, C. J. Drew, M. W. Egan, and B. Wolf, *Human Exceptionality,* 3rd ed., 1990, Needham Heights, MA. Allyn & Bacon. Reprinted with permission.

conductive hearing loss. Hearing loss caused by an impairment of the outer or middle ear that prevents transfer of sound to the inner ear.

sensorineural hearing loss. A hearing loss caused by damage to the inner ear or the auditory nerve.

Types of Hearing Impairments

There are two general types of hearing loss: *conductive* and *sensorineural.* **Conductive hearing losses** are due to blockage or damage to the outer or middle ear that prevents sound waves from traveling (being conducted) to the inner ear. Generally, someone with a conductive hearing loss has a mild to moderate disability. Some conductive hearing losses are temporary. In fact, we have all probably experienced a conductive hearing loss at some point in our lives. For example, have you ever experienced temporary loss of hearing due to change of air pressure flying in an airplane or riding in a car in the mountains? Preschoolers often experience a conductive hearing loss when they have head colds. Because of the infection, excessive fluid accumulates in the middle ear, interfering with the conduction of sound waves to the middle ear. With a mild loss, the individual can still hear almost all speech sounds, and can hear most conversations (Boone, 1987). If the hearing loss was caused by a head cold, once the ear infection clears up, the hearing difficulties also disappear. Many other conductive hearing losses can be corrected through surgery or other medical techniques.

The second type of hearing loss is a **sensorineural hearing loss.** Sensorineural loss occurs when there is damage to the inner ear or the auditory nerve (the eighth cranial nerve), and usually cannot be improved medically or surgically. Individuals affected by a sensorineural loss are able to hear different frequencies at different intensity levels; their hearing losses are not flat or even. Sensorineural losses are less common in young children than the conductive types.

Measurement

In order to understand how hearing is measured, let us review some terms and concepts about sound. Sound is produced by the vibration of molecules, through the air, water, wires, or some other medium. The number of vibrations per second

frequency of sound. The number of vibrations per second of molecules through some medium like air, water, or wires.

hertz (Hz). Units of measure for sound frequency.

decibels (dB). Unit of measure for intensity of sound.

pure sounds. Sound waves of specific frequencies used to test an individual's hearing ability.

audiometer. An electrical instrument used to measure the threshold of hearing using pure tones at different frequencies.

audiogram. A graph drawn from the results of hearing tests using an audiometer that charts individuals' thresholds of hearing at various frequencies against sound intensities in decibels.

hearing threshold. The point at which a person can perceive the softest sound at each frequency level.

air-conduction audiometry method. A method to test hearing using a pure tone sound generated by an audiometer.

determines the **frequency** of the sound. High frequencies are perceived through our ears as high pitch or tone. Low frequencies are perceived as low pitch. Frequency is measured in units called **hertz** (Hz). The normal ear hears sounds that range from approximately 20 Hz to 20,000 Hz. Our hearing has developed to hear speech sounds, which fall approximately in the middle of the human hearing range (primarily between 250 Hz and 4000 Hz). There are, however, sounds that humans cannot perceive, regardless of our hearing abilities. For example, some dog whistles use high frequencies that are beyond humans' hearing range.

Intensity, or the loudness, of sound is measured in **decibels (dB).** Softer, quieter sounds have lower decibel measurements. Louder sounds have higher decibel numbers. A decibel level of 125 or louder is painful to the average person. Decibel levels ranging from 0 to 120 dB are used to test how well an individual can hear different frequencies. A child with normal hearing should be able to perceive sounds at 0 dB. The scale used to assess hearing has been adjusted so 0 indicates no loss and numbers greater than 0 indicate the degree or amount of loss. Smaller numbers indicate mild losses, while larger numbers indicate moderate to severe or profound losses.

When audiologists test people's hearing abilities, they use **pure sounds,** sound waves of specific frequencies, at various combinations of hertz and decibels. Hearing is tested at various bands of pitch and loudness. By using an **audiometer,** an instrument that produces sounds at precise frequencies and intensities, audiologists can assess the ability to hear, in each ear independently. It is the machine that makes the sounds at the precise Hz and dB levels necessary to assess and measure a person's ability to hear. The results of this audiological assessment are plotted on an **audiogram.** An audiogram is a grid or graph. Along the top of the graph are Hz levels. The vertical lines each represent different levels of sound frequency or Hz. Each ear is tested separately. A **hearing threshold** is determined by noting when the person first perceives the softest sound at each frequency level. Sometimes, hearing threshold is reported only for the "better" ear. Sometimes, an average of an individual's scores at three different frequencies (500, 1000, 2000 Hz) is used. Any score below 0 dB represents some degree of hearing loss because the audiometer is set to indicate that a person has no hearing loss at 0 dB for various Hz levels. Those of you who have some knowledge of music might find Lowenbraun's (1988) explanation of Hz helpful. The frequency of middle C on the piano is at approximately 250 Hz. The next vertical line on the audiogram, 500 Hz, is approximately one octave above middle C; 1000 is two octaves above middle C, and so on.

To better understand hearing, let us review the audiograms of three children—Sue, Heather, and Travis. Sue's hearing is normal. She was tested by using pure tone sounds generated by an audiometer. Sue's hearing was tested by using the **air-conduction audiometry method.** Most children's hearing is assessed in this way either by a pediatrician at a "well-child" checkup or by a school nurse. You probably remember having your hearing tested this way. Earphones are placed over your ears, and you raise your hand when you hear a sound.

Sue's audiogram (Figure 10.2) displays the pattern of a child with normal hearing. The shaded area on this audiogram marks the area where speech sounds fall (sometimes called the "speech banana" because of its shape). Because Sue's hearing abilities lie above this area on her audiogram, the audiologist testing her hearing knows Sue can hear the speech sounds at the sound intensities measured during audiological assessment. Along the side of the graph are intensity levels measured in decibels. Horizontal lines represent different levels of loudness. Notice that a different code is used for Sue's right and left ears—O for the right ear and X for the left ear. Remember, each ear is tested independently. Sue's hearing threshold is marked on

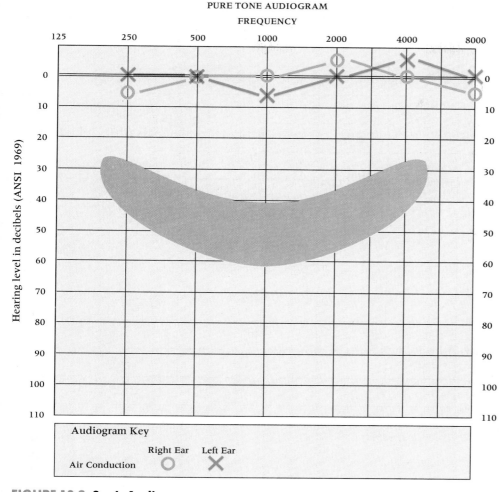

PURE TONE AUDIOGRAM

FREQUENCY

Audiogram Key

	Right Ear	Left Ear
Air Conduction	○	✕

bone-conduction audiometry method. Placing a vibrator on a person's forehead so sound by-passes the outer and middle ear and goes directly to the inner ear; tests for conductive hearing losses.

Sue's audiogram displays the pattern of a child with normal hearing. The shaded area on this audiogram marks the area where speech sounds fall. Because Sue's hearing abilities are marked above this area on her audiogram, she can hear the speech sounds at the sound intensities measured in the audiological assessment situation.

FIGURE 10.2 Sue's Audiogram

The authors wish to acknowledge the contributions of Dr. Richard Hood for his assistance in the preparation of the audiograms in this chapter.

her audiogram. As with most children with normal hearing, Sue's auditory thresholds (the points when she first perceives sound) are all approximately 0 dB.

Heather and Travis both have hearing impairments. Because they were suspected of having hearing losses, the audiologist testing them used two procedures: the air-conduction method (which was used to test Sue's hearing) and the bone-conduction method. The audiologist testing Heather and Travis used the air-conduction method for the first test. When it was apparent that the children had hearing losses, the audiologist wanted to know whether the loss was due to damage in the outer, middle, or inner ear. To determine this, the audiologist needed a second test using a different method. In the **bone-conduction audiometry method,** a vibrator is placed on the forehead so sound can bypass the outer and middle ear and go directly to the inner ear. When the bone-conduction thresholds are normal (near 0 dB) and the air-conduction thresholds are abnormal, the type of hearing loss is conductive. A conductive hearing loss is caused by problems of the outer ear or middle ear, which makes the transfer of sound to the inner ear impaired or impossible.

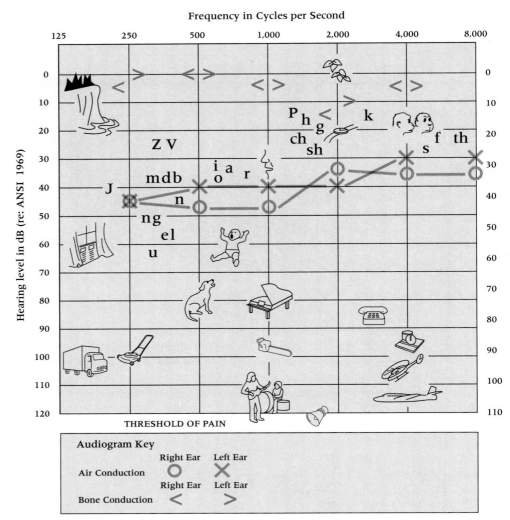

Travis's audiogram indicates that he has a conductive hearing loss that, with the amplification of hearing aids, is in the mild range. Travis's hearing abilities were plotted on an audiogram form designed by Northern and Downs (1984) to show where various speech and other sounds occur.

FIGURE 10.3 Travis's Audiogram

Source of audiogram form: *Hearing in Children*, (p. 7) by J. L. Northern and M. P. Downs, 1984, Baltimore: Williams and Wilkins. Used by permission.

Travis's audiogram, shown in Figure 10.3, indicates that he has a conductive hearing loss. The loss, of about 40 dB, and with the amplification of hearing aids, is in the mild range. Notice how flat the profile is for Travis's air-conduction test. However, the bone-conduction test reveals that when the middle ear is bypassed, his hearing is much closer to 0 dB. Travis's hearing loss either is temporary or can probably be corrected through surgery or other medical treatment.

Travis's hearing abilities were plotted on an audiogram form designed by Northern and Downs (1984) to show where various speech and other sounds occur. This type of audiogram differs from the type used to plot the results from Sue's audiological test (Figure 10.2). The audiogram designed by Northern and Downs is used by many audiologists to help parents better understand their child's hearing loss because the pictures on it show where different sounds fall. If the child's pattern is above the picture, then the sound should be heard. If the child's threshold falls below the picture, then the sound pictured cannot be perceived by that child. Without a hearing aid Travis, for example, could not perceive several sounds (z, v, p, h, g, k, and ch).

Heather has a sensorineural hearing loss, as indicated in her audiogram, shown in Figure 10.4. A sensorineural hearing loss is caused by a defect or damage to the inner ear and can be more serious than conductive hearing losses. Heather has a 30 dB loss. Notice the similarity of her scores from the air-conduction and bone-conduction tests. Heather's hearing was also tested with her hearing aids on. Notice that with the use of aids, Heather's hearing loss is no longer as serious; it is now at a mild functional level. Look at Heather's audiogram. What speech sounds is she unable to hear? How do her hearing abilities differ from Travis's? Now compare Travis's and Heather's audiograms to Sue's audiogram.

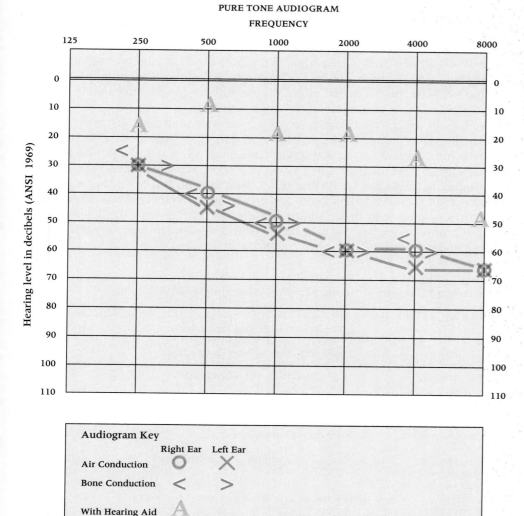

> Heather's audiogram indicates a moderate sensorineural hearing loss. Her hearing was tested through both the air-conduction and bone-conduction methods with and without hearing aids.

FIGURE 10.4 Heather's Audiogram

Significance

Experts vary on their definitions of hearing loss and on the point at which it has educational significance. Of course, all hearing losses are serious, but at some point a hearing loss substantially influences the way in which a child needs to be taught and how well the individual can use the communication modes of nonhandicapped peers. At what point is a hearing loss significant? According to Boone (1987, pp. 160–161), "the term *hearing loss* is used for individuals who experience a loss of sensitivity in the speech range greater than 25 dB." Others believe that even a loss of 15 dB can be educationally significant, affecting speech, language, and communication (Northern and Downs, 1984). The amount and type of an individual's hearing loss are related to the ability to understand information presented orally. These two factors affect how a student might be taught and the types of services needed. For example, a student with a moderate loss might not profit from typical instructional methods (lectures, oral directions) alone. But what constitutes a mild, or a moderate, or a severe hearing loss? Lowenbraun (1988), for example, considers losses from 20 dB to 60 dB mild to moderate; losses from 60 dB to 90 dB severe; and those greater than 90 dB profound. What does this mean? Conductive losses of 30 to 50 dB are relatively common, and would fall in Lowenbraun's mild to moderate range. Persons with this level of conductive hearing loss cannot, without a hearing aid, hear typical conversations. Clearly, this has considerable significance for how these persons communicate and learn from others.

To help us see the relationship between the degree of hearing loss and the types of related services a child might need, Moores (1987) created levels of hearing loss and recommendations for needed services at each level. At Level I (35–54 dB loss) and Level II (55–69 dB loss), the services of a speech/language pathologist and an audiologist are needed; at Levels III and IV (70–89 dB loss and 90 dB loss or greater), the services of an SLP, an audiologist, and an educator of the deaf are required. Table 10.1 provides another set of definitions and levels of hearing loss. This table is helpful because it provides explanations of how well individuals can hear for each level of hearing impairment.

TABLE 10.1. Correspondence among Measured Degrees of Hearing Loss and Descriptions of Ability to Understand Speech

Gallaudet Hearing Scale Score	Summary Descriptions of Items Included in the Gallaudet Hearing Scale	Classification of Hearing Impairments by Speech Comprehension Groups with Different Levels of Better-Ear Averages Proposed by the Committee on Conservation of Hearing Loss	Better-Ear Average
1	Usually can hear and understand whispered speech	No significant difficulty with faint speech	Less than 26 dB
2	Difficulty hearing and understanding whispered speech	Difficulty only with faint speech	26–40 dB
3	Difficulty hearing and understanding shouted speech	Frequent difficulty with normal speech	41–70 dB
4	Difficulty hearing and understanding shouted speech, but can usually hear and understand words spoken loudly into the better ear	Understands only shouted or amplified speech	71–90 dB
5–8	Cannot hear and understand any speech	Usually cannot understand even amplified speech	91 dB or more

Source: Characteristics of hearing impaired youth in the general population and of students in special educational programs for the hearing impaired, by P. Ries in *Deaf children in America*, p. 12, by A. N. Schildroth and M. A. Karchmer, 1986, Austin, TX, PRO-ED. Reprinted by permission.

HISTORY OF THE FIELD

As long ago as the days of ancient Greeks and the early Roman Empire, social leaders like Aristotle, Plato, and the Emperor Justinian wrote about issues facing people of their time who were deaf. Over the history of Western civilization attitudes toward people who were deaf have varied. Some societies protected them, others ridiculed, persecuted, and even put them to death.

Documents dating back to the 1500s report about physicians in several countries in Europe who worked with people who were deaf. Pedro Ponce de Leon (1520–1584), a Spanish monk credited with being the first teacher of students who were deaf, had remarkable success teaching his students to read, write, and speak. William Holder and John Wallis, who lived during the 1600s, are credited with beginning educational programs in England for individuals who were deaf. Like the Spanish before them, they advocated using writing and manual communication (a two-handed alphabet signing system) to teach speech. By the 1700s schools for the deaf were established by Henry Baker in England, Thomas Braidwood in Edinburgh, Abbé Charles Michel de l'Epée in France, and Samuel Heinicke in Germany.

In 1817 the first school for students who were deaf in the United States was started in Hartford, Connecticut. The American Asylum for the Education of the Deaf and Dumb (now the American School for the Deaf) was started through the efforts of Thomas Hopkins Gallaudet, a young divinity student who was sent to England and France to study about deafness so a school could be opened in this country. At this time, the French at the school begun by l'Epée, were experimenting with methods of manual communication, mainly sign language. Gallaudet was greatly influenced by the effectiveness of these methods and he brought Laurent Clerc, a Frenchman who was deaf and a well-known educator of the deaf, to the United States. Clerc is often credited with being the father of education for the deaf in the United States. Other Americans interested in deaf education also went to Europe and were impressed by the oral approaches in deaf education used in Germany. In most oral approaches of that day, the use of any form of manual communication or sign language was greatly discouraged.

The roots of the debate about whether the oral or the manual method of instruction and communication is better originate from the beginnings of education for those who are deaf in this country. The battles were initiated and fueled through the debates of Edward Gallaudet, Thomas Gallaudet's son, and Alexander Graham Bell. Each of these men had a deaf mother and a highly successful father. Bell invented the telephone, the audiometer, and worked on the phonograph. Gallaudet was the president of the nation's college for the deaf and was a renowned legal scholar. These two clashed. In 1883 and the next year, Bell wrote two papers critical of policies and practices that contributed to segregation of individuals who are deaf from the rest of society. He believed that residential schools for the deaf and sign language fostered segregation. Bell proposed legislation that would prevent two adults who were deaf from marrying, eliminate residential schools, ban the use of manual communication, and prohibit those who were deaf from becoming teachers of students who were also deaf. Gallaudet strongly opposed these positions in both his writings and in public debates. The battle between these two strong individuals and their opposing positions raged in Congress, and even influenced federal funding of teacher preparation programs. Gallaudet's position was supported by Congress, and he received an appropriation to establish a teacher preparation program that emphasized both the oral

Gallaudet University. America's federally funded university serving students who are deaf at the undergraduate and graduate levels.

and manual approach to education of these students. Although Gallaudet won support from Congress on this issue, the conflicts were not settled. In fact, for many years the oralist position was more popular, and the use of manual communication in any form was discouraged in classes for students with hearing impairments.

Horace Mann, a great leader in education and social reform during the late 1800s sided with the oral-only camp. He believed the oral-only method was best because the signing system of the manual method did not match English in grammar and structure. Throughout the late nineteenth century, and for most of the twentieth century, the oral-only position was the most commonly followed. It was not until the 1970s that a combined approach—called total communication—was widely adopted. Total communication uses oral and manual communication systems for the instruction of students who are severely and profoundly hearing impaired. The debate about oralism and a combined oral and sign language method for communicating and instruction continues today, however.

Formal education for the deaf in the United States in the nineteenth century took place primarily in residential schools. The deaf were sent to boarding schools, as were many nonhandicapped students in that day. From 1817, when the first school was started, to the eve of the Civil War in 1864, twenty-four schools for the deaf were in operation. **Gallaudet University** (first called the National Deaf Mute College) was founded in 1864. The overriding principle of this school was the right of all students who were deaf to an education. The educators believed these students can achieve and learn when expectations are high and a high-quality education is available to them.

Day schools gained in popularity later in the nineteenth century. However, since most American cities did not have enough students with severe hearing impairments to fill day schools, and because people assumed that living and learning with others with the same impairment was best for this group of people, residential schools remained the common type of school available for these students. Even today, most states have a residential school for students with severe hearing impairments.

PREVALENCE

How many people in the United States have hearing impairments? In 1987 almost 21 million people in the United States were reported with hearing problems (Hotchkiss, 1989). Of that total, only slightly more than 1 million were children under eighteen. The vast majority of people with hearing impairments are adults, with the greatest number over sixty-five. Hearing loss is a frequent part of the aging process. We know that hearing loss affects a person's ability to communicate no matter what the person's age. However, those who are prelingually deaf and those deafened as young children are seriously affected because their language was not fully developed before the onset of their hearing loss. Educators are most concerned, therefore, with how statistics are gathered on children who have hearing impairments. These numbers are very difficult to obtain. Why? Some states have carefully defined criteria for counting who is deaf, hard of hearing, and/or multiply handicapped. But not all states use the same criteria (also see the discussion of this issue for students who have visual impairments in chapter 9). In addition, the U.S. Department of Education reports children by their primary handicap. So, students who have mental retardation who also have a hearing impairment may be reported only in the mental retardation category or possibly in the multiply handicapped category, but not in the hearing impaired category.

These factors certainly affect, to different degrees, the number of students reported as having a hearing impairment. Here are some examples of how data about the numbers of those affected by hearing impairments differ. According to the *Annual Report to Congress on Implementation of the Education of the Handicapped Act* (United States Department of Education, 1989) during the 1987–88 school year, 0.14 percent of the entire school enrollment, or 56,937 students, were hearing impaired. However, Hotchkiss (1989), using the National Center for Health Statistics data from their national survey, reports that in 1987, 1,021,000 youth under the age of eighteen were hearing impaired. Why is there such a marked difference in the numbers? The difference might well be due to the way children are classified and differences in criterion for inclusion in this group.

There are some other interesting facts about those with hearing impairments in this country. Karchmer (1984) reports that 82 percent of the U.S. population is white, but only 62 percent of school-age youth with hearing impairments are white. Of all students with hearing impairments, 44 percent have a hearing loss in the profound range. He also indicates that 94 percent of students with hearing impairments became disabled before the age of three. The differences in percentages of those with hearing impairments by ethnicity are most likely due to limited access to medical care for people who are poor. The unfortunate commentary about these differences is that many of these cases of hearing impairments might have been prevented or lessened with proper and more timely medical attention.

IDEA requires each state to collect data about the number of children with disabilities served in the state. Since these counts were started, there has been a 20 percent decline in the number of students with hearing impairments receiving special education (Commission on the Education of the Deaf, 1988). In the year between the *Ninth* and the *Tenth Annual Report to Congress* (United States Department of Education, 1987 and 1988), the states reported a decline of 1632 students (or slightly more than 2 percent) who received special education because of hearing impairments. Gallaudet University's Center for Assessment and Demographic Studies, in their annual survey, also showed a decline of 3 percent (Schildroth and Hotto, 1988). We can give several reasons for this drop in numbers. Advances in medicine have prevented deafness in newborns and reduced the impact of hearing loss through improved early treatment. In particular, the rubella (German measles) vaccine protects women from this disease, which frequently causes hearing impairments in the child if contracted during pregnancy. Another reason for the decline in the number of students with hearing impairments who receive special education services is advances in audiological technology. Improved hearing aids have corrected the hearing problems of some children. Therefore, they might not need special services. A further decline in the number of children with hearing impairments is possible in the future, as more diseases and infections are prevented or detected earlier and more corrective surgical procedures are developed. However, unless children who live in poverty have improved access to needed medical services, the number might actually increase (see Concepts and Controversies in chapter 4).

CAUSES AND PREVENTION OF HEARING IMPAIRMENTS

It is not a surprise to learn that hearing impairments can result from various illnesses and injuries. For example, sustained loud noise can cause a hearing loss. We also know that some types of hearing impairments are the result of heredity. It was for

meningitis. A disease that affects the central nervous system and often causes hearing loss.

this reason that in the late 1800s Alexander Graham Bell proposed legislation that would ban two people who were deaf from marrying. Fortunately, he was unsuccessful. For both the medical and educational professions, understanding the causes of hearing impairments is useful. For educators, this information is crucial. Such knowledge can assist teachers in planning educational programs for specific youngsters. For example, if a child has a conductive hearing loss, hearing aids might be able to amplify sound sufficiently that the student can profit from oral instruction in the typical classroom. It is critical that the hearing aids be adjusted properly. Identifying the cause of an individual's hearing impairment helps medical professionals prescribe appropriate corrective procedures to cure or lessen the hearing loss. Researchers use this information to work on prevention, such as developing vaccines or corrective surgical procedures.

Causes

There are four major causes of hearing impairments. They are:

MATERNAL RUBELLA. Rubella (German measles) contracted by a pregnant woman is a devastating disease for an unborn child. Depending on when an expectant mother contracts this virus, the child may be born with a profound hearing loss, a visual impairment, or other disabilities alone or in combinations. As with other congenital hearing losses (those present at birth), hearing losses caused by maternal rubella are typically sensorineural with damage to the inner ear or the auditory nerve, resulting in a severe to profound hearing loss. Vaccines are available to prevent women of childbearing age from contracting this disease; therefore, the incidence of hearing impairments caused by maternal rubella have declined and could be eliminated.

MENINGITIS. Meningitis is a disease that affects the central nervous system (specifically the meninges, the coverings of the brain and spinal cord, and its circulating fluid). Most of the cases that involve a hearing loss are bacterial infections rather than the more lethal viral meningitis. This disease often results in a profound hearing loss and is often associated with other disabilities. Meningitis is the most common cause of postnatal deafness in school-age children and is one major cause of sensorineural hearing losses that are not present at birth. Vaccines do exist that will prevent the disease, but at present no national immunization program for meningitis exists.

OTITIS MEDIA. Infection of the middle ear and accumulation of fluid behind the ear drum is called otitis media. The condition can be corrected and treated through antibiotics and other medical procedures. If not detected, this condition may result in an overall language delay that could affect future academic learning. Otitis media results in a conductive hearing loss by damaging the outer or middle ear and usually results in a mild to moderate hearing loss.

HEREDITY. More than 150 different types of genetic deafness have been identified. Most likely, the unknown causes of deafness are genetic in nature. Genetic causes of hearing impairments are congenital and sensorineural. In some cases, particularly when there is a family history of congenital deafness, genetic counseling and prenatal testing might provide important information to the family.

It is important for educators to know the cause of a student's hearing impairment, the type and severity of the hearing loss, and whether the student is multiply handicapped. This information will help educators know what sorts of problems they and the student need to overcome to achieve success. For example, children with hearing impairments caused by maternal rubella are prelingually deaf. They lost their hearing before they were able to speak and understand language, and many have other handicaps as well. Students whose handicap is caused by meningitis usually have severe or profound hearing losses, but their hearing losses are acquired and they may have developed some speech and language before they became hearing impaired. The group with otitis media (ear infections) typically have less severe hearing losses (84 percent are in the mild to moderate range), and they tend to profit more from hearing aids because their hearing loss is conductive. Most children whose hearing losses are inherited are less likely to be multiply handicapped. Such information can help educators better plan appropriate educational programs for their students.

Today, the leading known causes of hearing impairments are heredity and meningitis (Hotchkiss, 1989). However, as Table 10.2 indicates, the cause is unknown in almost half the total population with hearing impairments. Even in these cases some researchers believe heredity and genetics are responsible for the hearing impairments of the majority of these unknown cases (Boone, 1987; Nance and Sweeney, 1975). Table 10.2 compares the percentages of students with hearing impairments across a

TABLE 10.2. Percentage Distribution of Causes of Hearing Impairments*

Cause	School Year 1972–73	1982–83	1987–88
Total, all causes	100.0	100.0	100.0
Cause unknown	48.6	39.5	48.8
Cause reported	51.4	60.5	51.2
Maternal rubella	17.6	16.3	5.2
Heredity	8.5	11.6	12.9
Meningitis	5.3	7.3	8.8
Otitis media	1.6	3.0	3.4
Other causes at birth			
Prematurity	5.2	4.0	4.8
Pregnancy complications	3.2	3.4	2.9
Trauma	2.3	2.4	2.4
Rh incompatibility	3.1	1.4	0.6
Other causes after birth			
High fever	2.3	3.1	2.9
Infection	1.5	2.7	2.5
Trauma	0.9	0.8	0.7
Measles	2.1	0.8	0.4
Mumps	0.6	0.2	0.1
Other causes	2.5	8.0	7.2

*Because some students had more than one reported etiology, the sum of the cause-specific percentages exceeds the total percentage of cases with known causes.
From Annual Survey of Hearing Impaired Children and Youth, 1973, 1983, 1988.

Source: Demographic Aspects of Hearing Impairment: Questions and Answers, 2d ed., p. 7, by D. Hotchkiss, 1989, Washington, DC: Center for Assessment and Demographic Studies, Gallaudet University.

cytomegalovirus (CMV). A herpes virus infecting 1 percent of all newborns each year; can result in severe brain damage and sensorineural hearing losses.

cochlear implant. Electronic microprocessor that replaces the cochlea and allows some people who are deaf to process sounds.

fifteen-year period. Otitis media, meningitis, and heredity are causes that have increased over time. Maternal rubella has decreased dramatically but unfortunately is still a contributing factor in the number of cases of children with hearing impairments today. (See the Concepts and Controversies in chapter 5 for further discussion of this issue.)

Over the years, there have been changes in the percentages of one cause versus another. For example, Brown (1986) reports that in 1964, 50 percent of children's hearing impairments were caused by maternal rubella. After 1964 the number of children who suffered hearing loss due to maternal rubella dropped markedly. It was at this time that a vaccine was discovered and used to prevent this disease. However, maternal rubella has not been completely eradicated, and so cases continue to be reported with hearing losses. Meningitis is currently the most common, known disease that causes hearing impairments in children. However, a new vaccine is now available for meningitis, and Riko, Hyde, and Alberti (1985) recommend that all children by the age of two be immunized. The widespread use of this vaccine should dramatically reduce the number of children who experience severe and profound hearing losses as a result of contracting meningitis. In future years we should see a drop in meningitis as a major cause of hearing impairments as we did for maternal rubella, if all children are immunized.

As we eliminate or reduce the incidence of some causes of hearing impairments, other causes are being discovered. For example, Pappas (1985) reports that congenital **cytomegalovirus (CMV)** infection, a herpes virus, infects 1 percent of all newborns or approximately 30,000 infants each year. Of that total, about 4000 babies will have a mild to profound sensorineural hearing loss and possibly other disabilities because of this virus. At present, no vaccine or cure is available to prevent or treat CMV; however, avoiding persons affected with the virus, ensuring the safety of blood used in transfusions, and good hygiene are important preventive measures (Pueschel and Mulick, 1990). As advances in medical technology continue, many of the unknown causes of hearing impairments will be identified in the future. Of course, the hope is that once the cause is identified, a cure or preventive technique will be discovered.

Prevention

Can this disability be prevented or corrected? Medical technology plays a role in prevention and treatment of hearing problems. As we have discussed, infection causes some hearing impairments. Some infections, if diagnosed and treated early, do not have to result in severe hearing impairments. Today, most conductive hearing losses that involve the middle ear can be treated either medically or surgically (Boone, 1987). Delicate surgical procedures can repair or replace poorly functioning small bones in the middle ear. Other medical advances might either prevent or correct hearing problems. For example, **cochlear implants** are now being performed on adults who are deaf but have an intact auditory nerve. The device called a cochlear implant is a new sensory aid with electronic microprocessors; it serves as an artificial cochlea. Such implants have helped people who are deaf to at least hear sound although they cannot understand speech. Technology will most likely improve with more experimentation. Cochlear implants use electrodes to stimulate nerve cells and these transmissions are interpreted as sound by the brain. This procedure is now being advocated for children over the age of two (Schmeck, 1988). Other such

TABLE 10.3. Possible Signs or Characteristics of Hearing Impairments

The child experiences difficulties in following oral instructions.
The child watches the teacher's lips very carefully.
The child turns an ear toward the speaker.
The child has a limited vocabulary.
The child articulates speech sounds poorly.
The child shows delayed language development.
The child does not respond to name when called from behind.
The child is inattentive during lectures or class discussions.
The child relies too much on classmates for assignments.
The child complains of earaches.
The child has "runny" discharge from the ears.
The child has frequent colds or sinus or ear infections.
The child turns radio or television on very loud.

advances, in the experimental stages, hold much promise for the reduction in the severity of many kinds of hearing impairments.

In some cases, hearing impairments can be easily prevented, but early detection is a key factor here. Once a hearing problem is identified and diagnosed, medical treatment and educational services can be provided. A more knowledgeable public, availability of good health care for all children, and better prepared preschool teachers, could prevent some hearing losses and provide treatment for others. What specific measures can prevent hearing loss? One way is to make the public aware of the importance of proper immunization. For example, although the number of children who are deaf because of maternal rubella has been reduced drastically, this disease is on the rise again. The public needs to be continually reminded of the importance of immunization, and children whose parents cannot afford vaccinations must also have access to them.

Although procedures to screen infants for hearing impairments are available (Turner, 1990), many infants with hearing impairments go undiagnosed until they are between the ages of three and six (Commission on Education of Deaf, 1988). The average age for detection of children with profound deafness is two and a half years (Swigart, 1986). These children need clinical and preschool services as soon as possible. Parents, pediatricians, and preschool and day care educators, and the general public, need to learn to diagnose children with potential problems. For example, preschoolers who do not respond to sounds in their environment as their normal peers do should be referred to specialists. Table 10.3 provides some signs or signals that children with hearing impairments might give to their teachers. Children who present some of the behavioral characteristics listed in this table might have a hearing loss and should be referred for an audiological examination. The attentive teacher who is looking for signals that might indicate a hearing impairment can help a child by making a referral to the school nurse or suggesting to the parents that the family doctor assess the child's hearing. Remember, early referrals can prevent a hearing loss or reduce its severity.

PROFILE OF CHILDREN WITH HEARING IMPAIRMENTS

Children with hearing impairments cannot be stereotyped. They are individuals with different learning styles and abilities. However, they share one common characteristic: Their ability to hear is limited. As we have mentioned earlier, the severity of the hearing loss and the age that the loss occurred determines how well a person will be able to interact with others orally. Clearly, students who cannot hear the communications of others well have a more difficult time learning through traditional instructional methods. This is most apparent for those who are deaf.

Academic Achievement

The academic achievement levels of students who are deaf are substantially lower than their peers without disabilities (Trybus and Karchmer, 1977). By age twenty, half of the students tested read below the mid-fourth grade level. Keep in mind that most newspapers are written at least at the fifth grade level. Trybus and Karchmer stated, "at best, only 10 percent of hearing impaired eighteen-year-olds nationally can read at or above an eighth grade level" (p. 64). In a 1983 study (Karchmer, 1984), only 25 percent of the adolescents were able to achieve academic achievement scores greater than fifth graders. Possibly because reading ability is directly related to students' level of hearing and degree of language acquisition, these students' achievement in mathematics seems to be much better than their reading abilities. Although the majority are not as proficient as their peers without disabilities, about 10 percent can perform mathematical calculations at grade level. However, Karchmer noted that once beyond the age of fifteen, few of these students continued to make academic progress.

Allen (1986) compared the reading and mathematics achievement test scores of two comparable groups of students with hearing impairments—one in 1974 and one in 1983. These students, ages eight to eighteen, all had mild to profound hearing losses and received special education services. Allen included over 12,000 children's scores from a standardized achievement test in his study, and found that the scores indicated improvement over time. The group's scores in 1983 were higher than those in 1974. However, the research showed significant differences in academic achievement between students who were not disabled and those with hearing impairments. These data are shown on two graphs in Figure 10.5: one for reading and one for mathematics. The graph for reading scores shows that the performance of students with hearing impairments in reading is substantially below their mathematical abilities. What do these graphs tell us? More emphasis needs to be placed on reading for these students, particularly since reading is an important means of acquiring information. Many technological advances developed to benefit people with hearing impairments, such as captioned television and films, require an ability to read well. These technological improvements might provide the motivation to learn to read. However, we cannot lose sight of the fact that students who are deaf must have more effective reading instruction in school to help improve their academic achievement.

Professionals identify two major educational goals for children who are deaf (Moores, 1987). These two goals are (1) to reduce the achievement gap between nonhandicapped students and students who are deaf and (2) to develop the speech and language skills to these individuals' potential. These goals are often in competition with each other. For example, programs for children with hearing impairments

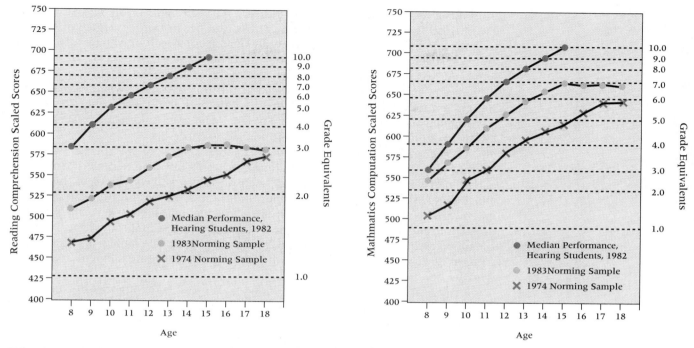

FIGURE 10.5 Mean Math and Reading Comprehension Scores for Three Groups of Students: 1974 Scores for Hearing Impaired, 1983 Scores for Hearing Impaired Students versus 1982 Scores for Nonhandicapped Students

SOURCE: Patterns of academic achievement among hearing impaired students: 1974–1983, by T. E. Allen in *Deaf children in America*, pp. 164–165, by A. N. Schildroth and M. A. Karchmer (Eds.), 1986, Austin, TX, PRO-ED, Inc. Reprinted by permission.

spend a good deal of time developing speech and language. As a result considerably less time is spent on academic subjects in these classes than in regular education classes (Moores, 1987). Academic subjects are given a lower priority than the development of speech and language skills. This contributes to the lower achievement scores noted for these youngsters. Supporting this theory are the results from a recent study conducted by Kluwin and Moores (1989), who found that the quality of instruction these students received influenced achievement test scores more than educational environments (for example, mainstreaming). Educators of the deaf need to discuss these issues openly. For example, should the school day be lengthened or the school year extended to devote sufficient time to all aspects of the curriculum? Should academic subjects be given a higher priority and should more time be devoted to these topics, thereby reducing the time spent on speech and language? Knowing that there is a high relationship between instructional time and academic achievement (Rieth, Polsgrove, and Semmel, 1979; Good and Brophy, 1986), how would you resolve this issue?

Speech Ability

As we know, many students with hearing impairments are unable to hear the communications of others well. Related to this, however, is their impaired ability to communicate with others. According to their teachers, less than 45 percent of students who are deaf have intelligible speech even though it might sound "different" from the speech of individuals without hearing impairments (Wolk and Schildroth, 1986). Intelligibility of speech is related to a number of factors: degree of hearing loss, the communication method the individual uses (speech only, sign only, speech and sign together), academic integration with nonhandicapped peers, cultural and linguistic background, and the presence of another handicap. It appears that the degree of hearing loss is the most crucial factor in determining whether a person's speech is intelligible. Of those students who are profoundly deaf, only 25 percent have intelligible speech (Allen, 1988). Students who have mild to moderate hearing losses, typically, speak almost like their nonhandicapped peers.

Another important factor that determines intelligible speech is the age when the hearing impairment occurs. A study found that children who became hearing impaired after age eight, when language acquisition is relatively complete, retain intelligible speech (Goehl and Kaufman, 1984). It is interesting to note that the individuals in this study retained excellent articulation abilities, but still sounded different to independent judges. These researchers suggest that though people who are moderately to severely hearing impaired can speak intelligibly, they still have patterns of rhythm, rate of speaking, and voice qualities that are different from those who are not hearing impaired.

A third factor affecting how well individuals speak is the manner of communication they use. For example, 90 percent of those who use oral speech as their primary mode of communication have intelligible speech, while only 7 percent of those who use sign language have intelligible speech. Also, 40 percent of those who rely on both speaking and signing in the classroom have intelligible speech. An interesting research study by Wolk and Schildroth (1986) showed that students with a profound hearing loss (greater than 91 dB loss) had a greater probability of having intelligible speech (73 percent), if their communication mode was speaking only. They also found that students who received some amount of integration, as opposed to those schooled in totally segregated settings, had better expressive communication skills, regardless of their degree of hearing loss.

The preceding discussion concerns students who are deaf or have profound and severe hearing losses. Those who have mild to moderate hearing losses are able to communicate more readily with the use of a hearing aid. Hearing aids, commonly available in America for more than thirty-five years, help students with mild to moderate hearing losses function in regular education classes. Most, however, need supportive services from speech/language pathologists. With extra assistance from special educators, these students can learn in regular education classes and achieve as well as most of their nonhandicapped peers.

ISSUES IN EDUCATION

For those members of our society who have disabilities, education is critical. Children who are disabled, and their families, need to receive an intensive educational experience as early as possible. Children with severe to profound hearing losses have much to learn, and a considerable amount of that learning will be challenging. Professionals in this field debate about a number of issues, such as where education should be delivered, how much speech and language development should be stressed in the curriculum at the expense of more traditional academic subjects, and what mode (oral, manual, or total) of communication is best. Regardless of such disagree-

---

American Sign Language (ASL). The sign language or manual communication system preferred by many adults who are deaf in this country.

Focus: Issues of Diversity

How can schools provide an appropriate education for youngsters who are a minority within a minority? It is difficult when children are culturally and linguistically diverse and deaf. Grant (1990) estimates that 15 percent of the hearing impaired population, approximately 7600 students, come from homes where languages other than English are spoken. In some regions of the United States, this figure may surpass 40 percent. These students' educational programs fall under two separate laws: the Bilingual Education Act and IDEA. The Bilingual Education Act requires that these students have instruction in two languages; one of which is English. IDEA mandates assessment and evaluation in the student's dominant language. For example, some children's home language is Spanish sign language; for others, it is a form of total communication using Spanish. Providing trained personnel who are bilingual and proficient in one or two forms of sign language can be difficult. With training, teachers, paraprofessionals, and other professionals can become available for students who are culturally and linguistically diverse and deaf.

ments, professionals agree: Education should begin at birth or at the time the hearing impairment was discovered for the individual and the entire family, particularly for those with severe hearing impairments. In this section, we discuss just what makes a first-rate educational program for children with hearing impairments. We also include some suggestions for teachers and other professionals to instruct these students more effectively. Throughout all of these discussions, think about how an array of professionals and services (see chapter 3 for a review) must be available and individually arranged for each student with a hearing impairment.

Education and the Preschool Child

The school services available to those with hearing impairments are varied and numerous. Preschool programs are important for children with hearing impairments especially for those with severe to profound hearing losses. Equally important are programs for the families of these children. Parents need to know how to help their child acquire language and communication skills, as well as a positive self-concept. They are primarily responsible for the child's integration into the family, neighborhood, school, and community. Finally, the family learns to understand how this handicap affects the individual members of the family. The training families require can best come from the professionals at an infant or preschool program. They can help parents cope with a range of issues from understanding the social and language development of their child to the proper care and fitting of hearing aids.

Young children, particularly those who are deaf, and their families need intensive educational efforts during infancy and the preschool years (Appell, 1982). Many families choose to learn some form of sign language or manual communication system, so they can communicate more fully with their child. Some professionals (Johnson, Liddell, and Erting, 1989) propose that infants and their families be taught **American Sign Language (ASL),** the manual language system widely used in the

Children who are deaf should be identified and receive intervention as early as possible. This child already has a hearing aid and an educational program that involves his whole family.

deaf community. They also suggest that individuals who live in the deaf community and are proficient in ASL help these children to acquire this form of manual communication as their "native" language. Many experts strongly suggest that parents of infants and preschoolers who are deaf use both manual and oral communication methods as they interact with their children (Lowenbraun, 1988; Moores, 1987). They recommend this procedure for all family members (grandparents, brothers, sisters) and family friends. Today, even infants can wear hearing aids, and learning to take care of such equipment is an important part of their growth process. With the further development of technology (discussed later in this chapter), these children will need to learn how to use sophisticated equipment and incorporate it into their daily living. This learning process needs to begin early in life.

What should a good preschool program look like? The early intervention curriculum should be comprehensive and have three main foci: the total development of the child within the context of the family, parental knowledge of normal child development and their child's hearing abilities, and support and skills to assist the child's assimilation into the family system (Bodner-Johnson, 1987). Fortunately, local school districts have begun to provide these early infant and preschool programs. Also, in many states, the residential center school for the deaf offers outreach preschool programs in local communities. These programs are most effective when an audiologist, an SLP, an educator of those who are deaf, and often a person who is deaf are included on the staff.

Education and the School-Age Child

The educational needs of two groups of students with hearing impairments are very different from each other. The challenges that students who are hard of hearing face are different from those of students who have more substantial hearing losses. Differences exist in the way they are taught, what they are taught, and, for some of these students, where they are taught. Therefore, we have separated the discussion about students with mild to moderate hearing losses and students with severe to profound hearing losses.

CHILDREN WITH MILD TO MODERATE HEARING LOSSES. Since the advent of PL 94–142 in 1975, more and more students with hearing impairments have been mainstreamed into regular education classes with generally positive results (Wolk and Schildroth, 1986). Mainstreaming seems to work well for students with a mild to moderate hearing loss. It is important for you to remember that most students with hearing impairments can hear satisfactorily with amplification (that is, a hearing aid), and therefore can attend school and function well with their nonhandicapped peers. As you know, in most schools information is presented orally, and students learn through a combination of textbooks, lectures, and class discussions. Children with mild to moderate hearing impairments can cope quite well with these methods as long as an array of supplemental services is available.

Along with educational benefits, students with hearing impairments acquire social skills in a regular classroom. Educators believe that when children with dis-

Tips for Teachers

1. Place the child as close to the speaker as possible.
2. Make certain that the child's hearing aid is turned on and functioning properly by listening through it.
3. Reduce the background noise as much as possible.
4. Articulate clearly, but do not talk louder unless you have an unusually soft voice.
5. Make certain to have the student's attention before talking or starting a lesson.
6. Do not exaggerate your lip movements.
7. Do not chew gum or cover your mouth when talking.
8. Do not turn your back on the class.
9. Use an overhead projector instead of a blackboard.
10. Avoid moving around the classroom while talking.
11. Speak slowly.
12. Repeat and restate information by paraphrasing.
13. Spend time talking to the child alone so you can become accustomed to each other's speech.
14. Avoid glare when talking or signing by not standing near a light source such as a window.

abilities participate in classes with their nondisabled peers they are more fully accepted socially, and all the children learn to interact positively. Unfortunately, some data indicate that these social interactions do not occur naturally for those with hearing impairments (Antia, 1985). Teachers need to encourage, support, and create opportunities for such interactions to occur. Many teachers have found that some teaching tactics have dual functions; they effectively assist in teaching a particular subject and they encourage social interactions. For example, the puzzle technique (sometimes called the jigsaw technique) encourages children to work together in a constructive fashion while solving a problem or completing a task. Many teachers and educators (Smith, 1989) report that using tactics like the puzzle technique result in better understanding of the content assigned because students share, discuss, and model for each other the steps they followed to arrive at the correct solutions to the problems posed to them. An illustrative application of the puzzle technique can be found in the accompanying Teaching Tactics box.

Educators have learned that, with certain modifications, students with hearing impairments can benefit from regular classes. There are a number of simple techniques and procedures to help students with mild to moderate hearing impairments profit more in oral communication situations (Burrow, 1983; Kampfe, 1984; Teitelbaum, 1981; Yater, 1977). Some of these are listed in this section's Tips for Teachers box. In addition to these tips, other modifications to the classroom routine can be helpful to the student with a hearing impairment. For example, the teacher can give the student handouts listing important points from lectures, films, or movies. A

Teachers need to create a supportive and integrated atmosphere, so all students feel part of the classroom community.

THE PUZZLE TECHNIQUE

Learning how to write is a very important skill that all students need to become proficient at executing. For some time in elementary and middle school, writing is a topic of instruction—a content area to be taught. As students progress through school, their writing is one way that they and their teachers assess the acquisition and mastery of other subjects. Writing continues to be important after school. Many jobs, ranging from clerical to managerial, require proficiency in writing. Unfortunately, writing is a skill not mastered by all students, whether they do or do not have disabilities. In academic subjects, students with hearing impairments tend to be behind others who do not share their disability (Allen, 1986; Trybus and Karchmer, 1977; Wolk, Karchmer, and Schildroth, 1982). By spending more time directly instructing students so they can use the skills required to write more efficiently and accurately, teachers help all their students. The puzzle technique is well suited to group writing and language arts instruction.

Marcia Bassett teaches language arts at Jefferson Middle School. She has been worried about the writing skills of her seventh graders. Other teachers too have told her that homework, in-class essays, and various assignments that require writing are unsatisfactory from this group of students. Ms. Bassett has twenty-eight students in this section with varying writing abilities. Some students have moderately acceptable writing skills, but the writing abilities of others is marginal at best. In addition, Mark, who has a moderate hearing impairment, is a member of this class. Mark's writing skills are of particular concern. To tackle this problem, Ms. Bassett has devised a special teaching unit that she calls "Solve the Puzzle." First, she clusters her students into seven groups of four students each. She assigns each group at least one student who is more capable in writing. She assigns Mark to the group that includes the class's best writer.

To prepare for the unit, Ms. Bassett wrote a number of short essays on different topics. They are topics from the students' other courses: ecology, American explorers, food chains, disruption on the playground, and social issues like apartheid. She then rewrote each essay, deliberately incorporating a substantial number of errors in spelling, punctuation, grammar, and capitalization. She duplicated copies of each essay for each class member plus seven extras. These essays are to serve as the materials the students use in their group activities.

Ms. Bassett begins each class session of this teaching unit by reminding the students of the importance of spelling, punctuation, grammar, and capitalization. She gives examples of each of these aspects of writing by showing the class errors they made in the previous day's class. The entire class works on the same essay during this period. In groups of four, they work to "solve the puzzle" of finding all the errors in one of the essays the teacher has prepared. Each student in a group has a different assignment: One student corrects all of the spelling errors, another looks for all of the punctuation errors, another the grammatical errors, and another the capitalization errors. After the four students have found errors of the types they were assigned, one student in the group then makes all of the corrections on a clean copy of the essay. As each student reports the errors that he or she found, the others verify the corrections and look to see if others were missed.

Each day the error-hunting assignments rotate. In this way each student has a chance to look for different types of errors on different days. *(continued)*

oral approach. One method of instruction advocated for students who are deaf, where they learn to communicate (both receiving and sending information) orally—not using sign language.

Teaching Tactics

(continued)

Ms. Bassett finds that all of the students' writing abilities improve greatly over the course of several weeks; it appears that they all profit by helping one another proofread written material. Mark's progress has been remarkable. He has learned how to proofread written assignments and find all four types of writing errors. Perhaps more importantly, he has developed a nice relationship with the other students in his small group. She has also observed comparable, supporting relationships develop among other students in other groups. This teaching tactic has served two functions: the students' writing skills improved and so, too, did their interpersonal relationships.

classmate can be asked to help by using carbon paper during lectures to make a copy of notes for the student who has a hearing impairment.

Teachers should also seek the help of specialists and others who can provide guidance so the learning environment is most efficient for all students in the class. Parents of students with hearing impairments can also give valuable information about their child's communication skills and special needs. For example, classroom teachers have found that the speech/language pathologist assigned to their school can offer many good ideas about activities that foster better speech and language. The specialist can also provide suggestions about classroom organizers that will assist students with hearing impairments gain more from traditional classroom settings. The child's parents can also help teachers come to a quicker understanding of their child's preferred learning styles. One child might profit from having a classmate serve as a resource to ensure that homework and other assignments are correctly understood. Another child might prefer to tape lectures to listen to more carefully in a quiet setting at home in the evening. Yet another student might benefit more by being able to do extra outside reading on specific topics. It is important to remember that each child is unique, and that teachers need to capitalize on each child's strengths, not just attend to their disabilities.

CHILDREN WITH SEVERE TO PROFOUND HEARING LOSSES. What are the best educational methods for students who are deaf? This question is being discussed and debated by those who are deaf and by professional educators. The debate centers not only on the best educational practices but also on where these students should be taught. Remember, the majority of students with hearing impairments have mild to moderate hearing loss and attend regular classes. This controversy does concern students who have very limited ability to use their hearing.

Three Teaching Approaches

Three different approaches are used to teach students who are deaf: speech (oral communication) only, sign (manual communication) only, and speech and sign (total communication). With the **oral approach,** children are taught to use as much of their residual hearing as possible (Ling, 1984b). They learn about amplification, how to speech read (lipread), and how to speak. The oral approach does not allow children to use any form of manual communication such as finger spelling or signing. In fact, even natural signing, such as using gestures, is discouraged. Those who follow the oral approach believe that individuals who are deaf must live and work in a world where most people hear normally and communicate through oral expression. Therefore, proponents of the oral approach believe that individuals who are deaf should learn to communicate as the majority do so they can more easily become part of mainstream society.

However, the oral approach programs have problems (Ling, 1984a). Some children in these programs develop excellent speech and can be educated in traditional settings. Others do not. According to Lowenbraun (1988), "for some children with severe and profound sensorineural hearing losses, the attainment of intelligible speech is an unreachable goal" (p. 345). Even for those who do attain intelligible speech, the process is arduous, slow, and difficult.

The second educational approach is manual communication. There are many forms of **manual communication.** American Sign Language (ASL) which is structured and formal, with its own linguistic rules and patterns is one widely used form of manual communication. (ASL is the form of manual communication used by Jamie MacAllister, whose story you read at the beginning of this chapter.) ASL is the preferred language of the adult deaf community and is widely used by those who are severely hearing impaired in the United States and Canada. It is used at Gallaudet University, the world's only accredited liberal arts university for postsecondary students who are deaf. However, ASL is not used by most teachers of the deaf in most elementary and secondary school settings. Only 3 percent of teachers for the deaf use ASL in their school classes (Woodward, Allen, and Schildroth, 1985). A recent study (Woodward et al., 1988) found that 35 percent of students with hearing impairments used oral communication in their classes. Differences in the use of oral communication related to the individuals' degree of hearing loss (11 percent with profound losses, 78 percent with less than severe losses). Those who do use manual communication more often use finger spelling, another form of manual communication, which more closely matches the grammatical form and structure of standard English. In **finger spelling** each letter of the alphabet has a sign. This system is efficient and has been used for centuries. An accomplished person can finger spell at a rate equivalent to typical speech. Finger spelling represents English. Words are spelled out, but the rules of grammar and language are the same as English speech. However, ASL is a language in its own, with its own linguistic rules and patterns. In a recent position paper, Johnson, Liddell, and Erting (1989) advocate the use of ASL at home and at school for children with severe hearing impairments. They maintain that ASL should be taught to these children as infants as their native language, and used in their primary grades as the language and linguistic foundation upon which other basic academic skills are taught. English, then, would be taught as a second language to these students. This would be a radical departure from current practices, but these professionals maintain that improved achievement scores would be one positive result.

Thomas Gallaudet, the founder of the American School for the Deaf, and Laurent Clerc, the school's first teacher, both advocated manual communication (Moores, 1987; Lane, 1984; Winefield, 1987). For this reason manual communication was widely used in the United States beginning in 1817. However, starting around 1870 and lasting to 1970 this approach became less popular. (See History of the Field earlier in this chapter.) Most teachers of the deaf were trained to teach their students

manual communication. Using the hands, not the voice, as the means of communication, as in sign language or finger spelling.

finger spelling. A form of manual communication where each letter of the alphabet has a sign.

through an oral-only approach and few of them knew signs themselves. Support for the oral-only approach was very strong. Some communities in Europe (for example, Milan) banned the use of signs in classes for the deaf, and there were proposals to do the same in this country (Moores, 1987). Although the oral approach became the major educational tool during this period, ASL was kept alive through the deaf community. It has become a symbol of their unity as a group of people: a clear representation of their culture and community (Padden and Humphries, 1988).

In the late 1960s, Roy Holcomb, a deaf educator and parent was dissatisfied with the oral approach. He developed a system now referred to as the total communication approach, using oral speech and manual communication (signing) together. The total communication approach encourages children to speak, but also allows them more options for receiving and sending messages. The philosophy behind this approach is that every child with a hearing impairment should be able to use whatever channels are available to learn and comprehend messages. Of those who use a total communication approach, 99 percent sign in an English code rather than using ASL, and 93 percent talk while they sign (Woodward, Allen, and Schildroth, 1985). The number of educational programs that use the total communication approach has increased dramatically in recent years (Ling, 1984a). It is the most commonly used system in classes for students who are deaf today.

Is there one best approach among these three for educating students who are hearing impaired? To better understand this issue let us consider research studies of children who are deaf and whose parents are also deaf. As we discussed earlier, many parents who are deaf use both signing and oral communication to teach their children who are deaf. Data from research studies indicate that these children when compared with children who have hearing parents are superior in language functioning, academic achievement, and social adjustment. Moores (1987) concludes that the combination of oral and manual communication assists in the development of these important skills and should be part of the educational program for every child with a severe or profound hearing impairment as early as possible. Other research studies support this position (Montgomery and Lines, 1976; Moores, 1985). Elementary schoolchildren with hearing impairments were presented information using sound alone. They understood less than half of what was said to them. However, when the information was presented using oral and manual communication they understood between 88 and 93 percent.

It is clear that the debate and confusion about the best mode of instruction for students with severe to profound hearing losses continues. It is a debate that has lasted for well over a hundred years, and promises to continue well into the future.

Educational Environments

At the national level, a full array of educational services is available for elementary and secondary students with hearing impairments. These services include regular education classrooms with specialized support services, resource rooms, special classes, special day schools, and residential center schools. More and more students with hearing impairments attend regular education classes at neighborhood schools (Schildroth and Hotto, 1988; Wolk and Schildroth, 1986) with fewer attending residential schools. At the same time, however, some parents are encouraged to send their children who are deaf to residential schools that are sometimes a great distance from home (Commission on the Education of the Deaf, 1988).

The controversy about LRE for students who are deaf is intense and complex. Some argue that students who are deaf should be grouped in order to create a large peer group who communicate with sign language (such as ASL) in a variety of activities throughout the day. Others maintain that these students should be educated in the mainstream.

Table 10.4, taken from the *Annual Report to Congress on Implementation of the Education of the Handicapped Act*, shows the percentage of students with hearing impairments, by each state, enrolled in each type of educational service. Find your state. Compare it to other states' patterns of service delivery. Which states serve the highest percentage of their students with hearing impairments in regular education classes? Which states have the highest percentages served in separate, special education classes?

How does the team decide which is the most appropriate service for a student with a hearing impairment? The answers to the following questions help the team make the decisions. First, how severe is the student's hearing loss? Is the student able to use speech? Can appropriate educational services be made available locally? Are the necessary support services available? It is clear that many factors must be considered when deciding a child's educational placement and program when developing an Individualized Educational Program (IEP) (Commission on the Education of the Deaf, 1988; Kampfe, 1984a, b). For example, Allen (1988) points out that students' speech intelligibility is strongly associated with placement: "Students with intelligible speech are more likely to be mainstreamed than are students with unintelligible speech" (p. 6). Some of these factors are found in Table 10.5.

In addition to states and local communities, the federal government also provides a variety of educational services for those who are deaf. The comprehensive set

TABLE 10.4. Percentage of Children Aged Six to Twenty-One Served in Different Educational Environments During the 1987–88 School Year by State: Hard of Hearing and Deaf

State	Regular Classes	Resource Room	Separate Classes	Public Separate Facility	Private Separate Facility	Public Residential Facility	Private Residential Facility	Homebound Hospital Environment
Alabama	18.11	39.92	40.33	1.23	0.41	.	0.00	0.00
Alaska	45.66	27.75	25.43	0.58	0.00	0.58	0.00	0.00
Arizona	1.65	51.60	9.13	20.13	0.00	17.49	0.00	0.00
Arkansas	14.20	35.98	11.74	11.93	0.76	25.19	0.19	0.00
California	23.79	4.97	64.60	5.98	0.66	0.00	.	.
Colorado	33.11	29.99	26.32	0.41	0.00	10.18	0.00	0.00
Connecticut	8.73	37.90	7.74	15.28	22.02	0.79	7.14	0.40
Delaware	17.80	24.08	15.18	28.27	0.52	13.61	0.52	0.00
District of Columbia	43.75	12.50	43.75	0.00	0.00	0.00	0.00	0.00
Florida	5.07	7.85	63.37	3.83	0.00	19.78	0.00	0.10
Georgia	0.88	41.58	26.50	8.94	4.63	17.32	0.16	0.00
Hawaii	16.59	27.35	45.29	8.52	0.45	1.35	0.00	0.45
Idaho	36.49	43.58	16.89	0.00	0.00	0.00	0.00	3.04
Illinois	14.14	17.47	56.81	3.09	0.35	7.86	0.25	0.04
Indiana	5.92	23.88	35.64	11.58	0.00	22.80	0.09	0.09
Iowa	36.96	26.92	26.36	0.42	0.00	9.07	0.14	0.14
Kansas	15.56	19.31	44.72	0.83	0.00	18.06	1.39	0.14
Kentucky	14.71	21.05	23.80	4.90	0.48	34.57	0.36	0.12
Louisiana	28.02	18.42	49.70	3.07	0.00	0.00	0.30	0.50
Maine	45.08	20.95	9.52	3.81	0.63	19.68	0.32	0.00
Maryland	33.25	8.99	29.94	3.65	0.68	23.24	0.25	0.00
Massachusetts	59.83	15.30	17.79	2.15	3.15	0.61	0.55	0.61
Michigan	35.89	15.79	35.10	7.42	0.00	5.72	0.00	0.08
Minnesota	27.50	45.99	21.46	3.07	.	1.89	.	0.09
Mississippi	10.70	43.12	40.67	0.92	0.31	3.98	0.31	0.00
Missouri	22.44	13.71	44.74	16.62	0.42	1.52	0.55	0.00
Montana	36.49	22.97	32.43	0.00	0.00	4.73	3.38	0.00
Nebraska	58.60	4.52	19.00	3.17	2.49	9.73	0.00	2.49
Nevada	6.72	11.94	79.10	0.00	0.75	0.75	0.75	0.00
New Hampshire	61.29	11.98	17.51	0.00	2.76	0.00	6.45	0.00
New Jersey	5.01	19.59	28.93	39.79	6.23	0.00	0.08	0.38
New Mexico	38.94	14.82	25.63	0.75	0.25	19.60	0.00	0.00
New York	15.97	17.19	21.43	9.66	29.89	2.53	3.01	0.32
North Carolina	36.65	18.91	17.10	1.23	0.00	25.95	0.00	0.16
North Dakota	34.03	19.44	15.28	0.69	0.69	29.86	0.00	0.00
Ohio	18.73	10.22	56.48	8.04	0.33	6.05	0.00	0.14
Oklahoma	28.34	15.58	31.01	5.93	0.59	18.10	0.30	0.15
Oregon	68.10	22.38	2.86	2.38	1.43	1.43	1.43	0.00
Pennsylvania	47.58	13.51	20.52	0.95	9.96	0.30	7.18	0.00
Puerto Rico	14.65	26.31	38.22	4.88	11.83	0.17	1.20	2.74
Rhode Island	16.67	12.96	6.79	62.35	0.62	0.00	0.62	0.00
South Carolina	36.77	18.65	30.10	0.73	0.00	13.75	0.00	0.00
South Dakota	44.48	32.07	0.34	1.38	0.00	21.38	0.34	0.00
Tennessee	33.59	24.62	11.85	10.64	4.56	14.59	0.08	0.08
Texas	4.40	47.73	32.50	13.13	1.61	0.03	0.03	0.57
Utah	31.41	22.38	40.61	0.00	0.00	5.60	0.00	0.00

TABLE 10.4. Percentage of Children Aged Six to Twenty-One Served in Different Educational Environments During the 1987–88 School Year by State: Hard of Hearing and Deaf (continued)

State	Regular Classes	Resource Room	Separate Classes	Public Separate Facility	Private Separate Facility	Public Residential Facility	Private Residential Facility	Homebound Hospital Environment
Vermont	56.18	3.37	0.56	1.12	1.12	0.00	37.64	0.00
Virginia	39.98	16.01	40.89	1.81	0.40	0.60	0.10	0.20
Washington	30.08	32.45	22.39	0.81	2.00	11.83	0.37	0.07
West Virginia	26.61	16.54	27.13	0.00	1.55	28.17	0.00	0.00
Wisconsin	52.85	12.95	28.50	5.18	0.00	0.52	0.00	0.00
Wyoming	53.25	30.52	9.74	1.30	0.00	3.25	1.95	0.00
American Samoa	0.00	0.00	100.00	0.00	0.00	0.00	0.00	0.00
Guam	13.04	34.78	52.17	0.00	0.00	0.00	0.00	0.00
Northern Marianas	.	.	.	.	.	.	.	.
Trust Territories	.	.	.	.	.	.	.	.
Virgin Islands	.	.	.	.	.	.	.	.
Bur. of Indian Affairs	.	.	.	.	.	.	.	.
U.S. and Insular Areas	24.41	20.86	35.19	6.91	3.84	7.60	0.96	0.23
50 States, D.C. & P.R.	24.42	20.86	35.16	6.92	3.84	7.60	0.96	0.24

NOTES: Data as of October 1, 1989.
  Annual.CNTL (LRXXNP1A)

Source: *Twelfth Annual Report to Congress*, p. A–65, by U.S. Department of Education, 1990, Washington, DC: Government Printing Office.

of federally supported educational services available to this group of individuals is amazing. The array of services extends from preschool programs through fairly comprehensive postsecondary programs. Two important examples of federally funded programs for school-age children are the Kendall Demonstration Elementary School and the Model Secondary School for the Deaf. The Kendall Demonstration Elementary School serves about 200 children who are residents primarily of Washington, D.C., and its surrounding suburbs. The Model Secondary School for the Deaf serves approximately 370 students from Washington, D.C., Delaware, Maryland, Pennsylvania, Virginia, and West Virginia.

The federal government also supports various types of postsecondary schools with programs for students with hearing impairments. Gallaudet University serves both undergraduate and graduate students and receives federal funding (Rawlings and King, 1986). The National Technical Institute for the Deaf (NTID) at the Rochester Institute of Technology in New York began offering technical and vocational degrees in 1968. Gallaudet and NTID serve a total of about 2900 students. Four regional, federally funded postsecondary schools—Seattle Community College, California State University–Northridge, St. Paul Technical Institute, and the University of Tennessee Consortium—serve a total of 662 students.

Other state and privately funded universities and colleges also offer special programs for students with hearing impairments. The 1986 College Guide lists 145 programs that educate 7031 students with hearing impairments (Rawlings et al., 1986). In 1964 there were only six college programs (excluding those that were federally funded) for these students (Rawlings and King, 1986). Over a three-year

TABLE 10.5. Placement and IEP Considerations

	Degree of Hearing Impairment	
	Mild to Moderate	Severe to Profound
Severity of loss	All hearing losses are serious, but usually youngsters with mild to moderate hearing impairments can remain in the regular education curriculum with consultative or supportive services from various experts like a speech/language pathologist and an audiologist.	Students with severe to profound hearing impairments require intensive instruction in areas not typically included in the regular education curriculum. These students must have a wide variety of supportive services available to them.
Potential for using residual hearing	Most students with mild to moderate hearing impairments have considerable levels of useful residual hearing that allow them to profit from hearing aids; therefore, allowing these students to benefit, with some adaptions, from typical oral methods of instruction.	The amount of useful residual hearing varies for each individual, but many students with severe to profound hearing losses have little residual hearing. Such students require considerable additional instruction in alternative communication modes and many modifications in the ways that instruction is delivered to them.
Academic achievement	The academic achievement levels of all students with hearing impairments tend to be lower than their nonhandicapped peers'. Students with less hearing loss who are not also multiply handicapped are usually not substantially below grade level, but might need some additional instruction on basic academic skills, possibly from a resource room teacher.	The academic achievement levels of students with severe to profound hearing impairments is considerably below their nonhandicapped peers' levels. These students need considerable instruction in basic language and communication skills, as well as intensive academic remediation.
Communicative needs	The hearing impairment of many youngsters with mild to moderate hearing losses goes undetected for a long time. If the hearing impairment occurred before or while the youngsters were developing language, it is likely that they will require speech and language development programs to provide them with the foundations needed for academic learning.	Youngsters with severe to profound hearing losses often benefit most from a total communication approach. For teachers to use this method of communication requires much training, and in many small, rural regions of our country this expertise is not available.
Preferred mode of communication	Students with mild to moderate hearing impairments need to become proficient using traditional oral methods of communication.	Many students with severe to profound hearing losses can learn (or retain) the use of oral language, and can use their residual hearing and develop fine speech (lip) reading skills to be able to understand oral communications. However, many of these individuals use manual communication. These individuals require the services of an interpreter for the deaf or technological equipment to communicate with others not proficient in signing.
Placement preference	The vast majority of students who have mild to moderate hearing impairments prefer to attend their neighborhood schools with their nonhandicapped peers.	Many students with severe to profound hearing impairments also prefer neighborhood schools. However, a significant number of students who are deaf prefer center schools where the other students in attendance share their deafness and their mode of communication.

period from 1982 to 1985, thirty-seven colleges added programs for students who are deaf (Rawlings, Karchmer, and DeCaro, 1987). Rawlings and King estimate that as many as 11,000 students with moderate, severe, and profound hearing losses attend institutions of higher education. Because there is no national registry of students with mild to moderate hearing impairments, it is impossible to determine how many of these youngsters attend college or university and complete academic degrees.

Of course, the quality and comprehensiveness of postsecondary school programs for those with hearing impairments vary. The Commission on the Education of the

Deaf (1988) reports that only a few of the programs available at state or private universities or colleges offer a full array of supportive services. Many of these programs have not educated the general faculty in the special educational needs of these students. As a result, there is a high dropout rate in many of these programs (estimates range from 59 to 79 percent). These data show that persons with hearing impairments, even those with little use of their hearing abilities, can successfully pursue a college education if provided with necessary support services. These programs need improved services to better meet the needs of these students.

FAMILY MEMBERS WITH HEARING IMPAIRMENTS

A HEARING DAUGHTER SHARES HER VIEW ABOUT GROWING UP WITH PARENTS WHO ARE DEAF

"I must have been about four the time Grandma Wells and I were cuddled up spoonwise in her bed. Grandma had her arms around me and the new ballerina doll I'd just received for Christmas. Grandma started humming, her voice, quiet and low, cracked. She breathed between words. Then her humming floated into a lullaby: 'Sleep, my child, and peace attend thee, all through the night. Guardian angels . . . Soft the waking hours are creeping, hill and dale in slumber steeping . . .'

"Mom and Dad picked me up from Grandma's the next day. That night as Mom tucked me into bed, I asked her to sing me a lullaby, even though I knew she couldn't.

"My parents are deaf. I can hear. And the fact of their deafness has made all the difference. It has altered the course of their lives, of my life, of their families' lives.

"In a way we were outsiders, immigrants in a strange world. With my two younger sisters and parents, it was as if we were clinging together for safety. There were unbreakable bonds between us. Yet there was also an unbroachable chasm, for despite my parents' spirit and their ability to get along, their world is the deaf, their deaf culture, their deaf friends, and their sign language—it is something separate, something I can never really know, but that I am intimate with.

"The best that can be said for deafness is that it's an invisible handicap. The worst, that it puts adults at the mercy of their hearing children, at the mercy of parents, at almost anyone's mercy. It is one of the cruelest and most deceptive of afflictions. It can emasculate men and devastate women. It is an impairment of communication. But it's not just the disfigurement of words and broken ears. It's most often a barrier between person and person.

"I acted as interpreter and guide for my parents the entire time I was growing up. I was an adult before I was a child. I was quiet and obedient around people because I didn't know what was expected of me. Outside our house speaking and hearing seemed to be valued more than anything. And that's what we had nothing of at home.

"I was the child who did all my parents' business transactions, nearly from the time I was a toddler. I spoke for my parents; I heard for my parents. I was painfully shy for myself, squirming away when the attention was focused on me, but when I was acting for my parents, I was forthright. I made their doctors' appointments. I interpreted in sign language for my mother when she went to the doctor and told him where it hurt and when he told her what medicine to take. I told the shoe repairman what was wrong with a shoe. I told the store clerk when we needed a different size. It was me the garage mechanic would hang up on when I called about a transmission for my father. I was usually the one to relay to Mom and Dad that a friend had died when we received a call. I was the one who had to call up other friends or relatives to give them bad news.

"A child doesn't know that his childhood is sad: it's just his life. I didn't realize that everyone didn't feel content at home and embarrassed and confused away from there. And it took me most of the first three decades of my life to figure out what those differences were between the deaf and hearing worlds."

Source: A Loss for Words (pp. 1–3) by Lou Ann Walker, 1986, New York: Harper and Row. Reprinted by permission.

A child with a moderate to profound hearing loss who is a member of a hearing family must learn a great deal. If this family member is an infant or preschooler when the hearing impairment was diagnosed or first identified, the family must first learn how to provide an optimal learning environment that can facilitate the development of many different types of skills, such as language, cognition, social and emotional growth, speech, and motor development. Most important, they will probably need help to gain the information, guidance, and support necessary to create a home environment conducive to maximal language acquisition. Somers (1984) believes that there are ten general goals that all families of young children with hearing impairments should strive to attain:

1. To understand the nature of the child's hearing loss
2. To understand the educational implications of a hearing loss
3. To understand the benefit of amplification
4. To understand the need for the child to utilize amplification
5. To understand the need to surround the child with language input and expand on the child's utterances in a meaningful way
6. To understand the need for consistent and continual audiological assessment
7. To understand the sequence of language development in the normally hearing child
8. To understand that a hearing-impaired child learns language in the same sequence as a child with normal hearing
9. To understand that the role of the parents is to flood the child with language geared to the youngster's interest and needs
10. To understand the need for developing a positive self-concept and appropriate social-emotional skills in their child (p. 185)

As we discuss throughout this book, the benefits of early educational experiences are great. For infants who are deaf, schooling should begin as soon as the impairment is identified. Schooling can take the form of a training program where professionals

Deaf theater groups perform throughout America. Many of these productions express deaf culture and are performed using American Sign Language.

work with both family and child, often in the child's home. This setting is conducive to working on the ten goals mentioned above. The Kendall School, part of Gallaudet University in Washington, D.C., provides a model program for infants. This home-based program stresses total communication, using manual communication simultaneously with oral speech. To accomplish this, members of the family of a child who is born deaf should learn sign language or manual communication as early as possible in the child's life.

American Sign Language (ASL) is not the only form of manual communication available, but it is the language of the deaf community in America. It is also the most binding element of deaf culture in our country. ASL is not a mere translation of oral speech or the English language; it is a fully developed language. In fact, seven states (Alaska, California, Connecticut, Maine, Michigan, Texas, and Washington) allow ASL as an option to meet the high school foreign language requirement, and the same is true at many colleges and universities (Wilcox, 1989). As the language of the deaf community, ASL is used in all aspects of their culture. For example, plays are written in ASL and performed by deaf theater groups around the world, and a base of folk literature has also developed over the years. Most certainly, members of the families of individuals who are deaf might well consider learning and becoming proficient in ASL. Or, they might elect to learn another form of manual communication such as finger spelling instead. Regardless of the form chosen, to use a total communication approach requires proficiency in some form of manual communication.

Modern technology has allowed for the production of many different types of visual and tactile devices to assist people with hearing impairments. These are discussed later in this chapter. Family members need to become sophisticated consumers of technology. The entire family needs to learn how to use and incorporate a wide variety of technology into their environment, but more important, they need to evaluate its ease of use, functionality, and merit. As more technology becomes available, more items are available to buy, and the total cost of such equipment can become burdensome to already strained family budgets. (See also the Concepts and Controversies section in chapter 9 for more discussion on the topic of paying for technological aids.) Therefore, careful use of family resources must also become a factor when equipment is selected.

Although language, social and emotional development, and technology are important to the overall development of children with hearing impairments, possibly the most important factor in these children's lives is acceptance by their families. Although some parents and other family members (grandparents, siblings, and extended family members) adjust quickly to the demands presented by a child with a hearing impairment, some struggle with a wide range of emotions and reactions like grief, guilt, and anger (Proctor, n.d.). Support groups that include professionals, family, friends, and other parents of children with hearing impairments provide a healthy way to deal with these emotions. Somers (1984) states a useful objective for these parents and families: "think of the child as a normal child who has a hearing impairment, not a hearing handicap" (p. 186). To achieve this goal, family members must find the proper balance between nurturing, developing independence, setting limits, and disciplining the child. The result will be the development of a healthy self-concept in the child.

ADULTS WITH HEARING IMPAIRMENTS

What is life like for adults who are hearing impaired? As is the case with most other groups of people with handicaps, these adults often do not hold jobs commensurate with their education, skills, and experience (Jacobs, 1980). Many find themselves in a situation like that of Stephen Bielik. Mr. Bielik is a computer expert who has difficulty holding a job. He believes that his deafness makes some supervisors uncomfortable. When this happens, people with disabilities often get laid off, and finding a comparable job is not easy (Forbath, 1990). Regardless, earnings do rise with level of education. According to a study from the National Technical Institute for the Deaf, students who receive associate of arts degrees earn 43 percent more than those with no college degree (Walter, Welsh, and Serve, 1988). Graduates holding bachelor's degrees earn 83 percent more than students who did not graduate. College graduates also hold more professional and managerial jobs than those who did not complete their degrees (Walter and Welsh, 1988).

In addition, many adults who are deaf enroll in continuing education programs. Over forty universities and colleges offer continuing education courses designed for these adults. In 1985–1986 an estimated 35,000 adults who are deaf took continuing education courses, many of them offered through Gallaudet University (Commission on the Education of the Deaf, 1988). Clearly, this increased interest will result in more programs. The increased demand will also challenge state universities and their continuing education divisions to become more responsive to this group of adult learners. Continuing education will also have a marked effect on the earning power of those who are deaf. Increased skills bring increased wages (Walter, Welsh, and Serve, 1988; Walter and Welsh, 1988).

The regular and systematic use of interpreter services in all aspects of society assures that people with severe hearing impairments are not excluded from everyday public and private events.

Adults who are deaf are also concerned about their rights as individuals and citizens. They are calling for more involvement of adults who are deaf on school boards and boards of trustees, particularly at schools for the deaf. They also want to be included as parent trainers, teachers, and members of IEP committees. These adults desire access to their rights and responsibilities as American citizens. For example, the Council for the Deaf sued Los Angeles County because it refused to pay for an interpreter for a juror who was deaf. Now these services are available so people who are deaf can serve on juries (*Albuquerque Journal,* 1989). Schools also must now provide sign language interpreters for parents who are deaf, so they can participate at school (*Education of the Handicapped,* 1990). The mental health field is another area where persons with hearing impairments find access difficult. In the past, persons who are deaf had trouble finding psychiatrists or mental health specialists who know sign language. Although the incidence of mental illness is no higher in the deaf community than it is in mainstream society, availability of services is more limited. However, because of recent advocacy and awareness of these problems, clinics—such as one based in a Philadelphia hospital—are now hiring personnel familiar with the deaf culture and proficient in the use of ASL (Solomon, 1989).

A widely publicized example of the new power and cohesiveness of these adults was seen in the controversy at Gallaudet University in 1988. The student body of this college protested against the selection of a president who was not deaf and did not know sign language. The protest drew international attention. The students sought and achieved their aim of having I. King Jordan, who is deaf, installed as president. Their actions also brought about the recall of several members of the college's board of trustees.

Many adults who are deaf (Jacobs, 1980) and professionals who work with this group of people (Lane, 1989) believe that people who are deaf face considerable discrimination. Discrimination and bias can present real problems that affect individuals' livelihood. For example, Michael Cousins, who is deaf, was unable to get a job driving a commercial truck after finishing first in his class. State and federal laws prohibited those who are deaf from working in this occupation. These laws did not account for differences in individuals' skills, nor do they account for newly developed technology like sensors that warn drivers of emergency vehicles. They ban an entire group of people solely on the basis of their disability. So far, the state law has been overturned, and Mr. Cousins hopes that the federal law will be changed as well (Riddle, 1988). But the deaf community faces formidable obstacles. In fact, Jacobs (1980) believes that "the real ills of deaf people lie more with minority group dynamics than with their deafness, and that these problems will not cease until the attitude towards deafness by the hearing majority changes" (p. 135). (See also the Concepts and Controversies section in this chapter.) Attitudes are changing. We now see total communication being used in homes of children who are deaf but whose parents are not hearing impaired. We now see interpreters at most public meetings. Television shows have been created by persons who are deaf for an audience of persons who are deaf (for example, "Deaf Mosaic"), and the Theater of the Deaf seems to increase in popularity each year. These are all positive signs, but more changes need to come.

TECHNOLOGY AND HEARING IMPAIRMENTS

For some time, a variety of electronic devices have been available for deaf people. Lights and vibrators can signal a crying baby, a doorbell or telephone ringing, or a fire alarm. Technology has dramatically affected the opportunities for persons with hearing impairments. Read the story of Lynn's first few waking moments on one typical school morning for an illustration of this point.

> Lynn, a first-year law student, wakes up when her special alarm clock shakes her bed. She turns off the alarm, climbs out of bed, goes downstairs, puts some bread in the toaster, and turns on the television and closed captioned decoder so she can read the morning news subtitles. A few minutes later, a light in the kitchen begins to flash wildly. She knows this means her visual smoke detector has gone off—burnt toast again. (Compton and Kaplan, 1988, p. 19)

Such innovations have changed the way people with hearing impairments live their lives, and as other uses of technology are developed, their lives will continue to change. Lynn uses technological equipment designed to improve communication and enhance awareness of environmental sounds. Such equipment is called assistive devices (Compton and Kaplan, 1988). Assistive devices include three categories of equipment: assistive listening devices, telecommunication devices, and alerting devices.

The technology of hearing aids has certainly advanced since these early 1890 versions.

assistive listening devices (ALDs). Equipment, like hearing aids, which helps individuals with hearing impairments use their residual hearing.

hearing aid. A device that intensifies sound to help people with hearing impairments process information presented orally.

Assistive Listening Devices

Hearing aids and other equipment that help people make better use of their residual hearing are called **assistive listening devices (ALDs).** For those with hearing impairments, the hearing aid is the most commonly used electronic device. This piece of equipment amplifies sound so the person can hear it more easily. For some individuals with hearing impairments, hearing aids allow them to hear well within the normal range. It has, therefore, enabled many students who are hard of hearing to attend regular education classes. For many people with hearing impairments, however, hearing aids do not sufficiently correct their handicap. For some of these people, additional technology is helpful.

Hearing aids were designed to be used in quiet places, where speech is the dominant sound in the environment. However, even in classroom settings background noise competes with sounds a student might want to focus on. In other settings, such as lecture halls, auditoriums, and recreational centers, background noise can mask all other sounds. Typical hearing aids amplify all noise, so everything becomes louder. For individuals with sensorineural hearing losses, this means that sounds that are perceived well without a hearing aid are amplified at the same level as those that are heard only faintly. Newer versions of the hearing aid are always being developed, and one day an aid will correct these problems. Although not yet readily available, digital aids are able to automatically reduce or eliminate background noise. They also self-adjust to enhance frequencies within the speech range and match an individual's hearing abilities at different sound frequencies and intensities. As an essential tool, the hearing aid needs special care. Table 10.6 summarizes information about the care and handling of hearing aids. Parents and teachers need to help young children learn to respect and care for their equipment.

FM transmission devices.
Equipment used in many classes
for students who are severely hearing impaired that allows direct oral
transmissions from the teacher to
each individual student.

audio loop. A device that directs
sound from the source directly to
the listener's ear through a specially designed hearing aid.

TABLE 10.6. Care of a Hearing Aid
Avoid dust, dirt, humidity. Do not drop the hearing aid. Keep the ear mold clean. Avoid hair spray. Do not leave the hearing aid in a hot place. Have the aid checked frequently by audiologist.

For some time, **FM (frequency-modulated) transmission devices** (auditory trainers) have been used by teachers and students in classrooms. When using
auditory trainers, the teacher speaks into a microphone, and the sound is received
directly by each student's receiver or hearing aid. This system allows students to
profit more from instructors' lectures. Background noise is reduced and teachers may
move more freely around the classroom without worrying about always having their
faces in full view of all of their students.

An adaption of this system, the **audio loop,** is an ALD that directs sound from
its source directly to the listener's ear through a specially equipped hearing aid or
earphone. Sound may travel through a wire connection or by using radio waves.

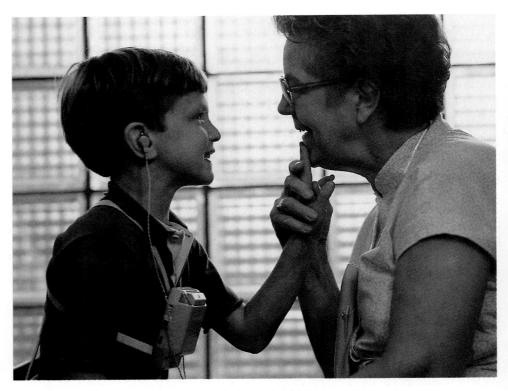

This student is using an FM transmission device during his language instruction.

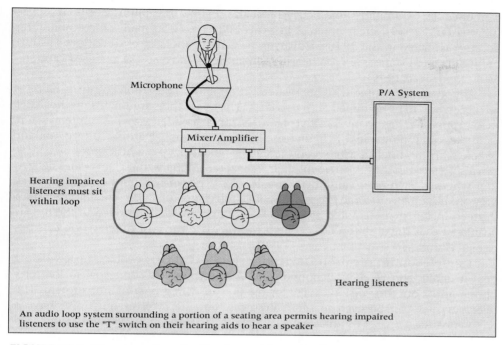

captions. Subtitles to print the words spoken in film or video, can be either closed or open.

open captions. Captions that appear on the television screen for all viewers to see.

closed captions. Captions are available for viewing, but can be seen on the television screen only with the use of a decoder.

Microphone

P/A System

Mixer/Amplifier

Hearing impaired listeners must sit within loop

Hearing listeners

An audio loop system surrounding a portion of a seating area permits hearing impaired listeners to use the "T" switch on their hearing aids to hear a speaker

FIGURE 10.6 Diagram of an Auditorium with an Audio Loop

SOURCE: Up close and personal: Assistive devices increase access to speech and sound, by C. L. Compton and H. Kaplan, 1988, *Gallaudet Today, 18,* p. 22.

Audio loops can be built into the walls of a room, as they are in some classrooms at Gallaudet University, or may be set up in a meeting room as the one in the diagram found in Figure 10.6.

Telecommunication Devices

Telecommunication and alerting devices are two types of assistive devices that take advantage of senses (sight, touch) other than hearing. Telecommunication devices use sight and hearing to improve communication and television listening.

Some years ago, **captions** were made available for television viewing. These are printed words that appear at the bottom of a TV screen like subtitles that translate foreign films. There are two kinds of captions: open and closed. **Open captions** are available for all viewers to see and were used with certain television programs in the 1970s. The "French Chef" with Julia Child was the first captioned television show; it appeared on public television in 1972. Because open captions were unpopular with the general public, **closed captions** became available in the 1980s. To view closed captions a person must connect the television set to a decoder.

Captioning is an important tool for people with severe to profound hearing losses. It allows them to have equal access to public information and entertainment. More than 125 hours of weekly television programming is now captioned (Commission on the Education of the Deaf, 1988). The Commission on the Education of the Deaf estimates that in 1987, more than 500,000 people in 150,000 homes watched

decoder. A device that allows closed captions to appear on a television screen.

Telecommunication Device for the Deaf (TDD). A piece of equipment that allows people to make and receive telephone calls by typing information over the telephone lines.

captioned TV. Although some believe that the quality of captions needs improvement (Clark, 1989), great progress in availability has been made since captioning became available in the 1970s. However, because of the cost of **decoders** ($200), only 10 percent of people with hearing impairments have access to closed captions (*New York Times,* 1990).

Advocates for people who are deaf have fought for legislation requiring all new television sets to be equipped with decoders. They base their arguments on the belief that captioning has many positive features for a broader viewing audience. For example, captioning might help increase literacy for people learning to read, and for people learning English as a second language. Older people who cannot hear well can also select captions to augment their TV listening. Finally, these advocates believe that when everything is captioned, people who are deaf will not be stigmatized as they are now. The outcome is now a law: All television sets with screens larger than thirteen inches manufactured after 1993 will have decoders installed in them. It is estimated that the addition of decoders will increase the cost of television sets between $3 and $10 (*New York Times,* 1990).

The **Telecommunication Device for the Deaf (TDD)** enables those who are deaf to make and receive telephone calls. A teletypewriter connected to the telephone prints out the voice message for the person with a hearing impairment. The teletypewriter can be used to send messages, but the receiver must also have a teletypewriter. This is, of course, a major drawback. However, newer, more advanced TDDs may solve this problem. The newer models use a microcomputer to turn the printed message into a voice message. Until these are available to the public, telephone relay systems are being developed in many communities to allow persons who are deaf to use the phone for everything from calling the doctor to ordering a pizza. When the person who is deaf uses a TDD in a relay system, an operator at a relay center places the call on a voice line and reads the typed message to the nonTDD user. A full conversation can be made using a relay system. Many businesses are adding TDDs to their workplaces. For example, TIAA-CREF, a large retirement plan company, has installed a TDD in their main office so policyholders who have TDDs can communicate directly with their agents. The benefits of the TDD system are remarkable. Soon, the speech of one person will be translated automatically into print for the person who is deaf and a person with unintelligible speech can type his or her message and have that synthesized into speech for the hearing receiver. Certainly, the future will see two-way systems of print-to-audio and audio-to-print communication.

DeafNet and Disabilities Forum are computer networks that provide electronic mail for people who are deaf. These network systems work like all other forms of electronic mail where individuals or groups can subscribe to a communication system that transfers printed messages to subscribers. Electronic mail allows individuals and groups with common interests to communicate by using computers and information sent over telephone lines. Smith (1988) reports that many students at Gallaudet enjoy using BITNET, a large international network of over 2000 computers housed at colleges, universities, and the federal government. Another advance that may benefit many individuals with severe to profound hearing impairments is the work currently under way to use computers to help students develop better speech (Mahshie, 1988). The intelligibility of their speech is a major problem for many people who are deaf (Allen, 1988). Researchers are developing gamelike instructional programs that will give people, through a video screen display, visual feedback of their sound productions. These programs can assist people in adjusting various aspects of speech such as pitch and loudness.

Alerting Devices

Alerting devices make people who are deaf become aware of an event or important sound in their environment. A flashing light, loud gong, or vibration can signal a fire alarm, doorbell, or telephone. The number of different alerting devices increases each year. One recently developed piece of equipment is the Quest Pager, which vibrates a wristband to signal or page the person wearing it (Smith, 1988).

The number of such devices that could be developed are only limited by our imaginations. Unfortunately, access to these helpful devices is also limited by finances. Although the cost of many individual technological devices has decreased over the years, the overall cost increases as more equipment is developed. For example, a speech synthesizer costs about $150, but you need a microcomputer to use with it. A decoder for captioned television costs $200. A TDD costs between $150 to $700, and altering signaling systems costs between $20 and $500 each. A hearing aid costs about $500, and cochlear implants cost about $20,000. As we discussed earlier, many adults who are deaf are underemployed because of their impairments. Over the course of even a few years, the expense of equipment can be overwhelming. (See Concepts and Controversies in chapter 9 for other points of view on this subject.)

> **alerting devices.** Devices that use sight, sound, or vibration to make individuals aware of an occurrence or an important sound.

Concepts and Controversies

Paternalistic Attitudes Held in Society

Harlan Lane, in a provocative article (1988), discusses the paternalistic attitude that American society has about people who are deaf. He defines paternalism as "a system under which an authority undertakes to supply the needs and regulate the conduct of those under its control" (p. 8). Under a paternalistic system, the benefactors perceive that others need their help, and the beneficiaries are forced into submissive roles that result in the necessity of the benefactors' dominance. He maintains hat these systems often become tense, dynamic relationships. The benefactors often do not understand the beneficiaries and cannot control them. The beneficiaries do not want this relationship. Lane believes that many persons who are deaf find themselves in a benefactor/beneficiary situation. Lane draws parallels between the situation of people who are deaf and that of Africans during periods of European colonial rule.

As one way to illustrate his point, Lane compares the words used by Burundi's Belgian rulers with those used in the professional literature about people who are deaf. For example, the European colonials described African people they colonialized as barbaric, depraved, impulsive, lazy, childlike, and servile. Terms used in the professional literature to describe people who are deaf include dependent, rigid, impulsive, stubborn, naive, and unfeeling. Such terms portray individuals who are deaf negatively and without basis in fact. Lane suggests that the use of these terms justifies the benefactors' roles of protection and involvement in their lives. After all, if either group of people were described as self-reliant, independent, mature, and smart, the benefactors would be unnecessary.

Lane continues his thesis to explain why the hearing community is so adamantly opposed to people who are deaf using sign language. Lane maintains:

> Like the colonizers and the colonized, the hearing establishment serving deaf people and deaf people themselves have two different points of view, two different conceptions of deaf people, and two radically different agendas . . . the half-million deaf Americans for whom this is a primary language believe it is the equal of English as a natural language and superior for instructing and communicating with deaf people. The hearing experts are frequently opposed to deaf teachers and block their entry into the profession; organizations of deaf people think they would be as good or better than hearing teachers and seek their admission.

> The truth is that there is a deep conflict between deaf people and those who profess to serve them in America. The fundamental divergence is that hearing experts generally do not concede to deaf people a major say in the conduct of deaf affairs, especially as their ideas are so contrary; deaf Americans, on the other hand do not see why hearing people should have the determining say in matters of deafness. So it is with the colonizers and the colonized.*

Using Lane's argument, draw parallels between the concept of benefactors and the student protests at Gallaudet. Can you think of other situations that can be explained by Lane's thesis?

SUMMARY

Most of us communicate with others through a process of telling and listening. This is one important way that we learn about the world we live in, subjects at school, and others' perspectives on issues and concerns. Those of us whose hearing is impaired have a more restricted ability to communicate, a difference that should determine the way these students are taught, the content of their curricula, and the related services they require for an appropriate education.

1. All hearing losses are significant. However, the severity of the hearing loss and the age when the loss occurs are two important factors that influence individuals' abilities to communicate with others orally and learn through traditional instructional methods. School-age children with hearing impairments can be divided into two groups: the deaf and the hard of hearing. The deaf are also divided into two groups. Those who are prelingually deaf typically lost their hearing at, during, or before birth, and those who lost their hearing after they had acquired some language are called adventitiously deaf.

2. There are two types of hearing losses: conductive and sensorineural. Conductive losses result in a flat profile on an audiogram, respond best to the use of hearing aids, and are caused by damage to the middle or outer ear. Conductive losses are also easier to correct using current medical technology. Sensorineural hearing losses are caused by damage to the inner ear or the auditory nerve (the eighth cranial nerve) and result in an uneven profile on an audiogram.

---

*Excerpted from "Is There a Psychology of the Deaf?" *Exceptional Children,* 1988, *55,* 7–19, by Horace Lane.

3. Hearing losses range in severity from mild to profound. Typically, students who are hard of hearing (with mild to moderate losses) profit from the use of hearing aids. With appropriate support systems, this group of students benefit from traditional educational programs. They attend their local, neighborhood schools with their nondisabled peers. They are taught by regular education teachers in classes where the standard curriculum is presented. Many of these students, however, need additional services from a variety of specialists: speech/language pathologists, audiologists, special education teachers. They may require some accommodations (seating assignments, handouts, peer assistance) to succeed in regular education classes. Also, their regular education teachers might need some guidance or training from a consulting teacher or speech/language pathologist. An expert, knowledgeable about hearing impairments, can be an important resource to both the teacher and the student.

4. Students with severe to profound hearing losses are often referred to as deaf. They can present a challenge to their families and teachers. Most of these individuals became disabled before they acquired language, so their abilities to develop speech and language were affected. They need very special educational experiences from the time their handicap is diagnosed.

5. Early intervention programs, where specialists work with both the infant or toddler and the family, help the child learn skills and the family adjust to the child's needs. They educate family members about speech, language, cognitive, and social development. Family members learn ways to encourage such development in children with severe and profound hearing losses. Children who are deaf, for example, do not develop language without effort. For many a total communication environment—where manual communication (sign language) and speech are used—results in the infant learning more because all channels available to send and receive information are used. For those who are not deaf themselves, implementing this approach requires the family to learn a new communication system. The family, as well as the preschool program, work as a team to provide an educational program that lasts all day long, every day.

6. Educational programs for students who are deaf must have special features. The students require intensive instruction to learn how to communicate with others effectively as well as to learn academic subjects. For many, developing intelligible speech is difficult. For most, academic achievement is not a guaranteed outcome of their educational programs. Because there are so many educational goals for these students, and limited instructional time, academic instruction often becomes a secondary goal. Professionals in this field also debate about the best communication mode to use when educating these youngsters. Some educators still maintain that the oral-only approach, not as popular today as in the past, is best because it stresses developing the students' facility with oral language. Others advocate the manual approach, where students are taught American Sign Language (ASL) as their native language and learn English as a second language. The majority today support the use of the total communication approach, in which signs support speech.

7. Many individuals who are deaf lead very productive lives. Many go to college or postsecondary schools. Those graduating hold higher paying and more prestigious jobs than those who do not graduate. A great number seek continuing education throughout their adulthood. Unfortunately, the support services needed for more to have successful educational and vocational experiences are not always available and the postsecondary dropout rate remains high. With future advances in technology, medicine, and improved educational services, more persons with deafness and severe hearing impairments will be prepared to be more active members of our society.

8. Technology has had a great impact on the lives of people with hearing impairments. First, assistive listening devices such as hearing aids allow many persons with mild to moderate losses to function independently in environments where oral communication is dominant. The hearing aid is continually being refined to accommodate individuals' specific hearing abilities. Second, telecommunication devices help individuals use both their sight and their hearing to improve communication and television listening. Certainly, the availability of captioned television has greatly broadened the world of those who are deaf. Finally, alerting devices help these people become aware of sounds and events in their environments by means other than sound. No doubt technological advances will continue at a remarkable rate in the coming years, and the diversity and availability of assistive devices will increase as well.

DISCUSSION QUESTIONS

1. List some technological advances that have helped persons who are deaf. Brainstorm other advances that might occur in the future that will assist these individuals at school and in daily life.

2. What are some common educational characteristics of persons who are deaf? How are these characteristics different for students who are hard of hearing? List the differences.

3. We discussed that many adults who are deaf are underemployed. Much of the new equipment and technology being developed is expensive and, therefore, unavailable to many of these individuals. How might local communities, states, and the federal government arrive at creative solutions to this problem?

4. This chapter presented several discussions about three different approaches to the education of the deaf—oral only, manual communication, and total communication. Consider all of the data presented. Which position do you advocate? Does your decision affect educational placement recommendations? If so, how?

5. People who are deaf are asking for more of a role in decisions made for and about them. In this chapter, we discussed two cases where the deaf community disagrees with others—the interpretation of the legal concept of least restrictive environment and the use of sign language. How do you think such disagreements should be resolved?

SUPPLEMENTARY BOOKS AND VIDEOS

Over the years people with hearing impairments have been included in fictional and nonfictional roles in both books and films. Below is a listing of such creative works that you might find of interest.

Books

Greenberg, J. (1988). *Of such small differences*. New York: Henry Holt & Company.

Kisor, H. (1990). *What's that pig outdoors? A memoir of deafness*. New York: Hill & Wang.

McCullers, C. (1970). *The heart is a lonely hunter*. New York: Bantam.

Sacks, D. (1989). *Seeing voices*. Berkeley: University of California Press.

Walker, L. A. (1986). *A loss for words: The story of deafness in a family*. New York: Harper & Row.

Videos

The videos listed below are available at many video rental stores. In addition, the television series "Deaf Mosaic," produced by Gallaudet University, is available through many cable networks nationally.

The miracle worker. (1962). United Artists.

The heart is a lonely hunter (1968). Warner Brothers/7 Arts.

Tin man (1983). Montage Films.

Children of a lesser god (1986). Paramount Pictures.

See no evil, hear no evil (1989). Tri-Star.

ALFREDO SERRANO, 15, was a recipient of one of the New Jersey Governor's Awards in Arts Education in 1988. A student at P.S. 32 High School in Jersey City, Alfredo has a learning disability. Many of his works have been exhibited throughout New Jersey, and he currently has paintings on display in the permanent Student Art Collection at the Jersey City Museum.

Chapter Eleven

PHYSICAL DISABILITIES AND HEALTH IMPAIRMENTS

*L*earning
Objectives

After studying this chapter, you should be able to:

- List the most common physical disabilities and health impairments in children

- Describe several ways in which physical disabilities could be prevented

- Describe five ways to minimize the effects of a child's absences from school

- Describe examples of high technology and low technology that might assist a child with physical disabilities or health impairments

- List the appropriate steps for helping a child who is having a seizure

*D*r. Paul Longmore, forty-four, is a historian and writer. Awarded an Andrew W. Mellon postdoctoral fellowship in the humanities, he is currently conducting research and teaching history at Stanford University. When he was seven years old, he contracted polio and has had a physical disability since then. The polio caused a severe curvature of his spine: When he lies down he must use a ventilator in order to breathe. He has no use of his arms, but can use his right hand. The damage caused by the polio has led to arthritis and as a result pain in Dr. Longmore's joints that increases as he gets older.

As a child, Longmore missed almost three years of school. For most of second grade, all of third grade, half of fifth grade, and half of sixth grade he was hospitalized for surgery, extensive therapy, or home in bed recuperating. *How did the long hospitalizations affect his schooling?*

I was affected in several ways, positive and negative. Academically, I became a very strong reader. My father had already taught me to read when I was four years old. When I became sick, because reading was something I could do independently and in bed, I read all the time. But to this day, I am poor in math and science. I missed so much math instruction—and I could not pick it up on my own—that I have never caught up.

Socially, the long absences really affected my interpersonal skills. Being by myself during those years, without any real connection to school and other children, I missed the opportunities and experiences that other children have to develop socially.

Psychologically, one of the biggest effects of the polio was that when I came back to school, I was ashamed of my body. Already I was getting clear messages that I was a less valued person because my body was damaged by the polio. For example, I hated having my picture taken. Every time my father tried to take a picture of me I ruined it by sticking my tongue out.

The overall effect of my physical disability was that I grew up so fast. As a very young child I faced difficult issues that most people don't have to face until they are quite old, if at all. I faced terrible sickness, isolation, pain, loss of independence, major changes in my body, and I even faced death. I had to contend with many adults, particularly medical professionals, who tried to control every part of my life, including whether I ate the Jello on my tray. Those struggles to gain autonomy taught me to trust my own judgment about what was best for me. They made me more independent-minded.

The emotional crises of hospitalizations and having to live with a disability caused me to be brutally honest with myself. You can't afford illusions when you have a major disability. At the same time, some adults treated me as though I was emotionally fragile, though I knew I was strong after what I had been through. Many adults also treated me as though I were incompetent and unintelligent. They underestimated me intellectually and emotionally. At every stage, I was given the message that I was less valued, less competent.

In elementary school, other students sometimes ridiculed me. As a teenager, I was devalued romantically. But the whole disability experience taught me to pay close attention to my own feelings and to read others' feelings.

Dr. Longmore also discussed his interaction with classmates:

I was in a separate special education room for several years in elementary school, ate at a separate lunch table, had different recess times, and was separated in many other ways. I remember thinking that I was 'segregated' and 'discriminated against' because of my disability, even before those words were introduced in the disability area. I remember, as an adolescent, first realizing the terrible impact of prejudice.

But, thanks to a sensitive special education teacher, the separation did not continue. At the end of sixth grade, when it came time to enter junior high school, Miss Gustafson called me over to her desk one day and said, 'You are a pioneer. If you don't succeed in the regular junior high school, they won't give these other children a chance.' I felt proud. Later, some of my friends have suggested that was too much burden to put on a young boy with a severe disability, but I have always appreciated the faith and trust she placed in me that day. I liked that feeling of responsibility.

We asked Dr. Longmore what accommodations he needed as a student and what advice he would give teachers who work with students who have physical disabilities and health impairments.

The accommodations were rather informal. Three friends from my church were given the same class schedule that I had and they would help with physical things like opening my locker, getting books out of my book bag, moving papers, and getting my lunch. My advice to teachers: Treat each child as an individual; pay attention to the child's uniqueness. Different individuals react differently to physical disabilities and health impairments, and need different things at different times. So, listen to the child. Remember that these children are struggling with the stigma of disability in addition to their physical problems, so you have to be sensitive to their attempts to negotiate their own identity as they grow up.

I think that the biggest problem is that children with disabilities are shut out of the experiences and opportunities that other children have and that allow human growth, the development of feelings of competence, and taking control of one's life. But children with disabilities, even if they can't have the *identical* experiences and opportunities that other children have, can have *versions* of those experiences. Children with disabilities can do things differently. It takes creativity on the part of the teacher and the child to provide the growth experiences and opportunities that all children need.

1. What was the longest period of time you were ever absent from school? What were your feelings when you returned? If you felt uncomfortable, how could a teacher have helped make your return more comfortable?

2. Why do you think issues of independence are so important to people with physical disabilities and health impairments?

3. Physical disabilities are a social experience in addition to a physical experience. How might the social climate of a school be improved for students with physical disabilities and health impairments?

4. Dr. Longmore believes that being shut out of experiences and opportunities is the biggest problem for children with disabilities. Why might that affect children so negatively?

Physical disabilities and health impairments should not cause individuals to be shut out of experiences and opportunities.

Our society seems obsessed with beauty and physical fitness. We are urged to purchase certain styles of clothes, special cosmetics and hair products, new exercise equipment, and even cars to make ourselves more attractive. Have you noticed messages about physical perfection in television shows, commercials, music videos, and movies? Have you heard your friends assign popularity ratings to others on the basis of physical appearance?

Sometimes we equate physical perfection with virtue or goodness, and equate imperfection with evil. Think, for example, of the characters in the story of *The Wizard of Oz*. Do you remember the beautiful Good Witch Glinda and the deformed Wicked Witch of the East? That symbolism has been repeated in many books and movies, including *The Hunchback of Notre Dame, Dark Crystal,* and *Star Wars* (see generally, Fiedler, 1978; Bogdan, 1988). You can list many more examples.

Children whose health is precarious often do not conform to the standards of strength and energy emphasized by the fashion, advertising, and sports and entertainment industries and so admired by our society. Unfortunately, the prejudices of society frequently are reflected in schools as well. Children whose appearance is unusual because of deformities or muscle problems, or whose ability to walk, not to mention to move athletically, is challenged by wheelchairs or braces may suffer prejudice and discrimination in school. Children who are unable to communicate verbally may find, even after learning to communicate skillfully with a computer or other device, that the people around them are too embarrassed or impatient to converse with them.

How can educators eliminate these prejudices in order to provide appropriate learning environments for all children? How can educators address the individual learning needs of children with health impairments and physical disabilities? We will consider these and many other issues in this chapter. First, we will describe the most common physical disabilities and health impairments. We will review the physical disabilities and health impairments most frequently encountered in school. They are HIV infection, asthma, cytomegalovirus, seizure disorders, cerebral palsy, spina bifida, spinal cord defects, traumatic brain injury, polio, muscular dystrophy, and multiple sclerosis. Many other conditions cannot be discussed here because of space limitations. However, when teachers welcome a student with a physical disability or health impairment, the student, family and physician, and other professionals in the school can give important information about the child's condition and ways in which the teacher can help assure an appropriate education for the child.

PHYSICAL DISABILITIES AND HEALTH IMPAIRMENTS DEFINED

A child with a physical disability has a problem with the structure or functioning of the body. A child with a health impairment has a limitation on the body's physical well-being that requires ongoing medical attention. In order to benefit from education these children require special services in school. These special services may include special teaching, scheduling, counseling, therapies, equipment, and technology. Children with physical disabilities and health impairments may be absent frequently from school because of fragile health or medical treatments. They may need special leg braces or wheelchairs; they may need adaptive equipment such as swivel spoons or pencils with extra grips; they may have physical needs such as assistance with medications, or with bladder catheterization, or during seizures. Some may present potential emergencies in which the teacher will be required to be familiar with emergency techniques. Some of these children also will face powerful emotional issues, such as their impending death or continuous physical dependence, many years before their young friends must face such issues.

Children with physical disabilities and health impairments generally fit within two categories discussed in the Individuals with Disabilities Education Act (IDEA): orthopedically impaired and other health impaired.

IDEA defines orthopedically impaired as

> [having] a severe **orthopedic** impairment which adversely affects a child's educational performance. The term includes impairments caused by congenital anomaly (e.g., clubfoot, absence of some member, etc.), impairments caused by disease (e.g., poliomyelitis, bone tuberculosis, etc.), and impairments from other causes (e.g., cerebral palsy, amputations, and fractures or burns which cause contractures). (section 300.5(6))

Other health impaired is defined as

> having limited strength, vitality or alertness, due to chronic or acute health problems such as a heart condition, tuberculosis, rheumatic fever, nephritis, asthma,

orthopedic. Related to a physical deformity or disability of the skeletal system and associated motor function.

neuromuscular. Involving both nerve and muscle, as in a neurological problem that affects the muscles, such as muscular dystrophy.

hydrocephaly. A condition in which excess cerebrospinal fluid is collected in the ventricles of the brain and can lead to an enlarged head.

sickle cell anemia, hemophilia, or diabetes, which adversely affects a child's educational performance. (section 300.5(7))

Some children's physical disabilities or health impairments appear in combination with other disabilities such as communication disorders or mental retardation. These children are often considered multiply handicapped. IDEA uses the term multihandicapped to mean impairments that coexist, or accompany each other (concomitant impairments):

> concomitant impairments (such as mentally retarded–blind, mentally retarded–orthopedically impaired, etc.), the combination of which causes such severe educational problems that they cannot be accommodated in special education programs solely for one of the impairments. The term does not include deaf-blind children. (section 300.5(5))

In this chapter, we will discuss three major types of physical disabilities and health impairments. These are (1) *impairments of health and diseases* such as asthma, cystic fibrosis, and HIV infection; (2) *neurological impairments,* in which the spinal cord or brain are damaged, such as spina bifida, cerebral palsy, and seizure disorders; and (3) **neuromuscular diseases** such as polio, muscular dystrophy, and multiple sclerosis. There is great diversity among these disabilities, perhaps more diversity than among any of the other disabilities treated in the chapters in this textbook.

The organization in this chapter on physical disabilities and health impairments reflects current understanding of their causes and effects. In the past, these disabilities were organized in other ways. For example, in earlier textbooks, because autism was believed to be a form of mental retardation, it might have been found in a chapter on mental retardation. Before the 1990 amendments to IDEA, autism was considered a type of physical disability or health impairment and would have been included in a chapter on physical disabilities. We discuss autism in chapter 8, Behavioral Disorders and Emotional Disturbance, because it is now a separate category in IDEA and because many of the special education intervention techniques used to teach individuals with autism are similar to techniques used with individuals with behavioral disorders and emotional disturbance. Similarly, because children with spina bifida often did not receive medical treatment for **hydrocephaly** (excess fluid collected in the brain) and frequently became mentally retarded, discussion would have been found in the chapter on mental retardation. Because students with cerebral palsy typically have difficulty with speech and often are difficult to understand, they were often misclassified as mentally retarded. While cerebral palsy is sometimes found in students with mental retardation, we have chosen to organize it within the chapter on physical disabilities since it is primarily a physical impairment.

Measurement

The measurement of physical disabilities and health impairments in individual students is extremely complex and requires input from many different professionals. Each professional uses a wide variety of assessment tools and techniques. A complete evaluation for a child with cerebral palsy, for example, would include a physician's evaluation, an evaluation by physical therapists and occupational therapists, evaluations by other professionals such as SLPs and technology experts (depending on the nature and severity of the physical disability), as well as a thorough academic, vocational, and intellectual evaluation by teachers and diagnosticians. The area of physical disability and health impairments, perhaps more than any other special education area, demands ongoing collaboration by practitioners from many professions for proper assessment and appropriate education.

Significance

Students with physical disabilities and health impairments must face many challenges. Physical disabilities and health impairments are often obvious, even at first meeting. As a consequence, individuals with these disabilities are forced to deal with the often negative or stereotypical reactions of others in addition to their own feelings about their appearance. They must also address the actual physical and medical requirements of their disabilities and accomplish the tasks of school and daily life. Special educators can help these youngsters meet these important challenges and shape satisfying lives for themselves.

Students with physical disabilities and health impairments, because of severe limitations on their mobility, communication, and energy, frequently require the assistance of many professionals over the entire course of their lives to maintain health and live independently. Special educators play an important collaborative role in providing the services the students need.

HISTORY OF THE FIELD

The history of physical disabilities and health impairments is as long as human history. Anthropologists have discovered skeletons with physical disabilities in grave sites over 11,000 years old (Frayer, 1987). The history of treatment is as long. Records of treatment for spinal cord injuries go back to prehistoric times (Maddox, 1987). The earliest documented treatment was the application of meat and honey to the neck. Beginning with Hippocrates (400 B.C.), treatment usually included traction or even a stretching rack to attempt to straighten the back or push in the deformity. Spinal surgery was used around A.D. 600, even though it was not until the mid-1800s that anesthesia became available and sterile techniques began to be used. Even with these medical advances, people with spinal cord injuries generally died soon after their injuries. New techniques of treatment and rehabilitation were not developed until World War II. These helped many more people survive their spinal cord injuries and their medical treatment.

Ancient descriptions of conditions such as cerebral palsy and epilepsy can be found. For example, William J. Little, an English surgeon, described the condition now known as cerebral palsy in well-researched case studies in 1861. Hippocrates recognized that epilepsy originated in the brain, but believed that it was caused by several factors: blockage of the normal passage of "phlegm" from the brain, cold phlegm being discharged into warm blood, and unequal heat distribution in the brain by sitting too long in the sun (Scheerenberger, 1983). Epilepsy continued to receive attention through the middle ages. It was frequently linked to mental retardation and individuals who exhibited epileptic seizures were treated in the same manner as those who exhibited mental retardation. Like mental retardation and behavioral disorders, epilepsy was often wrongly believed to have been caused by immoral conduct by the mother or evil possession of the individual.

The first American educational institution for children with physical disabilities was established in Boston in 1893: the Industrial School for Crippled and Deformed

Children (Eberle, 1922). The first public school classes for "crippled children" were established in Chicago at the turn of the century (La Vor, 1976). Later, schools were established in New York City, Philadelphia, and Cleveland.

While children with physical disabilities and other health impairments have always been with us, the causes of these disabilities and teachers' responsibilities have changed over the years. Concerns were different depending on factors such as the overall health status of children in society, the ability of medicine and science to address certain health problems, and general views toward children and health. For example, a text published in 1948, *Helping Handicapped Children in School* (Dolch, 1948), included chapters titled "Crippled Children" and "Health Handicaps." The chapter on crippled children focused primarily on heart trouble caused by rheumatic fever, measles, scarlet fever, and diphtheria. These diseases, once common, are now rare. Even when children get them, today the damage can usually be limited by the use of antibiotics and other medical advances. But other causes of physical disabilities now demand our attention. Dolch's 1948 chapter on "crippled children" closes by urging the prevention of physical disabilities by decreasing the accident rate, and by prenatal and obstetrical care for all mothers and medical care for all children—pleas that continue to be heard today. The chapter on health handicaps also addressed issues that were a sign of their time: infected and decayed teeth, chronic cold and bronchitis, glandular problems, tuberculosis, and malnutrition. While some of these problems are now less frequent in children, others may again be on the rise as more children live in poverty and unsafe circumstances.

The U.S. Congress passed significant legislation in this area after World War I and World War II. The Soldiers' Rehabilitation Act was passed in 1918 to offer vocational rehabilitation services to wounded soldiers. Two years later a similar law for civilians with physical disabilities was passed: the Citizens Vocational Rehabilitation Act (La Vor, 1976). (People with mental illness and mental retardation were not added to this law until 1943.) Additional advances were made following other wars such as the Vietnam War. Soldiers returned with physical war injuries so serious that employers, family members, friends, and the individuals forced major changes in order to reintegrate them into society. In 1965 the National Commission on Architectural Barriers was established to study the problems facing people with physical disabilities.

In the last twenty years, disability has come to be understood in political terms (Kriegel, 1969). People with physical disabilities have played an important part in changing the political, legal, and social climate for all individuals with disabilities. For example, although Section 504 of the Rehabilitation Act (prohibiting discrimination) had passed in 1973, it was not until a wheelchair sit-in in the office of Secretary Califano at the Department of Health, Education and Welfare (now Health and Human Services) four years later that the implementing regulations were passed. The passage of the Americans with Disabilities Act in 1990 is another example of the important role people with physical disabilities have played in improving society's response to all people with disabilities.

PREVALENCE

According to the *Twelfth Annual Report to Congress on Implementation of the Education of the Handicapped Act*, approximately 1 percent (41,514) of all children receiving special education services are categorized as orthopedically impaired; another 1.2

percent (46,639) have other health impairments. Thus, only approximately 2.2 percent of all children receiving special education services fall within the categories discussed in this chapter. We mentioned earlier that some children with physical disabilities and health impairments have coexisting disabilities that may cause them to be categorized as multihandicapped. The *Twelfth Annual Report to Congress* indicates that 1.6 percent (65,096) of children were in this category. As we discuss specific disabilities in this chapter, we will indicate the prevalence rate for each.

CAUSES AND PREVENTION OF PHYSICAL DISABILITIES AND HEALTH IMPAIRMENTS

Many physical disabilities and health impairments are relatively easy to prevent. Even if the condition cannot be totally prevented, the disabling effects can be lessened. For example, spinal cord injury in young children is most often caused by automobile accidents or child abuse. (A common site of spinal cord dislocation is in the lower back due to the effects of spanking.) The use of child restraints and safety belts can prevent many automobile accident injuries. Family support services and training in effective parenting techniques can help parents understand the harmful physical as well as emotional effects of physical punishment. In older children and adults, the most common causes of spinal cord injury are car accidents, falls and jumps, gunshot wounds, and diving accidents. Table 11.1 lists some common causes

TABLE 11.1. Causes and Prevention of Physical Disabilities

Motor vehicle accidents	Child restraints
	Safety belts
	Auto air bags
	Motorcycle helmets
Water and diving accidents	Diving safety
	Swimming safety
	Flotation devices
	Supervision
Gunshot wounds	Gun control and weapons training
Sports injuries (boxing, skiing, football)	Headgear
	Safe fields and slopes
	Conditioning/training
Child abuse	Family support services
	Parenting training
Poisoning/toxins	Safe storage of poisons
Diseases such as polio, measles	Vaccination
Premature birth	Prenatal care of mother
	Health care for infant
Prenatal disabilities	Prenatal diagnosis
	Prenatal treatment
HIV Infection	Abstinence or safe sex
	Avoid drugs, do not share drug equipment
Genetic disabilities	Genetic screening
	Protection from head injuries
Seizures	Medication
Hydrocephaly	Medical care and shunts

cystic fibrosis. A disorder of chronic lung infections and malabsorption of food.

acquired immunodeficiency syndrome (AIDS). A usually fatal medical syndrome caused by infection with human immunodeficiency virus.

TABLE 11.2. Possible Signs or Characteristics of Physical Disabilities and Health Impairments

Limited vitality and energy
Many school absences
Need for physical accommodations to participate in school activities
Physical presence but mental "absence"
Poor motor coordination
Frequent falls
Speech difficult to understand

---

and preventive measures of physical disabilities and health impairments. Table 11.2 lists some possible signs of physical disabilities and health impairments.

PROFILE OF CHILDREN WITH PHYSICAL DISABILITIES AND HEALTH IMPAIRMENTS: THREE CATEGORIES

In this section we will review three categories of physical disabilities and health impairments: (1) health impairments; (2) neurological impairments; and (3) neuromuscular impairments. For the major conditions within these categories we will discuss definition, incidence and prevalence, causes, prevention, and treatment.

Health Impairments

Conditions within the category of health impairments include fragile health, chronic diseases such as asthma and **cystic fibrosis,** and communicable diseases such as tuberculosis and cytomegalovirus (CMV). One of the most significant health impairments of children today is HIV infection. In this section we discuss HIV infection, asthma, and CMV infection.

HIV INFECTION. Human immunodeficiency virus (HIV) is a potentially fatal viral infection transmitted primarily through exchange of bodily fluids in unprotected sex or by contaminated needles. It is the virus responsible for the deadly **acquired immunodeficiency syndrome** (AIDS) and can be communicated to a child by an infected mother. Before blood-screening procedures were instituted, the virus was also transmitted in blood transfusions. The effects of the infection in children include central nervous system damage, additional infections, developmental delay, motor problems, psychosocial stresses, and death.

The number of infants and children with HIV infection increases every year. In 1988 the Centers for Disease Control reported 1065 cases of pediatric AIDS in the United States. Of those reported, 839 were infants and 226 were adolescents. Children with AIDS currently represent less than 2 percent of the total number of persons with AIDS, but their numbers are increasing dramatically. The Surgeon General of the United States estimates that perhaps two to three times that number of children are actually infected with HIV and predicts 3000 cases by 1991. Others predict much larger numbers, perhaps as many as 10,000 to 20,000. Clearly, an increasing number of children and adults will be infected by HIV until a cure is found and until more people refrain from high-risk behaviors or use preventive techniques.

In children under the age of thirteen, the cause of HIV infection can be traced primarily to the risk behaviors of their parents. Approximately 75 percent acquired the infection from their mothers before or at the time of birth, while 20 percent acquired the infection from blood transfusions. In contrast, the HIV infections of adolescents are caused primarily by their own risk behaviors.

How do we treat children with HIV infection? The treatment includes medical care, education, and developmental services. Many professionals are concerned about the risk to themselves as they work with children with HIV infection. Crocker and Cohen (1988) offer the following recommendations to allay their concerns:

1. There is not a serious concern regarding transmission of HIV infection in the setting of usual developmental services.

2. General admission [to services] is the expectation for the child with HIV infection.

3. Activities and handling for these children should be basically normal, consistent with their developmental status and personal health.

4. Caution is necessary regarding the known special susceptibility of such children to additional infections.

5. Improved attention to good hygienic practices is appropriate in all child care activities, including the generous use of handwashing; gloves are not necessary for schoolwork, therapy, feeding, diaper-changing, physical examination, or developmental assessment; bloody fluids deserve particular respect.

6. HIV antibody testing is not a usual component of the admission process; sharing of diagnostic information is limited by strict confidentiality requirements.

7. Individual programs should establish internal policy committees and staff training activities, with involvement of expert consultants as needed. (pp. 25–26)

Children with HIV infections participate in integrated developmental services and education.

asthma. A chronic condition of difficulty in breathing.

epilepsy (convulsive disorders). A tendency to recurrent seizures.

seizure. A spontaneous abnormal discharge of the electrical impulses of the brain.

ASTHMA.   One common type of severe difficulty in breathing is **asthma.** A person with asthma usually has labored, wheezing breathing that is sometimes accompanied by shortness of breath and a cough (Harvey, 1982). A combination of three events causes the wheezing: (1) tightening of the muscles around the bronchial tubes; (2) swelling of the tissues in these tubes; and (3) an increase of secretions in these tubes.

Asthma is one of the most common chronic diseases of children and is frequently encountered in the classroom. Harvey (1982) estimates that at least 2.5 percent of children have asthma.

The basic causes of asthma are unknown. Asthma is believed to be an allergic reaction to certain substances (allergens) in individuals who have a physical predisposition to asthma. The substances that can cause allergic reactions vary by individual; for some people it may be foods, for others plants or environmental pollutants.

A major aspect in the treatment of asthma is to eliminate the allergens from the child's environment. This may mean that the student will require special precautions concerning the air in the classroom, as well as restrictions on playing outdoors during recess, playing with classroom pets, eating certain foods (chocolate is an allergen for many people), and handling certain teaching materials. Considerations during an asthma attack are also necessary. Consultation with the student, the family, and the physician is necessary to monitor medications and to plan procedures for assisting the child during an attack.

CYTOMEGALOVIRUS (CMV).   Cytomegalovirus, a virus of the herpes group, is extremely common. Approximately 40 percent of children and most adults have been infected with the virus (Taylor and Taylor, 1989). Infection with the virus is usually harmless. However, if a fetus contracts the virus (the infection before birth is called cytomegalic inclusion disease), the infection may lead to brain damage. About 1 percent of all fetuses contract cytomegalic inclusion disease; 10 to 15 percent of the 1 percent of these babies develop a disability. It is important, therefore, for pregnant women who do not have antibodies to the disease to protect themselves and their unborn children from CMV infection.

CMV can be transmitted through bodily fluids. A vaccine is not yet available. It appears that pregnant women who work in child-care settings may have an increased risk of infection. Prevention strategies include washing hands frequently, disposing of diapers properly, and keeping toys and play areas clean. Prenatal testing can determine whether CMV infection has occurred (see chapter 4 for further discussion of prenatal testing).

Neurological Impairments

Neurological impairments are problems with the structure or functioning of the central nervous system, including the brain and the spinal cord. We discuss seizure disorders, cerebral palsy, spina bifida and spinal cord defects, and traumatic brain injury.

CONVULSIVE DISORDERS.   The most common neurological impairment encountered in the school is convulsive disorders or epilepsy. **Epilepsy** is a disorder in which the individual has a tendency to have recurrent seizures. **Seizures** are spontaneous abnormal discharges of the electrical impulses of the brain (Mullins, 1979). Seizures may involve the entire brain (generalized seizures) or only a portion of the

TABLE 11.3. Convulsive Disorders

Major types	1. Absence (petit mal)
	2. Tonic-clonic (grand mal)
	3. Complex partial (psychomotor)
Onset	1. Primary epilepsy (usually appears at a young age)
	2. Secondary (usually appears at an older age)
Stages	1. Preictal (aura)
	2. Seizure
	3. Postictal (resting)

absence seizure. A seizure in which there is a short lapse in consciousness.

tonic-clonic seizure. A seizure characterized by a stiff (tonic) phase in which the muscles become rigid, followed by a jerking (clonic) phase in which the arms and legs will snap.

aura. A signal of an impending seizure.

complex partial seizure. A period of automatic behavior resulting from discharge in a localized area of the brain, sometimes called psychomotor or focal seizure.

brain (partial seizures). The frequency of seizures may vary from a single isolated incident to hundreds in a day. Table 11.3 summarizes important information about convulsive disorders.

The three main types of seizures are (1) absence (petit mal) seizures, (2) generalized (tonic clonic or grand mal) seizures, and, (3) complex partial (psychomotor) seizures. **Absence seizures** are characterized by short lapses in consciousness. It may be difficult to determine that the person is experiencing anything out of the ordinary, and, in fact, the person may not even realize a seizure has occurred when it has passed. Typically, someone experiencing an absence seizure simply stares or shows small eye movements like fluttering of the eyelids. Because absence seizures are not dramatic, a teacher might wrongly assume the child is merely daydreaming or not paying attention.

Generalized seizures (most frequently **tonic-clonic seizures** traditionally referred to as grand mal) are the most serious type of seizure. They are characterized by convulsions and loss of consciousness. The dramatic behaviors exhibited may, at first, be frightening to the teacher and other students in the class. The child may fall to the floor. Usually there is a stiff (tonic) phase in which the muscles become rigid. This is followed by a clonic phase in which the arms and legs jerk. Other behaviors may accompany the seizure including teeth grinding, frothing due to inefficient saliva swallowing, and loss of bladder control. Seizures usually last less than five minutes, after which the individual enters the "postictal stage," and becomes relaxed, very sleepy, and disoriented.

Some children can anticipate their seizures because they experience a preictal stage or **aura** with heightened sensory signals of an impending seizure such as a peculiar smell, taste, vision, sound, or action, or a behavioral change before the onset of the seizure. It is helpful for an individual to know about his or her aura pattern in order to be able to assume a safe position or warn companions before the seizure begins.

Complex partial seizures (psychomotor seizures) are the result of discharge in a localized area of the brain. Because the unique electrical dysfunction is localized in the brain these are sometimes called focal seizures. After a period of automatic behavior, the child returns to normal activities. Sometimes the child's behavior during a psychomotor seizure is interpreted as misbehavior or clowning, leading to confusion on the part of the child, who is not aware of his behavior during a psychomotor seizure.

primary epilepsies. Predictable seizure disorders that appear at a young age, and appear to be hereditary.

secondary (lesional) epilepsies. Seizure disorders that appear at any age, and seem to be in response to particular damage.

cerebral palsy. A disorder of movement and posture caused by a defect in the developing brain.

About 1 percent of the population, approximately 2 million people in the United States, have epilepsy (Epilepsy Foundation of America, 1987). Approximately 200,000 persons have seizures more than once a month and approximately one-fourth of all patients with epilepsy continue to have seizures despite treatment (Penry, 1986).

Seizures may be caused by many conditions and circumstances and are divided into primary epilepsies (usually congenital) and secondary epilepsies (acquired). **Primary epilepsies** usually appear at a young age, occur in families where there is some history of epilepsy, have a stereotypical pattern of the seizure, and have a predictable response to specific medications. **Secondary (lesional) epilepsies** may appear at any age and result from accidents or child abuse, metabolic disturbances such as hypoglycemia, brain tumors and abscesses, lesions, brain injury, meningitis, or alcohol or drug withdrawal (Wannamaker et al., 1984).

Can epilepsy be prevented? In some cases, it can. Prevention of epilepsy can be accomplished by reducing risks of injury through seatbelts and helmets and by protecting the health of pregnant women so that their babies will be born well-nourished and healthy at full term. (Babies who are premature or fragile due to other causes such as poor nutrition are subject to a variety of problems including seizures.)

Treatment for epilepsy usually involves medication. The medication must be monitored so that the proper dose is prescribed for the child. Too much, too little, or the wrong medication can have serious effects. But even at the proper dose, medication has side effects such as drowsiness, lethargy, intellectual dullness, coarsening of facial features, behavioral changes, or sleep disturbances in the child. The teacher needs to be aware of the child's condition and the possible side effects of medication. The teacher then becomes an important member of the treatment team in observing, recording, and reporting behavior patterns that may be the result of medication.

CEREBRAL PALSY. Another neurological impairment frequently encountered in schoolchildren is cerebral palsy. **Cerebral palsy** is a condition in which the person is unable to fully control movement or motor function. This condition is a result of damage to certain areas of the brain during its development. Usually, the damage occurs close to the time of birth or within the first three years. The major source of damage is an incident that prevents sufficient oxygen from getting to the brain (United Cerebral Palsy Associations, 1986). Cerebral palsy is not a disease. It is, rather, a condition that is nonprogressive and noninfectious. Once it is acquired, it cannot be cured. Damage may occur before (prenatally), during (perinatally), or immediately after (postnatally) the child's birth. This is called congenital cerebral palsy. Occasionally, an individual will acquire cerebral palsy later in childhood. Acquired cerebral palsy is usually the result of brain damage resulting from accidents, brain infections, or child abuse.

The inability to fully control motor function may be apparent in one or more ways, depending on the precise location of brain damage, the degree of brain damage, and the extent to which the central nervous system is involved. Jerky movements, spasms, involuntary movements, and lack of muscle tone, alone or in combination, may result from cerebral palsy. Sometimes, the individual with cerebral palsy is multiply handicapped. Experts speculate that this can happen if the same damage to the brain that caused the cerebral palsy also caused another distinct disability or that the controllable motor function necessary for a skill like speech cannot be achieved due to cerebral palsy. Other disabilities that sometimes accompany cerebral palsy include seizures, sensory deficits such as abnormal sensation and

Communication is an important part of everyone's life. Some children with cerebral palsy require technology to communicate efficiently.

spasticity. An uncontrolled tightening or pulling of muscles.

athetoid. Purposeless and uncontrolled involuntary movements.

ataxia. Movement disrupted by impaired balance and depth perception.

perception, visual impairments, hearing impairments, speech impairments, and learning problems. Although mental retardation is present in some children with cerebral palsy, others function in the normal or higher intellectual range.

The ability to communicate effectively is a critical skill for all people, including people with cerebral palsy. Many individuals with cerebral palsy have trouble with verbal communication (see the story of Samantha Reid in chapter 5, Communicative Disorders). The disability makes it difficult to control the muscles required for spoken language, often making speech both very difficult to produce and difficult or impossible to understand. The same impairment may also make eating difficult and cause drooling and facial contortions. Nonverbal communication that depends on facial expressions and body language may be difficult for others to "read" in an individual whose body is subject to uncontrolled movements.

An individual's cerebral palsy is usually described by the types of cerebral palsy and the area of the body affected. The three main types of cerebral palsy are (1) **spastic,** in which the movements are very stiff; (2) **athetoid,** in which involuntary movements are purposeless and uncontrolled, while purposeful movements are contorted; and (3) **ataxic,** in which movements such as walking are disrupted by impairments of balance and depth perception. In addition, some individuals—especially infants and young children—have low (floppy) muscle tone.

Cerebral palsy is also classified according to the areas of the body that are affected

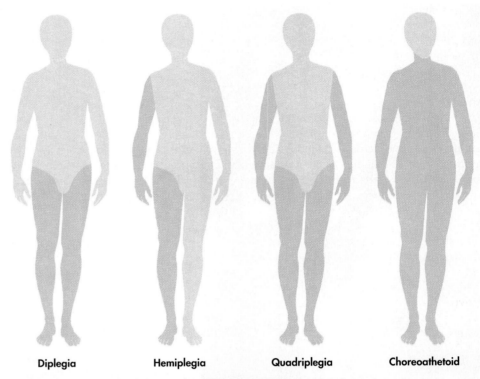

Diplegia   Hemiplegia   Quadriplegia   Choreoathetoid

FIGURE 11.1   Areas of the Body Affected by Cerebral Palsy

(see Figure 11.1) (Bleck, 1982):

monoplegia: one limb

hemiplegia: upper and lower limb on the same side

paraplegia: lower limbs only

diplegia: major involvement in the lower limbs and minor involvement in the upper limbs

triplegia: three limbs, usually both lower limbs and one upper limb

quadriplegia: major involvement of all four limbs

Thus, a child's disability might be described as "cerebral palsy, spastic hemiplegia." What do you learn from that clinical description? How might a child's cerebral palsy be described when there are involuntary uncontrolled movements in both legs?

The United Cerebral Palsy Association (1986) estimates that between 5000 and 7000 infants are born with cerebral palsy each year. In addition, 1200 to 1500 preschool children acquire the condition each year. The prevalence estimates of cerebral palsy are 500,000 to 700,000 children and adults in this country with cerebral palsy. The number of young children with cerebral palsy is decreasing, reflecting this country's improved ability to prevent the condition.

As we mentioned earlier, cerebral palsy is caused by damage to the brain, whether by impaired development, injury, or disease. It may be congenital (present at birth) or acquired. Let us look at this a little more closely.

In congenital cerebral palsy, a developing infant may have been deprived of necessary amounts of oxygen when something went wrong during birth. Circumstances such as a placenta separating from the wall of the uterus too early, a twisted birth position, knotting or kinking of the umbilical cord, or other problems of labor and delivery may cause brain damage. Cerebral palsy may also result from the effects of premature birth, blood type (Rh) incompatibility, the mother's infection with rubella or other viral diseases, and attacks by other dangerous microorganisms.

contracture. Joint stiffening, often because of muscle shortening, to the point that the joint can no longer move through its normal range.

Many cases of congenital cerebral palsy can be prevented. Parents who follow these simple measures can have babies who are born healthy. Women should achieve good health before they become pregnant and obtain early prenatal care while pregnant. Prenatal care can assure access to intensive medical care for the mother and infant when problems occur, provide diagnosis and treatment for diseases in the mother, such as diabetes, that can damage developing infants, and can help prevent exposure of the fetus to infections, viruses, drugs, alcohol, and other toxins. These efforts offer great promise in the fight to eliminate preventable disabilities.

Acquired cerebral palsy typically results from automobile or motorcycle accidents, brain infections such as meningitis, poisoning through toxins such as lead (ingested in paint chips from walls), serious falls, or injuries from child abuse. Prevention programs designed to promote the protection of children from injury can decrease the number of children subjected to brain damage and resulting cerebral palsy. The use of seatbelts, airbags, helmets and other protective devices can cut down on the motor vehicle injuries that can cause cerebral palsy. Adequate health care for children including proper immunizations and vaccinations, and protection from lead and other poisons can also help prevent acquired cerebral palsy. Proper child care, child supervision, and family support can help families avoid household accidents and family stresses that can lead to child injury. Improved vigilance against child abuse can prevent the terrible and all-too-frequent consequences in the lives of vulnerable children.

Although cerebral palsy cannot be cured, proper management or treatment can limit further physical damage, improve the child's functional skills, and offer opportunities for increased independence and autonomy. Since this condition affects motor functioning, management of cerebral palsy primarily addresses motor issues.

A variety of treatment services are available for children with cerebral palsy. The treatment is customized to the needs of the individual. For example, speech and language therapy enables the individual to accomplish schoolwork, communicate with teachers and students, and interact with family members and neighbors. Some students will, with the assistance of therapy, be able to communicate verbally. Others may never be able to speak well and will require augmentative communication tools such as language boards, computers, and voice synthesizers.

Mobility may be impaired in individuals with cerebral palsy. Even if they can walk, the walking may require such exertion and be so inefficient that the individual needs canes, crutches, or a wheelchair to get around. Students with cerebral palsy may also need braces or splints to help support the affected limbs and make them more functional or to prevent **contractures** that would eventually lead to bone deformities and further mobility limitations. Proper positioning of the body also requires special consideration. Many children need wedges, pillows, and individually designed chairs and work tables so that they can be comfortable, breathe easier, and avoid injuries, contractures, and deformities.

Some children with cerebral palsy need surgery to help improve their condition. In some cases, surgery may improve functional walking, limit the damage of progressively worsening contracting of muscles (contractures), and accomplish cosmetic improvements. For example, a child who has suffered contractures and now has twisted arms and legs because the needed physical therapy was never provided, may

myelodysplasia. A general term for spina bifida.

spina bifida. A developmental defect where the spinal column fails to close properly.

spinal cord. The cord that extends through the bony spinal column to the brain.

meninges. Membranes that cover the spinal cord and brain.

need to have ligaments or muscles surgically severed so that sitting upright in a wheelchair or lying straight in bed is possible.

Specially designed tools also serve to improve the way children with cerebral palsy accomplish ordinary activities of daily living such as eating and grooming. A toothbrush with a thick, easily gripped handle, a plate with suction devices on the bottom, a swivel spoon holder with a rubber ball to grasp, and other creative answers to motor limitations enable a child to accomplish activities independently. Students also want to fit in with their peers. Clothing that is stylish, fits easily over leg braces, and can be worn comfortably in a wheelchair is available.

MYELODYSPLASIA, SPINA BIFIDA, AND DEFECTS OF THE SPINAL CORD.

Myelodysplasia and **spina bifida** refer to the failure of the spinal column to close properly. The spinal column is the protective column through which nerves transmit critical messages from the brain to other parts of the body. This bony tube of vertebrae in the back encases and protects the nervous tissue of the **spinal cord** and its covering, the **meninges.** The spinal cord extends to and is connected to the brain. Occasionally, birth defects occur along the spinal cord. These can occur anywhere from the tailbone (coccyx) to the neck. The defects range in seriousness depending on how high the defect is along the spinal column (the closer to the neck, the more serious the impairment) and how much of the spinal cord material is involved in the damage. The defect may range from the absence of protective vertebrae to actual protrusion of the spinal cord and its covering. Because of the importance of the spinal cord and brain, the risks to the infant of a defect in the spinal column can be grave. Risks include the possibility of infection and further damage to the delicate nervous system, brain damage such as hydrocephaly (expansion of the brain ventricles as spinal fluid collects and does not drain properly), and paralysis.

Defects in which the spinal column or canal has not closed properly are referred to as spina bifida occulta, myelomeningocele, and meningocele (Bleck and Nagel, 1982). Spina bifida occulta is a defect where the bony protective arches of the spinal column have failed to develop. The spinal cord and its covering (meninges) are protected, if at all, only by skin. Spina bifida occulta in its mild form is very common and most people who have it do not even realize they have the condition (Mullins, 1979).

Spina bifida meningocele is potentially more serious, involving not only a defect in the spinal column but also some protrusion of the meninges. Meningocele indicates a skin sack protruding on the back containing some of the cord covering but not the cord.

Spina bifida myelomeningocele is the most serious of the forms of spina bifida because the back, the meninges, and the actual spinal cord are involved. Myelomeningocele indicates a skin sack protruding on the back containing a portion of the spinal cord and its covering that have escaped through a defect in the bony spinal column. Figure 11.2 shows how the body is affected by the types of spina bifida.

The material of the central nervous system damaged by spina bifida generally would have controlled the body areas below the location of the lesion. The parts of the body that would have been supplied by nerves branching from the spinal cord at this point or lower are likely paralyzed and deprived of sensations. The higher the lesion, the more areas of the body affected by the damaged nerves. In some cases where the lesion is very low on the spine, the child may not be paralyzed but will probably have some weakness in the lower legs and feet.

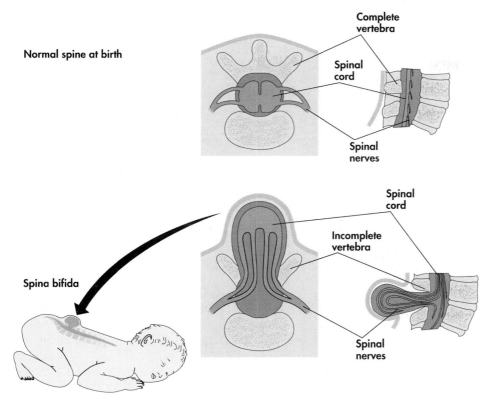

Normal spine at birth

Spina bifida

shunt. A tube to drain excess spinal fluid from the brain into a body cavity such as the abdomen.

FIGURE 11.2 How the Body Is Affected by the Types of Spina Bifida

Spina bifida occulta, spina bifida meningocele, and spina bifida myelomeningocele occur in approximately 0.1 to 4.13 of 1000 live births (Bleck, 1982). The causes of these spinal canal defects are not yet clear, although the presence of a virus or an unknown toxin during early fetal development has been suggested. The defect occurs very early in the development of a fetus, between the twentieth and the thirtieth day of fetal development, before a woman even knows she is pregnant.

Today, infants born with spinal column defects generally have surgery to repair the back to avoid infection. If the infection is not treated or if the infant contracts meningitis the effects can be devastating, including mental retardation (McLone, 1982). Surgical closure of the defect allows the infant's motor, sensory, and intellectual functioning to be preserved and a suitable environment for the child's neural tissue development to continue. The child's back also will look better and be easier to care for after surgery.

Although not all children with spina bifida have hydrocephaly, some of them do. Medical procedures for these children include the insertion of a **shunt,** or tube, to drain excess spinal fluid from the child's brain. The use of a shunt can prevent the brain damage that results when the brain ventricles fill up with the fluid and expand, stretching the child's head outward and squeezing and compressing the brain and nerves. Typically, the excess fluid is shunted into another place in the infant's body, for example the abdomen, where the body can safely absorb, process, and eliminate the fluid (see Figure 11.3).

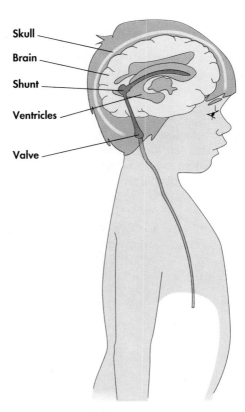

Skull

Brain

Shunt

Ventricles

Valve

FIGURE 11.3 Shunts Are Used to Draw Fluid from the Brain. This Procedure Prevents Brain Damage.

Without treatment, the future for a child with a major spinal cord defect can be bleak. With treatment, however, the child's prognosis is excellent. McLone (1983) reported that when all newborns with myelomeningocele received medical treatment, intellectual development was normal in 73 percent of the children. Urinary continence was achieved in 87 percent of them. Most of the children did not require wheelchairs. Of the children who required shunts to drain the excess spinal fluid, 48 percent did not require shunt revisions or repeated shunt surgery.

TRAUMATIC BRAIN INJURY. Finally, we discuss briefly traumatic brain injury. Traumatic brain injury is severe trauma to the head that results in lingering physical and cognitive impairments. Individuals who have traumatic brain injury can require many years of work to relearn simple tasks. Fortunately, advances in medical technology are making recovery possible in some cases.

According to the National Head Injury Foundation, approximately 500,000 cases of traumatic brain injury per year requiring hospital admission are reported. Approximately 100,000 of those victims die, and another 100,000 are debilitated for life.

Traumatic brain injury is the number one killer of people under thirty-four. The leading cause of traumatic brain injury is motor vehicle accidents. Among infants, however, child abuse accounts for 64 percent of head injuries.

Neuromuscular Diseases

POLIO. Poliomyelitis is a viral infection that attacks the nerve cells in the spinal cord that control muscle function. Before vaccines were developed in the 1950s and early 1960s, hundreds of thousands of people had contracted the infection in this country alone. The worst epidemic year in the United States was 1952, when 56,000 Americans contracted the infection.

With proper vaccination, polio can be easily and cheaply prevented. But because polio is no longer a common disease, many Americans ignore vaccinating their children and risk exposing their children (and themselves) to the virus. Many developing countries without adequate vaccination programs continue to see polio as the most common cause of physical disabilities in children (Werner, 1987).

The effects of polio infection range from cases where the child has what appears to be a cold and fever to mild to severe paralysis. We now know that effects can surface many years after the infection. The children who acquired polio in the epidemics of the 1930s, 1940s, and 1950s are now adults. We have learned that about 25 percent of them will develop post-polio sequelae, after effects consisting of deep fatigue, decreased muscle functioning, and increased pain in muscles and joints.

Polio does not affect intelligence. Franklin D. Roosevelt, for example, contracted polio in 1921 and went on to become president of the United States. Polio's effects on the body, however, can be quite serious. Paralysis, ranging from mild to severe, can occur. Contractures, or a shortening of muscles and tendons limiting limb movement, can be another complication of the paralysis, requiring therapy or surgery. When the child's weak joints must bear too much weight, deformities such as sway back and dislocated joints may occur. Improper muscle tone may interfere with breathing and lead to upper respiratory infections.

MUSCULAR DYSTROPHY. Muscular dystrophy is a neuromuscular disease in which the muscles progressively weaken. The muscle cells degenerate and are replaced by fat and fibrous cells. The most common type is Duchenne muscular dystrophy. The cause of muscular dystrophy is unknown, but it appears to run in families, usually transmitted by the mother's genes. Muscular dystrophy affects mainly boys. It is relatively rare, with an incidence of about 2 in every 10,000 people (Batshaw and Perret, 1986).

Although muscular dystrophy is not curable at this time and genetic counseling is the only known form of prevention, this does not mean that it is not treatable, however. Treatment consists of helping children stay strong, healthy, and active, and helping them lead as normal lives as possible. Most individuals with Duchenne muscular dystrophy eventually need wheelchairs, usually while they are still in elementary school. Fatigue becomes a problem as the weakening progresses.

MULTIPLE SCLEROSIS. Approximately 250,000 Americans have **multiple sclerosis,** a chronic disease in which the myelin covering of the nerve fibers in the brain and spinal column deteriorates. After the myelin is damaged, it is replaced with scar tissue that blocks and distorts the brain's messages.

Neither the cause nor a cure is known, but multiple sclerosis is not infectious. The most common theory is that it is caused by a virus that seems to trigger an autoimmune reaction in which the body's immune system attacks its own healthy myelin. The course of the disease is not predictable and is different in every person. Some of the symptoms include muscle weakness, loss of physical coordination, tremors, paralysis, spasticity, vision impairment, and fatigue. Intelligence is not af-

poliomyelitis. A viral infection that attacks the nerve cells in the spinal cord that control muscle function.

muscular dystrophy. Progressive muscle weakness that comes from problems in the muscles themselves.

multiple sclerosis. A degenerative nervous system disease leading to the loss of the myelin covering of nerves.

Focus: Issues of Diversity

The children of migrant agricultural workers, many of whom are culturally and linguistically diverse, are at highest risk for exceptionalities, including physical disabilities and health impairments (Baca and Harris, 1988). The Education Commission of the States Migrant Education Task Force (1970) reported that the life expectancy of migrant workers is forty-nine years compared to the national average of seventy-nine, the infant mortality rate is 25 percent higher than the average, lack of prenatal and postnatal care result in birth injuries and disabilities, and poor nutrition and poor access to health care lead to poor mental and physical development. Physical disabilities and health impairments could be prevented in many of these children.

fected, but the other symptoms may affect the individual's ability to communicate. Multiple sclerosis occurs primarily in adults.

ISSUES IN EDUCATION

Education and the Preschool Child

Great challenges face infants and toddlers with physical disabilities and their families during the critical early years. Whether the impairment is orthopedic or health related, early intervention programs focus on motor development, self-help in daily living, and social skills (Hanson, 1984). For example, children born with cerebral palsy may have reflex patterns that interfere with typical motor development, or abnormal oral reflexes that interfere with swallowing and eating (Orelove and Sobsey, 1987).

Parents play a critical educational role during these early years (Walker, Slentz, and Bricker, 1985). Much of the instruction for preschool children with physical disabilities and health impairments takes place in the home and is carried out by the parents. If the child's intervention program is to be successful, the parents' efforts and enthusiasm must be supported by the other members of the team.

Education for these young children initially centers on motor responses. Enlisting other team members such as the occupational therapist, physical therapist, and nurse, will enhance appropriate education. During this time, students often are put through a regimen of special exercises to develop motor skills. It may include strengthening weak muscle groups through the use of weights, or adapting to artificial limbs or orthopedic devices. Teachers and parents who are not yet trained or supervised should avoid exercising the child's limbs or putting the child through motor exercises until they have the training to conduct the exercises without risking harm to the child.

Because this is a time of tremendous physical and sensorimotor growth, normal motor patterns must be established as early as possible. For those children who already have abnormal motor patterns, the teacher must make sure not to encourage abnormal patterns (Campbell, 1987a, b). For example, the teacher should always position the child properly so that alignment, muscle tone, and stability (Orelove and Sobsey, 1987) are correct during any activity. If the child is not properly positioned, abnormal patterns will remain and possibly worsen. How does a parent carry

This child was properly positioned. and she is now ready for her reading activity.

this out? To properly position children with disabilities, parents need certain equipment, such as foam rubber wedges, Velcro straps, and comfortable mats. While some of this equipment is expensive, other items can be made rather inexpensively. Parents and teachers need to keep in touch with therapists to make certain they are working properly with their children.

After the child is properly positioned, parents and teachers should design and encourage activities that motivate the child to move in functional ways. Simply positioning a child on a wedge or bolster and then neglecting the child's learning wastes the child's time. Placing a rattle at the infant's eye level motivates the infant to swat it in order to hear the sound. The teacher can encourage stretching by placing a favorite food or toy at the limit of the child's reach so that the child must stretch in order to get it. This simple activity accomplishes three goals: (1) the child is learning appropriate motor patterns, (2) the child's body is properly positioned, and (3) the child is learning the relationship between movement and getting what she wants.

For some students with physical disabilities, establishing communication is difficult. Parents and professionals should acknowledge and reinforce every attempt at communicating. Sometimes it is difficult to determine how a child with severe disabilities is attempting to communicate; but an observant person can learn a great deal about the communication of a child, even when others wrongly believe the child does not communicate at all (Goode, 1979). In what specific ways does the child react to sounds? How do students respond to certain smells? Do they have different facial movements when different people enter the room? Do they gaze at certain objects more than others? How is anger expressed to the family? Through careful observation and experience, parents can recognize meaningful communication when others believed there was none. Parents and professionals should also remember that communication is a two-way street. Children learn to communicate with others by being communicated with: Talk to the child, express feelings with your face and body, play games together, and encourage the child to listen to tapes and the radio.

Education and the School-Age Child

As we mentioned earlier, each child with a physical disability or health impairment has individualized needs. When the child is ready to enter school, both the child and the child's family become critical members of the IEP team, providing recommendations for a program. Sometimes, simple schedule flexibility can make a big difference. For example, one teenager, with the rheumatic disease lupus, described one of the accommodations she needed at school:

> Still, school is difficult for me. Because my knees are weak, I can't carry a lot of books at one time. I have to have extra time between my classes so I can go back to my locker and get different books. I wanted to be a cheerleader this year but I didn't bother to try out because my knees were in such bad shape. I have dead bone in them from the prednisone. (Krementz, 1989, p. 51)

Allowing a student extra time between classes should be easy to accomplish. By listening to the student, a teacher can individualize accommodations.

Educators must also be aware of a wide variety of other potential obstacles to a student's education. Teachers need to learn how to assist a child with health care needs, how to deal with frequent absences, how to assist a child who is having a

Tips for Teachers

- Be alert to signs of fatigue in the child.
- Find teaching materials that can be adapted to the physical needs of the student.
- Use teaching materials and activities that are appropriate for the age of the student.
- Make sure that all areas of the room and school are accessible.
- Make sure materials, projects, or leisure activities are within the student's reach.
- Encourage personal privacy when assisting the student with hygiene.
- Include activities each day that the student can accomplish from a wheelchair.
- Lift only as much weight as you can.
- Post emergency instructions and telephone numbers.

seizure, how to make scheduling accommodations, how to address special issues relating to paralysis, how to adapt the class activities, how to adapt teaching techniques, and how to promote social integration. We discuss these issues below. Because of space constraints we can only touch briefly on these critical topics.

PROVISION OF HEALTH CARE IN THE CLASSROOM. Some children may need assistance with their medication while they are at school. Coordination among the child, the child's physician, the family, and the school nurse will be necessary so that the child takes the proper dose at the proper times and so that the effects of the type of medication and the dosage can be monitored and changed if necessary.

Some children may need assistance in the bathroom. Every school should have bathroom stalls that accommodate wheelchairs and braces, and should have accessible sinks, mirrors, towel dispensers, and door handles. Personal assistance for some children may be required. While older children with paralysis generally are able to accomplish their bathroom needs independently, through the use of self-administered clean intermittent catheterization (CIC), for example, many younger children will need the teacher's assistance. It is important to encourage personal privacy when helping a child with hygiene needs.

ABSENCES. Many children with physical disabilities and health impairments will be absent often from school because they need medical care or because they are too fragile to come to school on certain days. Asthma is one of the major causes of school absences, accounting for about one-fourth of all health-related absences. Other conditions associated with excessive absences are hemophilia, cystic fibrosis, nephrosis, leukemia, and sickle cell anemia (Shayne et al., 1987). How can a teacher help these children keep up with their classmates? Some schools provide a **home or hospital teacher,** use television or telephone hook-ups between the child and the classroom, make videotapes of special classroom activities, and allow classmates to take turns acting as peer tutors after school. These methods not only help the child's academic progress but also maintain a social connection to the teacher and the other students so that the child feels more comfortable about returning to the classroom later.

SEIZURES. Children with epilepsy fall within all ranges of intelligence. However, they have a higher rate of learning disabilities, mental retardation, or other disabilities than their peers without epilepsy. Even children whose IQs are normal may experience some problems caused by epilepsy or its treatment. These problems include lack of concentration, restlessness, fidgeting, or the possible side effects of medication. Children with frequent, prolonged, or severe seizures may even experience a decrease in intelligence (Svoboda, 1979).

Since teachers spend so much time with a child during the waking hours, they can provide important information on the characteristics of a child's seizure disorder. Teachers can help the child and the child's physician by monitoring the effects and dosage of seizure medication. Teachers should also be prepared to respond effectively to a child's seizure and to show other students and school personnel how to help a child experiencing a seizure. Table 11.4 provides some guidelines for managing seizures in school settings.

PARALYSIS. Teachers of children paralyzed with spinal cord defects need special training. For example, some children with severe cerebral palsy may need the teacher to physically move them from place to place or position them. The physical therapist

home or hospital teacher. A special teacher who teaches in the child's home or hospital when the child must be absent from school due to health problems.

TABLE 11.4. First Aid for Seizures

Convulsive or generalized tonic-clonic

According to the Epilepsy Foundation of America, the following steps are appropriate to assist a person experiencing a convulsive seizure or a generalized tonic-clonic seizure:

- Prevent the person from hurting himself or herself. Place something soft under the head, loosen tight clothing, and clear the area of any sharp or hard objects.
- Do not force any objects into the person's mouth.
- Do not restrain the person's movements.
- Turn the person on his or her side to allow saliva to drain from the mouth.
- Stay with the person until the seizure ends naturally.
- Do not pour any liquids into the person's mouth or offer any food, drink, or medication until the person is fully awake.
- Give artificial respiration if the person does not resume breathing after the seizure.
- Provide an area for the person to rest until fully awakened, accompanied by a responsible adult.
- Be reassuring and supportive when consciousness returns.
- While a convulsive seizure is not a medical emergency, occasionally a seizure may last longer than ten minutes or a second seizure may occur. This requires prompt medical attention in a properly equipped medical facility.

Nonconvulsive/complex partial

For nonconvulsive/complex-partial seizures, the following first aid is recommended:

- Do not restrain the person.
- Remove harmful objects from the person's path.
- Calmly try to encourage the person to sit down or encourage him or her away from dangerous situations. If the person does not respond to these measures, force should not be used.
- Observe but do not approach the person who appears angry or combative.
- Remain with the person until he or she is fully alert.

Source: Epilepsy Foundation of America, 1981, pp. 10, 12.

can instruct the teacher on the safest and most appropriate manner to transfer a particular child.

COORDINATION WITH OTHER PROFESSIONALS AND SCHEDULING. Teachers of students with physical disabilities and health impairments must be prepared to work cooperatively with the other professionals, such as speech/language pathologists, physical therapists, occupational therapists, counselors, and physicians participating in the child's education. Although it can be complicated, coordination is well worth the effort. A child who needs to work with other professionals may have additional absences from school.

ADAPTATION. The teacher also needs to be sensitive to the physical environment needs of the child. The student may require specially fitted chairs, desks, and work tables, and perhaps extra space for maneuvering bulky leg braces, crutches, or wheelchairs.

Many students also require specially designed tools to perform tasks for themselves. For example, some students with cerebral palsy will use pointers strapped to their heads because they have better control with their heads than with hand movements. Other children may need mouthpieces that allow them to hold pencils or crayons for their schoolwork. The physical therapist and occupational therapist can assist the teacher in developing these accommodations. Many students with severe physical disabilities require language boards or computers for communication.

This boy is enjoying a lively conversation as he is eating lunch with his friends.

Teachers must learn to interact with the child using whatever communication accommodations are required. Students, as part of their education, should learn to care for, store, and maintain their equipment.

MEALTIMES. Mealtimes must also be considered when planning the educational program for a child with physical disabilities or health impairments. Some children are susceptible to anemia, are unable to chew or to swallow, or lose their appetite because of medication. The school nurse or a nutritionist can help the teacher in these cases (Crump, 1987). Some children need special utensils such as a large-handled spoon or a plate held firmly to the table by suction cups. Children who have difficulty eating may be self-conscious about the problem. Their classmates may also be uncomfortable at the beginning. The teacher can create a comfortable, accepting atmosphere for eating. The important thing to remember is that, in addition to assisting the child to get essential nutrients, the mealtime experience should be a healthy, happy opportunity for social exchange (Perske et al., 1986).

TEACHING TECHNIQUES. For children who cannot move as fast and efficiently as others, the teacher must anticipate accommodations. For example, the child may need extra time for completing written assignments. The teacher may engage classmates to take notes for students who cannot write. Something as simple as taping children's workpapers to their desks and providing extra thick pencils might allow them to accomplish the task. These simple adjustments give a twofold message: (1) you are willing to give the student a chance, and (2) the student is important to you.

Imagine trying to take a timed test while your body goes through uncontrollable jerky movements! Testing presents difficulties for many children with physical disabilities. The risk is that, without accommodations, the test will merely measure the degree of physical difficulty experienced by the individual rather than actual intellectual or academic abilities. How can a teacher give a fair test? Oral testing is one way to obtain an accurate reading of the student's skill level. What other ways besides traditional timed tests might you use to assess the arithmetic abilities of a child with cerebral palsy?

INTEGRATION. Teachers of students with physical disabilities and health impairments, as do teachers in all areas of special education, make special efforts to assure that the students do not become isolated and segregated because of their disabilities. Recreation is one of the areas in which social integration can naturally occur. In addition to all the health benefits of recreation and exercise, recreational skills can allow children with physical disabilities to have fun with their classmates and can provide opportunities for enjoyment with their families. Many adapted toys and

Integration can occur in natural settings with typical toys.

games are available for people with physical disabilities. A frisbee, for example, has been specially adapted with two adjustable clips on the top so that people with limited hand movements can play. A child could play with other children, with his or her family, or with a pet.

Sports and fitness programs are available for individuals with physical disabilities. Little League Baseball has a Challenger Division for children with physical and mental disabilities. Workout tapes for individuals with a variety of disabilities, including for people who use a wheelchair, have also been developed.

Teaching Tactics

LEARNING TO EAT INDEPENDENTLY

Mr. Keyes is a consulting teacher who works with children with physical disabilities and orthopedic handicaps and their teachers. One student, Christopher, is seven years old and has cerebral palsy. Christopher has been struggling to feed himself, but trying to grasp the silverware and scoop food from the lunch tray is frustrating him.

Mr. Keyes read in last year's IEP that Christopher had been learning to hold a spoon, but that he had been successful only if the teacher held it with him. Mr. Keyes decided to extend that skill by trying to teach Christopher how to hold a spoon independently.

Mr. Keyes first observed Christopher attempting to grasp a spoon. It was clear that Christopher was motivated but that his cerebral palsy made it difficult for him to make the tight fist required to hold the spoon. Even when Christopher managed to get hold of the spoon, the tray scooted along the table as soon as Christopher attempted to scoop the food and food spilled over the sides whenever he got a scoop. This was so frustrating for Christopher that Mr. Keyes feared he would soon give up. Meanwhile, at home and at school, someone fed Christopher.

Mr. Keyes further observed that during other activities Christopher could hold some items. For example, Mr. Keyes saw Christopher grasp and lift the small juice can when they made juice in class. Mr. Keyes decided to try to adapt a handle as fat as the juice can on Christopher's spoon. Mr. Keyes taped some rubber onto the handle of the spoon.

Christopher was able to grasp this built-up spoon, and soon was attempting to feed himself. The problems of the scooting tray and spilling food remained, however. Mr. Keyes needed to solve those problems also. He found some small suction cups and glued them to the bottom of the tray so it would stick to the table. He also used some heavy aluminum foil to build up the sides of the tray so that the food wouldn't spill over when Christopher scooped his food.

With these changes Christopher's ability to eat independently improved. Later, Mr. Keyes discussed these adaptations with the occupational therapist. After evaluating Christopher and the adapted eating utensils, the therapist was able to provide eating utensils that looked more normal and did not need replacing and repairing as often. The occupational therapist also provided side head guards and a chin guard so that Christopher could hold his head steadier when he was eating. She even designed a guiding mechanism to assist Christopher to raise the spoon to his mouth.

Christopher's parents are pleased with the independence that these adaptations allowed their son. Of course, mealtimes now take longer, with Christopher feeding himself rather than being fed by someone else. The family has managed to schedule longer mealtimes to accommodate Christopher's new skill.

(continued)

Teaching Tactics

LEARNING TO EAT INDEPENDENTLY (continued)

They also look forward to going to restaurants more frequently and now carry an extra set of adapted silverware in the car for that purpose.

You can see that all the members of the IEP team had contributions to make as Christopher took an important step toward increased independence at mealtimes. Pleased with Christopher's success, the team is now working together to adapt his pencils, markers, and crayons so that he can do his homework independently. What else might they try to adapt?

As you think about Christopher, consider the questions Mr. Keyes asked himself. These questions can help you address the learning of children with physical disabilities and health impairments.

1. Does the problem interfere with independence?
2. Does the child attempt the skill at all?
3. Does the child have a related skill that can be built on?
4. Can we adapt the environment or a tool to accommodate the student?
5. Does the adaption allow more independence?
6. What can other members of the IEP team contribute?
7. How can the new skill generalize to other settings such as home or community?

Educational Environments

Children with physical disabilities have a right to schools that are accessible. (It is important to remember that this is also an issue for other people with disabilities who might need access to the school such as teachers, other employees, parents and grandparents, and guest speakers.) Accessibility means elevators large enough to hold wheelchairs, handrails along the corridors, chalkboards placed low enough so that children in wheelchairs can write on them, seating arrangements that can accommodate children with a variety of equipment, standing tables so that children can spend time out of wheelchairs, and playground equipment large enough to hold a child with leg braces. (See also the Concepts and Controversies section in chapter 9, Visual Impairments, for another interpretation of the term *accessible*.)

When considering the ways to make an educational environment accessible to a child with a physical disability, remember *all* of the places the child needs to go: the bathroom, the lunchroom, the playground, the gymnasium, the music room, the library, and so on. The child's educational activities should be chosen based on individual learning needs, not by where a wheelchair can and cannot fit.

Although it is generally understood that all children should attend school, children with fragile health may spend some of their education time at home or in a hospital. When they are in school, they may need extra rest and the support of devices such as ventilators, feeding tubes, and ostomy supplies. The quality of the educational environment for these children may be particularly critical since they may not be able to move easily between environments as children usually can. Their personal relationships also require attention. Since they may not have a large number of other children in the environment, they may need extra assistance establishing and maintaining friendships. When they are hospitalized, the professional faces may change daily, so continuity in school is critical.

FAMILIES OF CHILDREN WITH PHYSICAL DISABILITIES AND HEALTH IMPAIRMENTS

The families of children with severe physical disabilities and health impairments face special issues as they raise their children. Often the costs of the child's health care are staggering. Parents' own career decisions may sometimes be driven by questions about maintaining family health insurance. Even when health insurance is available, financial recordkeeping and filing for reimbursements can be complicated and cause a strain. If the child is eligible for government medical benefits, eligibility regulations may be complex. Some families find it necessary to move to a

CATHIE'S FAMILY: CATHIE, JAMIE, BETSY, AND SCOTTY THOMAS

Cathie Thomas is the single mother of three rambunctious young children. Cathie adopted Jamie (10), Betsy (7), and Scotty (4), one by one, as infants. "I met each of these children in my special education work. I fell in love with each one and I decided to make a family." The family lives in a cheerful home, toys underfoot, and two dogs adding to the sounds of children playing. The intense schedules of the four busy family members are contained in a much-consulted three-inch-thick appointment book. Cathie describes the typical day as "hectic."

Each of the children has serious physical disabilities, and Jamie and Scotty have other disabilities as well. All three children were born severely premature, three to four months early. None of their birth mothers had received any prenatal care.

Jamie has Down syndrome, bronchopulmonary dysplasia (a lung disease), mental retardation, a paralyzed vocal cord, severe communicative disorders, vision and hearing impairments, heart damage (ventral septal defect), respiratory distress syndrome, and severe sensory integration deficits.

Scotty has bronchopulmonary dysplasia and a neurological disorder that causes him to fall frequently. He also appears to have developmental delays, although since he is only four years old, it is difficult to make a diagnosis yet. Scotty's mother was required to use strong prescription drugs while she was pregnant. He was born sixteen weeks prematurely, at only twenty-four weeks' gestation.

Betsy is multicultural—her mother was Hispanic. Betsy does not have major intellectual impairments. Because she began to develop hydrocephaly at birth, she has a shunt from her brain to her abdomen to drain the excess fluid. In an earlier time, before shunts, that fluid probably would have caused her to develop severe hydrocephaly and mental retardation.

Each of these children had medical needs that would have been impossible for Cathie to pay for on her salary as a teacher. But because of their disabilities, Cathie was able to arrange subsidized adoptions so the state remains financially responsible for their medical care but Cathie is their legal mother. This arrangement coupled with the help of friends, family, and their church, has decreased the financial problems that often accompany severe physical disabilities.

When she adopted the children, Cathie was already living in a large city with many services for children with disabilities, and she was working in a special education classroom. She did not need to move from her home community and she was very knowledgeable in locating the services her children needed.

Cathie described one aspect of each of her children's unique needs:

Jamie has had many illnesses and eighteen surgeries over his ten years. None of the experts who saw him as a baby believed he would live; he was failing to thrive. This boy has suffered tremendous pain in his life—when he was an infant, he suffered through several surgeries without any anesthesia! I think he decided to live when he realized he had someone who loved him.

Jamie was on oxygen continuously until he was three years old. Even today he continues to miss a great deal of school because of his precarious health. But his teacher and I have agreed that sometimes we will send him to school even when he is sick, because if I kept him home every time he was sick, he would be home more days than he is in school. With his intellectual impairments, he just can't afford to miss that much school. Of course, they let him rest, and he stays rather quiet on those days, but at least he remains part of his class and stays connected to school. His teacher is very creative in helping him to be comfortable when he doesn't feel well while keeping him integrated with his classmates.

Betsy had a shunt from the time she was an infant. Children who have shunts cannot risk hurting their heads because the shunt may become dislodged and then another surgery would be required to reattach it. So she wore a protective helmet (with her frilly little dresses) for years. Betsy has always been so bright and beautiful, that I think many people didn't really believe she had a serious physical disability. So I was criticized as being overprotective for refusing to allow her to swing, ride a bike, go down the slide, play on the high beams, or do anything else that might cause her shunt to detach. She was not even allowed to play outside at school without a teacher by her side. Recently, she had a periodic CT scan on her head, and the physician discovered the shunt had detached. But her brain had begun to dispose of the fluid naturally. So he said to Betsy, "You don't have to wear the helmet anymore. You can do whatever you want to." Betsy immediately went outside and jumped on the monkey bars!

Scotty, because of his premature birth, has required constant oxygen since he was born. He has combined obstructive-restrictive airway disease and has been on oxygen his entire life. As a four-year-old, he carries his own oxygen tank with him everywhere he goes. Scotty and I decided that it would be easier for him if we lowered the handles on his tank so that he could drag it like a wagon. The company that supplies the oxygen didn't seem to mind that adaptation too much, but I think they wish that Scotty and I would stop gluing dinosaur pictures on his tanks!

About two years ago, Scotty really wanted to begin going down the slide at the playground. We discussed this in the team meeting, since it was rather difficult to figure out a way to safely get him and his oxygen tank down that twenty-foot slide. But his doctor came up with the idea that it would be fine for Scotty to unhook from the tank for the few minutes it would take to go down the slide, and then he could hook up again to resume his regular playing. It takes creativity to think of alternative ways to help these children to do the things that children do!

larger city in order to obtain necessary health care and therapies. Such a move may mean leaving a community in which they have long-term social ties and extended family.

If the child's treatment or health problems require absences from school, the family's routine may be disrupted when one adult has to stay home with the child. Similarly, it may require special planning and complicated arrangements to be able to go away for a weekend, for a family vacation, for time with other children, or time for parents alone.

Many homes and apartments are not yet designed for the range of physical needs of the entire population. If a child needs large equipment, a special bathtub, ramps, or other accommodations typical for an individual with physical disabilities, the family may have to move to an accessible apartment.

How do families cope with these problems? Around the country, families have joined together in support groups to address these common issues. Often families share creative ideas for helping the child with the disability to join in the activities of the family, such as inexpensive adaptations of toys, shared babysitting, exchanging information about helpful medical personnel, and accommodate physical disabilities in other ways.

ADULTS WITH PHYSICAL DISABILITIES AND HEALTH IMPAIRMENTS

Students with physical disabilities and health impairments have among the lowest dropout rates of all students in special education (U.S. Office of Special Education and Rehabilitative Services, 1989). As a result many have a greater chance of gaining a college education. An increasing number of colleges are genuinely accessible to people with disabilities, and many have special programs to assist students with physical disabilities and health impairments. In addition to accommodations for wheelchairs and other mobility devices, colleges should be prepared to allow extra time to take tests, and provide assisted methods for taking class notes and transcribing class tape recordings. The key is for colleges to provide individualized means for students with physical disabilities and health impairments to accomplish college work.

Independent living is the goal for adults with physical disabilities and health impairments. The "independent living movement," people helping themselves to live on their own, has had a great influence on the lives of people with disabilities (Crewe and Zola, 1983). Increasingly, adults with physical disabilities and health impairments take control of their lives and their jobs, establish friendships, have families, and exercise political power. Legislation such as the Americans with Disabilities Act (ADA) will have a tremendous impact on the ability of adults with disabilities to pursue their rights and end discrimination (see the discussion of legislation in chapter 1).

What is the life of an adult with physical disabilities like? Let us look at one story. Teddy Pendergrass, famous singer, wrote about his life as he recovered from a broken neck after a 1982 automobile accident:

> I ain't going to lie, this thing's a bitch. You go through living hell, through all kinds of anxieties, and you suffer enormous apprehensions about everything. At first you don't know how people will accept you, and you don't want to be seen. Given

high-tech devices. Complex technical devices such as computers.

low-tech devices. Simple technical devices such as homemade cushions or a classroom railing.

thoughts like that, you don't want to live. But—and that's a big but—you have an option. You can give it up and call it quits, or you can go on. I've decided to go on.

. . . It was a matter of months before I began to feel stronger. First, my self-image was nothing. You feel worthless because all of a sudden you aren't the way you once were. I cried a lot. I was angry. But you have to reorganize, take a stand, and the problem becomes not what you are going to do next, but how are you going to do it.

I felt that no one understood me. All they knew was that Teddy Pendergrass, the guy who had such a big image, was now a fallen man. It was tough for people to see that the man hadn't fallen, that the person was still there.

. . . Everybody's got something wrong with them. I see people looking funny at me in the chair. But how long can I sit around saying, "I hate it. I hate it!" My life's work has always been to achieve, and I don't see any reason why that should change; I still work a lot of hours.

. . . My first album since the accident, *Love Language,* was very beautiful and melodic, but it wasn't the music of that aggressive person who was sure and confident about what he wants to do. *Workin' It Back* [his subsequent lp] is upbeat. The cover picture says hello. The music is still celebrating life.*

TECHNOLOGY AND PHYSICAL DISABILITIES AND HEALTH IMPAIRMENTS

Modern technology can dramatically improve the ability of people with physical disabilities and health impairments to gain access to and control the world around them, communicate with others, and benefit from health care. When thinking about the adaptations that technology can allow an individual with physical disabilities and health impairments, consider not only **high-tech devices** such as computers, but also **low-tech devices** such as simple built-up spoons and crutches made from locally available materials (Vanderheiden, 1984; Werner, 1987). Technology does not have to be expensive, or even sophisticated—creativity and individualization are the keys to successful use of technology.

One of the most commonly used technological advances is the personal computer. "When used by a person with a disability, the computer has been likened to the six gun of western mythology—the great equalizer between people of different ability or strength" (Maddox, 1987, p. 223). Computers are used for many skills including augmentative communication, for writing and printing, practicing mathematics, and to create "smart rooms" where the thermostat, lights, music, and doors are controlled by a central computer panel.

Many adaptations are available for computers so that people with severe physical disabilities can use them. For example, computers can be operated by voice, mouthstick, sip-and-puff breath stick, a single finger, a toe, a headstick, or many other creative methods suitable to an individual's abilities. Computer disks and other technological tools are now common items in students' backpacks.

With computer skills, individuals have access to other environments and people: children might be hooked up to their classrooms on days when they are unable to attend school, they may be able to accomplish library research by hooking up to an

*"Teddy Pendergrass," from *Spinal Network* (1987) S. Maddox (Ed.). Boulder, CO: Spinal Network and Sam Maddox. Reprinted by permission.

rehabilitation engineering. Application of mechanical and engineering principles to improve human physical functioning.

gait training. Analysis and instruction of walking.

technology-dependent children. Children who probably could not survive without high technology devices such as ventilators.

ventilator. A machine to assist with breathing.

Advanced computer systems that are specially adapted to the abilities of individuals with physical impairments make almost anything possible.

information system, have access to the work of friends who also have computers, or communicate with students around the country from a central data base.

Rehabilitation Engineering

Rehabilitation engineering has brought the benefits of science and engineering to movement, seating, and walking problems such as those created by cerebral palsy. **Gait training** laboratories (special laboratories for walking) help many children by analyzing their normal and abnormal movements, and with the help of physical therapists and other specialists help to improve posture and balance.

Health Care

Advances in health care technology have helped many infants and children to survive and even recover from illnesses and injuries that just a few years ago were fatal. The development of sophisticated ultrasound technology has recently allowed doctors to perform surgery on babies even before they are born (Stark, Menolascino, and Goldsbury, 1988). Some of these children will continue to need technology as they grow up, and in fact might not be able to survive without it. This new category of **technology-dependent children** has greatly benefited from modern scientific advances. As they enter school, they will challenge the educational system. We already see children bringing portable **ventilators** and other machines on the bus to school (U.S. Congress, Office of Technology Assessment, 1987).

personal care attendant. An individual hired to assist with tasks.

Specialized health care that used to require a hospital setting, such as dialysis and oxygen therapy, is now often provided in the child's home. Home health care allows the child to stay with the family, attend school with the neighborhood children, and lead a more normal life. Adults with physical disabilities also hire **personal care attendants** to assist with cooking and eating, bathing and grooming, and personal hygiene.

Biofeedback is used increasingly to help individuals with physical disabilities learn new ways to function, deal with pain, and retrain muscles. Some have reported its use in controlling seizures.

Communication

We discussed the use of technology for communication in chapters 5 and 10. Children with physical and health impairments can also use these tools to communicate (see Samantha's story in chapter 5). But analysis of the communication needs of children with physical disabilities and health impairments will be different from the analysis of the needs of other children. For example, the technology needs of a child with normal intelligence but limited motor ability is different from an analysis of a child with profound mental retardation but average motor abilities.

For many children with physical disabilities, the following communication technology might be useful: head pointers, visual scanners, head switches, finger or toe switches. These tools might be used together with an electric typewriter, a computer keyboard, or an automated language board (Lambert, 1985).

In telecommunications the speaker phone is especially helpful to people with disabilities. This simple device makes telephone conversations comfortable for individuals who do not have the strength or mobility to hold a telephone receiver but who can otherwise communicate on the telephone. The speaker phone is another example of using easily available technology to address the individualized needs of a person with physical disabilities or health impairments.

Advanced technology opens the door of communication for those with physical disabilities. They can accomplish goals once thought impossible. For example, Ruth Sienkiewicz-Mercer, a woman with a severe physical disability and communication problems wrote her memoir *I Raise My Eyes to Say Yes* with the help of extensive communication boards.

Mobility

Mobility is an area where the benefits of technology are most obvious. Individuals with disabilities can choose from a wide variety of lightweight or electric specialized wheelchairs, including motorized chairs, computerized chairs, chairs in which it is possible to rise, wilderness sports chairs, and racing chairs. Electronic switches permit persons with only partial head or neck control or finger or foot control to move about independently. Driving a car is also possible (Risk, 1985). Imagine the freedom of movement such technology allows. Think about the increased privacy and personal independence that becomes possible.

Individuals may also select artificial limbs, personalized equipped vans, and electrical walking machines to enhance mobility. "Bionic" limbs have also become available. Myoelectric (or bionic) limbs are hollow, but contain a sensor that picks up electric signals transmitted from the individual's brain through the limb.

robotics. High technology mechanisms that perform motor skills.

This boy's bionic arm enables him to practice his cello.

Robotics is another area that holds promise for the future of people with physical disabilities. Robotics is the use of sophisticated devices to accomplish motor skills such as grasping. For example, robotic arms can manipulate objects by at least three directional movements: extension/retraction, swinging/rotating, and elevation/depression (Apostolos, 1985). Models of voice-activated robots are in the developmental stages but are estimated to cost about $300,000 (Moore, Yin, and Lahm, 1986). Might some of the actions that personal care attendants currently accomplish for people with disabilities be done by robots in the future? Manipulator robots have been successfully used in assisting children in such self-help activities as dialing a telephone, turning book pages, and drinking from a cup (Kwee, 1986). Costs, transportability, repairs, and training are currently roadblocks to the wide use of this type of technology (Heckathorne, 1986), but in the future such technology might become more economical and widely used.

Specially trained animals sometimes assist individuals with physical disabilities. Service dogs, for example, have been trained to pull a wheelchair, pick up things, open doors, push elevator buttons, turn lights off and on, and bring a telephone receiver. Capuchin monkeys, chosen for their small size and ability to perform tasks, were bred at Disney World and trained to assist people with physical disabilities. They can feed the individual, dial a speaker phone, and turn on the television, stereo, and even the VCR.

Graduation is a day for everyone to celebrate their accomplishments.

Concepts and Controversies

Inclusion Versus Segreation

Are separate special education classrooms or schools for children with physical disabilities and health impairments necessary? As we have discussed throughout this book, students with disabilities should be educated in the least restrictive environment. Sometimes, however, separate classrooms or even separate schools for students with physical disabilities and health impairments are proposed. Are they justified? Think about these questions in the context of what you have learned about physical disabilities and health impairments.

What is the purpose of separate classes or separate schools? Are they for the benefit of the child with disabilities or for the convenience of someone else? Perhaps the regular class teachers in the schools are uncomfortable about teaching children with physical handicaps. Frith and Edwards (1981) found that regular class teachers had many misconceptions about children with physical disabilities.

But it does appear that students with physical handicaps require some extra time from their teachers (Brullem et al., 1983). Might this justify keeping them in segregated classes?

Some argue that all of the special equipment and furniture needed by children with physical disabilities should be located in one place for the sake of efficiency. Others argue that it would be too expensive to make every school physically accessible, so only one school in the district should be accessible.

Think about the health care and nursing needs of some of these children. Might medical needs justify some separateness?

What are the arguments against separate classes and separate schools for children with physical disabilities and health impairments? Think about how heterogeneous this category of children is, ranging from children with seizures to children who require constant medical attention, from children with asthma to children with leg braces. Do they really have so much in common that they need to be in one place, separated from other students? How do you respond to the other arguments?

SUMMARY

Children with physical disabilities and health impairments have limitations that adversely affect their educational performance unless special education is provided.

1. These children's special education needs may include special teaching, scheduling, counseling, therapies, equipment, and technology. Children with physical disabilities and health impairments may be absent frequently from school because of fragile health or medical treatments. They may need special leg braces or wheelchairs, they may need adaptive equipment such as swivel spoons or pencils with extra grips, they may have physical needs such as assistance with medications or with bladder catheterization or seizure assistance. Some may present potential emergencies in which the teacher will be required to be familiar with emergency techniques. Some of these children also will face powerful emotional issues, such as their impending death or continuous physical dependence, many years before their young friends must face such issues.

2. Many physical disabilities and health impairments are relatively easy to prevent. Even if the condition cannot be totally prevented, the disabling effects can be lessened. For example, spinal cord injury in young children is most often caused by car accidents or child abuse. (A common site of spinal cord dislocation is in the lower back due to the effects of spanking.) The use of child restraints and safety belts can prevent many automobile accident injuries. Family support services and training in effective parenting techniques can help parents understand the harmful physical as well as emotional effects of physical punishment. In older children and adults, the most common causes of spinal cord injury are car accidents, falls and jumps, gunshot wounds, and diving accidents.

3. The most common neurological impairment encountered in the school is epilepsy. Epilepsy is a disorder in which there is a tendency to recurrent seizures. Seizures are spontaneous abnormal discharges of the electrical impulses of the brain, involving the entire brain or only a portion of it. The frequency of seizures may vary from a single isolated incident to hundreds in a day.

4. Cerebral palsy is a condition in which the person is unable to fully control movement or motor function. This condition is a result of damage to certain areas of the brain during development. Usually, the damage occurs close to the time of birth. The major source of damage is an incident that prevents a sufficient amount of oxygen from getting to the brain. Cerebral palsy is not a disease. It is, rather, a condition that is nonprogressive and noninfectious. Once it is acquired, it cannot be cured. Damage may occur before (prenatally), during (perinatally), or immediately after (postnatally) the child's birth. Occasionally, an individual will acquire cerebral palsy later in childhood. Acquired cerebral palsy is usually the result of brain damage resulting from accidents, brain infections, or child abuse.

5. Spina bifida refers to the failure of the spinal column to close properly. The spinal column is the protective column through which nerves transmit critical messages from the brain to other parts of the body. This bony tube of vertebrae in the back encases and protects the nervous tissue of the spinal cord and its covering, the meninges. The spinal cord extends to and is connected to the brain. Occasionally, birth defects occur along the spinal cord. These can occur anywhere from the tailbone (coccyx) to the neck area. The defects range in seriousness depending on how high the defect is along the spinal column (the closer to the neck, the more serious the impairment) and how much of the nerve material is involved in the damage.

6. Technology can assist many people with physical disabilities and health impairments to have improved health and lead independent lives.

7. The three major types of physical disabilities and health impairments are (a) impairments of health and diseases such as asthma, cystic fibrosis, and HIV infection; (b) neurological impairments, in which the spinal cord or brain are damaged, such as spina bifida, cerebral palsy, and seizure disorders; and (c) neuromuscular diseases such as polio, muscular dystrophy, and multiple sclerosis. There is great diversity among these disabilities.

DISCUSSION QUESTIONS

1. What other disabilities might occur in combination with a physical disability? Select several combinations of disabilities and analyze how the child might be affected in each.

2. When a child's movements are clumsy or jerky, it is sometimes difficult to participate with other children or the family in recreational activities. What recreational activities might you suggest in the IEP for a child in a wheelchair? Can the child share these activities with the family and enjoy them as an adult too?

3. Suppose a community planned a health fair on the prevention of physical disabilities and health impairments. What topics ought to be included?

4. Describe some inexpensive adaptations that an individual with physical disabilities might make to his clothing to make sitting in a wheelchair more comfortable.

5. Develop an outdoor recess activity for an elementary school class that can include children with and without physical disabilities.

SUPPLEMENTARY BOOKS AND VIDEOS

People with physical disabilities and health impairments have been portrayed in many books and films over a long period of time. You might find some creative works of interest in the partial lists found below.

Books

Brown, C. (1955). *My left foot.* New York: Simon & Schuster.

Callahan, J. (1989). *Don't worry, he won't get far on foot: The autobiography of a dangerous man.* New York: William Morrow.

De Ford, F. (1983). *Alex: The life of a child.* New York: Viking Press.

Gallagher, H. G. (1985). *FDR's splendid deception.* New York: Dodd Mead & Co.

Nolan, C. (1987). *Under the eye of the clock.* New York: St. Martin's Press.

Perske, R. (1986). *Don't stop the music.* Nashville: Abingdon Press.

Treves, F. (1923). *The Elephant Man and other reminiscences.* London: Cassell & Co. Ltd.

Videos

Mask (1985). MCA Home Video.

Gaby: A true story (1987). Tri-Star.

Born on the fourth of July (1989). Universal.

My left foot (1989). Miramax Pictures.

Edward Scissorhands (1990). 20th Century Fox.

GLOSSARY

ABC model. A framework for analyzing behavior that takes into account both the events that precede the behavior and the events that are subsequent to it; A = antecedent, B = behavior, C = consequence.

ability grouping. Placement of students with comparable achievement and skill levels in the same classes or courses, an arrangement often used in the education of students who are gifted.

absence seizure. A seizure characterized by a short lapse in consciousness.

academic achievement. The grade level at which a student functions in specific academic areas such as reading and mathematics, typically determined through standardized achievement tests.

acceleration. More rapid than usual passage by a student through a curriculum or grades of school.

accommodation. The focusing process of the lens of the eye.

acquired handicap. A disabling condition having onset after birth.

acuity. Degree of response to visual, auditory, or tactile stimuli.

adaptive behavior. Individual behavior that meets the standards of personal independence and social responsibility expected for age and cultural group; an essential component in the diagnosis of mental retardation.

advanced placement. Courses taken by high school students to earn college credit.

advance organizers. Written material or statements made by a teacher to focus students' attention on the upcoming lesson by previewing the material to be covered and providing a rationale for the importance of the information to be presented.

adventitious blindness. A severe visual impairment acquired after the age of two.

advocate. An individual, parent, or professional who promotes the interests of persons with disabilities.

age of onset. The age at which a handicap begins.

aggression. Hostile and attacking behavior, which can include verbal communication, directed toward self, others, or the physical environment.

AIDS. Acquired immune deficiency syndrome; see *human immunodeficiency virus.*

air-conduction audiometry method. A method used to test hearing using a pure tone sound generated by an audiometer.

alerting devices. Devices that use attention-getting sight, sound, or vibration to make individuals who are deaf or blind aware of an occurrence or an important sound.

alpha fetoprotein analysis. A prenatal diagnostic test in which the blood of the mother is analyzed for certain proteins.

American Association on Mental Deficiency (AAMD). An earlier name for American Association on Mental Retardation.

American Association on Mental Retardation (AAMR). The oldest and largest multidisciplinary mental retardation organization investigating and promoting the best practices for people with mental retardation; Seguin was first president in 1876.

American Sign Language (ASL). A fully developed natural language, one of the world's many signed languages; the sign language or manual communication system preferred by many adults who are deaf in the United States.

American Speech and Hearing Association (ASHA). See *American Speech-Language-Hearing Association.*

American Speech-Language-Hearing Association (ASHA). A professional organization concerned with communicative disorders.

Americans with Disabilities Act (ADA). Federal disability antidiscrimination legislation passed in 1990.

amniocentesis. A prenatal diagnostic test in which amniotic fluid is withdrawn from the mother's uterus and the cells are analyzed for possible genetic anomalies in the fetus.

analytic listening. Hearing, analyzing, and possibly interpreting another person's communication or verbal message.

anencephaly. A condition in which the brain fails to develop completely or is absent.

aniridia. Undeveloped iris due to lack of pigment, resulting in extreme sensitivity to light.

Annual Report to Congress on the Implementation of the Individuals with Disabilities Education Act. A report delivered to the federal government each year on students receiving special education in all types of educational settings.

anorexia. An eating disorder characterized by intense fear of gaining weight, disturbed body image, chronic absence or refusal of appetite for food, causing severe weight loss of at least 25 percent of body weight.

anoxia. Inadequate supply of oxygen to the body and brain, usually at birth.

anvil. One of the three tiny bones (ossicles) in the middle ear.

anxiety. A state of painful uneasiness, emotional tension, or emotional confusion.

aphasia. Impaired ability to use language or articulate ideas due to brain injury or stroke.

appreciative listening. Listening for the sake of enjoyment, such as listening to music.

appropriate education. A standard, required by IDEA, which guarantees that students with disabilities receive an educational program individually tailored to their abilities and needs.

array of services. A wide selection of services that are available so an appropriate education can be provided to each student with special needs.

arthritis. Pain and inflammation in joints.

articulation. The process of forming speech sounds.

articulation disorders. Abnormal production of speech sounds.

asphyxia. Deprivation of oxygen, often through near drowning or smoke inhalation.

assertiveness. Promoting one's own interest.

assessment. The process of determining the presence of a handicapping condition and students' current functioning levels through standardized testing procedures; also see *diagnosis*.

assistive devices. See *assistive technology*.

assistive listening devices (ALDs). Equipment, like hearing aids, that helps individuals with hearing impairments use their residual hearing.

assistive technology. Technological equipment designed to help individuals function in their environment.

Association for Children and Adults with Learning Disabilities (ACALD). See *Learning Disability Association of America*.

Association for Children with Learning Disabilities (ACLD). See *Learning Disability Association of America*.

Association for Retarded Citizens (ARC). An organization founded by parents of children with mental retardation to advocate, seek resources, and shape public policy.

associations. Mentally making relationships among and between items and/or concepts; professional, parent, and consumer organizations.

associative thinking. The ability to see relationships among differing concepts or knowledge bases.

assumed brain injury. A medical term referring to the possible cause of some learning disabilities, thought by special educators to be misleading because it gives the impression that nothing can be done about the condition.

asthma. A chronic condition causing difficulty in breathing.

astigmatism. An eye disorder that produces images on the retina that are not equally in focus.

ataxia. Movements disrupted by impairments of balance and depth perception.

athetoid. Purposeless and uncontrolled involuntary movements.

at risk. Children whose history (family, developmental, medical), physical characteristics, life circumstances, or environment suggest that without intervention they will be identified as having disabilities later in life; a category of preschoolers under the age of three who are suspected of having a handicap, and are eligible for special services without needing a specific label.

atrophy of the optic nerve. Reduced function of the optic nerve.

attentive listening. Focusing on one specific form of heard communication while ignoring others heard simultaneously.

attention deficit disorder (ADD). A condition characterized by hyperactivity, inability to control one's own behavior, and constant movement.

attention-deficit/hyperactivity disorder (ADHD). See *attention deficit disorder*.

attention deficits. Characteristics often associated with learning disabilities that impair learning; students do not pay attention to the learning task or to the correct features of the task.

attributes. Common characteristics or features of a group.

attributions. Explanations individuals give themselves for their successes or failures.

audiogram. A graph drawn from the results of an audiometer hearing test that charts an individual's thresholds of hearing at various frequencies against sound intensities in decibels.

audiologist. A specialist in evaluation, habilitation, and rehabilitation of hearing impairments.

audio loop. A device that directs sound from the source directly to the listener's ear through a specially designed hearing aid.

audiometer. An electrical instrument used to measure the threshold of hearing for pure tones of different frequencies.

auditory nerve. The nerve that carries messages received through the ear to the brain.

auditory threshold. See *hearing threshold*.

augmentive communication device. Equipment, such as a microcomputer with synthesized speech, that helps people communicate with others.

augmentive communication systems. A global term referring to a variety of alternative methods of communicating, for example communication boards, communication books, sign language, and computerized speech.

aura. A signal a person with epilepsy receives of an impending seizure.

autism. A severe disorder of thinking, communication, interpersonal relationships, and behavior.

aversive treatment. A noxious and sometimes painful consequence that would usually be avoided, for example electric shock, used for behavior modification.

backward chaining. See *chaining*.

barrier games. Games that encourage language development by having children describe objects while others guess what they are describing.

basic interpersonal communicative skills (BICS). The language of face-to-face conversational skills that can be acquired within about two years.

behavioral disorders. A condition of disruptive or inappropriate behaviors that interferes with a student's learning, relationships with others, or personal satisfaction to such a degree that intervention is required.

behavioral goals and objectives. Expected and desired learning outcomes for students; stated in measurable terms so the teaching and learning process can be evaluated.

behavior management. Systematic use of behavioral techniques, such as behavior modification, to control or direct responses.

behavior modification. Systematic use of the principles of learning, including rewards and punishment, to promote desired behaviors and discourage undesired behaviors in an individual.

bell-shaped curve. See *normal curve.*

biased responding. A predisposition to answer in a certain way regardless of the question.

bilingual. The capacity for using two languages, usually with differing levels of skill.

bilingual approach. See *bilingual maintenance approach* and *bilingual transitional approach.*

bilingual maintenance approach. Teaching partly in English using ESL strategies and partly in students' home language so that the students maintain proficiency in their home language while gaining proficiency in English.

bilingual transitional approach. Teaching partly in English using ESL strategies (especially math and science) and partly in students' home language (especially reading and writing) until they learn enough English to be able to get by without home language instruction.

Bill of Rights for Children with Communicative Disorders. Developed by Roland Van Hattum to help insure that the educational system meets the needs of children with communicative disorders.

blindisms. Inappropriate social behaviors possibly due to understimulation of infants with low vision.

bone-conduction method. A method used to test for conductive hearing losses where a vibrator is placed on a person's forehead so sound bypasses the outer and middle ear and goes directly to the inner ear.

braille. A system of reading and writing that uses dot codes that are embossed on paper, developed by Louis Braille around 1829.

brainstorming. An instructional activity where a group of students think of different ways items or information relate; used to develop thinking skills.

bronchopulmonary dysplasia. A type of lung disease that some premature infants get; the airways and actual lung tissue grow abnormally, making it difficult for the infant to breathe.

bulimia. An eating disorder in which the person chronically causes himself or herself to vomit after eating, limiting weight gain.

captions. Printed subtitles of the words spoken in film or video, can be either *closed* or *open.*

career education. A curriculum designed to teach individuals the skills and knowledge necessary in the world of work.

case manager. See *service manager.*

cascade of services. A model associating particular special education services and placements with severity of handicap, developed by Deno and his colleagues.

cataract. A cloudy film over the lens of the eye.

categorical. A system of labeling using specific classifications such as learning disabilities or mental retardation.

categorical programs. Classes available only to those students identified as having a specific disability, such as learning disabilities, mental retardation, visual impairments, hearing impairments, etc.

categorizing. A thinking skill involving grouping or classifying items or concepts into categories.

center schools. Segregated school settings that typically serve students with a particular type of handicapping condition (for example, visual impairments, hearing impairments); some of these schools are residential.

central nervous system dysfunction. See *presumed central nervous system dysfunction.*

central vision. The ability to see a field of vision greater than 20 degrees.

cerebral palsy. A disorder of movement and posture caused by a defect in the developing brain.

chaining. A strategy to teach the steps of skills that have been task analyzed; in the chain either the first step can be taught first (*forward chaining*) or the last taught first (*backward chaining*).

Child Find. An organized effort to locate and identify children with disabilities.

children at risk. See *at risk.*

chorionic villus sampling. A prenatal diagnostic test in which fetal cells are snipped from the developing placenta for genetic analysis.

chromosome. The rodlike body that carries the genes; normally, individuals have 22 pairs of autosomes and two sex chromosomes.

chunking. Clustering information into smaller pieces so it can be more easily remembered.

classification. A structured system that identifies and organizes characteristics to establish order.

classifying. Grouping items or concepts into categories marked by common characteristics.

clean intermittent catheterization (CIC). Inserting a clean tube (catheter) through the urethra to empty the bladder on a regular schedule, usually every three to four hours.

cleft palate. A congenital condition in which the roof of the mouth is not joined together, causing too much air to pass through the nasal cavity when the individual is speaking; although plastic surgery is helpful, a cleft palate results in a speech disorder requiring extensive attention from speech/language pathologists and other specialists.

closed captions. Captions or subtitles that show words spoken in film or video in print, these captions are available for viewing, but can be seen on the television screen only with the use of a decoder.

closed-circuit television (CCTV). Using a television for transmissions not accessible to the general public; sometimes only one camera and one television monitor are used.

cluster programs. A plan where gifted students spend a part of their day in the regular classroom on enriched or accelerated activities.

cochlea. Part of the inner ear that contains fluid and hair-like nerve cells that transmit information to the brain.

cochlear implants. Microprocessors that replace the cochlea and allow some people who are deaf to process sounds.

cognitive academic linguistic proficiency (CALP). The abstract language abilities required for academic work, usually requires about five to seven years to acquire.

cognitive behavior modification (CBM). Instructional strategies that use internal control methods (such as self-talk) in structured ways to help students learn how to learn; the approach was initially developed by Meichenbaum.

collaborate. To work cooperatively with other professionals providing educational services to students with disabilities. See *collaboration*.

collaboration. Group effort of special education teachers, regular education teachers, other service providers, and families working together to provide the best possible services and education.

communication. The transfer of knowledge, ideas, opinions, and feelings, either verbally or nonverbally, that allows people to interact with others on many dimensions.

communication board. A flat device on which words, pictures, or other symbols are placed to expand the verbal interactions of people with limited vocal abilities; high-technology versions are computerized and produce synthesized speech.

communication game. A way of conceptualizing communication as a game with at least two players (the sender and receiver) and a message.

communication process. The process used by people to communicate with others.

communication signals. Gestures, social formalities, or voiced messages that announce some immediate event, person, action, or emotion.

communication symbols. Spoken words or utterances, letters of the alphabet, pictures, or gestures used to relay a message; these usually refer to a past, present, or future event, person, object, action, or emotion.

communicative competence. How well an individual can communicate with others, typically gauged in terms of oral language.

communicative disorders. An impaired ability to function well in the communication process because of a speech or language disorder.

community-based instruction (CBI). A strategy of teaching functional skills in the environments in which they occur; for example, shopping skills taught in the local market rather than in the classroom.

community living arrangement. A home located in a typical residential neighborhood.

complex partial seizure. A period of automatic behavior resulting from discharge in a localized area of the brain, sometimes called psychomotor or focal seizure.

computer assisted instruction (CAI). Instructional programs focusing on a particular topic that supplement or replace traditional teacher-directed instructional methods and are delivered at least in part by using a computer.

computer enhanced instruction. Software programs that supplement traditional instruction, used primarily for drill and practice.

computer network system. Linked computers and telephone lines that allow people to communicate with each other and with various resources like research laboratories and major library facilities.

conceptualize. Generate questions and formulate abstract ideas.

conduct disorder. A type of behavioral disorder in which persistent, negative, hostile, antisocial behavior impairs daily life functioning.

conductive hearing loss. Hearing loss caused by an impairment of the outer or middle ear that prevents transfer of sound to the inner ear.

confidential school records. Private files of a student that are often not kept at the child's school; includes test scores, observations, a family history, and evaluations of social, academic, and other skills.

congenital. Present at birth.

congenital visual impairment. A severe visual impairment present at birth.

consulting teacher. A specially trained teacher who serves as a resource person to advise and provide instructional support to teachers who have students with disabilities in regular classrooms.

content. One of the three aspects of language; governs the intent and meaning of the message delivered in a communication.

continuum of services. Full range of educational services arranged in a stairstep fashion, where one level of service leads directly to the next one. See also *cascade of services* and *array of services*.

contracture. Joint stiffening, often because of muscle shortening, to the point the joint can no longer move through its normal range.

convergent thinking. The process of reaching conclusions by using known facts; using thinking skills associated with academic learning such as memory, classification, and reasoning.

conversations. Oral exchanges of ideas, opinions, feelings, beliefs, and sentiments.

convulsive disorders. A general term for seizure disorders and epilepsy.

cornea. The transparent, curved part of the front of the eye.

Council for Exceptional Children (CEC). The largest professional organization of special educators concerned with all exceptionality areas, founded by Elizabeth Farrell in 1922.

creativity. A form of intelligence characterized by advanced divergent thought, the production of many original ideas, and the ability to develop flexible and detailed responses and ideas.

critical thinking. Evaluative thinking; problem solving abilities.

cross-categorical. Classes available to students with a variety of disabilities usually according to level of severity.

cultural pluralism. All cultural groups are valued components of the society and the language and traditions of each group are maintained.

curriculum. A systematic grouping of content, activities, and instructional materials.

curriculum based assessment (CBA). A method of evaluating children's learning and the instructional procedures by collecting data on students' daily progress on each instructional task.

curriculum compacting. Saving time in the instructional day by reducing the time spent on typical academic subjects so enrichment activities can be included in the curriculum for the gifted.

cystic fibrosis. A disorder of chronic lung infections and malabsorption of food.

cytomegalovirus (CMV). A common herpes virus that usually causes few if any symptoms in an adult but can cause severe brain damage including sensorineural hearing losses to a developing fetus.

deaf. A profound hearing disability; a person who is deaf cannot understand sounds in the environment, such as speech and language of others, with or without the use of a hearing aid; hearing cannot be used as the primary way to gain information.

DeafNet. Electronic mail system for people who are deaf.

decibels (dB). Units of measure for intensity of sound.

decoder. A device that allows closed captions to appear on a television screen.

deducing. A thinking skill where a person comes to a conclusion from known facts or general principles; a type of convergent thinking.

degeneration of the macula. See *macular degeneration.*

deinstitutionalization. Decreasing the number of individuals with disabilities living in large congregate facilities.

delinquency. Illegal behavior, which may or may not be the result of a behavioral disorder, committed by juveniles.

demographics. Data used to describe the characteristics of a population or group of people.

demonstration. Showing someone how to solve a problem or execute a task by using a concrete example or sample problem.

depression. A state of despair and dejected mood.

desktop publishing. Using a piece of equipment, such as a microcomputer, to prepare written material in publication format and quality.

Developing Understanding of Self and Others (DUSO). A commercially available instructional program designed to increase language, cognitive, and social skills for students in the primary grades.

dexadrine. A drug sometimes prescribed for the management of hyperactivity.

diabetic retinopathy. Changes in the eye's blood vessels, caused by diabetes.

diagnosis. Process of identifying an individual as having a disability by using a series of standardized tests and observational procedures. See also *assessment.*

diagnosticians. See *educational diagnosticians.*

dialect. Words and pronunciation from a particular area or group, different from the language used by the normative group.

dignity of risk. Enhancing the human dignity of individuals by enabling them to experience the risk taking of ordinary life that is necessary for normal growth and development.

direct instruction. A method of teaching academic subjects; involves systematic instruction of the skill to be learned and the collection of data evaluating the effectiveness of the teaching procedure selected.

Directing Discourse. An example of an instructional material designed to increase adolescents' language and cognitive skills.

Disabilities Forum. A telemail system, provided by CompuServe for individuals in the field of disabilities.

discalculia. Impaired ability to calculate or perform mathematical functions.

discipline. Teaching students self-control; fostering self-management of behavior; teaching students to follow the rules of proper conduct.

discrepancy formulas. Formulas developed by state educational agencies or local school districts to determine the difference between a students' actual achievement and expected achievement based on scores from tests of achievement and intelligence.

discrepancy scores. The scores resulting from the application of a discrepancy formula; used in some states to determine eligibility for programs designed for students with learning disabilities.

disgraphia. Impaired ability to write.

distance education. The use of telecommunications to deliver live instruction by content experts to remote geographic settings.

distance senses. The senses—hearing and vision—that provide us with information external to our bodies; senses developed to help alert us to danger.

distractible. Having impaired ability to focus on a task, often characteristic of youngsters with learning disabilities.

divergent thinking. Using creative thinking skills such as fluency, flexibility, originality, and elaboration; usually, conclusions are reached by reorganizing information and developing a variety of responses.

Down syndrome. A chromosomal disorder that causes identifiable physical characteristics and usually causes delays in physical and intellectual development and puts individuals at high risk for communicative disorders and mental retardation.

dry eye. A cause of blindness that can be prevented through diet and nutrition.

due process hearing. A noncourt proceeding before an impartial hearing officer; when the parents and the special services committee cannot reach an agreement on the types of services and the educational program for a student, a third party settles the dispute.

dysfluencies. Aspects of speech that break the flow or pattern of speech such as hesitating, repeating, inserting fillers, or speaking too quickly; typical of normal speech development in young children.

dyslexia. Impaired ability to read, often caused by brain damage.

eardrum. The tympanic membrane, the part of the ear upon which sound waves and their vibrations fall and cause the ossicles to move; separates the outer and middle ear.

early childhood programs. Preschool, day care, and early infant school programs that involve students with disabilities and their families, designed to improve the speech, language, social, and cognitive skills of the students attending.

early intervention programs. See *early childhood programs*.

ecological assessment. Taking into consideration all dimensions of the individual's environment, including the individual.

educable mentally retarded (EMR). A term formerly used for people with mild mental retardation.

Education for All Handicapped Children Act (EHA). See *Individuals with Disabilities Education Act*.

educational diagnosticians. Professionals trained to test and evaluate individual children and youth to determine whether they are eligible for special education, and, if so, what special services they require.

educational placement. The location or type of classroom program (for example, resource room) arranged for a child's education; the setting in which a student receives educational services.

eighth cranial nerve. See *auditory nerve*.

elective mutism. Refraining from speaking, not the result of physical problems with the muscles and organs of speech production.

Eleven-sentence Paragraph. A teaching tactic that helps students organize their thoughts to produce structured written compositions.

emotional disturbance. A term used interchangeably with behavioral disorders.

encephalitis. A virus that causes an inflammation of the brain that can result in cognitive and language disabilities if left untreated.

English as a second language (ESL). English instruction in the classroom or in special pull-out classes until English proficiency is achieved.

English for speakers of other languages (ESOL). See *English as a second language*.

enrichment. A common approach to teaching gifted students where topics or skills are added to the traditional curriculum or a particular topic is studied in more depth.

enrichment triad/revolving door model. A model for education of the gifted, created by Renzulli, where students participate in activities planned to develop thinking skills, problem solving, and creativity.

eminence. A position of superiority; a term often used in reference to genius, particularly by individuals like Sir Francis Galton and Lewis Terman.

epicanthic folds. A flap of skin over the innermost corners of the eyes.

epilepsy. A disorder in which there is a tendency to recurrent seizures. See also *convulsive disorders*.

evaluation. Assessment or judgment of special characteristics such as intelligence, physical abilities, sensory abilities, learning preferences, and achievement.

evaluative thinking. Thinking skills involved in making comparisons, contrasts, and decisions.

exceptionalities. All categories of special education including gifted.

excess cost. Expenses for the education of a child with disabilities that exceed the average expenses of education for a child without disabilities.

externalizing behaviors. Behaviors, especially aggressive behaviors, directed toward others.

feeding tubes. Tubes through which nutrients are placed directly into the body.

fetal alcohol effects (FAE). A disabling condition in which full *fetal alcohol syndrome* (see below) cannot be documented by the pregnant woman drinking alcohol.

fetal alcohol syndrome (FAS). A condition where a baby is born with mental impairments, behavioral problems, and perhaps some physical disabilities caused by the mother drinking alcohol during pregnancy.

finger spelling. A form of manual communication used by people with severe to profound hearing losses where each letter of the alphabet has a sign.

flexibility. A characteristic of creative thinking; the variety of ideas produced by an individual.

fluency. Smoothness and rapidity in skills; this term is associated with quickness in thinking; in speech, the rate, flow, and pattern of oral speech; in reading, the rate of correct oral reading; also used synonymously with proficiency or mastery in a variety of academic subjects.

fluency disorder. See *stuttering*.

fluent English proficiency (FEP). See *full English proficiency*.

FM transmission devices. Equipment used in many classrooms for students with severe hearing impairments that allows direct oral transmissions from the teacher to each individual student.

follow-up. To provide later monitoring, evaluation, diagnosis, or treatment after the initial diagnosis or treatment of a condition; a type of research that studies the lives of adults who were identified as having a disability during childhood.

follow-up study. A longitudinal research study that usually analyzes the adult outcomes of people who were subjects in a research study when they were children.

form. One of the three aspects of language; the rule systems of language comprised of phonology, morphology, and syntax.

forward chaining. See *chaining*.

free appropriate public education (FAPE). A major standard set forth in PL 94–142, now called the Individuals with Disabilities Education Act (IDEA), which states that students with disabilities are entitled to a free appropriate public education which often includes supportive services and highly individualized educational programs.

frequency of sound. The number of vibrations per second of molecules through some medium like air, water, or wires.

full English proficiency (FEP). Ability to read, write, and speak English at a level appropriate to the environment and capacity of the individual.

functional skill. A skill or task that will be used in the individual's normal environment.

Future Problem Solving Program. A national competition and instructional program developed by Torrance and his colleagues to teach creative problem solving; students attempt to find positive solutions to real issues such as the nuclear arms race and water conservation.

gait training. Analysis of and instruction in walking.

Gallaudet University. America's federally funded university serving students who are deaf at the undergraduate and graduate levels.

gene. A functional segment of DNA, the basic unit of heredity carried on the chromosome.

General Education Initiative. See *Regular Education Initiative*.

generalize. The process of transferring knowledge or skills learned in one situation to untaught situations; the ability to expand upon knowledge by applying it to novel situations; the transfer of learning from particular instances to other environments, people, times, and events.

generalized seizure. A seizure characterized by convulsions and loss of consciousness; traditionally referred to as a grand mal seizure.

gifted. A term describing individuals with high levels of intelligence, outstanding abilities, and capabilities for high performance.

glaucoma. Fluid in the eye is restricted, causing pressure to build up resulting in damage to the retina.

goals. See *behavioral goals*.

grand mal seizure. See *generalized seizure*.

group homes. Apartments or homes in which a small number of individuals with mental retardation live together as part of their community and receive assistance from service providers.

habilitation. An individualized program of education, training, and supportive services designed to enhance the abilities of an individual with mental retardation.

hammer. See *malleus*.

hard of hearing. A mild to moderate hearing impairment; individuals with this level of hearing loss have sufficient residual hearing to hear and comprehend others' speech and oral communication when using a hearing aid.

hardware. Computer equipment.

Head Start. National, federally funded early intervention programs designed primarily to serve young children who live in poverty; these programs typically assist at-risk preschoolers by providing an accepting and responsive environment that encourages thinking and communication skills.

health impairments. Physical health problems limiting strength.

hearing aid. A machine that intensifies sound to help people with hearing impairments process information presented orally.

hearing impairments. An overall term that includes all levels of hearing losses.

hearing threshold. The point at which a person can perceive the softest sound at each frequency level.

hertz (Hz). Units of measure for sound frequency.

heterogeneity. Differentness among members of a group.

high achiever. A student who expects success and views it as an incentive to work harder.

high intelligence. A combination of traits such as the ability to understand complex relationships, to think abstractly, and to solve problems, is usually demonstrated by achieving scores on intelligence tests that fall two standard deviations above the mean, or approximately 130 and above.

high-tech devices. Complex technical devices such as computers.

home or hospital teacher. A special teacher who teaches in the child's home or hospital when the child must be absent from school due to health problems.

homogeneity. Commonality of characteristics among members of a group.

honors sections. Advanced classes for students who show high achievement in specific subject areas.

Hoover cane. Long, white cane used in the mobility and orientation system developed in 1944 by Richard Hoover to help people with visual impairments move independently through the environment.

human immunodeficiency virus (HIV). A virus that affects the immune system and impairs the individual's ability to fight infections; often develops into AIDS.

hydrocephaly. A condition in which excess cerebrospinal fluid collects in the ventricles of the brain; can lead to an enlarged head, compacted brain, mental retardation, and other disabilities.

hyperactive. Unable to sit or concentrate for long periods of time.

hyperactivity. A high level of activity that is irritating to others and distracting to self.

hyperopia. Farsightedness, condition that permits visual focus on objects at a distance but not close.

Hypertext. A computer program that can be used to modify textbook materials through rewording, defining vocabulary, and providing further explanations.

IDEA. See *Individuals with Disabilities Education Act.*

identification. To seek out and identify children with disabilities within special education categories.

Illinois Test of Psycholinguistic Abilities (ITPA). A test to identify students as learning disabled; intended to determine strengths and weaknesses of individual students; also thought to identify students' learning styles and preferences to assist in instructional planning.

imitation. Learning by watching and copying the behavior of others.

immersion. Teaching a second language through content area instruction in that language by using contextual cues and adjustments to each student's proficiency; compare to *total immersion approach.*

inactive learners. Students who do not become involved in learning situations, approach the learning task purposefully, ask questions, seek help, or initiate learning.

incidence. The number of new cases that occur within a certain time period.

incidental learning. Knowledge gained as a result of other activities and experiences not specifically designed to teach the knowledge learned.

incontinent. Lacking bladder and/or bowel control.

incus. See *anvil.*

independent study. A common approach to the education of the gifted that allows a student to pursue and study a topic in depth on an individual basis.

index crime. Behavior that is illegal regardless of the age of the defendant; compare to *status offense.*

Individual Transition Plan (ITP). A written plan that identifies the skills and supportive services that an individual needs to function in the community after schooling is completed.

Individualized Education Program (IEP). A written plan of instruction required by IDEA for every school-age youngster receiving special education; the plan must include a statement of the individual's strengths and weaknesses, long-term and short-term goals and objectives, and all special services required.

Individualized Family Service Plan (IFSP). A written plan required by IDEA for children under the age of three who receive special preschool programs; identifies and organizes services and resources to help families reach their goals for their children.

Individualized Habilitation Plan (IHP). A written plan used to provide educational and social services to individuals living in an intermediate care facility.

individualized instruction. Instruction planned to meet the individual needs of students where they are presented with instructional tasks reflecting their own pace of learning; pinpointing exactly what the student does and does not know and providing instruction based on that information.

Individuals with Disabilities Education Act (IDEA). Formerly referred to as the Education for All Handicapped Children Act (EHA); originally passed as PL 94–142 in 1975, amended in 1986 by PL 99–457 to also provide instruction and services to infants and toddlers, amended and reauthorized again in 1990 under PL 101–476, which strengthened transitional programs for adolescents and young adults with handicaps; ensures a free appropriate public education in the least restrictive environment for all children and youth with disabilities.

Individual Written Rehabilitation Plan (IWRP). A written plan used to provide vocational rehabilitation for adults with disabilities.

inference. Decision or opinion based on assumptions; a conclusion drawn by using reason.

information processing theory. The suggestion that learning disabilities are caused by an inability to organize thinking and approach learning tasks systematically.

infused. Incorporating or integrating enrichment activities developed for gifted students into a regular education classroom setting.

institution of higher education (IHE). A postsecondary school, typically a college or university.

instructional goals. A statement about learning that includes a result to be achieved after specific instruction.

instructional objectives. Statements about learning that relate to an overall goal; includes a description of the student's behavior, the conditions under which the behavior is to occur, and the criteria for acceptable performance.

integrated classes. Regular education classes where students with special needs learn alongside students without disabilities.

intellectual functioning. The actual performance of tasks believed to represent intelligence such as observing, problem solving, and communicating.

intelligence. A person's ability to think, often measured by standardized tests.

intelligence quotient (IQ). The numerical figure, with a score of 100 being average, obtained from a standardized test; often used to express mental development or ability.

interactive video. A computer-controlled educational device students use to view and hear instructional presentations and make choices regarding the pace and order of the presentations.

Intermediate Care Facilities for the Mentally Retarded (ICF/MR). Federally funded community-based living centers or group homes where individuals with mental retardation reside.

interdisciplinary instruction. An educational approach that involves studying a topic and its issues in the context of several different disciplines; sometimes used in the education of the gifted.

internalizing behaviors. Behavior that is withdrawn into the individual.

internships. Programs that place students, usually gifted high school seniors, in job settings related to their career goals in order to challenge them and apply knowledge in real-life skills.

interpreter. A person who translates languages; someone who translates oral speech into sign language, and sign language into oral speech for persons who are deaf.

iris. The colored part of the eye.

itinerant specialists. Specialists from various disciplines—special education, speech, occupational therapy, physical therapy—who work at different schools across the week, some travel great distances as they go from school to school.

itinerant teachers. See *itinerant specialists.*

jigsaw technique. See *puzzle technique.*

job coach. An individual who works alongside people with disabilities, helping them to learn all parts of a job.

job developer. An individual who seeks out, shapes, and designs employment opportunities in the community for people with disabilities.

Joint Committee on Learning Disabilities (JCLD). A committee representing a number of professional, parent, and consumer organizations concerned with learning disabilities: International Reading Association, Orton Dyslexia Society, American Speech-Language-Hearing Association, Council for Learning Disabilities, Division for Learning Disabilities (a division of the Council for Exceptional Children), Learning Disability Association of America (formerly ACLD), Council for Children with Communication Disorders (a division of the Council for Exceptional Children), National Association of School Psychologists.

judicial hearing. A hearing before a judge in a court.

Kendall Demonstration School. A model elementary school on the campus of Gallaudet University that serves elementary-age students who are deaf.

Kurzweil Reader. Equipment designed for people with severe to profound visual impairments that translates print into synthesized speech; the first of these print to voice systems was developed by Kurzweil in 1975.

L1. Dominant, or home, language.

L2. Language learned second.

labeling. Assigning an individual as belonging to a group; associating an individual with a specific handicapping condition.

language. The formalized method of communication used by people; includes the signs and symbols by which ideas are represented and the rules that govern them so the intended message has meaning.

language delay. When children do not develop skills as quickly as their age peers; some children with language delays are language disordered and require the special assistance of a specialist so they can ultimately use language proficiently.

language disorder. Difficulty or inability to master the various language systems and their rules of application, morphology, phonology, syntax, semantics, and pragmatics, which then interferes with communication.

lateral dominance. A theory that one hemisphere of the brain controls motor responses and preference for eye–hand coordination.

learned helplessness. A situation that occurs when individuals expect to fail, become afraid of taking risks or attempting tasks, and then do not become actively involved in learning; often a result of repeated failure or control by others.

learning disabilities. A handicapping condition where the individual possesses average intelligence but is substantially delayed in academic achievement.

Learning Disability Association of America (LDAA). An advocacy organization of parents of children with learning disabilities that provides information to the public, schools, and community programs, formerly called Association for Children with Learning Disabilities (ACLD) and Association for Children and Adults with Learning Disabilities (ACALD).

learning strategies. Instructional methods to help students read, comprehend, and study better by helping them organize and collect information strategically.

learning styles. The systematic strategies individuals use to gain new skills and information.

least restrictive environment (LRE). A major principle of IDEA which states that students with handicaps should be integrated and receive their education in the most normal setting.

legally blind. Visual acuity measured as 20/200 or worse in the better eye with correction, or peripheral vision no greater than 20 degrees.

legislation. Laws passed by a legislature or Congress and signed by a governor or president.

lens. Part of the eye located behind the iris, brings objects into focus.

Let's Talk. A commercially available instructional program that provides ideas and lessons to increase language and cognitive skills for adolescents.

life skills. Daily living skills used to shop and cook, and to organize, clean, and manage home.

Likert scale. A system used in questionnaires or surveys to provide a forced-choice answer along a scale of some dimension (such as, strongly agree to strongly disagree, or like to dislike); the numbering system typically used ranges from 1 to 5 or from 1 to 7.

limited English proficiency (LEP). Limited ability to read, write, or speak English.

limited English-speaking. A category of students whose ability to speak English is limited.

litigation. Lawsuits or legal proceedings.

local education agency (LEA). Typically a local school district, but may be a cooperative district or set of districts which are funded as a single unit.

longitudinal study. See *follow-up study.*

loudness. One of the two aspects of voice; refers to the intensity of sound produced while speaking.

low achiever. A student who expects failure and sees no value in expending effort to learn.

low vision. A mild to moderate visual impairment; visual acuity as measured between 20/70 and 20/200.

low-incidence disability. A disability that occurs infrequently; the number of new cases is very low.

low-tech devices. Simple technical devices such as built-up spoons or crutches.

macular degeneration. Damage to a small area near the center of the retina, which restricts field of central vision resulting in difficulties with reading and writing.

magnet school. A center school that serves children who do not live in the immediate neighborhood; some magnet schools are designed to serve children whose parents work in a nearby area; other magnet schools emphasize a particular theme (such as theater arts, math, and science).

mainstreaming. Including students with special needs in regular education classrooms for some or all of their school day.

manual communication. Any formal or established system of manual gestures used for communication such as finger spelling or American Sign Language.

malleus. Hammer, one of the three tiny bones (ossicles) in the middle ear.

marginal listening. When the auditory content is not the primary focus of one's attention, as when we are involved in a task but listening to background music.

maternal rubella. See *rubella.*

mean. The sum of all scores divided by the number of scores; the average.

mediational strategies. The means for transmitting or communicating information.

meninges. The membranes that cover the brain and spinal cord.

meningitis. Inflammation of the meninges; a disease that affects the central nervous system and often causes hearing loss.

meningocele. A defect in the spinal column through which meninges (covering of the cord) protrude.

mental age. An age estimate of an individual's mental ability; expressed as the average chronological age of children who can ordinarily answer the questions in the test correctly; derived from a comparison of the individual's IQ score and chronological age.

mental retardation. A handicapping condition that affects cognitive functioning and adaptive behavior.

mentorships. An approach to education of the gifted where a student is paired with an adult in order to learn to apply knowledge in real life situations.

metacognition. A cognitive behavior modification strategy in which students use self-management techniques to help them remember what they are taught by talking themselves through systematic problem-solving steps.

microcomputer technology. Computer hardware and software used in instruction.

Migrant Student Record Transfer Service (MSRTS). A nationwide computerized transcript and health record service for migrant students, located in Little Rock, Arkansas.

mild mental retardation. The level of mental retardation that usually includes individuals with IQs from approximately 50–55 to 70–75.

Mimosa Cottage Project. One of the earliest demonstration and research sites for students with mental retardation, located at a state-funded institution in Parsons, Kansas, where research demonstrated that institutionalized individuals with severe disabilities could learn a variety of tasks.

minimal brain dysfunction. A condition associated with learning disabilities; a result of functional problems of the central nervous system or brain damage that can impair individuals' ability to learn or succeed at academic tasks.

minority language student. Student whose dominant or home language is not English.

mnemonics. A learning strategy that assists people in remembering information by associating the first letters of items in a list with a word, sentence, or picture.

mobility. The ability to travel safely and efficiently from one place to another.

modeling. An instructional tactic where one person demonstrates how to do a task or solve a problem while another person observes and copies those steps; see also *demonstration.*

moderate mental retardation. The level of mental retardation that usually includes individuals with IQs from approximately 35–40 to 50–55.

morphology. Rules that govern the structure and form of words; the basic meaning of words.

motivation. Presence of internal incentives to learn or perform, influenced by previous success or failure.

multicultural. Reflecting more than one culture.

multihandicapped. Having more than one handicapping condition; the combination causes severe educational problems.

multiple sclerosis. A degenerative nervous system disease leading to the loss of the myelin covering of nerves.

multiply handicapped. Possessing more than one handicapping condition.

muscular dystrophy. Progressive muscle weakness that comes from problems in the muscles themselves.

myelodysplasia. A general term for spina bifida.

myelomeningocele. A defect in the spinal column through which meninges (covering of the cord) *and* the spinal column protrude.

myopia. Nearsightedness; inability to focus on objects at a distance.

National Education Association (NEA). One of the largest organizations for professional educators.

National Joint Committee on Learning Disabilities. See *Joint Committee on Learning Disabilities.*

National Technical Institute for the Deaf. A postsecondary school, located in Rochester, New York, which offers technical and vocational degrees to students who are deaf.

natural setting. The environment in which individuals of comparable age typically live, work, and play.

neonatal intensive care (NIC). A specialized hospital unit for infants who are in need of intensive medical attention because of prematurity or other health reasons.

neurological. Relating to the nervous system.

neuromuscular. A neurological problem that affects the muscles, such as muscular dystrophy.

noncategorical. An approach to special education that does not classify or differentiate among disabilities or exceptionalities in providing services.

noncategorical classes. Classes that are available to students with a variety of handicaps, usually arranged according to the levels of severity (mild, moderate, severe, profound) of individuals' handicaps.

nondiscriminatory testing. Assessment that properly takes into account a child's cultural and linguistic diversity.

non-English-proficient. Lacking sufficient proficiency in reading, writing, or speaking English.

non-English-speaking. Lack of expressive and/or receptive proficiency in English.

non-English-language background (NELB). Home language is not English.

nonverbal behavior. Physical or gestural communication or actions, like raising your hand for teacher attention, or smiling; body language, communications that do not use oral language.

nonverbal cues. Information that is physical or gestural, like smiling or raising your hand for teacher attention.

normal curve. Bell-shaped curve plotting the normal distribution of human traits such as intelligence in a population.

normalization. Making available to people with mental disabilities patterns of life and conditions of everyday living that are as close as possible to or indeed the same as the regular circumstances and ways of life of society.

nystagmus. Rapid, involuntary movements of the eye that interfere with bringing objects into focus.

objectives. See *instructional objectives.*

obturator. A device that creates a closure between the oral and nasal cavities when the soft palate is missing or damaged, used by people with a cleft palate.

occupational therapist (OT). A professional who directs activities designed to improve muscular control as well as develop self-help skills.

open captions. Captions that appear on the television screen for all viewers to see.

ophthalmologist. A medical doctor who specializes in eye disorders.

Optacon Reader. Provides a sensation of printed materials on a person's finger.

optician. A person who fills either ophthalmologists' or optometrists' prescriptions for glasses or corrective lenses.

optic nerve. The nerve that sends messages from the eye to the visual center of the brain.

optic nerve atrophy. Reduced function of the optic nerve.

optometrist. Professional who measures vision and can prescribe corrective lenses.

oral approach or method. One method of instruction advocated for students who are deaf where they learn to communicate (both receiving and sending information) orally without using sign language.

oral language. Communication through speech, usually the most efficient mode of communicating.

orientation. The mental maps people use to move through environments.

orthopedic. Related to a physical deformity or disability of the skeletal system and associated motor function.

orthopedically impaired. A category in IDEA of children with severe physical deformities caused by congenital abnormalities (such as clubfoot), diseases (such as polio), or other causes (such as cerebral palsy).

ossicles. Three tiny bones (incus, malleus, stapes) in the middle ear that transmit sound waves from the eardrum through the middle ear to the cochlea.

ostomy. A surgical opening in the abdomen through which the bowel or bladder can be emptied.

other health impaired. A category in IDEA of children who have limited strength due to health problems.

otitis media. Infection of the middle ear and accumulation of fluid behind the eardrum which can result in hearing impairments, communicative disorders, or learning disabilities if it becomes a chronic condition.

outreach programs. Specialized programs offered in local communities by residential schools or centralized agencies serving students with special needs.

overlearning. More or longer practice than necessary for the immediate recall of a task.

overtraining. See *overlearning*.

partial seizure. A seizure affecting only a portion of the brain.

partially sighted. See *low vision*.

passive learners. See *inactive learners*.

Peabody Language Development Kits (PLDK). A commercially available series of instructional programs that include prepared lessons aimed at improving language and cognitive skills.

Peabody Picture Collection (PPC). A set of picture cards that can be used to improve individuals' vocabulary and expressive language skills in teacher-prepared activities.

perceptual motor training activities. The training of motor, visual, or auditory skills in an effort to improve academic performance.

perceptual skills. Ability to decode stimuli and act accordingly.

personal care attendant. An individual hired to assist with tasks such as personal maintenance and hygiene, mobility, household maintenance, child care, cognitive and life management, or security and safety.

personal disturbance. See *internalizing behaviors*.

phenylketonuria (PKU). A metabolic disorder present at birth in which certain proteins are not absorbed by the body, causing damage to the central nervous system and leading to mental retardation; can be prevented by a special diet.

phonology. The rules within a language used to govern the combination of speech sounds to form words and sentences.

physical disabilities. Problems with the body that interfere with functioning.

physical therapist (PT). A professional trained to treat physical disabilities through nonmedical means such as exercise, massage, heat, and water.

pitch. An aspect of voice; the perceived high or low sound quality of one's voice.

PL 94–142. See *Individuals with Disabilities Education Act*.

polio. A viral infection that attacks the nerve cells in the spinal cord that control muscle function.

postlingually deaf. Individuals who lost their ability to hear after they developed language.

postsecondary education. Education, usually offered by an institution of higher education that comes after high school (e.g., community college, technical vocational school, college, university, continuing education).

potential English proficiency (PEP). Capacity to attain proficiency in English.

pragmatics. A key element of communication that deals with the relationships among language, perception, and cognition.

prelingually deaf. Individuals who lost their ability to hear before they developed language.

preschool programs. See *early intervention*.

President's Committee on Mental Retardation (PCMR). A committee of citizens appointed by the president of the United States to annually report to the president on issues related to mental retardation.

presumed central nervous dysfunction. A medical term referring to the cause of some learning disabilities; thought by some special educators to be misleading because it gives the impression that nothing can be done about the condition; some brain or neurological damage that impedes individuals' motor and/or learning abilities.

prevalence. The total number of cases at a given time.

prevention. The avoidance of the development of a disability.

primary epilepsies. Seizure disorders that appear at a young age, occur in families with some history of epilepsy, have a stereotyped pattern, and have a predictable response to specific medications.

problem solving. The process of searching out, analyzing, and evaluating facts using various reasoning and thinking skills in order to develop appropriate and effective solutions.

process/product debate. Opposing beliefs held by professionals in the field of learning disabilities that either perceptual training or direct instruction is the more effective instructional approach; this debate centered on the efficacy of two different theories of instruction and was held during the 1970s; the perceptual training approach was not supported by researchers.

profound mental retardation. The level of mental retardation that usually includes individuals with IQs below approximately 20 to 25.

projective tests. Psychological tests in which ambiguous stimuli are presented in order to elicit unconscious thoughts or feelings.

psychiatric disorder. Related to mental illness.

psychodynamic approach. Explores subconscious emotions, motivations, and feelings.

psychosis. A generic term for a severe major departure from normal acting, thinking, and feeling that interferes with everyday adaptation.

pull out programs for gifted students. The most common educational placement for gifted students; gifted students spend part of the school day in a special class.

punishment. Any consequence that results in a decline in the rate or strength of the behavior being punished.

Purdue Secondary Model for Gifted and Talented Youth. A high school curriculum developed by Treffinger and his colleagues that combines two approaches used in the education of the gifted: enrichment and acceleration.

pure sounds. Sound waves of specific frequencies used to test an individual's hearing ability.

puzzle technique. A teaching tactic where children work together to complete tasks which encourages sharing, discussion, cooperative learning, and modeling.

reason abstractly. Ability to think about ideas and concepts; ability to draw inferences or conclusions from known or assumed facts.

reflex. An involuntary movement in response to a stimulus.

regular class. A typical classroom designed to serve students without disabilities.

Regular Education Initiative (REI). A position held by some special educators that students with disabilities should be served exclusively in regular education classrooms and not be "pulled out" to attend special classes; an attempt to reform regular and special education so they are a combined system that maximizes mainstreaming.

rehabilitation engineering. Using mechanical and engineering principles to improve an individual's physical functioning.

related services. Services that may or may not be part of the classroom curriculum, but support classroom instruction, such as transportation, physical therapy, occupational therapy, and speech and language therapy.

residual vision. The amount and degree of functional vision that one retains despite a visual handicap.

resonance system. See *resonating system.*

resonating system. Oral and nasal cavities where voice is shaped into speech sounds.

resource program. Student attends a regular class for the majority of the day and goes to a special education class several hours per day or for blocks of time each week.

respirator. A machine to assist with breathing.

respiratory system. The system of organs whose primary function is to take in oxygen and expel gases.

response cost. Loss of privileges, rewards, or withdrawal of attention contingent upon inappropriate behavior; applied to reduce the occurrence of a behavior.

retina. Inside lining of the eye.

retinal detachment. Detachment of the retina that interrupts transmission of visual information to the brain.

retinitis pigmentosa. A genetic eye disease that leads to progressive blindness.

retinoblastoma. A tumor in the retina.

retinopathy of prematurity (ROP). A severe visual handicap caused by too much oxygen to an incubated infant; formerly referred to as retrolental fibroplasia.

retrolental fibroplasia. See *retinopathy of prematurity.*

reversals. Letters or words written or read backward.

reverse chaining. See *chaining.*

rewards. Reinforcement given when a student performs a task correctly.

Ritalin. A drug sometimes prescribed to help students with ADD focus their attention on assigned tasks and reduce their hyperactivity.

robotics. The use of sophisticated devices to accomplish motor skills.

rubella. Commonly known as the German measles; a virus that, when contracted by a pregnant woman, has significant and harmful effects on the fetus; when contracted by a young child this virus can lead to death or lifelong disabilities.

Sander's chart. A chart that explains the development of articulation in children by showing the ages when various speech sounds develop.

schizophrenia. A type of psychosis; a severe emotional disorder in which the individual becomes irrational, and often delusional and socially withdrawn.

school psychologists. Professionals trained to test and evaluate individual children to determine whether they are eligible for special education, and, if so, what special services they require.

scoliosis. Curvature of the spine.

secondary epilepsies. Seizure disorders that appear at any age; might be the result of accidents or child abuse, metabolic disturbances such as hypoglycemia, brain tumors and abscesses, lesions, brain injury, meningitis, and alcohol or drug withdrawal.

Section 504 of the Vocational Rehabilitation Act. A federal law that forbids discrimination in federally funded programs against people with handicaps.

segregated classes. Classes used exclusively for students with special needs; see also *self-contained special education classes.*

seizure. A spontaneous abnormal discharge of the electrical impulses of the brain.

selective attention. Ability to attend to the critical features of a task.

selective listening. Focusing on only one sound in an environment, such as a lecture.

self-advocacy. A social and political movement started by and for people with disabilities to speak for themselves on important issues such as housing, employment, legal rights, and personal relationships.

self-contained special education classes. Special classes where students attend for most of the school day and are mainstreamed into regular education activities on a part-time basis; special classes that provide intensive, specialized instruction; some of these classes are categorical for students who have the same handicapping condition (e.g., all having hearing impairments), and some cross-categorical where class members have different disabling conditions (e.g., several with mental retardation, several with learning disabilities, etc.).

self-management techniques. Strategies that assist students in identifying and solving problems independently.

semantics. The system within a language that governs content, intent, and meanings of spoken and written language.

sensorineural hearing loss. A hearing loss, often in the severe to profound range, caused by damage to the inner ear or to the eighth cranial nerve, also known as the auditory nerve.

sequencing. See *sequential thinking.*

sequential thinking. Those abstract thinking skills used to categorize and put items in order according to various dimensions (such as size, weight, length).

seriously emotionally disturbed. The term used in IDEA to categorize students with behavioral disorders and emotional disturbance.

service manager. The person who oversees the implementation and evaluation of an Individualized Family Service Plan.

setting demands. The behavioral requirements, both obvious and subtle, of an environment.

severe mental retardation. The level of mental retardation that usually includes individuals with IQs from approximately 20–25 to 35–40.

sheltered workshops. Special segregated workshops attended by some adults with disabilities.

shunt. A tube to drain excess spinal fluid from the brain into a body cavity such as the abdomen.

sign language. See *manual communication.*

signals. See *communication signals.*

Snellen chart. A chart used to test children's visual acuity, developed by Snellen in 1862.

social conventions. Cultural rules that govern how language is used in interactions with friends, families, employers, and figures of authority.

social integration. Participation in all facets of society—education, employment, recreation, used with reference to persons with disabilities participating alongside those who are not disabled.

social interactions. Skills and behaviors occurring between or among people involving social, rather than academic, relationships.

socially maladjusted. A category of children who are excluded from the definition of *seriously emotionally disturbed;* there is no widely accepted definition for this group of children but it is intended to distinguish children who are delinquent and socially deviant from those who are emotionally disturbed.

socioeconomic status (SES). The status an individual or family unit holds in society, usually determined by one's job, level of education, and the amount of money available to spend.

software. The programs that make the computers work for computer assisted instruction, word processing, or computer enhanced instruction.

sonography. A prenatal diagnostic test that uses sound waves to determine size, position, and possible abnormalities of a fetus.

sound localization. Being able to locate the source of sounds.

spasticity. An uncontrolled tightening or pulling of muscles.

spatial relations. Information regarding the space between objects.

special education. Individualized education for children with special needs.

special education array. See *array of services.*

special services committee. A multidisciplinary team, including school administrators, regular and special education teachers, diagnosticians, related service personnel, and the child's parents who follow the process of identification, planning, writing the IEP, and evaluating the child's progress in special education.

speech. The vocal production of language, considered the fastest and most efficient means of communicating.

speech disorder. Abnormal speech that is unintelligible, unpleasant, or interferes with communication; can be of several types—voice, speech, or fluency (stuttering).

speech/language pathologist (SLP). A professional who works with children with communicative disorders in a variety of roles and settings.

speech mechanisms. Includes the various parts of the body—tongue, lips, teeth, mandible, and palate—required for oral speech.

speech synthesis. Computer-generated speech; a new option with TDDs that allows a printed message to be translated into a voice message through the use of a microcomputer.

speech synthesizers. Equipment that allows a message entered into a microcomputer to be translated into a voice message.

spina bifida. A developmental defect where the spinal column fails to close properly.

spina bifida meningocele. A condition in which there is a defect in the spinal column and a protrusion of the meninges.

spina bifida myelomeningocele. A defect in the spinal column through which the meninges (the covering of the cord) and the spinal cord protrude.

spina bifida occulta. A spinal column defect where bony protective arches of the spinal column have failed to develop.

spinal cord. The cord that extends through the bony spinal column to the brain.

Sputnik. The first space satellite, whose launching by the USSR in 1957 provoked a renewed interest in the education of the gifted in this country.

state education agency (SEA). Typically a state's department of education or division of special education.

standard deviation. A statistical measure that expresses the variability of a set of scores.

standard score points. A measure common to all tests so the results can be compared.

stapes. One of the three tiny bones (ossicles) in the middle ear.

status offense. Behavior that is defined as a crime due to the age of the juvenile; compare to *index crime*.

statute. Law passed by a legislature or Congress and signed by a governor or the president.

stirrup. See *stapes*.

strabismus. Improper alignment of the eyes that results in two images being received by the brain.

stuttering. A fluency disorder; the lack of fluency in an individual's speech pattern, often characterized by hesitations or repetitions of sounds or words.

subgroups. The groups of individuals who cluster by various characteristics and are already identified as members of a larger group.

submersion. The child is placed with native English speakers in all-English classrooms with no special language assistance; sometimes called the "sink or swim" method; compare to *total immersion approach*.

substance abuse. The deliberate and nontherapeutic use of chemicals such as alcohol, tobacco, drugs, gasoline, cleaning fluids, and glue in ways that contribute to health risks, disruption of psychological functioning, or adverse social consequences.

substitutions. Articulation errors made when incorrect sounds replace the correct ones, such as saying "wed" for "red"; reading errors made when one phonic sound replaces another.

supportive services. Auxiliary services—such as adaptive physical education, speech and language, audiology, physical or occupational therapy—required by many students with handicaps.

symbols. See *communication symbols*.

syntax. Rules of grammar that govern the endings attached to words and govern the order of words in phrases and sentences.

talented. A term that describes individuals who show natural aptitude or superior ability in a specific area; does not necessarily imply a high or superior degree of intelligence.

talking books. Audio versions of books.

task analysis. The act of breaking a task or skill into its component parts for instructional purposes.

Tay Sachs. A fatal metabolic condition in which fats are not properly processed by the body.

teacher's language. An important part of the learning environment for students; teachers need to match their oral and written language with the understanding abilities of students.

technology. Advancement and development of machines and devices that has greatly impacted the habilitation and instruction of individuals with disabilities.

technology-dependent children. Children who probably could not survive without technology such as ventilators.

Technology Related Assistance for Individuals with Disabilities Act of 1988. A federal act that provides funding and allows for technical assistance to persons with disabilities as they select and use assistive technology.

telecommunication device for the deaf (TDD). A piece of equipment that allows people to make and receive telephone calls by typing information over the telephone lines.

telecommunication devices. Devices that use sight or hearing to improve communication, captions are examples of telecommunication devices.

telecommunications. Various electronic devices that allow students and teachers to access and send materials and information across long distances; see also *computer network system*.

test content. The items and tasks of a test.

test standardization. Scores of a large number of individuals are collected and analyzed so that the score of a single individual can be compared to the norm.

test validity. The extent to which a test actually assesses what it claims to assess.

The Association for Persons with Severe Handicaps (TASH). A professional organization that promotes educational, policy, vocational, and habilitative research and discussion of people with severe disabilities.

theoretical construct. A model based on theory, not necessarily on practice or experience.

thinking skills. See *associations; chunking; classifying; convergent thinking; divergent thinking*.

tonic-clonic seizure. A seizure characterized by a stiff (tonic) phase in which the muscles become rigid, followed by a jerking (clonic) phase in which the arms and legs snap; also called grand mal seizure.

total communication approach or method. A system of instruction for students who are deaf which employs both oral speech and manual communication together.

total immersion approach. The student is taught entirely in English, and no English instruction or home language instruction is provided; all other students are also non-native-English speakers of similar proficiency levels, and the teacher can speak the student's home language; not to be confused with *submersion*; compare to *immersion*.

toxin. A poisonous substance that can cause immediate or long-term harm to the body.

trainable mentally retarded (TMR). A term formerly used for people with moderate mental retardation.

transfer of learning. See *generalization*.

transition. A period when a person is making a change; in special education, it refers to the period between one setting to another, such as from preschool to school, from elementary to middle school, and from school to work; the process of moving from adolescence to adulthood, within the context of social, cultural, economic, and legal considerations.

trauma. An injury.

traumatic brain injury. A category of disability included in IDEA in 1990; an injury to the brain that impairs learning, behavior, or motor functioning.

trisomy 21. The most common cause of Down syndrome; this genetic anomaly occurs when a third chromosome attaches to the chromosome 21 pair.

tuberculosis. An infectious disease usually affecting the lungs.

tuberous sclerosis. A syndrome usually characterized by mental retardation, seizures, and tumors.

tunnel vision. Severe limitation in peripheral vision.

tympanic membrane. See *ear drum*.

ultrasound. A medical testing procedure in which sound waves bouncing off a body (such as a fetus) produce an image.

use. One of the three aspects of language; applying language appropriately in social context and discourse; includes pragmatics.

ventilator. A machine to assist with breathing.

vibrating system. The larynx and vocal folds where voice is actually produced.

visual acuity. How well a person can see at various distances.

visual efficiency. How well a person can use sight.

visual impairments. An overall term that includes all levels of visual losses.

visual perception. Ability to decode visual stimuli.

vocal symbols. Oral means of relaying messages, such as speech sounds.

vocal system. Activated by the respiratory system, so voice can be produced by the larynx and vocal folds.

voice disorder. Abnormal spoken language production; characterized by unusual pitch, loudness, or quality of sounds.

word processing. Using the computer to write and edit text.

written symbols. Graphic means, such as the written alphabet, used to relay messages,.

REFERENCES AND SUGGESTED READINGS

CHAPTER 1   THE CONTEXT OF SPECIAL EDUCATION

The Context of Special Education—General

Martin, E. (June 30, 1988). *Wu Song and the tiger.* Modified from speech, International Conference on Special Education, Beijing, China.

Singer, J.D., & Butler, J.A. (1987). The Education for All Handicapped Children Act: Schools as agents of social reform. *Harvard Educational Review, 57,* 125–152.

U.S. Department of Education. (1990). *Twelfth Annual Report to Congress on the Implementation of the Education of the Handicapped Act.* Washington, DC: U.S. Government Printing Office.

Special Education Defined

34 C.F.R. (Code of Federal Regulations) Section 300.14.

Cromwell, R. L., Blashfield, R.K., & Strauss, J.S. (1975). Criteria for classification systems. In N. Hobbs (ed.), *Issues in the classification of children* (Vol. 1) (pp. 4–25). San Francisco: Jossey-Bass.

Hobbs, N. (Ed.). (1975a). *Issues in the classification of children* (Vol. 1). San Francisco: Jossey-Bass.

Hobbs, N. (Ed.). (1975b). *Issues in the classification of children* (Vol. 2). San Francisco: Jossey-Bass.

Hobbs, N. (1975c). *The futures of children: Categories, labels, and their consequences.* San Francisco: Jossey-Bass.

Mercer, J. (1973) *Labeling the mentally retarded.* Berkeley: University of California Press.

Soder, M. (1989). Disability as a social construct: The labeling approach revisited. *European Journal of Special Needs Education, 4,* 117–129.

History

Aiello, B. (1976). Especially for special educators: A sense of our own history. *Exceptional Children, 42,* 244–252.

Barr, M.W. (1913). *Mental defectives: Their history, treatment and training.* Philadelphia: P. Blakiston's.

Barsh, R.H. (1965). *A movigenic curriculum,* (Bulletin No. 25). Madison, WI: Department of Public Instruction, Bureau for the Handicapped.

Dunn, L. (1968). Special education for the mildly retarded—Is much of it justifiable? *Exceptional Children, 35,* 5–22.

Eberle, L. (1922, Aug.). The maimed, the halt and the race. *Hospital Social Service, VI,* 59–63. Reprinted in R.H. Bremner (Ed.) *Children and youth in America, a documentary history: Vol. II, 1866–1932* (pp. 1026–1028). Cambridge, MA: Harvard University Press.

Frostig, M., & Horne, D. (1964). *The Frostig program for the development of visual perception.* Chicago: Follett.

Itard, J.M.G. (1806). *The wild boy of Aveyron.* (G. Humphrey & M. Humphrey, Trans.). (1962). Englewood Cliffs, NJ: Prentice-Hall.

Kanner, L. (1964). *A history of the care and study of the mentally retarded.* Springfield, IL: Charles C. Thomas.

Kauffman, J.M. (1989). *Characteristics of behavior disorders of children and youth.* (4th ed.) Columbus: Merrill.

Kephart, N. (1960). *The slow learner in the classroom.* Columbus: Merrill.

Montessori, M. (1912). *The Montessori method.* (A. George, Trans.). New York: Stokes.

Nazzaro, J.N. (1977). *Exceptional timetables: Historic events affecting the handicapped and gifted.* Reston, VA: The Council for Exceptional Children.

Roos, P. (1970). Trends and issues in special education for the mentally retarded. *Education and Training of the Mentally Retarded, 5,* 51–61.

Sarason, S.B., & Doris, J. (1979). *Educational handicap, public policy, and social history.* New York: The Free Press.

Scheerenberger, R.C. (1983). *A history of mental retardation.* Baltimore: Paul H. Brookes.

Seguin, E. (1846). *The moral treatment, hygiene, and education of idiots and other backward children.* Paris: J.B. Balliere.

The summer school for teachers. (1907, Feb.). *The Training School Bulletin, 36,* 17.

Prevalence and Incidence

Hill, P. (1982). *Educational policymaking through the civil justice system.* Santa Monica, CA: Rand Corporation Institute for Civil Justice.

Families

Bower, D., & Wright, V.K. (1986). *The rubberband syndrome: Family life with a child with a disability.* Lincoln: Nebraska Department of Education; Des Moines: Iowa Department of Public Instruction.

Turnbull, A.P., & Turnbull, H.R. (1986). *Families, professionals, and exceptionality.* Columbus, OH: Charles E. Merrill.

Legislation and Litigation

Americans with Disabilities Act of 1990, P.L. 101-336.

Ballard, J., Ramirez, B.A., & Weintraub, F.J. (1982). *Special education in America: Its legal and governmental foundations.* Reston, VA: Council for Exceptional Children.

Brown v. Board of Education, 347 U.S. 483 (1954).

Burlington School Committee v. Department of Education, 471 U.S. 359 (1985).

Education for All Handicapped Children Act (EHA), 20 U.S.C. sections 1400 et seq. and amendments.

Handicapped Children's Protection Act of 1986, 20 U.S.C. section 1415.

Honig v. Doe, 108 S.Ct. 592 (1988).

Irving Independent School District v. Tatro, 468 U.S. 883 (1984).

Mills v. Board of Education of the District of Columbia, 348 F. Supp. 866 (1972).

Pennsylvania Association for Retarded Children v. Commonwealth of Pennsylvania, 343 F. Supp. 279 (E.D. Pa., 1972).

Rehabilitation Act of 1973 Section 504, 19 U.S.C. section 794.

Rowley v. Hendrick Hudson School District, 458 U.S. 176 (1982).

Smith v. Robinson, 468 U.S. 992 (1984).

State ex. rel. Beattie v. Board of Education, 169 Wis. 231, 172 N.W. 153, 154 (1919).

Timothy W. v. Rochester, New Hampshire, School District. 1987–88 EHLR DEC. 559:480 (D.N.H. 1988).

Timothy W. v. Rochester, New Hampshire, School District. 875 F. 2d 954 (1st Cir. 1989), *cert. denied* 110 S. Ct. 519 (1989).

Least Restrictive Environment

Biklen, D. (1985). *Achieving the complete school: Strategies for effective mainstreaming.* New York: Teachers College Press.

Normalization

Nirje, B. (1969). The normalization principle and its human management implications. In R.B. Kugel and W. Wolfensberger (Eds.), *Changing patterns in residential services for the mentally retarded* (pp. 179–195). Washington, DC: President's Committee on Mental Retardation.

Nirje, B. (1976). In R.B. Kugel & A. Shearer (Eds.), *The normalization principle.* (rev. ed.), *Changing patterns in residential services for the mentally retarded* (pp. 231–240). Washington, DC: President's Committee on Mental Retardation.

Nirje, B. (1985). The basis and logic of the normalization principle. *Australia and New Zealand Journal of Developmental Disabilities, 11,* 65–68.

Perske, R. (1972). The dignity of risk. In W. Wolfensberger (Ed.), *The principle of normalization in human services* (pp. 194–205). Toronto: National Institute of Mental Retardation.

Wolfensberger, W. (Ed.) (1972). *The principle of normalization in human services.* Toronto: National Institute on Mental Retardation.

Supplemental Books and Videos

Books

Bower, E.M. (Ed.) (1980). *The handicapped child in literature: A psychosocial perspective.* Denver: Love Publishing.

Ferguson, A.M. (1981). *Children's literature—for all handicapped children.* ERIC doc. ED 234 541, EC 160 408.

Harp, H.D. (1984). *Understanding handicaps through reading: An annotated bibliography of children's books since 1975.* Monmouth: Oregon State University / Western Oregon State College School of Education.

Mullins, J. (1975). *Special people behind the 8-ball.* Johnstown, PA: Mafex Associates.

Stone, A.A., and S.S. Stone (1966). *The abnormal personality through literature.* Englewood Cliffs, NJ: Prentice-Hall.

Videos

Brownstone, D.M., & Franck, I.M. (Eds.)(1978). *Film review digest annual 1977.* Millwood, NY: KTO Press.

Halliwell, L. (1988). *Halliwell's filmgoer's companion.* (9th ed.) London: Grafton Books.

Klobas, L.E. (1988). *Disability drama in television and film.* Jefferson, NC: McFarland & Co.

Leonard, H. (Ed.). (1985). *The film index: A bibliography. Vol. 3: The film in society.* White Plains, NY: Kraus International.

Magill, F.N. (Ed.) (1989). *Magill's cinema annual 1989: A survey of the films of 1988.* Pasadena, CA: Salem Press.

Maltin, L. (Ed.). (1987). *Leonard Maltin's TV movies and video guide: 1988 edition.* New York: NAL Penguin.

Michael, P (Ed.). (1969). *The American movies reference book: The sound era.* Englewood Cliffs, NJ: Prentice-Hall.

Ozer, J.S., (Ed.). (1988). *Film review annual: 1988.* Englewood, NJ: Film Review Publications.

Shale, R. (1982). *Academy awards: An Ungar reference index.* (2d ed.) New York: Frederick Ungar Publishing.

The Video Source book, (1985). (7th ed.) Professional volume. Syosset, NY: The National Video Clearinghouse.

CHAPTER 2   MULTICULTURAL AND BILINGUAL SPECIAL EDUCATION

Multicultural and Bilingual Special Education—General

Baca, L.M., & Cervantes, H.T. (Eds.). (1984). *The bilingual special education interface.* St. Louis: Times Mirror/Mosby.

Baca, L.M., & Cervantes, H.T. (Eds.). (1989). *The bilingual special education interface* (2nd ed.). Columbus, OH: Charles E. Merrill.

Banks, J.A. (1988). *Multiethnic education: Theory and practice* (2nd ed.). Newton, MA: Allyn & Bacon.

Cummins, J. (1986). Empowering minority students: A framework for intervention. *Harvard Educational Review, 56,* 18–36.

Cummins, J. (1989). A theoretical framework for bilingual special education. *Exceptional Children, 56,* 111–119.

Skutnabb-Kangas, T, & Cummins, J. (Eds.). (1988). *Minority education: From shame to struggle.* Philadelphia: Multilingual Matters.

Multicultural and Bilingual Special Education Defined

Salend, S.J., & Fradd, S. (1986). Nationwide availability of services for limited English-proficient handicapped students. *The Journal of Special Education, 20,* 127–135.

Measurement

Bozinou-Doukas, E. (1983). Learning disability: The case of the bilingual child. In D. Omark & J. Erickson (Eds.), *The bilingual exceptional child* (pp. 213–232). San Diego: College-Hill.

Cegelka, P.T., MacDonald, M., & Gaeta, R. (1987). Promising programs: Bilingual special education. *Teaching Exceptional Children, 20,* 48–50.

Diana v. State Board of Education, No. C-70-37 Rfp (N.D. Calif. 1970).

Gonzales, E. (1989). Issues in the assessment of minorities. In H.L. Swanson & B. Watson (Eds.), *Educational and psychological assessment of exceptional children: Theories, strategies, and applications* (pp. 383–402). Columbus, OH: Charles E. Merrill.

Jones, R. (Ed.). (1988). *Psychoeducational assessment of minority group children: A casebook.* Berkeley, CA: Cobb & Henry.

Larry P. v. Riles, Civil Action No. C-70-37 (N.D. Cal. 1971).

MacMillan, D.L., Hendrick, I.G., & Watkins, A.V. (1988). Impact of *Diana, Larry P.,* and P.L. 94-142 on minority students. *Exceptional Children, 54,* 426–432.

Mercer, J.R., & Lewis, J.F. (1978). *System of multicultural pluralistic assessment: Student assessment manual.* New York: Psychological Corporation.

Parents in Action on Special Education (PASE) v. Hannon, 506 F. Supp. 831 (N.D. IL 1980).

Significance

Chinn, P.C., & Hughes, S. (1987). Representation of minority students in special education classes. *Remedial and Special Education, 8,* 41–46.

History of the Field

Bilingual Education Act of 1968, P.L. 90-247.

Bransford, L., Baca, L., & Lane, K. (Eds.). Special issue: Cultural diversity. *Exceptional Children, 40*(8).

Crawford, J. (1989). *Bilingual education: History, politics, theory, and practice.* Trenton, NJ: Crane.

Dunn, L.M. (1968). Special education for the mildly retarded: Is much of it justifiable? *Exceptional Children, 35,* 5–22.

Lau v. Nichols, 414 U.S. 563 (1974).

Mercer, J. (1973). *Labeling the mentally retarded.* Berkeley: University of California Press.

Poplin, M.S., & Wright, P. (1983). The concept of cultural pluralism: Issues in special education. *Learning Disability Quarterly, 6,* 367–371.

President's Committee on Mental Retardation. (1970). *The six hour retarded child.* Washington, DC: U.S. Government Printing Office.

Prevalence

American Council on Education and Education Commission of the States. (1988). *One-third of a nation: A report by the Commission on Minority Participation in Education and American Life.* Washington, DC: Author.

Cegelka, P.T., Lewis, R., & Rodrigues, A.M. (1987). Status of educational services to handicapped students with limited English proficiency: Report of a statewide study in California. *Exceptional Children, 54,* 220–227.

Council of Chief State School Officers. (1990). *School success for limited English proficient students: The challenge and state response.* Washington, DC: Author.

Quality Education for Minorities Project. (1990). *Education that works: An action plan for the education of minorities.* Cambridge: Massachusetts Institute of Technology.

U.S. Department of Education. (1990). *Twelfth annual report to Congress on the implementation of the Education of the Handicapped Act.* Washington, DC: U.S. Government Printing Office.

Causes and Prevention

American Council on Education, and Education Commission of the States. (1988). *One-third of a nation: A report of the Commission on Minority Participation in Education and American Life.* Washington, DC: Author.

Chan, K.S., & Rueda, R. (1979). Poverty and culture in education: Separate but equal. *Exceptional Children, 45,* 422–428.

Children's Defense Fund. (1988). *Vanishing dreams: The growing economic plight of America's young families.* Washington, DC: Author.

Gault, A. (1989). *Mexican immigrant parents and the education of their handicapped children: Factors that influence parent involvement.* Unpublished doctoral dissertation, University of Illinois at Urbana-Champaign.

Hanson, M.J., Lynch, E.W., & Wayman, K.I. (1990). Honoring the cultural diversity of families when gathering data. *Topics in Early Childhood Special Education, 10,* 112–131.

Reed, S., & Sautter, R.C. (1990, June). Children of poverty: Kappan special report. *Phi Delta Kappan, 71,* K1–K12.

Schorr, L.B. (1989). *Within our reach: Breaking the cycle of disadvantage.* Garden City, NY: Doubleday.

Profile of Children

Language and Communication

Chan, D.M. (1986). Curriculum development for limited English proficient exceptional Chinese children. *Rural Special Education Quarterly, 8,* 26–31.

Dubois, B.L., & Valdes, G. (1980). Mexican-American child bilingualism: Double deficit? *The Bilingual Review, 7,* 1–7.

Miller, N., & Abudarham, S. (1984). Management of communication problems in bilingual children. In N. Miller (Ed.), *Bilingualism and language disability: Assessment and remediation* (pp. 177–198). San Diego: College-Hill.

Cultural Differences and Behavior

Council for Children with Behavioral Disorders. (1989). White paper. Best assessment practices for students with behavior disorders: Accommodation to cultural diversity and individual differences. *Behavioral Disorders, 14,* 263–278.

Over protest, surgery ordered for boy. (1990, Feb. 23). *New York Times,* p. A-13.

Mobility

Baca, L., & Harris, K.C. (1988). Teaching migrant exceptional students. *Teaching Exceptional Children, 20,* 32–35.

Barresi, J. (1984). *Interstate Migrant Council: National policy workshop on special education needs of migrant handicapped students. Proceedings report.* Denver: Education Commission of the States.

Bilingual education. (1990, March 21). *Education Week,* p. 7.

Kozol, J. (1988). *Rachel and her children: Homeless families in America.* New York: Crown.

Salend, S.J. (1990). A migrant education guide for special educators. *Teaching Exceptional Children, 22,* 18–21.

Issues in Education

Cavazos asks bilingualism among teachers (1990, July 6). *The New York Times,* p. A-7.

Ortiz, A.A., Yates, J.R., & Garcia, S.B. (Spring 1990). Competencies associated with serving exceptional language minority students. *The Bilingual Special Education Perspective, 9,* 1, 3–5.

Education and the Preschool Child

Evans, J. (1983). Model preschool programs for handicapped bilingual children. In D.R. Omark & J.G. Erickson (Eds.), *The bilingual exceptional child* (pp. 321–340). San Diego: College-Hill.

Hanson, M.J., Lynch, E.W., & Wayman, K.I. (1990). Honoring the cultural diversity of families when gathering data. *Topics in Early Childhood Special Education, 10,* 112–131.

Otto, D.E. (1982). Language renewal, bilingualism, and the young child. In R. St. Clair & W. Leap (Eds.), *Language renewal among American Indian tribes: Issues, problems, and prospects,* (pp. 31–42). Rosslyn, VA: National Clearinghouse for Bilingual Education.

Education and the School-Age Child

Baral, D.P. (1979). Academic achievement of recent immigrants from Mexico. *NABE Journal, 3,* 1–13.

Collier, C., & Hoover, J.J. (1987). *Cognitive learning strategies for minority handicapped students.* Lindale, TX: Hamilton.

Cummins, J. (1984). *Bilingualism and special education: Issues in assessment and pedagogy.* San Diego: College-Hill.

Cummins, J. (1989). A theoretical framework for bilingual special education. *Exceptional Children, 56,* 111–119.

Garcia, S.B., & Ortiz, A.A. (1988). Preventing inappropriate referrals of language minority students to special education. New focus Series, No. 5. Wheaton, MD: National Clearinghouse for Bilingual Education.

Goldman, S.R., & Rueda, R. (1988). Developing writing skills in bilingual exceptional children. *Exceptional Children, 54,* 543–551.

Henderson, R.W. (1980). Social and emotional needs of culturally diverse children. *Exceptional Children, 46,* 598–605.

Plyler v. Doe, 102 S.Ct. 2382 (1982).

Ruiz, N.T. (1989). An optimal learning environment for Rosemary. *Exceptional Children, 56,* 130–144.

Skutnabb-Kangas, T. & Toukomaa, P. (1976). *Teaching migrant children's mother tongue and learning the language of the host country in the context of the socio-cultural situation of the migrant family.* Helsinki: Finnish National Commission for UNESCO.

Tikunoff, W.J. (1987). Mediation of instruction to obtain equality of effectiveness. In S.H. Fradd & W.J. Tikunoff (Eds.), *Bilingual education and bilingual special education: A guide for administrators* (pp. 99–132). Boston: College-Hill.

Educational Environments

Baca, L., & Amato, C. (1989). Bilingual special education: Training issues. *Exceptional Children, 56,* 168–173.

Cegelka, P.T., MacDonald, M., & Gaeta, R. (1987). Promising programs: Bilingual special education. *Teaching Exceptional Children, 20,* 48–50.

Families of Culturally/Linguistically Diverse Children with Exceptionalities

Dorris, M. (1989). *The broken cord.* New York: Harper & Row.

Miller, N., & Abudarham, S. (1984). Management of communication problems in bilingual children. In N. Miller (Ed.), *Bilingualism and language disability: Assessment and remediation* (pp. 177–198). San Diego: College-Hill.

Rosenthal, E. (1990, Feb. 4). When a pregnant woman drinks. *New York Times Magazine,* pp. 30, 49, 61.

Streissguth, A.P., LaDue, R.A. & Randels, S.P. (1988). *A manual on adolescents and adults with fetal alcohol syndrome with special reference to American Indians.* Washington, DC: Indian Health Service.

Culturally and Linguistically Diverse Adults with Exceptionalities

Technical Assistance for Special Populations Program (TASPP). (1989). *Selected resources on developing vocational programs for individuals with limited English proficiency.* Champaign: University of Illinois at Urbana-Champaign Site.

Technology and Multicultural and Bilingual Special Education

Barker, B.O. (1989). Technology in rural special education: An introduction. *Rural Special Education Quarterly, 9,* 2–3.

Clark, T.A., & Verduin, J.R. (1989). Distance education: Its effectiveness and potential use in lifelong learning. *Lifelong learning: An omnibus of practice and research, 12,* 24–27.

Condon, M., Zimmerman, S., & Beane, A. (1989). Personnel preparation in special education: A synthesis of distance education and on-campus instruction. *Rural Special Education Quarterly, 9,* 16–20.

Earl, G. (1984). *The Spanish Hangman.* Computer program. San Antonio, TX: Author.

Zemke, R. (1985). Microcomputer activities in a senior day care center. In C. Smith (Ed.), *Technology for disabled persons: Conference papers* (pp. 5–11). Menomonie, WI: Stout Vocational Rehabilitation Institute, University of Wisconsin–Stout.

Concepts and Controversies—English Only

Hays, C.L. (1989, Nov. 7). Immigrants' town is divided over official-language issue. *New York Times,* p. B-8.

CHAPTER 3   IFSP, IEP, ITP: PLANNING AND DELIVERING SERVICES

Special Education Services

Danielson, L.C., & Bellamy, G.T. (1989). State variation in placement of children with handicaps in segregated environments. *Exceptional Children, 55,* 448–455.

Deno, E. (1970). Special education as developmental capital. *Exceptional Children, 37,* 229–237.

Reynolds, M.C. (1962). A framework for considering some issues in special education. *Exceptional Children, 28,* 367–370.

U.S. Department of Education. (1989). *Eleventh annual report to Congress on the implementation on the Education for Handicapped Act.* Washington, DC: U.S. Government Printing Office.

U.S. Department of Education. (1990). *Twelfth annual report to Congress on the implementation on the Education for Handicapped Act.* Washington, DC: U.S. Government Printing Office.

Consultation

Friend, M. (Guest Ed.) (1988). Special issue: Dimensions of school consultation practice. *Remedial and Special Education, 9,* 5–58.

Heron, T., & Kimball, W.H. (1988). Gaining perspective with the educational consultation research base: Ecological considerations and further recommendations. *Remedial and Special Education, 9,* 21–28, 47.

Individualized Educational Programs—General

Algozzine, B., Ysseldyke, J.E., & Christenson, S. (1983). An analysis of the incidence of special class placement: The masses are burgeoning. *The Journal of Special Education, 17,* 141–147.

Boyle, J. (1987). *A survey of the state's efforts in gifted education: A report to the Wisconsin Department of Public Instruction.* Stevens-Point: University of Wisconsin.

Grossman, H.J. (Ed.) (1983). *Classification in mental retardation.* Washington, DC: American Association on Mental Deficiency (now Retardation).

Kroth, R. (1990). *A report of the referral and identification rate of students in the Albuquerque Public Schools.* Unpublished manuscript. University of New Mexico, Albuquerque.

Miramontes, O.B. (1990). Organizing for effective paraprofessional services in special education: A multilingual/multiethnic instructional service team model. *Remedial and Special Education, 12,* 29–36, 47.

Strickland, B.B., & Turnbull, A.P. (1990). *Developing and implementing Individualized Education Programs.* (3rd ed.). Columbus, OH: Charles E. Merrill.

Individualized Family Service Plans (IFSPs)

Furuno, S., O'Reilly, K.A., Hosaka, C.M., Inatsuka, T.T., Allman, T.L., & Zeisloft, B. (1979). *Hawaii Early Learning Profile* (HELP). Palo Alto, CA: Vort Co.

Johnson, B.H., McGonigel, M.J., & Kaufmann, R.K. (1989). *Guidelines and recommended practices for the Individualized Family Service Plan.* Washington, DC: National Early Childhood Technical Assistance System and Association for the Care of Children's Health.

Individualized Education Program (IEP)

Lambert, N., Windmiller, M., Tharinger, D., & Cole, L. (1981). *ABS-AAMD Adaptive Behavior Scale School Edition: Administration and instructional planning manual.* Washington, DC: American Association on Mental Retardation.

Lynch, E.C., & Beare, P.L. (1990). The quality of IEP objectives and their relevance to instruction for students with mental retardation and behavior disorders. *Remedial and Special Education, 11,* 48–55.

Smith, D.D. (1989). *Teaching students with learning and behavior problems* (2nd ed.) Englewood Cliffs, NJ: Prentice-Hall.

Individualized Transition Plan (ITPs)

La Mar, K., & Rosenberg, B. (1988). *Synthesis of individual transition plans: Format and process.* Sacramento: California State Department of Education.

Ludlow, B.L., Turnbull, A.P., & Luckasson, R. (1988). *Transitions to adult life for people with mental retardation: Principles and practices.* Baltimore: Paul H. Brooks.

Wehman, P., Moon, M.S., Everson, J.M., Wood, W., & Barcus, J.M. (1988). *Transition from school to work: New challenges for youth with severe disabilities.* Baltimore: Paul H. Brooks.

Least Restrictive Environment (LRE)

Anderegg, M.L., & Vergason, G.A. (1988). An analysis of one of the cornerstones of the regular education initiative. *Focus on Exceptional Children, 20,* 1–7.

Council for Children with Behavioral Disorders. (1988). *Position statement on the regular education initiative.* Reston, VA: Author.

Commission on the Education of the Deaf. (1988). *Toward Equality: Education of the deaf.* Washington, DC: Government Printing Office.

Dublinski, S. (1988). Letter to Madeleine Will. *Learning Disability Quarterly, 11,* 134–135.

Edgar, E. (1987). Secondary programs in special education: Are many of them justifiable? *Exceptional Children, 53,* 555–561.

Gartner, A., & Lipsky, D.K. (1987). Beyond special education: Toward a quality system for all students. *Harvard Educational Review, 57,* 367–395.

Keogh, B.K. (1988). Perspectives on the regular education initiative. *Learning Disabilities Focus, 4,* 3–5.

Smith, D.D. (1988). No more noses to the glass: A response. *Exceptional Children, 54,* 476.

Smith, D.D., & Bassett, D. (1991). The REI debate: A time for a systematic research agenda. In J. Lloyd, A.C. Repp, & N.N. Sing (Eds.), *Perspectives on integration of atypical learners in regular education settings* (pp. 150–173). Sycamore, IL: Sycamore Press.

Snell, M.E. (1988). Gartner and Lipsky's beyond special education: Toward a quality system for all students: Messages to TASH. *Journal of the Association for Persons with Severe Handicaps, 13,* 137–140.

Stainback, S., & Stainback, W. (1989). No more teachers of students with severe handicaps. *TASH Newsletter, 15,* 9–10.

Turnbull III, H.R., (1991). *Free appropriate public education: The law and children with disabilities.* (2nd ed.). Denver: Love.

Wang, M.C., & Reynolds, M.C. (1985). Avoiding the "Catch-22" in special education reform. *Exceptional Children, 51,* 497–502.

Will, M. (1986). *Educating students with learning problems: A shared responsibility: A report to the secretary.* Washington, DC: U.S. Department of Education, Office of Special Education and Rehabilitative Services.

CHAPTER 4   MENTAL RETARDATION

Mental Retardation—General

Blatt, B. (1987). *The conquest of mental retardation.* Austin, TX: Pro-Ed.

Gardner, H. (1983). *Frames of mind: The theory of multiple intelligences.* New York: Basic Books.

Gould, S.J. (1981). *The mismeasure of man.* New York: W.W. Norton.

Piaget, J. (1969). *The origins of intelligence in children.* New York: W.W. Norton.

Mental Retardation Defined

Doll, E.A. (1941). The essentials of an inclusive concept of mental deficiency. *American Journal of Mental Deficiency, 46,* 214–219.

Grossman, H.J. (Ed.). (1983). *Classification in mental retardation.* Washington, DC: American Association on Mental Deficiency (now Retardation).

Mercer, J. (1973). *Labeling the mentally retarded.* Berkeley: University of California Press.

Polloway, E.A., & Smith, J.D. (1983). Changes in mild mental retardation: Population, programs, and perspectives. *Exceptional Children, 50,* 149–159.

President's Committee on Mental Retardation. (1970). *The six-hour retarded child.* Washington, DC: U.S. Government Printing Office.

Sattler, J. (1988). *Assessment of children* (3rd ed.). San Diego: Author.

TASH Newsletter. (1987, August). Definition of the population TASH serves. *13 (8),* 5.

Thorndike, R.L., Hagen, E., & Sattler, J. (1985). *Stanford-Binet Intelligence Scale.* Chicago: Riverside.

Wechsler, D. (1974). *Manual for the Wechsler Intelligence Scale for Children–Revised.* Cleveland: The Psychological Corporation.

Zigler, E., & Hodapp, R.M. (1986). *Understanding mental retardation.* Cambridge, England: Cambridge University Press.

History

Barr, M.W. (1913). *Mental defectives: Their history, treatment and training.* Philadelphia: P. Blakiston's.

Blatt, B., & Kaplan, F. (1966). *Christmas in purgatory: A photographic essay on mental retardation.* Boston: Allyn & Bacon.

Deutsch, A. (1949). *The mentally ill in America: A history of their care and treatment from colonial times* (2nd ed.). New York: Columbia University Press.

Howe, S.G. (1866). On the proper role of state institutions for the disabled. Speech given at ceremonies on laying the cornerstone of the New York State Institution for the Blind at Batavia, Genessee County, New York. Batavia, NY: Henry Todd.

Itard, J.M.G. (1806). *Wild boy of Aveyron,* (G. Humphrey & M. Humphrey, Trans.). (1962). Englewood Cliffs, NJ: Prentice-Hall. Originally published Paris: Gouyon (1801).

Kanner, L. (1964). *A history of the care and study of the mentally retarded.* Springfield, IL: Charles C. Thomas.

Nirje, B. (1969). The normalization principle and its human management implications. In R. Kugel & W. Wolfensberger (Eds.), *Changing patterns in residential services for the mentally retarded* (pp. 179–195). Washington, DC: President's Committee on Mental Retardation.

Nirje, B. (1976). The normalization principle. In R. Kugel & A. Shearer (Eds.), *Changing patterns in residential services for the mentally retarded* (pp. 231–240). Washington, DC: President's Committee on Mental Retardation.

Perske, R. (1972). The dignity of risk. In W. Wolfensberger (Ed.), *The principle of normalization in human services* (pp. 194–200). Toronto: National Institute on Mental Retardation.

Rothman, S.M., & Rothman, D.J. (1984). *Willowbrook wars: A decade of struggle for social justice.* New York: Harper & Row.

Scheerenberger, R.C. (1983). *A history of mental retardation.* Baltimore: Paul H. Brookes.

Scheerenberger, R.C. (1987). *A history of mental retardation: A quarter century of promise.* Baltimore: Paul H. Brookes.

Wolfensberger, W. (1972). *The principle of normalization in human services.* Toronto: National Institute on Mental Retardation.

Prevalence, Incidence, Demographics

Baroff, G.S. (1986). *Mental retardation: Nature, cause, and management* (2nd ed.). New York: Hemisphere.

McLaren, J., & Bryson, S.E. (1987). Review of recent epidemiological studies of mental retardation: Prevalence, associated disorders, and etiology. *American Journal of Mental Retardation, 92,* 243–254.

U.S. Department of Education, Office of Special Education and Rehabilitative Services. (1990). *Twelfth annual report to Congress on the implementation of the Education of the Handicapped Act.* Washington, DC: U.S. Government Printing Office.

Causes and Prevention

Batshaw, M.L., & Perret, Y.M. (1986). *Children with handicaps* (2nd ed.). Baltimore: Paul H. Brookes.

Crocker, A.C., & Cohen, H.J. (1988). *Guidelines on developmental services for children and adults with HIV infection.* Silver Spring, MD: American Association of University Affiliated Programs for Persons with Developmental Disabilities.

Dietrich, K.N., Krafft, K.M., Shukla, R., Bornschein, R.L., & Succop, P.A. (1987). The neurobehavioral effects of early lead exposure. In S.R. Schroeder (Ed.), *Toxic substances and mental retardation,* Monographs of the American Association on Mental Deficiency, 8 (pp. 71–95). Washington, DC: American Association on Mental Deficiency.

Dorris, M. (1989). *The broken cord: A family's ongoing struggle with fetal alcohol syndrome.* New York: Harper & Row.

Evrard, J.R., & Scola, P.S. (1990). Preparation for parenthood. In S.M. Pueschel & J.A. Mulick (Eds.), *Prevention of developmental disabilities* (pp. 27–35). Baltimore: Paul H. Brookes.

Hanson, M.J. (1984). *Atypical infant development.* Baltimore: University Park Press.

MacMillan, D.L. (1982). *Mental retardation in school and society* (2nd ed.). Boston: Little, Brown.

Menolascino, F.J., Neman, R., & Stark, J.A. (Eds.). (1983). *Curative aspects of mental retardation: Biomedical and behavioral advances.* Baltimore: Paul H. Brookes.

Menolascino, F.J., & Stark, J.A. (Eds.). (1988). *Preventive and curative intervention in mental retardation.* Baltimore: Paul H. Brookes.

Patterson, D., Graw, S., Gusella, J., & Watkins, P. (1987). Somatic cell molecular genetics of chromosome 21. In S.M. Pueschel, C. Tingey, J.E. Rynders, A.C. Crocker & D.M. Crutcher (Eds.), *New perspectives on Down syndrome* (pp. 47–68). Baltimore: Paul H. Brookes.

President's Committee on Mental Retardation. (no date). *A guide for state planning: For the prevention of mental retardation and related disabilities.* Washington, DC: Author.

Pueschel, S.M., & Mulick, J.A. (Eds.) (1990). *Prevention of developmental disabilities.* Baltimore: Paul H. Brookes.

Pueschel, S.M., & Rynders, J.E. (1982). *Down syndrome: Advances in biomedicine and the behavioral sciences.* Cambridge, MA: Ware Press.

Streissguth, A.P. (1986). The behavioral teratology of alcohol: Performance, behavioral, and intellectual deficits in prenatally exposed children. In J.R. West (Ed.), *Alcohol and brain development* (pp. 3–44). New York: Oxford University Press.

Streissguth, A.P., & LaDue, R.A. (1987). Fetal alcohol: Teratogenic causes of developmental disabilities. In S.R. Schroeder (Ed.), *Toxic substances and mental retardation,* Monographs of the American Association on Mental Deficiency, 8 (pp. 1–32). Washington, DC: American Association on Mental Deficiency.

Profile

Bricker, D. (1983). Early communication: Development and training. In M.E. Snell (Ed.), *Systematic instruction of the moderately and severely handicapped* (2nd ed.), (pp. 269–288). Columbus: Charles E. Merrill.

DeVellis, R.F. (1977). Learned helplessness in institutions. *Mental Retardation, 15,* 10–13.

Donnellan, A.M., Mirenda, P.L., Mesaros, R.A., & Fassbender, L.L. (1984). Analyzing the communicative functions of aberrant behavior. *Journal of The Association for Persons with Severe Handicaps, 9,* 201–212.

Edgerton, R. (1967). *The cloak of competence.* Berkeley: University of California.

Harter, S., & Zigler, E. (1974). The assessment of effectance motivation in normal and retarded children. *Developmental Psychology, 10,* 169–180.

Kendall, C.R., Borkowski, J.G., & Cavanaugh, J.C. (1980). Metamemory and the transfer of an interrogative strategy by EMR children. *Intelligence, 4,* 255–270.

Lloyd, L.L. (Ed.). (1976). *Communication assessment and intervention strategies.* Baltimore: University Park Press.

Mercer, C.D., & Snell, M.E. (1977). *Learning theory research in mental retardation: Implications for teaching.* Columbus, OH: Charles E. Merrill.

Rosen, M., Floor, L., & Zisfein, L. (1974). Investigating the phenomenon of acquiescence in the mentally handicapped: I-Theoretical model, test development and normative data. *British Journal of Mental Subnormality, 20,* 58–68.

Sigelman, C.K., Budd, E.C., Spanhel, C.L., & Schoenrock, C.J. (1981). When in doubt, say yes: Acquiescence in interviews with mentally retarded persons. *Mental Retardation, 19,* 53–58.

Sigelman, C.K., Schoenrock, C.J., Budd, E.C., Winer, J.L., Spanhel, C.L., Martin, P.W., Hromas, S., & Bensberg, G.J. (1983). *Communicating with mentally retarded persons: Asking questions and getting answers.* Lubbock, TX: Research and Training Center in Mental Retardation, Texas Tech University.

Weisz, J. (1982). Learned helplessness and the retarded child. In E. Zigler & D. Balla (Eds.), *Mental retardation: The developmental—difference controversy* (pp. 27–40). Hillsdale, NJ: Erlbaum.

Zeaman, D., & House, B.J. (1963). The role of attention in retardate discrimination learning. In N.R. Ellis (Ed.), *Handbook of mental deficiency* (pp. 159–223). New York: McGraw-Hill.

Issues in Education

Early Education

Garwood, S.G., & Fewell, R.R. (1983). *Educating handicapped infants: Issues in development and intervention.* Rockville, MD: Aspen Publications.

Hanson, M.J. (1987). *Teaching the infant with Down syndrome: A guide for parents and professionals* (2nd ed.). Austin, TX: Pro-Ed.

Hayden, A. (1979). Handicapped children, birth to age 3. *Exceptional Children, 48,* 510–516.

Hayden, A.H., & Dmitriev, V. (1975). The multidisciplinary preschool program for Down's syndrome children at the University of Washington model preschool center. In B.Z. Friedlander, G.M. Sterrit, & G.E. Kirk (Eds.), *Exceptional infant: Assessment and intervention* (Vol. 3). New York: Brunner/Mazel.

Infant Health and Development Program. (1990). Enhancing outcomes of low-birth-weight, premature infants: A multisite, randomized trial. *Journal of the American Medical Association (JAMA), 263,* 3035–3042.

Skeels, H.M., & Dye, H.B. (1939). A study of the effects of differential stimulation on mentally retarded children. *Convention Proceedings: American Association on Mental Deficiency, 44,* 114–136.

Skeels, H.M. (1966). Adult status of children with contrasting early life experiences. *Monographs of the Society for Research in Child Development, 3*(3).

Weikart, D.P., et al. (1984). *Changed lives: The effects of the Perry Preschool Program on youths through age 19.* Monographs of High/Scope, Educational Research Foundation: No. 8. Ypsilanti, MI: The High/Scope Press.

School Age

Ayllon, T., & Azrin, N.H. (1964). Reinforcement and instructions with mental patients. *Journal of Experimental Analysis of Behavior, 7,* 327–331.

Ayllon, R., & Azrin, N.H. (1968). Reinforcer sampling: A technique for increasing the behavior of mental patients. *Journal of Applied Behavior Analysis, 1,* 13–20.

Brinbrauer, J.S., Wolf, M.M., Kidder, J.D., & Tague, C.E. (1965). Classroom behavior of retarded pupils with token reinforcement. *Journal of Experimental Child Psychology, 2,* 219–235.

Houghton, J., Bronicki, B., & Guess, D. (1987). Opportunities to express preferences and make choices among students with severe disabilities in classroom settings. *Journal of the Association for Persons with Severe Handicaps, 12,* 18–27.

Lent, J.R., & McLean, B.M. (1976). The trainable retarded: The technology of teaching. In N.G. Haring & R.L. Schiefelbusch (Eds.), *Teaching special children* (pp. 197–223). New York: McGraw-Hill.

Robinson, G.A., Patton, J.R., Polloway, E.A., & Sargent, L.R. (Eds.). (1989). *Best practices in mild mental disabilities.* Reston, VA: Division on Mental Retardation of the Council for Exceptional Children.

Shevin, M., & Klein, N. (1984). The importance of choice-making skills for students with severe disabilities. *Journal of the Association for Persons with Severe Handicaps, 9,* pp. 159–166.

Smith, D.D., & Lovitt, T.C. (1982). *The computational arithmetic program (CAP).* Austin, TX: Pro-Ed.

Smith, D.D., & Snell, M.E. (1978). Classroom management and instructional planning. In M.E. Snell (Ed.), *Systematic instruction of the moderately and severely handicapped* (pp. 20–73). Columbus: Charles E. Merrill.

School Age

Williams, P., & Shoultz, B. (1982). *We can speak for ourselves: Self-advocacy by mentally handicapped people.* Bloomington, IN: Bloomington University Press.

Smith, D.D. (1989). *Teaching students with learning and behavior problems* (2nd ed.). Englewood Cliffs, NJ: Prentice Hall.

Educational Environments

Brown, L. Branston, M., Hamre-Nietupski, S., Pumpian, I., Certo, N., & Gruenewald, L. (1979). A strategy for developing chronological-age-appropriate and functional curricular content for severely handicapped adolescents and young adults. *Journal of Special Education, 13,* 81–90.

Gaylord-Ross, R., Forte, J., Storey, K., Gaylord-Ross, C., & Jameson, D. (1987). Community referenced instruction in technological work settings. *Exceptional Children, 54,* 112–120.

Horner, R., McDonnell, J.J., & Bellamy, G.T. (1986). Teaching generalized skills: General case instruction in simulation and community settings. In R.H. Horner, L.H. Meyer, & H.D.B. Fredericks (Eds.), *Education of learners with severe handicaps: Exemplary service strategies* (pp. 289–314). Baltimore: Paul H. Brookes.

Snell, M., & Browder, D. (1987). Domestic and community skills. In M. Snell (Ed.), *Systematic instruction of persons with severe handicaps* (3rd ed.) (pp. 390–434). Columbus, OH: Charles E. Merrill.

Families

Kroth, R.L. (1985). *Communicating with parents of exceptional children: Improving parent–teacher relationships* (2nd ed.). Denver: Love.

Lobato, D.J. (1990). *Brothers, sisters, and special needs.* Baltimore: Paul H. Brookes.

Perske, R. (1988). *Circles of friends.* Nashville: Abingdon.

Turnbull, A.P., & Turnbull, H.R. (Eds.) (1978). *Parents speak out: Views from the other side of the two-way mirror.* Columbus, OH: Charles E. Merrill.

Turnbull, H.R., & Turnbull, A.P. (Eds.) (1985). *Parents speak out: Then and now.* Columbus, OH: Charles E. Merrill.

Adults

Braddock, D., Hemp, R., Fujiura, G., Bachelder, L., & Mitchell, D. (1990). *The state of the states in developmental disabilities.* Baltimore: Paul H. Brookes.

Hasazi, S.B., Gordon, L.R., Roe, C.A., Hull, M., Finck, K., & Salembier, G. (1985). A state-wide follow-up on post-high school employment and residential status of students labeled "mentally retarded." *Education and Training of the Mentally Retarded, 20,* 222–234.

How we lived and grew together: Interstate seminar on self-advocacy for persons with developmental disabilities. (1986). New Jersey Division of Developmental Disabilities; University Affiliated Facility, Rutgers Medical School; New York State Office of Mental Retardation and Developmental Disabilities; Pennsylvania Office of Retardation; Pennsylvania Developmental Disabilities Planning Council.

Ludlow, B.L., Turnbull, A.P., & Luckasson, R. (Eds.). (1988). *Transitions to adult life for people with mental retardation: Principles and practices.* Baltimore: Paul H. Brookes.

Technology

McLone, D.G., Czyzewski, D., Raimondi, A.J., & Sommers, R.C. (1982). Central nervous systems infections as a limiting factor in the intelligence of children with myelomeningocele. *Pediatrics, 70,* 338–342.

Menolascino, F.J., & Stark, J.A. (Eds.) (1988). *Preventive and curative intervention in mental retardation.* Baltimore: Paul H. Brookes.

Peuschel, S.M., & Rynders, J.E. (1982). *Down syndrome: Advances in biomedicine and the behavioral sciences.* Cambridge, MA: Ware Press.

Concepts and Controversies

Children's Defense Fund. (1990). *SOS America: A children's defense budget.* Washington, DC: Author.

CHAPTER 5   COMMUNICATIVE DISORDERS

Communicative Disorders—General

Boone, D.R. (1987). *Human communication and its disorders.* Englewood Cliffs, NJ: Prentice-Hall.

Cantwell, D.P., & Baker, L. (1987a). *Developmental speech and language disorders.* New York: Guilford Press.

Hubbard, K., & Kramer, L. (1990, Jan. 20). John Casey's ship comes in with a national book award for his novel about fishermen's lives. *People Magazine,* pp. 57–58.

Oyer, H.J., Crowe, B, & Haas, W.H. (1987). *Speech, language, and hearing disorders: A guide for teachers.* Austin, TX: Pro-Ed.

Rice, M.L. (1988). Speech and language impaired. In E.L. Meyen & T.M. Skrtic (Eds.), *Exceptional children and youth* (3rd ed.), (pp. 233–261). Denver: Love.

Shames, G.H., & Wiig, E.H. (Eds.). (1986). *Human communication disorders: An introduction* (2nd ed.). Columbus, OH: Charles E. Merrill.

Van Hattum, R.J. (1985). *Organization of speech-language services in schools: A manual.* Austin, TX: Pro-Ed.

Van Riper, C., & Emerick, L. (1984). *Speech correction: An introduction to speech pathology and audiology* (7th ed.). Englewood Cliffs, NJ: Prentice-Hall.

Communicative Disorders Defined

Committee on Language-Speech and Hearing Services in the Schools. (1982). Definitions: Communicative disorders and variations. *ASHA, 24,* 949–950.

Speech Disorders

Boone, D.R., & McFarlane, S.C. (1988). *The voice and voice therapy* (4th ed.). Englewood Cliffs, NJ: Prentice-Hall.

Gregory, H.H. (1986). Stuttering: A contemporary perspective. *Folio Phoniatrica, 38,* 89–120.

McReynolds, L. (1986). Functional articulation disorders. In G.H. Shames & E.H. Wiig (Eds.), *Human communication disorders: An introduction* (2nd ed.) (pp. 139–182). Columbus, OH: Charles E. Merrill.

Sander, E.K. (1972). When are speech sounds learned? *Journal of Speech and Hearing Disorders, 37,* 62.

Shames, G.H. (1986). Disorders of fluency. In G.H. Shames & E.H. Wiig (Eds.), *Human communication disorders: An introduction* (2nd ed.) (pp. 243–289). Columbus, OH: Charles E. Merrill.

Sheehan, J.G., & Martyn, M.M. (1970). Spontaneous recovery from stuttering. *Journal of Speech and Hearing Research, 13,* 279–289.

Wingate, M.E. (1962). Personality needs of stutterers. *Logos, 5,* 35–37.

Language Disorders

Carrow-Woolfolk, E., & Lynch, J.I. (1982). *An integrative approach to language disorders in children.* New York: Grune & Stratton.

Cuda, R.A., & Nelson, N. (1976). Analysis of teacher speaking rate, syntactic complexity and hesitation phenomena as a function of grade level. Presented at the annual meeting of the American Speech-Language-Hearing Association, Houston. As reported in G. Wallach & K. Butler (Eds.), (1984). *Language learning disabilities in school-age children.* Baltimore: Williams & Wilkins.

Gruenewald, L., & Pollack, S. (1984). *Language interaction in teaching and learning.* Austin, TX: Pro-Ed.

Lindfors, J.W. (1987). *Children's language and learning* (2nd ed.). Englewood Cliffs, NJ: Prentice-Hall.

Marvin, C. (1989). Language and learning. In D.D. Smith, *Teaching students with learning and behavior problems* (pp. 147–181). Englewood Cliffs, NJ: Prentice-Hall.

Mathinos, D. (1988). Communicative competence of children with learning disabilities. *Journal of Learning Disabilities, 21,* 437–443.

Mattes, L.J., & Omark, D.R. (1984). *Speech and language assessment for the bilingual handicapped.* Austin, TX: Pro-Ed.

Nippold, M.A. (1988). *Later language development: Ages nine through nineteen.* Austin, TX: Pro-Ed.

Prather, E.M. (1984). Developmental language disorders: Adolescents. In A. Holland (Ed.), *Language disorders in children: Recent advances* (pp. 159–171). Austin, TX: Pro-Ed.

Stevens, M.I. (1988). Pragmatics. In M.A. Nippold (Ed.), *Later language development: Ages nine through nineteen.* Austin, TX: Pro-Ed.

History

Moore, G.P., & Kester, D. (1953). Historical notes on speech correction in the preassociation era. *Journal of Speech and Hearing Disorders, 18,* 48–53.

Van Riper, C. (1981). An early history of ASHA. *ASHA, 23,* 855–858.

Weiner, P.S. (1984). The study of childhood language disorders in the nineteenth century. *ASHA, 26,* 35–38.

Prevalence, Incidence, and Demographics

Dublinske, S. (1981). Block grant proposal introduced: What does it mean? *Language, Speech and Hearing Services in Schools, 12,* 192–199.

Garbee, F.E. (1985). The speech-language pathologist as a professional. In R.J. Van Hattum (Ed.), *Organization of speech-language services in schools* (pp. 58–129). Austin, TX: Pro-Ed.

U.S. Department of Education. (1987). *Tenth annual report to Congress on the implementation of the Education of the Handicapped Act.* Washington, DC: U.S. Government Printing Office.

U.S. Department of Education. (1990). *Twelfth annual report to Congress on the implementation of the Education of the Handicapped Act.* Washington, DC: U.S. Government Printing Office.

Causes and Prevention

Anderson, C. (1972). *Society pays: The high costs of minimal brain damage in America.* New York: Walker.

ASHA Committee on Prevention of Speech-Language and Hearing Problems (1984). Prevention: A challenge for the profession. *ASHA, 26,* 35–37.

Bradley, A. (1990, May 16). Lack of funds halt measles-vaccination program. *Education Week,* p. 5.

Hilts, P.J. (1990, May 9). Fight measles stalls on money: U.S. runs out of funds for emergency vaccinations to fight the epidemic. *New York Times,* p. A-13.

Leonard, L. (1986). Early language development and language disorders. In G.H. Shames & E.H. Wiig (Eds.), *Human communication disorders: An introduction* (2nd ed.), (pp. 291–330). Columbus, OH: Charles E. Merrill.

Marge, M. (1984). The prevention of communication disorders. *ASHA, 26,* 29–37.

McWilliams, B.J., Morris, H.L., & Shelton, R.L. (1984). *Cleft palate speech.* Philadelphia: B.C. Decker.

Education

Aram, D.M., Ekelman, B.L., & Nation, J.E. (1984). Preschoolers with language disorders: 10 years later. *Journal of Speech and Hearing Research, 27,* 232–244.

Dudley-Marling, C., & Searle, D. (1988). Enriching language learning environments for students with learning disabilities. *Journal of Learning Disabilities, 21,* 140–43.

Neidecker, E.A. (1987). *School programs in speech-language: Organization and management* (2nd ed.). Englewood Cliffs, NJ: Prentice-Hall.

Nelson, N.W. (1985). Teacher talk and child listening—Fostering a better match. In C.S. Simon (Ed.), *Communication skills and classroom success* (pp. 65–102). Austin, TX: Pro-Ed.

Ray, R.A. (1986). *The 11-sentence paragraph.* Unpublished manuscript, Albuquerque, NM: Special Education Department, University of New Mexico, Albuquerque.

Smith, D.D. (1989). *Teaching students with learning and behavior problems* (2nd ed.). Englewood Cliffs, NJ: Prentice-Hall.

Snyder, L.S. (1984). Developmental language disorders: Elementary school age. In A.L. Holland (Ed.), *Language disorders in children* (pp. 129–158). Austin, TX: Pro-Ed.

Wallach, G.P., & Butler, K.G. (1984). *Language learning disabilities in school-age children.* Baltimore: Williams & Wilkins.

Early Intervention

Blank, M., Rose, S.A., & Berlin, L.J. (1978). *The language of learning: The preschool years.* New York: Grune & Stratton.

Casto, G., & Mastropieri, M.A. (1986). The efficacy of early intervention programs: A meta-analysis. *Exceptional Children, 52,* 417–424.

Fey, M.E. (1986). *Language intervention with young children.* Austin, TX: Pro-Ed.

Liebergott, J.W., Bashir, A.S., & Schultz, M.C. (1984). Dancing around and making strange noises: Children at risk. In A. Holland (Ed.), *Language disorders in children: Recent advances* (pp. 37–56). Austin, TX: Pro-Ed.

Mallory, B.L., & Kerns, G.M. (1988). Consequences of categorical labeling of preschool children. *Topics in Early Childhood Special Education, 8,* 39–50.

Paul, L. (1985). Programming peers' support for functional language. In S.F. Warren & A.K. Rogers-Warren (Eds.), *Teaching functional language* (pp. 285–307). Baltimore: University Park Press.

Reichman, F., & Healey, W.C. (1983). Learning disabilities and conductive loss involving otitis media. *Journal of Learning Disabilities, 16,* 272–278.

Smith, B.J., & Schakel, J.A. (1986). Noncategorical identification of preschool handicapped children: Policy issues and options. *Journal of the Division for Early Childhood, 11,* 78–86.

Stremmel-Campbell, K., & Campbell, C.R. (1985). Training techniques that may facilitate generalization. In S.F. Warren & A.K. Rogers-Warren (Eds.), *Teaching functional language: Generalization and maintenance of language skills* (pp. 251–285). Baltimore: University Park Press.

Wilcox, M.J. (1984). Developmental language disorders: Preschoolers. In A. Holland (Ed.), *Language disorders in children: Recent advances* (pp. 101–128) Austin, TX: Pro-Ed.

Instructional Materials

Blank, M., & Marquis, A.M. (1987). *Directing discourse.* Tucson, AZ: Communication Skill Builders.

Dinkmeyer, D., & Dinkmeyer, D. (1982). *DUSO-Revised: Developing understanding of self and others.* Circle Pines, MN: American Guidance Service.

Dunn, L.M., Smith, J.O., Dunn, L.M., Horton, K., & Smith, D.D. (1981). *Peabody language development kits (Rev. ed.). Levels P-3.* Circle Pines, MN: American Guidance Service.

Dunn, L.M., Dunn, L.M., Smith, J.O., Smith, D.D., & Horton, K. (1983). *Peabody picture collection.* Circle Pines, MN: American Guidance Service.

Hoskins, B. (1987). *Conversations: Language intervention for adolescents.* Allen, TX: DLM–Teaching Resources.

Plourde, L. (1985). *Classroom listening and speaking (CLAS).* Tucson, AZ: Communication Skill Builders.

Simon, C. (1981). *Communicative competence: A functional-pragmatic approach to language therapy.* Tucson, AZ: Communication Skill Builders.

Wiig, E. (1982). *Let's talk: Developing prosocial communication skills.* Columbus, OH: Charles E. Merrill.

Families of Children with Communicative Disorders

Casto, G., & White, K.R. (1987). *Early Intervention Research Institute: ERIC Abstract #25.* Reston, VA: ERIC Clearinghouse on Handicapped and Gifted Children.

Lindfors, J.W. (1987). *Children's language and learning* (2nd ed.). Englewood Cliffs, NJ: Prentice-Hall.

Simpson, R.L. (1990). *Conferencing parents of exceptional children* (2nd ed.). Austin, TX: Pro-Ed.

Adults

Cantwell, D.P., & Baker, L. (1987b). Prevalence and type of psychiatric disorder and developmental disorder in three speech and language groups. *Journal of Communicative Disorders, 20,* 151–160.

Hall, P.K., & Tomblin, J.B. (1978). A follow-up study of children with articulation and language disorders. *Journal of Speech and Hearing Disorders, 43,* 227–241.

King, R.R., Jones, C., & Lasky, E. (1982). In retrospect: A fifteen-year follow-up report of speech-language-disordered children. *Language, Speech and Hearing Services in Schools, 13,* 24–32.

Technology

Clymer, E.W. (1988). *Administrative applications of microcomputers for speech, language, and hearing professionals.* Rockville, MD: American Speech-Language-Hearing Association.

Fishman, I. (1987). *Electronic communication aids: Selection and use.* Boston: Little, Brown.

Hyman, C.S. (1985). Computer usage in the speech-language-hearing profession. *ASHA, 27,* 25.

IBM National Support Center for Persons with Disabilities. (1989). *Resource guide for persons with speech or language impairments.* Atlanta: IBM.

CHAPTER 6 LEARNING DISABILITIES

Learning Disabilities—General

Hallahan, D.P., Kauffman, J.M., & Lloyd, J.W. (1985). *Introduction to learning disabilities* (2nd ed.). Englewood Cliffs, NJ: Prentice-Hall.

Lovitt, T.C. (1989). *Introduction to learning disabilities.* Needham Heights, MA: Allyn & Bacon.

Mercer, C.D. (1987). *Students with learning disabilities* (3rd ed.). Columbus, OH: Charles E. Merrill.

Myers, P.I., & Hammill, D.D. (1990). *Learning disabilities: Basic concepts, assessment practices, and instructional strategies* (4th ed.). Austin, TX: Pro-Ed.

Robinson, S.M., & Deshler, D.D. (1988). Learning disabled. In E.L. Meyen & T.M. Skrtic (Eds.), *Exceptional children and youth: An introduction* (3rd ed.), (pp. 109–138). Denver: Love.

Vaugh, S., & Bos, C.S. (1987). *Research in learning disabilities: Issues and future directions.* Boston: College-Hill.

Wallace, G., & McLoughlin, J.A. (1988). *Learning disabilities: Concepts and characteristics* (3rd ed.). Columbus: Merrill.

Learning Disabilities Defined

Cartwright, G.P., Cartwright, C.A., & Ward, M.E. (1984). *Educating special learners* (2nd ed.). Belmont, CA: Wadsworth.

Hammill, D.D. (1990). On defining learning disabilities: An emerging consensus. *Journal of Learning Disabilities, 23,* 74–85.

National Joint Committee on Learning Disabilities. (1988). (Letter to NJCLD member organizations).

U.S. Office of Education. (1977). Assistance to states for education of handicapped children: Procedures for evaluating specific learning disabilities. *Federal Register, 42,* 65082–65085.

Identification of Students

Algozzine, B., & Ysseldyke, J.E. (1986). The future of the LD field: Screening and diagnosis. *Journal of Learning Disabilities, 19,* 394–398.

Algozzine, B., & Ysseldyke, J.E. (1987). In defense of different numbers. *Remedial and Special Education, 8,* 53–56.

Dangel, H.L., & Ensminger, E.E. (1988). The use of discrepancy formulas with LD students. *Learning Disability Focus, 4,* 24–31.

Ellenwood, A.E., & Felt, D. (1990). Attention-deficit/hyperactivity disorder: Management and intervention approaches for classroom teacher. *LD Forum, 15,* 15–17.

Forness, S.R., Sinclair, E., & Guthrie, D. (1983). Learning disability discrepancy formulas: Their use in actual practice. *Learning Disability Quarterly, 6,* 107–114.

Hooper, S.R., & Willis, W.G. (1989). *Learning disability subtyping: Neuropsychological foundations, conceptual models, and issues in clinical differentiation.* New York: Springer-Verlag.

Keogh, B.K. (1987). A shared attribute model of learning disabilities. In S. Vaughn & C.S. Bos (Eds.), *Research in learning disabilities: Issues and future directions* (pp. 3–18). Boston: College-Hill.

McKinney, J.D. (1987). Research on the identification of learning-disabled children: Perspectives on changes in educational policy. In S. Vaughn & C.S. Bos (Eds.), *Research in learning disabilities: Issues and future directions* (pp. 215–237). Boston: College-Hill.

McLeskey, J. (1989). The influence of level of discrepancy on the identification of students with learning disabilities. *Journal of Learning Disabilities, 22,* 435–438, 443.

Mercer, C.D., King-Sears, P., & Mercer, A.R. (1990). Learning disabilities definitions and criteria used by state education departments. *Learning Disability Quarterly, 13,* 141–152.

Rosas, C. (1990). *The overrepresentation of limited English proficient in the category of learning disabilities: A review of the literature.* Unpublished manuscript, University of New Mexico, Albuquerque.

Schumaker, J.B., Deshler, D.D., Alley, G.R., & Warner, M.M. (1983). Toward the development of an intervention model for learning disabled adolescents: The University of Kansas Institute. *Exceptional Education Quarterly, 4,* 45–74.

Tarnowski, K.J., & Nay, S.M. (1989). Locus of control in children with learning disabilities and hyperactivity: A subgroup analysis. *Journal of Learning Disabilities, 22,* 381–383, 399.

Ysseldyke, J., Algozzine, B., & Epps, S. (1983). A logical and empirical analysis of current practice in classifying students as handicapped. *Exceptional Children, 50,* 160–165.

History

Hammill, D. (1989). *A brief history of learning disabilities.* Austin, TX: Pro-Ed.

Hammill, D., & Larsen, S. (1974). The effectiveness of psycholinguistic abilities. *Exceptional Children, 41,* 5–14.

Kirk, S.A., McCarthy, J.J., & Kirk, W.D. (1968). *Illinois Test of Psycholinguistic Abilities* (ITPA). Urbana: University of Illinois Press.

Swanson, H.L., & Watson, B.L. (1989). *Educational and psychological assessment of exceptional children* (2nd ed.). Columbus: Merrill.

Prevalence, Incidence, Demographics

Gerber, M.M. (1984). The Department of Education's sixth annual report to Congress on PL 94–142: Is Congress getting the full story? *Exceptional Children, 51,* 209–224.

U.S. Department of Education. (1990). *Twelfth annual report to Congress on the implementation on the Education for Handicapped Act.* Washington, DC: U.S. Government Printing Office.

Causes and Prevention

Deshler, D.D., & Schumaker, J.B. (1986). Learning strategies: An instructional alternative for low-achieving adolescents. *Exceptional Children, 52,* 583–590.

Englemann, S.E. (1977). Sequencing cognitive and academic tasks. In R.D. Kneedler & S.G. Tarver (Eds.). *Changing perspectives in special education* (pp. 46–61). Columbus, OH: Charles E. Merrill.

Gibbs, D.P., & Cooper, E.B. (1989). Prevalence of communication disorders in students with learning disabilities. *Journal of Learning Disabilities, 22,* 60–63.

Hallahan, D.P., & Bryan, T.H. (1981). Learning disabilities. In J.M. Kauffman & D.P. Hallahan (Eds.), *Handbook of special education.* Englewood Cliffs, NJ: Prentice-Hall.

Lovitt, T.C. (1977). *In spite of my resistance . . . I've learned from children.* Columbus, OH: Charles E. Merrill.

Meichenbaum, D. (1985). Teaching thinking: A cognitive-behavioral perspective. In S.R. Chipman & J.W. Segal (Eds.), *Thinking and learning skills: Research and open questions* (Vol. 2). Hillsdale, NJ: Lawrence Erlbaum.

Reichman, J., & Healey, W.C. (1983). Learning disabilities and conductive loss involving otitis media. *Journal of Learning Disabilities, 16,* 272–278.

Swanson, H.L. (1987). Information processing theory and learning disabilities: A commentary and future perspective. *Journal of Learning Disabilities, 20,* 155–166.

Heredity

Decker, S.N., & Defries, J.C. (1980). Cognitive abilities in families of reading disabled children. *Journal of Learning Disabilities, 13,* 517–522.

Decker, S.N., & Defries, J.C. (1981). Cognitive ability profiles in families of reading disabled children. *Developmental Medicine and Child Neurology, 23,* 217–227.

Owen, F.W., Adams, P.A., Forrest, T., Stolz, L.M., & Fisher, S. (1971). Learning disorders in children: Sibling studies. *Monographs of the Society for Research in Child Development, 36* (4, Ser. No. 144).

Language skills

Cantwell, D.P., & Baker, L. (1987). *Developmental speech and language disorders.* New York: Guilford Press.

Wallach, G.P., & Butler, K.G. (1984). *Language learning disabilities in school-age children.* Baltimore: Williams & Wilkins.

Characteristics

Attention

Lenz, B.K., Alley, G.R., & Schumaker, J.B. (1987). Activating the inactive learner: Advance organizers in the secondary content classroom. *Learning Disability Quarterly, 10,* 53–67.

Torgesen, J.K., & Licht, B.G. (1983). The learning disabled child as an inactive learner: Retrospect and prospects. In J.D. McKinney & F. Feagans (Eds.), *Current topics in learning disabilities* (Vol. 1), (pp. 3–31). Norwood, NJ: Ablex.

Learned Helplessness and Attribution

Aponik, D.A., & Dembo, M.H. (1983). LD and normal adolescents' causal attributions of success and failure at different levels of task difficulty. *Learning Disability Quarterly, 6,* 31–39.

Borkowski, J.G., Weyhing, R.S., & Turner, L.A. (1986). Attributional retraining and the teaching of strategies. *Exceptional Children, 53,* 130–137.

Kleinhammer-Tramill, P.J., Tramill, J.L., Schrepel, S.N., & Davis, S.F. (1983). Learned helplessness in learning disabled adolescents as a function of noncontingent rewards. *Learning Disability Quarterly, 6,* 61–66.

Pearl, R. (1982). LD children's attributions for success and failure: A replication with a labeled LD sample. *Learning Disability Quarterly, 5,* 173–176.

Pearl, R., Bryan, T., & Donahue, M. (1980). Learning disabled children's attributions for success and failure. *Learning Disability Quarterly, 3,* 3–9.

Switzky, H.N., & Schultz, G.F. (1988). Intrinsic motivation and learning performance: Implications for individual educational programming for learners with mild handicaps. *Remedial and Special Education, 9*, 7–14.

Generalization

Ellis, E.S. (1986). The role of motivation and pedagogy on the generalization of cognitive strategy training. *Journal of Learning Disabilities, 19*, 66–70.

Rivera, D., & Smith, D.D. (1988). Using a demonstration strategy to teach midschool students with learning disabilities how to compute long division. *Journal of Learning Disabilities, 21*, 77–81.

Problem Solving and Thinking Skills

Collins, M., Carnine, D., & Gersten, R. (1987). Elaborated corrective feedback and the acquisition of reasoning skills: A study of computer-assisted instruction. *Exceptional Children, 54*, 254–262.

Social Skills

Blackbourn, J.M. (1989). Acquisition and generalization of social skills in elementary-aged children with learning disabilities. *Journal of Learning Disabilities, 22*, 28–34.

Bryan, T.H., & Bryan, J.H. (1986). *Understanding learning disabilities*. Palo Alto, CA: Mayfield.

Bursuck, W. (1989). A comparison of students with learning disabilities to low achieving and higher achieving students on three dimensions of social competence. *Journal of Learning Disabilities, 22*, 188–194.

Fox, C.L. (1989). Peer acceptance of learning disabled children in the regular classroom. *Exceptional Children, 56*, 50–59.

Gresham, F.M., & Elliot, S.M. (1989). Social skills deficits as a primary learning disability. *Journal of Learning Disabilities, 22*, 120–124.

Hoyle, S.G., & Serafica, F.C. (1988). Peer status of children with and without learning disabilities—A multimethod study. *Learning Disability Quarterly, 11*, 322—332.

Kistner, J.A., & Gatlin, D. (1989). Correlates of peer rejection among children with learning disabilities. *Learning Disability Quarterly, 12*, 133–140.

McKinney, J.D. (1989). Longitudinal research on the behavioral characteristics of children with learning disabilities. *Journal of Learning Disabilities, 22*, 141–150, 165.

Schumaker, J.B., & Hazel, J.S. (1984a). Social skills assessment and training for the learning disabled: Who's on first and what's on second? Part I. *Journal of Learning Disabilities, 17*, 422–431.

Schumaker, J.B., & Hazel, J.S. (1984b). Social skills assessment and training for the learning disabled: Who's on first and what's on second? Part II. *Journal of Learning Disabilities, 17*, 492–499.

Education

General

Bos, C.S., & Vaughn, S. (1988). *Strategies for teaching students with learning and behavior problems*. Needham Heights, MA: Allyn & Bacon.

Christenson, S.L., Ysseldyke, J.E., & Thurlow, M.L. (1989). Critical instructional factors for students with mild handicaps: An integrated review. *Remedial and Special Education, 10*, 21–31.

Lovitt, T.C. (1984). *Tactics for Teaching*. Columbus, OH: Charles E. Merrill.

Smith, D.D. (1989). *Teaching students with learning and behavior problems*. Englewood Cliffs, NJ: Prentice-Hall.

Early Intervention

Casto, G., & Mastropieri, M.A. (1986). The efficacy of early intervention programs: A meta analysis. *Exceptional Children, 52*, 417–424.

Gibbs, D.P. & Cooper, E.B. (1989). Prevalence of communication disorders in students with learning disabilities. *Journal of Learning Disabilities, 22*, 60–63.

Kroth, R. (1989). *The special education speed bump*. Unpublished manuscript, University of New Mexico, Albuquerque.

Lazar, I., Hubbell, V.R., Murray, H., Rosche, M., & Royce, J. (1977). *The persistence of preschool effects: A long-term follow-up of fourteen infant and preschool experiments*. Washington, DC: Office of Human Development Services, U.S. Department of Health, Education and Welfare.

Mallory, B.L., & Kerns, G.M. (1988). Consequences of categorical labeling of preschool children. *Topics in Early Childhood Special Education, 8*, 39–50.

Smith, B.J., & Schakel, J.A. (1986). Noncategorical identification of preschool handicapped children: Policy issues and options. *Journal of the Division for Early Childhood, 11*, 78–86.

Learning Strategies

Deshler, D.D., & Schumaker, J.B. (1986). Learning strategies: An instructional alternative for low-achieving adolescents. *Exceptional Children, 52*, 583–590.

Mastropieri, M.A., & Scruggs, T.E. (1988). Increasing content area learning of learning disabled students: Research and implementation. *Learning Disabilities Research, 4*, 17–25.

Mastropieri, M.A., & Scruggs, T.E. (1989). Mnemonic social studies instruction: Classroom applications. *Remedial and Special Education, 10*, 40–46.

Dropout

deBettencourt, L.U., Zigmond, N., & Thornton, H. (1989). Follow-up of postsecondary-age rural learning disabled graduates and dropouts. *Exceptional Children, 56*, 40–49.

Edgar, E. (1987). Secondary programs in special education: Are many of them justifiable: *Exceptional Children, 53*, 555–561.

Demonstration Plus Permanent Model

Blankenship, C.S. (1978). Remediating systematic inversion errors in subtraction through the use of demonstration and feedback. *Learning Disability Quarterly, 1*, 12–22.

Rivera, D., & Smith, D.D. (1987). Influence of modeling on acquisition and generalization of computational skills: A summary of research findings from three sites. *Learning Disability Quarterly, 10*, 69–80.

Families

Bower, D., & Wright, V.K. (1986). *The rubberband syndrome: Family life with a child with a disability.* Lincoln: Nebraska Department of Education; Des Moines: Iowa Department of Public Instruction.

Kroth, R. (1978). Parents: Powerful and necessary allies. *Teaching Exceptional Children, 10,* 88–91.

Simpson, R.L. (1990). *Conferencing parents of exceptional children* (2nd ed.). Austin, TX: Pro-Ed.

Adults with Learning Disabilities

Follow-up Studies

Aaron, P.G., Phillips, S., & Larsen, S. (1988). Specific reading disability in historically famous persons. *Journal of Learning Disabilities, 21,* 523–528.

Blalock, G. (1989). Transition education. In D.D. Smith, *Teaching students with learning and behavior problems* (2nd ed.), (pp. 302–331). Englewood Cliffs, NJ: Prentice-Hall.

deBettencourt, L.U., Zigmond, N., & Thornton, H. (1989). Follow-up of postsecondary-age rural learning disabled graduates and dropouts. *Exceptional Children, 56,* 40–49.

Edgar, E., Levine, P., Levine, R., & Dubey, M. (1988). *Washington State follow-along studies 1983–1987 students in transition: Final report.* Seattle: University of Washington, Experimental Education Unit.

Fafard, M., & Haubrich, P.A. (1981). Vocational and social adjustment of learning disabled young adults: A follow-up study. *Learning Disability Quarterly, 4,* 122–130.

Haring, K.A., Lovett, D.L., & Smith, D.D. (1990). A follow-up study of recent special education graduates of learning disabilities programs. *Journal of Learning Disabilities, 23,* 108–113.

Johnson, D.J., & Blalock, J.W. (1987). *Adults with learning disabilities: Clinical studies.* Orlando, FL: Grune & Stratton.

Kavale, K.A. (1987). The long term consequences of learning disabilities. In M.C. Wang, M.C. Reynolds, & H.J. Walberg (Eds.), *Handbook of special education: Research and practice* (Vol. 2), (pp. 303–344). Elmsford, NY: Pergamon.

Neubert, D.A., Tilson, G.P., & Ianacone, R.N. (1989). Postsecondary transition needs and employment patterns of individuals with mild disabilities. *Exceptional Children, 55,* 494–500.

O'Connor, S.C., & Spreen, O. (1988). The relationship between parents' socioeconomic status and education level, and adult occupational and educational achievement of children with learning disabilities. *Journal of Learning Disabilities, 21,* 148–153.

Smith, J.O. (1988). Social and vocational problems of adults with learning disabilities: A review of the literature. *Learning Disabilities Focus, 4,* 46–58.

White, W.J., Alley, G.R., Deshler, D.D., Schumaker, J.B., Warner, M.M., & Clark, F.L. (1982). Are there learning disabilities after high school? *Exceptional Children, 49,* 273–274.

College Students with Learning Disabilities

Beirne-Smith, M., & Deck, M.D. (1989). A survey of postsecondary programs for students with learning disabilities. *Journal of Learning Disabilities, 22,* 456–457.

Chronicle of Higher Education. (1988, June 1). Connecticut requires colleges to recruit disabled people. p. A-30.

Green, L. (1988, Aug. 1). Fairness, comfort of bar exams' special accommodations debated. *The National Law Journal,* p. 4.

Van Ness, E. (1989, April 9). As easy as 1-3-2. *New York Times, Education Life Supplement,* pp. 47–48.

Technology

Carnine, D. (1989). Teaching complex content to learning disabled students: The role of technology. *Exceptional Children, 55,* 524–533.

Cohen, A.L., Torgesen, J.K., & Torgesen, J.L. (1988). Improving speed and accuracy of word recognition in reading disabled children: An evaluation of two computer program variations. *Learning Disability Quarterly, 11,* 333–341.

Collins, M., Carnine, D., & Gersten, R. (1987). Elaborated corrective feedback and the acquisition of reasoning skills: A study of computer-assisted instruction. *Exceptional Children, 54,* 254–262.

Cosden, M.A., & Semmel, M.I. (1987). Developmental changes in microeducational environments for learning handicapped and non-learning handicapped elementary school students. *Journal of Special Education Technology, 8,* 1–13.

Higgins, K.K. (1988). *Hypertext computer assisted instruction and the social studies achievement of learning disabled, remedial, and regular education high school students.* Unpublished doctoral dissertation, University of New Mexico, Albuquerque.

Horton, S.V., Lovitt, T.C., Givens, A., & Nelson, R. (1989). Teaching social studies to high school students with academic handicaps in a mainstreamed setting: Effects of a computerized study guide. *Journal of Learning Disabilities, 22,* 102–107.

Kolich, E.M. (1985). Microcomputer technology with the learning disabled: A review of the literature. *Journal of Learning Disabilities, 18,* 428–431.

Messerer, J., & Lerner, J.W. (1989). Word processing for learning disabled students. *Learning Disabilities Focus, 5,* 3–17.

Moore, L.J., & Carnine, D. (1989). Evaluating curriculum design in the context of active teaching. *Remedial and Special Education, 10,* 28–37.

Morocco, C.C., & Neuman, S.B. (1986). Word processors and the acquisition of writing strategies. *Journal of Learning Disabilities, 19,* 243–247.

Stearns, P.H. (1986). Problem solving and the learning disabled: Looking for answers with computers. *Journal of Learning Disabilities, 19,* 116–120.

Trifiletti, J.J., Frith, G.H., & Armstrong, S. (1984). Microcomputers versus resource rooms for LD students: A preliminary investigation of the effects on math skills. *Learning Disability Quarterly, 7,* 69–76.

Medical Management of Hyperactivity

Axelrod, D., & Bailey, S.L. (1979). Drug treatment for hyperactivity: Controversies, alternatives, and guidelines. *Exceptional Children, 45,* 544–550.

Aman, M.G. (1980). Psychotropic drugs and learning problems—A selective review. *Journal of Learning Disabilities, 13,* 87–97.

Becker, R. (1988, Aug. 8). A hyperactive child's parents seek the right to say no to drugs. *People Magazine,* pp. 59–60.

Bradley, C. (1937). The behavior of children receiving benzadrine. *Journal of Psychiatry, 94,* 577–585.

Eaton, M., Sells, C.J., & Lucas, B. (1976). Psychoactive medication and learning disabilities. *Journal of Learning Disabilities, 10,* 403–410.

Patterson, G.R. (1965). An application of conditioning techniques to the control of a hyperactive child. In L. Ullman & L. Krasner (Eds.), *Case studies in behavior modification* (pp. 370–375). New York: Holt, Rinehart, & Winston.

Shafto, F., & Sulzbacher, S. (1977). Comparing treatment tactics with a hyperactive preschool child: Stimulant medication and programmed teacher intervention. *Journal of Applied Behavior Analysis, 10,* 13–20.

Sulzbacher, S.I. (1972). Behavior analysis of drug effects in the classroom. In G. Semb (Ed.), *Behavior analysis and education—1972* (pp. 37–52). Lawrence: The University of Kansas Support and Development Center for Follow Through.

Whalen, C.K., Henker, B., Collins, B.E., Finck, D., & Dotemoto, S. (1979). A social ecology of hyperactive boys: Medication effects in structured classroom environments. *Journal of Applied Behavior Analysis, 12,* 65–81.

CHAPTER 7 GIFTEDNESS AND CREATIVITY

Giftedness and Creativity—General

Callahan, C.M. (1981). Superior abilities. In J.M. Kauffman & D.P. Hallahan (Eds.), *Handbook of special education* (pp. 48–86). Englewood Cliffs, NJ: Prentice-Hall.

Clark, B. (1988). *Growing up gifted* (3rd ed.). Columbus, OH: Charles E. Merrill.

Davis, G.A., & Rimm, S.B. (1989). *Education of the gifted and talented* (2nd ed.). Englewood Cliffs, NJ: Prentice-Hall.

Feldhusen, J.F., & Treffinger, D.J. (1985). *Creative thinking and problem solving in gifted education* (3rd ed.). Dubuque, IO: Kendal/Hunt.

Gallagher, J.J. (1985). *Teaching the gifted child* (3rd ed.). Boston: Allyn & Bacon.

Gallagher, J.J. (1988). National agenda for educating gifted students: Statement of priorities. *Exceptional Children, 55,* 107–114.

Gardner, H. (1983). *Frames of mind: The theory of multiple intelligences.* New York: Basic Books.

Guilford, J.P. (1959). Three faces of intellect. *American Psychology, 24,* 469–479.

Laycock, F. (1979). *Gifted children.* Glenview, IL: Scott, Foresman.

Renzulli, J. (1978). What makes giftedness? Reexamining a definition. *Phi Delta Kappan, 60,* 180–184, 261.

Renzulli, J.S. (Ed.) (1986). *Systems and models for developing programs for the gifted and talented.* Mansfield Center, CT: Creative Learning Press.

Silverman, L.K. (1988) Gifted and talented. In E.L. Meyen & T.M. Skrtic (Eds.), *Exceptional children and youth: An introduction.* (3rd ed.), (pp. 263–292). Denver: Love.

Sternberg, R. (1985). *Beyond IQ: A triarchic theory of human intelligence.* Cambridge, England: Cambridge University Press.

Tannenbaum, A.J. (1983). *Gifted children: Psychological and educational perspectives.* New York: Macmillan.

Terman, L. (1925). *Genetic studies of genius* (Vol. 1). Stanford, CA: Stanford University Press.

Giftedness and Creativity Defined

Alvino, J., McDonnel, R.C., & Richert, S. (1981). National survey of identification practices in gifted and talented education. *Exceptional Children, 48,* 124–132.

Houseman, W. (1987). *The 1987 state of the states gifted and talented education report.* The Council of State Directors of Programs for the Gifted.

New Mexico State Board of Education (1988). *Educational standards for New Mexico schools.* Santa Fe: New Mexico State Board of Education.

Marland, S. (1972). *Education of the gifted and talented.* Report to the Congress of the United States by the U.S. Commissioner of Education. Washington, DC: U.S. Government Printing Office.

Characteristics

Commission on Tests (1970). *I: Righting the balance. II: Briefs.* New York: College Entrance Examination Board.

Hollingworth, L.S. (1942). *Children above 180 IQ, Stanford-Binet: Origin and development.* Yonkers, NY: World Book.

Grossberg, I.N., & Cornell, D.G. (1988). Relationship between personality adjustment and high intelligence. Terman versus Hollingworth. *Exceptional Children, 55,* 266–272.

Creativity

Krippner, S. (1967). The ten commandments that block creativity. *Gifted Child Quarterly, 11,* 144–151.

Renzulli, J. (1973). *New directions in creativity.* New York: Harper & Row.

Torrance, E.P. (1970). *Encouraging creativity in the classroom.* Dubuque, IA: Brown.

Torrance, E.P., & Ball, O.E. (1984). *Torrance tests of creative thinking, streamlined manual including norms and directions for administering and scoring figural A and B* (rev. ed.). Bensenville, IL: Scholastic Testing Service.

Torrance, E.P., & Torrance, J.P. (1978). Future problem solving: National interscholastic competition and curriculum project. *Journal of Creative Behavior, 12,* 87–89.

Treffinger, D. (1986a). Research on creativity. *Gifted Child Quarterly, 30,* 15–19.

Giftedness among Women

Benbow, C., & Stanley, J. (Eds.). (1983). *Academic precocity.* Baltimore: Johns Hopkins Press.

Eccles, J. (1985). Why doesn't Jane run? Sex differences in educational and occupational patterns. In F. Horowitz & M. O'Brien (Eds.), *The gifted and talented: Developmental perspectives* (pp. 251–295). Washington, DC: American Psychological Association.

Gallagher, S. (1989). Special issue on gifted females. *Journal for the Education of Gifted, 12,* 83–167.

Kerr, B.A. (1985). *Smart girls, gifted women.* Columbus, OH: Psychology Publishing.

Rand, D., & Gibb, L.H. (1989). A model program for gifted girls in science. *Journal for the Education of the Gifted, 12,* 142–155.

Reis, S.M., & Callahan, C.M. (1989). Gifted females: They've come a long way—Or have they? *Journal for the Education of the Gifted, 12,* 99—117.

Silverman, L.K. (1986b). What happens to the gifted girl? In C.J. Maker (Ed.), *Critical issues in gifted education: Vol. 1. Defensible programs for the gifted* (pp. 43–89). Rockville, MD: Aspen.

Giftedness among Minority Groups

Baldwin, A.Y. (1987). Undiscovered diamonds: The minority gifted child. *Journal for the Education of the Gifted, 10,* 271–285.

Bradley, C.L. (1990). *Creativity differences between reservation and urban Native Americans.* Unpublished doctoral dissertation. Texas A&M University, Lubbock.

Chinn, P.C., & Hughes, S. (1987). Representation of minority students in special education classes. *Remedial and Special Education, 8,* 41–46.

George, K. (1987). *A guide to understanding gifted American Indian students.* Washington, DC: Office of Educational Research and Improvement, granted to ERIC Clearinghouse on rural Education and Small Schools, Las Cruces, New Mexico. (ERIC Document Reproduction Service No. ED 284 715.)

Kirschenbaum, R. (1988). Methods for identifying the gifted and talented American Indian student. *Journal for the Education of the Gifted, 11,* 53–63.

Maker, C.J., & Schiever, S.W. (1989). Defining the Hispanic population. In C.J. Maker & S.W. Schiever (Eds.), *Critical issues in gifted education: Defensible programs for cultural and ethnic minorities* (Vol. 2), (pp. 1–4). Austin, TX: Pro-Ed.

Mistry, J., & Rogoff, B. (1985). A cultural perspective on the development of talent. In F.D. Horowitz and M. O'Brien (Eds.), *The gifted and talented: Developmental perspectives* (pp. 125–144). Washington, DC: American Psychological Association.

Poppe, R. (1989). *Gifted and talented education among Native Americans.* Unpublished manuscript, University of New Mexico, Albuquerque.

Renzulli, J. (1973b). Talent potential in minority group students. *Exceptional Children, 39,* 437–444.

Smith, T.W. (1990). *Ethnic images.* GSS Topical Report No. 19. Chicago: National Opinion Research Center, University of Chicago.

Tonemah, S. (1987). Assessing American Indian gifted and talented students' abilities. *Journal for the Education of the Gifted, 10,* 181–194.

Wakabayashi, R., Ayers, G., Rivera, O., Saylor, L., & Stewart, J. (1978). *Unique problems of handicapped minorities. The White House Conference on Handicapped individuals. Volume 1: Awareness papers, 23–27.* Washington, DC: U.S. Government Printing Office.

Handicapped/Gifted

Hirsch, S.P. (1979). *Young, gifted, and handicapped: Mainstreaming high-potential handicapped students into the Executive High School Internship Program.* Washington, DC: U.S. Office of Education.

Maker, C.J. (1977). *Providing programs for the gifted handicapped.* Reston, VA: Council for Exceptional Children.

Maker, C.J. (1986). Education of the gifted: Significant trends. In R.J. Morris & B. Blatt (Eds.), *Special education: Research and trends* (pp. 190–221). New York: Pergamon.

Silverman, L.K. (1986a). The IQ controversy: Conceptions and misconceptions. *Roeper Review, 8,* 136–140.

Whitmore, J.R., & Maker, C.J. (1985). *Intellectual giftedness in disabled persons.* Rockville, MD: Aspen Systems.

Gifted Underachievers

Rimm, S.B. (1986). *Underachievement syndrome: Causes and cures.* Watertown, WI: Apple.

Whitmore, J.R. (1980). *Giftedness, conflict, and underachievement.* Boston: Allyn & Bacon.

History

Galton, F. (1869). *Hereditary genius: An inquiry into its laws and consequences.* London: Macmillan.

Gardner, J.W. (1984). *Excellence: Can we be equal and excellent too?* (rev. ed.). New York: W.W. Norton.

Oden, M. (1968). The fulfillment of promise: 40-year followup of the Terman gifted group. *Genetic Psychology Monographs, 77,* 3–93.

Stern, J.D. (1988). *The condition of education: Elementary and secondary education* (Vol. 1). Washington, DC: U.S. Department of Education, Office of Educational Research and Improvement.

Prevalence, Incidence, Demographics

Branscomb, A. (1980, May). *Commerce Technical Advisory Board recommendations on learning environments for innovation* (Report of the CTAB to Jordan J. Baruch, Assistant Secretary for Productivity, Technology and Innovation). Washington, DC: U.S. Department of Commerce.

Cartwright, G.P., Cartwright, C.A., & Ward, M.A. (1989). *Educating special learners* (3rd ed.). Belmont, CA: Wadsworth.

Mitchell, B. (1982). An update on the state of gifted/talented education in the U.S. *Phi Delta Kappan, 64,* 357–358.

Mitchell, P., & Erickson, D.K. (1978). The education of gifted and talented children: A status report. *Exceptional Children, 45,* 12–16.

Sisk, D. (1981). Educational planning for the gifted and talented. In J.M. Kauffman and D.P. Hallahan (Eds.), *Handbook of special education* (pp. 441–458). Englewood Cliffs, NJ: Prentice-Hall.

Sisk, D. (1987). *Creative teaching of the gifted.* New York: McGraw-Hill.

Causes

Delisle, J.R. (1984). *Gifted children speak out.* New York: Walker.

Pressey, S. (1964). Concerning the nature and nurture of genius. In J. French (Ed.), *Educating the gifted child: A book of readings* (pp. 11–23). New York: Holt, Rinehart & Winston.

Education

General

Cox, J., Daniel, N., & Boston, B. (1985). *Educating able learners: Programs and promising practices.* Austin, TX: University of Texas Press.

Feldhusen, J., & Robinson, A. (1986). The Purdue secondary model for gifted and talented youth. In J.S. Renzulli (Ed.), *Systems and models for developing programs for the gifted and talented* (pp. 153–178). Mansfield Center, CT: Creative Learning Press.

Gallagher, J.J., Weiss, P., Oglesby, K., & Thomas, T. (1983). *The status of gifted/talented education: United States survey of needs, practices, and policies.* Ventura, CA: Ventura County Superintendent of Schools Office.

Hobson v. Hansen, 269 F. Supp. 401 (D.D.C. 1967, affirmed subnom. *Smuck v. Hobson,* 408 F. 2d 175 (DC Cir 1969).

Hubbard, K. (1983). "Richard III: The man, the myth, the reality": A unit of study for the gifted. *History and Social Science Teacher, 18,* 165–169.

Kutner, L. (1989, Oct. 5). Keeping a gifted child challenged in school: Special classes may not be the answer. *The New York Times,* p. B-4.

Kulik, C-L.C., & Kulik, J.A. (1984). Effects of ability grouping on secondary school students: A meta-analysis of evaluation findings. *American Educational Research Journal, 19,* 415–428.

Maker, C.J. (1986b). Integrating content and process in the teaching of gifted students. In C.J. Maker (Ed.) *Critical issues in gifted education: Defensible programs for the gifted.* Rockville, MD: Aspen.

Maker, C.J. (1989). Curriculum content for gifted students: Principles and practices. In R.M. Milgram (Ed.), *Teaching gifted and talented learners in regular classrooms.* Springfield, IL: Charles C. Thomas.

McDowell, L. (1989). *Prepackaged program experimentation assignment.* Unpublished manuscript, University of New Mexico, Albuquerque.

Renzulli, J.S. (1987). The positive side of pull-out programs. *Journal for the Education of the Gifted, 10,* 245–254.

Renzulli, J..S., & Reis, S.M. (1986). The enrichment triad/revolving door model: A schoolwide plan for the development of creative productivity. In J.S. Renzulli (Ed.), *Systems and models for developing programs for the gifted and talented* (pp. 391–428). Mansfield Center, CT: Creative Learning Press.

Renzulli, J.S., Reis, S.M., & Smith, L. (1981). *The revolving door identification model* (pp. 429–459). Mansfield Center, CT: Creative Learning Press.

Scheidemann, N.V. (1931). *The psychology of exceptional children.* New York: Houghton Mifflin.

Sisk, D. (1987). *Creative teaching of the gifted.* New York: McGraw-Hill.

Treffinger, D.J. (1986b). Fostering effective, independent learning through individualized programming. In J.S. Renzulli (Ed.), *Systems and models for developing programs for the gifted and talented* (pp. 429–460). Mansfield Center, CT: Creative Learning Press.

VanTassel-Baska, J. (1987). Point-counterpoint. The ineffectiveness of the pull-out program model in gifted education: A minority perspective. *Journal for the Education of the Gifted, 10,* 255–264.

VanTassel-Baska, J., Feldhusen, J., Seeley, K., Wheatley, G., Silverman, L., & Foster, W. (1989). *Comprehensive curriculum for gifted learners.* Boston: Allyn & Bacon.

Early Education

Bloom, B.S., & Sosniak, L.A. (1981). Talent development vs. schooling. *Educational Leadership, 39,* 86–94.

Goertzel, V., & Goertzel, M.G. (1962). *Cradles of eminence.* Boston: Little, Brown.

Karnes, M.B., Shwedel, A.M., & Linnemeyer, S.A. (1982). The young gifted/talented child: Programs at the University of Illinois. *Elementary School Journal, 82,* 196–213.

Families

Bloom, B.S. (1985). *Developing talent in young people.* New York: Ballantine Books.

Rimm, S.B. (1986). *Underachievement syndrome: Causes and cures.* Watertown, WI: Apple.

Stanley, A. (1990, May 7). Prodigy fights for chance to be doctor at 17. *The New York Times,* p. A-1.

Wernick, S. (1990, May 30). The highly gifted child: Hidden and often ignored. *New York Times, Education,* pp. B-1, B-8.

Adults

Hughes, H.H., & Converse, H.D. (1962). Characteristics of the gifted: A case for a sequel to Terman's study. *Exceptional Children, 29,* 179–183.

Nichols, R.C., & Astin, A.W. (1966). Progress of the merit scholar: An eight-year follow-up. *Personnel and Guidance Journal, 44,* 673–681.

Oden, M.H. (1968). The fulfillment of promise: 40-year follow-up of the Terman gifted group. *Genetic Psychology Monographs, 77,* 3–93.

Terman, L.M., & Oden, M.H. (1959). *The gifted group at midlife*. Stanford, CA: Stanford University Press.

Torrance, E.P. (1972). Career patterns and peak creative achievements of creative high school students twelve years later. *The Gifted Child Quarterly, 16,* 75–88.

Technology

Jenkins-Friedman, R., & Nielsen, M.E. (1990). Gifts and talents. In E.L. Meyen (Ed.), *Exceptional children in today's schools: An alternative resource book* (2nd ed.) (pp. 451–490). Denver: Love.

Tisone, J.M., & Wismar, B.L. (1985). Microcomputers: How can they be used to enhance creative development. *Journal of Creative Behavior, 19,* 97–103.

Yin, R. & White, J. (1984). *Microcomputer implementation in schools.* Washington, DC: Cosmos.

CHAPTER 8 BEHAVIORAL DISORDERS AND EMOTIONAL DISTURBANCE

Behavioral Disorders and Emotional Disturbance—General

Coleman, M.C. (1986). *Behavior disorders: Theory and practice.* Englewood Cliffs, NJ: Prentice-Hall.

D'Alessandro, M.E. (1987). "The ones who always get the blame": Emotionally handicapped children writing. *Language Arts, 64,* 516–522.

Haring, N.J., & Phillips, E.L. (1962). *Educating emotionally disturbed children.* New York: McGraw-Hill.

Hewett, F.M., & Taylor, F. (1980). *The emotionally disturbed child in the classroom* (2nd ed.). Boston: Allyn & Bacon.

Kauffman, J.M. (1989). *Characteristics of behavioral disorders of children and youth* (4th ed.). Columbus, OH: Charles E. Merrill.

McDowell, R.L., Adamson, G.W., & Wood, F.H. (Eds.). (1982). *Teaching emotionally disturbed children.* Boston: Little, Brown.

Nelson, C.M., & Rutherford, R.B. (1988). Behavioral interventions with behaviorally disordered students. In M.C. Wang, M.C. Reynolds & H.J. Walberg (Eds.), *Handbook of special education: Research and practice* (Vol. 2, Mildly handicapped conditions), (pp. 125–153). New York: Pergamon.

Quay, H.C., & Werry, J.S. (Eds.) (1986). *Psychopathological disorders of childhood* (3rd ed.). New York: John Wiley & Sons.

Behavioral Disorders and Emotional Disturbance Defined

Achenbach, T.M., & Edelbrock, C.S. (1978). The classification of child psychopathology: A review and analysis of empirical efforts. *Psychological Bulletin, 85,* 1275–1301.

Bower, E.M. (1960). *Early identification of emotionally disturbed children in school* (rev. ed.). Springfield, IL: Charles C. Thomas.

Bower, E.M. (1982). Defining emotional disturbance: Public policy and research. *Psychology in the Schools, 19,* 55–60.

Brophy, J.E., & Evertson, C.M. (1981). *Student characteristics and teaching.* New York: Longman.

Cullinan, D., Epstein, M.H., & Kauffman, J.M. (1984). Teachers' ratings of students' behaviors: What constitutes behavior disorder in school? *Behavioral Disorders, 10,* 9–19.

Forness, S.R., & Cantwell, D.P. (1982). DSM-III psychiatric diagnoses and special education categories. *Journal of Special Education, 16,* 49–63.

Gerber, M.M., & Semmel, M.I. (1984). Teacher as imperfect test: Reconceptualizing the referral process. *Educational Psychologist, 19,* 137–148.

Kauffman, J.M. (1980). Where special education for disturbed children is going: A personal view. *Exceptional Children, 46,* 522–527.

Smith, C.R., Wood, F.H., & Grimes, J. (1988). Issues in the identification and placement of behaviorally disordered students. In M.C. Wang, M.C. Reynolds, & H.J. Walberg (Eds.), *Handbook of special education: Research and practice* (Vol. 2, Mildly handicapping conditions), (pp.95–123). New York: Pergamon.

Measurement

Haring, N. (Ed.). (1987). *Assessing and managing behavior disabilities.* Seattle: University of Washington Press.

Walker, H.M., Severson, H.H., Todis, B.J., Block-Pedego, A.E., Williams, G.J., Haring, N., & Barckley, M. (1990). Systematic Screening for Behavior Disorders (SSBD): Further validation, replication, and normative data. *Remedial and Special Education, 11,* 32–46.

History

Beers, C.W. (1908). *A mind that found itself: An autobiography.* New York: Longmans, Green.

Bender, L. (1942). Schizophrenia in childhood. *Nervous Child, 1,* 138–140.

Berkowitz, P.H., & Rothman, E.P. (1960). *The disturbed child: Recognition and psychological therapy in the classroom.* New York: New York University Press.

Berkowitz, P.H., & Rothman, E.P. (Eds.) (1967). *Public education for disturbed children in New York City: Application and theory.* Springfield, IL: Charles C. Thomas.

Bower, E.M. (1990). A brief history of how we have helped emotionally disturbed children and other fairy tales. *Preventing School Failure, 35,* 11–16.

Bower, E.M., & Lambert, N.M. (1962). *A process for in-school screening of children with emotional handicaps.* Princeton, NJ: Educational Testing Service.

Brigham, A. (1847). The moral treatment of insanity. *American Journal of Insanity, 4,* 1–15.

Cruikshank, W.M., Bentzen, F.A., Ratzeburg, F.H., & Tannhauser, M.T. (1961). *A teaching method for brain-injured and hyperactive children.* Syracuse: Syracuse University Press.

Deutsch, A. (1949). *The mentally ill in America: A history of their care and treatment from colonial times* (2nd ed.). New York: Columbia University Press.

Healy, W., & Bronner, A.F. (1926). *Delinquents and criminals: Their making and unmaking.* New York: Macmillan.

Hewett, F.M. (1967). Educational engineering with emotionally disturbed children. *Exceptional Children, 33,* 459–471.

Hewett, F.M. (1968). *The emotionally disturbed child in the classroom.* Boston: Allyn & Bacon.

Hobbs, N. (1966). Helping disturbed children: Psychological and ecological strategies. *American Psychologist, 21,* 1105–1115.

Kauffman, J.M. (1976). Nineteenth century views of children's behavioral disorders: Historical contributions and continuing issues. *Journal of Special Education, 10,* 335–349.

Long, N.J., Morse, W.C., & Newman, R.G. (Eds.) (1965). *Conflict in the classroom: The education of emotionally disturbed children.* Belmont, CA: Wadsworth.

Redl, F., & Wineman, D. (1957). *The aggressive child.* New York: The Free Press.

Rhodes, W.C., & Tracy, M.L. (Eds.). (1972a). *A study of child variance: Conceptual project in emotional disturbance.* Ann Arbor: University of Michigan.

Rhodes, W.C., & Tracy, M.L. (Eds.). (1972b). *A study of child variance: Vol. 2. Interventions.* Ann Arbor: University of Michigan.

Rhodes, W.D., & Head, S. (Eds.). (1974). *A study of child variance: Vol. 3. Service delivery systems.* Ann Arbor: University of Michigan.

Rothman, D.J. (1971). *The discovery of the asylum: Social order and disorder in the new republic.* Boston: Little, Brown.

Scull, A. (Ed.). (1981). *Madhouses, mad-doctors, and madmen: The social history of psychiatry in the Victorian era.* Philadelphia: University of Pennsylvania Press.

Strauss, A.A., & Lehtinen, L. (1947). *Psychology and education of the brain-injured child.* New York: Grune & Stratton.

Prevalence

Center, D.B., & Obringer, J. (1987). A search for variables affecting underidentification of behaviorally disordered students. *Behavioral Disorders, 12,* 169–174.

Costello, E.J., Costello, A.J., Edelbrock, C., Burns, B.J., Dulcan, M.K., Brent, D., & Janiszewski, S. (1988). Psychiatric disorders in pediatric primary care. *Archives of General Psychiatry, 45,* 1107–1116.

U.S. Department of Education. (1990). *Twelfth annual report to Congress on the implementation of the Education of the Handicapped Act.* Washington, DC: U.S. Government Printing Office.

Whitaker, A., Johnson, J., Shaffer, D., Rapoport, J.L., Kalikow, K., Walsh, B.T., Davies, M., Braiman, S., & Dolinsky, A. (1990). Uncommon troubles in young people: Prevalence estimates of selected psychiatric disorders in a nonreferred adolescent population. *Archives of General Psychiatry, 47,* 487–496.

White, D., Pillard, E.D., & Cleven, C.A. (1990). The influence of state definitions of behavior disorders on the number of children served under P.L. 94-142. *Remedial and Special Education, 11,* 17–22, 38.

Causes and prevention

Anderson, C.W. (1981). Parent–child relationships: A context for reciprocal developmental influence. *The Counseling Psychologist, 4,* 35–44.

Ashem, B., & Janes, M.D. (1978). Deleterious effects of chronic undernutrition on cognitive abilities. *Journal of Child Psychology and Psychiatry, 19,* 23–31.

Brophy, J., & Good, T. (1970). Teachers' communication of differential expectation for children's classroom performance: Some behavioral data. *Journal of Educational Psychology, 61,* 365–374.

Profile of Children with Behavioral Disorders and Emotional Disturbance

American Psychiatric Association. (1987). *Diagnostic and statistical manual of mental disorders* (3rd ed. rev.). Washington, DC: Author.

Berdine, W.H., & Blackhurst, A.E. (Eds.). (1985). *An introduction to special education.* Boston: Little, Brown.

Center, D.B., & Wascom, A.M. (1987). Teacher perceptions of social behavior in behaviorally disordered and socially normal children and youth. *Behavioral disorders, 12,* 200–206.

Edgar, E. (1987). Secondary programs in special education: Are many of them justifiable? *Exceptional Children, 53,* 555–561.

Epstein, M.H., Cullinan, D., & Polloway, E.A. (1986). Patterns of maladjustment among mentally retarded children and youth. *American Journal of Mental Deficiency, 91,* 127–134.

Fagen, S.A., & Hill, J.M. (1987). Teaching acceptance of frustration. *Teaching Exceptional Children, 19,* 49–51.

Gottlieb, J., Alter, M., & Gottlieb, B.W. (1991). Mainstreaming academically handicapped children in urban schools. In J.W. Lloyd, A.C. Repp, & N. Singh (Eds.), The regular education initiative: Alternative perspectives on concepts, issues, and models (pp. 95–112). Sycamore, IL: Sycamore Press.

Gresham, F.M. (1981). Social skills training with handicapped children: A review. *Review of Educational Research, 51,* 139–176.

Mattison, R.E., Humphrey, F.J., Kales, S.N., & Wallace, D.J. (1986). An objective evaluation of special class placement of schoolboys with behavior problems. *Journal of Abnormal Child Psychology, 14,* 251–262.

Reiss, S., Levitan, G.W., & McNally, R.J. (1982). Emotionally disturbed mentally retarded people: An underserved population. *American Psychologist, 37,* 361–367.

Ross, D.M., & Ross, S.A. (1982). *Hyperactivity: Current issues, research, and theory* (2nd ed.). New York: Wiley.

Ruhl, K.L., & Hughes, C.A. (1985). The nature and extent of aggression in special education settings serving behaviorally disordered students. *Behavioral Disorders, 10,* 95–104.

Strain, P., Guralnick, M., & Walker, H. (Eds.). (1986). *Children's social behavior: Development, assessment, and modification*. New York: Academic Press.

Walker, H.M. (1984). The Social Behavior Survival program (SBS): A systematic approach to the integration of handicapped children into less restrictive settings. *Education and Treatment of Children, 6,* 421–441.

Walker, H.M. (1986). The Assessments for Integration into Mainstream Settings (AIMS) assessment system: Rationale, instruments, procedures, and outcomes. *Journal of Clinical Child Psychology, 15,* 55–63.

Williams, S.L., Walker, H.M., Holmes, D., Todis, B., & Fabre, T.R. (1989). Social validation of adolescent social skills by teachers and students. *Remedial and Special Education, 10,* 18–27, 37.

Autism

Batshaw, M.L., & Perret, Y.M. (1986). *Children with handicaps: A medical primer* (2nd ed.). Baltimore: Paul H. Brookes.

Cohen, D.J., & Donnellen, A.M. (Eds.). (1987). *Handbook of autism and pervasive developmental disorders*. Silver Spring, MD: Winston.

Donnellan, A.M., Mirenda, P.L., Mesaros, R.A., & Fassbender, L.L. (1984). Analyzing the communicative functions of aberrant behavior. *Journal of the Association for Persons with Severe Handicaps, 9,* 201–212.

Kanner, L. (1943). Autistic disturbances of affective contact. *Nervous Child, 2,* 217–250.

LaVigna, G.W., & Donnellan, A.M. (1986). *Alternatives to punishment: Solving behavior problems with non-aversive strategies*. New York: Irvington.

Lovaas, O.I. (1977). *The autistic child: Language development through behavior modification*. New York: Irvington.

McGee, J.J., Menolascino, F.J., Hobbs, D.C., & Menousek, P.E. (1987). *Gentle teaching: A nonaversive approach for helping persons with mental retardation*. New York: Human Sciences Press.

Issues in Education

Education and the Preschool Child

Cass, L.K., & Thomas, C.B. (1979). *Childhood pathology and later adjustment*. New York: Wiley.

Education and the School-Age Child

Barrish, H.H., Saunders, M., & Wolf, M.M. (1969). Good behavior game: Effects of individual contingencies for group consequence on disruptive behavior in a classroom. *Journal of Applied Behavior Analysis, 2,* 119–124.

Braaten, S.R., Simpson, R., Rosell, S.J., & Reilly, T. (1988). Using punishment with exceptional children: A dilemma for educators. *Teaching Exceptional Children, 20,* 79–81.

Carpenter, R.L., & Apter, S.J. (1988). Research integration of cognitive-emotional interventions for behaviorally disordered children and youth. In M.C. Wang, M.C. Reynolds, & H.J. Walberg (Eds.), *Handbook of special education: Research and practice* (Vol. 2, Mildly handicapped conditions) (pp. 155–169.) New York: Pergamon.

Fad, K.S. (1990). The fast track to success: Social-behavioral skills. *Intervention in School and Clinic, 26,* 39–43.

Haring, N.J., & Whelan, R.J. (1965). Experimental methods in education and management. In N.J. Long, W.C. Morse, & R.G. Newman (Eds.), *Conflict in the classroom* (pp. 389–404). Belmont, CA: Wadsworth.

Hewett, F.M., & Taylor, F. (1980). *The emotionally disturbed child in the classroom* (2nd ed.). Boston: Allyn & Bacon.

Hollinger, J. (1987). Social skills for behaviorally disordered children as preparation for mainstreaming: Theory, practice and new directions. *Remedial and Special Education, 8,* 17–27.

McDowell, R.L., Adamson, G.W., & Wood, F.H. (Eds.). (1982). *Teaching emotionally disturbed children*. Boston: Little, Brown.

Quality Education for Minorities Project. (1990). *Education that works: An action plan for the education of minorities*. Cambridge, MA: Massachusetts Institute of Technology.

Skinner, B.F. (1953). *Science and human behavior*. New York: Macmillan.

Smith, D.D. (1984). *Effective discipline*. Austin, TX: Pro-Ed.

Smith, D.D. (1989). *Teaching students with learning and behavior problems* (2nd ed.) Englewood Cliffs, NJ: Prentice-Hall.

Snider, W. (1990, Dec. 5). Fresno schools, Hmong refugees seek common ground. *Education Week, X,* 1.

Walker, H.M., McConnell, S., Holmes, D., Todis, B., Walker, J., & Golden, N. (1988). *The Walker Social Skills Curriculum: The ACCEPTS program*. Austin, TX: Pro-Ed.

Walker, H.M., Todis, B., Holmes, D., & Horton, G. (1988). *The Walker Social Skills Curriculum: The ACCESS program*. Austin, TX: Pro-Ed.

Wood, F.H., & Braaten, S. (1983). Developing guidelines for the use of punishing interventions in the schools. *Exceptional Education Quarterly, 3,* 68–75.

Educational Environments

Huntze, S.L. (1988). Cooperative interface of schools and other child care systems for behaviorally disordered students. In M.C. Wang, M.C. Reynolds, & H.J. Walberg (Eds.), *Handbook of special education: Research and practice.* (Vol. 2, Mildly handicapped conditions) (pp. 195–217). New York: Pergamon.

Knitzer, J., Steinberg, Z., & Fleisch, B. (1990). *At the schoolhouse door: An examination of programs and policies for children with behavioral and emotional problems*. New York: Bank Street College of Education; Washington, DC: Children's Defense Fund.

Knitzer, J. (1982). *Unclaimed children: The failure of public responsibility to children and adolescents in need of mental health services*. Washington, DC: Children's Defense Fund.

Nelson, C.M., Rutherford, R.B., & Wolford, B.I. (1987). *Special education in the criminal justice system*. Columbus, OH: Charles E. Merrill.

Adults with Behavioral Disorders and Emotional Disturbance

Carmody, D. (1990, Feb. 14). Colleges tightening discipline as disruptive behavior grows. *New York Times,* p. B-9.

Chess, S., & Thomas, A. (1984). *Origins and evolution of behavior disorders: From infancy to adult life.* New York: Brunner/Mazel.

ERIC Clearinghouse on Handicapped and Gifted Children. (1988). *Special Education Dropouts, Digest #451.* Reston, VA: Author.

Lichtenstein, S. (1987). *A study of the post-school employment patterns of handicapped and nonhandicapped graduates and dropouts.* Unpublished doctoral dissertation, University of Illinois at Champaign–Urbana.

Lichenstein, S. (1988). *Dropouts: Perspectives on special education.* Concord, NH: Task Force for the Improvement of Secondary Special Education.

Thomas, A., & Chess, S. (1984). Genesis and evolution of behavioral disorders: From infancy to early adult life. *American Journal of Psychiatry, 141,* 1–9.

Wolman, C., Bruininks, R., & Thurlow, M.L. (1989). Dropouts and dropout programs: Implications for special education. *Remedial and Special Education, 10,* 6–20, 50.

Technology and Behavioral Disorders and Emotional Disturbance

Campbell, M., Green, W.H., & Deutsch, S.I. (1985). *Child and adolescent psychopharmacology.* Beverly Hills, CA: Sage.

Sherrington, R., Brynjolfsson, J., Petursson, H., Potter, M., Dudelston, K., Barraclough, B., Wasmuth, J., Dobbs, M., & Gurling, H. (1988, Nov. 10). Localization of a susceptibility locus for schizophrenia on chromosome 5. *Nature, 336,* 164–167.

Moss, D.C. (1988, Nov.). Ritalin under fire. *American Bar Association Journal,* p. 19.

Suddath, R.L., Christison, G.W., Torrey, E.F., Casanova, M.F., & Weinberger, D.R. (1990, March). Anatomical abnormalities in the brains of monozygotic twins discordant for schizophrenia. *New England Journal of Medicine, 322,* 789–794.

Socially Maladjusted

Wood, F.H. (Ed.). (1990). Special issue: Issues in the exclusion of socially maladjusted students. *Behavioral Disorders, 15,* 139–189.

CHAPTER 9   VISUAL IMPAIRMENTS

VISUAL IMPAIRMENTS—GENERAL

Barraga, N.C. (1964). *Increased visual behavior in low vision children.* New York: American Foundation for the Blind.

Barraga, N.C. (1976). *Visual handicaps and learning.* Belmont, CA: Wadsworth.

Barraga, N.C., & Collins, M.E. (1979). Development of efficiency in visual functioning. *Journal of Visual Impairment and Blindness, 73,* 121–126.

Barraga, N.C., & Morris, J.E. (1980). *Program to develop efficiency in visual function: Source book on low vision.* Louisville, KY: American Printing House for the Blind.

Harley, R.K., & Lawrence, G.A. (1984). *Visual impairment in the schools* (2nd ed.). Springfield, IL: Charles C. Thomas.

Harley, R.K., Truan, M.B., & Sanford, L.D. (1987). *Communication skills for visually impaired learners.* Springfield, IL: Charles C. Thomas.

Kirchner, C. (Ed.). (1988a). *Data on blindness and visual impairment in the U.S.: A resource manual on social demographic characteristics, education, employment and income, and service delivery* (2nd ed.). New York: American Foundation for the Blind.

Moores, D.F. (1987). *Educating the deaf: Psychology, principles, and practices* (3rd ed.). Boston: Houghton Mifflin.

Rogow, S.M. (1988). *Helping the visually impaired child with developmental problems: Effective practice in home, school, and community.* New York: Teachers College Press.

Scholl, G.T. (1986). *Foundations of education for blind and visually handicapped children and youth: Theory and practice.* New York: American Foundation for the Blind.

Tuttle, D.W. (1988). Visually impaired. In E.L. Meyen & T.M. Skrtic (Eds.), *Exceptional children and youth: An introduction* (3rd ed.) (pp. 351–386). Denver: Love.

VISUAL IMPAIRMENTS DEFINED

Genensky, S.M., Berry, S.H., Bikson, T.H., & Bikson, T.K. (1979). *Visual environmental adaptation problems of the partially sighted: Final Report.* Santa Monica, CA: Santa Monica Medical Center, Center for the Partially Sighted.

Harley, R.K., & Lawrence, G.A. (1984). *Visual impairment in the schools.* Springfield, IL: Charles C. Thomas.

Kirchner, C., & Lowman, C. (1985). Sources of variation in the estimated prevalence of visual loss. In C. Kirchner (Ed.), *Data on blindness and visual impairment in the U.S.: A resource manual on characteristics, education, employment, and service delivery* (pp. 3–12). New York: American Foundation for the Blind.

HISTORY

Roberts, F.K. (1986). Education for the visually handicapped: A social and educational history. In G.T. Scholl (Ed.), *Foundation of education for blind and visually handicapped children and youth: Theory and practice* (pp. 1–18). New York: American Foundation for the Blind.

Sacks, S.Z., Rosen, S., & Gaylord-Ross, R.J. (1990). Visual impairment. In N.G. Haring & L. McCormick (Eds.), *Exceptional children and youth* (5th ed.) (pp. 403–446). Columbus OH: Charles E. Merrill.

Scholl, G.T., Mulholland, M.E., & Lonergan, A. (1986). Education of the visually handicapped: A selective timeline. In G.T. Scholl (Ed.), *Foundation of education for blind and visually handicapped children and youth: Theory and practice* (front and back cover). New York: American Foundation for the Blind.

PREVALENCE AND INCIDENCE OF VISUAL IMPAIRMENTS

Kirchner, C. (1983). Special education for visually handicapped children: A critique on numbers served and costs. *Journal of Visual Impairments and Blindness, 77,* 219–223.

Kirchner, C. (1988b). Federal data sources on blindness and visual impairment: An editorial assessment. In C. Kirchner

(Ed.), *Data on blindness and visual impairment in the U.S.: A resource manual on social demographic characteristics, education, employment and income, and service delivery* (2nd ed.) (pp. 35–43). New York: American Foundation for the Blind.

Kirchner, C., & Peterson, R. (1988a). Multiple impairments among noninstitutionalized blind and visually impaired persons. In C. Kirchner (Ed.), *Data on blindness and visual impairment in the U.S.: A resource manual on social demographic characteristics, education, employment and income, and service delivery* (2nd ed.), (pp. 101–109). New York: American Foundation for the Blind.

Kirchner, C., & Peterson, R. (1988b). Estimates of race: Ethnic groups in the U.S. visually impaired and blind population. In C. Kirchner (Ed.), *Data on blindness and visual impairment in the U.S.: A resource manual on social demographic characteristics, education, employment and income, and service delivery* (2nd ed.), (pp. 81–99). New York: American Foundation for the Blind.

Packer, J., & Kirchner, D. (1985). State level counts on blind and visually handicapped school children. *Journal of Visual Impairments and Blindness, 79,* 357–361.

U.S. Department of Education (1990). *Twelfth annual report to Congress on the implementation on the Education for Handicapped Act.* Washington, DC: U.S. Government Printing Office.

CAUSES AND PREVENTION

Benton, V., & Truelove, N. (1978). "Adopt a school"—A program of eye care for children. *Sight Saving Review, 48,* 77–80.

Cartwright, G.P., Cartwright, C.A., & Ward, M.E. (1989). *Educating special learners* (3rd ed.). Belmont, CA: Wadsworth.

Gates, C.F. (1985). Survey of multiply handicapped visually impaired children in the Rocky Mountain/Great Plains Region. *Journal of Visual Impairment and Blindness, 79,* 385–391.

Leary, W.E. (1988, March 30). Trial backs freezing as eye therapy. *New York Times,* p. 8.

National Society to Prevent Blindness. (1977). Signs of possible eye trouble in children (Pub. G-112). New York: Author.

New York Times (1989, July 18). Scientists report finding eye disease gene. p. C-5.

Poirier, R.D. (1984). Scorecard: An update on NSPB's planning system. *Sightsaving, 53,* 18–21.

Vaughan, D., & Asbury, T. (1986). *General ophthalmology* (11th ed.). Los Altos, CA: Appleton-Century-Crofts.

Werner, D. (1987). *Disabled village children.* Palo Alto, CA: Hesperian Foundation.

EDUCATION

Gallagher, W.F. (1988). Categorical services in the age of integration: Paradox or contradiction? *Journal of Visual Impairment and Blindness, 82,* 226–229.

Hodges, H.L., (1983). Evaluating the effectiveness of programs for the visually impaired: One state's approach. *Journal of Visual Impairment and Blindness, 77,* 97–99.

Lowenfeld, B. (1982). In search of better ways. *Education of the Visually Handicapped, 14,* 68–77.

Orlansky, M.D. (1977). *Mainstreaming the visually impaired child.* Austin, TX: Learning Concepts.

Scott, E.P. (1982). *Your visually impaired student: A guide for teachers.* Baltimore: University Park Press.

Silverstein, R. (1985). The legal necessity for residential schools serving deaf, blind, and multiply impaired children. *Journal of Visual Impairment and Blindness, 79,* 145–149.

Tuttle, D.W. (1981). Academics are not enough: Techniques of daily living for visually impaired children. *Handbook for teachers of the visually handicapped.* New York: American Printing House for the Blind.

Viadero, D. (1989, Nov.). Side by Side: With the help of her teachers and classmates, a gutsy blind girl thrives in the mainstream. *Teacher Magazine, 40–48.*

Early Intervention

ERIC (1987). Orientation and mobility for blind infants. *Research Resources on Special Education Council for Exceptional Children,* Abstract XIII. Reston, VA: Council for Exceptional Children.

Ferrell, K.A. (1986a). Infancy and early childhood. In G.R. Scholl (Ed.), *Foundations of education for blind and visually handicapped children and youth: Theory and practice* (pp. 119–136). New York: American Foundation for the Blind.

Ferrell, K.A. (1986b). Working with parents. In G.R. Scholl (Ed.), *Foundations of education for blind and visually handicapped children and youth: Theory and practice.* (pp. 265–274). New York: American Foundation for the Blind.

Harley, R.K., Long, R.G., Merbler, J., Wood, T.A., & Langley, M.G. (1986). *The development of a program in orientation and mobility for multihandicapped blind infants.* U.S. Department of Education Grant No. G008400665.

Joffee, E. (1988). A home-based orientation and mobility program for infants and toddlers. *Journal of Visual Impairment and Blindness, 82,* 282–285.

Klein, B., Van Hasselt, V.B., Trefeiner, M., Sandstrom, D.J., & Brandt-Snyder, P. (1988). The parent and toddler training project for visually impaired and blind multihandicapped children. *Journal of Visual Impairment and Blindness, 82,* 59–64.

Moore, S. (1984). The need for programs and services for visually handicapped infants. *Education of the Visually Handicapped, 16,* 48–57.

Stratton, J., (1977). *The blind child in the regular kindergarten.* Springfield, IL: Charles C. Thomas.

Warren, D.H. (1984). *Blindness and early childhood development* (2nd ed.). New York: American Foundation for the Blind.

Reading

Diesenhouse, S. (1989, Feb. 15). Welter of braille codes create "Tower of Babel." *New York Times, Education,* p. B-8.

Disability Rag (1988, Nov./Dec.). Some books now available on computer disk through club, p. 11.

Disability Rag (1989, July/Aug.). Kudos and raspberries: Kudos to Book of the Month Club, p. 37.

Ethington, D. (1956). The readability of braille as a function of three spacing variables. Unpublished master's thesis, University of Kentucky, Lexington, KY. As cited in Harley, Truan, & Stanford (1987).

Jones, J.W. (1961). *Blind children: Degree of vision and mode of reading.* Washington, DC: United States Office of Education.

Kirchner, C., Peterson, R., & Suhr, C. (1988). Trends in school enrollment and reading methods among legally blind school children, 1963–1978. In C. Kirchner (Ed.), *Data on blindness and visual impairment in the U.S.: A resource manual on social demographic characteristics, education, employment, and service delivery* (2nd ed.) (pp. 113–121). New York: American Foundation for the Blind.

Mangrum, T. (1989, Aug. 30). Quotes: I'm a lawyer. *American Bar Association Journal,* p. 30.

Mack, C. (1984). How useful is braille? Reports of blind adults. *Journal of Visual Impairment and Blindness, 78,* 311–313.

McDowell, E. (1990, Jan. 8). New markets are found for large-print books. *New York Times,* p. C-7.

Nolan, C.Y. (1967). A 1966 reappraisal of the relationship between visual acuity and mode of reading for blind children. *The New Outlook, 61,* 255–261.

Listening

Robinson, S., & Smith, D.D. (1981). Listening skills: Teaching learning disabled students to be better listeners. *Focus on Exceptional Children, 13,* 1–16.

Smith, J.A. (1972). *Adventures in communication.* Boston: Allyn & Bacon.

Advance Organizers

Deshler, D.D., Warner, M.M., Schumaker, J.B., & Alley, G.R. (1983). Learning strategies intervention model: Key components and current status. In J.D. McKinney & F. Feagans (Eds.), *Current topics in learning disabilities,* (Vol. 1) (pp. 245–283). Norwood, NJ: Ablex.

Lenz, B.K., Alley, G.R., & Schumaker, J.B. (1987). Activating the inactive learner: Advance organizers in the secondary content classroom. *Learning Disability Quarterly, 10,* 53–62.

Lenz, B.K. (1989). Set the stage for learning—Use advance organizers. *Strategram, 1,* 1–4.

Recreation

Albuquerque Tribune. (1989, Nov. 11). Blind runner depends on buddies' help. p. C-5.

Gaines-Carter, P. (1988, May 28). Helping the blind see the Capitol: Tactile maps point out landmarks and potential pitfalls. *Washington Post,* p. B-1.

Kelley, J.D. (Ed.). (1981). *Recreation programming for visually impaired children and youth.* New York: American Foundation for the Blind.

Martin, D. (1989, Aug. 26). A blind NY athlete, rejecting all limits, competes with tenacity. *New York Times,* p. 9.

Snouffer, E. (1989, Nov. 15). Wrestling with public's blind spot: UNM freshman adjusts to life on campus and on wrestling mat. *Albuquerque Journal,* pp. C-1–C-4.

Orientation and Mobility

Edwards, L.A., De'laune, W., Barber, A., Geruschat, D., Rieser, J., & Hill, E. (1985). *Orientation and mobility for low vision persons: A final report.* Philadelphia: Pennsylvania College of Optometry.

Hill, E.W. (1986). Orientation and mobility. In G.R. Scholl (Ed.), *Foundations of education for blind and visually handicapped children and youth: Theory and practice* (pp. 315–340). New York: American Foundation for the Blind.

New York Times. (1989, March 18). 9 budding ballerinas learn to dance without sight and without fear, p. 31.

Career Education

Bush-LaFrance, B. (1988). Unseen expectations of blind youth: Educational and occupational ideas. *Journal of Visual Impairment and Blindness, 82,* 132–136.

Irwin, J., & Macdonell, P. (1988). Access to transition services: Integral part of curriculum. *Journal of Visual Impairment and Blindness, 82,* 69–70.

Simpson, F. (1986). Transition to adulthood. In G.R. Scholl (Ed.), *Foundations of education for blind and visually handicapped children and youth: Theory and practice* (pp. 405–422). New York: American Foundation for the Blind.

Families

Ferrell, K.A. (1986b). Working with parents. In G.R. Scholl (Ed.), *Foundations of education for blind and visually handicapped children and youth: Theory and practice* (pp. 265–274). New York: American Foundation for the Blind.

Gullett, S. (1990, March 3). No sight, no problem: Family of 4 lives much like everyone else. *Albuquerque Tribune,* p. B-5.

Kroth, R.L. (1985). *Communicating with parents of exceptional children: Improving parent–teacher relationships* (2nd ed.). Denver: Love.

Simpson, R.L. (1990). *Conferencing parents of exceptional children* (2nd ed.). Austin, TX: Pro-Ed.

St. Peter, S.M., & Sexton, J.D. (1987). The impact of a disabled child: Familial stress and professional strategies. In A. Rotatori, M.M. Banbury, & R.A. Fox (Eds.), *Issues in special education.* (pp. 113–121). Mountain View, CA: Mayfield.

Adults with Visual Impairments

Albuquerque Journal. (1989, Oct. 17). State Depart. hires blind envoy. p. A-2.

Education Week. (1989, Oct. 11). Blind student in Georgia may compete in track meet, p. 2.

Edwards, L.A. (1986). *Rehabilitation of low vision individuals.* Washington, DC: Catholic University of America, D:ATA Institute.

Jernigan, K. (1983). Blindness: Disability or nuisance? In R.L. Jones (Ed.), *Reflections on growing up disabled* (pp. 58–67). Reston, VA: The Council for Exceptional Children.

Johnson, S., & Hafer, M. (1985). Employment status of visually impaired men and women. *Journal of Visual Impairment and Blindness, 79,* 241–244.

Kirchner, C., & Peterson, R. (1988c). Employment: Selected characteristics. In C. Kirchner (Ed.), *Data on blindness and visual impairment in the U.S.: A resource manual on characteristics, education, employment, and service delivery* (2nd ed.), (pp. 169–177). New York: American Foundation for the Blind.

NASDSE (1989, May 4). Visually impaired can receive student aid information on cassette. *SpecialNet,* Electronic Mail.

New York Times. (1989, Aug. 12). A phone card in braille, p. 16.

New York Times. (1990, Jan. 28). Enhancing television for the visually impaired, p. 24.

New York Times. (1990, May 9). A printer translates into braille, p. C-6.

Sorber, G. (1990, Aug. 2). Newsline dedicated. *Albuquerque Journal,* p. D-1.

Summers, L. (1989). Reimbursing adaptive technology. *NARIC Quarterly, A Newsletter of Disability and Rehabilitation Research and Resources, 2,* 1, 7–11, 17.

Technology-Related Assistance for Individuals with Disabilities Act of 1988. Catalogue No. 850. (Senate Rpt. 100–438). Washington, DC: U.S. Government Printing Office.

CHAPTER 10   HEARING IMPAIRMENTS

Hearing Impaired—General

Boone, D.R. (1987). *Human communication and its disorders.* Englewood Cliffs, NJ: Prentice-Hall.

Brown, S.C. (1986). Etiological trends, characteristics, and distributions. In A.N. Schildroth & M.A. Karchmer (Eds.), *Deaf children in America* (pp. 33–54). Austin, TX: Pro-Ed.

Commission on the Education of the Deaf. (1988). *Toward equality: Education of the Deaf.* Washington, DC: U.S. Government Printing Office.

Haederle, M. (1990). First year student challenges stereotypes. *UNM/Law: A Newsletter for Alumni and Friends, 3,* 8–9.

Karchmer, M.A. (1984). Demographics and deaf adolescents. In G. Anderson & D. Watson (Eds.), *Proceedings of the National Conference on Habilitation and Rehabilitation of Deaf Adolescents* (pp. 28–46). Washington, DC: National Academy of Gallaudet College.

Liben, L.S. (1978). The development of deaf children: An overview of the issues. In L.S. Liben (Ed.), *Deaf children: Developmental perspectives* (pp. 3–20). New York: Academic Press.

Lowenbraun, S. (1988). Hearing impaired. In E.L. Meyen & T.M. Skrtic (Eds.), *Exceptional children and youth: An introduction* (3rd ed.) (pp. 321–350). Denver: Love.

Moores, D.F. (1987). *Educating the deaf: Psychology, principles, and practices* (3rd ed.). Boston: Houghton Mifflin.

Northern, J.L., & Downs, M.P. (1984). *Hearing in children* (3rd ed.). Los Angeles: Williams & Wilkins.

Quigley, S.P., and Paul, P.V. (1984). *Language and deafness.* San Diego: College-Hill.

Schildroth, A.N., & Karchmer, M.A. (1986). *Deaf children in America.* Austin, TX: Pro-Ed.

Wolff, A.B., & Harkins, J.E. (1986). Multiply handicapped students. In A.N. Schildroth & M.A. Karchmer (Eds.), *Deaf children in America* (pp. 55–81). Austin, TX: Pro-Ed.

Deafness and Its Culture

Evans, A.D., & Falk, W.W. (1986). *Learning to be deaf.* New York: Mouton de Gruyter.

Gannon, J.R. (1981). *Deaf heritage.* Silver Spring, MD: National Association of the Deaf.

Lane, H. (1988). Is there a "Psychology of the Deaf?" *Exceptional Children, 55,* 7–19.

Padden, C., & Humphries, T. (1988). *Deaf in America: Voices from a culture.* Cambridge, MA: Harvard University Press.

Hearing Impairments Defined

Ries, P. (1986). Characteristics of hearing impaired youth in the general population and of students in special educational programs for the hearing impaired. In A.N. Schildroth & M.A. Karchmer (Eds.), *Deaf children in America* (pp. 1–31). Austin, TX: Pro-Ed.

History

Adams, M.E. (1929, Nov.). 1865–1935: A few memories of Alexander Graham Bell. *American Annals of the Deaf, 74,* 467–479.

Alby, J.F. (Spring 1962). The educational philosophy of Thomas Hopkins Gallaudet. *Buff and Blue Literary Number,* 17–23.

Gannon, J.R. (1989). *The week the world heard Gallaudet.* Washington, DC: Gallaudet University Press.

Lane, H. (1984). *When the mind hears: A history of the deaf.* New York: Random House.

Winefield, R. (1987). *Never shall the twain meet: The communications debate.* Washington, DC: Gallaudet University Press.

Prevalence, Incidence, Demographics

Commission on the Education of the Deaf. (1988). *Toward equality: Education of the Deaf.* Washington, DC: U.S. Government Printing Office.

Karchmer, M.A. (1985). A demographic perspective. In E. Cherow, N.P. Watkins, & R.J. Trybus (Eds.), *Hearing impaired children and youth with developmental disabilities* (pp. 36–54). Washington, DC: Gallaudet College Press.

Schildroth, A.N., & Hotto, S.A. (1988). Annual survey of hearing impaired children and youth: A tradition of discovery, 1987–88. *Annual Report of the Gallaudet Research Institute.* Washington, DC: Gallaudet University.

U.S. Department of Education. (1987). *Ninth annual report to Congress on the implementation of the Education for Handicapped Act.* Washington, DC: U.S. Government Printing Office.

U.S. Department of Education. (1988). *Tenth annual report to Congress on the implementation of the Education for Handicapped Act*. Washington, DC: U.S. Government Printing Office.

U.S. Department of Education. (1989). *Eleventh annual report to Congress on the implementation of the Education for Handicapped Act*. Washington, DC: U.S. Government Printing Office.

U.S. Department of Education (1990). *Twelfth annual report to Congress on the implementation of the Education for Handicapped Act*. Washington, DC: U.S. Government Printing Office.

Causes and Prevention

Allen, T.E. (1986). Patterns of academic achievement among hearing impaired students: 1974–1983. In A.N. Schildroth & M.A. Karchmer (Eds.), *Deaf children in America* (pp. 161–206). Austin, TX: Pro-Ed.

Hotchkiss, D. (1989). *Demographic aspects of hearing impairment: Questions and answers* (2nd ed.). Washington, DC: Gallaudet University, Center for Assessment and Demographic Studies.

Nance, W.E., & Sweeney, A. (1975). Genetic factors in deafness in early life. *Otlaryngologic Clinics of North America, 8,* 19–48.

Pappas, D. (1985). *Diagnosis and treatment of hearing impairment in children*. San Diego: College-Hill.

Pueschel, S.M., & Mulick, J.A. (1990). *Prevention of developmental disabilities*. Baltimore: Paul H. Brookes.

Riko, K., Hyde, M.L., & Alberti, M.B. (1985). Hearing loss in early infancy: Incidence, detection, and assessment. *Laryngoscope, 95,* 137–43.

Schmeck, H.M. (1988, May 5). Implants in inner ear can help deaf children, panel of experts finds. *New York Times, Health,* 22–23.

Swigart, E.T. (1986). *Neonatal hearing screening,* San Diego: College-Hill.

Turner, R.G. (1990). Recommended guidelines for infant hearing screening: Analysis. *ASHA, 32,* 57–61, 66.

Education

General

Allen, T.E. (1988). A demographic view of deaf students and mainstreaming in the United States. *Research at Gallaudet,* Winter/Spring, p. 6.

Antia, S. (1985). Social integration of hearing-impaired children: Fact or fiction? *The Volta Review, 87,* 279–289.

Burrow, E. (1983). *Special needs adaptions for Office of Education teachers*. Commerce, TX: Occupational Curriculum Laboratory, East Texas State University.

Grant, J. (1990). Bilingual education and the hearing impaired: Mandate and practices. In Civil Rights Commission (Ed.), *Rights of the hearing impaired*. Washington, DC: U.S. Government Printing Office.

Johnson, R.E., Liddell, S.K., & Erting, C.J. (1989). *Unlocking the curriculum: Principles for achieving access in deaf education.*

Gallaudet Research Institute Working Papers 89-3. Washington, DC: Gallaudet University.

Kampfe, C.M. (1984). Mainstreaming: Some practical suggestions for teachers and administrators. In R.H. Hull & K.I. Dilka (Eds.), *The hearing-impaired child in school* (pp. 99–112). New York: Grune & Stratton.

Montgomery, G., & Lines, A. (1976). Comparison of several single and combined methods of communicating with deaf children. In *Changing attitudes to communication*. Carlisle: British Deaf News, Supplementum. As reported in Moores, D.F. (1987). *Educating the deaf: Psychology, principles, and practices* (3rd ed.). Boston: Houghton Mifflin.

Sanders, D.M. (1988). *Teaching deaf children: Techniques and methods*. Boston: College-Hill.

Smith, D.D. (1989). *Teaching students with learning and behavior problems* (2nd ed.). Englewood Cliffs, NJ: Prentice-Hall.

Teitelbaum, M.L. (1981). Teachers as consumers: What they should know about the hearing impaired child. In M. Ross and L.W. Nober (Eds.), *Special education in transition: Educating hard of hearing children* (pp. 82–87). Washington, DC: Alexander Graham Bell Association for the Deaf.

Yater, V.V. (1977). *Mainstreaming of children with a hearing loss: Practical guidelines and implications*. Springfield, IL: Charles C. Thomas.

Achievement

Good, T.L., & Brophy, J.E. (1986). School effects. In M.C. Wittrock (Ed.), *Handbook of research on teaching* (3rd ed.), New York: Macmillan.

Kluwin, T.N., & Moores, D.F. (1989). Mathematics achievement of hearing impaired adolescents in different placements. *Exceptional Children, 55,* 327–335.

Rieth, H.J., Polsgrove, L., & Semmell, M.I. (1979). Relationship between instructional time and academic achievement: Implications for research and practice. *Education Unlimited, 1,* 53–56.

Trybus, R.J., & Karchmer, M.A. (1977). School achievement scores of hearing impaired children: National data on achievement status and growth patterns. *American Annals of the Deaf Directory of Programs and Services, 122,* 62–69.

Wolk, S., Karchmer, M.A., & Schildroth, A.N. (1982). *Patterns of academic and non-academic integration among hearing-impaired students in special education*. (Series R, #9). Washington, DC: Gallaudet College, Office of Demographic Studies.

Speech and Communication

Goehl, H., & Kaufman, D.K. (1984). Do the effects of adventitious deafness include disordered speech? *Journal of Speech and Hearing Disorders, 49,* 58–64.

Jordan, I.K., & Karchmer, M.A. (1986). Patterns of sign use among hearing impaired students. In A.N. Schildroth & M.A. Karchmer (Eds.), *Deaf children in America* (pp. 125–137). Austin, TX: Pro-Ed.

Wolk, S., & Schildroth, A.N. (1986). Deaf children and speech intelligibility: A national study. In A.N. Schildroth & M.A. Karchmer (Eds.), *Deaf children in America* (pp. 139–159). Austin, TX: Pro-Ed.

Woodward, J., Allen, T., & Schildroth, A. (1985). Teachers and deaf students: An ethnography of classroom communication. In S. DeLancey & R. Tomling (Eds.), *Proceedings of the first annual meeting of the Pacific Linguistics Conference* (pp. 479–493). Eugene: University of Oregon.

Woodward, J., Allen, T.E., Schildroth, A.N., & Karchmer, M.A. (1988). *A study of communication patterns in classrooms throughout the United States: Gallaudet Research Report.* Washington, DC: Gallaudet University.

Early Intervention

Appell, M.E. (1982). Early education for the severely handicapped/hearing impaired child. In B. Campbell & V. Baldwin (Eds.), *Severely handicapped/hearing impaired students* (pp. 181–197). Baltimore: Paul H. Brookes.

Bodner-Johnson, B. (1987). Helping the youngest ones. *Gallaudet Today, 18,* 8–11.

Ling, D. (1984a). *Early intervention for hearing-impaired children: Oral options.* San Diego: College-Hill.

Ling, D. (1984b). *Early intervention for hearing-impaired children: Total communication options.* San Diego: College-Hill.

Moores, D.F. (1985). Early intervention programs for hearing impaired children: A longitudinal assessment. In D. Nelson (Ed.), *Children's language* (Vol. V). Hillsdale, NJ: Erlbaum.

Somers, M.N. (1984). The parent–infant program at Kendall Demonstration School. In D. Ling (Ed.), *Early intervention for hearing-impaired children: Total communication options* (pp. 183–229). San Diego: College-Hill.

Postsecondary

Rawlings, B.W., Karchmer, M.A., & DeCaro, J.J. (1987). Postsecondary programs for deaf students at the peak of the rubella bulge. *American Annals for the Deaf, 132,* 36–42.

Rawlings, B.W., Karchmer, M.A., DeCaro, J.J., & Eggleston-Dodd, J. (1986). *College and career programs for deaf students.* Washington, DC: Gallaudet College.

Rawlings, B.W., & King, S.J. (1986). Postsecondary educational opportunities for deaf students. In A.N. Schildroth & M.A. Karchmer (Eds.), *Deaf children in America* (pp. 231–257). Austin, TX: Pro-Ed.

Walter, G.G., & Welsh, W.A. (1988). Characteristics and success of deaf college students in three types of educational environments. *American Rehabilitation, 14* (2), 8–11, 28–29.

Families

Proctor, L.A. (ND). *Growing together: Information for parents of hearing impaired children.* Washington, DC: National Information Center on Deafness.

Walker, L.A. (1986). *A loss for words: The story of deafness in a family.* New York: Harper & Row.

Wilcox, S. (1989). Foreign language requirement? Why not American Sign Language? *ERIC Digest,* ERIC Clearing House on Languages and Linguistics, Center for Applied Linguistics, Report (EDO-FL-89-01).

Adults

Albuquerque Journal. (1989, May 13). L.A. pays interpreter so deaf can be jurors, p. A–3.

Education of the Handicapped. (1990, Aug. 1). Court says schools must pay for sign language interpreter.

Forbath, P. (1990, Oct. 29). Disabled workers struggling to find acceptance. *Albuquerque Journal, Business Outlook,* p. 7.

Jacobs, L.M. (1980). *A deaf adult speaks out* (2nd ed.). Washington, DC: Gallaudet College Press.

Jones, L.M. (1983). The deaf: Handicapped by public ignorance. In R.L. Jones (Ed.), *Reflections on growing up disabled* (pp. 50–57). Reston, VA: The Council for Exceptional Children.

National Information Center on Deafness. (1987). *Career information registry of hearing impaired people: Directory 1986–1987.* Washington, DC: Gallaudet University.

Riddle, L. (1988, Nov. 9). Federal rule blocks way for deaf truck driver. *New York Times, National,* p. A-12.

Solomon, W.E. (1989, May 11). Treatment plan for deaf overcomes the language and culture barriers. *New York Times, Health,* p. B-9.

Walter, G.G., Welsh, W.A., & Servé, M.S. (1988). Providing a college education to deaf students: Why it pays. *American Rehabilitation, 14,* 16–19, 31–32.

Walter, G.G., & Welsh, W.A. (1988). Characteristics and success of deaf college students in three types of educational environments. *American Rehabilitation, 14,* 8–11, 28–29.

Technology

Compton, C.L., & Kaplan, H. (1988). Up close and personal: Assistive devices increase access to speech and sound. *Gallaudet Today, 18,* 18–23.

Levitt, H. (1985). Technology and the education of the hearing impaired. In F. Powell, T. Finitizo-Hieber, S. Friel-Patti, & D. Henderson (Eds.), *Education of the hearing impaired child* (pp. 120–132). San Diego: College-Hill Press.

Mahshie, J. (1988). Making strides: Speech training aids take a quantum jump with advanced computer technology. *Gallaudet Today, 18,* 14–17.

New York Times (1990, Oct. 16). Closed-caption law: Victory for the deaf. p. A-11.

Smith, D. (1988). Technology that teaches. *Gallaudet Today, 18,* 3–13.

Viadero, D. (1990, June 6). Television decoder touted as reading-instruction aid. *Education Week,* pp. 1, 27.

CHAPTER 11 PHYSICAL DISABILITIES AND HEALTH IMPAIRMENTS

Physical Disabilities and Health Impairments—General

Batshaw, M.L. & Perret, Y.M. (1986). *Children with handicaps: A medical primer* (2nd ed.). Baltimore: Paul H. Brookes.

Bleck, E., & Nagel, D.A. (Eds.). (1982). *Physically handicapped children: A medical atlas for teachers* (2nd ed.). New York: Grune & Stratton.

Bogdan, R. (1988). *Freak show: Presenting human oddities for amusement and profit.* Chicago: University of Chicago Press.

Fiedler, L. (1978). *Freaks.* New York: Simon & Schuster.

Fraser, B.A., & Hensinger, R.N. (1983). *Managing physical handicaps: A practical guide for parents, care providers, and educators.* Baltimore: Paul H. Brookes.

Maddox, S. (Ed.). (1987). *Spinal network: The total resource for the wheelchair community.* Boulder, CO: Author.

History

Dolch, E.W. (1948). Helping handicapped children in school. Champaign, IL: Garrard Press.

Eberle, L. (Aug. 1922). The maimed, the halt and the race. *Hospital Social Service, 6,* 59–63. Reprinted in R.H. Bremner (Ed.), *Children and youth in America, A documentary history: Vol. II, 1866–1932* (pp. 1026–1928). Cambridge, MA: Harvard University Press.

Frayer, D.W., Horton, W.A., Macchiarelli, R., & Mussi, M. (1987, Nov. 5). Dwarfism in an adolescent from the Italian late Upper Palaeolithic. *Nature, 330,* 60–61.

Kriegel, L. (1969). Uncle Tom and Tiny Tim: Some reflections on the cripple as Negro. *American Scholar, 38*(3), 412–430.

La Vor, M.L. (1976). Federal legislation for exceptional persons: A history. In F.J. Weintraub, A. Abeson, J. Ballard, & M.L. La Vor (Eds.), *Public policy and the education of exceptional children* (pp. 96–111). Reston, VA: Council for Exceptional Children.

Maddox, S. (Ed.) (1987). *Spinal network: The total resource for the wheelchair community.* Boulder, CO: Author.

Scheerenberger, R.C. (1983). *A history of mental retardation.* Baltimore: Paul H. Brookes.

Prevalence, Incidence, Demographics

U.S. Department of Education. (1990). *Twelfth annual report to Congress on the implementation of the Education of the Handicapped Act.* Washington, DC: U.S. Government Printing Office.

Causes and Prevention

Andersen, R.D., Bale, J.F., Blackman, J.A., & Murph, J.R. (1986). *Infections in children: A sourcebook for educators and childcare providers.* Rockville, MD: Aspen.

Profile of Children with Health Impairments and Physical Disabilities

Health Impairments

Children's Hospital of St. Paul. (1984). *CMV: Diagnosis, prevention and treatment.* St. Paul, MN: Author.

Council for Exceptional Children. (1986). *Report of the Council for Exceptional Children's taskforce on policy issues relating to the management of students with communicable diseases.* Reston, VA: Author.

Crocker, A.C., & Cohen, H.J. (1988). *Guidelines on developmental services for children and adults with HIV infection.* Silver Spring, MD: American Association of University Affiliated Programs for Persons with Developmental Disabilities.

Crocker, A.C., Cohen, H.J., Decker, C.L., Rudigier, A.F., & Harvey, D.C. (Eds.). (1989). *Public policy affirmations affecting the planning and implementation of developmental services for children and adults with HIV infection.* Silver Spring, MD: American Association of University Affiliated Programs for Persons with Developmental Disabilities.

Harvey, B. (1982). Asthma. In E. Bleck & D.A. Nagel (Eds.), *Physically handicapped children: A medical atlas for teachers* (2nd ed.) (pp. 31–42). New York: Grune & Stratton.

Hobbs, N., & Perrin, J.B. (1985). *Issues in the care of children with chronic illness.* San Francisco: Jossey-Bass.

Isaacs, J., & McElroy, M.R. (1980). Psychosocial aspects of chronic illness in children. *Journal of School Health, 50,* 318–321.

Luckasson, R. (1988). Public school education and children with HIV. In *AIDS: The legal issues* (pp. 188–205). Washington, DC: American Bar Association AIDS Coordinating Committee.

Mattsson, A. (1972). Long-term physical illness in childhood: A challenge to physical adaptation. *Pediatrics, 50,* 801–811.

Taylor, J.M., & Taylor, W.S. (1989). *Communicable disease and young children in group settings.* Boston: College-Hill.

Neurological and Neuromuscular Impairments

Bleck, E.E. (1982). Cerebral palsy. In E.E. Bleck & D.A. Nagel (Eds.), *Physically handicapped children: A medical atlas for teachers* (2nd ed.) (pp. 59–132). New York: Grune & Stratton.

Bleck, E.E. (1982). Muscular dystrophy—Duchenne type. In E.E. Bleck & D.A. Nagel (Eds.), *Physically handicapped children: A medical atlas for teachers* (2nd ed.) (pp. 385–394). New York: Grune & Stratton.

Bleck, E.E. (1982). Myelomeningocele, meningocele, and spina bifida. In E.E. Bleck, & D.A. Nagel (Eds.), *Physically handicapped children: A medical atlas for teachers* (2nd ed.) (pp. 345–362). New York: Grune & Stratton.

Epilepsy Foundation of America. (1981). *Seizure recognition and observation: A guide for allied health professionals.* Landover, MD: Author.

Epilepsy Foundation of America. (1983). *Preventing epilepsy.* Landover, MD: Author.

Epilepsy Foundation of America. (1987). *Questions and answers about epilepsy.* Landover, MD: Author.

Finnie, N.R. (1975). *Handling the young cerebral palsied child at home* (2nd ed.). New York: E.P. Dutton.

Head-injured students said inadequately served. (1988, April 20). *Education Week,* p. 15.

Mairs, N. (1986). *Plaintext: Essays.* Tucson: University of Arizona Press.

McLone, D. (1980). Technique for closure of myelomeningocele. *Child's Brain, 6,* 65–73.

McLone, D. (1983). Results of treatment of children born with a myelomeningocele. *Clinical Neurosurgery, 30,* 407–412.

McLone, D., Czyzewski, D., Raimondi, A.J., & Sommers, R.C. (1982). Central nervous system infections as a limiting factor in the intelligence of children with myelomeningocele. *Pediatrics, 70,* 338–342.

Mullins, J.B. (1979). *A teacher's guide to management of physically handicapped students.* Springfield, IL: Charles C. Thomas.

Penry, J.K. (Ed.). (1986). *Epilepsy: Diagnosis, management, quality of life.* New York: Raven Press.

Perske, R., Clifton, A., McLean, B.M., & Ishler Stein, J. (Eds.). (1986). *Mealtimes for persons with severe handicaps.* Baltimore: Paul H. Brookes.

Stores, G. (1981). Problems of learning and behavior in children with epilepsy. In E.H. Reynolds & M.R. Trimble (Eds.), *Epilepsy and psychiatry* (pp. 33–48). London: Churchill Livingstone.

Svoboda, W.B. (1979). *Learning about epilepsy.* Baltimore: University Park Press.

United Cerebral Palsy Associations. (1986). *Cerebral palsy— Facts and figures.* New York: Author.

Wannamaker, B.B., Dreifuss, F.E., Booker, H.E., & Willmore, L.J. (Eds.). (1984). *The comprehensive clinical management of the epilepsies.* Landover, MD: Epilepsy Foundation of America.

Werner, D. (1987). *Disabled village children: A guide for community health workers, rehabilitation workers, and families.* Palo Alto, CA: The Hesperian Foundation.

Issues in Diversity

Baca, L., & Harris, K.C. (Summer 1988). Teaching migrant exceptional children. *Teaching Exceptional Children, 20,* 32–35.

Education Commission of the States Migrant Education Task Force (1979). *Migrant health,* Report No. 131. Denver: Author.

Education

Education and the Preschool Child

Campbell, P.H. (1987a). Physical management and handling procedures with students with movement dysfunction. In M.E. Snell (Ed.), *Systematic instruction of persons with severe handicaps* (3rd ed.), (pp. 174–187). Columbus, OH: Charles E. Merrill.

Campbell, P.H. (1987b). Programming for students with dysfunction in posture and movement. In M.E. Snell (Ed.), *Systematic instruction of persons with severe handicaps* (3rd ed.), (pp. 188–211). Columbus, OH: Charles E. Merrill.

Epstein, S.G., Taylor, A.B., Halberg, A.S., Gardner, J.D., Walker, D.K., & Crocker, A.C. (1989). *Enhancing quality: Standards and indicators of quality care for children with special health care needs.* Boston: New England SERVE.

Goode, D.A. (1979). The world of the congenitally deaf-blind: Toward the grounds for achieving human understanding. In H. Schwartz & J. Jacobs (Eds.), *Qualitative sociology: A method to the madness* (pp. 187–207). New York: The Free Press.

Hanson, M.J. (1984). *Atypical infant development.* Baltimore: University Park.

Mrazek, D.A. (1984). Effects of hospitalization on early child development. In R.N. Emde & R.J. Harmon (Eds.), *Continui-ties and discontinuities in development* (pp. 211–225). New York: Plenum.

Orelove, F.P., & Sobsey, D. (1987). *Educating children with multiple disabilities: A transdisciplinary approach.* Baltimore: Paul H. Brookes.

Walker, B., Slentz, K., & Bricker, D. (1985). *Parent involvement in early intervention.* Washington, DC: D:ATA Institute.

Education and the School-Age Child

ACCH (Association for the Care of Children's Health). (1984). *Home care for children: An annotated bibliography.* Washington, DC: Author.

Bigge, J.L. (1991). *Teaching individuals with physical and multiple disabilities* (3rd. ed.). New York: Merrill.

Crump, I. (Ed.). (1987). *Nutrition and feeding of the handicapped child.* Boston: College-Hill/Little, Brown.

Graff, J.C., Mulligan-Ault, M., Guess, D., Taylor, M., & Thompson, B. (1990). *Health care for students with disabilities: An illustrated medical guide for the classroom.* Baltimore: Paul H. Brookes.

Krementz, J. (1989). *How it feels to fight for your life.* Boston: Joy Street/Little, Brown.

Mulligan-Ault, M., Guess, D., Struth, L., & Thompson, B. (1988). The implementation of health-related procedures in classrooms for students with severe multiple impairments. *Journal of the Association for Persons with Severe Handicaps, 13,* 100–109.

Shayne, M.W., Walker, D.K., Perrin, J.M., & Moynihan, L.C. (1987). Health-impaired children deserve a break. *Principal, 66(3),* 36–39.

Snell, M.E. (Ed.). (1987). *Systematic instruction of persons with severe handicaps* (3rd ed.). Columbus, OH: Charles E. Merrill.

Educational Environments

American National Standards Institute (1971). *American National Standard specifications for making buildings and facilities accessible to, and usable by, the physically handicapped* (ANSI A117.1–1961 R1971). New York: Author

Families

Goldfarb, L.A., Brotherson, M.J., Summers, J.A., & Turnbull, A.P. (1986). *Meeting the challenge of disability or chronic illness: A family guide.* Baltimore: Paul H. Brookes.

Kaufman, J., & Lichtenstein, K.A. (1986). *The family as care manager: Home care coordination for medically fragile children.* Millersville, MD: Coordinating Center for Home and Community Care, Inc. (CCHCC).

Adults

Burbach, H.J., & Babbitt, C.E. (1988). Physically disabled students on the college campus. *Remedial and Special Education, 9(2),* 12–19.

Crew, N.M. & Zola, I.K. (1983). *Independent living for physically disabled people: Developing, implementing, and evaluating self-help rehabilitation programs.* San Francisco: Jossey-Bass.

Lifchez, R., & Winslow, B. (1979). *Design for independent living: The environment and physically disabled people.* Berkeley: University of California Press.

Thomas, C.H., & Thomas, J.L. (1986). *Directory of college facilities and services for the disabled* (2nd ed.). Phoenix, AZ: Oryx Press.

Technology

Health Care

Singer, J.D., Butler, J.A., & Palfrey, J.S. (1986). Health care access to use among handicapped students in five public school systems. *Medical Care, 24,* 1–13.

Stark, J.A., Menolascino, F.J., & Goldsbury, T.L. (1988). An updated search for the prevention of mental retardation. In F.J. Menolascino & J.A. Stark (Eds.), *Preventive and curative intervention in mental retardation* (pp. 3–25). Baltimore: Paul H. Brookes.

Surgeon General of the United States. (1987). *Surgeon General's report: Children with special health care needs* (GPO 184–020/65654). Washington, DC: U.S. Government Printing Office.

U.S. Congress, Office of Technology Assessment. (1987). *Technology-dependent children: Hospital v. home care, a technical memorandum* OTA-TM-H-38 (GPO 052–003–01065–8). Washington, DC: U.S. Government Printing Office.

Communication

Capozzi, M., & Mineo, B. (1984). Nonspeech language and communication systems. In A.L. Holland (Ed.), *Language disorders in children* (pp. 173–209). San Diego: College-Hill.

Lambert, H. (1985). A communication system for the nonvocal physically impaired person. In C. Smith (Ed.), *Technology for disabled persons: Conference papers* (pp. 40–42). Menomonie, WI: Stout Vocational Rehabilitation Institute, University of Wisconsin–Stout.

McDonald, E.T., & Schultz, A.R. (1973). Communication boards for cerebral palsied children. *Journal of Speech and Hearing Disorders, 38,* 73–88.

Schiefelbusch, R.L. (Ed.). (1980). *Nonspeech language and communication: Analysis and intervention.* Baltimore: University Park Press.

Vanderheiden, G. (1984). High and low technology approaches in the development of communication systems for severely physically handicapped persons. *Exceptional Education Quarterly, 4,* 40–56.

Mobility

Apostolos, M. (1985). User acceptance of a robotic arm. In C. Smith (Ed.), *Technology for disabled persons: Conference papers* (pp. 43–47). Menomonie, WI: Stout Vocational Rehabilitation Institute, University of Wisconsin–Stout.

Heckathorne, C.W. (1986). Augmentative manipulation. In R. Foulds (Ed.), *Interactive robotic aids—One option for independent living: An international perspective* (pp. 40–43). Monograph 37. New York: World Rehabilitation Fund. EC 200 463.

Kwee, H.H. (1986). Spartacus and Manus: Telethesis developments in France and in the Netherlands. In R. Foulds (Ed.), *Interactive robotic aids—One option for independent living: An international perspective* (pp. 9–17). Monograph 37. New York: World Rehabilitation Fund. EC 200 463.

Moore, G.B., Yin, R.K., & Lahm, E.A. (1986). Robotics, artificial intelligence, computer simulation: Future applications in special education. *Technological Horizons in Education, 14*(1), 74–76.

Risk, H.F. (1985). Force capabilities of the physically handicapped at selected automobile driving controls. In C. Smith (Ed.), *Technology for disabled persons: Conference papers* (pp. 15–27). Menomonie, WI; Stout Vocational Rehabilitation Institute, University of Wisconsin–Stout.

Weiss, L. (1983). *Access to the world: A travel guide for the handicapped.* New York: Facts on file.

Woolridge, C., & Russell, G. (1976). *Head position training with a cerebral palsied child: An application of biofeedback techniques.* Toronto: Rehabilitation Engineering Research, Crippled Children's Center.

Concepts and Controversies

Brullem, A.R., Barton, L.E., Barton, C.L., & Wharton, D.L. (1983). A comparison of teacher time spent with physically handicapped and able-bodied students. *Exceptional Children, 49,* 543–545.

Frith, G.H., & Edwards, R. (1981). Misconceptions of regular classroom teachers about physically handicapped students. *Exceptional Children, 48,* 182–184.

PHOTO CREDITS

Cover and chapter opening art provided by VERY SPECIAL ARTS. The publisher and authors of this text would like to extend a very special thanks to the Very Special Arts Education Office in Washington. Since 1974 Very Special Arts (VSA) has provided training and experience in every art form to people with disabilities. As writer Edith Wharton said, "There are two ways of spreading light: to be the candle or the mirror that reflects it."

Art & Photo-Research provided by Photosynthesis.

page 10: John Stuart / The Image Bank; page 11 left: Culver Pictures; page 11 right: The Mary Evans Picture Library; page 12: Brown Bros.; page 13: The Museum of the City of New York; page 28 top and bottom: The New York Times; page 41: Lawrence Migdale; page 44: M. Bartlett / Woodfin Camp & Assoc.s; page 50: Lawrence Migdale; page 52: John Running; page 60: Lawrence Migdale; page 64: The New York Times; page 74: Susan Fish; page 86: L. Merrim / Monkmeyer Press; page 88: W. McIntyre / Photo-Researchers Inc.; page 90: B. Seitz / Photo-Researchers Inc.; page 97: S. Pick / Stock, Boston; page 102: Lawrence Migdale; page 104: Lawrence Midgale; page 131: Mike Jackson / The Picture Group; page 134: R. Hutchings / Photo-Researchers Inc.; page 140: Elliott Varner Smith; page 142: M. Ruiz / The Picture Group; page 150: G. Zucker / Stock, Boston; page 155: W. McIntyre / Photo-Researchers Inc.; page 156: B. Seitz / Photo-Researchers Inc.; page 163: B. Daemmrich / Stock, Boston; page 167: C. Gupton / Stock, Boston; page 177: Courtesy of the American Speech, Language, and Hearing Association; page 187: S. Niedorf / The Image Bank; page 189: R. Friedman / Black Star; page 201: Bob Daemmrich; page 216: S. Grant / The Picture Cube; page 225: B. Daemmrich / Stock, Boston; page 228: B. Barnes / Stock, Boston; page 232: S. Frisch / Stock, Boston; page 236: J. Rodriguez / Black Star; page 245: D. Dietz / Stock, Boston; page 260: Richard Howard / Offshoot Stock; page 271: Lawrence Migdale; page 278: G. Molteni / The Image Bank; page 283: David Dempster; page 288: P. Thomann / The Image Bank; page 293: S. Niedorf / The Image Bank; page 303: Brent Jones; page 308: Lawrence Migdale; page 310: North Wind Picture Archive; page 311: Brown Bros.; page 318: O. Franken / Stock, Boston; page 319: Lawrence Migdale; page 324: S. Grant / Stock, Boston; page 330: B. Daemmrich; page 345 left and right: Craig Blouin / Offshoot Stock; page 353: R. Sidney / Monkmeyer Press; page 354: G. Tourdjman / The Image Bank; page 364: B. Daemmrich / The Image Works; page 365: Elliott Varner Smith; page 371: J. Chenet / Woodfin Camp & Assoc.s; page 374: R. Isear / Photo-Researchers Inc.; page 383: B. Daemmrich; page 402: N. Benn / Stock, Boston; page 404: Will McIntyre / Photo-Researchers Inc.; page 409: B. Daemmrich; page 415: B. Daemmrich / The Image Works; page 417: B. Daemmrich / The Image Works; page 419: North Wind Picture Archives; page 420: L. Downing / Woodfin Camp & Assoc.s; page 432: B. Barnes / Stock, Boston; page 439: Black Star; page 443: P. Bates / The Picture Cube; page 451: B. Daemmrich; page 455: G. LeDuc / Monkmeyer Press; page 456: B. Daemmrich / Stock, Boston; page 463: L. Johnson / Black Star; page 465: B. Laing / Black Star; page 466: B. Barnes / Stock, Boston.

AUTHOR INDEX

SUBJECT INDEX